LECTURES ON ARCHITECTURE

BY

Eugène-Emmanuel Viollet-le-Duc

Translated by Benjamin Bucknall

IN TWO VOLUMES

Volume I

DOVER PUBLICATIONS, INC.

NEW YORK

Published in Canada by General Publishing Company, Ltd., 30 Lesmill Road, Don Mills, Toronto, Ontario.
Published in the United Kingdom by Constable and Company, Ltd.

This Dover edition, first published in 1987, is an unabridged republication of the work as first published in English by Sampson Low, Marston, Searle and Rivington, London, in 1877 (vol. I) and 1881 (vol. II) (original French edition, *Entretiens sur l'architecture*, completed 1872 in two text volumes and an "Atlas" of engraved plates). In the present edition: the 38 double-page plates have been reproduced directly from the "Atlas" (A. Morel et Cie, Paris, 1864) rather than from the London edition, to achieve greater quality; the French labeling of these plates has been translated into English (for the first time); plates XXVII and XXVIII (originally monochrome in the Paris and London editions) and XXXVI (originally in full color in both those editions) appear here in black-and-white; some of the plates have been slightly relocated for reasons of space; the numbering of the plates has been somewhat regularized, and the list of plates made more complete; the erratum bound in to the London edition has here been corrected directly in the text, and a number of new corrections made.

Manufactured in the United States of America
Dover Publications, Inc., 31 East 2nd Street, Mineola, N.Y. 11501

Library of Congress Cataloging-in-Publication Data

Viollet-le-Duc, Eugène-Emmanuel, 1814–1879.
Lectures on architecture.

Translation of: Entretiens sur l'architecture.
Originally published: London : Sampson Low, Marston, Searle, and Rivington, 1877–1881.
Includes index.
1. Architecture. I. Title.
NA2520.V5613 1987   720   87-20087
ISBN 0-486-25520-4 (pbk. : v. 1)
ISBN 0-486-25521-2 (pbk. : v. 2)

TABLE OF CONTENTS.

LIST OF PLATES.

TRANSLATOR'S PREFACE.

I HAVE undertaken this translation with the sanction of the author, under the conviction that, although his admirable work is already widely known and appreciated, there are many to whom an English version would be acceptable.

The general reader as well as the student will find these Lectures highly interesting and instructive. The author has a profound knowledge of his subject, and discusses it from a strictly philosophical point of view ; but he elucidates it so ably that any person of average mental culture can comprehend him. Clearing the ground of that confusion of ideas which has hitherto so unhappily obscured elementary conceptions of Art, he discusses its nature and origin, referring the latter to instinctive tendencies ; and proceeds to show that none of the various forms of Architecture can lay an exclusive claim to artistic excellence. Tracing architectural art from its beginnings, he follows it through the Greek and Roman Periods and the Middle Ages down to the days of the *Renaissance*. He adduces evidence in the course of his investigation to prove that the development of Art is independent of that of other branches of civilisation, and illustrates the immutable principles upon which that development depends. He then shows the application of these principles to the novel requirements of modern architecture, exemplifying several new and admirable methods of construction, and pointing out the course which beginners in Architecture should pursue in their elementary studies, and subsequently in composition.

While every page of the work illustrates important truths in Art, or in Nature as related to it, the author never loses an opportunity of insisting upon those which are liable to be forgotten. While commenting on faults, he shows how to avoid them, by referring to the misconceptions in which they have originated; and calls special attention to the notion of "Revival," as it is commonly understood, and which in its essence is clearly akin to the justly depreciated *Renaissance.* He condemns it as the fundamental error of our times, which renders fruitless so much earnest labour and enthusiasm, and effectually hinders the formation of a *School of Architecture.* In exposing this fallacy he proves that a reproduction of the mere forms or methods of the past must be devoid of genuine vitality, and that it is to *analysis and the application of principles, and not to the imitation of forms,* that we must look for a true revival.

If these Lectures were attentively read by our young architects, we should, I am persuaded, soon observe an improvement in Architecture; we should have better construction and more sensible work, less pretension and more Art. Nor can their perusal by amateurs fail to raise the standard of criticism.

With regard to the translation itself I have endeavoured to follow out the principles laid down by Dr. Newman :—" While every care must be taken against the introduction of new, or the omission of existing ideas in the original text, yet in a book intended for general reading, faithfulness may be considered simply to consist in expressing in English the *sense* of the original, the actual words of the latter being viewed mainly as *directions into* its meaning, and scholarship being necessary in order to gain the full insight which they afford; and next, that, where something must be sacrificed, precision or intelligibility, it is better in a popular work to be understood by those who are not critics, than to be applauded by those who are."

I wish to take this opportunity of expressing my deep obligations to Mr. John Sibree, M.A. Univ. Lond., for the assistance he has rendered me by his able and careful revision of my manuscript for the press. My thanks are also due to my friend Mr. Charles Wethered of Stroud, for his helpful advice, sympathy, and encouragement during the progress of a work undertaken in the midst of professional engagements not always the most favourable to literary pursuits.

BENJAMIN BUCKNALL,

ARCHT.

THE AUTHOR'S PREFACE.

RATHER more than a year ago, yielding to the earnest solici-
tations of my friends and brother architects, I determined
upon opening a studio for pupils and delivering a course of lectures
on Architecture. The undertaking appeared to me to have no
particular interest except for those who should wish to frequent
the studio or attend the lectures. In my simplicity I thought
that all I had to do was to hire a studio and set about preparing an oral course to the best of my ability. But in the
Republic of Arts (a Republic after the fashion of that of Venice)
matters are not so easily managed. At the outset rooms were
freely offered for my lectures, and everybody expressed a willing-
ness to send me pupils. But when *I* was ready, the rooms were *not :*
I was urged to make a beginning, and received many fair words,
but no material aid. Now I am a very indifferent petitioner ;
so, after some attempts—not very persistent, I must confess—I
went home and quietly waited. I soon understood the reason of
this decline of interest. Certain Professors of the *École des beaux-
arts* and of the *Bibliothèque impériale* wished to do me the honour
of attacking my "tendencies" by preventive measures. A professional work which I am just publishing, and whose scope
embraces only one of the phases of architectural art, was regarded
by a Professor of Archæology, deeply versed in the study of Greek
antiquities,—a clever and erudite man,—as designed to be the
vehicle of exclusive and therefore "dangerous" dogmas. The
learned Professor is especially displeased (why, does not appear)
at my having drawn attention to an art foreign to his studies,
but which belongs to us as much as Greek art belonged to the

Greeks, or Roman art to the Romans. In disputing our claim to a strictly lawful right, however, the author of the clever tirade of which this work was the object, brought nothing really to bear against my opinions but simple assertions to the contrary. This was something, certainly ; but for us who have our compasses in our hands and geometry at our service, it is not enough. Perhaps, before protesting on behalf of imperilled civilisation, and setting up for its champions, it would have been more reasonable to examine whether, after all, the barbarians were really at the gates. A cry of alarm where there is no enemy at all, or when his forces and means of attack are unknown, can only serve to throw an army into confusion. My friends began to intimate a general rising in arms—a fierce impending conflict ; and both sides were hoping for a goodly sight of broken lances. Now tumult is the foe to study ; and I love study and detest tumult. I therefore allowed the storm to blow over ; which, meeting no resistance, spent its rage in vain. I put the manuscript of my lectures back into my portfolio, and gave my mind to other matters. And now I an perfectly willing to leave the professional chair to those who occupy it with an ability to which I do not aspire, and an authority which is indisputable.

Our art gains nothing by these fruitless strifes, which turn upon words rather than things ; while by engaging in them artists lose a little of that good sense which is so needful to us all. But there are eternal principles which it is the duty of each of us, according to his several capacity, to exalt above those passions of the Schools that are so unworthy to occupy the attention of sincere and earnest men. Renouncing the honours of a chair which I foresaw would only prove an arena for controversies I had no leisure to carry on, and which I deem useless at the best, I have resolved to offer to my friends, my fellow-architects, my pupils, and my provincial and foreign correspondents, whose sympathy and encouragement are to me such a valuable support, these *Lectures on Architecture.* The indulgent readers to whom I have just referred, and even those to whom an adversary is perhaps necessary to give them an opportunity of displaying their zeal for what they deem the "good cause"—that of Civilisation and Progress—will, I trust, acknowledge that my chief object is Truth, and that, if I am liable to any accusation, it is that of not belonging to any school. It is true, that alone is enough to array them all against me.

In the present day "specialities" alone are recognised. It is not imagined that a savant, an artist, or a man of letters can move in a wide circle. Each is confined within a narrow sphere, beyond which he cannot pass without losing a great part of his importance in the eyes of the public. If an artist, for instance, has in the course of his profession manifested certain preferences (and who is there that has not preferences?), immediately he is classed, "labelled," as it were: he is not consulted or employed, or his capacity acknowledged, except within the range which those predilections are supposed to have marked out for him. If he protests against the limitation which opinion imposes upon his knowledge and tastes, his protest is unheeded. His adversaries, or those who regard themselves as such, if he endeavours to take a single step in their direction, are eager to thrust him back within the narrow circle traced around him; for every one thinks it his interest to make his neighbour's sphere as narrow as possible, and is ready to declare him a trespasser the moment he ventures beyond it. These sentiments appear to me perverse in themselves, hurtful to the interest of Science, Art, and Letters, and unjust to individuals. I will not, however, undertake to criticise sentiments against which I have long deemed it vain to struggle: it is evident that *my* range seemed too wide, seeing that it has been so vehemently contested.

My hesitation in offering to the public general ideas on Architecture arose from the following dilemma: "Either my teaching must limit itself to the circle to which I am supposed to be restricted, and will thus rest on too narrow a basis, and in fact be more dangerous than useful; or, in advancing beyond that circle, I shall lose the confidence which every author or professor ought to inspire in those who read or listen to him, if he wishes his instructions to be profitable."

Hence the scruples which have long restrained me,—scruples which the kindly persistent solicitation of my brother architects has at length succeeded in overcoming. Induced by their too flattering estimate of my powers, and by the consideration that many persons who have not and who never have had any practical acquaintance with Architecture, take it upon themselves to teach it to us from their professional chair or their writing-desk; and observing that among my fellow-architects, those alone who are best entitled to be heard, keep silence or nearly so on the principles of their art, refrain from imparting their knowledge, and

appear to wait for light to break forth from some other quarter,
—I have ventured to undertake this novel task, not without
diffidence: for, in my view, a course of lectures on Architecture
must embrace a wide field of studies—research into the history
of Nations, an examination of their Institutions and Customs,
and a proper estimate of the various influences that have raised
them to distinction or effected their decay. Merely to present
to attentive readers the architectural forms characteristic of the
nations with whose arts we are acquainted, without pointing out
the causes by which their peculiarities have been determined,
their connection with the national genius, and their relative
influences,—without inquiring into the " why and wherefore " of
the various systems of architecture to which these forms are
subordinated,—would have been to present a sterile compilation
of the numerous works which all can now easily procure, or at
least consult in our public libraries: it would have been to teach
nothing to those who possess these works, and to introduce confusion into the minds of those who are just entering on the study.
And this confusion is most injurious in the teaching of the Arts,
as it is in every department of instruction—a fact only too well
attested in our times. To select one of those systems of architecture for discussion, while setting aside or wilfully ignoring
the others, would have been a course the more reprehensible in
my view, as I have never ceased to condemn it in others. It
will therefore be no matter for surprise that I should have mis-
trusted my powers, and entered with timidity upon a path so
thickly strewn with difficulties.

One thing alone sustains me and gives me hope—the respect
I entertain for Truth, and the love of an art to which I have
devoted my life, and which has ever been the object of my
homage, under whatever conditions it may have originated, and
in whatever form it may have presented itself. I have said to
myself: " If my lectures should have no further result than to
induce in our students a respect for the past, and a habit of
founding their judgment not on prepossessions but on careful
and thoughtful examination; if, moreover, they should foster
the spirit of method among artists, I shall have done good
service." I know how desirous our rising generation of architects
are to learn and to know; how little fruitless discussions are to
their taste; how imbued they are with the practical spirit of our
age, which duly estimates the value of time, and demands a

style of teaching that shall be at once liberal, invigorating, and free from prejudice.

This is what I propose to myself in treating of Architecture : to inquire into the reason of every form,—for every architectural form has its reason ; to point out the origin of the various principles that underlie them, and to trace the logical consequences of those principles, analysing their most typical developments so as to exhibit them with their merits and defects ; and, finally, to call attention to the application which can be made of the principles of ancient Art to the requirements of the present day : for the arts never die ; their principles remain true for all time ; humanity is always the same ;—however its customs and institutions may be modified, its intellectual constitution is unchanged ; its faculty of reasoning, its instincts and sensations, proceed from the same source now as they did twenty centuries ago : it is moved by the same desires and the same passions ; while the various languages it employs do but enable it to express in every age the same ideas and to call for the satisfaction of the same wants. I must insist upon it that if any of my readers are disposed to believe that I am maintaining principles favourable to one school rather than another, they are mistaken, and my lectures will prove them to be so. I have not taken pen in hand to promote the triumph of a system or to refute theories ; I leave this task to those who, while they fancy themselves defending the interests of Art, are for the most part only obeying the passions of the moment. I am contemplating a different object,—the knowledge of the True ;—the development of the immutable principles of our art, as variously applied by differently constituted civilisations. I shall not conclude in favour of one form of architecture to the prejudice of the rest ; neither shall I conclude by saying : "You have heard the claimants ; make your choice !" For this would, in fact, be to arrive at no conclusion at all ; whereas all instruction, to be useful, demands, if not a positive conclusion, at least direction and method. If students are to learn a science or an art, with a view to its practical application, they reasonably ask that the road be traced out for them. The teacher who indicates to us all the possible paths without showing us the preferable one, with the reasons for selecting it, does not fulfil his function : he introduces confusion and obscurity into minds that have come to seek order and light. But the road indicated must not be a narrow one : it must be wide and free for all, that each may follow it according to his tastes, his inspirations, and his particular genius.   This road—the only good, the only free one, the only one that does not lead to false conceptions—is the road marked out for all ages by human reason ; that which has been followed with varying tread, and in their several fashions, by all the great artists of ancient and modern times.

"Prove all things," says St. Paul,[1] "and hold fast that which is good."   This is my motto, and I shall be faithful to it.   Misapprehension of my views may have led some to attack what they do me the honour to call my "doctrines."   I shall reply simply by my teaching.   If this maintains its ground, the anticipative criticisms to which it may be subjected, those "*indictments for tendencies*" that have been brought against me, will at no distant date be forgotten.   If, on the contrary, it is destined, like so much else, to fall into oblivion, to what purpose would it be to reply to attacks directed against views which nobody will remember ?

[1] First Epistle to the Thessalonians.

PARIS, 1860.

LECTURE I.

WHAT IS BARBARISM ?—WHAT IS ART ?—IS ART DEPENDENT ON DEGREE OF CIVILISATION ?—WHAT SOCIAL CONDITIONS ARE MOST FAVOURABLE TO THE DEVELOPMENT OF THE ARTS ?

MODERN criticism has divided the History of Art into periods of greatness—of splendour—and periods of barbarism. It cannot be doubted that there have been epochs when the Arts developed themselves with singular energy, when they were held in honour, loved, and cultivated ; others at which they have fallen into disregard, or even contempt, have ceased to be cultivated, and have left only vague and scarcely discernible traces of their existence. But is it reasonable to confound the social barbarism of a nation or an age with barbarism in Art ? Is not this an error, resulting, like so many others, from a misapplication of terms ? May not a people be " barbarous " from the modern point of view,—*i.e.* uncivilised, superstitious, fanatical, subject to irregular and incalculable impulses, and governed by imperfect laws, and yet possess arts in great perfection ?

Is man in becoming civilised, refined, tolerant, moderate in his tastes, and well-informed,—such in fact as our social conditions can make him,—thereby rendered more apt and capable in the domain of Art ? Philosophy, gentle manners, justice, and politeness, constitute a state of society in which it is agreeable to live ; but this state may be unfavourable to the development of Art.

The word *barbarous* has two meanings. It signifies, on the one hand, *rude, uncultivated;* on the other hand, *cruel.* A very " barbarous " people may be very gentle, while a very civilised people may be very cruel, and consequently barbarous. Cruelty is an instinct of human nature which civilisation succeeds more or less in suppressing. It is therefore unnecessary to take this form of barbarism into consideration, especially as the arts are not influenced by it. History gives us only too many examples of acts of cruelty committed by nations among whom the arts had reached their highest degree of perfection.

While the Parthenon was being erected at Athens, the Greeks were giving themselves up to all the cruelties of the Peloponnesian war. While the Romans were making their pastime of the deadly combats of slaves who had no cause to hate each other, and were condemning human beings to be torn by wild beasts in the circus for the diversion of an idle populace and the satisfaction of a brutal curiosity, they were building admirable monuments and civilising barbarous nations. At a later date, Christians slaughtered and burned each other for a difference of opinion respecting a dogma or a text ; yet they covered the East and the West with inimitable works of Art. In the very middle of the seventeenth century, the *Parliaments* were still sending to the stake rogues or fools who made pretensions to sorcery,—a piece of cruelty beyond question ; yet this century witnessed the erection of Versailles, and the Hôtel des Invalides, and possessed poets and artists whose works we never cease to admire. We may then once for all exclude from the discussion the word *barbarous* in the sense of *cruel.* It remains for us to consider the term as meaning *not civilised.* Ought we to conclude from the fact that a nation is uncivilised, or that only faint indications of its future culture are as yet perceptible, that its arts are barbarous ? We think not.

The point of interest when the arts are in question is, not whether such or such a period in the history of humanity was more or less civilised,—or, if we will, more or less barbarous,— than another ; but whether the period under consideration was more or less favourable to the development of the arts. It is certain that the different branches of a civilisation do not shoot forth all at once ;—that the development of Institutions, of Governments, of the Sciences, of Letters and the Arts, is not simultaneous. Were these various functions of the body social to present themselves simultaneously, it would follow that since our institutions, our administration, and our scientific discoveries are superior to those (for instance) of the seventeenth century, our modern dramas and comedies ought to surpass the tragedies and comedies of Racine and Molière ; while our painters should leave far behind them those of Italy in the sixteenth century, since Julius II. did not travel by railway, and Charles V. had no electric telegraphs to transmit his mandates to all the provinces of his vast empire.

The value of Art is independent of the element in which it originates and flourishes. Art cannot be barbarous, for the simple reason that it is Art. It has its infancy, which may give promise of the noblest development ; it has its old age, ever recalling its past. It is really barbarous only in ceasing to be Art ;—when it degrades itself by belying and violating its own

principles ; when it slavishly follows the caprices of that fantastical queen we call Fashion ; when it becomes the plaything of
a people without fixed ideas or convictions ; and when no longer
reflecting national Manners and Customs, it is but an encumbrance,—a thing of mere curiosity or luxury.

Yes, Art has its youth and its decrepitude.   Its maturity is
like that of all earthly things,—a moment, a point of time,—
the inappreciable interval between progress and decline.   Is Art,
then, barbarous in its youth ?   Is it barbarous in its decrepitude ?
This is the real question.   Individuals and Nations,—which
are but individuals united by a community of Customs and Institutions,—are evidently nearer to absolute barbarism in their
infancy than when they have reached the culminating point of
their civilisation.   Nations fall back into barbarism when those
springs are worn out which, while they serve to unite these
bodies, establish harmony and an equal balance between their
different parts ; just as the old man, whose organs cease to perform their functions with regularity, falls into a second childhood
and no longer enjoys the full use of his faculties.   Is Art necessarily subject to the same revolutions ?   We believe not.   But
before we proceed further, let us clearly understand what Art
is ; for there is nothing like defining terms to arrive at the knowledge of Truth.

It is not our intention to give one of those definitions comprised in two or three lines, the principal merit of which consists
in displaying their author's wit, but which are understood only
by persons as clever as himself.   We think it necessary to give
our definition somewhat at length : for many talk of the arts,
who would find it very difficult to tell us what Art really is.

The Middle Ages recognised seven " Liberal Arts ;" but at
present some of these, viz., Theology, Astronomy, Geometry, and
Medicine,—with due deference to the SORBONNE, the OBSERVA-
TOIRE, the ÉCOLE POLYTECHNIQUE, and the FACULTY,—rank as
sciences.   We shall therefore confine ourselves to MUSIC, ARCHI-
TECTURE, SCULPTURE, and PAINTING.   Our reasons for placing
the arts in this particular order are, that man naturally uttered
sounds before he built houses ; built houses before he sculptured
them, and sculptured before he painted them,—for a sharpened
flint was all he required to carve wood or soft stone ; whereas
the extraction of colours, whether from mineral or vegetable
substances, and their subsequent application, involves a course
of reasoning and observation needing time for its accomplishment.
Should this order, however, clash with the susceptibilities of any
of our readers, we need not insist upon it.   As regards Poetry
and the Drama, they naturally class with Music.   These four
arts are sisters ; the first two, Music and Architecture, twins :

for it will be observed that they do not originate in the imitation of natural objects, as do Sculpture and Painting.

The arts are, in their origin, natural cravings, which, to obtain their satisfaction, assume a form subordinate to certain instincts of the soul,—instincts which long observation converted into rules. Man very early recognised that words and signs alone are not sufficient to express all his feelings ; and therefore sought to impress his fellows by giving to his voice certain inflections and modulations,—a rhythm which would render his thoughts more vividly. Modulation of the voice is not taught to infants ; and yet before they are able to speak, they express their wants or feelings by a certain rhythm, and a particular series of sounds, whether born in Paris or Pekin. They assist these tones and this rhythm by expressive gestures understood by every one. Already we are in presence of Art. Animals cannot use gestures to assist their cries ; which moreover express only immediate feelings, such as joy, pain, terror, weariness. But man foresees, hopes, remembers ; and his voice, obeying his will, expresses the feelings which he desires to communicate to his fellows ; though the cause or the object of his prevision, his hope, or his remembrance, may be unknown to his hearers. Say to an assembly, "Your houses are being pillaged, your wives are being murdered," in the same tone in which you would say, "Let us go to supper," —no one will stir. But if the tone of your voice be in keeping with your words ; if that tone be seconded by an expressive gesture,—a gesture evidently inspired by the sentiment which animates you,—you will soon see the crowd moved and fired by your own feelings of indignation.

And it is especially important to note that Art in this primitive form acts much more strongly upon men in their primitive state than on men highly civilised. The latter will reason. Your voice may be expressive, your accent pathetic, your gestures true and forcible ; but in spite of the art you have employed in your modulation and manner, they will say : "Whence has he got this very unlikely piece of news ?"

From modulation to melody the way is short, and forthwith Music is born. Let us now take Architecture, which we have placed second in the rank of age.

Building a hut with branches of trees is not Art ; it is merely the supplying of a material want. But to hollow out a dwelling in a declivity of soft rock ;—to divide the excavation into compartments of different sizes according to the number and habits of the occupants ;—to leave pillars for the support of the ceiling, and to enlarge them at the top for the greater security of the suspended mass above ; then gradually to cover these walls and pillars left in the solid with gravings and signs intended to commemorate an event, such as the birth of a child, the death of a father or of a wife, or a victory gained over an enemy,—this is Art.

More need not be said to make it clear that Music and its derivatives, Poetry and the Drama, with Architecture, are the only arts in which primitive man,—actuated by the desire of propagating his ideas, preserving his remembrances, or imparting his hopes, by associating them with a form or a sound,—displayed certain creative faculties inherent in his nature.

Sculpture and Painting are to Architecture what the Drama and Poetry are to Music,—its derivatives, its necessary consequences.

A man of greater intelligence and strength than his neighbours has killed a lion. He hangs its skin above the doorway of the cave which he inhabits. This commemorative spoil perishes; he therefore cuts in the stone, as best he can, something which resembles a lion, that his children and neighbours may preserve the remembrance of his strength and courage. But he wishes this sign, destined to perpetuate the memory of his valour, to be seen from afar,—to attract notice. He has observed that red is the most striking of all colours; he therefore daubs his sculptured lion with red. To all who see this image it plainly says: " Here is the dwelling of the strong man who knows how to defend himself and his." This is Art. Here it exists entire, complete, needing only to perfect its means of execution.

Our primitive hero dies. His family hew out a cell in the rock wherein to deposit his remains, and above it they carve a man fighting with a lion. The figure of the man will be large, that of the lion small; for the relatives of the deceased wish passers-by to know that the father or the husband represented was a man of might. True, a little man who kills a great lion is more courageous than a man of great stature who overpowers a wild beast of small size; but this is a complex idea which does not enter into the mind of the primitive artist. In all the ancient sculptured monuments of India, and even of Egypt, the conqueror is represented as of colossal size and the enemies he has vanquished as pigmies.

In tracing things thus *ab ovo*, our design is to make it well understood what Art is, and that in essence, if not in form, Art is not dependent on degree of civilisation.

In the vestibule of St. Peter's at Rome there is an equestrian statue by Bernini of the emperor Constantine, who had his father-in-law hanged, his brother-in-law strangled, his nephew's throat cut, his eldest son beheaded, and his wife smothered in a bath; who threw to the beasts all the Frank chiefs conquered on the borders of the Rhine, and completed the destruction of what remained of the institutions of old Rome, which never recovered its ancient grandeur.

Truly, the red lion sculptured on the doorway of the barbarian, or the combat figured on his tomb, is more in conformity with the principles of Art, than is the statue of the emperor Constantine in the vestibule of a Christian church. The lion may be a misshapen image, and the statue of Constantine an admirable work; but that does not affect the question,—the quality of the execution being altogether irrespective of the immutable principles of Art.

When, however, a highly gifted people, while religiously preserving those immutable principles, possesses a taste for the Beautiful with the practical means of reproducing it in palpable forms, we may truly say of it: "This is an artistic people."

Once in the course of history such a people existed, in a corner of Eastern Europe. Yet, politically, the Athenian people may be reckoned one of the most capricious; their unstable institutions appear to us barbarous; their ideas of administration were vague and unpractical to a degree; they had but slight regard for their word; they maintained slavery; their populace was envious and grasping; their public men for the most part deceitful and corrupt; they knew nothing of printing, steam, electric telegraphs, or railways. Yet their orators, their poets, their philosophers, their architects, and their sculptors, have maintained a position superior to that of any which the most civilised ages, our own included, have been able to boast.

The further we advance, the more clearly we shall perceive that we must refrain from hasty conclusions. Thus, *à propos* of the Greeks, it is certain that this people had but very inaccurate ideas of the structure of the human body compared with those which we possess: anatomical science was less advanced in the time of Pericles than it is in our own; and we are not aware that the Athenians had schools of dissection. Still, without wishing to depreciate the merits of contemporary artists, why is the statuary of the Greeks so much superior to that of our own time? It is evident then that Art is not dependent on Science; neither is it dependent on the political condition of a country.

The governmental machinery of our modern civilisations is evidently more complete and better organised than that which regulated the primitive civilisations of Greece and of the Greek Archipelago; but this does not prevent the *Iliad* and the *Odyssey* from maintaining their rank as superior to all other poems, either of the past or of the present. Hence we may conclude that Art is not dependent on the political state of a nation. Whatever may have been the power of Rome and the grandeur of its institutions, we have good reason to doubt whether its police organisation was so effective as that of Paris, London, or Vienna. Even in the times of the Emperors, it was not safe to venture out of the Eternal City without an escort; and it would often have been dangerous for a Roman gentleman to go to his villa in the environs. And if such was the state of the capital, what must have been that of the provinces? In the present day, any one of us may travel alone through France, and even through a great part of Europe, without risk of encountering a single highway robber. Yet Rome was then building, not only in the city itself, but in Gaul, in Germany, in Spain, in Africa, and in Asia, monuments of Art distinguished by a majestic grandeur which impresses even the rudest minds.

If Augustus could visit Paris, he would no doubt admire our police organisation,—the order which reigns at all hours of the day and night in this populous city, and the complicated though invisible machinery of our Municipal Administration; but if he went to the opera, he would take us for a nation of puppets. He would wonder how people who possess every comfort at home, could of their own free will submit to be crammed, for four hours together, into little wooden boxes overlaid with paltry ornamentation and gilding, to hear one or two hundred singers and instrumental performers make an intolerable din, and to see dancers whirl about on a few square yards of flooring among strips of painted canvas. He would wonder still more how it could possibly have come into any one's head to light these things and these people from below,—to place an artificial sun beneath their feet, in contravention of the immemorial use and wont of nature.

If he visited our railway-stations and most of our large establishments of public utility, would he not fancy us a nomadic people, erecting our buildings in a slight and temporary fashion, with a view some day to their transport elsewhere? What would he say if he saw us constructing at the same time, and in the same city, public buildings, some of them with pointed and others with flat roofs,—houses upon slender iron props, and palaces on stone basements of a formidable thickness? Certainly Augustus would consider us a people devoid of any idea of Art. He would be wrong. But it is plain that Art is not dependent on civilisation.

Many of my readers will say: "You teach us nothing new; these are truths with which all are familiar." If indeed these are familiar truths; if it be an admitted fact that the production of epochs in Art depends on the *nature*, not the *degree* of civilisation, we must resolve once for all to cease confounding advancement in civilisation or industrial progress with that of the Arts; we must be content to judge the Arts independently of the laws, the prejudices, or the more or less barbarous customs of a people: we must no longer conclude that because a nation is superstitious, fanatical, and oppressed, its arts are therefore inferior to those of another nation which is liberal, cultivated, and well governed ; we must banish all such commonplaces as, *e.g.* "The Arts of those barbarous times ;"—for the Arts of those barbarous times may be superior to such as belong to periods greatly advanced in civilisation.

Should our study of *any* phase of the Arts of former ages be met with the objection, "You are carrying us back to barbarism ;" —the reply is obvious, that *all* periods of ancient Art—from the early Indian to that of Louis xv.—incur the same opprobrium ; for no one will dispute the superiority of our present social state to the civilisations of antiquity, of the Middle Ages, and of the last three centuries.

We must be consistent. Either the Arts follow step by step the material and moral progress of civilisation,—in which case, we live in the age most favourable to the Arts, since we enjoy the benefits of civilisation in a higher degree than any preceding period, and consequently we must regard all Art anterior to our time as relatively barbarous ;—or else the Arts are independent of moral and material civilisation, and in this case we have nothing to guide us in our preference of one form of Art to another but individual taste and caprice. Now both these conclusions rigorously deduced are false. The Arts may be highly developed and perfected under a very imperfect civilisation ; and rightly to estimate their relative worth we must judge of them according to certain laws, the origin of which we shall have occasion to point out ;—laws which belong exclusively to the Arts, and are independent of the state of civilisation to which nations may attain.

We, more than any other civilised nation, are prone to found our ideas age after age on phrases that have obtained popular currency ; to regard as undisputed and indisputable truths a few ill-considered words, uttered by a clever man totally unacquainted with the study and practice of Art, but whose words are taken up and repeated by successive generations of unthinking people.

We have certain ideas which resemble the jingles taught us by our nurses, repeated by one generation after another, but whose original meaning has been lost. But if you venture to say to the multitude, "You are mistaken ; you employ a word in a sense that does not belong to it ; restore its true significa- tion : is not its etymology so-and-so ? You will thus be able to make a more rational and consistent use of it, and avoid being taken for ignorant people uttering words without knowing their proper meaning ;"—you are immediately anathematised as a corrupter of youth,—daring to call in question things consecrated by immemorial usage. In vain do you protest that your intentions are good, your assertions true : in vain do you appeal to common sense, and furnish proofs of your position. "Anathema !" Two centuries ago you would have been burned,— your books, at any rate. It is no longer the custom to burn people or books ; but you will be considered a dangerous person, —at the very least a troublesome, cavilling busy-body. You have wished to restore its proper signification to a corrupted word. You are accused of desiring to alter the language,—to take it back to barbarism. You have tried to make Discourse accord with Logic. You are charged with trying to make people speak to-day as they spoke six or seven centuries ago. Why these contests, this acrimony, when by once seriously examining both sides of the question, truth and unanimity might be secured ? But in the domain of the Arts and of Science every one has his "*settled view;*" and will hear of no change in it, whatever new ideas or new information may supervene. People will fill a hundred pages to prove that they are right, while *one* would suffice to show that they are wrong. Scaliger asserts that all wars originate in *bad grammar.* He is perhaps right ; and in like manner we might say that all disputes on questions of Art arise from the want of a proper understanding as to what we mean by Art.

Art is an instinct—a craving of the mind which, in order to express itself, employs various forms : but ART is unique, as REASON, WISDOM, PASSION are unique. ART is a single fountain diffusing itself through many channels. The orator, the poet, the musician, the architect, the sculptor and the painter even, do but seek in different ways the expression of one and the same feeling, present in the soul of every competently endowed man. So true is this, that the artist, whether he be poet, musician, architect, sculptor, or painter, can express in his own peculiar language, and can communicate to the crowd feelings of an exactly similar nature,—can touch one and the same chord in the soul ; for though each art has a language of its own, the impressions they produce in man are limited, and are always reproduced irrespective of the language adopted.

The Arts act upon the senses, and the senses give birth in different ways to a similar series of impressions. For instance : the sight of sorrow, the accent of sorrow, and the representation of sorrow, will all produce the same feeling,—that of pity. My meaning will be readily conceived by those who have long practised and who love the arts ; but it may be only vaguely comprehended by some of my readers, and must therefore be developed ; particularly as some have made a perverse application of this property common to the various forms of art, by affecting to make some of those forms express ideas completely foreign to

Art—*e.g.* philosophical or metaphysical ideas; and I am anxious that my meaning should not be mistaken.

Which of us has not experienced, at least once in his life,—whether in listening to a poet or a musician, or in viewing a monument, a bas-relief, or a painting,—certain emotions, such, for instance, as a sense of grandeur, of sadness, of secret dread, of pride, joy, hope, or regret? It would even appear that the farther the arts are removed from the imitation of nature, the more they are calculated to strike certain deep-seated chords in the soul,—leaving a profound and lasting impression. The accent and action of an orator, a mere gesture, a musical phrase, or the sight of a noble building, will often produce such a perturbation of the nerves that tears start to the eyes, and we experience a sensation of heat or cold; though we are unable to describe the nature of the feeling which moves us. This feeling is our artistic instinct, which is touched by some one of the various expressions of Art.

Let us analyse this feeling; let us seek its source, and examine one by one those secret fibres of the soul which are endowed with the instinct of Art. Natural phenomena produce in our minds, through the senses, certain impressions which are essential to our nature, and are independent of the physical effect. Thus, a perfume will remind us of a person, an event, a place. If the repetition of an accessory and purely physical sensation, such as that of smell, can replace us in the mental situation in which we found ourselves when we previously experienced that physical sensation, it is because there exist within us certain intimate relations between the senses and our imagination. But though our senses are various, our imagination is one: one portion of the mind is not appropriated to smell, another to sight, and a third to hearing: one and the same chord in the soul may therefore be struck by an impulse that reaches it through the ear and through the eye.

The noise of the sea, the murmur of the wind, the rising or the setting of the sun, the aspect of a rugged declivity or of verdant meadows, darkness or light, awaken in the soul moral sensations and reveries which are independent of our material reality, and which we shall call poetical for want of a better word. These sensations owe their character simply to the combination of the purely physical impression coming from without with ideas drawn from within. Thus the roaring of the waves of the sea is but a sound of which we know the cause; yet we could listen to it for hours. Why does this sound awaken in us a peculiar feeling which is neither joy nor sadness, nor impatience nor weariness? It is because this grand harmony develops in our mind certain feelings which are already there in

a latent state. Now, let us suppose that Art, speaking in the
language of the musician, recalls to you the harmony of the
waves,—in an instant your mind is again filled with the same
thoughts which occupied it when you were on the sea-shore;
nay more, it brings back to you the majestic spectacle of that
waste of waters, and you seem even to inhale the fresh odour of
the beach. Suppose again that, during those hours passed in
listening to the murmur of the waves, you were under the
influence of some happy or some sorrowful event; the same
feeling of joy or of sorrow which you then experienced will be
awakened by the musician.

It will be readily allowed that those thoughts which arose
in your mind on the sea-shore can be recalled by the musician or
the poet. The architect possesses the same power :—which may
seem more remarkable still. The musician by his own peculiar
language,—the harmony of sounds,—recalls to your mind the
grand spectacle of the sea : the poet by awakening in your
imagination ideas analogous to those which caused your reveries
on the strand, seems to transport you back to that strand. The
architect also by means of his peculiar language can place you
again under the influence of the same impression. If he traces
beneath the sky a long horizontal line along which your eyes
may range without interruption, your mind will be affected by
a sense of grandeur,—of calm,—which will arouse in it ideas
analogous to those caused by the sight of the sea.

We *see* the ocean, we *hear* the noise of its waves ; and we can
therefore understand by what artifice the musician, acting upon
the hearing, and the architect upon the sight, can recall, each in
his own language, the effect produced on our senses by the sea.
But we do not hear the rising of the sun ; how then is it possible
that a symphony can arouse in the soul the same emotions as are
caused by this daily phenomenon ? Why do we frequently say,
" That piece of music breathes a delightful freshness. This
is marked by a character of gloom which oppresses the soul"?
How can sounds be "fresh" or "gloomy"? Yet such is the
fact ; unhappy those who do not comprehend this seeming
nonsense of the language of the arts !

Take a person into a low, far-stretching crypt, arched upon
numerous short and massive pillars : although he can walk erect
and breathe with ease, he will incline his head, and none but
melancholy thoughts and gloomy images will present themselves
to his mind ; he will experience a sense of oppression, a longing
for light and air. But take him into a building vaulted at a
lofty height and flooded with light and air ; he will direct his
gaze upwards, and his face will reflect the feelings of grandeur
which crowd into his mind. This is a phenomenon which any
one may observe.

Watch persons entering a low dimly-lighted chamber; they will not first direct their gaze towards the ceiling so close above them, however richly decorated; but they will direct it horizontally, and at length let it fall upon the ground. And unless you call attention to it, they will depart without knowing whether the ceiling is ornamented or not. Observe, on the contrary, those entering the basilica of St. Peter's at Rome;—from the very threshold their eyes are turned upwards to the enormous dome which crowns the edifice. The pillars of the church are covered with marble; magnificent tombs adorn the walls: yet they do not see these, but continue to advance—still seeking to penetrate the depths of the immense cupola. You have to remind them more than once that they are passing sculptures unheeded and treading on porphyry, before their eyes even alight upon these objects—which are nevertheless near enough to be minutely appreciated. Thus then, long horizontal lines, low or lofty ceilings, a dark or brilliantly lighted chamber, will give rise in the soul to emotions of a widely different nature. This is natural and evident; all can understand it. But the human mind is complex; and by means of a deep-seated faculty, the workings of which we cannot comprehend, it establishes certain relations between sights, sounds, and ideas, which, however wonderful, are none the less real; since we find them recognised by all the individuals that compose a crowd in the same place and at the same moment. Thus (for we must reason familiarly if we would be understood), why, in music, does the *minor key* awaken in the mind different ideas from the *major?* It may be said that there is a *minor* and a *major* in all the arts, as also in the infinite details which constitute each of them severally.

A man blind from his birth was asked if he could form an idea of the colour red? " Yes, " he answered, " red is like the sound of a trumpet. " There exists then a close reciprocity between the various expressions of Art. And why? Because all these expressions derive their origin from the self-same source. An artistic people is one that has equally understood all the different languages of Art. An architect who can listen to a melody or a poem, or view a sculpture or a painting, without experiencing emotions as lively as those he would feel in viewing a building, is not an artist, but a mere practitioner; the same may be said of the musician, the poet, the painter, and the sculptor. This connection between the various fibres of the soul which vibrate at the touch of Art, is so intimate that all human beings, especially primitive human beings,—children,—naturally employ metaphor when they wish to excite in the minds of others the feelings which they themselves experience. Only those races which have been endowed with a feeling for Art have succeeded, by combining its various expressions, conformably to a common principle, in producing those grand effects whose cause we can now scarcely understand, but which have nevertheless exercised so powerful an influence that their memory still dwells with us after the lapse of ages.

With a people thus happily constituted, everything became an expression of Art, tending with a wonderful union and harmony towards the complete expression, in the same place and at the same moment, of one and the same idea. So much so that if ever the slightest discord, the least forgetfulness of principles, found its way into that atmosphere of Art, a hiss of disapprobation immediately arose from the crowd. Those who first comprehended the power residing in this union of the various expressions of Art, invented the Theatre, which is simply the assemblage of all those expressions. And from that time the theatre became one of its most indispensable institutions to every people endowed with a feeling for Art.

Yet what a bold idea was that of uniting in the same place the various expressions of Art, to produce in the multitude a single feeling, a homogeneous emotion (if I may use the term), blending these diverse expressions into a kind of symphony in which each of them was to combine in producing at a given moment an harmonious, complete accord! And how successful was this bold essay among the Greeks! How well they understood it, and what powerful emotions it excited among that highly gifted people! And have we not preserved the remembrance of such a concert of the arts, and of their influence on the multitude, in times less remote from our own?

Were the Middle Ages ignorant of this intimate correlation of the different languages of Art, when they raised those grand churches in which the sight of imposing ceremonies, music, and the voice of the orator, all seemed to unite in directing the mind towards one thought?

If Classic Antiquity possessed the power of producing in the highest degree of grandeur this combined display of the arts, the Middle Ages were not less gifted with the same instinct, or genius, if I may so term it ; and this we shall have occasion to demonstrate.

Thus then from a philosophical point of view, Art is unique— Art is but one—though it assumes divers forms, in order to act on the human mind ; and when those divers forms are brought into harmony in one place and at the same time—when they spring from the same inspiration, and employ in order to affect the senses the means peculiar to each—then it is that they produce the most vivid and lasting impression which it has been given to the thinking being to experience.

I remember an extremely vivid emotion of my childhood which is still fresh in my mind, though the incident in question must have occurred at an age which generally leaves none but the vaguest recollections. I was often intrusted to the care of an old servant, who took me wherever his fancy happened to lead him. One day we entered the church of Nôtre-Dame ; and he carried me in his arms, for the crowd was great. The cathedral was hung with black. My gaze rested on the painted glass of the southern rose-window, through which the rays of the sun were streaming, coloured with the most brilliant hues. I still see the place where our progress was interrupted by the crowd. All at once the roll of the great organ was heard ; but for me, the sound was the singing of the rose-window before me. In vain did my old guide attempt to undeceive me ; the impression became more and more vivid, until my imagination led me to believe that such or such panes of glass emitted grave and solemn sounds, whilst others produced shriller and more piercing tones ; so that at last my terror became so intense that he was obliged to take me out. It is not education which produces in us that intimate connection between the different expressions of Art.

Those times which have been favoured by the possession of Art,—Art in its immutable essence,—and have had the power to express it in the various languages through which it reveals itself, have been, and will always remain, epochs in Art. The duration of one of these epochs may be short, but that does not diminish the value, any more than the short duration of a flower can take away from the sweetness of its perfume, the brilliancy of its colours, or the exquisite delicacy of its petals.

There are several misconceptions respecting the scope and purport of the subject under discussion which must be cleared away. " The veterinary art," for example, and " the art of verifying dates," are quite foreign to it. In the affectation of applying the term universally, the origin of Art has been forgotten. Art is of noble birth, but it is easily debased. We lay it down then as a principle, that just as Morality and Reason are each indivisibly *one*, so Art is indivisibly *one*. Their institutions are various and mutable, but amongst all nations morality is the same, and the method of reasoning the same. All human beings are born barbarians ; but they possess an aptitude for comprehending the invariable rules of morality, and an aptitude for reasoning and employing their reason for self-preservation, for defence, possession, and enjoyment. These three faculties,— that of comprehending the Arts, of teaching and practising Morality, and of acting according to Reason,—belong exclusively to man.

A dog makes no distinction between a post and a statue,

between a painting by Titian and a piece of blank canvas; and if birds ever pecked at painted grapes it must have been because Greek birds were decidedly different from ours. If, as the story goes, Alexander's horse neighed on seeing his master's portrait, Alexander's horse must have been something more than a brute. But there is no savage that does not see in a statue the representation of a being with which he is acquainted. But will the savage distinguish between a statue by Phidias and a block of stone that pretty closely resembles a man? No.

He will connect but one idea with both of these images, an idea entirely independent of its value in point of material execution. As a child he was told, "This rudely carved block is the god who rules the fate of battles, who will give thee victory over thine enemies if thou wilt bring him fruits every day." This block, shapeless though it be, is in his eyes a superior being: he endows it with feelings, he fears it, he sees it in his dreams, he sees it in battles; his imagination gives it form and passions. If the savage be a Hindoo or an Egyptian, he will soon aspire to make his god in material form such as his imagination depicts him. Nor is it an imitation of the beings with whom he is familiar that will satisfy him. To what purpose would be a mere copy of nature? To realise his ideal he puts an animal's head on the body of a man; gives his god ten arms, and paints him red or blue. He has been struck with the haughty, noble, or fierce expression of some bird of prey: he takes the principal features and exaggerates them: he instinctively exceeds the lineaments which nature has traced, and he places this head upon the body of his god of battle. No one dreams of objecting, and the myth is accepted by all. But to be permanently respected, the deity must be colossal; it must be imposing in point of size and semblance of physical power as well as in virtue of the combination of ideas which gave it birth; or it must be enclosed within a darksome place, far from vulgar observation: it is hewn in a rock or placed in the innermost recess of a narrow crypt approachable only by traversing several successive grottos, diminishing as we advance. He who embodies this idea of divinity assumes that his fellows will be struck with awe and respect in penetrating into these subterranean chambers. He experiences these feelings himself, though the idol is the work of his own hands. Whilst he is labouring at it he will be influenced only by the thought of embodying a product of his imagination; he will see nothing beyond his chisel and his stone; but from the day when his idol is completed and placed in its grotto he will fear it quite as much as his neighbour who has had no hand in the work, and will worship it with the same devotion. The artist becomes the dupe of his own creation; he loses sight of the rough stone which he has carved into shape, and sees only the realisation of his idea. The material labour is no more remembered : and his work is as much *his* god as it is that of his brethren.   Nor let it be imagined that this tendency of the human mind exists only under the conditions of primitive culture : it is natural to all human beings, and exists in all generations.   The intelligent child that makes a doll out of a piece of wood will associate with this rough image ideas and feelings which it cannot entertain towards the handsome doll fresh from Giroux's : it gives the doll a name, and takes it to bed with it : sometimes (and we have often remarked the fact) the image thus made is nothing but a strange medley of indescribable forms, some dream of that childish mind which it longs to express, and which none else can render aright.   And this desire, this craving, is Art.   Art is therefore the form given to a thought ; and the artist is he who in creating that form succeeds in conveying by it the same thought to the minds of his contemporaries. To the architect, Art is the expression in the world of sense, the embodiment visible to all, of a craving that has thereby found its satisfaction.

Even in our present civilised state, do we not see children or uncultivated persons prefer an imperfect conventional picture to a really good engraving, and attach to this inferior production ideas which a more finished work fails to suggest to them ?   Now is this tendency to be despised as the result of ignorance ?   We think not.   It is a feeling springing from a pure source ; a natural craving : without proper guidance it leads, it is true, to barbarism.

This instinctive craving, which impels men to make idols, must be defined : it arises from a combination of ideas :—(1) There is the attachment we feel to the product of our own skill and labour,—the feeling of vanity which accompanies a sense of creation ; (2) the idea of special sanctity which the object requires by consecration ; (3) the consciousness of having embodied the idea of divinity in creating something that transcends nature.   The Hindoo who has made a monster with an elephant's head and ten arms, is persuaded that the object he has produced is supernatural, and consequently divine.   His neighbours on beholding this idol will experience a feeling of dread : to them it will be the expression of the power of the divinity.   All nations have begun by making monstrosities before attempting to imitate nature.   Among the Greeks the earliest heads of Medusa have an enormous mouth, and tusks like the wild boar.   But when a nation like the Greeks unites with those primitive instincts in which Art originates, the love of the Beautiful, and moreover an aversion for what is ugly, inharmonious, discordant, and vulgar,—that people reaches the acme of

Art. The Greeks ended by making of the hideous Gorgon's head a mask of surpassing beauty : yet the sculptor always kept the same object in view, that of inspiring dread ; but as the world around him became more refined and intelligent, he perceived that deformity and exaggeration caused disgust rather than fear, and eventually succeeded in embodying for the multitude the idea of a being malevolent and terrible and yet not hideous. Nor did progress rest here : he became aware that the refined intelligence by which he was surrounded could be affected only by what was beautiful,—that beauty was the only garb in which his ideas would be favourably received.

A generation thus favoured in respect of Art may indeed, from the standpoint of our civilisation, be regarded as barbarous. It may have been given up to fanaticism, swayed by prejudice, and governed by very imperfect laws ; it may have lived under a tyranny insupportable in our eyes ; it may have possessed no well-regulated governmental machinery or police ; it may have held half its population in slavery, and have been torn by civil discords. But all this did not prevent Art from becoming a language universally understood.

We have endeavoured to show how the first glimmerings of Art dawn upon mankind. Imagination is its source ; the imitation of nature is its means of expression. Man cannot create, strictly speaking ; he can but bring together and unite the elements of the divine creation,—combining them into what may be called a secondary creation. But here we must make a distinction. Imagination would produce only vague and shapeless fancies if man did not possess a regulator within, obliging him to give to his fancies the semblance of reality. This regulator is his reason, or rather (for our language has no one word to express it) his faculty of reasoning.

This natural faculty enables him to see that the farther the creations of his imagination are removed from the reality of nature, the more necessary it becomes to give cohesion and harmonious form to the material combination destined to make those creations intelligible. Imagination conceives a centaur,—*i.e.* an impossible being, unlike anything that nature has ever produced,—an animal with four feet and two arms, two pairs of lungs, two hearts, two livers, two stomachs, and so on. A Red Indian may conceive such an absurdity ; but only a Greek would be capable of giving,—with the aid of the regulative faculty within,—a form of apparent reality to this impossible being. His reasoning faculty has led him to observe how the different parts of an animal are united and welded together ; he will therefore join the vertebral column of a man with that of the horse, the shoulders of the horse will give place to the hips of the man. He joins the abdomen of the man to the breast of the quadruped with such perfect address that the most experienced critic would imagine he was contemplating a correct and delicate study from nature. The impossible becomes so like reality that even now we think of the centaur as living and moving, as well known to us as the dog or the cat. The physiologist,—Cuvier in hand,—comes and proves that this creature, which you know as well as if you had seen it running in the woods, could never have existed,—that scientifically, it is a chimera,—that it could neither walk nor digest,—that its two pairs of lungs and its two hearts are the most ridiculous of suppositions. Which would be the barbarian, the savant or the Greek sculptor? Neither : but the criticism of the savant shows us that Art and the Knowledge of facts,—Art and Science,—Art and Civilisation,—may hold their course utterly apart. What matters it to me as an artist that a man of science proves to me that such a being cannot exist, if I have the consciousness of its existence ; if I am familiar with its gait and its habits ; if my imagination pictures it in the forests ; if I endow it with passions and instincts ? Why rob me of my centaur? What will the man of science have gained when he has proved to me that I am taking chimeras for realities ? Most certainly the Greeks of Aristotle's time knew enough of anatomy to be aware that a centaur could not actually exist ; but they respected the Arts in an equal degree with Science, and would not suffer the one to destroy the other,—a sufficient proof, be it observed, that we have in them a people which, for us artists at any rate, is not barbarous. In the statuary of the Greeks, how many irregularities does science disclose to us ! how many faults does the anatomist discover ! Whence then that nobility which casts a halo around these works ? How is it that a Greek statue in a museum full of competing objects of interest,—though mutilated, out of place, in a false light, and mounted on a pedestal often absurdly inappropriate,—still maintains an aspect of grandeur which makes all neighbouring sculpture seem clumsy and vulgar ? Are we to suppose that the Athenian women were all queenlike in their mien and in the delicacy and beauty of their forms? Certainly not. It was Art that imparted to those forms their inimitable air of distinction ; by Art, in fact, they were re-created.

Art, the same essentially, may present itself amongst other nations, in a different type of civilisation, provided always that it proceeds in the same manner, having its origin in the imagination of man, and using nature only as an instrument, with whose recondite appliances it must be well acquainted, but of which it must not be the slave. The sculptor who created the centaur, succeeded in giving his fiction an air of reality, by attentively studying the mechanism and the minute details of actual creation.

It was through his exceedingly close and delicate observation of nature that the sculptor obtained for his secondary creation recognition by all—by the poet even, who endows this being with distinctive manners, habits, and feelings. But are we to suppose that such creations belong only to primitive culture ? Does not Art exercise its functions in our day in giving verisimilitude to fictions ? and does it not always proceed in the same manner ?

You are a poet or novelist, for example : you wish to give reality to a fable ; you imagine something impossible,—a ghost, for instance ; but you know that your readers do not believe in ghosts ; how then will you contrive to make the story gain such a hold upon their minds as to leave the impression of a real event ? You will take pains to describe the locality of the fiction, to give an air of reality to every detail ; you will draw a picture in which every object shall have a palpable form, each of the *dramatis personæ* a clear and definite physiognomy and character ; in short, you will leave nothing vague or undefined ; and when your scene is thus prepared and your readers brought before it and made in imagination actors in your drama, you will introduce your apparition. Then all that would otherwise have seemed improbable in your story will assume an aspect of reality striking in proportion to the fidelity to nature which characterised your preliminary descriptions. This is Art.

Helen in the Iliad would be simply odious, in spite of her beauty, and the expedition against Troy one of the most ridiculous of enterprises, if the poet had not been an artist in the true sense of the word. Had he described the charms of Helen, comparing her to the lily and the rose, the reader would have remained unmoved, and would have despised Helen, her lover, her husband, and all the Greeks and Trojans together. The poet does better than describe to us the ivory whiteness of her skin and the sapphire of her eyes. He shows us Trojans seated in the repose and dignity of age, giving vent to bitter reproaches against the wife of Menelaus, the cause of their protracted sufferings and the loss of so many valiant warriors. Helen passes ; and instantly the old men rise and stand speechless in the presence of her majestic beauty. Art can produce nothing finer or more sublime than this. After this passage, there is not a reader of the Iliad who does not excuse Paris, or who fails to comprehend the fury which animates so many heroes; the origin of the war no longer seems ridiculous, and all its miseries and disasters are attributed to Destiny alone.

The Greeks, then, will always remain the kings of Art. They have enlarged, and, more than this, have elevated the senses, the instincts, the passions, and the feelings of man in always approaching them by their nobler side. They are never vulgar, even in depicting the most vulgar actions and objects. Their imitators have approached more or less nearly to this nobility in Art without attaining it; for, to equal them, it is not enough to know the secret of their art; the sympathy of a whole people, the same favourable atmosphere, would be requisite. *Odi profanum vulgus, et arceo*, says Horace; but Horace is an expatriated Greek surrounded by barbarians. No Athenian poet, architect, or sculptor could have said, " I hate the profane vulgar, and repulse them," for there were no barbarians in Athens.

The Art which we find in the poetry and sculpture of the Greeks meets us also in their architecture; for a people cannot be called artistic, unless Art pervades all the forms to which its hands and its intellect have given birth. Moreover, architecture, with music, is one of the forms of art in which man's creative faculty develops itself most independently. It has not, in fact, to seek its inspiration in natural objects, but to follow laws laid down with a view to satisfy certain requirements. Who makes these laws? Human reason, man's faculty of reasoning.

How and why does Art come to obtrude itself in the satisfaction of a physical requirement? Because Art is born with man, and is perhaps his primary necessity, when his natural tendencies are not diverted from their proper course. The following incident came under our own observation. A child breaks his dog's dish; his father says, " That is very stupid of you: Fido will no longer be able to be fed through your carelessness, and he will be starved to death : go to the market and buy another with your own money." The child is taken to the market; all the dishes he sees are painted, and he is unwilling to buy one. He goes back to his father and says, " I have not bought a dish for Fido."—" And why not?"—" Because all the dishes were covered with painted flowers; and if I give one of them to Fido, he will look at the flowers and forget to eat." There is more roguishness than *naïveté* in this ; but though the child has his own ends to serve in reasoning thus, he makes Art lend its influence to aid his argument, and thus renders a striking homage to it. Nobody has taught him that flowers painted on a dish could divert attention from the food that was on it ; it is an observation of his own ; he has discerned for himself that Art is a power,— that it engages the imagination. It is this artistic sentiment inherent in man which leads him to ornament his dwellings and the temples which he raises to the Deity, whether he has been born in a savage or a civilised condition.

Education alone can stifle this innate feeling, and unfortunately it too often effects this lamentable result in times which flatter themselves that they are not barbarous. The æsthetic instinct is perhaps the most delicate of human instincts ; for man possesses it as soon as he begins to see and to feel: it is easy to taint its purity; but to develop it is a difficult task at all times, particularly so under the conditions of a civilisation such as ours, which assumes to regulate the course of every individual according to certain conventions and dogmas.

Art among a given people cannot be directed; the utmost that can be done is to provide for it an atmosphere favourable to its development. This is a truth which Greek culture thoroughly comprehended, and this constitutes its greatest glory,—a glory that will not perish while the world endures.

Our age suffers from one disadvantage which we cannot remedy: we come too late. The ancients, by coming before us, have forestalled us in the possession of those simple and beautiful ideas which might otherwise perhaps have been our own. We cannot reduce things to one homogeneous system as they could; our task as artists is a very difficult one. We retain a multiplicity of antiquated notions and customs which belong to a bygone civilisation, together with the wants, customs, and requirements of our own times. Nevertheless we enjoy, like the ancients, the power of reasoning, and to a certain extent that of feeling; and it is on these two faculties that we must rely in our search after the True and the Beautiful. I am persuaded that the taste of the present generation might be improved by its acquiring the habit of reasoning. Observe in how many cases Reason confirms the judgment pronounced by Taste. Often—perhaps always— what we call taste is but an involuntary process of reasoning whose steps elude our observation. Acquiring taste is nothing else than familiarising ourselves with the Good and the Beautiful; but to familiarise ourselves with the Beautiful we must know how to *find it*,—that is to say, how to distinguish it. Now, it is our reasoning faculty that must help us to do this. We behold an edifice which at once attracts admiration, and we say, "What a beautiful building!" But this instinctive judgment does not content us who are artists. We ask ourselves, "Why is this building beautiful?" We want to discover the causes of the effect it produces on us, and to discover these we must have recourse to reason. Accordingly, we try to analyse all the parts of the work which charms us, that we may be able to proceed synthetically, when we in our turn have to construct. This analysis is difficult in the present day, perplexed as we are by prejudices, and by systems, every one of which assumes to be absolutely true. We shall, however, try to keep ourselves free from the influence of these prejudices and systems.

I think I have now made it plain how a people may be barbarous and yet possess arts in high perfection: how the *presence* of Art in any work of man may be recognised, and how it happens that Art may be found in a cottage or a grotto while it may be altogether absent from a palace or a temple of the most colossal dimensions. It remains for me to show what are the social conditions most favourable to the development of Art. It must be left to the following discourses to do full justice to the question, which requires to be treated at length. For the present, I must confine myself to laying down a few general principles.

The conditions under which the Arts have flourished or decayed have presented themselves in every form of society :—in the theocracy of Egypt, the changeable and capricious government of Greece, the rigorously organised dominion of Rome, the oligarchic or anarchical Republics of Italy, and under the feudal yoke of the Middle Ages. Art is, then, in no way influenced by what we term the form of government. On the contrary, the Arts develop themselves with vigour when they are, so to speak, riveted to the manners and customs of a people, and are their truthful expression. They decline when their connection with the habits of the nation is severed : when they become, as it were, a separate State or Institution, a kind of special study or culture. Then their sphere begins gradually to narrow, until we see them confined within the limits of the schools, and adopting a language no longer understood by the multitude. Art then becomes a stranger, occasionally entertained, but not the associate of everyday life. At last, it is dispensed with altogether, as being an encumbrance rather than a help ; it assumes to rule, but has no longer any subjects.

In order to live, Art must be free in its outward expression, though strictly regulated as regards principles ; it dies when its principle is disregarded, and its expression enthralled. Greek art died when the genius of its people was stifled by subjection to the Roman power,—when they undertook to build at Athens edifices like those of Rome. In times less remote we see the arts of the Middle Ages following step by step the manners of the people among whom they flourish ; we see them in the sixteenth century participating in the great intellectual movement of that period ; and under Louis xiv. they are still the living expression of the manners of the time; though, like these manners, they are exceptional,—a sort of theatrical representation which ended with the reign of that prince. Since then, our manners have been singularly modified, while Art has remained where it was in the seventeenth century as to its forms,—at least, so we are told. As to its principles, they have been scattered to the winds ; of this, our readers shall judge for themselves.

I observe that all the early civilisations exhibit nearly the same creative power in Art ; that they have all the same physical and intellectual cravings, in the expression of which they follow a similar order of simple and very limited ideas. Under the conditions of this primitive culture, the task of the artist is comparatively easy; he is not obliged to load his memory with those numberless details which now stifle the ardour of our early enthusiasm; nor is he bound to know all that *we* have to learn. It is easy to acquire a knowledge of the first of all sciences— that of the human heart—when all spend their lives in the fields or in places of public resort, and take part in everything that is going on,—as is the case among nations whose civilisation is in its infancy. Feelings, passions, vices, virtues, tastes, and wants are more plainly expressed among men in a primitive condition than among those who live in the midst of a highly advanced civilisation.

The artist, who to become such must have been an observer, benefits by a state of society whose simple mechanism is continually before his eyes. Thus, only to mention those ancient nations of whose arts we can accurately judge,—the Egyptians, the Eastern and Western Greeks and the Etruscans,—we discover in their statuary and painting an appreciation of *gesture*, the truthfulness and delicacy of which excite our highest admiration, and seem incapable of being surpassed. The same characteristics present themselves during the twelfth century in the West. Certainly the French painters and sculptors of the twelfth century did not learn their style from the bas-reliefs of Thebes or borrow it from Greek or Etruscan vases; but they obtained it by proceeding in the same manner as the artists of Egypt, Greece, and Etruria.

The observation of the Egyptian, the Greek, the Etruscan, and the Frenchman was directed to the same appearances. Now gesture (since this is the point we are considering) cannot be represented by the plastic arts, except when it is the expression of a feeling of a homogeneous kind,—in one word, a *simple* feeling; and simple feelings are only to be found among men in a primitive condition. In a highly civilised society human feelings are always complex and divided.

The death of his wife affects the savage only as the loss of a being with whom he has been accustomed to live; but to the sorrow which such an event occasions in the civilised man succeed other feelings,—perplexities, expectations of fortune originating or vanishing as its consequence, and all the details incidental to a change in a very complicated existence. How can so many different feelings be expressed by a single gesture? In fact, the gestures of men are a fair index of their grade of civilisation. Highly civilised men cease to employ them. But to what must the plastic artist then have recourse? He imitates those interpretations of gesture with which his predecessors in less civilised times have supplied him; so that, besides the disadvantage of imitating an interpretation, this second-hand copy appears false and exaggerated, and the artist fails to make himself understood. He affects *Style,* and discourses about it among people who have no idea what Style is; whereas, the primitive artist, without knowing it, infused Style into his works, and made himself perfectly understood.

Our remarks with regard to gesture apply to all else that belongs to the domain of Art. The architect has little difficulty in building a temple to the Divinity when that Divinity is a myth,—the impersonation of a passion or a principle, or even when it is a part of the organisation of the universe; for this myth has a palpable form, a visible appearance; it has attributes; such and such features harmonise with it, others do not. But to raise a temple to God,—as conceived by Christians,—is a much more difficult task; for in Himself He unites all things, He presides over all; He is the Beginning and the End; He is Immensity. How then can a dwelling be made for Him who is omnipresent? How can this abstract idea of the Divinity be interpreted in stone? and how can men be led to conceive of a building as the dwelling-place of the God of Christians? Yet the artists of the Middle Ages attempted this, and not without success. How did they set to work? They made their Christian church an epitome as it were of the Creation,—an assemblage of all created things, visible and invisible,—a sort of universal Epic in stone. If the undertaking was difficult, who shall censure those who attempted it?

We of the present day should therefore be modest, and hesitate long before bestowing the epithet "barbarous" on those who preceded us in the paths of Art. I am not one of those who despair of the present and look back on the past with regret. The past is past; but we must search into it sincerely and carefully; seeking not to revive it, but to know it thoroughly, that we may turn it to good account. I cannot admit that a reproduction of the forms of ancient art, of medieval art, or of that of the academies of Louis xiv., should be enforced upon the present,—simply because these forms were the expression of the manners of those times, and because our manners in the nineteenth century bear no resemblance to those of the Greeks or Romans, or to those of the feudal times, or of the seventeenth century; though the principles which guided the artists of the past are always true, always the same, and will never change as long as men are moulded of the same clay.

Let us then strive to submit ourselves anew to those unchangeable principles ; let us ascertain how our predecessors interpreted them in forms which were the real expression of the manners of those times ; and then we may freely pursue what is called the Path of Progress. Let us investigate, and use our reason as a guide, since this faculty at least remains to us amidst the chaos of modern times.

In our second Lecture we shall enter upon the main body of our subject. My readers will, I trust, excuse the length of this Introduction.

LECTURE II.

IN the preceding Lecture I endeavoured to give a definition of Art as I comprehend it,—to show how it develops itself, how it proceeds, and what are its various expressions. We must now limit the scope of our investigation, and occupy ourselves more especially with one of the forms of Art, namely, Architecture. I shall speak only incidentally of Architecture as it existed in times anterior to the Greek epoch ; my chief aim being to trace out for my readers the systems employed by the Western Nations,—those nations whose intellectual endowment and political and industrial growth have always tended towards the realisation of the one idea of incessant progress. The Greeks were the pioneers of Western Civilisation ; the first to throw off those swathing-bands by which the Oriental world seemed to be bound itself, and to wish to bind the rest of mankind for ever.

Let us then proceed at once to the consideration of our subject.

In Greece and in the Greek colonies there still exist monumental remains of great antiquity, and of immense interest to the Archæologist ; but with which I am not sufficiently familiar to expatiate on their history, origin, structure, or destination. I should not wish to incur the reproach of discoursing on subjects with which I am but imperfectly acquainted. Other instructors, far better versed than myself in archæological studies, will give to the world, elsewhere, the result of their researches ; and any remarks that I might offer respecting monuments which I have not examined, sketched, explored, or analysed, and of which I can only form an idea from the descriptions of others, or the

engravings that have been published, would have no such claim
to attention as the erudite discussions of those who have devoted
long years to their investigation. I shall confine myself as far
as possible to what I have seen,—to that, namely, which an
architect can duly appreciate and exactly describe. I must say,
moreover, that before venturing to pronounce opinions respecting
the origin, characteristics, defects, progress, and decline of any
art, I should require to have had leisure to study that art for
some time, to penetrate its mysteries, and to understand its
language. Having only a slight respect for preconceived ideas,
and not being gifted with the happy faculty of discoursing on
subjects with which I am not familiar, I prefer to be silent
on those topics,—a course which my readers will doubtless approve.

Many authors and professors have asserted that the stone
and marble temples of Greece exhibit in their structure the
tradition of a wooden construction. This hypothesis may be
ingenious, but it does not appear to me to be based on an
attentive examination of these monuments. Those who originated
it had no acquaintance, or at any rate a very superficial acquaintance, with the architecture of the Greeks, and, as always
happens in such cases, the authors who afterwards treated the
subject, found it easier to repeat that hypothesis than to examine
critically whether it should be accepted or questioned. " The
Greek temple," say most of the authors who have written on
the architecture of that nation, " derives its origin from a timber
building : the columns are trunks of trees stripped of their bark ;
the capitals, blocks of wood serving as caps projecting to receive
the beams : the triglyphs are the ends of the ceiling joists of the
portico : the slanting cornice-drip, the ends of the rafters of the
roof on which a board had been nailed ; and so with all the rest."
At first sight the theory appears plausible ; one difficulty,
however, meets us at the onset, which is this :—The primitive
timber edifices were circular in form : they were composed of
trunks of trees whose lower ends were planted in a circle, and
their tops brought together in a cone. Vitruvius himself,—an
author worth consulting for his antiquity,—Vitruvius, who
relates all the stories that were, as we may suppose, current in
the schools of his day respecting the origin of the Ionic and
Corinthian capitals,—Vitruvius, an indifferent critic, notwithstanding the respect we owe him,—in speaking of the primitive
wooden cabin, is far from ascribing to it the forms adopted by
the Grecian Doric temples. These are his words in the third
chapter of his second book :—" The men of early times, planting
forked trunks of trees in the ground and interlacing them with

branches, made walls which they plastered with clay. Some forming blocks of dried clay, constructed walls with these ; and then laying pieces of wood across they covered the whole with reeds and leaves as a shelter from the rain and the burning rays of the sun ; but as these coverings did not long withstand the bad weather of winter, they inclined the roofs, taking care to plaster them with clay that the rain might escape more readily."

And here the text of Vitruvius becomes still more interesting : "Now, in proof that the earliest buildings were constructed in this manner, we have the fact that precisely similar ones may be seen at the present day, among foreign nations, such as those of Gaul, Spain, Portugal, and Aquitania, where the houses are covered with shingles of split oak or with twigs. Among the inhabitants of Pontus and Colchis, where forests abound and trees are consequently plentiful, the buildings are constructed in the following manner :—Trunks of trees are laid lengthwise on the ground to the right and to the left, with a space between them equal to their length. Across the ends of these the natives lay other trees so as to enclose the whole space intended for the habitation. They then place on the four sides (of the square) more trees, which rest one upon the other at the corners, and thus keeping them plumb with those below, they pile them up to the required height of the tower. The spaces left between the trunks are filled in with chips and clay. For the roof they place trunks cut shorter and shorter in regular steps on each side, till they come to a pyramidal apex; and covering the whole with leaves and clay they form a hipped roof in their rude fashion. But the inhabitants of the country districts of Phrygia, who have no forests from which to draw their materials, hollow out small natural mounds, and then after making through the side, as well as circumstances allow, a hollow path to enter the cavity, they plant in the ground all round this cavity stout poles inclined together in a conical form and bound at the top ; they cover these with twigs and stubble, and heaping earth over this cone, they form habitations which are warm in winter and cool in summer. In other countries they cover the houses with reeds. . . . At Athens may still be seen a most curious relic of antiquity,—the roof of the Areopagus, composed of mud ; and in the Capitol the hut of Romulus, covered with thatch, is an existing illustration of this primitive mode of building." These examples show clearly enough that the primitive wooden hut bears not the slightest resemblance in its construction to the Greek temple ; for its form is almost always that of a cone or a pyramid. Indeed, the first idea which occurs to a man who desires to build himself a habitation with trees, is to fix them in a circle in the ground, and unite them at their summit. Even at the present day the savage tribes of Africa adopt this method.

But to come to details. Let us imagine that a man unacquainted with the resources of the art of building desires to place pieces of timber across the tops of wooden posts or uprights. Let us suppose that this man is intelligent, as the native tribes or aborigines of Greece undoubtedly were; and that he had already invented the axe at least, if not the saw and the mortising tool. The first idea that will occur to him with the view of getting the posts in line—which is essential if he means to connect them by a cross-piece—will be to square them; for it is

Improbable primitive timber construction.

not easy to place the trunks of trees in a straight line while in their natural form, which always presents some twist or inequality. Our intelligent workman then (for we must not forget that he *is* intelligent) has remarked that timbers bearing on their extremities, in a horizontal position, bend under their own weight, and still more if they are loaded; he therefore inserts between the top of his upright and the horizontal piece, the beam or lintel,—an intermediate piece to lessen its bearing. Will he employ for this purpose a square parallelopiped of wood, such as is shown at A figure 1,—a block of wood very difficult to procure, from its width being greater than the diameter of the uprights, and especially difficult to cut and fashion without the aid of the saw? Certainly not; for in addition to other objections, this capital, this square parallelopiped, will give but very little aid in supporting the bearing of the beams. He will not take so much trouble to obtain such an insignificant result, he will cut a piece of wood of some length, equal to the upright in width, and placing it between the head of the latter and the beam, he will succeed in effectually supporting the bearing of the beam, by means of the two considerable projections B, as indicated in figure 2. This is veritably a timber construction, and is such as we see imitated in stone in the ancient monuments of India, and even in those recently discovered at Nineveh. The square upright presents four awkward angles; the primitive constructor cuts them away and ultimately forms an octagonal prism—the cylindrical form is the very last a carpenter adopts for vertical supports, since it is that which requires the longest process,—the squaring of the wood being of primary

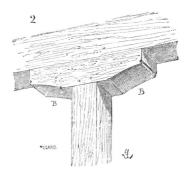

Probable primitive timber construction.

necessity in timber framing. An ordinary working carpenter would tell us this; and we may observe in passing, that it is always desirable, when endeavouring to establish theories respecting the origin of particular forms in art, to consult the crafts whose ordinary methods recall primitive modes of proceeding.

The primitive architecture of the nations of the remote East (the common source of all the arts) presents to us more than any other, both in its general configuration and in its details, veritable imitations in stone of a wooden structure; and these imitations are carried so far that even in monuments hewn in the rock, the Hindoo architects have made the ceilings simulate planks and joists. Many of the Chinese houses, to take another example, have wooden porticoes, the eave-plates of which are carried on posts accompanied by struts formed of curved timber, as shown in figure 3.

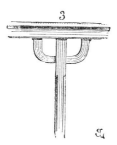

Chinese timber construction.

Now, in the crypts of Ganesa, at Cuttack, in India, may be seen pillars left in the solid rock which are of this form, figure 3 *bis.*[1]

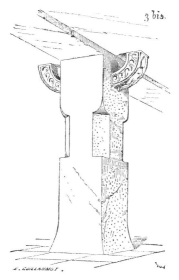

Stone pillar in imitation of timber construction, Cuttack, India.

[1] See *The Illustrated Hand-book of Architecture:* Being a concise and popular account of the different styles of Architecture prevailing in all ages and countries; by J. Fergusson. London, 1855, vol. i.

Others again, in one of the temples of Ajunta, present this form of structure, figure 3 *ter.*

Stone pillar in imitation of timber construction, Cuttack, India.

In both these examples the curved struts and the projecting caps which carry the beam, all hewn out of the solid rock, are evidently the tradition of a timber framing. The transition from the square of the base to an octagon, and then, in the example 3 *ter* to a sixteen-sided polygon, with the return near the top to the octagon and the square, is far more suggestive of processes applicable to fashioning and framing timber than of those employed in working stone. This is evident to all who have

endeavoured to contrive a timber support that shall be at the
same time stiff, firm on its base, and as much lightened as the
nature of the material will admit.

We all know the capitals of the ruins of Persepolis : many of
these affect the form indicated in figure 4. Now, in the same

4

Stone Capital—Ruins of Persepolis.

country,—in Assyria and Persia—peasants' huts of modern date
may be seen whose ceilings are carried on forked posts such as are
shown in figure 5, which beyond all doubt represent the origin of
that form of the stone capitals of Persepolis. This forked shape
has a double advantage ; it not only supports the beam or lintel in
front, but it also affords a resting-place between the two branches

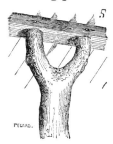

Forked Post.

of the fork for a piece of timber at right angles to the front,—serving
as a beam for the support of the floor joists which thus find their
place in the depth of the lintel. Figure 5 *bis* illustrates this
primitive disposition of a wooden structure in which the constructor had sought to do without the framing by mortise and
tenon which came into use when tools and the other appliances
for construction were improved. These are the wooden buildings
that must have been imitated in stone by the tribes of Asia. The
remains of their monuments, whether built of masonry or hewn
in the rock, prove this fact in the clearest manner possible. But
these methods of procedure have no connection with the Greek

temple. Shall we seek yet more striking examples, if such are possible? Let us consider those tombs in Asia Minor hewn in the living rock, and of which any one may form an idea by

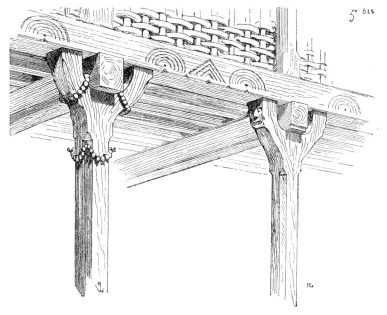

Ancient Asian timber construction.

referring to the engravings of them executed from the drawings of M. Texier—those crypt-like sepulchres whose portals represent and might be taken for timber constructions. The primitive edifices of Central America present to the attentive eye the very

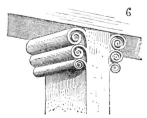

Form of ancient stone Capital suggested by carpenter's work.

same peculiarities;[1] for all civilisations in their commencement proceed in the same manner.

The imitation of construction in wood appears even in the

---

[1] Among others, those of Chunjuju, and of Zayi.

.

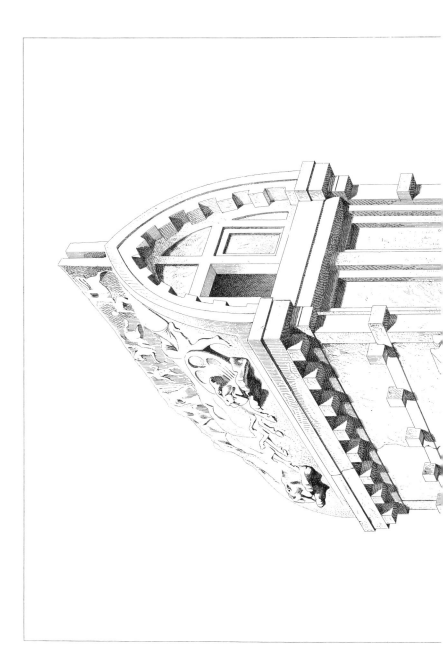

E. Vuillet. Le Bar. del.

L. Gaucherel. sculp.

Plate I.   Lycian Tomb (British Museum)

minutest details of these primitive edifices of the East : for instance we frequently see at the tops of pillars a succession of rolls one over the other presenting a decoration of the character shown in figure 6.

Is it not evident that these rolls are nothing more than the curled chips cut from the wooden post by the carpenter in the process of squaring it ? The ornaments represent strings of berries and a variety of those gravings which are so easy to execute upon wood, and of which all primitive peoples, who have abundant leisure, are so prodigal. Passing from details to the examination of complete buildings, we find in India certain sacred edifices of stone which are singularly suggestive of the wooden pyramid described by Vitruvius ;—a collection, namely, of tree trunks or of bamboos placed horizontally one upon another, and set back in steps from the base to the summit ;[1]—others which nearly resemble in shape immense baskets formed of bamboo interlaced, and adorned with garlands of berries, little figures, loops, and rings.

In India houses are still constructed with bamboo lattice-work

7

Indian lattice-work building.

placed upright, plastered with tempered clay and covered also with lattice-work thatched with leaves, straw, or rushes (figure 7). In the same country this very form is found reproduced in stone buildings of extreme antiquity. As a conclusion to this general review of timber constructions, let us look at that Lycian sarcophagus in the British Museum, which is a reproduction in a lasting material of a form of monument such as was undoubtedly made of wood in that country, at a very remote period. Is it not plainly an immense shrine of carpentry-work of which the pieces, the joinings and the notchings are apparent,—and even the very bearers by which it was to be carried ? Let us attentively examine the drawing, Plate I., of this curious monument, cut in three blocks of stone. Would not any one suppose it to be a production of carpentry, composed of posts, rails, spars, and

[1] The temple of Barolli, the pagoda of Canaruc, etc.

pannels ? Is it not evidently a wooden cover placed upon a sarcophagus hewn out of a block of marble ? If this tomb is not of
an extremely early period, as the sculpture upon it would lead
us to believe, it only demonstrates more clearly that when the
populations of Asia Minor and of Greece did imitate wooden
constructions in stone they expressed those constructions most
frankly : Here the modillions or mutules are not returned round
the ends as in the Greek temple : the uprights are square
instead of cylindrical ; the roofs are veritable framed gables
supporting the purlins that carry the roofing, which is curved and
not slanting, quite in conformity with the primitive notion of a
wooden building. The ridge itself represents two planks sculptured upon the sides which are exposed to view. The spars that
form the intermediate floor are made to clasp the longitudinal
rail to prevent any giving ; the spars of the upper floor are fixed
between two clips. The feet of the four uprights are held
on the two bearers by means of keys conspicuously indicated.
This monument reveals to us a very curious fact :—in the first
place, we see that in the early days of these nations the dead
were placed in a sarcophagus of stone or marble, which was
covered with a coffer or shrine of wood ; and next it shows us
that the Greek temple is a stone construction, and not the imitation of a construction in wood.

Here let me observe that although the immense Eastern
Continent, extending from China to the Caspian, the Black Sea,
and the Persian Gulf, owing to its lofty mountains, its noble
rivers, the wonderful fertility of its valleys, its extensive marshes
and favouring climate, furnished at all times a considerable
quantity of every kind of timber, such could never have been
the case with Greece. I willingly admit that its soil, barren
at present, may once have produced forests. But what were
these woods compared with those which grew so luxuriantly on
the continent of India ? Did Greece ever possess those gigantic
bamboo canes so well adapted for constructive purposes ? If
there ever existed in Greece forests of timber fit for building,
they must have been quickly destroyed. Let us then look at
the Greek Temple.

In the first place, what is the programme ? It is required to
build a *cella,*—an enclosed chamber,—and to surround it with
porticos, as well for its protection as to afford shelter. Nothing
can be simpler. Four walls with openings for doorways, and a
succession of vertical supports surrounding them, carrying lintels
which are sheltered by a projecting cornice :—over all, sloping
roofs to throw off the rain on the two sides which have no doorways. Reason alone has dictated this disposition. What, then,
are the means of execution ?

The architect seeks for a quarry in the immediate neighbourhood ; and he will find one at hand, for Greece and Sicily abound
in materials of a calcareous nature, and the Greek cities are
generally built on plateaus or the slopes of hills, and possess an
Acropolis,—that is to say, a rock naturally or artificially escarped,
—around which the habitations and public buildings are grouped.
Mountains and promontories which furnish abundant materials
exist in close proximity. Having secured his quarry, however,
the architect has none of those powerful appliances which
mechanical science has rendered familiar to us ; the arms of his
slaves are his only force ; he therefore endeavours to avoid as
much as possible the difficulties which accompany the transport
of very heavy blocks. Nevertheless, the employment of
materials of considerable dimensions is just what is prescribed to
him by the traditions of the art in the form in which he is
acquainted with it,—the art as he has received it from Egypt
and the East : the only system he recognises is that of the
column and lintel ; he is therefore obliged to seek some method
by which he may reconcile the exigencies of this form of art with
the means of execution placed at his disposal. This is how he
proceeds :—the difficulties by which he is surrounded will not
discourage him ; on the contrary, they will become the most
effective stimuli to his artistic genius. *Art* will profit by them.
The Greek architect thinks, and with reason, that the Cella of
his temple may be built with materials of small dimensions ; it is
merely a wall with two apparent faces,—one in the interior, the
other on the exterior of the temple. Two faces,—consequently,
from his point of view, two stones ; the construction of a wall of
ordinary strength, with materials which do not constitute its
whole thickness, but are composed of ashlar slabs having only
one external face, like two thick paving-stones set back to back,
would be wrong from the point of view of the constructor,
though right from that of the logician : now the Greek is above
all things a logician ; he therefore prepares in the quarry slabs of
ashlar, or stones intended to have only one external face. With
these ashlar slabs he will build his Cella. But he is aware that
these two faces form two unconnected walls ; so at regular
intervals, to tie them together, he inserts bonders, that is, long
stones forming parpaings. He requires vertical supports,—in
other words, columns ; he perceives that these isolated piers, to
present the appearance of perfect stability, should be composed
of blocks as large as possible. The quarries and the means of
transport at his disposal rarely enable him to erect monolithic
columns. He selects in the quarry the thickest beds he can find,
near to a declivity where the calcareous strata crop out. Upon
the upper surface of these beds he traces a circle whose diameter

is that of his intended columns : around it he sinks a deep trench wide enough for the stone-cutter to stand in ; and thus from the rock itself he detaches a cylinder. Having reached the lower surface of the bed, and completely worked out the excavation on the side of the declivity, he upsets the cylinder, that is, turns it over on its side, and then rolls it down as a huge disk to the foot of the escarpment. There he sinks a square hole in the centre of each circular face of the disk, and in these holes he fixes two pivots or axles ; then by means of a timber frame and cables he rolls the column drums to the site of the temple.

Thus it was the difficulties attendant on the obtaining of his material that first obliged him to adopt the cylindrical form for the largest-sized blocks as being the most easy of transport. This is no hypothetical description ; for any one may see the quarries near Selinuntum in Sicily, which were used by the inhabitants of that Greek colony. In this place, which even now goes by the name of *Cava di Casa* (building-stone quarry), are exhibited all these successive operations. Here may be seen, still unmoved from their calcareous bed, cylinders of enormous size,—no less than twelve feet in diameter and from seven to ten feet in height ; others which have rolled by their own weight to the foot of the hill,—others again on the road to their destination, with the square holes sunk in the centre of their circular faces. The cruel destruction of the populous city of Selinuntum by the Carthaginian invaders caused these blocks to be left in the very act of transportation ; and no ruin can excite a more lively emotion than these still fresh and vivid traces of human labour, interrupted, as it were, but yesterday.

But it is not only the columns of the temple which require blocks of great bulk. The lintels that will bear from column to column must also be of considerable size if the temple is of large dimensions. In the extraction of these blocks the Greek architect will proceed in the same manner as when he was preparing to build the walls of the Cella ; he will compose them of two long stones placed side by side, leaving a vertical joint between the two, with their faces one on the exterior, the other on the interior of the portico. Experience soon shows him that this method presents an advantage independent of the facilities it affords to the transport of the blocks. It must be observed that all calcareous stones, marble included, are liable to have flaws, or ruptures across the bed, which are invisible at the time of extraction, but which discover themselves under the strain of superincumbent weight, and occasion a fracture which in a lintel is irremediable ; whereas two lintels placed side by side, have two chances to one in favour of resistance, for if one of them is defective, its twin brother may withstand the strain, and thus prevent an immediate fall. And in point of fact this method is employed without exception by the Greek architect whenever he employs calcareous stones whose strength is not very considerable, such as those of Sicily. The materials for his temple being all brought to the site, the architect will elevate and place them in position by means of very ingenious contrivances. Thus, for the cylindrical drums of the columns he will make use of the square hole cut in the centre of one of the beds, and, giving it a dove-tail section, he will suspend them by means of the *lewis;* or, working back the rounded surface a little, he will leave two projecting tenons which

Greek mode of hoisting the lintel stones.

will serve him as a catch for the rope, by whose aid the stones will be lifted one upon another; for as these blocks are laid close fitting, without either wedges or mortar, they will reach the place of their destination in a suspended position,—and when once set, it will be no longer possible to displace them. All the means of suspension must then be so contrived as to leave their bed joints entirely free. The capitals will be easily raised vertically by means of the projecting corners of the abacus. As to the blocks composing the lintels which are laid end to end,— which are long and not very thick, and have two joints neces- sarily hidden, one or two faces in view, and an under bed or

soffit also in view,—they must be secured and hoisted by the two
ends ; the architect will prepare for the suspension of these by
sinking in the two vertical end joints of each block a channel
deep enough for a strong rope to pass freely through it as shown
in figure 8. When the stone is raised to its place he will withdraw the rope from its groove. The Greeks attained wonderful
perfection in the setting of close-jointed masonry. In this kind
of masonry the blocks could not be wheeled on stages of scaffolding at different heights, and let down upon wedges with the
crow-bar, according to our method ; they had to be brought
exactly over their intended position, in order to be lowered
gently and carefully into place. Had they rested awry on their
bed, the hoisting engines would not have been strong enough to
detach them again, by reason of the close adhesion of the two
horizontal perfectly plane and close-fitting surfaces. The only
means by which it was possible at that time to secure this
accuracy in setting, was the use of immense cranes which were
successively brought and stayed first over each column, and then,
—when all these were erected,—over the spaces between the
columns, in order to hoist the lintels, triglyphs, metopes, cornices,
etc. We must remember, *à propos* of this, that the Greeks are
a maritime people, and that, as such, they must have very early
possessed engines of construction which were intelligently, simply,
and perfectly combined.

Having briefly described the material means of its execution,
let us now proceed to the examination of the building itself ; let
us watch the construction of a Greek temple. The walls of the
Cella being built, and the columns raised, the architect perceives
that the horizontal blocks,—the lintels which have to bear from
one column to another,—may on account of their length, give
way under the weight they carry ; so, upon the summit of the
columns he places projecting blocks,—in a word, *capitals.*

The abacus of the Grecian Doric capital is square ; two of its
fronts, by their wide projection, support in an equal degree the
bearing of the architrave ; but the two others—those which face
outside and inside—support nothing. If the Grecian Doric
capital had been designed in imitation of a wooden capping,
these two interior and exterior projections, extending beyond
the face of the beam, would have had neither object nor meaning,
as I have previously explained. In a stone construction, however,
these projections are amply justified. In fact, the largest blocks
composing the Grecian Doric order are necessarily the architraves or lintels, bearing from column to column ; for if the
columns can be raised in drums more or less numerous, it is quite
otherwise with the architraves, which must have a length equal
to the distance between the centres of the columns, and a height

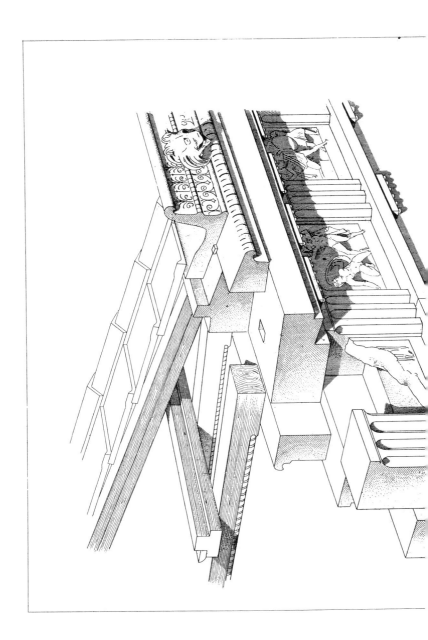

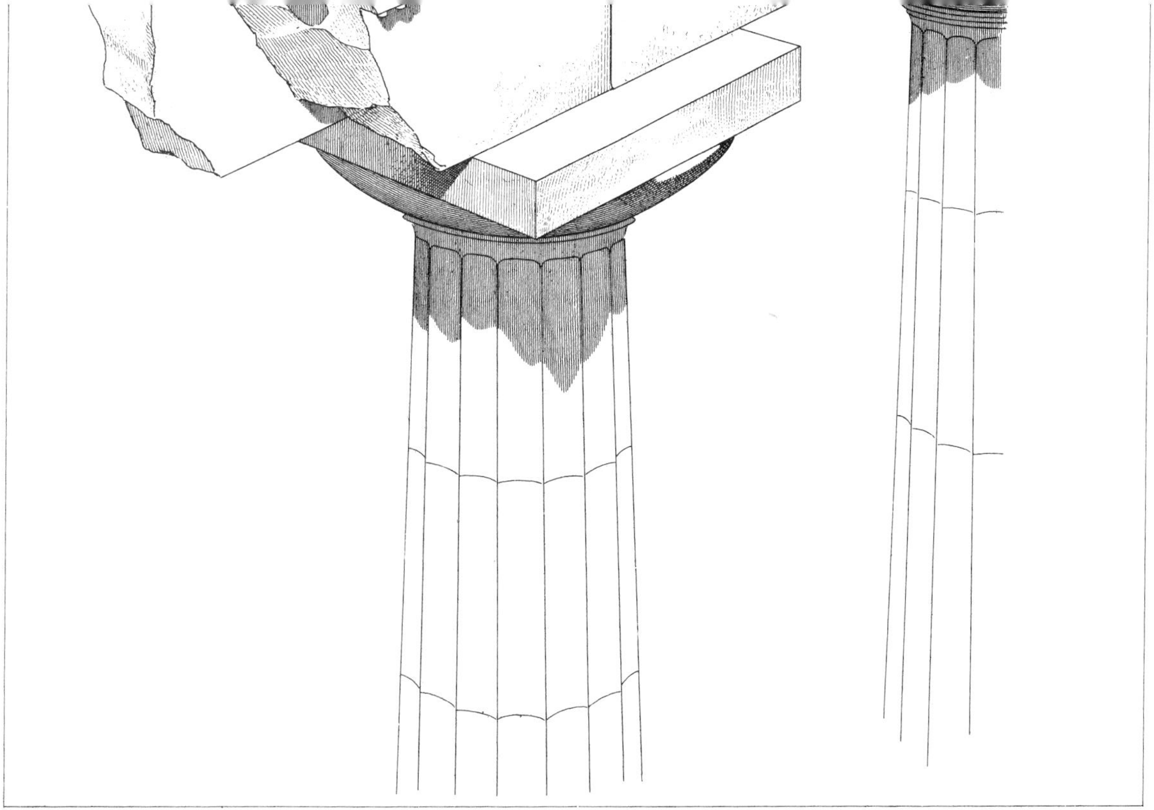

E. Viollet Le Duc del. — L. Gaucherel sculp.

PLATE II. Doric

sufficient to present a great resistance. But we have just seen that these blocks are lifted by their two concealed ends, and laid with close joints. To lower such weighty blocks exactly upon their resting-places, that is, upon the abaci of the capitals, it was essential that the operation should be performed with skill, precision, and certainty, so as not to risk a deviation of the column from the perpendicular. The interior and exterior projections of the capital then became extremely serviceable ; they afforded means for placing balks of timber along the back and front, which kept the columns in line, and rendered them mutually supporting ; they also enabled the stone-setters to stand on either side of the lintel, without need of other scaffolding, to guide the blocks and lower them gently on to the capitals without danger of mistake, because the two balks had left between them just the space of those lintels.

We should observe that all the primitive builders are chary of scaffolding ; they do not like, and the Greeks least of all, to perform labour which is to all appearance useless, that is to say, which is to leave no trace. Some of the Greek temples remain unfinished, and may still be seen as they were left in course of being dressed down,[1] that of Segesta for example ; and it will readily be perceived, even by those who are but little versed in the practice of our art, that the materials which compose these buildings were raised by the simplest means as regards their suspension and setting, and that the builders have endeavoured as far as possible to make the building itself serve as a scaffolding, by providing projections as resting-places for timbers laid longitudinally or transversely as the case required. Moreover, these builders take good care never to elevate large blocks when they can avoid it. Above the lintels or architraves there are no longer found any but stones of comparatively small dimensions ; and it is evident that to avoid too great expense and difficulty, the Architecture itself cedes to the means of execution. The frieze which surrounds the architrave is merely a succession of small blocks, between which are placed slabs on edge, with a filling in at the back, often in several layers. The cornice projects but little, and does not bond over the whole thickness of the frieze ; it has only just tail sufficient to prevent its overbalancing. (See Plate II.) But the builder, while economising his materials, compensates by his intelligence for any defect they may present in point of strength or durability ; for instance, he observes, that according to a physical law, the

---

[1] The Greeks erected the columns of their temples, and other parts requiring equal accuracy of outline, with blocks which, with the exception of their beds and joints, were only roughly hewn into shape ; and these were afterwards dressed down to the required form, in the same way as the French masons proceed now when they are building with soft stone.—(*Translator's note.*)

rain-water follows the under horizontal surface of the cornice projection ; he therefore makes it a drip, that is, he gives a slant to this under surface in order to oblige the water to drop the moment it reaches the edge.

These are improvements in which man's faculty of reasoning only has taken part. It might be supposed that he would rest content here. Not so. Art intervenes in its turn. The building is erected beneath a clear sky, through which, during ten months of the year, a brilliant sun pours down its light. The artist quickly observes that the cylindrical pillars of his temple appear, by an optical delusion, larger at their summit than at their base. This is as shocking to his reason as it is to his sight ; he converts these cylinders into truncated cones. The requirement of stability had, perhaps, already obliged him to adopt this diminution of the shafts. He further observes that the intermediate blocks,— the capitals supporting the lintel,—seem to crush the column by their mass ; he leaves them their square form in the upper part, where it answers to a requirement of stability, and works away the under part in such a manner as to pass from the shaft of the column to the square abacus with a curve.

The artist, however, is not yet satisfied with his work : the columns appear flat when in full light, faint and ill-defined when in shade. He therefore re-works the surface of the shaft in a series of vertical facets ; and it is not long before he decides to hollow out these facets so as to form flutings sufficiently deep to catch the oblique rays of light on their edges, yet not deep enough for these edges to be inconvenient or dangerous to persons passing. And thus the sun's rays, by repeating on each of the shafts a series of vertical lights and shadows, restore to them the importance which they lacked while they were merely cylindrical. The artist's own feeling, moreover, tells him that to impress the eye with the value which a particular form should assume, the principal lines of that form should be repeated ; just as the musician feels that if he would impress the ear with a particular phrase, it must be repeated several times in the course of his composition. Now the vertical line of the column increases in importance in proportion to the number of times this line is reproduced upon its surface. The artist, however, also knows that nothing more is needed than to make himself understood, and that he must not fatigue the senses by a too frequent repetition : he therefore sinks in the shaft of his column only the number of flutings required by the effect contemplated.

The columns, their capitals, and the lintels being now in place, the architect, as I have just observed, is no longer compelled to employ materials of large dimensions : he may place on the architrave of his temple blocks of moderate size ; and this he does not fail to do. First, over each joint of this architrave crowned by a fillet, and over the centre of each intercolumniation he places blocks at some distance apart so as to weigh on the architrave as lightly as possible. But the artist is a Greek; he is anxious that his judicious combination should be manifest—comprehended by every one. On the external face, therefore, of each of these stones, which stand between the architrave and the cornice, and form, as it were, so many small detached pillars, he cuts a triglyph: in other words, he sinks on their visible surface upright flutings which express, as he feels, something which *supports weight;* and his feeling is the more correct, and his reasoning the more just, inasmuch as he proceeded in a precisely similar manner when he sought to express the function of vertical support in the columns. The triglyph is also a vertical support, and this he distinctly indicates.

The Greek architect possesses the merits and the failings of the reasoner: he insists upon making it apparent to every eye that the various parts of his edifice have each a useful and necessary function; he will not have it said that he has sacrificed anything to caprice; he is not content with knowing that his building is solid,—he must make it appear such. But though he never conceals the means he employs, his artistic instinct leads him to invest each part of his edifice with a form admirably adapted both to the place it occupies and the effect it is designed to produce: his good taste forbids that pedantic repetition which wearies the public, and gives it a disgust for Reason by the very abuse or excess of reasoning.

To close the openings which remain between the triglyphs, the architrave, and the cornice, he inserts therein slabs set on edge and recessed back; previously requesting his brother, the statuary, to sculpture bas-reliefs upon these stones thus enframed between the triglyphs, architrave, and cornice. Plate II. illustrates the general arrangement of this so truthful construction; —which is not, as I judge, the tradition of the timber framing of some remotely distant age, as some have contended,—but a veritable stone construction. The columns, by their cylindrico-conical form, the capitals with their square abacus, the entablature with its triglyphs, its inserted metopes, and its throated cornice, and the way in which all these members rest upon one another, indicate stone throughout,—quarried, worked, hoisted, and made manifest by reason of its nature and of the function which it fulfils. Wood also plays its part in the Greek temple; but it is a part altogether secondary,—quite distinct from the stone construction. The Greeks had too much good sense ever to have placed upon the architrave, or the beams,—admitting that the architraves were primitively beams of wood,—joists

whose scantling would be given by the triglyphs, merely to cover
—what? A portico of seven or ten feet in width.
———Every fact, moreover, without exception, comes in to disprove
this supposed origin. The joists of the wooden ceiling of the
portico, or the lintels and marble slabs intended for its covering,
and which form a ceiling, are never placed on the architrave, but
invariably on the frieze,—that is to say, above the triglyphs;
the space reserved for them and the projection on which they
rested are still to be seen in every existing temple. This space
indicates only timbers of a scantling proportionate to their bearing,—namely, from 6 to 9 inches square, or a resting-place just
sufficient to receive the horizontal slabs of marble when that
material takes the place of timber-work.

Just as the triglyphs are taken for the ends of joists, so the
rain-drip of the cornice is supposed to represent the rafter-ends.
But even if this hypothesis has a semblance of probability on the
two lateral sides of the temple,—what possible signification could
rafter-ends have on the fronts below the pediments? We have
too high an opinion of the good judgment of the Greek artists to
allow that they could ever have committed so flagrant an offence
against reason and common sense. If the rain-drip did indicate
the projection of the rafters beyond the frieze, they would not
have put a similar drip at the base of the pediment. And
beneath the projections of the cornice of this pediment they
would have placed indications of the ends of the purlins; since,
according to the belief in question, they so scrupulously represented in their stone construction each single piece of timber.
Plate I., representing a Lycian tomb, which is really an imitation
of a wooden construction, exhibits no such absurdity: the purlins
are plainly indicated on the gable ends, and the joists of the
ceiling which supports the roof are not returned along the fronts
of these gables; they only exist on the lateral faces.

The Greek temples are buildings of stone in which the system
of the lintel is worked out in accordance with reason and taste:
why not take them simply for what they are? why contend that
Greeks, the inventors of logic—men gifted with refined æsthetic
sensibility,—amused themselves with simulating in stone a construction of wood,—a thing essentially monstrous? That such
imitations have occurred among the Hindoos, that they have influenced the architecture of the Assyrians and of the inhabitants
of Asia Minor, is possible; but to suppose it among the Western
Greeks is to misunderstand their genius altogether.

It is by explanations such as these of the derivations of
Ancient and Medieval architecture,—more ingenious than well-
considered—that the course of architectural study has come to
be misdirected, and consequently the mind of the architect per-

verted. In explaining buildings we think it a commendable principle to take them for what they really are, and not for that which we should wish them to be. This supposition that the Greek temple is an imitation in stone of a wooden hut is of the same order as that which refers the architecture of our Gothic churches to the forest avenues of Gaul and Germany. Both are fictions well adapted to amuse the fancy of dreamers, but very hurtful, or at best useless, when we are called upon to explain the derivations of an art to those whose vocation it is to practise it.

The triglyphs fulfil the purpose over the architraves of a clerestory. They are uprights of stone, relieving the pressure on the architrave, as we have said, by their separation and the space intervening between them. It would even appear that originally the intervals between the triglyphs were often left open.

In the tragedy of *Iphigenia in Tauris*, Orestes and Pylades wish to gain an entrance into the temple of Diana to carry off the statue of the goddess. Pylades proposes to penetrate into the cella through the openings left between the triglyphs. " Look," he says to Orestes, " into the interval of the triglyphs, where there is space enough for the body to pass through."[1] This translation word for word from the Greek text does not say " between the triglyphs;" but the speakers are not architects, and in common parlance we might say " in the triglyphs," or " in the interval of the triglyphs," as we now say " in the balusters," meaning " between the balusters of a balustrade." This passage of Euripides possesses a double interest for us : for the reference here cannot be to the intervals left between the triglyphs placed over the columns, as through these the two heroes would have only gained entrance into the open portico, and it was easier to pass between the columns than through the holes left between the triglyphs : evidently the text must refer to the triglyphs placed on the wall of the cella, where indeed they are often to be found. May not these openings left between the triglyphs placed at the top of the cella wall have been intended to admit light and air into the inner enclosure? This hypothesis would favour the supposition that the cella was completely covered in.

Let us revert to the structure of the Greek temple. The Greek architect recognises the necessity of symmetry : it is an instinct of the human mind ; but he does not allow that this instinct should over-ride reason. In building his temple he began with the cella,—the enclosure reserved for the divinity,— making it an independent construction, a walled enclosure of

---

[1] *Iphigenia in Tauris*, line 114,—
    " Look within the triglyphs," etc.

inconsiderable dimensions, around which he placed the columns of his portico, leaving between this enclosure and the columns a space for perambulation wide in proportion to the size of the cella. He troubles himself little as to whether the centres of the pilasters at the corners of the cella (the antæ) correspond with those of the columns of the portico. He has perceived that practically this coincidence of centres cannot be appreciated. His sole concern is so to arrange his columns that the wooden ceiling may rest upon the wall of the cella and the internal friezes of the portico. This consideration is his only guide. His reason leads him still further to disregard what are called the rules of symmetry; the angles of his portico engross his attention, he sees their isolated columns, which have to support a heavier weight than the rest, he foresees that if one of the architraves bearing on this angle should happen to break, it will have the effect of forcing the column outwards. Reason suggests to him the prudence of allowing a less space between the angle-column and the two neighbouring ones than he has allowed between the other columns of the portico, and of increasing the diameter of this angle-column ; and what his reason suggests, that he follows, despite of the rules of symmetry. This difference between the centres of the columns enables him to put a triglyph at the angle of the frieze (which is equally accordant with reason, since the triglyph is a point of support, and if points of support are anywhere necessary they are especially so at the corners of a building), without thereby sensibly increasing the spaces between the three last triglyphs.

These difficulties in the general arrangement being solved, the architect proceeds to the consideration of details : he has observed that when it rains, the water trickles down the vertical face of the external cornice, and mingling with the dust, leaves brown stains which darken the crown of his edifice, whose extreme verge he desires to see stand out lustrous against the azure of the sky. He lays on this cornice a gutter of marble or terra-cotta, furnished at regular intervals with projecting gargoyles,—and thus succeeds in throwing the water off from the face of the cornice : but this gutter, itself exposed to the rain, soon becomes weather-stained, and he overlays it with carving or painting to render this defect less apparent. The more the born artist observes, the wider does the field of observation extend itself before him. Now the observation of the artist and that of the savant differ in their results. The savant observes in order to compare,—to draw conclusions,—in a word, *to know.* The artist observes, but he does not stop at conclusions : his conclusions lead him on to augment, modify, or neutralise the effects produced by physical laws,—to struggle in concert with or in opposition to them. The artist observes that a cylinder brightly illumined presents only one light and one shade : he modifies this effect by distributing the light and shade by means of flutings ; and thus compels the natural light to round his columns. He observes that the wide abacus of his capital casts, during the greater part of the day, a lengthened shadow over the top of the column, and that this shadow, rendered very transparent by the direct reflection of the light on the ground below, is so luminous that the junction of the capital with the column can no longer be distinguished ;—that this effect gives an appearance of weakness and indefiniteness which deprives this member of the architecture of the appearance of solidity it ought to preserve above the vertical lines of light and shadow produced by the flutings ; he then sinks several deep lines at the point of junction of the capitals with the columns ; and to give these lines greater vigour of effect he paints them a dark tone, and so destroys an effect of shade that shocks his artistic sense. He observes that the reflected lights in shadows produced by a vivid light are themselves luminous. He has observed that the shadow under the abacus whose faces suddenly arrest the light is hard,—that the transition is abrupt,—that the summit of the column is lost to the eye, and that the architrave has the appearance of resting,— not upon a substantial form, but upon a void ; still he must maintain for the capital a very decided projection ; his constructive reason requires it. How then does he proceed ? He seeks and discovers that profoundly considered and delicately rendered form,—the circular torus supporting the abacus :—he curves this torus sharply inwards at its junction with the abacus, in such a manner that at the points of the tangent the rounded edge of the torus shall catch a strong light, which, reproducing that of the abacus, fades away in graduated half tints towards the neck. In this way he blends the over vivid light of the abacus with the too complete shadow which is cast by it : again, unsatisfied with the first result, he gives his curve an inclined, almost conical, form, as far as the neck, in order that its surface may receive as much as possible the lights reflected from the ground on the neighbouring walls illuminated by the sun. And thus by means of a delicate observance of light, of shadows, and of reflections, he utilises these natural effects with incomparable intelligence, to satisfy the requirements of his eye, and to preserve, even in appearance, the forms which his reason has led him to adopt as the best and the most solid.

Every student of Architecture is more or less familiar with the Greco-Doric order, and can easily verify the justness of the observation of the Greek architect. With regard to the forms adopted in Greek Architecture for the exterior of the building, it is evident that their generating principle was the sun. The Greek artist perceives that, seen from a certain distance, the columns of his temple, though fluted, do not stand out distinctly against the wall of the cella when they are illuminated from a direction perpendicular to it;—that their lights merge into the light which falls upon the cella, and that the shadows cast by the columns on the upright wall behind them completely derange, in appearance, the harmonious distribution of the solids and voids,—that is to say, of the columns and the spaces between them. The architect then calls to his aid the Painter, and bids him overlay this posterior wall with some strong colour which absorbs the light,—a brown or a red,—and to avoid any contradiction, even in appearance, with the actual structure of his edifice, he requires him to trace on this wall, at even distances, and with a light colour, fine horizontal lines,—which recall to the eye the fact that the wall is built in horizontal courses,—and, seen between the columns, whose bright lines are all vertical, serve to distinguish very clearly the posterior construction from the anterior supports. So necessary was this application of colour to the exterior of buildings in a country where the atmosphere is of marvellous transparency, that if we view the temple of Theseus at Athens (for instance) in full sunshine, now that it has lost its paintings, we shall find it impossible to distinguish the lights of the column from those shed on the walls of the cella;—these lights on different planes mingle together and appear as if thrown upon one single surface.

If we take separately all the members of a Greek temple and study them individually, as well as in their direct relation to the whole, we shall invariably perceive the influence of those intelligent and delicate observations which attest the presence of art, —that exquisite sentiment which subordinates every form to reason, not indeed to the dry and pedantic reason of the geometrician, but to reason as directed by the senses and by observation of the laws of nature.

This very brief review of the modes of procedure among the Greek artists makes it sufficiently evident that if the Parthenon is in its place at Athens, it is but an absurdity in Edinburgh, where the sun prevails over the mists only for some days in the year;—it sufficiently proves to us, we believe, that had the inhabitants of Edinburgh been gifted by nature with senses as acute as those with which the Greeks were endowed, they would have proceeded in a manner quite different from that in which the latter proceeded on the shores of the Ægean or the Mediterranean. ART does not therefore reside in this or that form, but in a principle,—a logical method. Consequently no reason can be alleged for maintaining that one particular *form* of art is Art, and that apart from this form all is barbarism; and we are justified in contending that the art of the Iroquois Indians or that of the French in the Middle Ages may not have been barbarous. What is desirable to ascertain is, not whether the Indian or the Frenchman has more or less nearly approached the forms of Greek Art, but whether they have proceeded in the same manner as the Greeks;—and whether, being in a different climate,—having other wants and other customs,—they have not necessarily, for the very reason that they did proceed like the Greeks, departed as far from the forms adopted by the latter, as their climate, their requirements, and their customs differed from the climate, requirements, and customs of the Greeks. No one in the present day seriously recommends the *imitation* of the forms of Greek art in the province of Architecture;—does it therefore follow that the study of these forms is useless? Certainly not. To the architect that study is indispensable; but indispensable with the condition that it shall not confine itself to the forms, but advance to the discovery of the principle,—the principle common to all the Arts. It is barbarism to reproduce the Greek Temple in the streets of London or Paris,—for the transplanted imitation of this building denotes an ignorance of the principle which guided its erection, and *ignorance is Barbarism.* It is barbarous to neglect the thorough and careful study of Greek art; for Greek art is that which most perfectly subordinated form to the modes of thought and feelings recognised by the people among whom it originated,—principles not invented by it, but which it fully comprehended and unerringly pursued. It is also barbarous to ignore in modes of art foreign to the Greek mode the true principles which they exhibit.

The preceding remarks have already made it evident how, in the structural details of their buildings, the Greeks subordinate symmetry to the dispositions which reason has suggested, when these dispositions cannot be reconciled with it. But it is not only in the details of their Architecture that this fact presents itself; it is apparent also in the general conformation of their architectural arrangements. The Erechtheium of the Athenian Acropolis is a most striking illustration. It consists, as every one knows, of a group of three halls, or temples, two of which communicate with three porticos of different elevations : two are of the Ionic order, and the entablature of the third is supported by Caryatides. It would be impossible to find, even in Gothic Architecture, which is supposed to be so little restrained by the laws of symmetry, any building of a character more fantastic, or more " picturesque," to use a modern phrase. Several causes led to these irregularities; the ground could not be disturbed, since the building was intended to cover the Fountain which Neptune caused to issue

from the earth by a stroke of his trident, and the olive-tree produced by Minerva. It was a sacred spot, situated at the northern
extremity of the plateau occupied by the Acropolis, and at a point
where the rock begins to decline towards the north before it
forms an abrupt descent. The architect of the Erechtheium was
obliged to regard the natural levels of the rock ; but he gratified
his ingenuity in profiting by the inequalities of the ground,—in
proposing to himself an original problem,—in showing that it is
quite possible to erect a building of pleasing appearance while
deviating from the commonplace rules of symmetry ; it seems as
if he had even delighted in seeking difficulties in order boldly to
overcome them,—not by disguising the irregularities of his plan
and elevations, but, on the contrary, by bringing these irregularities into relief by a great variety in the disposition. This small
Greek building is justly considered a master-piece : but what
architect in our days would venture to emancipate himself so
completely from the rules of symmetry, even though he qualified
this defect,—if defect it be,—by exquisite grace in the details
and by beauty in the execution ? This audacity might and would
be permissible at Athens, because the artist knew that he was
surrounded by a people itself sufficiently artistic to comprehend
the motives which prompted so bold a conception ; for while
every *new idea* was discussed at Athens, he who had acted solely
in conformity with his reason and the inspirations of his tastes
was sure of being able to defend his cause and render it
triumphant.

The Erechtheium is completed ; the scaffolding which surrounded it is removed, and now I can imagine that I see some
Athenian critic (and such were not wanting among the
argumentative and impressionable population of that city,
disposed to indulge in epigram and raillery), that I see him
stand out from the curious crowd, and say to the architect :
" Why this diversity of levels, these three buildings in conjunction which seem to have been brought together by chance ?
What means this lower portico whose entablature abuts against
the antes of the cella ? I see three frontispieces, one in front of
the cella, another lower, placed on one side and forming a projection, or return facing the other end of the principal building,
as if the second portico were too large for the place it occupies.
I turn round and discover another portico, low and small,—its
cornice supported by Caryatides, and built, not centrically with,
but at the angle of the cella. What confusion ! Could any one
looking at the edifice in one of its aspects, form any idea of its
appearance from the others ? On one side a great door gives
entrance to a narrow chamber, while on the other, a small door
at a higher level also opens into the same chamber. Is the

public money intended to be spent on works which satisfy neither taste nor reason?" To this harangue the Athenian architect would have replied: "Athenians,—the person who has spoken with so little reflection is probably a stranger, since he requires to have explained to him the principles of an art in the practice of which you excel every other people. He has certainly not troubled himself to look around him, or taken many steps either in the City or on the Acropolis, before passing judgment upon an edifice with whose site and sacred destination he is unacquainted. For his instruction, if not for yours, I will explain the reasons which have guided me, so as to make it clear to him that an Athenian architect, who cares for his reputation, and still more for the glory of Athens, does nothing without having maturely considered the arrangements and the design which he should adopt for the buildings whose construction is confided to him. I have had to provide, as you are aware, three temples, or rather two temples united in one; one consecrated to Erechtheian Neptune, another to Minerva, and a smaller one to Pandrosus; but this is not the proper place for the discussion of sacred things. You know whether I could dare to disturb the venerated ground which I was pledged to protect; the two sanctuaries dedicated to Neptune and Minerva are as you see under the same roof, although they stand on ground of different levels, the fountain of Neptune being situated above the olive-tree of Minerva. But look, Athenians, at the part of the Acropolis on which we stand; observe that we are nearly close to the ramparts of the northern side, and that the ground falls at this point; that only fifty paces distant to the south stands the great temple of Minerva. On the eastern side, in front of the cella dedicated to Neptune, I have erected a portico on the same plane as the temple itself, and which forms with it a complete whole. But on the north side what need was there to raise my portico, which serves as entrance to the sanctuary of Minerva, to the same height as that of Neptune? On this side it was necessary to provide an ample shelter open to that aspect which is so desirable in a place scorched by the heat of the sun, and to dispose it in such a manner as to leave a space of sufficient width for the defenders of the ramparts. I have taken as my centre for this portico the door of the vestibule leading to the sanctuary of Minerva. To shelter and protect this portico from the southerly wind I have, as you see, prolonged the wall of the cella. . . . I am taken to task for having lowered the northern portico,—for not having ranged its cornice on a level with the cornice of the two sanctuaries; but do not you perceive that in so doing I have given importance to the principal building,—to the sacred place; and that desiring to give to this portico great depth and width, for the reasons pointed out before, if I had raised its entablature, to the level of that of the cella, the accessory would have overpowered the principal, and for you Athenians who live in the lower part of the town, near the temple of Theseus, the view of the sanctuaries of Neptune and Minerva would have been shut out by this accessory through the effects of perspective?   Moreover, do you not see that I have been thus enabled to give a becoming proportion to this portico, and to bring the apex of the roof under the cornice of the cella, which is necessary for the efficient clearance of the water?

" And now let us pass on to the southern side where the rock rises ; should I build for Pandrosus an edifice that might have come into competition with the porticos of Minerva and Neptune ? Should I not indicate to strangers the two main entrances to my building, which includes three separate temples?   Was it not desirable to give a less monumental character to this third portico,—to make it a kind of annex ?   But more than this, look at the immense columns before us of the great temple of Minerva. Which of the orders would not have appeared mean in view of that majestic portico of the Parthenon ?   By placing a cornice upon Caryatides I avoided any comparison, any sort of similitude, which might have suggested the thought that you, Athenians, can do nothing more in the present day than reproduce in miniature what past ages have created.   Moreover, had I adopted the Ionic order for this portico, no delicacy in the execution nor grace of detail could have made it compare with the majestic grandeur of the order of the temple of Minerva.   There is a principle of our Art which you comprehend as well as I do,— that we should always avoid, more especially in sacred things, any appearance of parsimony or meanness.   We must not give occasion to strangers who come to Athens, and who, viewing the Acropolis from a distance, see two temples near together,—the one large and imposing, the other diminutive, yet nearly alike in form,—to say : What great god's temple is this, and what lesser god's temple is that by its side ?   You see, Athenians, that in my endeavours to erect here sanctuaries worthy of the divinities, I have, by means of exceptional, and even, if you choose so to call them, singular, yet well-considered arrange- ments, obviated those comparisons so detrimental to the respect we owe to the gods.   Perhaps I might have obtained the praise of him who criticises my work, if, paying less regard to the general aspect of the Acropolis, I had built a temple divided in its interior, but outwardly recalling time-honoured forms—such, for instance, as those of the temple of Theseus ; but let me ask you what kind of figure that miniature of the Parthenon would have made in this place, even were its composition still richer and more elegant? whereas, by adopting for the irregular building which I have just completed, an order of a delicate character, and by covering it with finely wrought sculptures, I withdraw attention from its irregularity, by engaging the spectator in the examination of details. Observe, besides, the play of sunlight among these inequalities; and what a perfect shelter the portico of the Caryatides, exposed as it is all day to the burning rays of the sun, affords by very reason of its lowness. If you look at these statues, which at a little distance seem only the size of life, and then turning, contemplate the portico of the temple of Minerva, enveloped in shadow, would you be likely to institute a comparison between them? And when you have admired the majestic grandeur of that portico, will not your eyes return to rest with pleasure on this porch of the Pandroseium?" Thus, perhaps, would the architect of the Erechtheium have spoken, and the Athenians would assuredly have approved his words.

One essential quality of Greek Art is clearness; that is to say, speaking only of Architecture, the distinct expression of the purpose, the requirements, and the means of execution. Clearness, the inseparable companion of taste, pervades not only the structure of Greek buildings, which is invariably simple, easy to understand, and free from everything that is doubtful or untruthful,—but likewise the details—the monumental sculptures or paintings which seem to combine with the Architecture, not for the purpose of dissimulating, but of rendering its forms more evident. Never in Greek buildings does the sculpture alter an outline or the profile of a member; it is merely there as a light embroidery whose faint projection is insufficient to destroy the line: sometimes, even, it is merely a graving heightened by colour; for in that climate the clearness of the atmosphere and the brilliancy of the sunlight render visible the smallest details from a great distance. Decorative sculpture diminishes in projection according as the surfaces over which it extends are directly exposed to this light. If the bas-reliefs placed in the metopes, and the statues in the tympanum of the façades have a considerable projection, it is because these sculptures are always enveloped in the shadow of the cornice-drip when the sun is high above the horizon, and are therefore only lighted by reflection; when the sun is low the bas-reliefs are lighted almost horizontally, and cast only slight shadows, so that their great projection cannot disturb the main lines of the architecture.

If we examine the delineations of Greek buildings of which so large a number has been published, we shall see that decorative sculpture occupies but a very secondary place,—that it is subordinated to the forms of the profiles. The Greeks were,

above everything, lovers of form, and they rejected whatever
tended in any degree to impair its harmony and unity. It was
this instinct which, in statuary, led them to prefer the nude.
They appear to have draped their statues only in conformity
with some religious conventions; but they emancipated themselves from these rules as soon as they could. The earliest
statues of Venus were completely draped according to prescription; but the instinct of the Greeks was more influential than
their religious dogmas, and even as early as the time of Pericles
the sculptors had already ceased to regard them.

The Greeks were a people *sui generis,*—a colony of artists;
and, as I have said before, no barbarians were to be found among
them. As long as they were independent of foreign influence
they maintained the language of the Arts pure from all alloy,
free from any compromise, and they were certain of being
understood. In our day we find ourselves under very different
conditions, and are obliged to make endless concessions, in order
to make ourselves intelligible. In the province of Art there is
no longer any authority, because there are no longer any convictions. We have schools, or rather coteries, which dispute
about principles they do not observe, because no one would
admit them in their rigorous application. Some maintain that
the study of the Arts of Classic Antiquity should alone be held in
honour among us; though when they build they disregard the
principles of those arts; others, less exclusive perhaps, but quite
as illogical, require that the rising generation be instructed in
the arts of the Middle Ages and of the Renaissance, while in
practice they ignore the elementary rules of these arts, and
content themselves with reproducing mere appearances which
satisfy the generality until *fashion* demands something different.

Amid this singular state of confusion and controversy, all study,
to be profitable, must be undertaken with discernment and with
a view to a practical result. Now, more than ever, time is
precious;—and the most assiduous labour, the most learned
researches, do but lead to the bitterest deceptions, unless we bring
into this labour and these researches a spirit of enlightened
criticism; unless we cast off those miserable rags of prejudice to
which, for nearly two centuries, we have clung as our only befitting garment. The study of Greek antiquity is, and probably
ever will be, the surest means of initiating youth into the knowledge of the arts,—the most solid foundation of taste, and consequently of good sense, for one cannot exist without the other;
it teaches how to distinguish truth from sophistry,—it enlarges
without confusing the mind. However poetical the imagination
of the Greek, it never leads him beyond the limits of the true;
his object above all is to be clear, to be understood, to be human;

for he lives among men, and to man he refers everything. As for ourselves, in the present day, we admire the various manifestations of art among the Greeks ; but the reproduction of those manifestations is beyond our power ;—we live a different life. But their principles, embodying eternal truth, we may appropriate to ourselves ; we may, in a word, reason as they did, though we do not speak the same language.

If the study of Greek art is necessary for the Architect, the study of Roman art is not less so, although the principles followed by the Romans differ from those admitted among the Greeks.

The genius of the Roman people differs materially from that of the Greeks. The Roman is essentially an administrator and a politician ; he is the founder of Modern Civilisation : but is he, like the Greek, an Artist ? Certainly not. Is he possessed of that instinct inherent in the organisation of some favoured beings which leads them to clothe all their conceptions in forms which are the direct emanation of Art ? No. He proceeds quite otherwise. If we analyse the buildings of the Greeks generally, as we just now briefly analysed a Greek temple, we shall invariably discern that acute intelligence, that delicate perception which knows how to turn every difficulty and every obstacle to the ultimate advantage of Art, even in the most minute details. The analysis of a Roman building reveals to us instincts and objects of a different nature. The Roman only regards the whole,—the satisfaction of a requirement : he is not an artist ; he rules,—he administrates,—he constructs. Form is for him merely the outer dress with which he clothes his constructions, without troubling himself to consider whether that dress is in perfect harmony with the body it covers, and whether all its parts are in conformity with a principle. These are subtleties which he does not stop to consider ; provided only the garment be ample and lasting, worthy of the thing it clothes, and that it reflects honour upon him who has caused it to be made, he cares little whether or not it fulfils the conditions of art which are sought after by the Greek.

It will be well to trace exactly the line of demarcation which separates Greek from Roman art. A thorough acquaintance with the qualities peculiar to these two civilisations will enable us better to appreciate the development of the arts of modern times ; —to estimate the value of what we have already derived, and of that which we may yet gather from each of them : for if we are Latins in our language, our policy, and our habits of life, we are somewhat Greek in the constitution of our minds and our genius.

The indigenous or aboriginal Greek populations made use of arts anterior to themselves ; but they succeeded in appropriating them and in establishing principles by subordinating those arts to their own peculiar taste which had its foundation in human reason. They neither invented any type of Architecture nor any system of construction; but they applied the principles of logic to Architectural Art, and this they never derived from the Eastern races nor even from the Egyptians. In this the Greeks are the Fathers of the Western world;—it was they who opened the way of progress. Though lovers of form, they never sacrificed principle to it until their genius was stifled under Roman domination; but then they were no longer Greeks. Under the Empire, Roman civilisation resembled a vast ocean which engulfed not only the barbarism, but also the original genius of every people. Under the Roman yoke the Greeks became merely skilful practitioners,—a fact which proves that among the Greeks, as is the case among other less gifted peoples, autonomy was the indispensable condition for the development of the arts. The Roman, as a necessary result of his administrative and political organisation, assimilated to himself and made Roman everything that he touched.

Such, however, was the innate strength of the Greek arts, that we find their traces throughout the Roman dominion to the end of the Lower Empire and even beyond; for we may follow them still through the Middle Ages. This we shall have further occasion to observe, and it is by no means the least interesting of the considerations presented by the history of Architecture and of the arts which spring from it.

The Architecture of the Greeks accurately reflects the intellectual condition of that people; and while, as remarked in our first lecture, the arts develop themselves independently of the political condition of nations or the degree of their civilisation, they are inherent in their genius. The Greeks constituted a society or an assemblage of societies rather than what we now understand by a nation. Although they were the first to manifest sentiments of patriotism,—sentiments unknown among the Eastern nations even at the present day,—the feeling scarcely extended beyond a love of the city,—that is to say, of an association of individuals bound together by common interests. They were strong enough to resist the Persians, whose armies were only hordes,—slaves rather than soldiers; but they were quickly absorbed into the vigorous political organisation of the Romans.

We fall into error in undertaking to pronounce on the history of nations according to our modern ideas. The patriotic feelings of an Athenian in no way resembled those of a Roman citizen or of a Parisian in the nineteenth century. Now this condition of *association*, rather than of nationality, is peculiarly favourable to the development of the arts. It is not only in Athens or Corinth that we find a proof of this. The Republics of Italy in the Middle Ages,—Venice, Florence, Pisa, Sienna, for example,—which present a social condition analogous to that of the Greek cities, were so many brilliant centres of Art. We must pursue our theme a little further. In a Greek city such as Athens, all the citizens took part in public affairs, and had a direct personal interest in them, as being all members of the same society; all were mutually acquainted, and their interests were less widely separated than they have come to be among our populations. Patriotism among them was therefore the sodality existing among the members of an association rather than the sentiment as developed in Rome and among the nations of Modern Europe; which is directed to the conservation of the political unity of an assemblage of provinces occupying a vast territory, often to the detriment of individual interests. Now when men who are influenced by the spirit of association all take, or imagine they take, a share of responsibility in public affairs, such an association effects very great results in everything it undertakes: 1st, because mutual responsibility facilitates control; 2dly, because, as each member supposes himself responsible for all the acts of the society, his vanity is exacting and watchful; 3dly, because individual members increase their importance by means of the party which they soon gather around them; and then party-leaders became rivals, unhappily perhaps for the public welfare, but very advantageously for the development of intellectual labours, and consequently for intellectual progress; 4thly, because the general approbation,—that which we call public opinion,—is the only power to which appeal can be made; and to gain the support of that power its adhesion must be secured, and incessant efforts made to enlist its favours. The Athenian democracy had the advantage of leisure; all business was carried on through the instrumentality of slaves. The Athenians passed their days in the places of public resort, beneath the porticos, or in the gymnasia, conversing, philosophising, and exchanging ideas on a thousand subjects of high discourse. We must not forget that the population of Athens and its neighbourhood did not exceed thirty or thirty-five thousand free men, of whom twenty thousand at most took part in the affairs of the republic; the ten or fifteen thousand others were soldiers or sailors, frequently absent from the country, to which they brought information and new ideas. We may suppose that every cultivated city of Greece governed itself in the same manner. We find in Greece only one aristocracy,—that of Sparta; and this aristocracy did not recruit itself like that of Rome,—no one could become a Spartan. The only satisfaction which his social position afforded the Spartan was that of pride: he was compelled to be poorer, worse clothed, and worse fed than those who were subject to him. He disdained every occupation but that of war and military exercises; and not until a very late date could a Spartan of the highest birth engage in politics. The Spartan aristocracy had no knowledge whatever of the arts; and we shall shortly see that the aristocracy of Rome, though differently constituted, was equally incapable of exerting any influence over the arts, and in fact, never attempted to do so. The democratic constitution of Athens, possible in a city, and among a small population, though in itself, I allow, far from durable, and full of the elements of danger, was nevertheless a social condition which enabled the Arts to develop themselves with great energy.

And why? Because it is necessary to please—not merely a coterie, or a ruler, or even a well-disposed committee, but everybody: and "everybody" is hard to please,—inclined to be critical and argumentative, especially among the Greeks. But if the task is hard, the reward for him who succeeds is great; for a triumph decreed by public opinion is the only one that can really flatter the artist. When works of art appeal to the judgment of an entire people, and the instincts and education of that people are such as to render its judgment sound, then the artist is independent; for who would dare to restrain him in giving expression to his thought when he can appeal to the general suffrage? But when, on the contrary, the arts become, so to speak, a part of the machinery of government; when they are "administered," as among the Romans, they may produce great works, may attain magnificence, and become the perfect expression of material requirements; but they lose that savour of individuality which penetrates,—that originality which charms while it moves the soul.

And such is the weakness of human nature that art, while following the independent and individual track which we have been describing, sinks rapidly from originality into affectation; good sense soon degenerates into subtlety; reason into sophistry. In studying the history of Greece, we find a succession of strifes, of fresh and never-ending rivalries. Considered from a political point of view, this history is no other than that of a group of colonies at war with one another, and a prey to internal anarchy. The Greek cities were not united even by the bond of a common religion. And yet, in the midst of a social state so imperfect from our point of view, the arts penetrated everywhere; they alone reigned, were respected, and steadily progressed.

Even in the heroic times it appears that Art was the sole bond of union among the Greeks. Theseus, king of Athens, instituted the festival of the Panathenæa, to induce the people of Attica, by a kind of religious confederation, to recognise Athens as their metropolis. It was the same with all the institutions of this people; they assume an artistic form in order to obtain recognition by the multitude. The Greek mythology is but a poetical form in which the phenomena, the forces and changes, of nature are variously figured. The Greeks were not the inventors of Mythology. I have already observed, and I repeat it : the Greeks did not invent ; they gave a peculiarly beautiful and well-adapted form to the principles which they found developed around them, or existing before them. Their religion and their arts are identical, and invariably proceed by way of synthesis. And the Athenians, who were the most religious of all the Greeks, were also the most inclined to make Art predominate over everything, or rather to transform everything into a work of Art. Among the Greeks, every event, fact, and phenomenon,—all that was good, all that was evil, all that existed in the material or immaterial order of the world,—found expression in the language of the arts ; and that, too, with a refinement of observation, a logical sequence, a simplicity and energy of expression, which seem more than human. But faculties so precious as these can only be developed in a perfectly homogeneous society, all of whose members are animated by a similar intelligence, understand one another, and are equally sensible to the various expressions of art.

If we open the pages of Pausanias we shall find that even in his time the productions of Greek Art were considered worthy of veneration. That writer often speaks of cities then nearly deserted, but where the inhabitants respected the remains of their former splendour ; where the ruined temples still retained the statues of their gods or goddesses, though they were often made of material that was fragile, or of a nature to tempt cupidity. At every turn we find a public monument commemorating some sacred remembrance ; but to confine ourselves to the subject of these Lectures, what we as Architects should most particularly observe in these Greek cities is the manner in which they are laid out, indicating that their builders had from the beginning an idea of Art. It might be an exaggeration to assert that this idea of Art was the first requirement to be satisfied ; and yet, if we observe the position of the buildings, compare their respective dimensions, and note the " picturesque " manner in which they are grouped, it becomes apparent that consideration of outline and general effect materially influenced the choice of their ground.

It is only when we remember how very little considerations of this nature are appreciated in the present day,—how little they influence the decisions of our modern city authorities,—that we begin to realise with sadness the wide abyss which separates us from those ages when the arts were loved. We call ourselves a civilised people ; yet what, for the most part, are our cities, and what in a few centuries will they become, when in all probability the vulgar demand for the satisfaction of material requirement will have utterly swept away the few remaining relics of former ages? What are the cities of the New World? and what the great manufacturing towns of England? That which we call civilisation has led us in the nineteenth century to make wide streets, and to line them with houses of uniform appearance. Our towns and cities have thus become deserts for thought; they have the weari- some monotony of solitude without its grandeur. What is there throughout these vast chessboards of streets to suggest historical associations? Where is there a centre of repose for the distracted mind of the spectator? On what point shall his attention be fixed? Where does he find the indication that a hundred generations have trodden the same ground before him? Not indeed that I regret the fetid and tortuous streets of our old towns, with their houses seemingly brought together haphazard, —their labyrinths of alleys, their public buildings obscured by booths and disfigured by dirt,—accumulation without order,—an indescribable chaos: yet in this chaos there was at any rate the imprint of man, of his labour,—the memorials of his history,— something more than the indications of the merely material interests of the time.

I can well understand why it is that minds in sympathy with Art in the present day (and they are much more numerous than is generally supposed, though they are often perhaps only half conscious of this instinct) so gladly fly from these deserts of stone, of wood, and iron,—deserts indeed to them!—and hasten to refresh themselves amid the ruins of Athens, Syracuse, or Pæs- tum; for these dead cities are to them more peopled than are the streets of Lyons or of Manchester.

The Greeks were sensible that a people gifted with a lively imagination should be addressed in a language calculated to strike the imagination, that this sentiment should be gratified, and that the satisfaction of simply material wants would not content them. If the Greek cities in their present ruined state still preserve the fragrance of art in the midst of their decay, it is because among the Greeks art was not a mere decoration —a superfluity: it was the ruling principle from the basement upwards; the genius under whose auspices the city was founded.

Let us look at Agrigentum, one of the finest of the Dorian colonies; and first observe with what care the site was chosen. Near to a well-sheltered harbour there rises a range of calcareous hills running parallel with the sea: the Greeks made this chain of hills the rampart of the city on the side most exposed to attack. They shaped the summit into the form of thick walls pierced with gateways. The rocky ridge was converted into a wide rampart, on the top of which were several temples built parallel with the walls; thus presenting to strangers coming from the port a long line of buildings of very various dimensions, resting upon an enormous basement of hewn rock. Between this natural rampart, thus turned to such admirable account, and the Acropolis, which stands beyond and commands the surrounding country, is a valley in which the city is built,—the dwelling-houses perfectly sheltered from the north and the south-east winds, both of which in Sicily are disagreeable. The Acropolis contained temples, of which, however, very few traces remain. The city was bounded on the south also by a long range of calcareous hills whose summits were shaped by the hand of man, and adorned with a belt of temples standing out in bold relief against the sky,—and on the north by the Acropolis joined to other hills of less elevation, itself also crowned by noble monuments.

At Selinuntum, another Dorian colony of Sicily, we find the temples built upon two plateaus, between which lay the port. Not only was the site of these buildings selected with great judgment and taste, but the buildings themselves were all raised on wide basements, or rather steps of large size, intended to separate and distinguish them from the private buildings around. The Greek architect, faithful to his principle of using nature as a means, and of making her enter largely into his artistic works, examined with acute intelligence the formation of the ground upon which he had to build. If he wished to form a theatre, for example, he seeks along the rocky hills,—so numerous in the countries where he builds his cities,—some natural hollow with an aspect suitable for the actors and the spectators : he then cuts the terraced benches and the *præcinctures* in the living rock, and afterwards completes by building what the formation of the ground does not supply. We have nearly perfect examples of these dispositions among the numerous theatres of the Peloponnesus, and in that of Syracuse. More favoured by climate, the Greeks, in their public monuments, were not limited by those requirements of enclosure and shelter which form the chief consideration of builders in the North. If provision was desired for a large assemblage of people, an enclosure surrounded by colonnades, or some space in the rock simply disposed and favourably situated, fully sufficed them ; and they excelled in imparting an air of simple grandeur to these works, without ever striving for effect. To look at them, nothing could seem more simple :— there is no appearance of effort; we experience none of that wonder and tension of mind which is often felt in viewing the monuments of an extinct civilisation ; on the contrary, we discern and feel the evidence of life in every Greek work, even those of which few traces have been left us.

Unfortunately, we possess scarcely any remains of the civil and domestic architecture of the Greeks, except these vestiges hewn in the rock. The buried cities of Herculaneum and Pompeii —especially the latter—may, however, aid our imagination in transporting us into the midst of a Greek city, and living for a brief moment among its ancient inhabitants. All existing remains, —the curious relics of Pompeii, some scattered fragments of domestic architecture, a few paintings, and the just discernible traces of the city of Segesta,—serve plainly to show that the Greek habitations were as little varied in their plan of arrangement as were their religious edifices. But it is not variety in design that forms the chief recommendation of Greek Architecture. A good plan once found, the Greek Architect did not think it necessary to modify it in any sensible degree. His good taste prevented his seeking anything out of the way, fantastical, or astonishing. The true lover of Art is never satiated ; for him a good thing is always new and admirable, or at any rate agreeable. The Greek artist felt this ; and in perfecting his works he did not change either the principle or the theme. He merely strove to infuse more refinement into the execution ; and even when he fell into the abuse of refinement,—when grace had changed to affectation, delicacy to stiffness, and care to over-minuteness,—we shall still discover, beneath this senility of form, the vital energy of the principle. The Greeks, even when they became the paid artists of their too powerful neighbours, the Romans, long preserved the freshness of the principles which rule their Arts. By slow degrees, however, even these remnants of vitality are extinguished, and, under the Emperors, the Greeks fell to the level of mere practitioners. In our next Lecture we shall explain the causes of this decline.

LECTURE III.

COMPARISON BETWEEN GREEK AND ROMAN ARCHITECTURE—PECULIARITIES
OF DIFFERENCE—THEIR CAUSES.

THE chief characteristic of the Roman people is, as we
have already observed, their genius for organising and
governing. The earlier conquering nations with whose history
we have some acquaintance were anything but civilisers; their
conquests had no other object than the acquisition of slaves and
treasure; they lowered rather than raised the countries they
subjugated. The Romans may have been sometimes rapacious
masters, more eager to enrich themselves than to spread the
light of civilisation among the nations they subdued; but such
was not the prevailing character of the Roman conquests. We
need not recall the history of the long and bloody strife which
preceded the ultimate triumph of the Romans over the nations
of Italy;—a war more social than political, since the question
at issue was the preservation of the wealth and influence of a
handful of patrician families, on the one hand, and, on the other
hand, the effort of the people to emancipate themselves from a
condition bordering on serfdom, and to conquer the rights of
citizens. This history has been written, and written well, by one
of the most distinguished of our literary contemporaries, M.
Mérimée; who, under the modest title of *Essais sur la guerre
sociale*, brings most vividly before us the terrible contests of the
latter period of the Republic, and reveals to us (although that
is not the object of his work) the various sources whence the
Romans derived their arts. In the early days of the Republic,
the Romans had no Art of their own, as had the Egyptians, the
Orientals, and the Greeks. The true view of their history
exhibits to us a people inconsiderable in number, governed by
a few patricians, intent upon aggrandising themselves at the expense of their neighbours,—a kind of land-pirates, all animated
from the beginning by a common impulse of conquest and
plunder, with little or no appreciation of the enjoyments afforded
by the cultivation and love of the arts. Rome, however, was

placed in the very midst of populations among whom the arts
had attained a wonderful development. Etruria and Campania
were covered with sacred, public, or domestic edifices, whose
excellence in point of art is attested by remains of the greatest
beauty. The Etruscans, even at a period so remote that we can
hardly now fix its date, already employed vaulting, although it
was not known to the Greeks. Whence did that people derive
this mode of roofing their buildings ? We cannot say ; moreover, any hypothesis that we might be able to suggest would have
for us simply an archæological interest, while it would lead us
beyond the limits we have laid down for ourselves. It is sufficient to observe here that vaulting was employed by some of the
peoples of Asia long before the times with which we are now
concerned in the West. The discoveries recently made at
Nineveh have brought to light buildings vaulted with tempered
clay or earth rammed upon a form, the banding arches of which
are faced with glazed bricks moulded in shape of voussoir. The
Romans adopted with peculiar intelligence everything useful
which they found amongst the foreigners with whom they had
relations. Thus their soldiers adopted the arms of various
nations,—the Samnite buckler, the Spanish sword, and so on.
Cæsar in *Sallust* says : " Most of our countrymen, when they
saw anything serviceable among their allies, or their enemies,
studiously applied it to their own use on their return home."[1]

From the Etruscans they took the circular arch formed with
jointed stones ;—from the peoples of Campania, the general plan
of their sacred edifices, the Greek orders, and the arrangement
and ornamentation of their dwellings. They borrowed, therefore,
from two separate sources ; they tried to combine two diametrically opposite principles,—that of the Greek lintel, and that of
the Etruscan arch : in so doing they plainly show that their ideas
of the arts were only those of pirates, whose procedure is dictated by pride rather than taste, and who adorn themselves
with spoils of various origin, and which in combination are pain-
fully incongruous.

That delicate faculty which led the Greeks to observe every
moral and physical phenomenon with incomparable nicety,—a
faculty which with this people held the place of Science, and enabled it to exceed the most perfect productions of Science, was
not developed among the Romans. Their genius was of a different type ; they were pre-eminently politicians, legislators, and
administrators : their arts necessarily took a direction quite other
than those of the Greeks. We see at Rome a very powerful
aristocracy, possessing admirable political traditions, and con-

---

[1] " . . . Majores nostri . . . quod ubique apud socios aut hostes idoneum videbatur, cum
summo studio domi exsequebantur."

stantly recruiting itself from every class, even from its opponents.
The Roman senate was the strength of Rome, and it directed
everything. The senators were either the descendants of ancient
families, or men who had distinguished themselves in the public
service. The way to participation in public affairs lay through
the senate ; and public affairs to a Roman meant either war or
the administration of conquered provinces, or the practice of
law—namely, pleading and judging. Now, not one of these oc-
cupations is favourable to the cultivation of the arts. Public
employment was the ambition of every Roman citizen ; and so
strong was this tendency at Rome, that towards the latter period
of the Republic, the inhabitants of the Latin territory consisted
of only two very distinct classes,—functionaries and slaves :—
the former, possessors of the soil, entirely occupied with the
management of their property, or (and this more especially) with
political intrigues ; the latter reduced to an abject condition,
addicted to theft and all the vices engendered by slavery, ignorance, and indolence. As to the free plebs of Rome, it was the
most barbarous, the most brutal, and the most venal populace
that ever filled a large city ; utterly unscrupulous, superstitious,
and open to bribery and therefore at the mercy of the cleverest,
the most stirring, and, above all, the wealthiest members of the
ancient families. The Greeks were industrious and commercial,
sensitive to physical and mental beauty, exceedingly fond of
discussion and controversies, proud of and delighting in what
ennobled them as men,—in their poets, their orators, and their
artists. A remarkable fact in the history of peoples is this co-
existence in the same individuals of an aptitude for commercial
pursuits,—the matter-of-fact calculations of the merchant,—with
an exquisite sentiment in works of Art ; the fact that the vanity
of the prosperous trader did not stifle among them those most
true principles of art which we designate as taste : it is remarkable that a nation should so recklessly suffer every principle to
be questioned,—worship a man one day, and with inconceivable
fickleness ostracise him the next ; should advance in the path
of progress (as we term it) with unheard-of rapidity ; pass in a
few years through every system of philosophy, every form of
government, lay the foundations of every science and make war
with all its neighbours ; and yet be able, amid this chaos of ideas,
systems, and passions, to maintain in art a regular and logical
advance ; to give it a form new, original, and beautiful, without
letting itself be drawn into those vagaries which in modern times
we call fashion.
    There is a fact which exhibits the prodigious activity of this
people, at the same time merchants and artists. Just before the
battle of Salamis, 480 B.C., the Athenians had no longer any city ;

the whole of their territory was devastated; nothing was left them but their ships. Twenty years afterwards they had built the Parthenon; and Æschylus, who had fought at Salamis, was bringing on the stage his tragedy of the *Persæ*, in which he makes the barbarian king act a noble and heroic part. Undoubtedly this is an adroit flattery of the conquerors; but it is still more conspicuously the mark of a refined taste, secure of sympathy among the multitude. Could we affirm that such an experiment would not be hissed among ourselves, and that a form of flattery so honouring to the conqueror and to the conquered would be appreciated?

Greek Art has its youth and its decadence, but it never for an instant deviates from its course: it is *one*, whereas all other outgrowths of the intelligence and restless passions of this singular people, come forth by chance, spring up and destroy each other. The Roman people exhibit a very different spectacle: they have but one idea, the dominion of the world: and this idea is so rooted in the mind of the Roman citizen that within the space of two centuries he succeeded in conquering three-fourths of Europe and the whole of Western Asia and Northern Africa; notwithstanding the alarming symptoms of decay which even at the end of the Republic, presaged a dissolution of ancient pagan society. The machinery employed by the Roman to effect this result is simple: the Roman citizen constitutes himself sovereign whenever a territory is reduced to subjection; he takes possession of the *ager publicus*—the public domain of his enemies,—and allots it; then he encourages the immigration of colonists among the conquered people; he assures the Romans and their allies of a subsistence in the country subjugated, and these having become proprietors guard and defend themselves, and very soon found colonies which are altogether Roman. If the Roman bestows the title of ally upon a country, he takes it under his guardianship, engages it to assist him against more distant enemies, makes it serve his interests and enter into his vast organisation. In this way the prestige of the Roman power spread gradually over the whole surface of the then known world,—dividing, flattering, protecting, or chastising the barbarian peoples, as its interests required. The Romans had political unity, the Greeks had not; because, as I have previously remarked, the Greek cities were only societies or associations, whereas Rome was the centre of a vast government hierarchically founded,—the crowning of an edifice that nothing could shake except a social revolution and a deluge of barbarians.

This very brief review of the Roman political system is necessary to enable us to understand what Roman Art is; for, as already stated, the Romans are a political people, and then arts are to them an instrument, a means, not an enjoyment, as among the Greeks. The Roman rejects everything that does not enter into his vast system of organisation ; and he troubles himself but little to know whether a particular form of Art is in harmony with the principles of the branch of art to which it belongs : he will not, like the Greeks, proceed to discuss whether his observations are logically deduced ; he will not interest himself in a profile or a play of light and shade ; he only requires one thing, which is that his work be Roman,—that it be an evidence of greatness, of power, and, in special, a work that shall accord with his system of political organisation,—above all, a work of utility, exactly fulfilling the programme laid down for it. He plans roads, bridges, rivers ; brings water into cities by means of immense aqueducts, and constructs amphitheatres that serve as places of assembly, and which are virtually town-halls as well as buildings devoted to public amusement. Little matters it to the Roman whether the people subdued by or in alliance with him preserve their own religion, provided they conform to his laws : more than that, he actually incorporates the gods of his vassal peoples with the phalanx of Roman Deities, and thus he attaches to his fortunes the populations whose arbiter he has become, by the strongest of human ties,—religion and established institutions. And his procedure is the same in the arts. The Roman finds among the Greek communities artists and craftsmen of superior skill ; he takes them into his service, he pays them, he allows them to ornament his buildings according to their taste ; but for him the Greek artist is only a workman. As to the general plan of his buildings, the system of construction, the style, he as a Roman assumes to himself alone the right to dictate them from the Euxine to the farthest shores of Britain. We cannot fail to perceive the dignity of this mode of regarding Architectural Art, or to observe how decidedly it is in conformity with the spirit of modern governments. But is it in harmony with the character of the populations of Western Europe, with our own French character, with our habits and traditions ? We may be permitted to doubt it, for in France (as among all nations gifted with the sentiment of Art, whose imagination is stronger than their will, and whose minds constantly require sustenance and willingly follow a chimera, if that chimera presents to their eyes a sentiment or an idea), independence of mind, inquiry, criticism, and discussion, have been elements necessary for the development of her arts. The proof of this is that we see them flourish when they are left unhampered, and decline and languish in times when it is sought to dictate their expression or regulate their development.

To preclude misunderstanding I must here more fully explain

my meaning. Art is a religion, or rather a belief: now every belief may be recognised or may be merely tolerated by the political estate of a country, or again may develop itself independently of that estate. In the first case, Art is neither impelled nor obstructed, it advances freely and proudly, it makes laws and is hampered by none ; in the second, it is subservient, it is geared into the political machine ; in the third case, it clothes itself in mystery, it has its secrets, and proceeds by imitation. With the Greeks, Art is sovereign, its rule is undisputed, its principles can exhibit the frank simplicity which characterises every operation of the mind that is unopposed and unconstrained. With the Romans, Art is made subservient to the interests of the state, conforms to its requirements, and becomes simply an instrument, a means to an end. In the West, during the Middle Ages, and especially in France, Art isolates itself ; it has a language of its own, it advances silently, is modified and advances independently of the circumstances that surround it.

Our Lectures will, I venture to hope, bring to light the relations that existed and still exist between the arts and the political element of ancient and modern civilisations. I say that still exist, for we have before us at the present time a spectacle full of instruction for those who calmly watch the discussions that are raised in the domain of the arts. On the one side we see the advocates of the arts of antiquity, on the other the apostles of Medieval art. I speak of artists who have convictions, who are defending principles ; it must be understood that I consider as excluded from the lists those who interest themselves for every form of Art alike,—not that I despise their judgment, but because this general and altogether material admiration cannot fail gradually to lead us into indifference. Now in these two opposing camps we see something more than artists ranged, some beneath the banner of Antiquity, others beneath the banner of the Middle Ages ; here are two great principles before us,—two principles that since the days of ancient Greece have never ceased to be at deadly strife, a strife still far from being at an end : these principles are, on the one hand, the subservience of individual intelligence to political interest ; on the other hand, the independence of the human mind in all that concerns the conscience and intellectual inspirations. I repeat it,—the contest is not ended ; and I see no disadvantage in its continuance, for in any case it injures no one ; but it is well to know what we are fighting for, against whom and with whom. The exclusive advocates of Antiquity have for a long time regarded the Greeks and Romans as ranged beneath the same banner, whereas the arts of these two civilisations proceed from diametrically opposite principles ; the Greek arts are free and independent, the Roman arts are <u>enthralled</u>; and if the barriers placed between the two camps, ancient and modern, were thrown down, there is every reason to believe that the Greek artists would have a much more cordial understanding with those of the Middle Ages than with the Romans, who have been ranked as their allies, while in reality they are only their oppressors.

The Roman institutions are in harmony with the character of the Roman people, or rather, the Roman people are in themselves an institution,—a vast administration and political machine, perfectly adapted to the time and its requirements. Its arts are but one of the expressions of that peculiar system, a system exceptional in the history of the Western world. Let us take a glance at this history before, but more particularly after, the Roman era : we behold a totally different spectacle ; we see the people almost continually at war with their governing institutions. During the Middle Ages, for instance, in France we see the Gallo-Roman populations subjugated by barbarians, and never losing an opportunity of rebelling against the institutions to which they are subjected. The Feudal system—which is altogether German—is repugnant to these populations. The Theocracy is as odious to the descendants of the conquerors as it is to the original inhabitants. The royal power, as soon as it becomes in some degree established, makes use of these conflicting elements to weaken each in its turn,—it presides at rather than tries to end the combat. In such a condition of society what becomes of Art ? Who concerns himself about it ? Who thinks of dictating formulas for it ? No one assuredly. It is left to take care of itself ; it pursues its own steady and patient course, making its way wherever it can, aloof from these strifes. At first it finds a refuge in the cloister, but there it is soon stifled under the monastic system. It frees itself from that restraint with the same energy we see displayed in the establishment of the *Communes.* The then existing governments—if the strange medley of institutions which reciprocally obstruct each other deserve the name—have not the sagacity to perceive that Art is a powerful element in Civilisation ; they use it without seeking to make it subservient. It would appear as if Art was then the only refuge of liberty. Thus, in the midst of a society drifting irresolute between the several powers, falling from one extreme into another,—engaging in the longest and most cruel struggles,—we see Art following its regular and systematic course, without the slightest deviation, as with the Greeks we saw it pursuing its steady career amid the confusion and contests of Greek society. How is it that among us in the Middle Ages, as among the Ancient Greeks, Art advances so unerringly along the path it has laid down ? Because it governs itself, because it submits to inquiry and criticism within itself, because it proceeds by an uninterrupted course of deductions, because its movements are free, and no one thinks of subjecting it to routine, that is to say, to an academical formula ; because it gathers from every source, and has no other guide than reason and public opinion !

Greek society, like the industrial class of the Middle Ages, develops itself along with commerce and the arts; and the arts, like commerce, cannot exist without liberty.   The Romans were not traders, neither were they artists ; their position as regards the subject nations was quite different from that of our modern governments : for them, conquerors of the world, all must be Roman, or be nothing ; and in order to insure this supremacy among peoples who, for the most part, were in a lower condition as to civilisation, especially in all that concerned military and political institutions, their first act, after the conquest by arms, was to organise the Roman system among the vanquished or newly allied.   All colonising peoples who, as the result of their talent in this respect, have retained their colonies, and made them contribute to the greatness and power of the mother country,—the English of the present day, for example,—have always employed nearly the same means.   Their programme was as follows : complete religious liberty, civil rights, rights of proprietorship, tribunals chosen by the subject cities, with right of appeal to the Roman magistrate, who intervened in questions only to moderate local abuses, and to show that the Roman government was better than the government it replaced ; a central power protecting without obstructing by any complicated administrative machinery ; military service of the conquered or allied populations, and (which more nearly concerns our subject) public works of great importance—roads, bridges, canals, clearing of land, town walls, aqueducts, harbours, civil buildings, basilicas, pretoria, theatres, baths, permanent camps, vast storehouses, sewers, fountains, etc.   As soon as the Roman has become master of a country, he employs his armies, which are arranged with that view, to cut roads, drain marshes, and form camps ; then he makes numerous requisitions of workmen, and very soon the towns wear an altered appearance : they are completed or modified in plan ; they are surrounded by walls ; the public buildings within and around them are constructed according to a uniform method ; and in a few years, or even in a few months, the Gallic or German town has become a Roman city, in which the Roman citizen, as well as the native inhabitant, finds all that is to be obtained in Rome itself.   It is easy to understand how readily, by the application of such a system, the conquered people would be led to conform to Roman ways and customs,—would lose their local traditions, and almost their nationality itself. Besides, the Romans did really introduce civilisation, regular government, wealth, and prosperity among semi-barbarous peoples; it is not surprising, therefore, that the latter soon forgot habits and customs that were found to be inferior to those for which they were indebted to the conquerors. This short review has been necessary to give a clear idea of the position occupied by Art in a system which was altogether political and administrative;—it was, and could be, only a very secondary one.

The genius of the Roman, as we see, has no analogy whatever with the genius of the Greek. The Greek is perpetually analysing and discussing, he never stands still, he is unwearied in research, is ever striving for perfection, he explores everything; nevertheless he is the slave of a logical principle that is based on his reason, his observations, and on his craving for harmony. In the domain of thought, his philosophers will propound systems the most antagonistic; the field of intelligence is for them not limited even by absurdity,—for, when the immaterial side of nature is concerned, by a rigorous sequence of logical deduction, that may be demonstrated as a possibility which common sense alone shows you to be impossible,—the non-existence of motion, for example, or of being itself. But, in the material domain, logic cannot lead to vagaries of this kind, for matter confronts us, visible and palpable, with its properties and its irrefragable laws. A Greek Architect may find various, even absurd, reasons for the law of gravitation; but he cannot ignore those laws,—he knows that he cannot infringe them. He may err as to the causes, but not as to the effects; for the Greek architect is, above all things, an attentive and acute observer, and is correct in the application of his observations. A Greek sculptor will not be acquainted with the mechanism by which the blood circulates, or with the exact functions of the bones and muscles; but he will observe the human body in its palpable and visible outward form, with such perfect intelligence that he will give his statue the actual lines and movements of nature,—will even exceed nature, —will, so to speak, correct and complete it, without disregarding its laws. The Greek architect will put a capital upon his column, but he will not set his column upon a base, for this base would incommode the passers-by; or, if he does put a base, it will be, like the column, circular in plan, and he will take care to raise the edge a little from the ground not to be in the way of the feet; all these methods proceed from the observation and the rigidly correct application of visible natural phenomena.

Let us pass on from details. Here is a most important fact, and one that merits our whole attention. In our last Lecture we saw how the Greek builder proceeds when he erects a temple, and by what course of logical sequence he ultimately succeeds in composing that collective architectural distribution which we designate ORDER,—that is, accordance of the isolated points of support with the thing supported. This distribution found,—all these parts placed in their due relation to each other, first, by the promptings of necessity, and secondly, through careful consideration of their relative effects, their functions, and the nature, apparent and hidden, of the materials,—the Greek architect, having attained proportions,—a correlation of the architectural members that satisfies both his reason and his senses, which are of exquisite delicacy,—is convinced that he has produced a work which cannot be modified without offending reason and the senses, since it is nothing other than the combined result of these faculties. He is quite as certain of the justness of his reasoning as the geometrician is of the truth of his demonstration ; he is sure that his senses are perfect, because they speak to him in a language that is understood by all his fellows : in a word, he has confidence in his reason and in his genius, and he will not admit that reason and genius can solve a given problem in two ways equally good and simple. Sceptical as a philosopher, he is no sceptic as an artist : he regards matter as susceptible of definite scientific treatment, which he verifies by experiment. If he is ignorant of its composition, he has remarked the effects of its strength, its weight ; of the light and shade upon its surface, and of its resistance to external action. The result he has obtained is then for him the only possible one. From this assurance respecting the Good and the Beautiful in the Greek mind,—given a concurrence of circumstances,—to the exact reproduction under similar conditions of this same Perfect and Beautiful, the deduction is natural and logical ; and thus, accordingly, reasons the Greek : "Since I have established an architectural ORDER whose parts are all in their necessary places,—since I have succeeded in making these various combined members produce an effect satisfactory both to reason and to the senses,—this order is order in its ideal perfection. If I take away one of its members,—if I alter the relation they bear to one another,—I destroy my work ; but my work is perfect, therefore I ought to preserve it intact. How have I proceeded in order to arrive at this perfection ? First, I placed myself under the guidance of my reason : that told me how I should put transverse stones upon vertical supports ; what space I should leave between these supports ; how I should tie my portico to the wall of the cella, and how I should shelter the whole. Then my senses suggested the forms and proportions that should be given to my building, and how I should ornament them. My work is, therefore, good in all respects ; it has *unity ;* it has its principle of harmony, independently of the dimensions, for the dimensions do not change the proportions; accordingly, whether I have to erect a portico of thirty cubits in height, or one of only ten cubits, the relative proportions of the different parts of this portico, namely, of the columns, their openings, and the entablature, cannot be changed. Therefore, my order is a unique type whose proportions I shall reproduce irrespectively of the size."

This is how the Greek architect reasons; and if the soundness of reasoning may be estimated by the length of time it has been applied, the Greek must have reasoned admirably. In fact, the Greek Order or Orders, once found, preserve their relative proportions irrespectively of the dimensions; and this method applied among the Romans, with certain modifications which we shall have occasion to discuss, was completely abandoned only by the architects of the Middle Ages. Greek architecture has its module dependent on itself. Medieval architecture has a module external to itself,—the human size. Roman architecture forms a transition between these two methods, and this transition results from the preference given by the Romans to utility and the satisfaction of material requirements, over the instinctive and abstract forms of Greek Art.

We have very briefly reviewed the state of Roman society, and the system adopted by Rome in the vast territories she had acquired: her architecture is the faithful transcript of her policy, and for that reason it presents us with an inexhaustible subject of study,—a source of instruction to be found nowhere else; but this study must be conducted with discernment, by considering Roman architecture in its real form, and not in the details by which, with a stoical indifference, its structure is invested. In Greek architecture the visible external form is the logical result of the construction; Greek architecture may be best compared to a man stript of his clothes, the external parts of whose body are but the consequence of his organic structure, of his wants, of the framework of his bones, and the functions of his muscles. The man is so much the more beautiful as all the parts of his body are in harmony with their purpose, and, with nothing superfluous, they yet suffice for their functions.

Roman architecture, on the other hand, may be compared to a man clothed: there is the man, and there is the dress; the dress may be good or bad, rich or poor in material, well or ill cut, but it forms no part of the body; if well made and handsome it merits examination; if it restrains the man's movements, and its shape has neither reason nor grace, it is unworthy of notice. In Roman architecture we have the structure,—the veritable, substantial, and useful construction devised to meet the requirements of a plan laid down by a master-hand; and we have also the covering,—the adornment,—which is independent of the structure, as the dress is independent of the man's body. To the Roman, whose tendencies are mainly political, its form is a question of secondary importance. He demands but one thing from the appareller of his buildings, which is, that the dress shall do him honour. Otherwise, it is a matter of indifference to him whether it is structurally logical, whether it exactly interprets the essential constructive forms of the edifice,—whether it is the fit and true casing of those forms, and whether it explains their purposes. The Roman occupies a position above, or, if we will, beside the Greek reasoner ; he does not understand him.

I have sometimes been accused of laying too much stress on reason in Architecture, and of undervaluing sentiment ; and what I have just said might perhaps give a certain plausibility to this reproach if I were not to develop my meaning. What then, in reference to Art, is sentiment ? Is it not simply an involuntary action of reason which education has grafted upon instinct ? A shepherd's dog is only a wolf whose instinct is directed by its brute reason, which education has developed ;—instead of eating the sheep, it watches to prevent their being stolen or worried. Our instinct prompts us to utter various sounds ; our sentiment tells us that some intonations are false, while others are true ; and why ? Is it not because reason has reacted on our instincts ? Why is a note false ? Why in Architecture are some proportions inharmonious ? Is it not, then, reason that acts upon our senses independently of our will,—to regulate, and to make of them that which we call sentiment ? Were not the Greeks a people who reasoned to such a degree that reasoning landed many of their philosophers in paradoxical absurdities ? Now, this race of reasoners was also the nation most gifted with the instinct of Art ; they were the first who, in Architecture, established the orders, —that is to say, who could turn instinct into a law,—the law of proportions. Previous to the Greeks we find every nation that has left architectural monuments evidently guided by the same instinct,—this innate desire to establish certain relations and diversities between the parts of a building ; but we know of none that ever gave to this instinct the authority of a law, and a good law, since it has never been modified without detriment to the effect produced on the senses. All the buildings in the world, from farthest East to West, —I refer of course only to those worthy of note,—produce on those who look at them a double impression. Admiration, pleasure, is excited ; but besides this, the perplexity, the confusion that is felt on looking at a thing which it requires an effort of the mind to understand. Under this complex impression, unless he is stimulated by a strenuous desire to learn, the spectator is bewildered, and passes on without trying to understand. Of styles of building the Greek alone produces a simple impression; no effort is needed for knowing and understanding it; it is as clear to the first comer as to the accomplished artist. What it means it says at once, and to all; and strangely enough, this singular and admirable quality seems a defect in the eyes of those who are in the habit of regarding architecture as a series of puzzles. I have sometimes heard it asked: "In what respect is the Parthenon beautiful?" It might as well be asked: "In what respect is an unclothed, well-formed young man beautiful?" To this question the only reply would be, "An unclothed man is beautiful because he *is*, because, without any effort of the mind, —without consideration—we know that he moves, that he is vigorous, that he feels, sees, thinks,—in a word, that he is complete, that he has unity." By means of their law of the Orders, the Greeks, in their architecture, succeeded in producing on the senses this simplicity of impression. The Greek building needs neither to be explained nor to be elucidated: it is beautiful because it cannot be otherwise, as the man is beautiful because he is perfection. I do not believe it possible to attain to this perfection otherwise than by employing reason to satisfy the instincts.

Vitruvius, no great philosopher, but yet imbued with Greek ideas on Art,—which, like a true Roman, he only superficially reflects,—begins his third book on the temples with a chapter in which he undertakes to establish an analogy between the proportions of the human body and those of the temples and the orders which compose them. This chapter of Vitruvius does not in fact establish anything; we cannot draw from it any conclusion whatever : but it lifts a corner of the veil which conceals from us the philosophy applied by the Greeks in their architecture, if instead of trying to find in the structure of the human body a metrical scale, such as Vitruvius supposes with a view to establish proportions between the parts of an architectural distribution, we try to find a method. We must not forget that the Greeks made man the centre-point of everything, and that no people ever studied him better from a psychological and material point of view. In order to establish laws for architectural proportions, as the Greeks did, it was essential to find a basis, or point of departure: for proportions are in the first instance merely arbitrary relations,—instinctive wants that cannot be strictly defined. Now the Greeks, though poets, were not men to rest content with mere vague ideas; they must apply a definite form or principle to everything, even in the immaterial world. Their mythology is a most evident proof of this.

If a treatise on architecture by Ictinus had been preserved we should perhaps have had a precise explanation of this analogy of the human body with architectural composition in general, and with the Orders in particular. In default of this work we will try and reason as Ictinus might have done. Of organised beings man is the most complete; and this relative perfection is so evident and so real that he has become the ruler over all. He is the ideal of structure; if, therefore, we would construct, we should take him as our model, not as to the form to be given to the things constructed, but as to the method applicable to these constructions. Man excels all living creatures in beauty, because his structure is in perfect harmony with his wants, his functions, and his intellectual impulses. Consequently, if the building is to be beautiful, its structure must rigorously follow this principle. There are many creatures with certain organs more perfect than those of man; many are stronger or more nimble; but none present so complete a combination of physical faculties in harmonious accord with material and intellectual necessities. For the construction, therefore, of a perfect building, this accord, this analogy between the requirements and the external form must be found. From this point of view the structure of the human body might certainly have been considered by the Greeks as indicative of a good method to be followed when architecture had developed, and it was necessary to find for it a form of beauty that should explain the structure, and be in harmony with it. But, as I have already said, the Greek is above everything an observer and a lover of form; what he sees in the human body is not what *we* find there,—we who as anatomists subject everything to analysis; he simply observes with an incomparable intelligence that the bones are moved by groups of muscles which cover them and which are encased in an elastic tissue; he studied osteology only through the play of the muscles and the cutaneous envelope; he does not dissect these different parts of contemporaneous origin in order to examine them separately; but he knows exactly their functions and their relations,—in a word, their appearance. Accordingly, when he builds, he gives to every member of his architecture this harmonious relation in accord with its function,—he preserves that economy and propriety in arrangement which is so charming in the human body. Thus there may be some truth in the spirit if not in the letter of his text when Vitruvius speaks of the influence of the human form upon Greek architecture. I think we should be wary of fanciful ideas in the philosophical study of a positive art such as Architecture. With my readers' permission I will substantiate the principles I have been describing by the examination of certain forms in Greek architecture that serve to establish them.

In the structure of every organic being, and especially in that of man, whatever be the movement or the posture, not only is the osteological system always apparent, but it presents salient points connected by curves, convex or concave, according to the nature of the fleshy parts that exist between them. The more energetic the movement, the more nearly do these curves approach to a straight line. The Greeks understood and observed this rule in Statuary, as might have been expected; and they appear to have been the first to apply it in Architecture. Previous to them, the Egyptians, in the profiles of their architecture, certainly had in

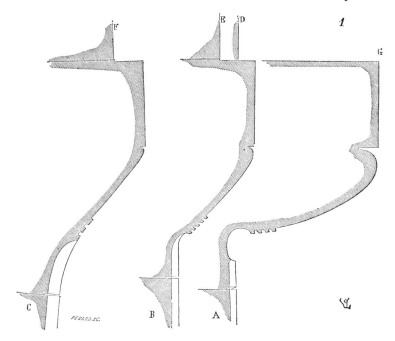

Successive forms of the Doric Capital.

view an imitation of the vegetal system. Their capitals, for instance, evidently reproduce the curves of flowers or fruit. It is not so with the Greeks : their profiles recall much rather the curves formed by the muscles attached to the ends, and covering the intermediate spaces, of the bones. When the artist desires to give an appearance of strength to any member of his design, he is careful, in tracing his profiles, to adopt the vigorous lines which the human body assumes when the muscles are strained by violent movement or effort. Accordingly, he does not trace his profile by any mechanical means, such as the compass ; his hand is guided only by an exquisite sense of the forms he has observed and knows so well. The line of the Doric capital, for instance, in the most ancient Greek buildings, has a rather decided curve (fig. 1, section A).[1]

The more the artist reasons on his art, the more he tries to perfect the expression by which he would interpret his meaning; he is led to strengthen the original expression,—to render it clearer: the line of the early Doric capital soon appears to him deficient in vigour, and insufficiently expressive of a support; he gradually modifies it to the form of section B;[2] then he continues the column into the capital, and ceases to make of the torus beneath the abacus anything but a simple cone, as shown in section C.[3]

Thus, following out his course of reasoning, the Greek architect passes, by an imperceptible transition, from the capital A, whose torus resembles a cushion,—a soft body interposed between the column and the abacus,—to the capital C, whose profile, firm to rigidity, is truly that of a strong support, directing the whole weight of the abacus, and that which it carries, upon the shaft of the column.

If we examine these sections attentively, we shall see that the reasoning of the builder and the feeling of the artist go hand-in-hand. The architrave bearing on the capital A, the most ancient of the three, has its face at D, *i.e.* vertical with that of the shaft. Already the builder of the Parthenon has felt his sense offended by the sight of this projection, D G remaining useless after the erection ; he therefore advanced the face of the architrave resting upon his capital to E,—that is, he made it overhang, and thereby gave vigour to his capital. Soon after, the Greek architect still further advances the face of the architrave F beyond the face of the column, and strengthens the expression of support given to the capital.

It is plain that if the Greeks did not imitate timber work in the construction of the stone or marble edifices whose remains are extant, neither did they imitate vegetable forms in the details of these buildings as the Egyptians always did, as the Romans attempted to do, and, later on, the artists of the Middle Ages.

I have said that the Greeks were the first to establish certain laws of proportion which we designate as *Orders* or distribution of parts ; but we must not thence conclude the Greek Order or Orders to be absolute in proportions observed. These laws did not among them hamper the liberty of the artist. Far from it ; they were not absolute but relative ; and although we may be able to establish certain proportions between the different members of the Doric order at the same period, there is nevertheless

---

[1] From the Acropolis, Selinuntum.
[2] From the Parthenon.   [3] Temple of Ceres, Eleusis.

great freedom and endless variety in the application of these rules ; the Doric order is always the Doric order, as a man is always a man ; but one is stout, another slight ; this one is short and sturdy, that one is tall and thin. This variety does not destroy relative proportions nor relative harmony : what the Greeks never do, whether we look at their statuary or their architecture, is to place the head and trunk of a Hercules upon the legs of a Bacchus,— a heavy and massive entablature upon columns slight and wide apart. They carry this study of the relations that should exist in a composition, that is in all the parts of the same edifice, into the smallest details. Not only do these ratios, these relations exist between the principal members of a design—between the columns, the capitals, the entablatures, the distances of the points of support, the voids and the solids,—but also between the pro- files—their shape, their projection ; they are even regarded (as far as we are able to judge) in the colouring of these buildings.

In the construction of their more important buildings the Greeks usually employed but two orders, the Doric and the Ionic. If we compare these two orders, it is easy to see that each pos- sesses a harmony of its own, though both are derived from the same principle. The structure is the same, the fashion only varies. Grave and simple in its design and general proportions, the Doric order presents a similar gravity and simplicity in its smallest details ; effect is obtained, as we have already shown, by the contours, the outlines, the play of light and shade upon large surfaces, and by the form of the mouldings. The Ionic order, on the other hand, elegant in its general proportions, preserves this elegance in the details, in the greater number and fineness of its mouldings, the more delicate and less sparingly distributed ornamentation. The Doric order seems to be designed for buildings of the largest size, or which, from their situation, should be viewed from a distance ; the Ionic seems more adapted to edifices intended for closer view, so as to engage the eyes by the delicacy of the details. It might almost be said that the Doric order is male and the Ionic female ; and yet neither of them ever departs from the general rules which the Greek architect has deemed obligatory in the orders or in the composition. If the columns in the Ionic order are slighter than in the Doric, they are covered with a greater number of flutings : their capitals are adorned with sculpture and are made more important ; the members of the entablature are more numerous, and the shafts of the columns stand upon circular bases ; for the instinct of the Greek artist made him feel that in ornamenting the capitals and working the columns more finely, he could not place them abruptly upon the pedestal,—that a transition was necessary. Most of the general principles are found equally applied in both orders ;

the *antes* never have capitals like those of columns ; for the Greek has too much good sense to put on a flat pilaster, or on the top of a wall, the capital which he considers appropriate for a column or a shaft whose section is circular. In both orders the structure is the same ; only in later times did the Greek suppress in the Doric order certain subordinate members of the construction,— the triglyphs, for instance.

It must not be supposed that the adoption of orders neces- sarily fettered the Greek architect ; principles do not destroy the individual liberty of the artist, who is ever seeking to improve, and never thinks he has reached absolute perfection. We have endeavoured to explain the importance he attaches to effect ; with what nicety he observes the play of the lights and shadows upon the surfaces, and the picturesque detaching of the outlines upon the sky. The Greek artist is gifted with senses too refined to allow him to follow blindly an imperious law. If symmetry is admitted by him it is rather as a principle of coun- terpoise than as a geometrical rule. It would never have entered into the mind of a Greek artist to give a similar appearance to two buildings intended for different purposes. The remains of their monuments and the valuable description of Pausanias prove that the Greeks never admitted the miserable expedient of modern architects who think to produce a grand general effect by conforming all the buildings of a public square, whatever be their separate destination, to the same design. The Greek observes nature and proceeds as she does ; if she has her laws, she also has infinite variety. A Greek architect to whom we might endeavour to point out the beauty of the symmetrical designs of our great modern architectural conceptions,—of those façades, exactly alike, of buildings that differ in their internal arrange- ments and in their orientation,—would regard us with pity and might say to us, " Why, since you believe that beauty resides principally in symmetry, do you not ask Heaven to make the sun rise and set in the east and in the west at the same time, so that your buildings may be lighted on both sides at once ? In nature everything proceeds by contrasts : she proves to you that Good only manifests itself when in contrast with Evil,—that Light cannot exist without Shadow,—that a thing is great only by its relative size,—that there exist not two beings of the same kind exactly alike ; yet you think to attain to the Good and the Beautiful by changing the natural order of things,—by substitut- ing Uniformity for Variety. I observe a square surrounded by buildings ; this is a court of justice, that a minister's palace, the next contains offices or rooms for the clerks, the fourth is a bar- rack, the fifth a bank, the sixth a place devoted to public amuse- ments. You tell me so, and I am willing to believe it ; but unless you write over the doors of the various places what they contain, how shall I know? This side of the square is exposed all day to the sun, that side remains in shadow; yet I see on the side in shadow the same porticos as on the side in light. I see that the clerks' rooms have windows like those of the concert-hall. I see the same ornaments carved on the friezes of these six buildings, the same emblems on their summits; and you who proceed in this unreasonable way and in order, as you allege, to conform to the rules of Art, you affect to be imbued with our spirit. You have never then visited Attica, or the Peloponnesus, or our colonies. Or do you pretend to be inspired by our arts, because I see here columns surmounted by Greek capitals and entablatures?—orders placed here and there with no apparent object? Do you think that Architecture consists in repeating upon a front parts you have taken from us and which you copy but indifferently? I do not know what people you are, but you are not Greeks, nor even Romans. Our architects did not proceed in this fashion. They had rules certainly, but rules to be interpreted, not servilely followed as a flock of sheep follows in the same track under the leading of the shepherd. The Greek architect who was intrusted with the execution of a building sought in the first place to fulfil exactly the conditions laid down for him; he wished the purpose of his building to be made evident to all, not only by the general arrangements but by the sculpture which adorned it; he laid it out with due regard to the aspect most desirable for the function of its several parts; he would not have ornamented a building intended for the accommodation of clerks as he would the palace of a chief magistrate, or an assembly room. A lover of his work, studying it in every particular, continually re-examining and improving it, he wished to leave nothing imperfect; he would not have masked clumsy partitions of deal or lath and plaster behind splendid fronts; he would have quitted his work with regret, fearful of having forgotten some detail, of having neglected some out-of-the-way corner, or of having left some handle to the critic. Then do not say that you follow in our track if you have robbed us of some few rags with which you deck yourselves, like the savages who imagine they inspire respect by throwing over their shoulders a piece of crimson cloth. You understand neither our spirit nor our language. Those who preceded you by a few centuries in this city, and whom you call barbarous, resembled us much more than you do. If they spoke a language different from mine I nevertheless know that they reasoned, that they felt and knew how to express what they wanted to say. I hear that our artists are highly spoken of in your schools. Is it in joke? Do you believe that you pay them a compliment by ignoring their intelligence or their intellect, while you adopt their dress,—a dress unsuited to you, and which you don't know how to wear?" An ancient Greek brought to Paris or London in the present day might say a great deal more; but this may suffice.

Having gained some acquaintance with the Greek spirit in its action on the arts, let us now consider that of the Roman.

The Roman people has at command numerous armies which it can employ in public works, and a slave population at least double that of the citizens. So much for labour. Its conquests and the way it administers them bring a stream of wealth into its treasuries. With the labour it will erect buildings: with the wealth it will pay artists and buy costly materials. Its political and social constitution makes of the erection and decoration of buildings two distinct operations. The method of the Roman, who is eminently practical, consists in the employment of means for building in accordance with his social condition. If he is able (and his wealth nearly always renders him so) he will clothe his building in forms of splendour: but first he provides an incredible number of labourers and sets them to work. Now every man, provided he has strength of arm, can break stones, make lime, wheel sand, mould and bake bricks; no instruction is needed for the execution of these preliminary works. Armies or slaves collected from every part of Europe are capable of it. Thus thinks the Roman, and he acts accordingly. With these means, then, what is the most convenient method for erecting large buildings? Assuredly not that of quarrying with much labour and trouble stones of great size and proportionate weight, difficult of carriage, requiring skilful masons to work them, and complicated machinery to raise and set them, a great expenditure of time, and a special staff of workmen. With the Roman this mode of building is quite exceptional. His customary plan is very different. With numerous, and for the most part ignorant, labourers at his command, he will accumulate vast quantities of small materials,—will mould bricks, burn lime on the site, and draw sand; then the architects will set out the walls and the piers; thousands of labourers, kept at work with military discipline, by foremen under the supervision of directors, will mix the mortar and carry the stones, the gravel, and the bricks; while out of this multitude a few special workmen will build up the faces, and the labourers will fill in the masonry with solid concrete. When the spring of the vaulting is reached the science of the architect will enter in; he will prepare wooden centres. There is no lack of timber: the provinces of Gaul and Germany are covered with immense forests. Upon these centres he will lay close-fitting planks, and, this operation completed, the same masons and labourers will come and encase this wooden form with their bricks, rubble, and mortar. A skilful head, a few carpenters, a few good masons, and some thousands of labourers, may thus erect a building of the largest size in the course of a few months. Nothing in our day more nearly represents the Roman method of building than our great Railway works ; their most artistic constructions were raised in the same manner, by employing a few skilful craftsmen and thousands of labourers working blindly but under a regular and severe supervision, according to particular rules established by experience. In support of what I have said, and in proof of the indifference of the Romans as to the decoration of their edifices, how many public buildings might be cited that have remained simply in the rough ?—though the Romans had several centuries in which to complete their artistic covering. At Rome the Great Gate that serves for the issue of the Claudian water,—a triumphal arch,—an edifice designed with architectural pretension, is not dressed down ; and what deserves special remark is that this Great Gate, built by Tiberius Claudius, son of Drusus, was restored, as well as the aqueduct, by Vespasian and by Titus his son. The founders, as well as the restorers of this magnificent aqueduct, thought proper to recall their munificence by inscriptions, but failed to give this public work its finishing strokes. Before engraving his name upon an edifice built at his expense, a Greek would have desired first to see his building finished, and worthy of transmitting to posterity its founder's taste and love for the arts. Even in the Coliseum there are parts where the dressing is only roughed in. But it is more especially at a distance from the capital that this neglect appears. The amphitheatre at Nîmes in Provence is not entirely dressed down, and the great aqueduct called the Pont du Gard has never been, except at a few points. In every province of the empire proofs may be seen of this indifference to artistic form. The chief concern of the Roman is the plan of his edifice, that is to say, the exact situation of each service of the building he desires to erect, —the relative dimensions of the parts, either as to surface or height ;—and in addition to this (what we who affect to be Roman scarcely think about) the orientation, the selection of the site, the way to profit by the irregularities of the ground, and economy. The Roman is never parsimonious, but he is economical ; that is to say, he will not permit waste either of space or of materials ; he cannot comprehend the artist who works, like the Greek or the master builder of the Middle Ages, for himself alone ; he expects the sculptor whom he employs to work for the public, and demands that his wealth shall do honour to him—the Roman : moreover, he does not call in the artist until the material requirements are satisfied ;—once again the artist is only an appareller. The Roman scarcely troubles his head about the form or finish of the details ; he prefers to cover his building with costly marbles, rich in colour, valuing them in proportion as they are rare and difficult to work : here he betrays the taste of the parvenu.

How very unlike is this method of production to that of the Greeks ! Among them all the workmen are artists. Do not ask them for buildings in which man plays the part of a machine. Of mortar they do not use a cubic yard throughout their buildings ; their foundations are laid with dry stones, hastily ; they avoid this mechanical and unseen labour as much as possible, and where they can, they place their buildings on the rock,—a foundation which in their territory abundantly exists. Of the constructions above ground, however, they aim to show every part ; the mason has his feeling of pride quite as much as the statuary ; he desires that *his* stone should be *seen*,—that at least one of its faces should be exposed to view. If the Greek does not make use of vaulting, it is not so much because he is ignorant of it—that we can hardly admit,—as because this mode of construction requires strong abutments, heavy bulks of masonry ; and he dislikes employing human labour to construct an inert mass of which a great deal is out of sight, necessitating tedious and mechanical labour. Whatever the advantages of a vaulted building, these advantages, in the view of the Greek, cannot compensate, if I may use the expression, for the humiliating labour in the abutments : besides, the soil of Greece, while rendering foundations unnecessary, afforded a great abundance of most excellent building materials. If marble happens to be wanting, as in Magna Græcia and in Sicily, he covers the stone he employs with a fine stucco laid on with remarkable care and skill, and paints this stucco in a way to bring out his work, to embellish it ; for the Greek is pre-eminently artistic ; he respects what he produces, and is unwilling that a single detail of his work should be lost to the eye.

When the Roman has erected his building in the manner just described, if he can find capable artists and can procure marbles,—even though it were at great expense and from the most distant countries,—as soon as the necessary conditions of his programme are fulfilled, he overlays his construction with costly material cut into thin slabs, ornaments it with string courses, and attaches to it columns and entablatures. On the vaulting he lays carved stucco work, painted and gilt : in fact, in material effect he apes the Greek as much as he can. But the Greek buildings are small, whereas the Roman buildings are large and lofty ; the Roman superimposes the Greek orders ; and, which is still more worthy of remark (and here the indifference of the Roman for Greek rationalism shows itself), the Greek orders support architraves only, while the Roman hardly ever employs in his public buildings anything but the arch and the vault; builds up engaged columns against the piers of his arches, and over the archivolts he puts *architraves* on his columns; that is to say, he makes use of the Greek composition as a frame serving to ornament the necessary part of his construction;—a strange blunder, which plainly shows how the Roman separates the construction from the decoration,—regarding the latter as a mere luxury,—a dress whose use or origin is of slight concern to him.

It is in this application to their buildings of Greek forms in contradiction with Greek construction that the Romans should not be imitated; yet we must say that since the period of the Renaissance this has been the starting-point of our study of Roman architecture; to such a degree, everywhere and always, are true principles,—though obviously conformable to reason and good sense,—disregarded even by those who ought to acknowledge and observe them as axioms. Nothing certainly can be more opposed to good sense than putting a lintel over an arch, since the office of the arch being in itself to relieve, it should on the contrary be placed over the lintel which can hardly carry itself. The weak thing should not protect but be protected by the strong. This is an invariable rule. The country women who go to market in the town carry their shoes in their hand all the way, and do not put them on till they enter it; any one may have observed this fact. What should we think of a person who should conclude from this that shoes are made to be carried in the hand when we walk, in order to be put on the feet when we sit down? Who would like to adopt this custom, and who would regard as barbarians the people who put on shoes to walk? The form of the foot may be faultless, the shoe perfection; but it will not be less true that shoes are made to be worn on the feet and not carried in the hand. It is not sufficient to admire the productions of antiquity: we should inquire in the first instance whether they are fitted for their place: and certainly a lintel upon engaged columns surmounting an arch would greatly shock a Greek of the time of Pericles. He would not fail to ask, on seeing these ill-assorted constructions combined, "Whether the lintel had not been broken, and whether, in order to support it, piers had not been afterwards built against the columns and an arch put as an under-pinning;" but when it came to be told him that this construction was so designed, and that it is an architectural composition, we fancy the Greek would shrug his shoulders. We are not now Greeks, and may not shrug our shoulders every time such blunders present themselves. But we may always reason, and need not accept Roman architecture

as it has come down to us in the gross : we may distinguish the
Roman buildings, admirable in themselves, from their borrowed
wrapping; and this we set ourselves to do.

While acknowledging the advantages appertaining to both
Greek and Roman architecture, we need not confound the two
in a common admiration; we may distinguish them as the
expression of different, and even opposite principles ; may see in
the former the most liberal and refined interpretation of noble
human instincts ; in the second, the absolute subordination to
material requirements, and to the organisation of a powerful
state. All that remains to us of Greek architecture is a small
number of buildings, almost entirely in ruin, and of the same
nature ; they are beyond criticism ; we can only admire these
relics of a wonderful art, and seek therein those forgotten vital
principles which I have endeavoured to bring again to light.

This, however, is not the case with Roman architecture.
It is found in works of every kind, from the Roman road and
the aqueduct to the triumphal arch and the votive column. The
history of the Roman people from the end of the Republic is
perfectly familiar to us,—more so, certainly, than our own ; and
its laws and customs are clearly ascertained. It is possible, then,
if not easy, to follow the advance of the arts step by step through
the history of this great people, inasmuch as the arts among the
Romans, like their religion, are scarcely more than the instruments of their unvarying policy. "It was neither fear nor piety
that established religion among the Romans," says Montesquieu,
" but the necessity under which all societies lie of having one. . ."
And further on, "I find this difference between Roman legislators
and those of other peoples, that by the former the religion was
made for the state, and by the latter the state for the religion."
This passage may be equally well applied to the Arts ; the
Romans had arts because they considered that it was proper for
every civilised state to have arts ; it was a matter of convention,
not of conviction, as with the Egyptians and the Greeks. And
observe that when the Romans build a temple,—a sanctuary for
the Divinity,—they take its plan and design from the Greeks ;
they have no temple properly their own, like the Egyptians and the
Greeks. The State religion of Rome was a Greek importation.
In mythology, the two peoples had the same ideas,—the deifica-
tion of natural forces ; but myths appear in very different forms.
Thus, for instance, to illustrate this difference, the god *Sterquili-
nius* (of manure), the symbol of Productive Power among the
Romans, corresponds to Eros (Love) among the Greeks. But
when buildings for the service of the State are in question, the
Roman legislator steps in ; he commands ; he knows what he
wants, and only borrows from other people the dress of his build-

ing. This, moreover, he shapes to his liking. He does not permit the artist to fetter him with his principles : he cares not to untie the Gordian knot,—he cuts it. He acts in reference to the arts as Claudius Pulcher, on the eve of a naval battle, treated the superstition of his soldiers. The sacred fowls, on being consulted, would not eat, which was a bad omen. "Since they will not eat," said he, "let them drink ; " and he had them thrown into the sea. While to the artist by conviction Art is a religion, a lively, ardent faith, it is merely a fettering prejudice to all who are not artists. Imagine a number of Architects, Sculptors, and Painters, all obedient to inflexible principles, living in a state that has no single conviction in respect of Art ; endless difficulties would arise. The Romans, pre-eminently politicians, legislators, and administrators, could not permit such restraints in their social body. Among them, artists are either slaves or freedmen,—or at most, citizens designedly kept in a position of obscurity. They will rather make a Prefect of a flute-player than of an architect. It is a matter of indifference to the Roman whether the architect employs this or that order, cornice, or moulding in his building. But the moment he attempts to reason,—to urge certain principles on which he feels bound to act as paramount to the will of the Edile ;—should he refuse, for example, to give three stories to an edifice which would be in better proportion with only two,—whatever authority he might invoke, or however excellent the reasons he might allege,—the Edile would command him peremptorily to obey, and not to amuse himself by disputing with him on the principles of his art ; for he, the Roman, recognises no authority except the interests of the State. A well-known incident shows what were the ideas of the Romans in reference to art. Mummius Achaicus, giving orders for the conveyance from Greece to Rome of some valuable works of art, stipulated that, if a certain painting by Zeuxis were injured, the careless or guilty persons should be bound to re-produce it. It is uncertain how artists were treated by the Roman authorities, or what degree of independence they were allowed ; thus we can only conjecture ; but we know what were the opinions of those authorities respecting certain sects of religion whose position was that which artists professing in-flexible principles amid Roman society would have occupied.

No government was ever more tolerant than the Roman ; it admitted all religions on the condition of their being tolerant themselves : only the Egyptian, the Jewish, and the Christian religions were proscribed by it, because they were all three sup-posed to be intolerant, and were considered dangerous to the State. For some time no distinction was made between them ; because, in the view of the State, among the Egyptians, the Jews, and the Christians, the priests formed a separate body independent of the civil authority,—making a distinction between the spiritual and the temporal, in modern parlance. The Romans repressed the worship of Bacchus, for example, not as a religious worship, but as opposed to public order; just as the State in modern times accords liberty of worship, but cannot permit any religious body to cause scandal or disorder in public. At Rome, the priest or diviner was one of the civil authorities. " In our city," says Cicero,[1] "the kings, and the rulers who have succeeded them, have always sustained a twofold character, and have governed the State under the auspices of religion." If the Roman government entertained these views concerning the practice of religion, still more decidedly would it maintain them in reference to the arts, which it considered of far less importance. We shall not here undertake to show, from the Art point of view simply, whether the Roman was right or wrong;—whether, under the oppression of civil authority, Art could develop itself or would of necessity gradually fall into disregard. Our only object here is to present such evidence as may enable our readers to perceive the wide difference that separates Greek from Roman Art. Our task, moreover, is not to write the political history of nations, but to point out in what degree the Arts,—that of Architecture in particular,—reflect the moral life, and the institutions of the peoples among whom they are developed. In point of religion, the Greeks were less tolerant than the Romans; witness the death of Socrates, the persecution of Alcibiades for having desecrated the Athenian Hermæ, and, as having the same bearing, the fact that the Peloponnesians did not join the Greek army till the day after the battle of Marathon, because they had to celebrate a religious festival; their civil institutions were far from being characterised by the strength and wisdom which distinguished those of Rome : they had no steadfastness or consistency of purpose or action ; and yet this state of things was wonderfully favourable to the development of the arts. If we were constrained to draw rigorous conclusions from all this, those conclusions would be sad, for they would tend to nothing less than this, that the more wise, powerful, and well-regulated the institutions by which nations are governed, the less capable are the arts of freely manifesting their proper vigour, and producing works in perfection. No one, perhaps, reasoned thus in the presence of Louis xiv. ; but the feeling which led this prince to cover France with public buildings in the Roman style was perfectly in agreement with his principles as an absolute monarch,—as head of the national unity : Roman architecture alone could be in harmony

---

[1] *De Divinatione*, Lib. i. c. xl. See the *Dissertation sur la Politique des Romains dans la religion.* —Montesquieu.

with his political system ; and he would have had little toleration for the sentiment that if a nation wishes to have arts, it must allow a certain degree of liberty to artists in matters of art. We say once for all : when man is in question, with his various feelings and relations, and the products of his reason and feelings, the conclusions of a rigorous logic are seldom correct. We must take account of the infinite variety of human instincts ; the contradictory elements of which man is composed ; his traditions, prejudices, and temperament. Nevertheless, there are certain laws of mental phenomena as exhibited by the nations of the earth, which survive the ages ; which manifest themselves in spite of revolutions and religious differences, and which remain always the same. Those two opposing principles in the development of the arts, whose originating causes among the Greeks and the Romans we have just pointed out, are and will be always in the field ; and we shall see how, in ages long subsequent to their first appearance, they act upon architecture. We ask then,—Is it not puerile, with history before us and these powerful currents of human intelligence which it presents, to discuss the pre-eminence of this school or that, to anathematise one form of art, and to deify another ? Truly, we have something better to do.

I cannot too frequently repeat it: ART is unique. Its essential characteristic is the harmony it presents with national manners, institutions, and genius. If it assumes different forms, it is because this genius, those manners and institutions vary ; if, in the course of time, it seems to return to the point whence it set out, it is because an analogous phenomenon presents itself in the national institutions, manners, and genius. If it has missed its way, and is seeking it in every direction, do not let us call out to it, "This is the only right course,—that which I have chosen." Let us content ourselves with illuminating its path, and diffusing light over the whole field ; let us aid it by attentive study, by earnest and faithful analysis ; but let us not impel it to the right or to the left, under the pretence of conducting it in the true path. The study and the love of Art,—not of *one* form of art, —and research into its true principles, are the only means to which the wise will recur when art seems to decline, or to have lost its way.

We have just spoken of national *genius;* but what is national genius ?—I wish to leave nothing indefinite in the minds of my readers,—to avoid those vague words which favour ambiguity ; for we ought to have a clear understanding on all points. In social organisms there are three distinct elements : the element which we call the genius of a nation, the customs it adopts, and the institutions to which it submits of its own free will or by compulsion. The ancient nations with whom we are familiar,—

the Greeks and Romans,—so different from each other, have each their own genius in perfect harmony with their customs and institutions. Such harmony has not always been preserved subsequent to the establishment of Christianity. The frightful disorder caused by the invasions of the barbarians on the continent has left profound traces visible even now, and which it will take long to efface. Hence those monstrous contradictions, both in the Middle Ages and in modern times, between the genius of the peoples, the institutions which govern them, and the customs they adopt. Hence also an incessant tendency on the part of those peoples to follow the inspirations of their own genius, and the violent methods adopted to stifle those inspirations which often conflict with the institutions to which they have been obliged to submit.

This short digression is necessary to explain what I mean by the genius of a people. The genius of a people is none other than the mode in which it expresses its physical and moral requirements. The genius of the Greek people leads it to give prominence to its conceptions, and to clothe them with a rational form. The genius of the Roman people leads it to subject everything to considerations of public interest,—to what we call the government. The Greek subordinates his institutions to his genius : while the very genius of the Roman nation is submission to its institutions. "*Morituri te salutant, Cæsar.*" This phrase, "Those doomed to death salute thee, Cæsar," is the truest expression of the Roman genius. Athens had its Socrates ; Rome could not have had such a man. Socrates is an Athenian at Athens ; he is listened to, he is dangerous, he undermines beliefs by subjecting them to discussion ; he is put to death : he would not have been a Roman at Rome, would not have been listened to, would not have been dangerous. At Rome it was the Gracchi that were considered dangerous. Still more, Spurius Mœlius, who, having distributed corn gratis to the people in a time of famine, was killed by Servilius Ahala, as aiming by this means at a popularity dangerous to the State. It was not philosophers, it was reformers of the social constitution, or those who put themselves in opposition to the civil law, that were regarded as dangerous at Rome. The harmony that exists between the arts of the ancients, and the genius and manners of the nations whose history is known to us, is so complete ; those arts reflect so faithfully that national character which was closely allied to their institutions, that the study of these arts is the only one that can be deemed elementary, and that ought before all others to occupy the attention of youth,—whose place, in fact, none other can fill. And if we may refer to our own position in regard to educational arrangements, we should say that all among us who have carried their studies as far as the Middle Ages and the Renaissance of the sixteenth century have not been able to do so with advantage till after they have studied Pagan antiquity. We should regard the exclusive study of Medieval Art as a step towards barbarism.   But we deem narrow and insufficient a course of instruction limited to Pagan antiquity ; and we consider illogical a curriculum that should leave unnoticed certain phases in the history of the arts, and that should leap at once from the age of the Cæsars to the age of Francis i., Julius ii., Leo x., and Henry ii.   While it is correct to regard the Arts among the Greeks and Romans as closely bound up with the institutions by which these nations were governed ; while it is reasonable and instructive to study them from this point of view, we fall into error if we insist upon establishing similarly intimate relations between the arts and the institutions of the Middle Ages.   At this epoch in our history, the genius of the people is almost always in conflict with the institutions that govern them. The arts are among the liveliest expressions of this struggle ; and as a direct consequence of this, the methods pursued, instead of being simple as among the ancients, are complex, and require to be sought out and scrutinised with care, and require the lights of criticism and analysis.   Are we to say that this study is superfluous ?   On the contrary ; in our judgment it must contribute to the development of the mind, to give us that suppleness of the intellect which is so necessary to us in the present day, in that complicated social condition which, bristling in every direction with contradictions incessantly renewed, presents a *résumé* of the traditions of the past and the physical and moral needs of the moment,—a social condition in which everything is fluctuating, unsettled, continually submitted to fresh investigation,—in which the genius of the nations seeks for definitive expression through doubts, systems, and revolutions,—in which institutions tend no longer to oppress this genius, but to reach a state of harmony with it as the result of so many experiments.

Our programme, then, is marked out.   If it is an extensive one, it is not our fault ; it is the time in which we live that requires it to be so ; it will, at least, not be blamed as narrow. We shall examine in succession that grand unity of principle which characterises the arts of Rome as far as they are truly Roman,—next the various elements which effect the destruction of this unity ; the influence of the spirit that proceeds from Christianity upon Architecture ; the new order that is established in the midst of the chaos of the first centuries of the Middle Ages,—first in the bosom of the cloisters, then, in the twelfth century, in the political world ; the relations and diversities that exist between this new order and the genius of the peoples, the secret, persistent, independent progress of the arts in the midst of political systems completely opposed to this progress, and the depression which is the consequence of this permanent condition of struggle ; for the arts of the Middle Ages form a kind of freemasonry, which, like all other isolated organisations, became narrow and sterile.   We shall follow the great movement of the Renaissance, its strange contradictions, and its effort to reach a result opposite to that which it originally contemplated.   And lastly, the means by which we may derive profit in the present day from the labours of so many generations,—the application of the principles which guided them.

We shall conclude this Lecture by replying to any of our contemporaries who challenge us to adopt a new style of Art proper to our times, as follows : " First render our time other than it really is,—a compound of the traditions of Classical Antiquity, of the influences of the spirit of Christianity, of the long struggles of the Middle Ages between the genius of the peoples and the results of the barbarian conquests, of the efforts made by the clergy and by royalty to secure absolute power, and of the incessant protests of the subordinate classes against feudal tendencies,—protests repeated with singular persistency in a direction opposed to these tendencies by daily labour.   Blot from our memory the Reformation, that enormous accumulation of learning and criticism.   Render us something other than the descendants of our ancestors.   Prevent the ages of scepticism from having an existence, and from having by that scepticism undermined all traditions and subverted all systems ; find, upon the soil of ancient Europe, a spot not covered by a ruin,—give us thoroughly homogeneous institutions, customs, and tastes that are not bound up with the past,—sciences that are not the result of the labours of our predecessors.   Make us, in fact, capable of forgetting all that was done before us.   Then we shall have a new art, and shall have produced that which was never seen before ; for, if it is difficult for man to learn, it is much more difficult for him to forget."

LECTURE IV.

ROMAN ARCHITECTURE.

THE general principles of Architectural Art, as understood and practised by the Romans, which were briefly referred to in the preceding Lecture, require further elucidation; for, however simple a style of architecture may be, that art comprises elements too varied, requirements too diversified, and necessities too absolute, to allow it to be reviewed without entering deeply into the numberless details which combine to form its visible manifestations. As I have already remarked, the outward form of Greek architecture was simply the result of a construction in logical accordance with the requirements and the means, an attentive observation of the effects produced by light and shade, and a sense of harmonious proportion.

Let us quit Greek architecture for the present. Its so remarkable productions will be often again referred to in the course of these Lectures; for it is the fountain whence, for more than twenty centuries, every human work has derived inspiration through widely different channels. Greek architecture—of which, unfortunately, we possess so few examples—will, in our use of it, serve the purpose for which it is really adapted in view of the requirements of the present, *i.e.* as the most positive and perfect type of the principles to which I shall constantly have occasion to call the attention of my readers. Roman architecture, as I have previously explained, depends on a principle diametrically opposite to that which governs Greek architecture. Its structure is merely a means for the satisfaction of a want; it is not, as with the Greeks, Construction made Art.

Among the Greeks Construction and Art are one and the same thing; the form and the structure are intimately connected: among the Romans we have the construction, and we have the form which clothes that construction, and is often independent of it. And yet the Romans borrowed much from the Greeks, as we shall presently see.

Greek architecture always proceeds by the combination of vertical and horizontal lines and surfaces. Roman architecture adds to these two elementary principles the arch and the vault, —the curved line and concave surface. From the times of the Republic we find it making use of this new element, which soon becomes the dominant principle, and which ends by subordinating the other two.

But I must first point out where the Romans borrowed from the Greeks, and the modifications introduced by their peculiar genius in the adaptation. The Romans had no religious architecture of their own; in constructing their temples they took the general plan and the Orders from the Greeks. The Greeks had composed three Orders, or rather three types of architectural distribution, each of which had its own particular proportions and ornamentation : these were the Doric, the Ionic, and the Corinthian orders. Of these three, the richest, the most elegant, and probably the least ancient, is the Corinthian : the Greek architects, however, down to the time of Pericles, show a marked preference for the Doric and Ionic orders ; in their great temples they usually adopt the Doric. The Corinthian order, of which there are few examples of a period previous to the Roman Empire, seems to have been applied by the Greeks only to buildings of small size, such, for instance, as the little votive edifice of circular form at Athens, called the *Choragic Monument of Lysicrates.* The Romans, subsequently to the Republic, employed the Corinthian order by preference, in the composition of their temple porticos. These destined masters of the world were like all parvenus : for them the veritable expression of Art resided less in purity of form than in apparent costliness. The Roman had but little appreciation for the fine curve of the Doric capital ; his character led him to prefer richness of sculpture to this exquisite delicacy of outline ; he was wealthy, and he wished to appear so. At Rome the Corinthian order was soon the only one applied to religious edifices, because, being the richest, it was considered the most imposing. But the limited scale of most of the Greek temples scarcely accorded with the Roman genius, which, from the earliest times of the Empire, sought to fill its cities with immense buildings : it therefore increased the dimensions of the order in question. In adopting the Greek orders, the Roman architect,—pre-eminently a builder,—displays his peculiar genius. The Greek columns are usually formed of drums of stone or marble, superimposed with extreme care ; for the Greek considers, rightly enough, that in its function a column indicates a monolith. If the mechanical means at his disposal did not permit the quarrying, transport, and raising of blocks of very great size, he compensated for this deficiency by greater finish in the execution; moreover, when the materials he employed were coarse, he coated them, as we have said, with a fine stucco, tinted,—giving, when he thought it desirable, an effect of homogeneity to what was really a combination. The Roman architect, on the other hand, works his column in a single block of stone, marble, or granite. In adopting the Corinthian order, whose shaft is comparatively slighter than that of the Doric, and considerably increasing the dimensions of his column, he was naturally induced to make the shaft a monolith. The Doric column has no base, whereas the Ionic and Corinthian have one; but these bases have no square plinth; their circular torus rests immediately on the ground. Certainly no Greek would ever have dreamed of placing at the foot of a column a block with sharp corners, obstructing the passage, and endangering the feet of persons entering the porticos. Before long the Roman puts a base to the columns of all the orders adopted by him; this base has a square plinth; he requires a bed under his monolithic column; it is indispensable for the resting of the enormous block. This bed he shows; he gives it a considerable footing. He finds the Doric order too simple, too severe. The sun is less brilliant in Italy than in Attica and Sicily; he adds a moulding to the abacus of his capital; he substitutes for the fine sinkings and the sharp listels in the neck of the Greek Doric capital, a projecting astragal. In place of the Greek profile, suggested in its delicate tracing by the artist's feeling,—the torus whose curve cannot be geometrically defined, —he puts a torus whose curve is a quarter of a circle. His architects have not leisure to study purity of line; his stone-dressers have not time for these refinements; it is less trouble to describe a quarter of a circle with the compass than to find an indescribable curve. When, in the Greek Doric order, the frieze presents a square return, the architect takes care to put a triglyph at the angle, and to lessen the two intercolumniations adjacent to this angle. The Roman desires absolute symmetry; for him it is a law. All the intercolumniations are therefore made equal. The triglyphs of the Doric order are placed over the centre of the columns. This arrangement leaves a half metope, with a square return at the angles,—in other words, a hollow beneath a corner: this is contrary to reason, but the requirements of symmetry have been satisfied, and the Roman often mistakes the laws of symmetry for artistic feeling. The Greek admits no rules other than those of reason; but reason reflects, considers, and cannot be tied: this does not suit the legislative spirit of the Roman. By proclaiming symmetry as one of the first laws of art, he saves himself endless trouble and uncertainty; for every one understands the laws of symmetry, and is apt to apply them. But observe this : the Roman who applies these laws to the forms of art,—to the apparel of his buildings,—will boldly and rationally emancipate himself from them when it becomes a question of the satisfaction of requirements ; *e.g.* in the several arrangements and minor details of his public buildings. Here we have one of the characteristic features of Roman architecture, and to this we would direct our reader's attention.

In referring to the Greek orders adopted and modified by the Romans, not as people of taste, but as wealthy, and desirous of displaying their wealth, it is not my intention to describe these orders and their more or less absolute proportions, or to repeat that which has already been said a hundred times, and which every young architect may readily find for himself elsewhere, if not in his own library. We possess but one author of the Augustan age who treats of architecture, namely Vitruvius. And being the only one, we may conclude that he is the best ; though it does not follow from this that he is excellent,—that his authority is absolute,—that he cannot make mistakes, or that he is exhaustive. I am not sufficiently versed in the language of the Augustan era positively to affirm that the text of Vitruvius has been tampered with, or that some missing portions were filled in according to its own ideas by the Renaissance. Judging as an architect, if not as a latinist, I should be inclined to think so. Besides other things, his statements respecting the proportions of the orders appear to me directly contradictory to the evidence afforded by the buildings of his time. Vitruvius sometimes ascribes strange origins to the Greek orders ; from which we should imagine that, to him at least, the reasons which guided the Greek architects were unknown. There is, however, a passage in Vitruvius relating to the Greek Doric order which is deeply interesting, and which was certainly not tampered with by the latinists of the Renaissance ; for they were unacquainted with the Greek temples, or at any rate too little acquainted with them to have made these remarks. The passage is interesting from the fact that we there see a Roman architect of the time of Augustus ascribing reasons by no means Greek, in fact altogether Roman, for certain dispositions adopted by the Greeks, to which we have previously referred ; and that even then the laws of symmetry seem to have been regarded as imperative.

Here is the translation of this passage : [1]—

"Several ancient architects have asserted that the Doric order is unsuitable for Temples, since it presents difficulties and incongruities with respect to symmetry. Tarchesius and Pytheus

---

[1] *De Ratione Dorica*, Lib. IV. cap. 3.

have asserted this, as well as Hermogenes ; for the latter, having at his disposal a great quantity of marbles for the purpose of building a temple of the Doric order to Bacchus, changed his plans, and adopted the Ionic order. The objection is not that the Doric order is wanting in beauty or grandeur, but that the arrangement of the triglyphs and the spaces between them is awkward in execution; for it is *essential* that the triglyphs should come over the centre of the columns, and that the metopes which are left between the triglyphs should be as high as they are broad ; the triglyphs, however, that are put at the corners cannot come over the centre of the columns. Thus the metopes which are next the corner triglyphs cannot be square, but must be oblong, and be each of them broader by half the width of the triglyph. Those who wish to get metopes of equal size all along the frieze must necessarily lessen the last intercolumniation at the angle by a space equal to half the width of a triglyph. Now, whether the metope be widened, or whether the space of the last intercolumniation be narrowed, the effect is bad. This consideration of symmetry prevented the ancients from making use of the Doric order in their sacred edifices."

I do not think that this was the actual reason which induced the Greeks to prefer in some cases the Ionic to the Doric order ; much more probably it was the constant desire of that people to seek fresh combinations, to emancipate themselves from routine, to introduce progress everywhere ; the craving for perfection which soon led them into affectation, and, as a natural consequence, into decline. Vitruvius seems to me mistaken when he says that it was to render the metopes equal to one another that the Greek architects gave the intercolumniations next the angle in the Doric order a less width than the others ; for they would thus have sacrificed a feature of general arrangement to a detail of minor importance, which is opposed to common sense. If we study their architecture we shall see that the Greeks did not trouble themselves about so unimportant a matter. But in any case, this passage from Vitruvius throws light on the spirit of the Roman architect ; he loves formulas, and wishes to apply them to everything, even to matters that depend only on reasoning and artistic feeling. But in the time of Augustus, and even long afterwards, the Romans employed for the garniture of their buildings Greek artists, who paid little attention to formulas when these were in contradiction either with their reason or their instinct : accordingly, there are no Roman orders that illustrate the formulas given by Vitruvius,—still less are there any identical with them. The relative proportions of the orders in Roman edifices are modified according to the nature of the materials, the position of those orders, the size of the buildings, the number of the columns, etc. The Roman orders obey one imperious law, that of symmetry ; it is the only one that accords with the temperament of this people, and with its legislative character. The Roman spirit, however, requires other concessions. We have seen how the refined and essentially artistic nature of the Greek people led it, in the expression of architectural forms, to combine effects and gradations of an extreme subtlety, without any excess or sacrifice of style. What I have said of the fluting and the capitals of the Doric order sufficiently illustrates the exquisite sense of the Greek in all that belongs to Art.

It cannot be repeated too often,—the Greeks present us with artists of taste, surrounded by people of taste ; they know how to express the truth with moderation, and are sure of being understood ; among them there are no barbarians.

The Roman, on the contrary, *insists ;* he must insist to make himself understood ; he influences and he has to influence the vulgar ; he would be great,—colossal ; he would inspire the multitude with awe ; he well knows that refinement in art would be thrown away upon the various peoples,—for the most part uncultured,—who live under his rule. He has a contempt for the nervous grace which is the character of Greek art : what he wants is the expression of wealth and grandeur ; and the Greek, in becoming his workman, soon loses the delicate taste for which his nation is distinguished, to respond to the imperial vanity of his masters. Nevertheless, in the hands of the Greek artist, the dress of the Roman buildings is marked for a long time by singular excellence of execution. If the Greek is obliged to cover it with ornaments, these preserve something of their native grace and sobriety. It is only by degrees that refinement of execution makes way for profusion. But later on I shall have to discuss more fully the system of decoration applied to Roman architecture, and to call attention to the beauty and freedom of execution by which the decorative sculpture is distinguished, first among the Greeks and subsequently during the last period of the Roman Republic and the first years of the Empire. For the present we will confine ourselves to that part of the architecture which is veritably Roman, namely, the structure of the buildings.

The Romans very early adopted two distinct modes of construction, which nevertheless were subsequently combined in their buildings ; these are,—construction with masonry and construction with rubble and brick. The first is only employed by them as a thick casing of large stones laid close-jointed without mortar, tied together with dowels and cramps of metal, or even sometimes of wood ; behind which are thrown in masses of small stone imbedded in excellent mortar. The vaultings are likewise formed in the same manner by means of principal arches of worked stone or brick maintaining a filling in of concrete.

This system of construction obliges the Roman architect to adopt arrangements in plan which are peculiarly his. There are massive piers forming points of support destined to carry the weight of the vaultings. In these constructions there are no walls, properly speaking, but separate points of strength, connected by partitions which are comparatively thin, as they have

1

Roman system of Construction.

nothing to carry. From this principle result dispositions which are admirably adapted to the arrangements required in edifices of vast size containing a great many different services; for instance, large chambers surrounded by small ones,—a number of rooms varying in form, surface, and height, passages and staircases, etc. As an example, let us suppose a programme of which the conditions are the construction of a principal hall surrounded by rooms of dimensions less both in surface and height : the Roman architect builds four main piers (fig. 1) ; from one to the other of these piers he throws barrel arches at the height he thinks suitable for the outer rooms ; continuing up his piers at the angles, he will construct a groined vaulting formed by the intersection of two cylindrical vaults. He will complete his edifice by building thin exterior walls, and if necessary other interior walls to separate the four rooms annexed to the great central chamber. Beneath the vaulting, and above the four barrel arches, he will be able to get openings for lighting the principal chamber. Putting lean-to roofs over the lower arches, and a roof with four gables and four valleys over the groined vaulting, he will thus obtain a construction equally simple, substantial, and durable.

Little as the Roman cares about cost of labour, he nevertheless possesses a mind too well regulated, has too much good sense, is too good an economist, to waste anything in unnecessary work. As a builder his calculations soon convince him that the piers supporting the vaulting of the large chambers and the arching of the four small ones would present the same strength with less material ; he hollows the piers as shown in fig. 1, by leaving on two of the sides next the small rooms recesses semicircular in plan and vaulted in form of quarter sphere, beneath the springing of the barrel vaults. Thus he adds to the space of the four small rooms. A construction of this sort,—which in fact is merely composed of rubble work with brick facings,—does not admit either within or without of any decoration resulting from the structure. But the Roman would be magnificent ; he is not content with having rigorously satisfied the requirements of a programme, but would embellish his construction ; he will, for example, set up a portico against one of the fronts of the building. This portico certainly has a use ; but it forms no part of the original conception of his work. He will therefore call in artists, and will procure monolithic columns,—blocks of immense size ; for his appliances are powerful, and when he desires to appear wealthy, he spares no cost. The structure of the building we have just described is his,—it is his own art ; the adventitious decoration he will borrow from the Greek.

We have not, however, in the buildings now in question, the front face of a detached temple whose outline is seen against the sky ; backed by these masses of brickwork the refinements of the Greek Doric order,—its lines so carefully considered in reference to the light and air which surround them,—its pediments whose angle is very obtuse in order not to crush the ordonnance beneath,—all those niceties of an art which delights in the finish of the smallest details, and which exists only for itself, would be thrown away and appear simply ridiculous. We cannot tell whether the Roman feels this ; probably he does ; but assuredly the Greek understands it. He will then adopt an order that is richer, but one whose lines are less delicate than those of the Greek Doric. He will take the Ionic order, or rather the Corinthian ; for the last, despite its elegance, presents more numerous reliefs and profiles,—striking effects and lively contrasts which will throw it out more clearly against the solid mass of the building. Within, the Roman will have the vaulting overlaid with fine stucco, and divide it into compartments, in order to make its real size apparent. This stucco will be carved, in a manner however appropriate to the material ; that is to say, it will only admit of a flat ornamentation, adapted to receive painting and render it effective. He will cover the lower part of the wall with slabs of coloured marble divided by slightly projecting mouldings ; for he is unwilling to destroy the aspect of unity which an interior illumined by a diffused light should preserve. While desirous that the external dress of his building should present striking projections which will throw broad shadows in due proportion to the magnitude of his construction, —he will prefer for its interior garniture an effect of quiet and unbroken richness. The Roman has therefore a taste of his own which is not to be despised,—far from it. The peculiar taste of the Roman people, in reference to art, deserves appreciation, as it may serve to guide us in the present day : and for this reason, that our institutions, our laws, our administration, and our manner of governing have very many points of agreement with the government, the administration, the laws and institutions of the Romans ; our language is derived from the Latin, and our constitution is substantially Roman ; though our character, our sentiments, our cast of mind as Frenchmen singularly resemble those of the Athenians. We possess some of their good qualities and nearly all their defects ; their language,—with which we are now unfortunately so little familiar,—seems to enter into ours as a seasoning. A municipal proclamation may be composed in words of only Latin derivation ; but we cannot investigate or enter the domains of intelligence, philosophy, or science, or give expression to new ideas, without using words derived from the Greek and employing the Greek dialectic.

The co-existence of these two elements, Greek and Roman, among us, renders it interesting to examine what constitutes Roman taste and to define its nature. As I have often remarked, —the Greek is a poet, an artist ; whereas the Roman rules and governs, and possesses the taste which appertains to this vocation. This taste is founded upon a profound knowledge of men and of the various qualities which distinguish them ; he knows how to employ persons in the capacity for which they are best fitted, how to bring human faculties under discipline and to make them combine for an end conceived by himself alone ; he knows that he is the head, and as the head he governs,—never stooping to take the place of the members. His taste consists in a persistent fidelity to the position he has won for himself in the world. It was by adhesion to this policy that the Romans were able to continue so long masters in everything, despite the evident symptoms of dissolution. They maintained political supremacy through their toleration of every religion, and indifference to dogmas ; by investing the magistrates with both civil and religious functions, and by subordinating everything to the law of the State. When the Emperors, having become Christians, took upon themselves to maintain religious theses in ecclesiastical synods, the Empire received its death-blow,—the great Roman corporation was dislocated. Observe how Constantine, with whom commences the last period of the decline of the Roman Empire, still expresses himself in the edict which he, conjointly with Lucinius his brother-in-law, promulgated at Milan, A.D. 313 : " We give every one the liberty to follow that religion which he prefers, in order that the blessing of heaven may descend upon us and upon all our subjects ; we declare that we have given the Christians free and absolute permission to practise their religion, with the understanding that all others shall have the same liberty, to secure the tranquillity of our reign." It is true that Constantine was not then a Christian. The Romans controlled the arts by following exactly the same course,—by the imposition of formulas which necessity dictated,—by the adoption of a system of architecture in conformity with their social state, but without entering upon what is more especially the province of the artist, namely, the details of his art—the form with which he invests it.

The Romans have that characteristic of true grandeur which consists in the absence of exaggeration, the rock fatal to greatness ; they are simply great, without effort or affectation ; they never outstep propriety. Roman taste is then a mean between very opposite principles,—a fixed resolution to go right on and to produce what it considers suitable and necessary by employing those principles and making them conduce to one determinate result. Louis XIV., in whom something of Roman grandeur was reflected, attempted an approximation to the models in question ; but what a difference ! How miserable and insincere, for example, seem to us now the disputes respecting art which were carried to the very footsteps of the throne, when the appointment of Bernini or Perrault for the completion of the Louvre was under discussion ! The dignified sentiment of the Roman in respect of art is then a lesson for us which we cannot too intently study.

We shall see how the example was followed or disregarded by subsequent generations, and how rapidly the arts developed themselves in the first case, and how quickly they declined in the second.

Let us return to the structure of Roman Architecture,—to the method of construction it preferred. The Greek method, since it permitted only the vertical support and the lintel, could afford but very little variety in the conception of its plans. Whether the interior spaces were covered by lintels and slabs of stone or timber-work, these means did not allow the erection of vast halls, —the bearing of the timbers employed horizontally being very limited,—that of stone still more so. Accordingly, Greek edifices intended to contain a great number of people were merely enclosures open to the sky. The climate of Greece favoured these primitive arrangements, the grandeur of which we do not dispute, but which were not suitable for the Romans, whose dominion under the Emperors extended from Italy to Germany, Gaul and Britain. But the system of construction of which we have just given an example (fig. 1) permitted the covering in of vast spaces, and that in a durable manner, with means that were simple and easy of application everywhere ; for gravel, brick-clay, and limestone are everywhere to be found. In case of necessity the Roman method of building could dispense altogether with dressed stone-work. The attention of the Roman architect is directed first of all to the arrangement of the plan ; as becomes a people which must and will impose determinate arrangements in accordance with its social and political state.

In fact, if we look at buildings veritably Roman, such as the baths, palaces, villas, and other great public works, what first strikes us is the purely original dispositions of plan. These buildings present an agglomeration of chambers which have each their due dimensions ; their points of support have an importance merely relative to these dimensions ; and this collection of different services forms a whole whose parts stay each other,—the smallest supporting the largest, advantage being ingeniously taken of the openings between the points of support. It is desirable to note how in these vast establishments space is economised,—how the constructive masses are hollowed when this can be done without sacrifice of solidity,—and how the interior configuration of the plan is adapted to its destination. If from the plan we proceed to examine the sections and elevations, we see that the heights of the chambers are in due relation to their perimeter ; and yet the whole together forms but one building, like a hive composed of cells of various sizes. Here it is that the Roman genius exhibits itself ; here the Roman is himself and borrows from no one ; from these productions it is that we should seek instruction that will be serious, profitable, and eminently fruitful, and not those architectural forms which the Romans merely borrowed from the Greeks when they wanted to build temples to the gods.

It is not our intention to give a course in Archæology, but in Architecture, and we need not examine the modifications, more or less happy, introduced by the Romans in the plans and arrangements of the Greek temple when they thought fit to adopt it. The study of these could not have any practical object; however interesting it might be, it is not within the limits to which we confine ourselves. Let us then only examine in Roman architecture what is Roman, for the field is already only too vast.

As early as the Republic the Romans erected several small buildings, circular in plan, covered with hemispherical vaults of concrete. It is thus that the cella of the temple of Vesta at Tivoli is constructed; but at the beginning of the Empire, this kind of construction received a development unknown till then. Magnificent baths were first built by Agrippa at Rome in the Ninth Region. Did he build at the same time the immense circular hall known as the Pantheon, which was close to the baths, though it had no direct communication with them? Did he find this hall existing, and did he attach the baths to it? Both hypotheses are equally admissible; certain it is that Dion affirms the Pantheon to have been completed by Agrippa in the 729th year of Rome, twenty-four years before our era; but this completion concerns the portico erected afterwards before the door of the Rotunda, as proved by the inscription still to be read on the frieze of the portico. Whether Agrippa erected the Rotunda, or whether he only decorated the interior with a splendid ordonnance in marble, and the exterior with a portico of grey granite and white marble—what we can easily prove, and what it concerns us to show, is how the construction or the building of this hall and its decoration form two distinct parts. Thus enriched by Agrippa, the Rotunda was consecrated to Jupiter the Avenger, as Pliny informs us. The diameter of the hall within is 142 feet 9 inches, and the circular wall that carries the vault is 18 feet thick; which is about $\frac{1}{8}$th of the internal diameter. The height from the pavement to the crown of the vault is 147 feet; the internal diameter is thus nearly the same as the internal height of the entire building. The circular wall is not solid: besides the entrance opening, it is hollowed within by four oblong recesses and three large semicircular niches.

Between these main recesses are disposed eight semicircular cells in the thickness of the wall, at the floor level; and at the level of the springing of the vault sixteen other hollow spaces, which would be open to the exterior if they were not closed by walling about four feet thick. For solidity and duration no con-

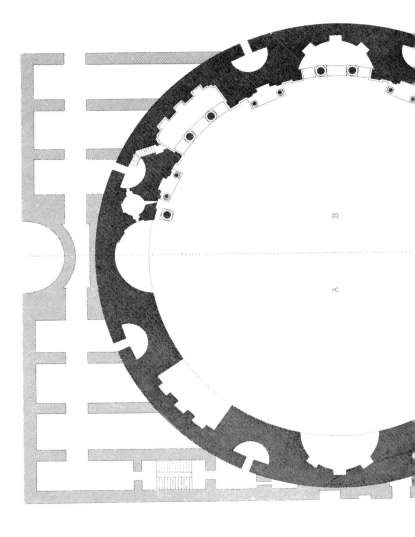

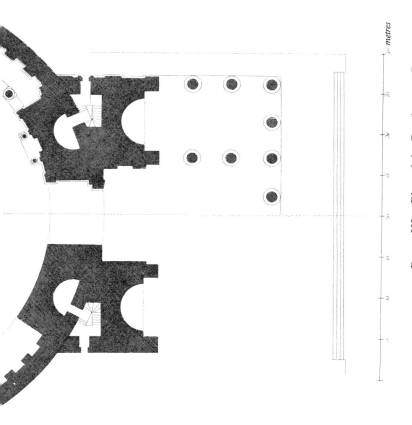

metres

PLATE III. Plan of the Pantheon at Rome

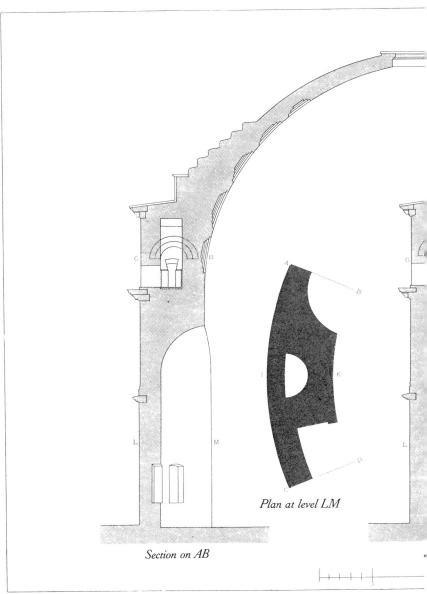

E. Viollet-Le-Duc del.

Plan at level LM

Section on AB

PLATE IV.   Sections of the Pantheon at Rome

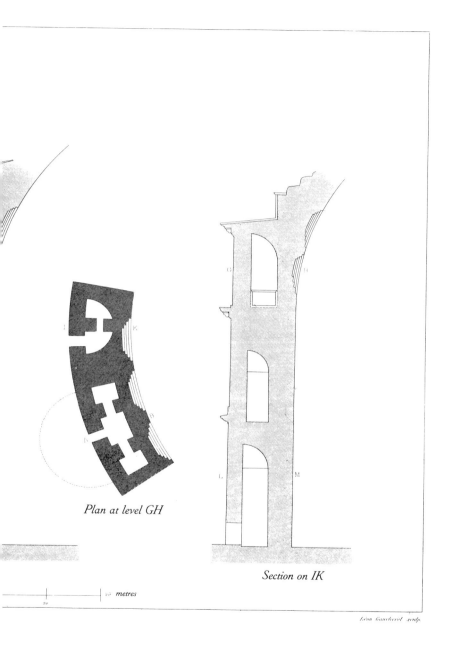

Plan at level GH

Section on IK

| | *metres*

Léon Gaucherel sculp.

struction could be more rationally conceived : the whole is faced
with large bricks, according to the Roman method ; and the thickness filled in with solid rubble concrete, with string-courses of
marble. The spring of the vault is at 74 feet 6 inches from the
floor level,—that is to say, about midway of the whole interior
height. We have a reason for giving these dimensions : they
serve to show that the Romans had certain formulæ applicable
to the interior spaces of buildings,—that they established certain
fixed proportions between the breadths and heights of these spaces,
and that already they subordinated the external appearance of
their edifices to the dispositions adopted within. But we shall
presently advert again to this method of the Roman architects.
The hemispherical vault which crowns the hollow cylinder formed
by the wall of the edifice, is built, as I said just now, of brick and
concrete ; the bricks serve the purpose of ribs imbedded in the
thickness of the vault, which is lightened by five rings of compartments sunk in its interior concavity. This hemispherical wall,
by reason of the vacancies contrived in its thickness, is in reality
nothing more than a combination of relieving arches which direct
the whole of its pressure upon sixteen main piers. We have here
obviously a complete system of construction imposing laws upon
architecture, before the architect gives a thought to the decoration of his building.

Let us now look at the plan of the Rotunda of Agrippa (Plate
III.) At A the plan shows the marble columns and coverings
adorning the interior removed ; at B this decoration is indicated.
It is easy to see that the marble decoration does not belong to the
structure,—that it is merely a screen-work of columns set against
and in no way contributing to the strength of the edifice : the
grandeur of the design is independent of the decoration ; this
might be disposed in any other way. The portico is an annex,
—one building against another building. The columns of a single
block which compose it, and the lintels which they carry, have
no sort of relation to the system of construction adopted in the
Rotunda, which is entirely composed of concave surfaces counterthrusting each other with great ingenuity. The internal structure
of the building certainly presents a fine field for the decorator ;
but consign this interior to ten different architects, and you will
have as many different decorations ; and I must confess that I am
not one of those who unreservedly admire that which has been
adopted. What every one may perceive is, that here there is not,
as in the Greek edifice, an intimate and forced alliance between
the construction and the dress which it receives. Let us, then,
examine the structure of this immense Rotunda (Plate IV.) :
we see with what care the architect has avoided useless masses of
material ; how even the vacant spaces contribute to the strength

of the circular wall, by directing the pressures upon determinate points, and by multiplying the resisting surfaces. At the height of the springing of the vault (see plan at level GH) a series of buttresses dividing the vaulted semicircular cells, and of barrel arches concentric with the circular wall, strongly maintain the great hemispherical dome. A construction solid throughout would have possessed less force of resistance; it would have been heavier, and have required a much greater quantity of material.

What I have said respecting Architectural Art among the Greeks and the Romans is sufficient to indicate to us the course we should pursue in the study of these forms of Art respectively. According to the Greek mode, it is impossible to separate the structure from the visible appearance,—the form,—the Art, in fact; while in following the Roman method, we must often separate the builder's work from the artistic wrapping with which that work is invested. Does it follow that, because these methods start from opposite principles, the one should be lauded and the other contemned? or,—which is more irrational still,—that they should both be regarded with undiscriminating admiration or dislike? Certainly not : we should analyse them both, and adopt from the former what is truthful, logical, deeply thought out, or delicately felt and expressed ; from the latter, what it has of grandeur and good sense, and what is applicable to our modern civilisation, whose tendency is to reduce everything to formulæ,—a result of the unity of our institutions and of our manners. I have given a summary notion of what is veritably Roman in the Rotunda of Agrippa ; but what I cannot convey by a drawing, or by a technical description, is the general effect produced by this immense interior on the mind of the spectator. I should first observe that, in my opinion, the interior decoration of the building,—which, be it remarked, was altered several times,—detracts from, rather than adds to, the grandeur of the effect produced by the purely Roman conception. Multiplicity and prominence of detail in a building,—especially when their use is not apparent,—lessen the impression of its grandeur. Details distract the mind, and cause it to lose sight of the principal object. In a Greek temple, the details, which are always subordinated to the general ordonnance—to the structure,—are not at first perceived. Hence it is that the Greek temples, though generally small, leave an impression of grandeur, which is still further increased by the image left on the memory ; so true it is that, in the Arts, and in Architecture especially, it is very difficult to combine opposite principles, and to prevent them, when we attempt a combination, from injuring each other. Leaving out of consideration the excellence of the details, and the perfection of their execution, I should rather the Roman had preserved to the Rotunda of the Thermæ of Agrippa its genuine aspect,—that this hall had received a decoration which would have allowed its simple and beautiful structure to be clearly manifest. In my opinion, the lower order which cuts the recesses at two-thirds of their height, the attic which masks their arching, and that division into two zones of a homogeneous piece of construction rising from the floor to the springing of the cupola, lessen the effect of this beautiful composition instead of adding to its grandeur. In that decoration I recognise the artist and the workman of real talent,—I see the transplanted Greek; but they are no longer at home in their work; they stand in my way; they do not comprehend the majestic design of the Roman, and oblige me to analyse before I can understand it.

In the Pantheon, where Roman Art is apparent, its designs are not in harmony with the decoration applied by the Greek artist. The compartments of the cupola, for instance, which, indubitably belonging to the structure of the Roman building, are hollowed in, like large cells, above the string-courses, cornices, and divisions of marble,—by their imposing character overpower the decoration below. One need not be a builder to feel that they belong to the general structure of the design; while the part below, upon which they seem to rest, is merely an immense wainscot of marble set up against the interior surface of the cylinder. I shall be met with the objection that these compartments were probably decorated with ornaments of metal, of which traces have been found; but these ornaments would only have given them a still more imposing character, accentuated their forms, and thrown them into stronger relief against the concavity of the hemisphere. Beneath this decoration, so impressive, so distinct, and so grand in its scale, what effect could be produced by that repetition of pannels in marble, of slightly projecting pilasters, of capitals of columns, whose height scarcely equalled half the diameter of the roses which must have adorned the back of the sunk compartments?

In a hall, whose members are all on a large scale, I can understand a wainscot of marble or of wood which, by its height and delicacy of detail, should recall at the base the size of the human figure; but I cannot understand a wainscot 80 feet high. In covering the interior of his Rotunda—probably as an after-thought— with decoration in marble forming a splendid composition beneath the vault, Agrippa makes a display of magnificence, but not of taste; and here it is that the Roman often sins: he is wealthy,— magnificent;—he affects to love the Arts, because he comprehends their power; but he wants the taste,—the sure and delicate taste,—of the Greeks when at home and free to follow their own inspirations. Remember the saying of a Greek sculptor to his fellow-artist : "Thou couldst not make thy Venus beautiful; thou hast made her rich." How is it that Roman ruins produce so profound an impression? Because, in their forlorn nakedness, they exhibit only the essential character of Roman Architecture. One of those halls of Caracalla's Baths whose walls are shattered, whose piers are laid bare, and which exhibit to the astonished sight the gigantic mechanism of the Roman structure, would produce a less effect perhaps if we saw it draped with its useless columns, its marble veneering, its decorations for show. What, in the Pantheon at Rome, is it that produces the most lively impression? It is that immense vault which derives all its decoration from its very structure ;—it is that single opening for light, 26 feet in diameter, perforated in its summit, through which the zenith is seen, and which throws upon the pavement of porphyry and granite a large circle of light. It is there that the genius of the Roman appears in full strength. So great is the elevation of this orifice above the floor, that its enormous opening scarcely affects the internal temperature. The most violent storms scarcely send down a breath of air on the head of a person standing beneath its orbit ; and when it rains, the drops are seen falling perpendicularly down upon the pavement of the Rotunda, on which they describe a circle of wet. The cylinder of rain-drops, falling from that height through the space of the building, renders sensible the immensity of that space. It is in conceptions like this that the Roman is really grand ; because they are the outgrowth of his own genius, and because for their execution he borrows from no one, nor asks the aid of any artist whose nature is foreign to his. When, on the other hand, the Roman wishes to erect a Greek temple, he takes richness of detail or of material as a sign of grandeur ; in every part of his work he falls below that simplicity and purity of conception which characterises the Greek. When the Greek comes and adds his art to the Roman building, he diminishes its grandeur ; and, lost in an alien element, he forgets his own principles, and devotes himself to the refinement of details. He is merely the skilful slave of a master who does not understand him, and to whom he cannot make himself understood. It must be said in praise of the Roman, that he is never guilty of hypocrisy : this vice, which has become so common in the Arts since the seventeenth century, is beneath him. I say "this *vice*," but incorrectly ; I should rather say "this *resource*." The rich casing with which the Roman covers his building is more or less in harmony with the structure ; to him it is evidently an affair of minor importance. He treats the question of Art with a sort of kindly indifference which is not without its charm, for it bears the mark of true grandeur. But let there be no misconception :

when the Roman wishes to be artistic,—at his own time, and in his own manner,—it is not easy to find his equal. Of this we have a remarkable example in a monument known to all, which is traditionally admired on no clearly understood ground, and which, from an Art point of view, is generally somewhat falsely appreciated,—I mean Trajan's Column. I do not know whether the Greeks had conceived anything of the kind among their home-sprung designs in Art: I doubt it, for in this conception the Roman is manifest; we find here the ideas of order and of method, and the consciousness of supremacy among the nations, carried to the degree of sublimity. In this idea of writing the history of a conquest upon a spiral of marble, surmounted by a statue of the conqueror, there is something foreign to the Greek spirit. The Athenians were too envious to render such honour to a man; and in politics they had not those ideas of order which are interpreted in so forcible a manner by the column in the Forum of Trajan. From its base to its summit, this column bears the imprint, so to speak, of the political and administrative genius of the Romans. The four faces of the square socle are covered with bas-reliefs representing groups of arms of the conquered people. Above the doorway leading to the spiral staircase which mounts up to the abacus of the capital is an inscription supported by two winged Victories. On the cornice at the angles of the socle, four eagles hold in their claws wreaths of laurel. The torus of the base is itself a large crown. Then round the length of the shaft there winds a sort of frieze like a ribbon, on which are sculptured, in the most admirable manner, the incidents of Trajan's first campaign. About the middle of the column, a Victory in bas-relief traces the acts of the conqueror upon a shield. Then begins the series of bas-reliefs representing the second campaign, and which was carried up to the bottom of the capital; whose profile, in form somewhat like the Greek Doric, is enriched with an egg ornament. A circular pedestal supporting the statue of Trajan terminates the whole. If the conception is beautiful, the construction is worthy of it. The column is composed of enormous blocks of white marble, in which the stairs with their newel are hollowed out. The capital is a single block, and the pedestal is formed of eight pieces of marble. The column of Trajan renders very apparent the profound distinctions that exist between the Greeks and Romans in their works of art. The curious descriptions of Greece by Pausanias call attention to statues, votive monuments, and bas-reliefs sculptured by such or such an artist, at the order of such or such a personage, to commemorate a particular event,—as frequently presenting themselves in the streets or the Acropolis of its various cities. These Greek cities must, therefore, have closely resembled museums in

the open air,—collections of works of art surrounding and filling
the principal buildings.   To the Roman, all this is placed in the
class of mere amusement.   With him, when he wishes to produce
a work of art, it is a condition that it be formally sanctioned,
that it should present a complete whole, that it should have the
importance of a law—a political or administrative act,—and
possess its clearness and methodical spirit.   The artist retires
from view,—the monument is, in fact, a *senatus consultum*.   When
with large and lofty ideas like these we have their successful
expression, as in the column of Trajan, I admit that—to my
taste at least—Greek Art is excelled, if not in its form, at least
in its spirit.   But the expression must be successful ; for a mere
written decree is a nobler production than a tasteless public
monument which imperfectly interprets a political idea.

But let us revert to those structures designed for public
utility which constitute veritable Roman Architecture.

The Roman building has this peculiarity, that it cannot be
studied by itself ; it is always in connection with a vast system ;
it is never, so to speak, detached ; it is a part of a whole.   In the
political organisation of the Romans, everything is connected ;
everything—even religion—combines for one and the same end ;
and it is the same with their architecture.   Accordingly, the
edifices which are most characteristic of the Roman spirit are the
Thermæ, the palaces, the theatres with their vast appendages, and
the *Villæ*,—which were a kind of town of buildings presenting in
miniature all that was essential to the material and mental life
of the Romans.   The Roman is everywhere and always a
Roman *citizen ;* and as soon as he can do so, even as an individual
proprietor, he surrounds his dwelling with the various services
that are essential to the Roman *civitas.*   If he is wealthy enough
to build a villa according to his conception, it will comprise not
only the buildings of a private residence,—not only the dependencies which compose a large establishment at once rural and
military, but the Basilica, the Thermæ, the Theatre, the Library,
the Museum, and Temples, intended for the use of the public.
It is therefore in these groups of associated buildings that we
shall seek to ascertain the essential principles of Roman Architecture,—to discover the general methods and the processes in
detail which are adopted in it.

We shall first consider that which is the essential part of a
Roman edifice,—the plan.   Let us compare, for instance, the
plans of two public buildings whose purposes are quite distinct,—
Barracks and Thermæ.   There are still to be seen in Rome, at
the N.E. end of the Sixth Region, and in the Adrian villa at
Tivoli, the remains of great camps or permanent quarters for
troops.   These establishments consist of a square enclosure having

four gates, and around which on the interior are disposed a suite
of rooms vaulted with barrel arches upon partition walls at right
angles to the enclosure,—and in the middle a certain number of
detached buildings also consisting of similarly vaulted rooms set
against a longitudinal wall.   In the centre is a square building,
—the Pretorium,—intended to lodge the commander-in-chief;
in the mid-length of one of the enclosure-walls is a temple in
which were kept the military insignia, which among the Romans
were sacred objects, to which worship was rendered.   Nothing
could be simpler : no arrangement could better indicate its
special use.   Each corps has its separate building, conveniently
placed.   Figure 2, which gives the plan of the great Pretorian

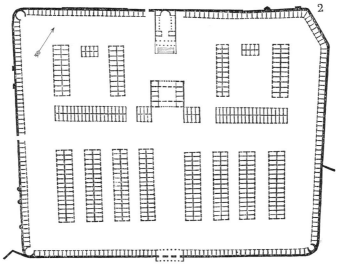

Plan of a large Roman Camp.

camp of the Sixth Region of Rome, sufficiently shows this.   The
mode of construction may be seen in Figure 3.

Sanitary precautions moreover are observed with remarkable
care.   If ranges of these cells are built along an escarpment, as
at the Adrian villa of Tivoli, the walls built against that escarpment are doubled, to keep out the damp.   The Roman does not
spare ground, but he never occupies it uselessly ; he likes
symmetry,—his military and civil organisation favours it,—but
not to the degree of sacrificing utility to it.

Let us now examine specimens of the Thermæ, in which we
shall see the capacity of this people for forming a complete whole,
admirably conceived and executed, consisting of very various
services, and in which a certain costliness of construction and

decoration must be adopted. Everybody knows the purpose of the Thermæ. During the early periods of the Republic, the Romans had no other baths but small establishments supplied with water from wells or the Tiber; but A.U.C. 441 Appius Claudius caused the water of the spring of Præneste to be brought into the city by means of aqueducts. Later rulers followed his example, and the Romans soon after built public and private baths in imitation of those of the Greeks.

Under the Emperors, these buildings were numerous; and the greater part of them included within their boundaries not only *Piscinæ* and halls for hot and cold baths, but gymnasia, halls of assembly, libraries, gardens, promenades,—everything, in fact,

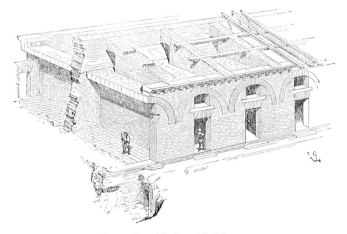

Construction of the Barrack buildings.

that contributed to satisfy the senses and the intellect. Every one could take his bath and go wherever he pleased in these establishments for a small fee. It will be easily imagined that in a populous city, they would be always filled, however numerous they might be. Many of the Romans passed the greater part of their day in the Thermæ. Under the Antonines, Rome already possessed three immense establishments of this kind,—those of Agrippa, those of Titus, and those of Caracalla.

Later on, Diocletian and Constantine built some in their turn. It must be remarked that a whole town might have been enclosed within the boundary of each of these Thermæ; and if we examine their plan we find no confusion, no useless or wasted space, but order everywhere,—the traces of a programme well carried out, —arrangements simple but cleverly combined with a view to satisfy the requirements of the case. Let us analyse this programme. At the entrance is an open space to give plenty of room for passing in or out ; opening on this space are chambers for those who come to take baths at certain hours. These chambers, considerable in number, are each entered by ante-rooms in which the bathers left their clothes in the charge of slaves. A portico enabled them to enter and quit these chambers under cover.

Even within the enclosure of the Thermæ we find a garden refreshed by fountains, furnished with seats,—*exedræ* for persons who wished to rest and converse,—ample apartments for rhetoricians and philosophers. We observe large open promenades for those who desired to take exercise away from the crowd ; closed halls for academical discussions ; *palæstræ* or open gymnasia in which various games were practised ; lecture-halls (*academiæ*), open and closed ; porticos for the directors of the exercises when they wished to escape from the noise of the palæstræ ; store-rooms for the sand used by the wrestlers, for oil, linen, wood, and so forth ; large open spaces or xysti for the games which required ample space,—such as ball or quoits ; rising seats for the spectators of these games, and numerous apartments for the employés of the establishment.

The following services are all to be found without and around the principal buildings of the Thermæ ; reservoirs for water ; one or several vestibules within the establishment itself, according to the number of entrances ; rooms for leaving clothes in charge of specially appointed slaves ; dressing-rooms adjoining ; rooms where the body was anointed with oil on leaving the warm baths previously to entering the open gymnasia ; halls disposed for conversation ; the cold-water bath,—a vast basin under cover, entered from the vestibules ; tepid baths and temperately warmed halls large enough to permit the practice of various kinds of exercise, with accommodation for spectators ; heated apartments admitting to the warm-water bath,—an immense basin of warm water deep enough to swim in ; and a smaller basin for those who wished to take their bath away from the crowd. Near to these a tepid room and bath for those who come out of the *caldarium* or warm bath, serving as a transition between the temperature of the warm chamber and the outer air ;—cool rooms for the purpose of effecting this transition ; apartments for exercise for those who have come out of the baths ; rooms for discussion, for rhetoricians and philosophers, closed and warmed apartments leading to the *sudatorium*,— chambers heated to a high temperature, that could be regulated at will, with warm-water basin, reservoirs, stoves, furnaces, etc. etc. ; hall for instructing pupils in gymnastics ; and libraries.

Not only does this programme suppose a building whose

extent exceeds that of the most considerable edifices with which
we are acquainted, but it also necessitates arrangements that are
altogether peculiar : it combines compartments of very considerable and very restricted dimensions ; it obliges the architect to
place together apartments greatly varying in extent and height.
In other words, it presents difficulties the most serious an architect can have to encounter.   Yet we find builders who erected
barracks on plans of the utmost simplicity, or even naïveté, meeting this programme, bristling with difficulties, with incomparable skill, fidelity, and judgment.

And it is in following out a rigorous and logical principle that
they will succeed in satisfying all these various requirements.

Let us select from among the Thermæ of Rome those which
have been most thoroughly studied, and which contain all the
services we have just specified.   Let us take the Thermæ of
Antoninus Caracalla, delineated with so much care and judgment
by a Professor whose loss all deplore,—the learned and modest
Blouet.   Let us examine the ground plan of this establishment
(Plate V.)   Profiting by the disposition of the ground, the architect has formed an immense plateau, A B C D.   At the front, on the
entrance side G, are the cells for separate baths, with porticos and
easy stairs.   These bath-rooms present a succession of barrel
vaults in two stories, recalling the arrangement of the rooms in
the Pretorian barracks ; each one includes an anteroom described
in the programme, and a basin large enough to contain several
persons.   The enclosure of the Thermæ is entered by a large
principal opening in the centre at G, and by several secondary
openings along the palæstræ.   On passing within the entrance
may be perceived, amidst an immense space divided into gardens,
walks, etc., the group of buildings constituting the principal
services of the establishment.   This group presents a symmetrical
mass ; in fact, the architect concluded that in order to avoid
crowding, the secondary services should be repeated, and that
the principal services, requiring immense halls, could be single ;
since crowding cannot occur in very large spaces, however great
the multitude.   Now, what are these principal services ?—(1) the
cold-water bath ; (2) the tepid bath ; (3) the warm bath with
its heated vestibule.   At E the architect placed the cold bath ;
at F the tepid bath and temperate chamber ; at I the warm
bath with its vestibule.   The three great services are thus well
marked ; they occupy the centre of the edifice, and guide the
distribution of the whole ; for it is evident that the architect first
considered the relative dimensions that must be given to these
halls—both as to extent and height beneath the vaulting—to
accommodate the number of persons they were designed to hold.

The other services are grouped around these three great

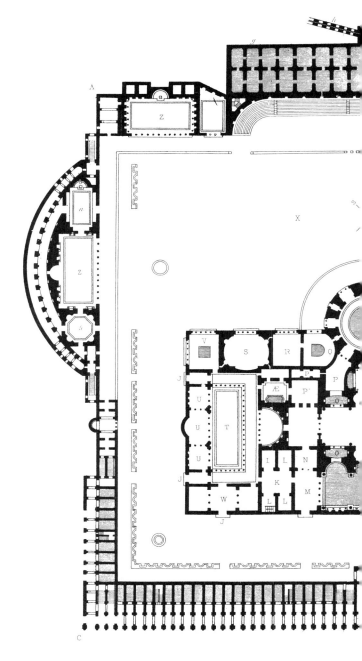

E. Viollet-Le-Duc del.

PLATE V.   Plan of the Baths of Caracalla

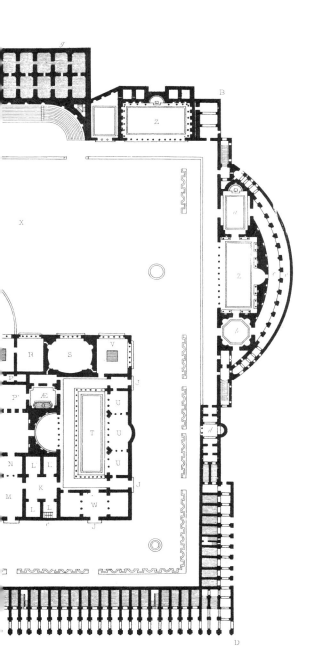

principal divisions. The architect remarks with excellent reason that a building which is liable to be crowded at certain times should, to avoid confusion, present several entrances. At J he provides two entrances ; he plans two halls, K, for persons to undress in, with the annexes, L,—vestiaries for the custody of the clothes, and for the slaves who have charge of them outside the passage-way ; and the rooms L, for anointing and for stowing the sand intended for the wrestlers. From these two halls K, those who wished to plunge into the cold water basin, or only to be spectators of the swimming exercises, could enter the covered spaces M. The cold-water basin K is open to the sky ; for cold water in a covered place is insalubrious ; besides, it is not necessary to shelter from the rain people who are bathing in cold water. Rooms intended for persons wishing to repose or converse are contrived at N. Hence the bathers enter the tepid hall F (*tepidarium*), likewise divided into three sections : one,— the principal,—for exercises ; and the two others,—the lateral ones,—for the spectators.

Smaller basins are placed in the recesses O, and in the middle of the two lateral sections. At P are reserved two courts for the furnaces and reservoirs of warm water. In the middle of the hall F you enter the second tepidarium Œ, which serves as vestibule to the warm-water bath (*caldarium*). The two passages which give entrance from the vestibule into the caldarium are compara- tively narrow and indirect, in order to prevent the entrance of the external air and of draughts. The warm-water bath is an immense circular hall covered by a very lofty hemispherical dome, so that the warm-water vapour may not be condensed on the basin. In the recesses left in the wall of the circular hall are placed smaller basins for solitary bathers. Openings furnished with glazed lattice-work admit light to the lower and upper story of the *caldarium.* The bathers who wish to make their way out find at Q the temperate rooms with basins of tepid water, which serve for a transition between the temperature of the *caldarium* and that of the external air. And thus those who go out cannot inconvenience those who enter. Next follow cold rooms, K, opening into the outer gardens. From these cold rooms there is an entrance through the open spaces, S, used for exercises, and by narrow passages into the small rooms which precede the *sudatorium* Æ. Reservoirs for the caldrons are contrived in the spaces P′P′. At the extremities are planned vast peristyles, T, with *exedræ* for those who desire to walk, discuss, or listen to the rhetoricians ; then come the spaces U, intended for the instruc- tion of the pupils in gymnastics. Two special vestibules with libraries, are disposed at W. In the angles, at V, are placed cold- water basins for the service of those who practise exercises in the xystus, x, which is terminated by a wide range of rising seats, Y, for the spectators of the games.

On each side of the xystus are the palæstræ, z, with the academical halls, a, and those intended for discussions, b; the portico for the gymnastic masters is at c. Apart in a quiet place, are the rooms, d, in which the professors of philosophy and rhetoric meet for their conferences. Lastly, rooms for the slaves —the bath servants,—are at e, with apartments above. Immense reservoirs in two stories are disposed at g; at h is shown the aqueduct which supplies the water.

It may be objected that if the programme is exactly observed, it is because that programme has been suggested by the building itself. This remark would not be just; for if we examine the plans of the Thermæ of Agrippa, of Titus, of Diocletian, or of Constantine, we shall find this programme equally well observed, with noteworthy differences in the laying out.

Besides, that is not the question; what we would examine is the admirable distribution of this plan, whose general and minor dispositions I have been describing. Observe how ingeniously these various services are distributed in the general block of the plan; look at this plan,—notice the orientation; see how the architect has placed all the warm rooms in a south-west aspect; how he has projected the vast rotunda of the *caldarium* beyond the line of the plan by more than half its diameter, in order that it may get the sun's rays at all hours of the day. See again how in such a large space the architect economises his ground; how cleverly he fits the rooms into each other, making use of all the spaces afforded by the construction; how he stays and supports these masses of building, sustaining the largest and highest by means of those which are less in surface and in height. See how well the thrusts of the vaultings are contrebutted; how clear and intelligible is the plan; how each part occupies just the position and the space suitable for it; how cleverly the issues are contrived;—wide and numerous where the crowd is likely to gather,—smaller, indirect, and deep, so as to form a screen, where the draughts might be uncomfortable or dangerous. From what peoples had the Romans learned the admirable arrangements of these plans? From themselves,—by simply satisfying their own requirements. How did they set about constructing this assemblage of buildings combined to form a single whole? In the simplest manner, and that which in point of economy was most suited to their social state. The walls, and the enormous piers of the buildings in question, are by no means adapted to a construction in worked stone. Here the Romans have no occasion for this material, whose transport is so difficult and costly, and which requires considerable time to work, mount, and lay: they

employ only brick and rubble.   The faces are made with triangular bricks, with their largest edge outside ; in the middle,
concrete, well mingled, of large gravel and excellent mortar.   At
intervals, however, for the purpose of regulating the progress of
the construction and insuring the levels, a course of large flat
bricks is built in, 4 feet 9 inches apart.   Relieving arches of brick,
built into the construction, direct the pressures upon the principal
points of support.   In the vaulting, the band arches are of large
bricks, usually in two rings, and the filling-in of concrete, composed of mortar and pumice-stone.   But in order safely to ram
this concrete on the planking of the centres, the builders began
by laying upon these planks two courses of wide bricks flatways,
breaking joint, like an arching of quarry work under the vaulting.
This construction,—at once so simple, so economical, and so ready
of execution,—being conceived and executed, the architects
erected their porticos with columns and entablatures of marble ;
the walls and piers are everywhere—in the interior at least—
covered with slabs of marble up to a certain height ; as to the
vaultings, the tympanum, and the back of the niches, they are
overlaid with stucco and mosaics.   And thus this enormous mass
of concrete and brick is clothed in a splendid dress of precious
materials, paintings and surfaces of mosaics, composed of vitrified
pastes of various colours.   In all the rooms, pavements of marble
mosaic are laid upon an isolated bed, resting on ranges of small
pillars connected by a flooring of large bricks laid double ; these
marble pavements are not only dry and perfectly healthy, but
they can be warmed underneath by means of hot currents produced by furnaces.

Our costly means of construction,—the quarries of useless
stone we accumulate in our buildings, and, side by side with
this prodigality, the extreme poverty of the details of the
interior construction,—the plaster and composition work,—these
are, it must be admitted, very barbarous modes of procedure, if
we compare them with those of the Romans, at once so simple,
truthful, and rational.   At enormous cost we pile up in our
edifices stone upon stone ; we expend all our resources in
working and carving them.   We draw upon our quarries as if
they were inexhaustible, to erect buildings of limited size ;
and when we have made such efforts, with such a useless
expenditure of strength, and have raised walls which in our
climate are always damp (stone being only too good a conductor
of moisture), we have not sufficient means left to clothe and
adorn these expensive buildings with beautiful and lasting
material.   We therefore call to our aid plaster, composition,
ornaments, and deal ; and thus we cover with rags a body
precious in itself, but whose value is concealed from all, and

rendered useless. If we affect to be Romans,—profess to owe our arts to the Romans, and call our architecture the offspring of theirs,—we should at least imitate them in what they did that was wise and rational ;—not erect with stone blocks buildings such as they judiciously constructed with concrete and brick ;—seek less the form of their architecture than its structure, which was so well adapted to that form ;—be sincere like them, and not dupe ourselves by aping their architecture if we no longer adopt their means of execution. It must not be imagined that this substitution of materials merely entails useless expenditure,—that its only inconvenience is the disregard of a principle : it presents disadvantages appreciable by all. These great Roman buildings, constructed as we have described,—composed so ingeniously of groups of different services judiciously brought together within a narrow compass, the smaller rooms profiting by the intervals left between the points of support necessitated by the elevation and extent of the larger,—possess an advantage of which I have not yet spoken : these great buildings, I say, preserve in their interior an equal and agreeable temperature which would be very advantageous in a climate like our own. There exists at Rome an immense edifice, whose general plan and system of construction recall the great halls of the Thermæ ; I mean St. Peter's. Now, in this building, which exceeds in content other celebrated buildings, the temperature is nearly the same in summer and in winter ; soft and cool in summer without being damp, and mild and dry in winter. That is a consequence not only of the disposition of the plan, which is Roman in character, but of the nature of the construction,—thick walls of concrete and brick, which transmit neither the heat nor the damp cold from without ; they serve as a non-conductor to the external temperature.

In France our stone buildings are dangerous in summer on account of the coolness which their surfaces preserve ; in winter they are icy cold.

If we examine the sections and elevations of the Thermæ of Caracalla, we find immense openings formerly furnished with frames of bronze, enclosing panes of glass, alabaster, or simply lattice-work. But we also observe that these lights open towards the most favourable points of the compass, making the most of the sun's heat, and avoiding the cold and damp aspects. In fact, the Romans attached great importance to the orientation of their buildings. Vitruvius touches several times upon this subject in the course of his treatise ; he even indicates the way to lay out the streets of a town, so as to render the dwellings convenient, and to avoid great draughts of air. He says, Book VI. chap. i. : " That a building may be well designed,

E. Viollet Le Duc del.

PLATE VI.   Existing State of the Frigidarium of the Baths of Caracalla

Viollet-Le-Duc del.

PLATE VII.   Restored View of the Frigidarium of the Baths of Caracalla

regard should first be had to the climate (the region—the latitude—as we should say), for the same arrangement will not suit in Egypt and in Spain ; it must be different in Pontus and in Rome.   In northern countries the buildings should be vaulted, well closed in, and their openings small, facing a warm aspect.   On the other hand, in southern countries, subject to the burning heat of the sun, the openings should be large, and face the north and north-east, to avoid the heat : thus the inconvenience resulting from natural extremes will be obviated by Art."   The Romans, however, when they became masters of the world, adopted everywhere the same mode of construction, because, in fact, their methods were applicable everywhere ; but they were careful to dispose their rooms and the openings for admitting light, heat or coolness, according to the locality.

Before leaving the Thermæ of Caracalla, I will attempt to give an idea of these vast and beautiful constructions, by repre- senting the actual state, in ruins, of one of their grand internal dispositions (Plate VI.) and the restoration of this portion of the Thermæ (Plate VII.)   I have chosen for representation the *frigidarium*, marked E in the plan,—one of the most original and magnificent conceptions of this beautiful whole.   The views (in its actual state, and as restored) are taken from the same point w.   It is easy to verify here the truth of what we have said concerning the architectural method adopted by the Romans ; namely, that the construction is not essentially connected with the decoration,—that this construction may be and is erected first, and the architectural decoration introduced when the building is up.   In Plate VII., which gives the restoration of the *frigidarium* open to the sky, may be seen above the three great arches at the back, the openings which light the centre hall F, and the *tepidarium* beneath the triple-groined vault covering that hall.

I have thought it desirable to present as an example of Roman building a construction of a somewhat advanced period in the history of that people, so as to enable my readers, in studying Roman architecture, to enter directly upon what is truly original in it.   Are we, then, to conclude that Roman architects always proceeded in this manner ?   Certainly not.   In the time of Augustus, if Vitruvius is to be credited, wood still played an important part in Architecture, not as a temporary means of supporting vaulting,—not as centres,—but as permanent, in the coverings of buildings.   The majority of the temples of Rome which were not circular,—those whose plan and structure were borrowed from the Greeks,—were covered with timber roofs. The naves of Basilicas were not vaulted, but covered in with boarded roofs.   It was not long before the burning of Rome under Nero that the Romans nearly everywhere abandoned timber coverings in favour of vaulting in masonry. Yet, before that Emperor's time, the Baths of Agrippa and the Pantheon were built, and the system of construction we have just described was known and employed.

The great circular hall of the Baths of Caracalla presented more than one point of resemblance to the Rotunda of Agrippa; but if the details of its architecture were less pure, and executed with less nicety and elegance, it must be admitted that in point of composition the *caldarium* of Caracalla excelled the Pantheon, as far as we can judge from the remains now to be seen. Its construction, freer and better expressed within as well as without, is of a character to excite our admiration. This is easily seen by examining the conscientious work of the late M. Blouet on this edifice, or rather group of edifices.

In their vaulted buildings the Romans seem to have particularly preferred two especial dispositions: the circular arrangement, closed in by a hemispherical dome, and the arrangement in bays, which we see adopted for the great central tepid hall of the Baths of Caracalla, in the Baths of Titus and of Diocletian, and in the building known as the Basilica of Maximus or of Constantine. The Romans invented only two kinds of vaulting : the hemispherical vault, and the cradle or semi-cylindrical vault ; the intersection of two cradle vaults suggested to them the groined vault. These three systems sufficed for everything ; and the combinations of their plans are simply the necessary result of these methods. If they build a circular hall, they cover it with a hemisphere ; if a semicircular hall, they cover it with a quarter sphere; if an oblong hall, the lateral walls of whose longer sides are thick or well abutted by contiguous buildings, they cover it with a cradle vault, which is nothing more than a longitudinal half-cylinder ; if a square hall whose angles only present a perfect resistance, they cover it with a groined vault. If the oblong hall is very wide,—if its side walls have to be pierced by large openings, thereby presenting only isolated points of support, they divide it into square bays (generally three, in order to get a central bay) ; and they cover it with three groined vaults,—that is to say, a longitudinal half cylinder intersected by three half cylinders of equal diameter with the first.

This disposition, at once broad and simple, directs the weight of the vault on the piers—a kind of buttresses ornamented most frequently inside by a column which receives the starting of the groining. Fig. 4 will clearly explain the whole of this construction. The Roman here employs the column as a rigid pillar (for this column is always a monolith),—as a sort of vertical stay set plumb beneath the springing of the vaults, and intended to serve as a point of support incompressible and light in appearance.   But here we observe that the Roman has not the correct taste of the Greek, or rather, that he but rarely troubles himself about questions of Art.   He surmounts this column with its complete entablature,—that is to say, with architrave, frieze, and cornice.   Now though it is rational to put an entablature upon a column which carries a horizontal construction, it is scarcely so to leave it this member when it acts as a vertical stay for the starting of a vaulting ; for then we ask of what use is this entablature, and what is the meaning of a cornice,—that is to say, a projection,—above a column placed inside a building. The great projection of these cornices, interposed between the narrow springing of the groining (whose width is that of the diameter of the column, seldom more) and the column itself, has the effect of destroying the unity of aspect which should be presented by a large hall whose vaulting is, as it were, only the arching of the walls.   But, as I have previously said, the Roman takes the orders from the Greeks ; he employs them without troubling himself as to their actual intention ; he takes the Greek order in its completeness, without considering the formation of its separate parts ; he takes it as a whole,—he does not analyse it.   If he wishes to form a screen between two rooms, as we often see in the Thermæ, he takes a small complete order, and puts it up as one would put up a railing or a balustrade.   Fig. 4 shows at A one of these secondary orders.   He will put a small Corinthian order beside a large Corinthian order ; their members and profiles are pretty nearly the same ; the one is but a diminutive of the other.   Hence it results that the large order seems colossal, or the small order appears dwarfed.   Inventive and ingenious as the Roman is when he builds, his invention is proportionately barren when he wishes to decorate : all the wealth he displays serves only to render more apparent his poverty, or rather his indifference, in matters of taste ; for the more precious the materials used, the more essential is it that the forms they assume should be varied.   In the Baths, the Roman is altogether Roman, and what he borrows from the Greek to ornament these magnificent establishments is, in view of the whole, of such secondary importance as to excuse me from enlarging upon the details in question.

It is certain that the Greek called in to decorate the interior of the halls of the Thermæ would be much embarrassed, and would hardly know how to dispose his delicate architecture —derived from principles opposed to those of the Roman builders—amid these immense Roman masses ; yet the merit of the architectural decoration must be admitted, for it has a grandeur of its own.   Fig. 4 shows how the Roman is able to cover his building of brick and concrete with a magnificent dress; how he hides an ordinary but nevertheless perfectly rational construction beneath stucco and painting, and how he can combine the precious materials which serve to clothe the surbases of his buildings, and which enter into the composition of the orders, with the stucco and the painting that cover them. The examples given in Fig. 4 and Plate VII. will render evident the merits of his achievement.

But in the employment of means the Roman edifices do not follow this principle exclusively. Their decoration and their construction are not always so independent of each other: of some of them,—the Basilica for instance,—the plan, construction, and decoration are only the product of a Greek tradition. There, at least, the two principles are not in contradiction; and the Basilica must be regarded by us as a subject for study which we ought not to neglect; for we shall presently see how this building was transformed among the western peoples in the Middle Ages, and became one of the types most habitually followed.

If Roman architecture varies little in the decorative envelope with which it clothes its construction, none is more fertile as regards the arrangement of plan or the structure.

The various programmes of Roman edifices as rendered by the architect present clearly-marked and distinct arrangements. It is impossible to mistake Thermæ for a theatre, a theatre for a basilica, or a basilica for a temple. The exterior aspect of their buildings never presents anything but the envelope of the actual content; their plans are simply the expression of the requirements of the case, and they never sacrifice these principles to what is now-a-days called "Architectural Effect." The first consideration is to find the simplest and most exact rendering of the scheme, the second, to invest the forms dictated by utility with the outward show of power and riches. If the schemes are vague, if the requirements indicated are not defined with sufficient rigour, as in the basilica, for example,—a building of a miscellaneous order, promenade, market-hall, exchange, tribunal, debating-hall, and antechamber,—then we see architects varying their plans, and differing in the manner of interpreting the programme; but if, on the contrary, the programme is perfectly definite,—if it is imperative both as regards the whole and the details of the disposition in question, then we see the edifices designed to respond to them reproducing with very little variation the forms which experience has pronounced the best.

Such, for instance, are the amphitheatres, the circuses, and the theatres. Look at the Coliseum of Rome, the amphitheatre of Verona, and the arenas of Nîmes and of Arles. In general

MODE OF BUILDING OF THE ROMANS.

arrangement, in plan, and in exterior aspect these buildings are identical. The same constructive processes are employed in their erection. The Romans took the idea of amphitheatres—at any rate, of amphitheatrical performances—from the Etruscans ; the Greeks adopted them only after the Romans had united Greece with the Empire. In the time of the Gracchi the Romans were content with wooden benches or scaffolding for the games of the circus, and the people got what places they could. But under the Emperors there was a wish to render these constructions durable, but especially to provide for an immense concourse of spectators, giving each a convenient place from which he could see what was going on in the arena.

The object of the amphitheatres is too well known to render it absolutely necessary to notice it here ; they were erected to enable a considerable number of spectators to see contests of gladiators, wild beasts, and even naval combats. " The Etruscans," says Quatremère de Quincy in his *Dictionnaire historique d'architecture*, "given up to a variety of superstitions, seem always to have indulged a sombre spirit, a harsh and sullen temper, and gloomy presentiments in connection with them. Thunder and lightning and every kind of natural portent suggested to their imagination angry deities whose wrath must be appeased by blood. It was in these superstitious ideas that the sanguinary combats in question originated; for they were not in Etruria, as afterwards at Rome, the mere pastime of an idle and cruel populace. In Etruria it was religion that presided at these games, it was religion that built amphitheatres."

Those primitive amphitheatres of the Italiot peoples were only excavations in the earth, whose sides were surrounded by slopes for the spectators—such was the amphitheatre whose remains may be seen at Pæstum,— or more frequently scaffolding extemporised at the time the games were held. This simple arrangement led to the erection by the Romans of immense edifices in masonry. For we must remark here in passing, that while the Romans during their sway replaced mere earthworks or wooden tiers of seats by masonry, the primitive form of these earthworks was rigorously adhered to. The theatres of the Greeks are usually placed on the sides of a hollow of a hill ; the Greeks, choosing a favourable locality, used to cut out in the rock the *præcinctiones* and ranges of seats, and surmount them by woodwork,—building the stage partly of stone, partly of timber framing. Such was the theatre of Syracuse, whose entire ranges of seats hewn in the rock may still be seen ; and such was that of Ephesus. But the Greeks had no amphitheatres : the savage spectacles for which they were constructed did not suit the taste of that refined people, who sought an emotional stimulus in the dramatic development of the passions and in poetic fictions rather than in the barbarous reality of a massacre. The Romans, on the contrary, were eager for the sanguinary spectacles of the Etruscans,—originally, perhaps, through the prompting of certain religious principles, but before long as an occupation and distraction for the idle populace of great cities. Nevertheless they did not fail to sustain their character in giving to these structures— whose origin must be referred to a fanatical race—regular, I may even say *official*, arrangements, such as were perfectly appropriate to their object, tending to avoid confusion and disorder ; for though the authorities tolerated, and even shared, the cruel instincts of the populace, they insisted that these instincts should at least display themselves in an orderly fashion, and always beneath the eyes of their magistrates. This was one of their means of government. The Romans did not seek to render the people moral, to foster humane feelings among them, but to regulate and direct their barbarian instincts. They did not endeavour to repress even the coarsest passions of the multitude, but only insisted on their not finding vent except in accordance with certain laws of order and police ; they preferred to satisfy those barbarous instincts with a legally regulated aliment rather than see them developed in the Forum.

The largest amphitheatre that was ever constructed was that at Rome known as the Coliseum, and which was capacious enough to contain one hundred and twenty thousand spectators. And it is worth remarking that the Coliseum was begun and finished by the two most humane and enlightened Emperors of Rome,— Vespasian and his son Titus ; and with such despatch, that the whole work is said to have been completed in two years and nine months. We may therefore conclude that these two Emperors reckoned the amphitheatre among those public buildings whose erection was of the greatest importance to the city of Rome. Whatever might have been the passion of the Emperors for vast and splendid monuments, we can scarcely admit that two of the wisest of them would have devoted enormous sums to the construction, and have been so urgent for the completion, of an edifice whose utility was not deemed of pressing importance. The earliest amphitheatres of the Italiot cities are only mounds of earth arranged round a circular or elliptical arena ; at the top of these mounds was placed a wooden scaffolding to allow a larger number of spectators to see the sanguinary spectacles exhibited at the bottom of that great basin. To gain a position on the slopes the spectators were obliged to ascend to the top of the ridges and then re-descend the slopes. Besides this inconvenience, these mounds had the disadvantage of sacrificing an enormous extent of ground ; for outside the slope they must have an incline of 45 degrees at least to keep them from falling in and to allow the spectators to reach their summit. That is to say (Fig. 5), for an arena whose diameter across the space destined for the games and for the public was equal to AB, A′B′, the whole space BC, DA, A′F′, B′E must be sacrificed. Now, I have already said that however liberal the Romans were in the arrangements for their public buildings, they were perhaps the first who attached great importance to the value of land, and who endeavoured, though without parsimoniousness, to limit their edifices to the space absolutely required for them. We have seen

5

coupe sur OP

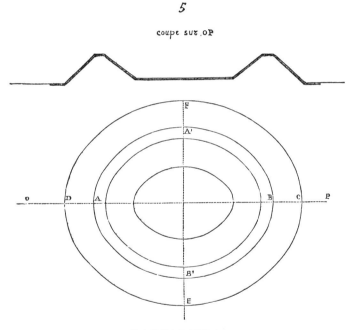

Early Italiot Amphitheatre.

already how economical was the distribution of the areas occupied by the buildings and the various services in the case of the Thermæ. At Rome itself, during the last period of the Republic, the population was so closely packed together, and the public buildings were so large and so numerous, that it was necessary to restrain within the strictest limits the areas allotted to buildings of all kinds.

Prompted by this necessity the Romans established for themselves a law from which they never deviated even when space was not wanting. When they began, like the Greeks, to build theatres, and, like the Italiot peoples, amphitheatres, they made their edifices first of wood, in a mere temporary fashion, as is done now in Spain, and even among ourselves : but the frequent occurrence of fires, the difficulty of keeping such piles of timber-work in repair, and their want of durability and solidity, soon induced them to build theatres and amphitheatres of masonry. Pompey's Theatre at Rome, of which only vestiges remain, was one of the first built of durable materials. Amphitheatres likewise soon came to be constructed in masonry, not only at Rome, but in almost all the cities of the provinces.

In constructing their amphitheatres the Romans preserved the form of those primitive earthworks which had served as their type ; that is, they built ascending tiers of stone benches around an elliptical arena ; but suppressing the exterior slopes, they encircled these tiers with a wall pierced by numerous arches arranged in stories, so as to form beneath the benches themselves flights of steps and passages by which an immense number of spectators could enter and take their place in the different ranges, and readily quit them again. The flights of steps, regularly disposed in sections, gave access to the seats by openings called *vomitoria*. The arenas of Arles, of Nîmes, and of Verona, but especially the amphitheatre of Vespasian (the Coliseum) at Rome, must be seen if we would gain an idea of these vast buildings, so judiciously arranged as a whole and in the numerous details of their construction,—buildings in which no room is lost, in which everything concurs for the accomplishment of the given programme, and in which the structure is contrived with strict economy, while it is made to last for ever. Here, better than elsewhere, we can appreciate the cellular system of Roman construction, whose principle consists in erecting and sustaining enormous masses by means of points of support and walls isolated from each other, united and stayed by a succession of vaults one above another. The entire construction of the amphitheatres consists simply of a succession of cross walls tending to the centres of the ellipse, covered by ramping vaults following the rise of the steps and carrying the tiers of benches. The enclosing wall bound together and supported by these numerous cross walls has little but its own weight to carry ; properly speaking, it is only an envelope which may be removed without injuring the solidity of those tiers of benches which are the principal object. This is so true that at Verona, for example, though that exterior wall has been almost entirely destroyed, the amphitheatre is still made use of for certain public fêtes.

At Pola, in Illyria, may still be seen a vast amphitheatre which was probably begun under Diocletian ; there, the ranges of seats and stairs were of wood, and only the exterior elliptical wall of stone. We have here the primitive amphitheatre of the Republic encased by a circle of masonry. It is probable that this expedient had been often adopted in the provinces, principally in well-wooded districts; it was an economical and ready method of erecting a building of prime necessity to the Romans, since it served for meetings of the people as well as for public games. The amphitheatre of Pola is one of those examples which show how the Romans always adopted the simplest and readiest means of carrying out the vast arrangements required by their civilisation : how, while remaining faithful to those arrangements which seem to have had the rigour of laws, they were able to make their style of architecture comply with the materials, the time, or the resources they had at their disposal, according to locality and circumstances. The stone casing of the amphitheatre of Pola, well preserved and constructed with wonderful skill and that solidity which characterises every Roman building, is one of the most remarkable examples of Roman architecture, not as regards the details, which are only roughed in or scarcely finished and of mediocre style, but in virtue of the perfect adaptation of the whole structure to its uses. It furnishes one more proof of the indifference of the Roman to perfection of form, to study and care in respect of detail,—in fact to that which was the chief consideration with the Greeks.[1]

The range of seats in the amphitheatre of Flavius Vespasian (the Coliseum) was originally surmounted by a wooden gallery or portico specially reserved for the women ; but this gallery having been burned was restored in marble with a ceiling in wood by Heliogabalus and Alexander Severus. Of this higher portico there remain only some débris of columns and capitals. The Coliseum is known to every architect—at any rate through drawings and engravings—especially through the admirable labours undertaken at Rome by one of our brother architects, M. Duc, in investigating this immense edifice. It would be unprofitable to attempt a detailed description which after all would be of less service than the most imperfect drawings ; I shall therefore only remark upon certain general arrangements which will assist us to understand the Roman method of procedure when a perfectly definite programme was presented. What strikes us at once in looking at the plan of the Roman amphitheatres, is the elliptical form given to the arena and consequently to the *præcinctiones* of the seats which surround it. It is certain that some imperative reason dictated this arrangement, for it would have been a much more simple matter to draw a circular than an elliptical

---

[1] See the general drawing and description of the details of the amphitheatre of Pola, in the fourth volume of Stuart's *Antiquities of Athens* (translated into French by L. F. F., and published by Landon. Paris, Bance, 1822).

plan, and it would have been easier of execution. To make the cross walls which divide the flights of steps and support the *præcinctiones* radiate from the foci of an ellipse, was a difficulty which the practical architect would have avoided unless constrained by absolute necessity.

In the Roman theatres, the tiers of benches are arranged in a semicircle in front of the stage.

It would seem therefore that for an amphitheatre it would have been sufficient to join two ranges of a theatre—that is, to form a perfect circle : thus the two orchestras would have composed the central arena. But we must observe that in the Greek and Roman theatre the stage is not a single point; it is a long extent of space towards which the eyes of the spectators are directed. The actors were necessarily distributed along the stage, whose length was much greater than its depth. In the arena of the amphitheatres this was not the case. If this arena had been circular, the spectacle, whatever it was, would have tended towards the centre ; and as a considerable number of men and animals had to figure in this space, it was necessary in order to prevent confusion, to offer to the actors in these sanguinary dramas an oblong area which by its very form would oblige these very actors (who, be it observed, could not choose their position, since the exhibition was frequently only a frightful mêlée, in which wild beasts played the principal part) to divide and spread themselves along it.

The crowd of spectators had then a tolerably extended line to contemplate, instead of having their eyes fixed on a single point. The combats would cover a wider field and have a freer scope. If two bodies of men were to contend with each other, an oblong arena would be more suitable for the manœuvres of their miniature battles than one of circular form; moreover, the amphitheatres and theatres were not devoted exclusively to public games and scenic representations : the people assembled there whenever a piece of news was to be communicated to them, an oration to be delivered or an election to take place,—in a word, whenever an occasion presented itself of calling them together ; and with the political system adopted by the Romans, these occasions were not unfrequent. For the amphitheatres therefore the elliptical was preferred to the circular form as more suitable both for spectators and for harangues and popular gatherings. The reason of my calling particular attention to this arrangement—which, be it observed, underwent no further modification when the acme of advantage has been reached—is to give special prominence to the dominant characteristic of a Roman building, which is invariably the simplest results of a well-studied and exact observation of the requirements of the case, never subordinating considerations of primary importance to what in our day are put forward as laws of Architecture, and which, in fact, for the most part, serve only to fetter and to embarrass. Innumerable difficulties present themselves in erecting so vast an edifice as the Coliseum on an elliptical plan. In the first place, difficulties in the planning, next in the setting out, and lastly in the construction ; difficulties regarding the general disposition and the details : for to build an edifice of this kind on a circular plan it is enough to set out on the paper or on the ground a section,—a fourth, an eighth, a sixteenth of the whole ; but on an elliptical plan a certain number of these sections, forming a fourth of the ellipse, must be separately studied. These difficulties do not deter the Roman architect when he has to satisfy the conditions of a programme based upon an exact study of the object of the building. In fact it is those general dispositions of Roman buildings which are contrived with such profound insight that deserve our chief attention as examples ; for in the case of no other nation have those arrangements dictated so absolutely the general form, or rather the structure, of the architecture.

The Roman is never in uncertainty ; his position indicates a very advanced civilisation, which submits everything to reasons of state. He commands as a master who knows exactly what he wishes and what he needs ; and he knows how to make himself obeyed, because he knows how to make himself understood. Subsequently to the Roman period we no longer find in architectural art anything clearly defined ; we have no longer governments commanding the arts, but artists interpreting, as best they may, the vague ideas that are suggested to them ; they may achieve remarkable results, but they cannot attain to that cogent reason, that unity of purpose which are the essential characteristic of architecture among the Romans. Even now, in spite of our civilisation, in spite of the strength of our institutions, our ideas in Art are vague and confused ; we do not know what we want, and our public monuments are no sooner finished than we find them grossly defective, and perceive that we must modify or rebuild them at great expense. Our artists dispute about Style,—are engrossed by one particular school of architecture—condemn or approve such or such a form of Art,—adopt or repudiate such or such a tradition;—but as for the broad and true way of appreciating Architecture becoming to a great people, it hardly occurs to them ; —happy if they are allowed to carve the profiles they prefer, or to put columns or pinnacles here and there according to their fancy. As we are said to be of Latin race, let us resemble them at least in their excellencies. I fear, however, that we approach nearer to those Roman-Greeks of Byzantium who were disputing about the light on Tabor while the armies of Mahomet II. were storming their ramparts.

Reason among the Romans does not proceed as among the Greeks. The Greek will allow himself to be carried away by his feeling as an artist,—by what he will regard as the necessity of subordinating material requirements to established rules of Art. The Roman will never allow the rules of Art—the love of the absolutely beautiful, if we choose to call it so—to take precedence of the satisfaction of those requirements. Let us take a striking example. Look at the Propylæa of Athens or of Eleusis ; should we not suppose them to be temples ? Does not the exterior aspect of these gates of citadels recal the front of a sacred edifice so as to be absolutely confounded with it ? If it were not for the three doors pierced in the wall, behind the entrance-portico, we might take these erections for the anterior part of a temple. The Romans never gave to the entrance of a citadel the semblance of a temple. With them each edifice takes a form which is simply the real expression of its object ; and if the details of the architecture—*i.e.* the decoration—should sometimes contrast with the general form, this adventitious adornment has not such an importance as to affect substantially the mass of the building as dictated by the programme.

We shall soon see in what forms this Roman principle was developed, and how it was abused ; for all principles, however good and true, are destined to perish, through the very abuse of their application.

We shall also see later on how in ages in which it has been presumed that Roman architecture was being revived, the essential qualities of that architecture were neglected in favour of that which did not really belong to it,—that mere envelope, namely, with which the Romans associated only ideas of luxury and superficial propriety.

LECTURE V.

METHODS TO BE FOLLOWED IN THE STUDY OF ARCHITECTURE—THE ROMAN
BASILICAS—DOMESTIC ARCHITECTURE OF THE ANCIENTS.

IN exploring the course of a river we start from its mouth, not
from its source ; we ascend the current and investigate its
shores, widely severed at first, and contracting by degrees.
We observe its tributaries and study their banks, rapids, and
cataracts, up to their respective fountain-heads. We thus gain
a knowledge of the nature of the waters of the principal current,
what substances they carry down with them, the causes of their
increase and decrease, the shores they water, and the origin of
the various springs that feed them. But no one has ever taken
it into his head to begin with the source of a river and to follow
its descent. It is the same with the study of the arts, when to
purely practical investigations we would add the inquiry into
their origins,—those principles, often mutually opposed, to which
they owe their birth. It is not our fault that we are the successors of the Asiatics, the Egyptians, the Greeks, the Romans, the
nationalities of the Middle Ages and the revivalists of the
Renaissance. Now ever since the sixteenth century it has been
admitted that the study of Architecture is virtually Archæology,
—that is, the knowledge of the arts of former times and the
examination of the practical appliances indicated by experience
and tradition. This is unfortunate ; but there is no help for it :
and such being the state of the case, it appears to me by no means
reasonable to say to students : " You will explore this river not
from its mouth to the sources of its several tributaries, but
only between the mouths of this and that particular tributary ;
for only in this part of its course are its waters clear and its banks
fertile." " But how do you know this," it may be replied,
" since, above and below this section which you choose to mark
out, explorations have still to be made ; or, if they have been
made, they are not connected with a systematic course of observations allowing us to compare the studies of various sections,
and to express an opinion as the result of this comparison ? "
The Renaissance displayed more enthusiasm than reflection in its

devotion to Pagan Antiquity; its procedure was like that of the discoverers of some buried city, who fall into raptures over the beauty of every fragment, and heaping its remains together without order, do not wait to discover whether they belong to one or to several buildings,—whether they are of the same age, and what is their relative value as works of Art. That vanity of which all have some share invariably disposes them to attach particular importance not only to what they produce, but to that which they have accidentally discovered. "This pebble is more beautiful than yours, because *I* picked it up." I am far from blaming this naïveté of *amour propre* which is common to humanity, for it has been the occasion of all the research for and discovery of those *chefs-d'œuvre* that would otherwise be lost to us : but when many pebbles have been collected, labelled, and classed, it may surely be allowed us to distinguish those which contain precious stones from so many others whose only merit is that they have found their way into the collector's bag. Admiration, enthusiasm, is necessary for the artist—a passion which ought to characterise him ; but this passion should be devoted to worthy objects, otherwise its fire is soon extinguished without having produced anything but a transient flame. Love a noble intelligence, an elevated soul, and you will soon reflect the excellencies of the being that has charmed you ; but if your love is addressed to a vulgar intellect or an abject soul, however pure and ardent that love may be, you will bear through life the shameful traces of your error. In the arts, selection and examination are therefore of supreme importance to youth entering on a course of study ; and we must observe that selection is more difficult now than formerly in proportion to the greater number of objects presented. Our libraries and museums enable us to contemplate architectural monuments covering nearly the whole earth, belonging to all ages and all civilisations ; but we do not possess a method : for I should not be justified in dignifying with this title the exclusive preferences of certain coteries which have no longer the will or the energy necessary to vitality, and the remnant of whose existence manifests itself only by restlessness and caprice without aim or result.

When archæological knowledge was less extensive, the methods were simple ; for instruction must in the nature of the case be circumscribed by the limits of that knowledge. Thus, for example, it is worth while observing how the Classical texts and the remains of the architectural monuments of Antiquity were interpreted during the three centuries that preceded us. The translators and commentators of Vitruvius in the sixteenth century do not scruple to give to their restorations of the edifices described by this author the aspect of the public buildings of their day. The Italian school, at that time considerably pedantic in its tastes, insisted on being more antique than the ancients, and gave to its restorations a monumental appearance in accordance with certain rules to which it did homage,—rules happily never followed during the antique period, which, like all good epochs in Art, maintained its liberty. In Louis xiv.'s time we find Perrault translating Vitruvius and composing architectural designs in the Classical style, the structure of which is impossible, and whose form recals only too vividly the hybrid architecture of his time. Subsequently the aversion to Medieval Art was so strong that it caused the rejection of certain principles of Classical Architecture for no other reason than that the Middle Ages had known how to apply them and derive advantage from them. Whatever may have been said in their defence by the distinguished men who wrote on Architecture during the last century, or even at the commencement of the present, we cannot look with any respect on those puerilities or that unreflecting exclusiveness. We shall find in the French translations of Vitruvius in the sixteenth century specimens of the Renaissance, in Perrault architecture of the age of Louis xiv., in the Italian commentators the architecture of Vignola or Palladio,—but not Classical structures. These men, and the age in which they lived, had the good fortune to be possessed of artistic if not archæological genius, though they prepared the way for archæological knowledge. Their position was better than ours, I allow ; but I remark again,—we have not chosen our age : we are born into it, and must take it as it is, and live its life.

I think it above all things desirable that young students of Architecture should be taught to reason,—that their minds should be habituated to analysis and examination. The contrary is the case at present : the majority of those who are preparing to become architects have quitted their classical studies before completing them ; for it is supposed, and not without reason, that the study of Architecture requires considerable time, and that it cannot be commenced too soon. But these immature intellects are not in a condition to choose the food that best suits them. There would be no great danger in this, if the course of instruction possessed unity, simplicity, and logical consistency ; if—as was possible two centuries ago—we could conscientiously teach certain conventional forms whose value no one disputed ; if we would limit ourselves to the study of particular authors or particular architectural examples. But we do not live in that golden age of professorial annals when teaching, restrained within narrow limits, had not the unwelcome prospect of seeing its recipients wandering to the right and left, and gleaning good grain and bad outside the limits of the school. Novel objects have presented themselves and are presenting themselves continually. It no longer takes six weeks to reach the Eternal City : Africa and Asia are "at our doors :" photography inundates us with representations of the architectural monuments of all countries and of every age,—irrefutable witnesses of the labours of man through long centuries and in every climate. The academical method which was wise and rational in the time of Louis XIV., and was made to suit the requirements of its day, has been overwhelmed by an intellectual deluge. Works on Architecture fifty years ago would have occupied but a single shelf in a library, whereas they now fill an entire hall. Pupils possess, or may possess if they will, those sources of instruction which were formerly locked up in the cabinets of masters, and exhibited only to the select few. The old barriers are worm-eaten and trodden under foot, in spite of eloquent protests ;—whelmed in the flood of those productions which in the shape of treatises, engravings, photographs, and casts, fill our cities and find their way to the pupil even in his master's studio, undermine his systems, contradict his teaching, and attack his principles. What then is to be done ? Shall we interdict the issue of books, photographs, and engravings, and forbid our pupils to travel by railway or steamboat ? Shall we return to barges and stagewaggons ?—draw a sanitary cordon around our schools, and imprison our pupils within its limits ? There is no middle course between this absolute restriction and the determination to grapple resolutely with the conditions of the age in which we live, and to make use of the materials which it so lavishly offers us. Let us make a bed for the torrent, since we cannot arrest its course.

The supposition that while the arts of the past are illustrated in so many forms around them, our students will be content to ignore five or six centuries of that Past,—that they will not see nor study them,—is a singular illusion : it seems to me the wiser course to show them what they can gain from those arts, and what they ought to disregard. Must we then describe *seriatim* all the architectural monuments of Classical Antiquity, those of the Middle Ages and of the Renaissance,—pointing out the defects and excellencies,—in order to indicate to our alumni what to study and what to reject ? No, certainly ; such a review, even if conducted with the most scrupulous care, could only give the ideas of the master individually, and would throw confusion into minds ready to seize the mere appearance and to rest satisfied with forms without a clear understanding of the principles that originated them. It is, then, by teaching our students to reason on what they see,—by instilling into them principles that are true for all the arts, and for all time, that we can aid them to guide themselves amid those specimens of Art with which they are so abundantly supplied,—to choose the good and to reject the bad. Another consideration must not be forgotten : there is something more dangerous to Art, if possible, than even confused views, viz., sophistry. While we as artists are willing to see only through our own glass, and hope to persuade our alumni that this glass is the only good one, the republic of arts abounds in amateurs more zealous than enlightened, who, without any practical knowledge of the arts, assert that they are acquainted with the right way, and presume to point it out to everybody else. One such instructor has seen the Parthenon, or has brought to light some portions of an edifice of classic date : he knows nothing of the church in his own village, but he would persuade you that Greek art suffices for all our requirements. Another has never quitted his native province ; but he will maintain that the cathedral which adorns it is the only one displaying " Christian feeling." A third regards the architecture of the world as having commenced under Augustus, and terminated with Constantine. A fourth asserts that only the architects of the Renaissance were able to combine the excellencies of classical art, and that we should keep strictly to their guidance. Each will maintain his thesis by the most powerful reasoning ; but none will have the support of Reason, since not one of them knows how one stone is laid upon another, how a piece of timber-framing is combined, or for what purposes brick or stone-work is the more appropriate. Each school of artists applauds the sophism which flatters its passion or its interest, without perceiving that in thus surrendering itself to the judgment of those who have no practical knowledge of the subject, it lays itself open to condemnation the very next day from other critics, whose opinions are equally unauthoritative. Let us settle our differences for ourselves, and, in spite of the proverbial obstacles to harmony between those of the same profession, let us maintain a good understanding with each other ; bearing in mind that we are all necessarily subject to the same laws, and that we ought to know what they allow, and what they prohibit.

My readers will not do me the injustice of supposing that I presume to interdict all unprofessional criticism of our art. We ought to submit to the scrutiny of the public ; and I do not wish that the body of architects should form an exclusive society of initiated members, forbidding the examination and criticism of its teaching and its works. No ; I desire only that, in the midst of the anarchy prevailing in the domain of Art, the various schools or sections of schools should base their respective claims to superiority on something more substantial than opinions pronounced by amateurs more or less well-informed,—that they should have recourse to good reasons, supported by facts, rather than listen complacently to commonplace generalities respecting the various forms of Art ; for a single word from a practical man is often sufficient to destroy a whole scaffolding of superficial argumentation. I anticipate what will be said,—indeed, it would not be for the first time,—" You are degrading the function of the Architect to that of the mere mason : you concede too much to practical considerations : Architecture is something more than the art of collecting and combining materials in a substantial and convenient form : Architecture is the sister of Music and Poetry,—is bound to give a wide scope to imagination, to inspiration, to taste, and to subordinate even the material laws involved to that divine afflatus which breathes upon the musician and the poet." Granted : but however inspired a musician in our day may be, if he is unacquainted with the inexorable laws of harmony he will produce nothing but an abominable charivari,—however inspired the poet, if he is not conversant with grammar and prosody he must keep his poetry to himself. Unfortunately, however, for us architects, though every one can detect a mistake in grammar, or a limping verse,— though every ear is offended by a false note or an inharmonious chord,—it is not thus in Architecture : very few recognise a defect in proportion or scale, or the disregard of the most ordinary rules. Sheltered by this ignorance on the part of the public, every kind of licence can be indulged in,—of which we see too many examples every day.

It is not any chance aspirant to fame that can get his opera performed or his poem published ; or if this sometimes happens the director and the publisher soon repent of having granted, the former his theatre, the latter his presses. But a bungler may persuade the public that he is an architect ; he may be allowed to build and a knowledge of the constructive art is not so commonly diffused as to prevent the public from occasionally approving a design that has neither reason nor beauty to commend it. We may have various opinions respecting the method of expressing our ideas in Architecture,—the form we prefer to give to our conceptions,—but we are all agreed as to the validity of the rules dictated by good sense and experience, and by the inexorable laws of Statics. Well then, if the method of architectural instruction is to be decided upon, let us begin by recognising this agreement, and not raise useless questions respecting form, which after all have only a secondary importance. Let us teach our pupils how each period of Art has endeavoured to comply with those invariable laws ; how a given programme should be realised ; and let us not flaunt before the eyes of youth those

preferential or exclusive prepossessions which, being founded in
neither reason nor taste, have the disadvantage of bringing before
the public questions insoluble for it, but which it will presume sum-
marily to decide by the aid of feeling and superficial knowledge.
I wish that this appeal on behalf of concord should be heard ; it
would be so if each were willing to examine the real opinions of
his colleague, instead of imputing to him those with which he is
vulgarly credited.   If this desirable understanding existed,
architectural teaching, instead of declining and falling into
confusion, would certainly retrieve its position.   Our students,
instead of being, as they now are, partisans in contests whose
importance they blindly exaggerate, would know that in our
art, emphatically, there is but one sure path,—that indicated by
knowledge and reason ; we should not suggest to them the
deplorable expedient of excusing themselves from serious, pains-
taking, practical study, under the pretext of sharing the sentiments
of such or such a school.   I do not assert that Architecture
is an art derived from reason only,—a branch of pure science, in
short ; but in a case of peril we ought to make a point of bending
our energies towards that part where the danger is.   When the
house is on fire we do not discuss the question whether it is
built according to the rules of Vignola or after the pattern of
Gothic habitations ; we run for water.   In the present day the
question is not whether one form of art shall be supreme over all
the rest ; it is out of our power to make it so ; I have stated why.
The great point is to impart to youth a sure method of appreciating their respective values ; and this method is reasoning and
analysis,—true science, which classes and selects after having
compared,—it is instruction in practical appliances, without
exclusiveness, without prepossessions, without vain theories.
The time is past when whole centuries of history could be
ignored : and if some slowly-moving intellects still fancy that
their silence benefits the arts, it is a pure illusion, for this course
only stimulates research : their very silence is a provocation, and
every provocation tends to intensify the feeling it has aroused.
To make a pretence of concealing what everybody has the means
of knowing, or of ignoring a state of feeling universally prevalent,
has been the infatuation possessing all systems during the period
of their decline : in politics it has occasioned violent revolutions ;
in the Sciences and the Arts it is opening a door to extravagance,
to audacious ignorance, and to senseless reaction,—to confusion
of thought and forgetfulness of elementary principles.   In ages
of transition and productivity, such as ours, I believe that the
only means of aiding that productivity (and what can we do
more ?) is to examine everything in good faith, and without
passion, and to take a fair account of the state of our knowledge ;

and if we presume to direct our contemporaries,—we, who are but atoms in the general current,—let it be with the help of our best guide,—our reason,—our faculty of comparison and deduction. If the guide is not infallible, it has at any rate the power of lighting up the road at every step, and enabling those who follow it to recognise and rectify its errors. This is less dangerous than silence ; for silence is darkness, and in darkness every one stumbles.

In conclusion, then, I will add,—First, that the time is come when teaching can be no longer exclusive ; that to insist on maintaining what we regard as good and sound doctrines is to propose to imprison the mind of the student within a boundary-wall which may have been wide enough a hundred years ago, but which exists no longer,—it is to perpetuate a condition of fatal confusion,—to ignore an enormous mass of acquired knowledge and of useful research and labour. Secondly, that in the state of uncertainty into which the acutest minds have fallen with regard to doctrines, it is not so much the forms of Art that we must teach youth as its invariable principles,—that is, the grounds of its existence, its structure and methods, and the changes these have undergone to suit new requirements and habits : what we ought to reject are vague theories, systems based on mere traditions, and which cannot appeal to a logical concatenation of facts, and those so-called inviolable formulas which have never been adhered to during the brilliant periods of Art. When there is a lack of faith among men (I mean real faith,—that which does not dispute about its object) only one guide remains to them,—their reason,—the sense of the True and the Just. The instrument is an imperfect one, I allow ; but it is better to make use of this than to have none. Modern pride has taken the place of the fatalism of the Ancients and the submission of the Middle Ages: let us take account of this intellectual change in the republic of arts, as governments do in the art of governing the present generation. It is amusing, certainly, to observe that the leaders of the schools who accuse us of wishing to effect a retrograde movement act as the Athenian authorities or medieval guilds would perhaps have done, and that we are obliged to assert the independence of reason in the arts. Voltaire pointed out much graver inconsistencies in his time ; we need not, then, despair of the future.

It is in reasoning, therefore, as it seems to me, that we must exercise the artists of our generation ; and I am convinced that by habituating them to reasoning we shall succeed in some measure in improving their taste. Every man who is a born artist possesses his art by *intuition ;* but calculation and experience are called in to show that this intuition is correct. We have here an example of a very singular mental operation : reflection wakes up in our minds many old ideas; all at once a new one arises, we know no more how or why than we know how, from the union of the sexes, a new individual is born. It is certain, however, that, to produce a phase of Art veritably our own, we must arouse ideas, not stifle them; we must bring them into view under all their aspects by ratiocination; we must try them by comparison and intellectual friction. The Ancients had the advantage over us of not possessing an enormous mass of materials of which we are obliged to take account; they had also the privilege of an education in perfect harmony with their social condition; while ours is only a crude farrago of obsolete traditions which no one believes, and of novel sciences which are manifestly at issue with those traditions.

Let all who choose to do so commiserate our age to their heart's content; there is reason for commiseration, and we ought to be allowed to indulge it freely; but, for myself, I consider our age as good as any other, and I take it as it is. If all will do the like, it will have Arts of its own: we have only to use our reasoning faculty a little, and to cease to fancy that we are still living under Louis XIV., and that M. Lebrun is *Surintendant des Beaux Arts* in France.

In the preceding Lecture we discussed the vaulted Roman edifices,—edifices characteristic of the peculiar genius of that people,—a genius reflecting the sense of duration, possession, and power. These, however, were not their only buildings. At the close of the Republic and the commencement of the Empire, the Romans were not yet inspired by that sense of incontestable superiority which, at a later period, caused them to adopt in their public buildings certain uniform methods which they insisted upon everywhere, in spite of local habits and foreign influences. The treatise of Vitruvius, though quite Roman in its character, and notwithstanding his attachment to formulas, still indicates a certain freedom in the art of building which deserves thorough study. There is a description of Roman buildings of which we have not yet spoken that presents peculiar arrangements and structure,—the Basilica.

The name *Basilica* is Greek, and means *Royal House.* It is probable that the word came from Asia, and that, with the successors of Alexander,—the Macedonian kings established in the East,—this form of building itself originated. It was probably their *Divan*—the place where they administered justice. Vitruvius makes no distinction between the Greek and the Roman basilica, but we have already had occasion to remark that Vitruvius appears not to have had an exact idea of Greek architecture and its arrangements in detail. He contents himself with observing " that the basilica contiguous to the forum or public

place ought to be situated in the warmest aspect, so that the
merchants who frequent it during the winter may not be incon-
venienced by the severity of the cold." He adds, that "its
breadth should never be less than the third of its length, nor
greater than the half, unless the nature of the locality prevents
these dimensions from being adopted." Here Vitruvius, as his
custom is, lays down certain formulas of proportion which are
not generally observed, and which he himself is the first to disregard in building the basilica of Fano. Let us continue. " If,"
says he afterwards, " the space destined for the building is longer,"
—that is, if its length is more than thrice its breadth,—" *chal-
cidica* are raised at its extremities, as in the basilica Julia Aqui-
liana ; the columns of the basilica will be as high as the width of
the portico, and the breadth of the latter will be the third of the
central space (nave), and the columns of the higher story will
be smaller than those of the ground-floor. The height of the
screen (*pluteus*), extending between the columns of the gallery,
should be one-fourth of the height of the columns themselves,
that persons walking in those upper galleries may not be seen
by the merchants on the ground-floor. As to the architraves,
friezes, and cornices, their proportions will be deduced from those
of the columns, as we have pointed out in the third book." I
have translated this passage, following as nearly as possible the
Latin text, which is clear and precise, but not fully explanatory.
In fact, Vitruvius does not inform us whether this building is
surrounded by a wall, whether it is closed, or how it is covered ;
and his text leaves this point quite undetermined. When he
proceeds to describe the basilica whose construction he superintended at Fano, he speaks of the walls, discourses at some length
on the disposition of the columns of this edifice, their proportions,
and the plans adopted in building the upper gallery ; and, remarkably enough,—as I said above,—he does not observe in this
construction any of the rules he has just laid down, either in the
design as a whole or in the details.

This is his text : " The length of the vault, *testudo* (it is
certain from what follows that Vitruvius does not here allude to
a vault of brick or rubble, but to a covering of timber-work),—
the length of the vault between the columns is one hundred and
twenty feet; its breadth, sixty feet ; the portico which surrounds
the central nave is twenty feet wide between the columns and
the walls ; the height of the columns, including their capitals, is
fifty feet, their diameter five feet ; at the back of the columns
are pilasters twenty feet high and two feet and a half wide, for
the support of the beams which carry the floor of the portico.
Above these pilasters are others eighteen feet high, two feet
wide, and one foot thick, to receive the beams which carry the

rafters of the upper portico, whose lean-to roof is placed some-what lower than the vault (the covering of the nave). The spaces remaining between the beams (of the lean-to roof of the upper portico), on the pilasters and on the columns, are left open for light in the intercolumniations."

The brevity of this last passage renders the text obscure, but we will endeavour to explain it :—

"The columns in the direction of the breadth of the vault, including those at the angles, are four in number on each side. Lengthwise, on the side facing the Forum, the number is eight, —including those at the angles ; but on the opposite side there are only six, the two central ones being omitted in order not to obstruct the view of the *pronaos* of the temple of Augustus, which is placed in the middle of the side wall of the basilica facing the centre of the Forum and the temple of Jupiter. In the temple of Augustus is placed the tribunal, in shape a semi-circle whose curve is incomplete, being only fifteen feet in depth, with a chord of forty-six feet. This tribunal was thus placed in order that the merchants who have business in the basilica may not interfere with the pleaders who are occupied with the magis-trates. Upon the columns all round are placed lintels formed with three beams two feet thick, at each third column (on the inside opposite the Forum) these lintels return and bear across on to the *antæ* which project from the *pronaos* (of the temple) and adjoin the semicircle on the right and left. Upon the lintels over the capitals (of the columns) are built supporting piers three feet high and four feet square. On these piers all round (the building) are laid coupled beams well joined, two feet in thickness, on which are placed across the tie-beams and principal-rafters opposite the frieze which is upon the antæ and the walls of the *pronaos*. These principals carry the roof which covers the whole basilica, and that which is in the middle of the *pronaos* of the temple. Thus a pleasing effect is produced by the resulting two-fold disposition of the roof, forming a ridge outside and a vault within. This method of construction saves considerable labour and expense ; for the ornament over the architrave, the ordon-nance of the upper columns and the parapets, are suppressed. Yet these columns which rise continuously to support the lintels that receive the roofing give great dignity and magnificence to the edifice."

Vitruvius naturally enough assumes his work to be good, and I esteem his opinion of it sound. He gives us ample evidence of the freedom of the Ancients in their architectural compositions, —a peculiarity belonging to all the best periods of Art. Half a century ago, Vitruvius, in the name of the rules of Roman architecture, would not have obtained for his design for the Fano basilica any mention at the *École des Beaux Arts*. What do I say? He would have been excluded from the competition!—sent to the lowest form to learn Roman architecture from Vignola or Palladio. Not put a complete entablature on the columns! surmount their capitals with wood lintels and with timber framing resting on pads! back the columns with pilasters! What heresy! what neglect of all rules! Twenty-five years ago the basilica of Fano would have passed for the work of a *romanticist*. And I think I remember that even then, if peradventure this edifice was mentioned among critics, it was with a sigh; it was passed over lightly,—glanced at with that delicate consideration we are accustomed to show to those aberrations to which even the most distinguished artists are sometimes liable. But who, then, is to be trusted, if the only special author left by antiquity abandons in the edifice he is building, and the only one of which he gives a description, the rules laid down by himself,—those rules so carefully transcribed in the books of the architects of the Renaissance, and which they themselves have not followed in practice? Can Architecture be an art whose forms are arbitrary, and whose principles alone are invariable? Have we for two centuries been going astray, in imposing certain forms as invariable,—as the highest expression of taste,—and in neglecting the study of those principles to which the ancients themselves seemed to attach the greatest importance? Is it possible, then, that the architects of the Middle Ages, so faithful to their principles, and so free in the adoption of forms, approached more nearly to antiquity than the *Grand Siècle*—the age of Classicism *par excellence?* What an upsetting of all received ideas! and how provoking it is that we cannot invoke prescription for ideas, even if false, as we invoke it in favour of proprietorship of doubtful title!

Nevertheless, all who are not absolutely devoted to the rules laid down by theorists, though little observed by practical men, will find in the description of the edifice at Fano, built and described by Vitruvius, a peculiar disposition which is deserving of serious attention. In the first place, the *Chalcidicum*—the tribunal—is placed on one of the long sides. Within, the building has but one height of columns, divided by the floor of the galleries. The columns are not surmounted by a complete entablature, but they have appendages in the form of pilasters which carry the floors of the galleries and their roof. The capitals of the columns detach themselves above these lean-to roofs, enabling the light to enter between them, into the interior. They only support lintels of wood, short stone pillars, and the wall-plates of the timber roof which is exposed to view. Vitruvius, rationalist as he is, asserts that this saves great trouble and expense! He thus, with the most candid air, condemns the

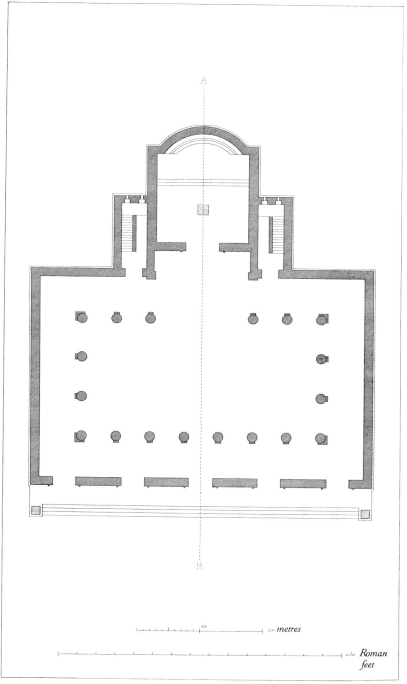

Plate VIII.   Basilica of Fano—Plan

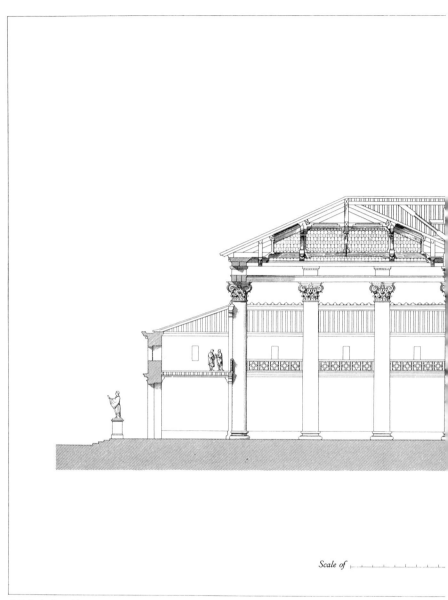

Scale of ├──┴──┴──┴──┴──┴──┴──┴

E. Vallet Le Duc del.

PLATE IX.   Basilica of Fano—Section on line A B of Plan

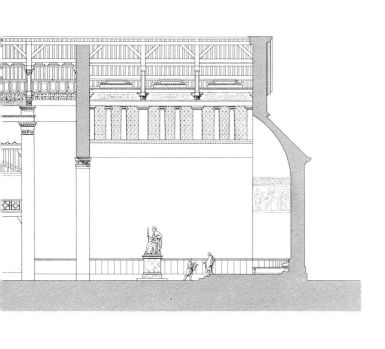

metres

Roman cornice; yet it is in the reign of Augustus that he writes in this manner. Were, then, sound doctrines not enforced at that time? No: Architecture still preserved that liberty, that freedom of action which were its noblest prerogatives among the Greeks and in the latter days of the Roman Republic; it had not made formulas take the place of Art; it appertained to artists, and had not yet become a part of the great political and administrative machinery of the Roman Empire.

Neither the plan nor the section of the basilica of Fano can be drawn in two ways. Vitruvius is careful to give us the dimensions of the principal parts of his building. Plate VIII. shows the plan, and Plate IX. the section of this basilica.

To illustrate the disposition of the pilasters on the back of the columns and bearing the floor of the gallery as well as the lean-to roof which covers it, I give (Fig. 1) some sections of these columns at different heights.

At A is seen the base which is not yet placed on the square socle so inconvenient in a much frequented place, but adopted later on without exception in the Ionic, Corinthian, and Roman Composite. At B is the capital carrying the floor of the gallery, with the notching out above for the passage of the longitudinal piece of timber C, indicated in the section D. At E starts the upper pilaster; on its sides are seen the holes for the tenons of the wooden balustrade F, occupying the place of the *pluteus* of the basilica composed of two superimposed orders. At G, the capital of the upper pilaster intended to support the timber plate H, shown in the section D, and which carries the upper ends of the rafters of the lean-to roof K. The column, below the capital, is slightly cut away for the passage of this plate, and to overlap the crest tiles of burnt clay so as to prevent the rain-water from finding its way in. At L is shown this plate with the notching in of the rafters, covered in, first with brick quarries, then with tiles M, with their overlaps and cresting ornamented on the interior face NN'. The capital P, copied from one of the fine capitals of the Augustan period deposited in the museum of St. John Lateran, receives the triple lintel of timber O.

That is all very clear in the text, and no great effort is required to explain by figures what Vitruvius meant. As to the system of timber roof adopted, the author, it must be admitted, gives us only a very vague idea; and there no longer exist any ancient timber roofs that could be given as examples. Moreover, there is one arrangement of the plan which singularly complicates the framing of this roof. Vitruvius is at the pains to tell us that opposite the *pronaos* of the temple of Augustus, he omitted two columns, that he returns at right angles the beams bearing on the two last remaining columns, so as to make them rest on

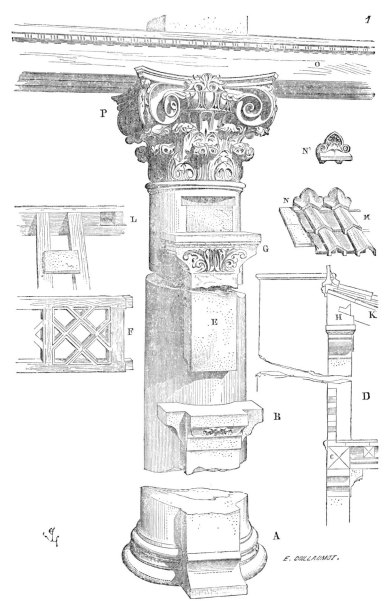

Construction of the Temple of Fano.

PLATE X.   Basilica of Fano—System of Roofing

the antæ which project from that *pronaos*. The principal nave returns, then, at right angles like a transept towards the entrance of the temple. He also tells us that his roof is provided with tie-beams, that it is cased inside, and has two eaves without, and that it returns opposite to the *pronaos*. The basilica is very wide (sixty Roman feet).[1] It required a principal above each column, and we cannot suppose there were diagonal principals in the void left opposite the *pronaos*. That arrangement would have had a very disagreeable effect, and would have been deficient in strength. We can hardly suppose any other than a single system of framing (according to the data given us by the ancient methods) with the plan drawn by Vitruvius. This system must have consisted of a succession of principals regularly distributed over each column of the nave, the foot of the two principals opposite the entrance of the *pronaos* resting on the tie-beams of two principals coupled together at right angles to the first, making a return of the roof towards the temple. These tie-beams placed in the prolongation of the wall-plates resting on the little piers of the two last columns must have been strongly suspended to the principal rafters by pendants and stayed by corbelling. I have endeavoured to give an idea of this singular disposition in Plate X., adhering as much as possible to the methods of carpentry indicated in the antique paintings of Pompeii and in the bas-reliefs of the column of Trajan. The timber-framing of the Middle Ages will also afford us great help in our endeavours to become acquainted with the art of carpentry as it existed among the Romans. Of all the processes of building-construction, timber-framing is certainly that in which ancient traditions were most faithfully preserved; for even in the most barbarous times works in carpentry never ceased to be executed in the West, and, as early as the time of Cæsar, the Gauls passed for being very clever in the art of working and framing wood. Our roof, Plate X., must be supposed ceiled with boarding according to the custom of the Romans, and as indicated in one part of this engraving. It is probable that the ends of the nave were not hipped—as that would have complicated the construction of the roof, and was not customary among the ancients—but closed with gables of open frame and lattice-work, as shown in Plates IX. and X.

Timber construction played an important part in this kind of edifice, so original in its arrangement. The remains of ancient basilicas and the description of the edifice of Fano give us reason to suppose that the Romans allowed themselves great freedom in the construction of their public buildings in the time of Augustus.

---

[1] The Roman foot found at Herculaneum being 11 inches and $\frac{4}{5}$ (English measure), 60 Roman feet would make about 59 feet.

The few Greek monuments to which the name of basilicas can be given, present themselves some remarkable arrangements which do not appear to have been adopted by the Romans. The basilica of Pæstum, and the building at Thoricus to which a similar function may be assigned, present a line of columns down the centre which formed two galleries or interior deambulatories, without reckoning the exterior porticos. These last buildings rather resembled open marketplaces than closed edifices like the Roman basilicas; and we do not find in them the place for the tribunal which appears in all the Roman basilicas. The Romans however ever under the Empire were not slow in giving to their basilicas, as to all the other edifices which they built at that period, a great degree of magnificence. The basilica situated in the forum of Trajan, built at Rome by a celebrated architect, Apollodorus of Damascus, was a structure as remarkable for its size as for the richness of the materials employed. This basilica, of which the remains are still to be seen, and of which certain ancient medals show us the exterior façades, consisted of five naves,—a very wide one in the centre, and four narrower ones on the wings, supporting the galleries of the story above. The tribunal was a vast hemicycle, whose diameter spanned the width of the whole five naves, and the porticos as well as the galleries were in front of it. A single entrance, with a portico and vestibule, opened at the end opposite to the tribunal, and three entrances at the south on the forum of Trajan. As to the celebrated column erected by the senate and people of Rome in honour of this prince, it was in a small court situated along the front opposite to the forum. This court opened into the two libraries destined for Greek and Latin books, and which were reached by two doors made in the two extremities of the northern wall of the basilica. The brick walls of the basilica were covered with a thick facing of white marble, at least in their lower part. The columns of the five naves were of grey granite, placed on bases of white marble and surmounted by Corinthian capitals of the same material. The ceiling was covered with plates of gilded bronze. The three principal porticos adjoining the forum on the south side were crowned, as antique medals show us, by *quadrigæ* and statues. The pavement, which is still visible, is composed of large marble slabs antique-yellow and violet. It is certain that this edifice was not vaulted, but covered by timber roofs.

Was the tribunal covered? If it was so by a vault in form of quarter sphere, how could this vault be connected with the galleries and the walls which they carried? The forms of the basilica scarcely agree with this hemicycle, which occupies the nearly entire width of the five naves. Such an arrangement does not seem feasible of execution, and perhaps the interval left between the aisles and the tribunal was open to the sky. For however we may conceive of the construction of the basilica and its wooden roof, we cannot understand how this wooden roof came to abut against the demi-cupola of the tribunal.

As I do not wish to suggest any hypothesis, I shall not seek to discuss the means of solving the question; and in citing this example, I intend simply to show how in certain cases the Romans used to vary their conceptions while remaining faithful to the general requirements of their social condition. We could perhaps find the key to the basilica of the forum of Trajan in those Persian palaces, all of which exhibit, on one of the sides of the courts surrounded by porticos, a hemicycle of large relative dimension, covered by a vault in form of quarter sphere. It is certain, moreover, that the modern East has preserved certain Roman traditions. Many buildings are erected there in modern times which are destined for a variety of purposes, like our Palais-Royal in Paris. The mosques and bazaars greatly resemble the Roman basilicas in the multiplicity of purposes they fulfil, and in the splendour of their interiors. We have in them edifices originating in the vanity of sovereigns who wished to attach their names to public works of a durable and magnificent order, and which were adapted to attract the multitude, and to unite them, so to speak, in their works; certainly, monuments of this kind did not originate in a Republic. Whatever, therefore, the Greek basilica may have been, we must recognise a distinction between it and the Roman basilica. Besides, as I have already remarked, it was the architectural arrangements of their temples only that the Romans took from the Greeks; whenever the public service was in question the Roman borrowed from no one, he created and modified the plans he had sketched according to the requirements. And since the basilicas were buildings intended for divers purposes, and as these purposes may vary or have more or less relative importance according to time and place, the Roman varied his plan *ad infinitum.*

The import of the opinion expressed respecting the public buildings of the Empire must not be misunderstood. Their arrangements are not so absolutely fixed as to exclude all variety; the principles only of the public Roman edifices from the time of Augustus downwards are immutable; but a principle, however absolute, may in its application assume various forms; we have a proof of this still later on, during the Middle Ages. I would observe, too, that it is not only to public buildings that architecture is applicable; it plays an important part in private life; and though we have only a very vague idea of what the habitations of the Greeks may have been, it is not the same as regards the Latins.

It cannot be too often repeated that during all the periods of history with which we are acquainted, there exists an intimate relation between the manners, the habits, the laws, and the religion of the nations and their arts. Perhaps our own age forms an exception ; of this posterity will judge ; but it is certain that (for example), during the period of Roman Antiquity comprised between the close of the Republic and the fall of the Empire, architecture strictly followed the various movements of Roman society. In our fourth Lecture we dwelt upon the methods followed by architects during the Imperial period, because in fact it is only during this period that the arts of Rome are truly Roman ; but just as the Republic is about to close, how interesting is it to observe the relations that exist between the arts and the manners of the times ; how many charms are there in this transitional architecture which is no longer Greek, but which is not yet that of the Empire ! What a favourable time for the arts was that in which lived a Cicero, a Lucullus, a Servius Claudius, a Sallust ! Certainly the house of Cicero at Tusculum must have been, compared with what the magnificent *villæ* of the Emperors and of their favourites afterwards were, a very modest abode ; but with what a delicious perfume of Art must those walls have been impregnated which were so beloved by the last citizen of the Republic ! To him who has some acquaintance with Classical Antiquity, what he says of it in his letters, and the care which he displays, as a man of taste and intellect, in embellishing this habitation, indicate treasures of elegance and exquisite arrangement ; for he nowhere dwells upon the richness of the marbles or the paintings ; he does not speak of his country house with the vanity of a parvenu who has no other aim in view than to eclipse some neighbour by his luxury ; he dwells only on the comfort he enjoys there, the collections of objects of Art which he fondly enumerates, and the advantages of the site. We observe, moreover, that he confides in his architect : although as much a Greek as a Roman, he does not enter into discussion on the forms of Art ; but it is clearly evident that he has an eye for them. Would we have an example of his respect for the decisions of the artist to whom he confides the works in connection with his house, we may look for it in one of his letters to Atticus, in which he says to his friend : " Know that in blaming my windows as too narrow, you are finding fault with Cyrus (his architect) ; happily it is only with the architect. When I was saying the very same thing to him he pointed out to me that wide windows looking into a garden did not offer a prospect so agreeable to the sight. For let A be the eye of the spectator, B and C the object he sees, D and E the rays proceeding from the eye to the object ; you understand what follows." This unfinished demonstration is all in Greek, and it is evident that Cicero only repeats what the architect, probably a Greek, might have said to him; a demonstration to which he seems scarcely to have paid attention, and which is of no great account with him. He adds further on, after an epigram directed to the Epicureans (Atticus belonged to that school): "If you find anything to criticise in other parts, I shall always be prepared with a tolerable justification, unless I can make a change for the better at small cost." It is difficult to cite a passage giving us a livelier conception of the relations existing between a Roman citizen—the first man of the Republic of that day, a man of so pure a taste and so acute an intellect—and his architect. It is evident that the *élite* of Rome at that time had a passion for the arts : but as they were sufficiently intelligent to perceive that the Greeks were their masters, they believed they could not do better than rely on the judgment of their artists. Moreover, does not Cicero write to his friend to purchase for him statues in Greece, where he was living, and to provide for their reaching him in good condition ? How much is it to be regretted that of this period of transition, in which the Greek arts were intermingled with the regular habits of Roman life, only so few remains are extant ! There must have been at that time in architectural works that freedom and elegance which are superior to richness,—a freedom of which we find some relics in the description which Vitruvius gives us of his basilica, but which entirely disappear under the Emperors. It was exactly the architecture appropriate to the state of society at the close of the Republic,—a social condition abounding in contrasts, highly civilised and very elegant, but which had not yet sunk into that moral thraldom in which we see it plunged a century later. In default of extant architectural monuments, what help could not architects of our day derive from the attentive study of that Roman society with which we have so many points of resemblance, and which—must we confess it ?—is so superior to us in an intellectual point of view ! With the aid of the slight remains we possess, and an exact acquaintance with men and things as we find them during the final period of the Republic, and by calling to our aid the study of the manners and the history of our own country, it would be possible to draw our arts out of that miserable rut in which we see them more deeply sinking every day. But to attain such a result we must have the courage to recognise that our modern teaching is unsatisfactory, that the antiquarian savans who write or speak on architecture are not architects, and that the architects who profess this art are not sufficiently versed in the knowledge of the history and manners of Classical Antiquity or of the Middle Ages. We should perhaps have an art of our own if we knew ourselves,—if we knew what we are, and what we may reasonably expect from our age.

The advantage arising from the study of Antiquity (and it is certainly a considerable one) is its ennobling effect on the minds of youth ; but to insure this result, that study must not be stolidly limited to forms,—as has been the case for two centuries in what has a relation to architecture, but which, in fact, has a higher aim. We must investigate the social condition of the Greeks and Romans, that of the Romans especially,—so grand, and so firmly based, in spite of its abuses and errors ; we must not merely enter the Roman house, but also become acquainted with him who inhabits it, appreciate his tastes, and live his life, to comprehend the perfect harmony that exists between the man and his habitation. Now-a-days, when every person and every thing are out of their place, when all the members of society make it their object to go out of their proper sphere, to produce a contradiction between their apparent and real existence, the part the architect has to play becomes more and more difficult, since it is not for him to set himself up as a moral censor, still less to become the agent of a kind of sumptuary police. Nevertheless the mental elevation of an architect, his exact knowledge of civilised societies, the commendable examples and the good reasons he is able to furnish, have a greater influence than appears to be imagined ; but it is not by passing his time at Rome or Athens in restoring for the thousandth time the Theatre of Marcellus, the *Porticus Octaviæ,* or the Parthenon, in shading in with painful care a bit of an entablature or of a capital in his studio at the Villa Medici, that the architect, on returning home, will be able to gain an influence over the mind of a capricious or irresolute client, or be in a position to base his advice on simple and solid reasons, to which, in the long-run, none but an imbecile can refuse to yield.

We have cast a glance over the public buildings of the Romans, and have been able to appreciate,—leaving questions of form out of consideration,—how liberally and scrupulously the requirements were satisfied, how clearly the exterior of the edifice explained that which it contained ; how the means employed were exactly those which suited the existing state of society ; how luxury and opulence never sank into a false refinement, but participated, on the contrary, in that grandeur which characterised the Roman people,—a grandeur free from affectation and bombast. If we descend into the private life of the Roman citizen, if we see him in his home, we find a very different state of things : when a Roman citizen is rich enough to build a theatre, a portico, or public baths, he adopts the *official* architecture, if I may call it so,—that which suits the public ;—but if he builds for himself —for his family—he does not seek to make a show, or to dazzle the multitude, he only asks for the satisfaction of his individual tastes,—to erect a habitation agreeable to himself and those he loves. Such at least were the habits of Roman citizens at the close of the Republic. At a later date, vanity—the wish to make a show—modified the tendencies of the Roman in this respect; but then the fall of ancient society was evidently approaching. Not only do the houses of Pompeii in their exterior preserve, all of them,—the richest and largest as well as the smallest,—an appearance of uniform simplicity, but the means of construction and the materials are the same in both classes. We also find this feature in all the oriental cities. When an individual is rich, and can afford to have apartments filled with statues and pictures, he makes a point of keeping this magnificence to himself, and avoids attracting the gaze of the envious. These habits were natural in a Republic; and citizens who had spent several millions of sesterces on an aqueduct or a circus for the city in which they lived, inhabited houses which made no more show than those of their less opulent neighbours. We may even suppose that their custom of concealing from the public the interior wealth of private habitations contributed to develop among the Romans that attachment to their *villæ*, where they could venture to manifest their taste for luxury and comfort, without fearing the criticisms of the *plebs* or their neighbours. We find the traces of this feeling of envy at Rome towards citizens who built pleasant abodes, in the life of Cicero, when he was compelled to quit Rome in consequence of the intrigues of the party of Clodius; the first thing his enemies do, as soon as he is gone, is to demolish his houses. Such violence on the part of an infatuated rabble in a city so often agitated by factions, necessarily compelled the richer citizens carefully to conceal their domestic comforts and luxuries. The programme of a private dwelling at Rome differed, therefore, from the programmes of public buildings, not only in virtue of their respective requirements, which, in the nature of the case, were different, but also in that aspect which was more closely related to Art. While the Roman thought that he could never do too much to make the public monuments externally conspicuous in grandeur and importance, he thought it, on the other hand, his duty to hide from the public the splendour of his private abode. We may easily understand, therefore, how little the Roman cities would resemble ours, and how greatly the apparent simplicity of private habitations would enhance the magnificence of the public buildings. Those cities would evidently gain in picturesque effect through this contrast; and the ideas of their inhabitants were affected by it. The associations of sight, like those of the other senses, result in abiding impressions; and it is certain that the effect produced by splendid public edifices, situated among dwellings of uniform appearance, presenting only simple lines and a grave and unpretentious exterior, was of a nature to elevate the mind, and to make it more capable of appreciating works of Art.   The Romans passed the greater part of their time away from home.   In the morning, the influential citizens used to receive the clients who assembled in the *atrium* of their houses to await their patron's levée.   He would go out with them ; for, under the Republic, the attendance of a large train of clients was a means of securing for the patricians an influence in public affairs.   Thus accompanied, he would proceed to the forum, or to those vast porticos which, at several points of the city, served as promenades and as a rendezvous for business ; he would occupy himself with public engagements, which made continual demands upon his attention ; and then repair to the baths or the games of the circus or the amphitheatre ; and at evening return home.   Then his house was open to a few friends only.   His domestic luxury was therefore strictly private ; the apartments constituting the Roman house were small, opening into interior courts and porticos ; no one outside could know what was taking place in the habitation of a Roman citizen.   Architecture had strictly complied with this condition.   We cannot be astonished that men whose birth, or fortune, or position involved them in all the intrigues of parties struggling for power, should have felt the need of that calm which rural life afforded.   Thus the attachment of the Romans to the country was general under the Republic, and only increased during the first years of the Empire. At Rome, a notable citizen known to every one was obliged to imprison himself in his house if he wanted to enjoy a little repose ; out of it he was assailed by friends, clients, partisans, or rivals, and was unable to be neutral and indifferent amid the perpetual stir of factions.   Men who, like Cicero—for example— had as much love for study as ambition (characteristics which, although of an opposite nature, are often met with in the same individual), experienced from time to time the necessity of giving repose to their minds by going away from Rome ; and it is especially in their country houses—their *villæ*—that the true character of the domestic architecture of the Romans makes itself perceptible.

    I cannot imagine, indeed, how those ideas of symmetry as characterising Classical architecture applied to private dwellings, which have prevailed from the sixteenth century downwards, should ever have gained currency ; for I do not find a trace of it either in buildings or authors.   At Pompeii there is not a single house whose plan or elevations are subjected to the rules of symmetry.   Cicero and Pliny speak much in their letters of the aspect, position, and arrangement of several apartments of their country houses ; but of symmetry not a word.   In fact, these dwellings were a combination of halls, porticos, chambers, galleries, etc., whose position was determined by the light, the wind, the rain, the shade, and the prospect,—all of them conditions which exclude symmetry.   The detailed description which Pliny gives of his Laurentine country-house to his friend Gallus is, in this respect, one of the most curious of literary monuments.   The invariably practical spirit of the Roman makes itself visible throughout the course of this letter ; the decoration, the mosaics, the marbles, and paintings he says nothing about ; but he insists in every line, on the prospect, the direction in which the apart-ments open, the arrangements special to each, the cool freshness of some and the mild temperature of others, the varied aspects of the country and the sea, the profound quiet of the places reserved for study and meditation, the comely appearance and comfortable condition of his slaves, the pieces of water and the gardens.   He does not mention orders, or casings, or cornices.   In this charming letter not a tinge of vanity makes itself visible. He likes his house, he has had it arranged according to his taste, he finds real gratification in it,—and his was a mind of so dis-tinguished an order, he was so accomplished a Roman gentleman, that this habitation could not but be a *chef-d'œuvre* of elegance and taste ;—yet in discussing its merits with his friend it does not become the occasion of the slightest vanity.   If we ought to follow the Romans in anything, it should assuredly be in their intellectual probity, their true elegance, their judicious love of moral and physical well-being, rather than in those conventional formulas to which homage was rendered during the pompous and conceited reign of Louis XIV., and which are paraded as the regen-erated traditions of Classical Antiquity.   Ought not those who love Classical Antiquity, who admire its productions and linger with delight amid that accomplished Roman society whose most trifling vestiges we eagerly explore,—ought not they, I say, ener-getically to repel the false interpretations put upon its arts ? For myself, I must emphatically assert that the hybrid Antiquity with which we are deluged is quite as repugnant to me as a *tête d'expression* by Coustou or Coysevox on the torso of the Venus de Milo.   Is it not a dangerous error to affiliate on the ancients certain ridiculous laws under which ignorance and mediocrity find shelter,—those inexorable laws of symmetry, of compositions of order uniformly applied everywhere ; when, on the contrary, we find in the works of Antiquity only one dominant law,—the sincere and true expression of the requirements of the case, together with a freedom restrained only by reason and taste, which is nothing other than the habit of reasoning applied to the feeling of Art ?

I think Horace could scarcely restrain a smile if, standing before the château of Versailles, he were told that this immense symmetrical barrack (and why symmetrical ?), pierced with rows of windows and decorated with columns and pilasters, was the *villa* of a sovereign.   Let us love and study Classical Antiquity ; love and study, if you will, the architecture of the *Grand Siècle* ; it has its merits and its grandeur : but do not let us confound works that are not only dissimilar but diametrically opposed in principle and in expression ; above all, let us beware of contending that the latter were inspired by the former.   We might as well assert that Puget sought his types in Ægina.   That the architects of the time of Louis XIV. thought they were following the traces of the Ancients,—that they said so in good faith,—must not be charged against them as a crime ; we ought to respect in the past even its illusions ; but it is unpardonable that such nonsense should be repeated in our days by mere traditional prescription.

Pliny the Consul had not only his villa in the environs of Ostia, on the sea-shore ; he also possessed a very beautiful country house in Tuscany, surrounded by delightful gardens ; he gives a description of this also to his friend Apollinarius.   In a different climate, a different locality, we find a different pro-gramme ; these two pleasure-houses present arrangements peculiar to each, suggested by the situation, the advantages of aspect, scenery, water, and the habits of the country.   Yet on the shore of Ostia as on the slope of the Apennines, in Tuscany, we find still the Roman dwelling, with its numerous services, its porticos, its halls commanding their several aspects, its baths, its studies, its separate apartments for strangers or friends, its xystus, its gymnasium for physical exercises, its rooms for large gatherings, its summer and winter apartments, its lodgings for the freedmen and the slaves.   All these various services are disposed, not to comply with an academic plan, but comformably to the taste of the master, and to suit his daily habits.

We have observed the Roman in his public buildings sub-mitting to the rules of symmetry ; there he studies appearance ; he is building for the public, and he understands that symmetry is a powerful means of exhibiting his grandeur ; to the multitude he is a magistrate ; but at home he lays aside this *official* charac-ter, he builds to suit his own taste,—for himself alone.   For one apartment he courts the warm rays of the sun ; in another he carefully avoids them : he turns to account all the advantages of the situation ; he looks for real convenience, and never allows himself to be guided by the vanity of the modern proprietor, who desires above all things that his country seat should be distinguished as an architectural composition, if he has to suffer for it every day of his life.   The Roman in his country abode (the one he prefers, however ambitious he may be) provides for intellectual and material needs, with admirable judgment and delicate taste; he takes physical well-being into consideration, hygienic arrangements,—his family's health and his own; but he must have a library, quiet apartments for study, such as will allow him to give himself up sometimes to that tranquil meditation which is necessary to intellectual health; he has his gymnasium for the mind as well as the body. Luxury and decoration are in his house not left out of consideration, but to them he never sacrifices *comfort* or convenient arrangements. In fact, he knows how to be a private man, as he knows how to be a public man; he is not carried away by an irrational passion for luxury any more than by the exercise of power. Let us then be Romans : I ask for nothing better; but not Romans with periwigs *à la Louis Quatorze* and high-heeled shoes; let us take example by their *savoir-vivre*, their clear and well-balanced intellect, their practical philosophy, their attachment to the arts as men of acute general intelligence rather than as artists,—not imagine that we imitate them by setting up rows of columns without knowing why, lodging ourselves in palaces magnificent to the view of passers-by, but inconvenient, gloomy, absurd, and full of unseen discomfort to their inhabitants. The château and manor-house of the Middle Ages approach far more closely to the Roman villa and Roman house than the country seats of the two last centuries; for the men who built those châteaux and manor-houses made it their chief consideration to lodge themselves in the most agreeable, healthy, and secure fashion, and troubled themselves very little as to whether one wing of their habitation was shorter or longer than the other, or whether one of its main blocks was higher or lower than its neighbour.

Let us try to form a conception of that residence so dear to Pliny the Consul,—his Laurentine villa. It was only seventeen miles from Rome, on the sea-shore, pretty near to a small city of Latium. "It is," says the Consul, "large enough for my convenience, and does not require a costly maintenance. In the first place, there is an entrance-hall (*atrium*), simple in character without being mean; thence you enter a circular portico enclosing a small but pleasant court; there you are sheltered from the weather, for the porticos are protected by transparent screens (glazing or *lapis specularis*), and still more effectually by the projection of higher roofs. This second court communicates with a third and larger one, into which opens the dining-room jutting out on the sea, so that when the African (south-west) wind blows and the waves have lost their first violence, they gently wash the base of the walls. This room is pierced on all sides by doors, and windows as large as the door, so that, front and sides included, you see three seas, and at the side you enter by, the great court with its portico, the small circular court, then the entrance-hall, and beyond that the woods and mountains. On the left of the dining-room is a large secluded room, then another smaller one open on one side to the east, on the other the west. It is on this side that there is a view of the sea, not so close as from the dining-room, but, on the other hand, a more tranquil one. Outside, near the dining-room, the building forms an interior angle which retains and intensifies the lively warmth of the sun. This place is very agreeable in winter, and serves as a gymnasium for my servants during that season. No other winds are heard there but those occasioned by the clouds that disturb the serenity of the sky. Another room has been connected with the one just mentioned: it is vaulted apse-fashion, and its windows are arranged so as to catch the rays of the sun at all hours of the day. There are placed closets in the thickness of the walls, forming a kind of library filled with those choice books which are always re-perused with pleasure. There is a sleeping apartment separated from this room only by a passage wainscoted with wood, so as to diffuse warmth on all sides. All the rest of the building on this side is reserved for the use of my freedmen and slaves, and is so neat and clean that my guests might lodge there." On the other side there are apartments and another dining-room ; then a suite of bathing-rooms consisting, according to custom, of the *frigidarium*, the sudatory, the perfuming chamber, a *tepidarium*, and a warm bath, looking over the sea. Not far off is a tennis-court exposed to the greatest heat of the sun towards the close of the day. Near this are two summer-houses, two stories high, surmounted by terraces that may serve for dining-rooms, and from which can be enjoyed an extensive view of the sea, of its shores adorned with mansions, and of the garden planted with box, rosemary, fig-trees, and mulberry-trees, and intersected by vine-covered trellises. On this garden another dining-room and suite of rooms open, then a large room, "after the style of the public buildings," with windows on both sides looking over the sea and the gardens. A *xystus* perfumed by violets extends in front of this gallery and shelters it from cold winds. Another very secluded suite of rooms is built at the end of the gallery ; and this is Pliny's favourite retreat ; he describes each apartment minutely, and dwells upon their advantages in point of position and prospect ; there were to be found rooms for taking one's siesta, a warm-air chamber, a study, and everywhere cool shade or sunshine at pleasure. Indeed, Pliny is not so unwise as to consider symmetry in all these arrangements, and to put himself to inconvenience for the sake of displaying regular façades to passers-by. Each apartment was built on that spot, and with those dimensions which were most suitable for it,—some placed at the ends of others,—some projecting, others retreating; these were small and low, those large and lofty : there were some vaulted or wainscoted, pierced with many windows, or having none; but the aspect and the view always dictate the plan, and internal requirements the elevations. These *villæ* were only an assemblage of buildings attached, or consolidated by bearing-walls with roofs of their own, windows smaller or larger according to their several purposes, and an internal and external decoration suitable to the function of each. There was no resemblance in this to the regular plans of public establishments, for the Roman had too much good sense to give to private habitations the appearance of an edifice destined for a public function. The Roman wished to have in his country abode, on a reduced scale, all that he was accustomed to find in one of the cities of the Republic. These habitations were intended to resemble well-arranged villages; they preserved the appearance of such in their exteriors. If classical authorities did not demonstrate the truth of this view, it would be sufficiently confirmed by a glance at ancient paintings representing country seats, and of which a considerable number are extant. They present us with picturesque groups of buildings of all forms and sizes, connected by porticos, each with its own roof, looking in various directions for the sake of the sunshine or the prospect, or retiring under the shade of trees or hills. Our old abbeys, castles, and manor-houses of the Middle Ages literally conform to this so rational programme, and we shall have occasion to observe this resem- blance; these latter buildings, therefore, approach more nearly to the traditions of classical antiquity than our large uniform structures of recent centuries, unless architecture consists merely in the imitation of an order or a profile, and is not a rational system of general arrangements, a true expression of the requirements, customs, and manners of a given phase of civilisation.

At his country house the Roman citizen proposed to himself to assemble around him all that is needed for the satisfaction of mind and body,—a worthy conception, certainly; and he realised it as far as his resources allowed, in the practical spirit that was characteristic of him. In the country, space is not so grudged as in the city; and while at Rome the houses were five stories high, in the rural districts the buildings consisted for the most part of a single floor only. What was the good, in fact, of people's perching one over the other when there was plenty of space around their houses? Do we go into the country to be climbing stairs all day, or to walk about and expatiate in a wide *surface* of ground, and to enjoy repose and silence? What are rural charms if we are shut up in a great stone box, in which we hear servants incessantly going up and down to answer bells, the noise of doors opening and shutting, visitors walking about in their rooms, the orders of the mistress, the cries of children, and that constant movement from which you cannot escape in cities? I repeat it, instead of borrowing from the Romans a few scraps of architecture, to which they attached at most a merely relative importance, let us, if we propose to resemble them in anything, copy chiefly their so judicious application of the art to their requirements and habits.

The profound judgment of the Roman is not less conspicuous in the manner in which he constructs his houses and villæ than in the general arrangements and details of his habitations; rubble, concrete, bricks,—these may be regarded as his usual materials; a few marble columns for porticos, if he is rich enough to allow himself this luxury; casings of the same material in the interior parts of the basements exposed to damp, and everywhere else coatings of stucco well made and painted,—and lintels and linings of wood. While the Romans construct their public buildings so as to last for centuries, the consideration that guides them in erecting their houses—and it is a reasonable one—is that private dwellings are destined to be renewed almost every fifty years. The greater part of the houses discovered at Pompeii are very slightly built, the remains of ancient *villæ*, so numerous in the environs of Rome, show us only buildings erected in the simplest and most economical manner. All the splendour of these dwellings consisted in decorations painted on plaster, pavements and casings of marble, and a variety of detached objects, such as vases, statues, marble fountains, and articles of bronze or costly wood inlaid with ivory and metal. The Roman evidently found no pleasure in piling up enormous masses of stone to make himself a habitation; he preferred to employ his resources in arranging the various halls composing his villa in the most agreeable manner as regarded the view or the aspect; in filling them with handsome furniture and a number of rare objects,—with mosaics, paintings, Greek statues, and manuscripts collected at great cost. He wished to enjoy coolness in summer and warmth in winter; he wished for a supply of water in every part of the house, and apartments appropriated to every function of life; he wished that his *family*, that is, his relatives, freedmen, and slaves, should enjoy their comforts as well as himself, and that in these rural abodes order should reign everywhere, produced not by a constraint insupportable both to him who imposes it and those who submit to it, but by wise foresight and well-ordered administration. In these residences the slaves were certainly much better lodged and treated than are our servants; they had their separate

quarters, their hall for exercises or games, and their own baths;
—social status apart, they were freer, more happy, and subjected
to a better hygiene than are the dependants of a man of wealth
in the present day. It is true that they constituted a form of
wealth, and that their master had an interest in keeping them in
strength and health. We can understand how men habituated
to that free, tranquil, and regular life which they had secured
for themselves in the country, should have been impatient of the
restraints of great cities; as soon therefore as a Roman citizen
had acquired a sufficient fortune to be able to build himself a
villa, he lived at Rome as little as possible, and even within the
enclosure of the great city itself many citizens had built themselves palaces which were in fact veritable *villæ*, that is to say with
all the services, outbuildings, and dependencies that were necessary to the easy and luxurious life of the Roman. On examining
a plan of ancient Rome on which are traced the remains of the
public edifices, we ask ourselves where were the houses in which
lived the vast population of the Great City,—where lived that
multitudinous *plebs* which filled the Campus Martius, the circuses,
and the amphitheatres? The public buildings, the palaces, the
porticos, the squares, occupy at least two-thirds of the surface
comprised within the enclosure of the city. Corporally the
masses were heaped together in houses several stories high;
their *life* was in the places of public resort. This populace was
moreover not very great, compared with that of the great cities
of modern times; Rome, having become the centre of government of the then known world, contained an enormous number
of public edifices constructed on a colossal scale. Space failed
then, and under the Emperors immense buildings were destroyed
to make way for new constructions; palaces and important
establishments had to be swept away to erect edifices more suitable to the wants of the day. Never has any people demolished
so much for the sake of rebuilding. Under the Antonines
whole quarters were removed to provide a site for immense
establishments; yet even to the close of the Empire, public and
private gardens were still to be found in many points of the city.
We have nothing in the Europe of the present day which can
give the idea of such a city. In the country all round the walls,
even to a distance of four or five miles, rose a vast number of
villæ, small and great, and in addition vast public establishments
along the roads,—temples, tombs, hostelries, and porticos for
travellers; while through this sea of habitations and architectural monuments interspersed with gardens wound those long
aqueducts which poured whole lakes of water from the mountains
into the heart of the metropolis. At present the remains
of these constructions *extra muros* are concealed beneath a

sterile winding-sheet; but if this be pierced at any chance point, we find, here a wall, there columns, mosaics, pavements, basins, cellars,—in fact an entire city outside the city.

Even at the close of the Empire, there was a deficiency of inhabitants to animate and people so many public and private edifices. Robbers attacked the traveller at the very gates of Rome; for in any case a people is required to constitute a city, and there was no longer a Roman people. The expansive power of the Romans had so firmly established itself in distant regions, that many rich citizens were living at their villæ in Gaul, Africa, the Peloponnesus, and Asia; while at the gates of Rome bands of slaves and ruined *coloni* were pillaging the country houses abandoned by their proprietors. But while living in these distant regions, these Romans were transmitting to various nations their customs, manners, and method of building; and we still find, in the East especially, architectural traditions left by them and preserved almost without modification. While the houses built by the Persians and the Arabs exhibit arrangements almost identical with those of Roman dwellings, at Rome and throughout Italy their memory has been long lost, and nothing less resembles an ancient palace than the Palazzo Farnese, or a *villa* of the times of Augustus or Tiberius, than the Villa Pamphili or the Villa Albano.

Already towards the later times of the Empire, and even before Constantine, Architecture had been debased. At Rome artists were wanting, if not workmen. New monuments were being decorated with fragments torn from older edifices; the Arch of Constantine was enriched with bas-reliefs and statues taken from the Forum of Trajan. The art of sculpture had fallen into oblivion, and notwithstanding all their power the Emperors were reduced to the necessity of pillaging the edifices of their predecessors; they were beginning the work of the barbarians and destroying admirable monuments to erect constructions whose style was already coarse, and which were clothed with decorations wanting in taste and miserable in point of execution. This is a fact which lays bare before us the weak side of the Roman system of architecture. The Romans had in their constructions so utterly divorced building from Art—they had so decidedly made of Art a mere envelope,—a dress, as we have said before,—that Art, thus treated as a stranger, soon lost the consciousness of its own importance; artists were wanting at Rome towards the close of the Empire; the workmen themselves no longer knew how to cut marble and stone; so true it is that power and money do not suffice to produce artists.

In the West, from the time of Constantine downwards, we

behold only a long series of devastations consummated by the barbarians. During this melancholy period, Art took refuge in the East, at Byzantium ; there it acquired renewed energy in the midst of Greek traditions ; it borrowed from the Asiatic civilisations and was transformed. We shall soon see how Roman art, transplanted and modified by Asiatic influences, long enlightened Western Europe ; how it reacted on Asia and the southern shores of the Mediterranean ; how by means of commerce it returned in its new form to the point whence it had started ; how it became mingled with the traditions which itself had left on the soil of Gaul and Italy ; and how it adapted itself to the genius of the barbarian races.

This study possesses no mere archæological interest ; it may, as I think, facilitate the productive travail of those modern arts which have yet to be born. It is in this light that I shall exhibit it. If we succeed in getting rid of inveterate prejudices ; if we become acquainted with the elements that have constituted our art for several centuries and the adaptation we have been able to make of those elements to our own genius, we shall have traced out for all minds that have preserved some degree of independence the road to be followed in the future.

We must not suppose that Christianity changed the social aspect of the Ancient World in a single day ; no physical or social revolution takes place in our world without transition, and the more distinctly the new principles differ from those that are abandoned, the longer and more laborious that transition is. Some superior intellects might have passed at once abruptly from Paganism to Christianity ; but the multitude, though becoming Christian in name, worship, and actions, must have long remained pagan in its usages, manners, and customs. Thus slavery prevailed over all Europe long after the Christian law had been recognised. This antagonism between tradition and the new law was the cause of protracted struggles. Hardly had Christianity become the State religion of the Empire when there arose on all sides schisms and heresies without number,—schisms and heresies which were in fact only the protest of pagan manners and pagan philosophy against the new religion.

We may observe the same distracted condition in the arts, and as these were at the time in question intimately connected with religion, they were long uncertain as to the way they should proceed. It should be remarked that though a whole nation may be induced to adopt a dogma, it is not possible to decree a form of art, especially if the art requires for its expression,—as architecture does,—the aid of a multitude of artists, artisans, and workmen. Christianity at its birth made use of pagan arts; it could not do otherwise; it was only slowly that manners and customs, becoming modified by degrees, sought for new expressions, which were long contested. We must therefore expect to find tentative efforts,—schisms in the arts,— intervening between Classical Antiquity and the Middle Ages. Faithful to the programme which I have traced out for myself, I shall endeavour to conduct my readers to those invariable principles which are able to lead us to a practical result,—the knowledge of that which is adapted to our own genius and our own times.

LECTURE VI.

WAS Christianity favourable or unfavourable to the development of the arts ? Supposing the world had not been enlightened by its divine rays, could Pagan Art have modified itself? could it have risen again after having once fallen? Have the civilisations of Christian origin arts of their own? Does Art with them inevitably tend towards decline? or is it destined to be always progressive? To give an answer to these questions, a brief review of ancient and modern civilisations is necessary. The civilisations of Antiquity (I speak, be it understood, only of those with which we are acquainted) attain more or less rapidly to a complete development, and then decline to rise no more. Civilisations of Christian origin waver for a long time irresolute ; they have their moments of brilliancy and their periods of obscurity, but they never fall so low as to be unable to collect vigour sufficient to start again upon a new career ; they constantly renew their energies in an inexhaustible fountain of active principles ; we see them slumber, but they never die. After an existence of eighteen centuries, based on the ruins of the past, having survived torrents of blood, despite the most monstrous excesses, despite ignorance with its retinue of error, fanaticism, prejudices, disorder, revolutions, wars, tyranny and anarchy, the West, so far from being exhausted, seems to live with a renewed life. The trials it has endured have weakened neither its intellectual vigour nor its material preponderance in the affairs of the world. Shall we admit that Art alone does not share this vital force of the modern societies of Western Europe, —that it does not participate in the impulses by which those societies are moved,—that it is a faculty by itself,—that it may perish amid a civilisation which continually revives after every fresh trial ? Possibly: let us examine this last question. Either Art is independent of modern Western civilisation, or it is one of the expressions of that civilisation. If independent, modern society has no need of it,—it does, or will do without it; but it can be proved without much difficulty that Art is one of the most powerful forces of Western civilisation. Many are ignorant, or affect ignorance, of this : but it is none the less a fact. To confine ourselves to France, it is plainly manifest that our share of influence in this little globe of ours is due, not to our agriculture, which only suffices for our own sustenance (and we should be thankful that it does so); nor to our manufactures, which, from a material point of view, are inferior to those of our neighbours the English; nor to our pecuniary resources, for we are not purchasers of political influence ; nor yet to our arms, for force of arms, by itself—when it is not used in support of fruitful ideas—only excites distrust;—moreover, after fighting for centuries, our only gain is the having proved that we fight well, and that when occasion offers we fight for principles. Our veritable arms, our real strength, are to be found in our ideas and their various expressions, which are but the different forms of art. The whole world reads our books, and comes to our *modistes* for its fashions. It is the art pervading all we produce that constitutes our real influence. Art, then, is one of the elements of our civilisation ; if, therefore, we are not as a nation rapidly declining,—if, on the contrary, we are progressing,—there is no reason why our arts should decline; if they do, our artists alone are responsible for it.

I admit that in what appertains to Architectural Art we are far from rightly appreciating our own times,—what they demand, and what they reject. We are just at the same point with regard to Architecture that the Western World at large was at the time of Galileo in regard to the sciences. The conservators of *the fixed principles of beauty* would, if they had the power, willingly confine, as a dangerous maniac, him who should attempt to prove that there exist principles independent of form; —that, while principles do not vary, their expression cannot be permanently riveted to one invariable form. For nearly four centuries we have been disputing about the relative value of ancient and modern Art ; and during these four hundred years our disputes have turned not upon principles, but upon ambiguous terms and figures of speech. We architects, shut up in our art—an art which is half science, half sentiment,— present only hieroglyphics to the public, which does not understand us, and which leaves us to dispute in our isolation. Shall we never have *our* Molière to treat us as he did the doctors of his time ? May we not hope some day (while still admiring them) to part company with Hippocrates and Galen ?

I believe that no one feels more confident than I do in affirming that in our art there is no invention ; we can only submit to analysis elements already known,—combine and adapt them, but not create : our art prescribes such strict limits in its means of execution that we must necessarily have recourse to the past in order to originate in the present. In Architecture we have the study and the application of what we have gathered to the matter in hand : we have here two distinct operations of the mind. Were all the *chefs-d'œuvre* of the past stored in the mind of one man, if he were not provided with a method enabling him to compose with the aid of these *chefs-d'œuvre*,— if he did not know how to make use of them,—he would only be able to produce fragmentary copies badly pieced together,—servile imitations, inferior, in point of art, to the work of the barbarian who has learned nothing.

In Architectural Art, moreover, there are two distinct elements which should always be considered, namely, necessity, to which we must submit, and the work of the artist's imagination. Necessity imposes the programme : it says, I want a dwelling ; I want air and light. But what is the work of the imagination ? What is imagination ? It is the power given to man to unite and combine in his mind things that have struck his senses. Even abstractions must clothe themselves with a form before the imagination of man can conceive them. A geometrician drawing a line on the board says, " A straight line is the shortest distance between two points." The pupil does not dispute this axiom ; his mind comprehends it at once, for his imagination represents to him two points and a straight line joining them. Again, he is told, "A point has neither length, breadth, nor height ; a line is merely a succession of points ; it has therefore only length." His mind may admit this abstraction, but his imagination, which is only the product of memory, always represents to him two visible points and a visible line. The mind admits the infinite, but no human imagination can picture it to itself. A man born without hands, deaf, and blind, could have no imagination. When an architect hears the words, " I want a hall," his memory at once recalls some hall that he has seen. If it is added, " I wish the hall to be lofty," his memory exerts itself and brings to his recollection a certain lofty hall. If, finally, it is said, " I wish it to be freely accessible and well lighted," his memory again takes wing, and he sees a hall fulfilling these conditions. All these operations of the mind take place in less time than is needed to describe them. The architect is left to himself ; the programme is given him and he must work it out. Then his memory presents in a confused mass all that it has been able to retain : at this point reason intervenes, compares, chooses here and there, rejects this or that ; and then the imagination begins to compose, and presents the hall complete in the architect's mind. Perhaps it does not resemble any that his memory has presented to him, yet it could not have been conceived without the aid of memory.

Memory,—that is, the faculty of representing to the mind's eye what we have seen, heard, or felt,—has been called the passive imagination ; the faculty next called into play—that of combining these sensations, and forming with them a new conception—the *active* imagination. The brutes possess the first ; man alone is gifted with the second. For instance, swallows know that they must build their nest at such a time, and in such a situation ; but all swallows' nests have resembled each other ever since swallows have existed. Man knows that he must make himself a shelter ; but in the course of a few centuries he advances from the mud cabin to the palace of the Louvre. And why ? Because man reasons, and his *active* imagination is nothing more than the application of reasoning to the *passive* imagination. " It is a different sort of imagination," says Voltaire,[1] " from that which the vulgar call (as they do memory) the foe of judgment. On the contrary, it cannot act except with profound judgment; it is continually combining its impressions and correcting its errors ; it builds up all its edifices with order. Practical mathematics call imagination into play in a surprising degree, and Archimedes had at least as much imagination as Homer." We should not then repeat with the vulgar that reason stifles imagination, and that, if we would be original, our memory should not have too many materials at its command. In order to originate, the judgment must arrange the elements gathered by the *passive* imagination. Form your judgment, learn to reason, and then, perhaps, you will attain originality. The imagination does not, it is true, act among primitive men—barbarians—as it acts in the brain of civilised and cultivated men ; for the *passive* imagination of barbarians represents objects to them imperfectly or obscurely : it is a mirror which enlarges or distorts what it reflects ; while among highly civilised men the memory is clear and exact,—a sort of dry catalogue. The result of this difference in their idiosyncrasies is, that in the primitive man the *passive* imagination is poetical, and its active counterpart weak and little developed ; on the other hand, the memory of the cultivated man presents things under their actual aspect, whilst his active imagination may be highly developed, and very poetical. That my meaning may be understood, suppose a man whose mind has been developed by civilisation to observe a weight oscillating at the end of a cord. His passive imagination presents to him nothing more than the fact—he does not attribute this phenomenon to any supernatural influence—to him it is no demon that impels the weight backwards and forwards : his

[1] *Philosophical Dictionary.*

active imagination intervenes and tells him, "Here is a law; this weight oscillates because it is under the influence of two forces, one accidental, which has moved it from its normal position, the other obliging it to return to that position, which it does gradually. This last force, therefore, is the law compelling the weight to stretch the cord in a direction perpendicular to the horizon; there is therefore an attraction obliging this weight to tend to the centre of the terrestrial globe." Another observer having fastened a ball to the end of a string makes it describe a circle by a movement of his hand. He sees that the rotatory movement given to the ball always keeps the string tight,—that the string becomes tighter in proportion to the rapidity of the motion. His passive imagination reminds him that the moon turns round the earth, and the planets round the sun; then his active imagination suggests to him a centrifugal and centripetal force. But let us apply the principle to our own subject. A barbarian has been in Rome; he has seen all kinds of buildings, and returns to his native country. His uncultivated memory recalls these edifices, and the sculptures and paintings that adorn them. He has certainly not remarked the relations that exist between the various members of the architecture; he has been much more struck with the details of the sculpture and the subjects portrayed in painting than with the proportions, the judicious use of the materials, and the well-carried-out programme. The objects seen by him assume in his memory strange forms, like those which pass in dreams. What is great leaves on his mind the remembrance of something gigantic: if he has seen large masses lifted by powerful machines, these machines assume monstrous shapes in his fancy; the sculptures are animated; the paintings look and speak. On returning to his native country, he desires to assemble his recollections. His passive imagination is feverishly excited; he too would build; but the active imagination sleeps, and can scarcely help him to produce from so many lively and poetical impressions some rude buildings in which everything is confused, everything misplaced. A few centuries afterwards there comes a civilised man, who calmly and critically examines these rude attempts: his passive imagination assembles them, but draws no conclusion from them. When he wishes to build, the *chefs-d'œuvre* of art are reflected on his mind: but we cannot create with *chefs-d'œuvre*, we can only admire and copy them. When, therefore, among these pure recollections,—which are, as it were, a correct measure of the value of things,—his memory recalls those rude essays—an expression, feeble, it is true, but still an expression of a work conceived by passive imaginations profoundly stirred—these rude images begin to lose their barbarous features; the active imagination of the cultivated man seems to possess itself of the passive imagination of the barbarian. In his turn he sees no longer what the barbarian *did*, but what his brain pictured to him, and he sees it with the power to reproduce it.

There are times when man needs some of the barbarian element, just as the soil needs manure ; for production requires a process of mental fermentation, resulting from contrasts, from dissimilarities, from a disparity between the real and the ideal world. The periods most fruitful in intellectual products have been periods of the greatest agitation (it must be understood that I include the arts among intellectual products—with no offence to those who produce "works of art" as a velvet weaver makes yards of velvet),—periods in which the student of history finds the greatest contrasts. If a society attains to an advanced degree of civilisation, in which everything is balanced, provided for, and adjusted, there ensues a general equality of well-being,—of the good and the proper,—which may render man materially happy, but which is not calculated to arouse his intellect. Movement, struggle, even opposition, is necessary to the arts ; stagnation in the mental order, as in the physical, soon induces decay. Thus Roman society placed in the centre of the West, and absolute mistress of the known world, became enfeebled and corrupted, because discussions and contrasts were wanting. Morals and Art decline, simply because everything in this world which does not renew itself by movement and the infusion of foreign elements, becomes subject to decay. Ideas are like families : they must be crossed if we would not see their vitality enfeebled.

What themes shall the poet find amid a perfectly well-ordered, well-governed, well-behaved society, where all have the same number of ideas, and of the same kind, on every subject ? Extremes and contrasts are necessary to the poet. When a man of strong feelings sees his country invaded; when he is the witness of shameful abuses; when his sense of right is outraged; when he suffers or hopes,—if this man is a poet, he is inevitably inspired ; he will write and arouse emotions in others : but if he lives in the midst of a polished, tolerant, easy-going community, by whom extremes alone are regarded as want of taste—what will he find to say ? He will perhaps describe the flowers, the brooks, the verdant meadows, or, stimulating his imagination to a fictitious warmth, he will plunge into the domain of the unreal, the un-natural, the impossible ; or, on the other hand, he will give expression to an undefined longing, a groundless disgust of life, and sufferings for which no adequate cause can be alleged. No ! —the true poet, sounding to its depths this social condition, apparently so calm and unvaried, will seek in human hearts feelings which never die, wherever man is to be found : beneath the uniform garb in which all the members of this community are dressed, he will find various passions, noble or base; he will compel us to recognise again those contrasts whose manifestations we seek to suppress : thus and thus only will he make himself heard and read. The more civilised and regular society becomes, the more is the artist compelled to analyse and dissect passions, manners, and tastes,—to revert to first principles—to lay hold of and display them in naked simplicity before the world,—if he would leave a deep impression upon this externally uniform and colourless society. Hence it is more difficult to be an artist in times like our own, than among rude, unrefined, people, who openly display their good or evil passions. In primitive epochs, *style* imposed itself on the artist ; now, the artist has to acquire style.

But what is style ? I am not speaking now of style as applied to the classification of the arts by periods, but of style as inherent in the arts of all times ; and to make myself better understood, I remark that independently of the style of the writer in each language, there is a style which belongs to all languages, because it belongs to humanity. This style is inspiration ; but it is inspiration subjected to the laws of reason,—inspiration invested with a distinction peculiar to every work produced by a genuine feeling rigorously analysed by reason before being expressed ; it is the close accord of the imaginative and reasoning faculties ; it is the effort of the *active* imagination regulated by reason. I said in a previous page :—the *passive* imagination of a Greek presents the idea of a man on a horse ; his active imagination suggests the combination of the two in a single being ; reason shows him how to weld the torso of the one to the breast of the other : he creates a centaur, and this creation has *style* for us as well as for the Greek.

A distinguished writer lately remarked that in architecture, " style is first the period, next the man."[1] This definition appears to me to confound what are conventionally designated *the styles* with style. There are periods which have their style, but in which style is wanting. Such for instance is the Roman period under the last Emperors of the West. There is a Louis XIV. style, a Louis XV. style, and some have lately discovered even a Louis XVI. style. Nevertheless, one of the characteristics of Architectural Art at the close of the seventeenth and during the eighteenth century is the absence of style. " Terms should be defined," says Voltaire ; and Voltaire is often right. Style proper and style as an archæological indication are two widely different things.

Style consists in a marked distinction of form ; it is one of the

[1] " *Traité d'Architecture*," by M. Léonce Raynaud, vol. ii. p. 86.

essential elements of beauty, but does not of itself alone constitute
beauty. Civilisation dulls those instincts of man which lead
him to introduce style into his works, but it does not destroy
them. These instincts come into play involuntarily. In a certain
assembly you remark one person in particular. This person may
not possess any of those striking characteristics which constitute
beauty; the features may not be regular; yet, attracted by a
mysterious influence, your gaze continually reverts to the
individual in question. However unaccustomed to such observation you succeed in explaining to yourself the reasons which
impel you to satisfy that instinctive attraction : the first thing
that strikes you is a marked line,—a harmony between the frame
and the muscles ; it is an *ensemble* in some cases irregular, but
which excites in you sympathy or antipathy. Your attention
is engaged by a contour, by certain forms of the bones which are
covered with muscles in harmony with those forms, the manner
in which the hair grows on the brow, the junction of the limbs
with the body, the concordance between the gestures and the
thought ; you have soon arrived at settled ideas as to the habits,
taste, and character of that person. Though seen for the first
time,—a stranger to whom you have never spoken,—you build up
a whole romance on the individual in question. Of animated
beings only those who have *style* possess this mysterious power of
attraction. Individuals of the human race are so often spoiled
by an artificial education, and by moral and physical infirmities,
that it is rare to find one of them possessing style : the brutes,
on the contrary, all exhibit this harmony,—this perfect conformity
between the outward form and the instinct—the breath which
animates them. Hence we may say that the brutes have style,
—from the insect to the noblest of the quadrupeds. Their
gestures are always true ; their movements always plainly indicate a want or a definite purpose, a desire or a fear. Brutes
are never affected, artificial, or vulgar ; whether beautiful or ugly
they possess style, because they have only simple feelings and
seek their ends by simple and direct means. Man,—especially
civilised man,—being a very complicated animal, and altered in
character by an education which teaches him to resist his
instincts, must make a retrospective effort,—shall I say,—to
acquire style ; and Alceste is right when he prefers to the sonnet
of Oronte the lines :—

> " Si le roi m'avait donné
> Paris sa grand' ville."

Every one is of Alceste's opinion ; but this does not hinder
the Orontes of their day from composing vapid sonnets, or
architects from overlaying their buildings with ornaments devoid
of reason and of style.

In the present day we are no longer familiar with those simple and true ideas which lead artists to invest their conceptions with style ; I think it necessary therefore to define the constituent elements of style, and in so doing, carefully to avoid equivocal terms, and those meaningless phrases which are repeated with the profound respect that is professed by most people for what is incomprehensible. Ideas must be presented in a palpable form,—a definite embodiment,—if we would communicate them. Clearly to understand what style as regards form is, we must consider form in its simplest expressions. Let us therefore take one of the primitive arts,—one of the earliest practised among all nations, because it is among the first needed, —the art of the coppersmith, for example. It matters little how long it took man to discover the method of refining copper, and of reducing it to thin plates, so as to make a vessel with it fit to contain liquid. We take the art at the time when he had discovered that by beating a sheet of copper in a particular way he could so model it as to give it the form of a vessel. To effect this, all the workman needs is a piece of iron as a point of support, and a hammer. He can thus, by beating the sheet of copper, cause it to return on itself, and of a plane surface make a hollow body. He leaves a flat circular bottom to his vessel, so that it may stand firm when full. To hinder the liquid from spilling when the vessel is shaken, he contracts its upper orifice, and then widens it out suddenly at the edge, to facilitate pouring out the liquid ; the most natural form therefore—that determined by the mode of fabrication—is this (fig. 1). There must be a means

FIG. 1.—Primitive form of copper vessel.

of holding the vessel : the workman therefore attaches handles with rivets. But as the vessel must be inverted when empty, and has to be drained dry, he makes the handles so that they shall not stand above the level of the top of the vessel. Thus fashioned by methods suggested in the fabrication, this vessel has style : first, because it exactly indicates its purpose ; second, because it is fashioned in accordance with the material employed and the means of fabrication suited to this material ; third, because the form obtained is suitable to the material of which this utensil is made, and the use for which it is intended. This vessel has style, because human reason indicates exactly the form suitable to it. The coppersmiths themselves, in their desire to do better or otherwise than their predecessors, deviate from the line of the true and the good. We find therefore a second coppersmith, who wishes to alter the form of the primitive vessel in order to attract purchasers by the distinction of novelty ; he gives a few extra blows of the hammer, and rounds the body of the vessel which had hitherto been regarded as perfect (fig. 2). The form is in fact new, and all the town wish to have vessels made by the second coppersmith. A third coppersmith, perceiving that his fellow-townsmen are taken with the rounding of the base, goes still further, and makes a third vessel (fig. 3), which is still more popular. This last workman, having lost sight of the principle, bids adieu to reason, and follows caprice alone ; he increases the length of his handles, and advertises them as of the newest taste. This vessel cannot be placed upside down to be drained without endangering the shape of these handles ; but

Fig. 2.—Modified form of copper vessel.   Fig. 3.—Bad form of copper vessel.

every one praises it, and the third coppersmith is credited with having wonderfully improved his art, while in reality he has only deprived a form of its proper style, and produced an unsightly and relatively inconvenient article.

This history is typical of that of style in all the arts. Arts which cease to express the want they are intended to satisfy, the nature of the material employed, and the method of fashioning it, cease to have style. The style of Architecture during the declining years of the Roman Empire and that of the eighteenth century consist in the absence of style. We may follow custom in saying, " The style of the arts of the Lower Empire," or of the reign of Louis xv. ; but we cannot say : " The arts of the Lower Empire, or those of the reign of Louis xv., *have style*," for their defect (assuming it to be such) is that they dispense with style, since they show an evident contempt for the form really appropriate to the object and its use. If a Roman matron of the period of the Republic were to appear in a drawing-room filled with ladies dressed in hooped skirts, with powdered hair and a superstructure of plumes or flowers, the Roman lady would present a singular figure ; but it is none the less certain that her dress would have *style*, while those of the ladies in hooped skirts would be in (the style of the period), but would not possess *style*. Here then we have, I think, an intelligible starting-point for the appreciation of style. Are we then to suppose that style is inherent in one form alone, and that women, for instance, if they wish their dress to have style, must dress themselves like the mother of the Gracchi? Certainly not. The satin and the woollen dress may both have style; but on the condition that the shape of neither is at variance with the forms of the body; that it does not ridiculously exaggerate the former nor hamper the movements of the latter; and that the cut of the dresses in each shows a due regard to the special qualities of the material. Nature invariably exhibits style in her productions, because however diversified they may be they are always subject to laws, —to immutable principles. The leaf of a shrub, a flower, an insect—all have style ; because they grow, are developed, and maintain their existence according to laws essentially logical. We can subtract nothing from a flower, for each part of its organism expresses a function by taking the form which is appropriate to that function. Style resides solely in the true and marked expression of a principle and not in an immutable form ; consequently, as nothing exists except in virtue of a principle, there may be style in everything. I have already remarked, and I repeat it lest it should be forgotten :—discussions on art turn on ambiguities. They tell you in the schools that Greek art has the impress of style ; that that style is pure,—complete, namely, and without alloy ; copy the Greek form therefore if you wish your art to have style. As well might it be said :— The tiger or the cat has style ; disguise yourself therefore as a tiger or a cat if you would lay claim to style. Instead of this it should be explained why the cat and the tiger, the flower and the insect, have style, and the instruction should run thus:—Proceed as nature does in her works, and you will be able to invest with style all that your brain conceives. True, this is not easy amidst a complicated civilisation, greatly embarrassed to know what suits it,—subjected to traditions and prejudices through habit rather than from conviction,—swayed by fashion,—*blasé*,—sceptical and little inclined to accept the true expression of a principle, but it is not impossible.

The notion that a very advanced civilisation necessarily precludes style in Art is, in my opinion, a very singular one. It is always possible to give to the arts this element which is essential to their splendour and duration. To do this we must have recourse to matter-of-fact reason. I will explain myself. Among primitive peoples the mind of the artist can produce nothing but works possessing style, because this mind or imagination proceeds nearly in the same way as nature. A want or a desire manifests itself, and man employs the most direct means of satisfying it. At that early epoch style resides in the simplicity of the means employed by the artist; but in France, in the year of grace 1859, we are far removed from such a state of things. We have hardly learned to read and write when we are set to work to translate Greek and Latin classics, and to commit to memory Corneille, Boileau, and Racine; our teachers are careful to explain to us the beauties of these poets and writers; and if we are intelligent we comprehend the explanation given to us, but not the excellence pointed out to us; so that, imbued with instruction of this kind—which in other respects I am far from blaming—if on leaving college we wish to express an idea that has occurred to us, we first ascertain (if we have been diligent students) how Cicero, Horace, or Boileau would have given a literary or poetic turn to the idea in question. Our education thus inclines us to clothe our own conceptions in a style which belongs to writers whose merits we have been taught to appreciate. But in the domain of letters it is obligatory

"Que toujours le bon sens s'accorde avec la rime;"

because every one reads, and most people desire to understand what they read. The poet or writer of the present day who "from heaven has received the secret influence"—without forgetting Cicero or Virgil, Racine or Voltaire—soon becomes conscious that he should express his ideas not by a slavish adherence to the forms or terms employed by those authors, but by proceeding as they did. Instruction aids the writer of real merit, without fettering his genius, because the judgment of the public serves him as a guide. But in Architectural Art this touchstone of common sense is wanting. Architecture offers the same aspect to the public as a book does to those who cannot read. They can admire the binding and the typography, but that is all. The book may contain the grossest absurdities, but that is of the slightest possible concern to him who is unable to decipher its characters. Deprived therefore of the guidance of public opinion, our young architects have recourse to works of Classic Antiquity, and what are called the best modern periods. We go to Rome or to Athens, and having imbued our imagination with the magnificent examples of Classic Antiquity seen beneath a brilliant sky, we find ourselves again among the fogs of the Seine, and are asked to build an edifice answering to new requirements—an edifice the like of which exists neither in Greece nor in Italy. It must also be observed that if the works of Virgil, Horace, and Cicero have been handed down to us entire and pure of alloy, it is not so with the architectural monuments of Antiquity,—the mutilated remains of an art of which no book, no description, explains to us the true meaning, the originating motives, the relations with the manners and ideas of the builders. It is true that the passions and all the mental workings of humanity are the same in all ages ; but does it therefore follow that Napoleon the First, for instance, had the same ideas respecting men and things as Alexander ? And it is precisely these differences in the relations of men with each other and in their ideas, that have and ought to have a considerable influence on Art, and especially on Architectural Art. A Greek or a Roman may have attached to certain forms particular ideas which are lost to us ; as soon therefore as those ideas ceased to be current, the forms which were destined to recall them became meaningless.

I fully admit that beauty is unique ; that, to quote the language of an author of the day apropos of Architectural Art : " The good is the essential basis of the beautiful." But then we must be agreed as to what the good is. In the view of most people the good consists in the habitual use of a certain idea or form, although that form or that idea may not be good as compared with others. We judge a method or a custom to be good because that method or custom is familiar to us ; though in comparison with another method or custom that is unknown to us they may be bad, or at least inadequate for their purpose. It was good to navigate with sails before the power of steam was known ; now-a-days that method—formerly excellent—is not good as compared to that furnished by modern appliances. We may say as much of the ideas, systems, and principles which regulate art. When ideas, systems, and principles are modified, the forms corresponding should be modified also. We admire a hundred-gun ship of war, rigged as a sailing vessel ; we perceive that there is in this work of man—the principle being admitted —not only a wonderful product of intelligence, but also forms so perfectly adapted to their purpose, that they appear beautiful, and in fact are so ; but however beautiful these forms may be, as soon as steam-power has supervened, they must be changed, for they are not applicable to the novel motive force ; hence they are no longer *good;* and on the principle just now cited they will no longer be beautiful for us. Since in our days, when we are subjected to an imperative necessity, we subordinate our works to that necessity, we are so far capacitated for acquiring style in art, which is nothing more than the rigorous application of a principle. We erect public buildings which are devoid of style because we insist on allying forms derived from traditions with requirements which are not in harmony with those traditions. Naval engineers in building a steam-ship, and machinists in making a locomotive, do not endeavour to reproduce the forms of a sailing vessel of the time of Louis XIV., or of a stage-coach : they simply conform to the novel principles with which they have to deal, and thus produce works which have a character, a style of their own, as indicating to every eye a definite purpose. The locomotive, for example, has a special physiognomy which all can appreciate, and which renders it a distinct creation. Nothing can better express force under control than these ponderous rolling machines; their motions are gentle or terrible; they advance with terrific impetuosity, or seem to pant impatiently under the restraining hand of the diminutive creature who starts or stops them at will. The locomotive is almost a living being, and its external form is the simple expression of its strength. A locomotive therefore has style. Some will call it an ugly machine. But why ugly ? Does it not exhibit the true expression of the brute energy which it embodies ? Is it not appreciable by all as a thing complete, organised, possessing a special character, as does a piece of artillery or a gun ? There is no style but that which is appropriate to the object. A sailing-vessel has style ; but a steamer made to conceal its motive power and looking like a sailing-vessel will have none ; a gun has style, but a gun made to resemble a crossbow will have none. Now we architects have for a long time been making guns while endeavouring to give them as much as possible the appearance of crossbows, or at any rate that of arquebuses ; and there are persons of intelligence who maintain that if we abandon the form of the arquebuse we are barbarians, —that Art is lost,—that nothing is left for us but to hide our heads in shame.

But let us leave metaphors. Here (fig. 4) is a piece of masonry of the best Roman period,—that, namely, during which the construction of buildings in Rome was intrusted to Greeks : it is the wall of the circular cella of the temple of Vesta, on the banks of the Tiber. The columns of this temple are monostyles of marble, and the wall of the cella is faced externally with the same material ; but at that time marble was too scarce a material to be lavishly used. The wall is therefore composed of alternate thin courses of marble, A, and a facing B, likewise of marble, with a backing—for economy's sake—of blocks of calcareous local stone—travertine. All these pieces are bonded together with iron cramps. On the inside these courses of travertine were coated with painted stucco. Here then we have a wall,—a simple wall whose construction possesses style. These alternate thin courses, serving as bonds for the facing, these sinkings which plainly mark the shape of each piece,—which indicate the method employed,—form without effort a decoration full of style, because the eye readily comprehends the strong and rational

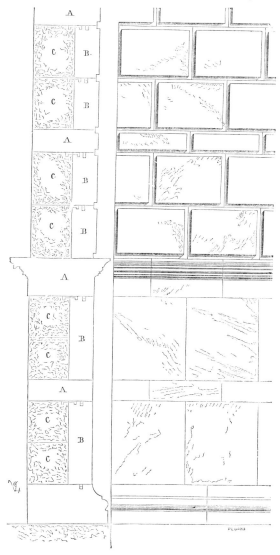

Fig. 4.—Example of Roman Masonry.

structure it expresses. Pleased with the firm and elegant appearance of this simple wall-face, our architect on his return to Paris is desirous of reproducing it. But he builds with stone,

not with marble ; he is supplied from the quarry with courses of
equal height and of one or two yards in length.   Will he amuse
himself by cutting up these large blocks into little pieces to
simulate that construction which was dictated by the smallness
of the slabs ; or, resting content with a mere appearance, will he
make sinkings where there are neither beds nor joints ?   In the
first case his construction will be bad and expensive ; in the
second he will utter a lie in stone.   In either case his construction will not have style, because it will not be in accordance with
the nature of the materials employed, and the manner of employing them in Paris.   A Roman-Corinthian monolithic isolated
column of marble or granite has style, because the eye, ascending
this huge block of stone from base to summit without perceiving

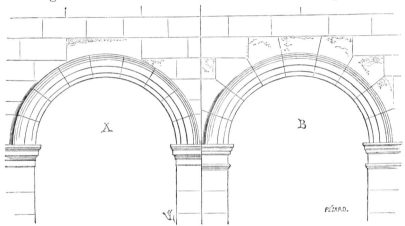

Fig. 5.—Arches Extradossed and not Extradossed.

a single joint, comprehends its rigid function, which is perfectly
indicated by the material and its homogeneity.   But a Corinthian
column composed of courses of stone, like those of the Madeleine,
or the Pantheon in Paris, has not style, because the eye is
disquieted at seeing such slender points of support formed of
small stones piled one on the other.   When you change the
material or the manner of employing it, you should change the
form.   When you change the scheme you should change the
arrangements of the plan.   A moulding has no style in itself :
its style consists in its being adapted to the function it fulfils or
the place it occupies.   The Romans, though inferior to the Greeks
when the application of style to the object is in question, are yet
very superior to us.   Thus, for example, when they build a range
of arches supporting a wall, they give the arch-stones the requisite
strength, and they denote these arches by mouldings which indicate to the eye their thickness and strength (fig. 5 A) ; that is,

the arch-stones are extradossed, and the decorative moulding is confined to these voussoirs. We consider these arches very beautiful, and attempt to make archivolts similar to them ; but, —barbarians that we are—we joint them as indicated at B. What meaning however can there be in the mouldings of the archivolt, whose voussoirs jut out beyond it and fit into the courses of masonry above ? They are simply absurd. The architect seems to say to the public : " You admire the Roman arches of such or such an edifice ; I have copied them exactly : admire mine also." The public, however, does not admire ; it cannot explain why, nor does it understand the difference between an extradossed arch and one whose voussoirs are built into the courses of the wall above ; but it is instinctively offended by a contradiction between this jointing and the decoration, and it reasonably turns away to admire the old Roman model. It must be admitted that the Romans were the first to forget the true principles of style, and here we need not imitate them.

At the present day, style has quitted the arts and taken refuge amid industrial pursuits ; but it might be restored to the arts if we would introduce into our study and appreciation of them a little of that good sense which we apply to the practical affairs of life. It would seem, however, that the more rationally we act with respect to the industrial arts, the further we go astray from reason when the fine arts are in question. We who in the construction of our machines give each of their component parts the requisite strength and shape, introducing nothing superfluous or which does not indicate a necessary function,—in our architecture accumulate irrationally forms gathered from all quarters—the result of contradictory principles—and call this Art ! I often hear architects lamenting that our great industrial development tends to stifle Art, and that the special schools of applied science encroach on the *Ecole des Beaux Arts.* But whose fault is that ? Let architects learn to reason on what they are commissioned to do—let them apply analytical methods to their designs ; let them cease to think that style consists in decorating a façade with Greek columns or Gothic pinnacles, without being able to give a reason for the adoption of these forms,—and they will soon regain for art the ground it is daily losing. It is true that to obtain this result, so desirable, so essential I may say, to the veritable progress of art, courage, perseverance, and conviction are necessary ; we must cast aside, without scruple or false shame, the commonplaces which from our infancy have been inculcated upon us as laws ; the judgment must be formed and constantly consulted. We must endeavour to proceed like the Greeks : they invented nothing, but they transformed everything. Let not our admiration of them limit itself to copying their work as a mere scribe copies a manuscript without reading it; let us read the book and grasp its spirit before transcribing the letter.

Every artist, musician, architect, sculptor, and painter, may, through a profound knowledge of the resources of his art, and by a right use of reason, imbue his works with style; for every artist who knows and observes succeeds in analysing style—in ascertaining its constituents; and from analysis he proceeds to synthesis. Even the artist who possesses only sound practical knowledge, and is devoid of genius (and let us wisely cherish the belief that we all belong to this class), is capable of comprehending style, and of investing his works with this quality, which will alone insure their recognition by posterity. Having come late into the world, it is extremely difficult for us of this generation to conceive new ideas: but it would be a great point gained to maintain style in our art productions; and as style depends only on the application to an object of the reasoning faculty, this is possible. Observe, I do not confound style with *mannerism;* mannerism is to style what affectation is to grace. Some privileged natures are born with that gift which we call grace; but observation, habituation to the beautiful and the good —which is in fact taste—lead men to be graceful in what they do and say; while mannerism is the superficial imitation of style without the appreciation of it.

The artists of our time, and its architects in particular, have the weakness—for such I deem it—to believe themselves geniuses; at any rate they act so as to give that impression. When they design, they mistake the vagaries of an imagination too full of remembrances, but without determinate ideas, for the inspirations of genius; thus they produce monstrosities. Eclecticism is a commendable method only when it is subordinated to a wise discrimination, guided by certain knowledge, and based on settled principles. If Eclecticism lays hold of a wavering mind, which has not taken time to imbue itself with principles by a rational study of Art, it becomes an evil; for in that case it necessarily precludes style, since while admitting indifferently all its various expressions it knows not how duly to apply a single one. The Egyptian, the Greek, the Roman, the Byzantine, the Gothic architectures have style; but the expressions are different in each, because each proceeds from a principle peculiar to itself. How then, if you have not a settled principle, could you imbue your works with style? It is very easy to say: "Collect from every quarter; furnish your brain with everything that seems to you good; then—then—design!" But I have no guide; you have not habituated me to reason; all the treasures in my brain present themselves at once, and I have equally at the point of

my pencil Egyptian and Greek temples and vaulted Roman
buildings, arches and lintels, round arches and pointed arches;
you told me to collect from every quarter: very good, if I had
merely to make a collection; but if I am to produce, what shall
I do with all these acquirements? Where shall I begin, and
where end? Amongst all these good things, which are the
best,—which ought to take precedence of the others? If we
are habituated to proceed by reflection,—if we have a principle,
—every work of design is possible, if not easy; it follows a
well-ordered methodical course, whose results, if not masterpieces, are at least good works, appropriate to their purpose, and
capable of possessing style. I do not know whether poets,
musicians, and painters, are suddenly inspired to write an ode,
to compose a sonata, or paint a picture: I am inclined to think
not; because no poet, musician, or painter of genius has informed
us of such revelations. The sacred fire does not kindle by
itself: to raise it to a glow we must collect wood and coals,
properly arrange our materials, blow, and blow sometimes with
long-continued effort, before we can expect even the first scintillations. Then, it is true, if the hearth has been well prepared,
the fire gradually begins to diffuse a grateful warmth, to sparkle
brightly and burn steadily; but I repeat it—this requires some
pains. When an architect is called upon to erect a building, a
confused scheme is probably laid before him—for written programmes are generally such;—and it rests with him to bring these
elementary instructions into something like order. Various
requirements and services have to be provided for, and these must
have his first and separate consideration: the architecture—that
is to say, the casing of these various services—must not yet be
thought of: he will content himself for the present with simply
putting everything in its place; he will observe in each part of
the scheme some chief point, and will give it importance, and thus
his intricate and complicated labour gradually becomes simplified
(for simple ideas are the last to be reached). Then having duly
considered these several parts he endeavours to combine them,
and again his task is one of simplification: but the *ensemble* of
parts, simply connected, does not satisfy him; he feels that this
body lacks unity; the junctions are apparent; they are awkward.
He tries again; puts that on the right which was on the left; that
in front which was previously behind: in fact he changes the
disposition of details in his plan a hundred times. Then (I am
supposing him to be a conscientious architect, who loves his art
and spares no pains to attain perfection) he reflects—laying
aside the sheets covered with the results of his previous labour.
Suddenly he thinks he perceives in his scheme a general ruling
idea (observe, no one has suggested it to him beforehand).

Light breaks in upon him. Instead of considering his design in detail, in order to plan the general arrangement, he reverses the process. He has gained a primary conception of the entire edifice, and of the way in which the various services should be subordinated to a simple and comprehensive arrangement. Then those details which had so much puzzled him take their natural place. The generating idea once found, the secondary ideas fall into their proper order, and present themselves when they are wanted. The architect has mastered his scheme ; he has a complete hold of it ; he recomposes it in an orderly fashion ; he completes and perfects it. But if during this process of thought he has been thinking about " orders,"—about the works of Greeks or Romans,—of Pierre de Montereau,—or Mansard, he is lost ; he is overwhelmed with reminiscences. What really valuable work can he accomplish if at the beginning he is thinking of taking one bit from the Parthenon, another from the Baths of Caracalla, the Sainte-Chapelle or the Invalides ? No ; the true architect has not been occupying himself with these monuments of the past. Having secured his plan, the building shapes itself in his mind ; he sees how he has to construct it ; the ruling idea of the plan re-presents itself in the elevation. The conditions of stability and the methods of construction indicate to him the external appearance. He must give a form, but he does not wish to be accused of imitating Roman architecture, that of Louis the Fourteenth, St. Louis, or Francis the First. He is greatly embarrassed. He makes an essay upon paper—" No ; this resembles such or such a building—no ; that order reminds one of such or such a portico—no ; these windows are copies of such or such a palace. But why trouble myself in this way ? Here I have my structure, my building, my means of stability : why not simply express what these render necessary ? " Then a kind of carcass or skeleton assumes shape in his mind ; the interior arrangements manifest themselves externally ; the idea of the plan freely reappears in the elevation : this shell indicates the parts which should be enriched and those which should be eliminated. This is how the architect designs. Now comes into play the function of the artist : for it is not sufficient for the architect to be clear-headed, and for the expression of his thought to be evident : that expression must be clothed in agreeable forms ; the eye must be attracted and pleased if we would be understood. The observant artist whose passive imagination has collected numerous examples, chosen and classified with discernment,—has remarked that in all the arts, including architecture, there is but a limited number of means for expressing ideas : he has remarked that grand effects are obtained by very simple methods of procedure applied to a ruling idea ; that there are modes of exciting emotions in architecture as in music and poetry; that we cannot with impunity depart from the laws imposed by human feeling,—laws which are to the sight what Moral Law is to the soul,—a natural regulator, independent of the different forms of civilisation; that the merit of the artist consists in observing these laws without reproducing forms previously employed, and that, after all, these laws are independent of such or such forms. Later on I shall revert to this highly important side of art,—the rules imposed by the sentiment of form. At present I confine myself to following the architect through the first part of his labour, up to the point when, in order to continue to invest his work with style, it no longer suffices him to have definite well-arranged ideas, and to know how to express them clearly.

Let us now see how the Greeks, whose example we must always respect, proceeded when ancient art, in its decline, had become only the pale copy of itself; how they became once more the imitators of Western arts, and how they modified that Roman art which had prevailed over all Europe and a part of Asia.

Under the immediate predecessors of Constantine, the Romans had already shown a decided inclination to place the centre of empire in the East. In Greece, on the shores of the Bosporus, in Syria, and even in Persia, they had built considerable cities and erected palaces and dwellings on an extensive scale, such as Rome herself never possessed. In these countries they had gradually become habituated to Asiatic magnificence; and though they were politically the masters of the East, they allowed Oriental taste to influence their arts. When at last they had settled at Byzantium, the Romans found there the elements of a Renaissance; if they did not desire it they were at least not opposed to it. A new form of worship was taking the place of paganism, and everything was concurring to render this revival one of the most brilliant epochs of art. Up to this time Christianity,—sometimes persecuted, sometimes tolerated, —had no art of its own; ancient art sufficed it; it made use of edifices already existing, scarcely caring to accommodate their form or arrangements to its special use. The Roman basilica, was, and naturally so, the building most suited for Christian assemblies; and I think it may be asserted that the arrangements of the Roman basilica—which was an edifice erected for civil purposes—exercised a decided influence on the earliest distinctly Christian ceremonial. But be this as it may (for it is a question foreign to our subject) the Christians did not lay claim to any peculiar art, but were satisfied to avail themselves of the services of such architects, sculptors, and painters as were at hand, in building and decorating their religious or civil edifices. The dwelling of a Roman who worshipped Christ differed in no respect from that of a Roman who worshipped Jupiter; each possessed slaves, and one lawful wife, who with her attendants and children lived in a part of the house especially assigned them; both spent the greater part of the day in places of public resort, which were the same for both, except that the Christian worshipped in his church and the Pagan in his temple. Before Christianity could influence the arts it must have affected the manners and habits of individuals both in public and in private. Now among the Latin converts no such change had taken place; while among the Greeks, on the contrary, with their peculiar sensitiveness to philosophic and religious ideas, Christianity had powerfully aroused the intellectual faculties, and had given occasion to numberless writings and discussions which affected public opinion to such a degree that the Roman Emperors living amid this Greek society soon began to busy themselves with supporting this or that heresy or dogma,—contrary to the wise traditions of imperial policy. It was then that this new religion began to influence the arts also. As there were discussions on points of doctrine, so there were also disputes respecting the representation of divine persons and saints: such representation was condemned or approved, and when approved it was decided that the images should be hieratic,— that the Church should adopt a consecrated form. The Emperors themselves took part in these controversies respecting forms, as they did in theological discussions; the age of the Antonines already belonged to a remote past. The West was on the point of falling into the hands of the barbarians; the Roman edifices which covered the soil of Gaul, Italy, and a part of Spain, were destroyed or despoiled; and a profound darkness, destined to last for centuries, was overspreading countries that had been once occupied by powerful and industrious cities.

At Byzantium, the Emperors, renouncing henceforth all influence over the affairs of the West, were living in the midst of luxury; sharing, as I have just stated, the restless passions of the Greek population among which they had settled. Art meantime was being transformed: the Romans carried their system of vaulting with them to the shores of the Bosporus,— if they did not find that architectural feature already there (I mean to say they only imported a method of construction): as to their architecture (to which, as we have seen, they attached little importance) they let the Greeks manage this according to their own taste; and they, with their usual subtlety of invention, proceeded by degrees to modify it essentially. First they abandoned the Roman orders consisting of columns with their complete entablatures; no longer employing the column except as a rigid supporting member to carry, not lintels but arches: soon they abandoned the Corinthian and Composite capitals as not affording a sufficient bearing surface to receive the springing of the arches, and as too slight and delicate in character to sustain the masses of construction with which they were loaded ; they therefore expanded the capital, enlarged its abacus, and covered its visible faces only with fine and slightly projecting sculpture such as could not detract from its solidity. Aiming at surprising effects—architectural *tours de force*—they sought to raise the Roman hemispherical vault on four piers by means of *Pendentives ;*[1] and, as in St. Sophia, to give to these cupolas, thus supported on four isolated piers, dimensions until then unknown. Justinian, to whom the erection of this colossal church is attributed, was much interested in the work, and visited it daily. Its cupola, which fell in almost immediately after its completion, was finally seated upon its four pendentives, when Justinian exclaimed (it is said), " Glory be to God, who has judged me worthy to complete this work ! I have conquered thee, O Solomon !" It is of little importance whether these words were actually uttered by Justinian, but it is of great significance that contemporary historians have imputed them to him ; for this plainly indicates the changes that had been wrought in the mind of the masters of the empire. At Rome none of the Emperors seem ever to have spent any of their time on the site of building-works, and certainly none were known to have regarded the construction of a building as an important affair of life. The Greeks of classic antiquity boasted greatly of their public monuments ; they were very proud of them, but the Romans scarcely mention theirs : they are content to build and make use of them. We find a new sentiment therefore gaining possession of the minds of the inhabitants of the Eastern Empire in the sixth century ; this sentiment, foreign to the Latin character, and originating in the vainglory of the Greeks,—this tendency to hyperbole in the creations of art,—had a considerable influence on the progress of the arts ; an influence which produced unexpected results a few centuries later. We may note that at Byzantium, Roman art, renovated by the Greek element, prospered for a considerable time, and became divided into branches whose various ramifications I propose to investigate.

The rise of numerous heresies in the very bosom of the Church, shortly after Christianity had been recognised as a religion of the Empire, is a notorious fact. Nestorius, Bishop of Constantinople, one of the leaders of these heresies, was exiled in the year 431. Compelled to retire to the city of Panopolis, on the right bank of the Nile, he was followed and surrounded by numerous disciples who revolted at the injustice which they supposed to have been

---

[1] Pendentives are the concave corbelled out surfaces which form the transition from the square plan below to the circular plan above, whence springs the dome.—(*Translator's note.*)

done him in his being made a victim to the influence of St. Cyril. Later on this body of heretics met with a favourable reception from the followers of Mahomet, who found among the proscribed, men familiar with the knowledge of ancient Greece, acquainted with the arts, and accomplished in all the known sciences. It is highly probable that they were employed in the works of art undertaken by the Mahometans when they settled around the provinces dependent on the Eastern Empire ; for as warriors who had recently quitted their native deserts, they had no artists or workmen among them. Thus as early as the fifth century, one of the branches of this tree that had sprung from the union of Greek and Roman arts flourished in Asia, in Egypt, in Arabia, and in the north of Africa, and was destined soon to spread even into the southern parts of the West. The only part of Italy that remained to the Byzantine Emperors after the invasion of the barbarians was the exarchate of Ravenna ; and in that city, in the middle of the sixth century, that is to say shortly after the building of St. Sophia, they erected the Church of San Vitale. This was almost the only Byzantine landmark planted on the Italian soil. In the course of the eighth century, Leo the Isaurian, who was elect d Emperor of the East in 717, having embraced the heresy of the iconoclasts, issued many edicts with a view to the suppression of the sacred images. He carried his fanaticism to such an extent as to persecute all who were engaged in the study of the arts; he abolished the schools of sacred literature and burned the libraries. The painters and sculptors took refuge on the shores of Italy, and were scattered through the whole country. It was among these emigrants that Charlemagne found artists to aid him in developing the revival of art which he projected. By this path the Byzantine arts were penetrating into the West, while through the Arabs who had by this time gradually extended along the African coast, they invaded the extremity of Western Europe by way of Spain. The Mahometan Arabs had only developed the arts they received from the Nestorians.

The Eastern Empire in the eighth century, though menaced and enfeebled, was thus unconsciously engaged in spreading the influence of its arts throughout Latin Europe, at this time sunk in the grossest barbarism. Meanwhile Roman architecture, which had left so many remains in Italy and Gaul, was reacting against this foreign influence with more or less success. In Italy, the old Latin genius was very reluctant to admit these Byzantine innovations. Even in Gaul the Roman traditions were still sufficiently powerful to cause them to be only modified, not destroyed, by the Byzantine element.

I do not undertake here to write the history of Architecture, but simply to enable my readers to form an idea of the condition of the arts in Europe and a part of Asia at the moment when the traditions of antiquity were about to undergo an important change in spirit and in form. In the absence of extant monuments and reliable authorities, it seems to me useless here to enter upon the question whether the Visigoths and Lombards had arts peculiar to themselves.[1] However ingenious the hypotheses that have been suggested, they are only hypotheses, and I shall abstain from noticing any of them : besides, why should we ignore obvious facts ? The arts of the ancient Latin world are perfectly familiar to us ; those of the Byzantine Greeks have left manifest traces at various points of the continent of Europe ; the products of the intermingling of these two forms of art are before our eyes, and indicate plainly the elements of which they are composed : why therefore ascribe to a barbarous people influences in art which could have been due only to a long series of traditions ? Barbarous nations, whatever may have been their natural endowments, can only possess arts after they have become civilised ; and they become civilised only by the long practice of the arts which they have borrowed from their neighbours or which they have found in the country they have invaded. In instructing themselves thus, they may give a new character to the models they copy, but they do not invent : they will in fact adhere to the models as closely as possible ; if they corrupt them or copy them unskilfully, it is unintentionally. I do not know of a single monument in Northern Italy that can be attributed to the Lombards ; or if there should be such, I venture to affirm that it resembles a Latin construction or approaches the Byzantine type. Only want of skill on the part of the imitator in reproducing the type could have added a barbarian element to the work,—using that word in its ancient acceptation—that is, *foreign*. But if no Lombard remains exist, there are buildings erected by the Visigoths, which have left conspicuous traces in the archæological record of the early middle ages. Yet after all, these are only buildings in the Roman style, rudely executed. To attribute to barbarians of any race an expansive influence, in the presence of those Latin traditions and monuments which were still so conspicuous a feature in Italy and

---

[1] The following is what Gregory the Great says of the Lombards : "Wherever the Lombards are we see nothing but mourning, and hear nothing but lamentation ; cities, castles, and fields are devastated, and the country is a desert." M. Léonce Raynaud, in his *Traité d'Architecture*, seems to confound the Lombards with the people afterwards known under that name, and who were in fact the Latin population which had been invaded by the Lombards. We have here one of the equivocations by which our subject is obscured. Far from erecting Churches, the Lombards were intent on destroying them. The few churches that were built in Upper Italy during the dominion of the Lombards are the work of the Latin population, which amid these melancholy days of invasion had still preserved the corporation of the *magistri comacini*.

Gaul, and of those Greek Byzantine arts which were then shedding a brilliant lustre, would be scarcely less absurd than to maintain that the Italian Renaissance of the fifteenth century was called forth by the Swiss or the Westphalians.

But I deem it useless to dwell longer upon a question which, though decided in the negative many years ago on substantial grounds, has, I scarcely know why, been lately revived. In political history the most important events—those which have exercised a powerful influence on the destiny of nations—are sometimes attributed to trivial causes. I distrust this theory in its application to general history, and as applied to that of the arts I reject it altogether. The progress of the arts is deliberate, continuous, logical : great results are produced only by strenuous, persistent, and regular effort ; by traditions perpetuated or revived, but whose course can be readily traced with a little investigation. If the political world exhibits sudden revolutions and startling changes, we never observe such in the arts, and least of all in the art of Architecture. We find a people making new laws, or quitting one form of worship for another; because a law is only a convention, and a form of worship is dictated by doctrines which the civilisation of the period recognises : whereas the arts, and architecture in particular, depend essentially upon manners, traditions, the habits of daily life, and industrial pursuits and methods, which no human power can modify except as the result of a long series of studies and experiments. We see Europe becoming Christian, yet for a long time preserving its ancient manners and customs, and consequently the architecture of pagan antiquity. It was necessary that Christianity should change manners ; more than this,—that a torrent of barbarians should overspread Italy, Gaul, and Spain, for several centuries ; that Roman traditions should be lost before the foundations of a new art could be laid : and even then those foundations could have no other basis than the débris of Roman arts. Above all it was essential that the ideas by which the successive phases of civilisation were guided should take a new course. At Byzantium, the degenerate Roman genius was absorbed by that of the Greeks, which was more active and more fitted to receive Christianity. In the West, Christianity found itself in the presence of primitive barbarians, and was able to mould them more easily and quickly than it could the old Roman organisation. If therefore we would discover the new impulse imparted to literature and the arts, it is to Byzantium we should look, or at least to the influences that emanated from the Eastern Empire. The ancient Greek spirit is therefore one of the earliest constituents of the genius of the middle ages.

I have already called attention to the distinction between

the Greek and the Roman spirit : the Greek reasons, discusses, investigates, with untiring energy ; indulging a restless activity of thought, and stopping short of fixed conclusions : his comprehensive intellect, however, makes him aware of the danger of this incessant intellectual movement, so that when the Greek can attach himself to something material—a form—he pronounces it unalterable. While the Greeks of Byzantium are discussing impalpable abstractions,—doctrines philosophical and religious,—they insist on giving a hieratic form to the plastic arts ;—a strange contradiction,—a singular contention between the instinct and intellect of this people. Their instinct leads them to give a fixed embodiment to material beauty, so that the tradition of it may not be lost ; while their intellect urges them to follow every path of research and invention. Seated midway between Asia and the West, this nation is endowed with double faculties : it carefully preserves the beautiful in art,—the beautiful regarded as immutable in form,—sometimes indeed obstinately ; while leading the way, even for the moderns, in the immense domain of science, dialectics, and rigorous examination in the moral sphere. In its procedure in art it remained antique ; in intellect it was modern. The Greeks, like all nations that have taken the lead in civilisation, always inclined to put themselves in opposition to the dominant influence that lay nearest them. Thus in the days of Classic antiquity,—wedged in among the unprogressive nations of Asia,—the Greeks soon presented the image of movement, intellectual, philosophical, commercial, and æsthetic. When, on the other hand, the Roman power established itself among them, they had no longer to fear the enervating influence of the East ; the East at their back, through a circle of very extensive radius, had been subjugated by the Empire ; the West, on the contrary, was falling into disorder, barbarism, and the profoundest darkness ; it was threatening the civilised world. This was the quarter in which danger was to be feared. And so the Greeks, who in the presence of Oriental immobility had in ancient times made themselves Occidentals, became Orientals in presence of Occidental barbarians, as if to protect, by rendering them in their turn immovable, the conquests of civilisation, intelligence, and art. Whether by instinct or deliberate intention, therefore, we must regard the Greeks as the great initiators of European civilisation, both for the ancient world and for Christian times. During the reign of barbarism in Europe,—viz., from the fifth to the twelfth century—the Greeks were the jealous, exclusive conservators of literature, arts, and industry ; not allowing any change to be made, even among themselves, in the sacred deposit ; as if they had conceived the idea of transmitting it through this melancholy interval, intact to more prosperous ages. The very people which from Augustus to Constantine had been urging art into every path of fantastic caprice, which seemed to have forgotten the essential constituents of style, and which was more and more sacrificing all higher considerations to refinements in mere mechanical execution ; this people, I say, as soon as it finds itself confronted with barbarism, not only pauses in the path of decline, but by a supreme effort, which is certainly worthy of admiration, returns to the pure sources,—the original types ; it reconstitutes those types with due consideration of the requirements of the times ; fixes them, and avails itself of the remains of the powerful organisation of the Roman Empire to prevent them from being altered, as far as its influence extends.   The Emperor being in the East the *Pontifex maximus* of the new religion, as he had been at Rome that of the old, we find him becoming the Supreme Head in regard to doctrine, and to Art declared immutable as dogma.   It was to this depository, guarded with religious care, that the West came for many centuries to seek the germs of its arts, sciences, and industry ; and when these germs had been developed, the Eastern empire, enfeebled by that very immobility to which I have referred—effete, and dissolute—was overwhelmed in its turn by the flood of barbarism ; so true is it that in this world nations, like the individual, have a task to fulfil, and when this task is accomplished they must disappear.

I have endeavoured briefly to explain how Greek art influenced the early middle ages ; I must now show how its influence acted in the West, and how modern arts were thence developed.   I remarked above that the Byzantine Greeks after the establishment of the Empire among them, retraced their steps and abandoned that path of freedom which art had followed since the time of Pericles, to shut themselves up in hieratic forms in the presence of the barbarism of the West.   No people ever understood what style in the arts is better than the Greeks : with them it was an affair of instinct, still more emphatically of reason.   From the time of Pericles, and after the Peleponnesian war, Greek art, while preserving its admirable skill in execution, was tending more and more towards realism.   Soon, absorbed in the irresistible power of Rome, the Greeks became the amusers, the artists, the tamers, of the Roman colossus. Comprehending at once that though they had been able to conquer and govern the East, they were powerless against the political organisation of the Romans, they contented themselves with the task of introducing the arts, philosophy, and literature, among their rude protectors ; but while imparting the most precious thing they had to bestow to masters who were but little susceptible to the charms of art, their art lost that delicate perfume which can only be exhaled in a favourable medium.   It is impossible to tame a barbarian (and to the Greek the Roman was a barbarian) without becoming something of a barbarian one's-self; and woe to the artist who submits to a master who has no idea of art ! The Greeks therefore, as sensible men, did not waste their time discussing questions of style with the Romans, for they well knew that they would not be understood ; but while submitting to the rigorous conditions imposed upon them, they contented themselves with the function of decorators : their aim was only to gratify the pompous tastes of their masters, —to charm them, if possible, by a brilliant, if not refined, execution. What otherwise could they do under Roman government, but obey and endeavour to become Romans themselves ? But when Christianity became the religion of the Roman Empire established at Byzantium, the Greeks resumed their leading position in the arts. Preserving that part of Roman architecture which really belongs to the Romans—the structure itself—they set about modifying the decoration. In what way they accomplished this we shall endeavour to discover presently. In construction they venture on those bold essays which are in accordance with their genius ; but these essays are systematic,—they are the result of calculation and reason rather than of caprice and fancy. Such a school, based on principles that were rigorously observed, could not fail to become the best of schools for barbarous nations ; especially if those nations were endowed with original genius, and were not embarrassed by influential traditions. Charlemagne was the first who undertook to revive the arts in the West ; but all that he was able to accomplish was a somewhat rude repro-duction of buildings entirely Oriental in their origin. But he introduced artists, grammarians, manuscripts, textile fabrics, and furniture from Byzantium or Lombardy, at that time influenced by Byzantine art ; and barbarous nations were thus made acquainted with the productions of a very advanced civilisation,— an importation which did not cease until the West had in its turn developed an art of its own. In order to form schools of artists, Charlemagne could have recourse only to men profes-sionally devoted to study—the clerical body. The Franks, who owned the soil by right of conquest, were too much occupied with warfare, and with maintaining possession of their domains, to think of cultivating the arts. The inhabitants of the towns were exclusively occupied with maintaining and defending them-selves ; and as regards the coloni and serfs their precarious position was a bar to the study of the arts or the acquirement of industrial skill. The monks, on the other hand, who enjoyed a comparative tranquillity and independence, soon formed schools of art, whence issued not only architects, but sculptors, painters, and artisans, whom the greater abbeys used to send to their dependencies. The focus of this intellectual radiation was that part of Gaul which bordered the Saone, the Marne, the Rhine, the Loire, and the Seine. During three centuries—from the ninth to the twelfth—this was the district from which the earliest ideas of art were diffused through Western Europe,— Italy included ;[1] notwithstanding the opinion that the arts of the West had no other origin than Italy, ever since the commencement of the Roman Empire. The monuments and records of the times in question are proofs that admit of no refutation. Italy was during that period, comparatively speaking, sunk in anarchy, and exposed to miseries of every kind; so that it was by no means in a condition to produce architects, still less sculptors and painters. If convents or churches had to be built in Italy, artists from the Clunisian brotherhood were sent for, or the services of Greek exiles were called into requisition. At the end of the tenth century the Venetians were engaged in building the Church of St. Mark ; they adopted a Greek plan— an ornamentation executed by Greeks,—and used columns and slabs of marble which they had carried off from the coasts of Greece, at that time exposed through the weakness of the Eastern Empire to the insults of pirates of all countries. In the north of Italy they still continued to erect public buildings during the tenth and eleventh centuries ; but the remains of these edifices exhibit a very indefinite character—feeble traditions of the ancient Roman architecture, mingled with features borrowed from Eastern artists. As regards the southern part of the Peninsula, we hardly know what occurred there during this period in which it suffered so much. The Moors settled in Sicily were ravaging its coasts. Rome, which had been long in a state of ruin, survived only amid the débris of its former splendour ; if it continued to build, it was only by heaping together the fragments that were strewn on every side : nothing that could be called art existed. This country, which had been exposed to continual devastation during several centuries, without commerce or manufactures, a prey to invasion from every quarter, separated from the East, and with no inherent vitality, in all its aspects, presented the most melancholy picture. On the other hand, between the Eastern Empire, and Southern and Central Gaul, extensive commerce had been carried on ever since the tenth century; Venetian agencies, through which the monetary transactions of Europe were then carried on, existed at Limoges, and corresponded with the East by the ports of the Mediterranean, and with the North by those of the Western coast. During the tenth and the eleventh centuries the intercourse

---

[1] See the *Dictionnaire raisonné d'Architecture* (by M. Viollet le Duc), articles ARCHITECTURE and ARCHITECTURE MONASTIQUE.

with Constantinople was incessant, and the arts of the West
derived advantage from its frequency.

Let us inquire, however, what were the peoples among which
the arts of the East thus came to exercise their influence, and
under what circumstances. When the Goths, the Franks, and
the Burgundians, successively invaded the Gallic soil, from the
mouths of the Rhine to the shores of the Mediterranean, and
round to Brittany, they found Roman art everywhere among
the people of the country. Having devastated the private and
public buildings of the cities, they were compelled to provide
themselves with a lodging, and after no great lapse of time to
make preparations for defence. These conquerors therefore
adopted the plan either of repairing, to the best of their ability,
what they had ruined, or of imitating the buildings that remained
standing. In the West, therefore, the Roman style of building
was never abandoned. It was not the invaders who erected the
buildings required : they were obliged to have recourse to the
artisans of the country, and they possessed none other than
Roman traditions. But when, after the anarchy that followed,
the invasion was succeeded by something like a settled government, a taste for luxury was soon manifested by the new
possessors of the soil ; the rude edifices that had been built—
the last vestiges of Roman architecture—required decoration ;
they therefore availed themselves of the services of Oriental
artists, and still more of articles that could be imported from the
East,—such as furniture, cloths, utensils, and jewels. While
therefore they preserved the Western Roman style of building,
the sculptors and painters from the time of Charlemagne forwards
clothed their buildings with a decoration copied from the articles
imported from the East. A silk orphrey might serve as a model
for the sculpture of a frieze ; a casket or a diptych might furnish
the types for bas-reliefs, decorating tympanums, or capitals.
Thus Roman architecture was clothed in some particulars with
a new garb, while at other points it endeavoured to reproduce
the ancient Western remains that were scattered through the
country. Byzantine art influenced Gaul in unequal proportions
during the ninth and tenth centuries. At Perigueux, for
example, at the close of the tenth century, a church was being
built which was Byzantine in plan and form, but Roman in its
decorative details ; a few years later, on the Loire, and on the
banks of the Seine and the Oise, edifices were being erected
which were almost entirely Roman in plan and structure, while
their ornamentation was evidently derived from an Oriental
inspiration.

The period during which this intermingling in various proportions of Roman traditions and Oriental importations was

effected, is that which is conventionally called in France *l'époque romane* (the Romanesque period). But there is no more of homogeneity in the Romanesque style, if we consider the extent of country assigned to its prevalence—viz., from the Alps to the Atlantic, and from the English Channel to the Mediterranean— than there was between the various provinces comprised within these widely separated boundaries ; so that when the style termed Romanesque is spoken of it is desirable to specify whether that of the West, that of the Rhine, the Saone, or the Marne, or that of Normandy, of the Ile de France, or of Poitou is intended. These various styles exhibit, however, features of consanguinity which belong essentially to the genius of Western Europe. I have had occasion to treat this question with greater precision elsewhere.[1] I have stated—believing that no one would contest the position—that there is a French Archi- tecture of the Middle Ages. It is evident that in speaking of a French Architecture of the Middle Ages, I meant a Western or Gallic Architecture, seeing that during a considerable part of the mediæval period there was, strictly speaking, no such country as France. Not anticipating that this opinion would be contested, I took no precautions to sustain it ; I was aware that well- informed foreigners, who were certainly not any of them disposed to concede to us more than is our due, recognised and studied a French Mediæval Architecture ; and it never occurred to me to doubt its existence. I find, however, that this question must be treated afresh ; though if it concerned only our national vanity, —since art is cosmopolitan,—I would not urge my opinion further : but something more important than mere puerile vanity is at stake ; a question of life or death is involved, of decline or progress, for Western art. It is not a mere party struggle that has to be waged—a breach to be made in the " classic " dogmatism of the *Ecole des Beaux Arts ;* the end to be attained is the re- habilitation of a phase of art that has not been worthily appreciated,—the product of our Western genius, elaborated for us and by us, as the result of long efforts and struggles, which though pacific are glorious enough to excite our admiration and sympathy. I have endeavoured in these Lectures to give promin- ence to the relations that have always existed between the genius of the peoples with whose character we are acquainted and their arts ; but I must be understood as intending by peoples—and ambiguity should if possible be avoided in such questions—not populations as marked out by political limits,—mere agglomera- tions of men having no connection in point of race or community of ideas, but associations swayed by one dominant intellectual tendency, impelled by the same temperament—shall I say because

---

[1] See the *Dictionnaire raisonné de l'Architecture française.*

affinity of race and similarity of character binds together the members of such associations. The civilisations both of ancient and modern times have been established in two very different ways; and as it is always desirable to give a name to phenomena, in the intellectual as well as in the physical world, I shall distinguish them as the *Sympathetic* and the *Political* civilisation respectively. I call that Sympathetic Civilisation which arises among an agglomeration of men of the same race or races that have certain affinities with each other. These civilisations are the only ones that have arts proper to themselves: the Greeks furnish us with the most remarkable example of this form of civilisation. By Political Civilisation I understand that which is introduced through the preponderating influence—the influence, gained by arms, skill, or commerce—of one people (sometimes a mere handful of men) over vast territories occupied by races that have no natural relationship to the conquerors or to each other. Such was the civilisation of ancient Rome. The Romans formed a political and administrative body rather than a nation; it is not proper to speak of *the Roman people;* there was no Roman people (for I shall not dignify with that name—under the Empire at least—the *plebs* that filled the streets of Rome); there was only a Roman organisation—a Roman government. Similarly there was not, properly speaking, any Roman art: there was only an organisation of arts belonging to foreign *peoples,*—a very perfect organisation, I allow, but which was not, and could not be, the expression of the genius of a people; and which presents at every period of its existence, as we have seen, and shall see in the sequel, the strangest contradictions. It would be useless, I think, to extend this examination of the nature of the various forms of civilisation, and of their influence on art; but in looking around us in Europe we see its importance demonstrated in the present day—in fact, more clearly than ever. Looking through the course of centuries, with the invasions and political catastrophes they have witnessed, we see these questions of races and nationalities rise again with as much warmth and vividness as ever; and is it not unreasonable to suppose that we who constitute the nation which most typically embodies the idea of a civilisation resulting from unity of sentiment—from the affinity of races fused together by a community of thought—have no art of our own? Can we suppose that this characteristic unity,— this unity which has been the soul of the nation's progress—has not manifested itself externally by any visible sign?

The Romans who had been engaged for six hundred years in subjugating the Italiots became the masters of Gaul in less than fifty. This fact proves to us that notwithstanding the dissimilarities which Cæsar has clearly exhibited, there had been for a long period a certain degree of homogeneity between the tribes of Gaul. The Roman supremacy in Gaul was not contested until the close of the Empire; and certainly the tendency of its administration was to introduce unity among the Western provinces. Barbarians diverse in language and customs invaded Gaul from various quarters ; settled in it contended with each other for mastery, made it a scene of warfare, and for several centuries directed all their efforts to destroying such unity as might exist among its various tribes. The feudal system, which assumed a tolerably regular form under the successors of Charlemagne, seemed invented expressly to produce a lasting separation, not only between the provinces but the fiefs themselves ; nevertheless, from the eleventh century downwards, we observe a slow but persistent tendency of the various tribes towards national unity. This tendency appears not to have been arrested for a single day. Those western tribes therefore who formed what the Romans called Gaul had a particular genius, in the same way as the Greeks had theirs. Can we then imagine why, since they alone of Western peoples were endowed with such a lively genius —a genius indicating a common origin—they alone should not have possessed a form of art of their own ? How could this contradiction be explained if we attempted it ? But no explanation is attempted ; a decision is pronounced *ex cathedrâ;* and those who are the first to recognise the constant tendency of the Gallic populations towards national unity, with singular inconsistency deny that those populations had an art of their own. They do their best to prevent the existence of an art specifically French being generally recognised, and to represent the idea that there is such an art as the ingenious dream of certain theorists. The obstinacy with which the idea is rejected may lead us to detect the principal grounds of so singular an antagonism. This very obstinacy demonstrates the importance of removing all that still tends to obscure the truth ; persistent unwillingness to admit an idea is that which generally proves such an idea to be fertile in consequences. But where are we to look for the causes of this opposition ? Among persons who are not artists we may discover them in the horror which the people at large feel for mediæval institutions in France; as if the arts were the consequence of these institutions, and did not, on the contrary, form one of the most vivid expressions on the part of the people of the soil of a reaction against an odious régime ; while among artists, those causes are to be referred to a false, irrational, incomplete system of instruction, and to the dislike of studies which, quitting the beaten path, involve unceasing search for the True, the knowledge of our national genius and instincts, and the use of judgment rather than formulas : they arise—and we cannot shut our eyes to the fact—from the torpor of minds habituated to dispense with their power of reasoning and to believe that inspiration is only phantasy ;—whereas, on the contrary, inspiration is the result only of profound calculation, of slow and studious labour.

I do not deny that the institutions of the Middle Ages are connected with gloomy associations in the pages of history, and not without reason ; but the artists who appeared among us were the first apostles of the enfranchisement of the oppressed classes ; it was they who first raised themselves by labour and knowledge ; it was they who first aroused the activity that distinguishes modern times from the torpor of the declining period of ancient civilisation and the barbarism of the first Christian centuries. Their works are, as it were, a visible protest against the prevailing ignorance. We must not confound the cry of the oppressed with that of the oppressor, under the pretext that in the mêlée it is impossible to distinguish them.

In that corner of Western Europe which is called France, therefore, I find—and only there during the Middle Ages—the elements that tend to constitute Art, because these elements existed in the minds of the people. Everywhere else in Europe I behold cities, associations of merchants, political constitutions more or less complete, and individuals displaying brilliant qualities; but I do not see countries presenting tendencies to national aggregation, impelled by the same sentiments towards intellectual unity and by the same faith in the future. So that it is in France especially that the Christian idea applied to the arts is seen developing itself in the most decided manner.

But what is the Christian Idea as applied to the arts ? Christianity, together with a new form of worship and a new religious system, introduced amidst the ancient Latin world the germs of incessant progress, of a struggle against material influences, of a moral and physical enfranchisement, of political and social consolidation, of equality, and of a reaction against brute force. The character which the Greeks of classic times had played in contrast with Asiatic immobility, a character whose action had been interrupted by the strong hand of Roman power, was to be resumed by the Christians of the West ; and, as the same causes produce analogous results in history, the Arts of the West, though starting from principles quite the opposite of those of ancient Greece, were destined to proceed in the same way,— to possess a style of their own based on reason and analysis, to shed a brilliant light around them, to advance without a moment's interruption, to become the initiators of further developments, and to decay rapidly through abuse in the application of those very principles. But—and in this also it resembles Greek art —this western Mediæval art, notwithstanding its short duration, was to become an inexhaustible source of instruction for all who should be willing to avail themselves of it in modern times.

But it will be urged, " We are Latins !" By dint of reiterated assertion we have come to believe this. Because our language is derived from the Latin, and our laws are partly copied from those of the Romans, and because for the last three hundred years we have been building very poor imitations of Roman edifices, we fancy that we are Latins. Let us investigate this matter. The Romans were not and made no pretension to be artists ; they themselves did not practise the arts ; all their artists were Greeks, as I have, if I do not deceive myself, clearly demonstrated ; the Roman was only a constructor ; he did not trouble himself about the form which his constructions should assume. As soon as a method of construction appears to him satisfactory, we find him repeating it again and again, even to the latest times of the Lower Empire. The Roman does not discuss questions of principle in reference to art ; he is never an enthusiast : the nation to which he belongs is a nation of politicians, legists, and administrators ; it is not commercial, nor manufacturing, nor scientific, nor philosophic ; those among the Romans whom we find occupying themselves with philosophy and science all have recourse to Greek intellect ; the Roman cares little about enlightening the human race or supplying it with ideas and principles ; it is enough for him to govern it,—taking it just as it is ; he organises it politically but does not civilise it. But what has been our character in the West from the time when we quitted a state of barbarism till the seventeenth century? Exactly the contrary : we have been bad politicians, sorry civilians, indifferent administrators ; we have not only not governed others, but have been scarcely able to govern ourselves. On the other hand, even in the twelfth century, Paris had its schools, and all Europe was flocking to them, to pursue the study of Greek philosophy. It was at Paris in the thirteenth century that the Encyclopædic movement was commenced—a movement that has lasted down to our own times ; it was at Paris that intellectual effort endeavoured to pierce the darkness of the Early Mediæval period. We dispute about everything and apropos of everything ; we reason, we analyse, we write, we investigate with restless activity. We have an art that sprang from Roman traditions and Byzantine influences,—Romanesque art cultivated in the cloisters ; in a few years we quit this for a new phase of art, practised exclusively by laymen—an art based on geometry and the observation of laws hitherto unknown—the equilibrium of forces ; and this art continually advances : it soon transcends its original aim. The lower classes combine and obtain privileges by force or address ; we become merchants, agriculturists, and manufacturers. We cover a good part of Europe with our productions and writings ; we have, like the Romans, an ambition to make conquests, but we have never had the capacity to retain them, because our own social element, our country, our habits, and sympathies are essential to our existence. To Englishmen (for example) England is everywhere where Englishmen are to be found, and this is the source of strength to their empire ; but for us France is to be found nowhere but *in* France. The Romans made war with no other object than to secure or extend their material power, to colonise barbarous countries, and—to enrich themselves. They not only took from the conquered peoples their money or the produce of their soil, but adopted their customs when they thought them desirable ; they gave them in exchange a protection which was sometimes illusory,—forms of government and administrations, colonists, prefects, roads, bridges, canals, and public buildings. We, on the contrary, have not adopted from the nations among whom we have been in contact their customs or ideas, but have often left them ours. If then it be true that we are Latins, I would ask in what respect we resemble them.

Dating from the eleventh century, we find Western Europe collecting the works of Classic Antiquity, appropriating them, and making them the foundation of all study ; but this did not prevent it from producing a new order of art strictly its own, and utterly alien to the principles of Latin art. It has long been asserted that the Crusades exercised a considerable influence on the arts of the West. But facts evidently contradict this opinion. The first Crusade took place in 1096, the second in 1147 ; and it was precisely during the twelfth century that the arts of Architecture and Sculpture underwent a transformation, which, so far from bringing them nearer to Oriental art, removed them further from it. These questions, generally treated by persons who have no practical acquaintance with the Arts, have been examined in a superficial manner : dates are confused, and hypotheses are formed from mere appearances : the erroneous view thus derived is repeated, and is ultimately adopted as unquestionable truth. It then becomes difficult to correct opinion by the examination of facts. We will, however, make the attempt. More than a mere archæological question is involved in this study, and I shall not attempt to conceal from the reader that I have a further aim in this inquiry. I think it important to the arts of modern times to make them acquainted with their origin, and thence infer the direction in which progress can be really hoped for. This I consider the only means of leading them to a fruitful unconstrained development : we must know what we are, in order to know what we should and can do. This is a principle which ought to be engraven in the mind of every artist.

No sooner was Western art disengaged from barbarism than it manifested tendencies opposed to the fundamental principles of Roman art. This movement commenced where the arts were practised after the revival attempted by Charlemagne : it commenced in the cloisters, and in particular was contemporaneous with the epoch at which the monastery of Cluny was at the height of its greatness—the eleventh century. We find these Western monks during this period not only seeking new combinations of plans, but a system of construction based on laws which the Romans did not know or refused to recognise. In the statuary and painted decorations it is perfectly obvious that they had recourse to Byzantine examples.

Both in arrangement of plan and in construction, the architects of the West, as early as the tenth century, aimed to conciliate two conflicting principles, and thus entered at once into opposition to the laws laid down by the Romans. The Roman ground-plan plainly indicated whether the edifice was vaulted or covered with a timber roof. When the edifice was vaulted—like the greater part of the Baths of Caracalla, for instance—the plan was solid ; it presented masses locking into each other so as to present resistance to thrusts in every direction ; it is a cellular system of construction. When it was not vaulted it conformed to the Greek plan, and consisted only of longitudinal walls and points of support vertically weighted, and therefore slight. The Greek ground-plan was easy to trace, and required but a small amount of materials ; it was simple and economical : the Roman plan, on the contrary, required complicated and scientific combinations, and involved considerable expenditure on account of the enormous masses of material which it called for; conformably with the Roman method of building, it required to be carried out with rapidity,—with the co-operation of a very great number of appliances for labour and transport, and with a great stock of materials simultaneously conveyed to the site. The monks and nobles of the tenth and eleventh centuries did not possess those immense resources which the Romans had at command in all parts of the empire ; they therefore abandoned the Roman ground-plan and adopted solely the simpler arrangement of the Basilica, or of unvaulted buildings like those of the Greeks. It was not long, however, before they recognised the utility of vaulting, especially in damp and variable climates. Timber roofs were liable to be burned, or to decay rapidly ; and architects soon became desirous of replacing them by vaulting : but they would not on that account abandon the simple distribution of ground-plan, whether for religious or secular edifices. Here, then, we have at the outset two opposing principles confronting each other. I will not here trace the history,—which is a long one,—of the efforts made by what is called Romanesque Art, to reconcile them, having done this in another work.[1] It will be sufficient to point out the characteristic phases of this development. We remark first an increase in the thickness of the longitudinal walls, in order to resist the thrust ; a method soon found to be insufficient and expensive in large buildings. Next the distribution of the thrust on certain points by means of groined vaulting, and the strengthening of these points of resistance by piers. And, in order not to encumber the interiors, a direction of all the oblique lines of thrust on piers, frankly erected outside : which was tantamount to raising a building and keeping it up by means of points of support independent as it were of the building itself,

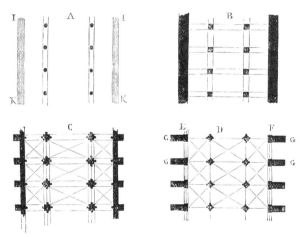

Fig. 6.—Transition from the Roman to the Gothic Ground-Plan.

just as shores might be. Lastly, stability given to these independent points of support rather by heavily weighting them than by a wide area of base. These successive experiments ended in results very far removed from the simple principles of Greek or Roman art, whether in its Latin or Byzantine form.

A diagram will explain the transformations which the ground-plan of the ancient timber-roofed Basilica underwent before arriving at the vaulted basilica of the thirteenth century (fig. 6). A is the plan of a Roman hall or basilica with a nave and two aisles, roofed with timber. The Romanesque architects desired to replace the timber roofing by vaulting ; they gave, as at B, greater thickness to the walls and pillars ; but these precautions were insufficient : the walls gave out, and the building tottered. They then, as at c, instead of the continuous round-arched vault,

---

[1] See in the *Dictionnaire*, etc. the articles ARCHITECTURE and CONSTRUCTION.

established groined vaulting, opposite the thrusts of which they projected exterior buttresses. It was soon perceived that the walls between these buttresses were useless, and the plan D was the result. In reality the building occupied only the space comprised between EF. On the outside, therefore, were erected the buttresses G, against which were directed all the oblique thrusts. The longitudinal walls IK of the plan A were thus divided into sections, and these sections placed at right angles to their original position; the same superficial area being occupied in plan by the solids, but strong lateral resistance permitting the construction of vaulting. To all appearance this was simple enough; nevertheless it involved an entire revolution in the art of building. It was a complete rupture with the ancient methods. It required no less than three centuries for this new principle whose consequences were capable of expansion *ad infinitum*, to become definitely established. And while the system of construction was being thus modified, the forms of Art were undergoing transformations which are apparent to the most careless observer.

The architectural orders invented by the Greeks composed the structure itself; that is to say, in the architecture that accorded with these orders there was only one mode of structure; therefore the structure of the Greek edifices and their appearance were essentially united. It would not be possible to despoil a Greek building of the order which forms its principal decoration without destroying the building itself. A glance at the remains of Greek edifices suffices to show us that the Doric or Ionic orders adopted by the architects constitute these buildings. The Greek orders are none other than the structure itself, to which that form was given which was most appropriate to its function. In the orders adopted from the Greeks the Romans saw only a decoration which might be removed, omitted, displaced, or replaced by something else, without the structure to which the decoration was applied being thereby seriously affected. Of course, I do not refer now to Roman temples built conformably to Greek types. I think I have made this characteristic of Roman architecture sufficiently manifest. The Romans, however, influenced as they were by a thoroughly practical spirit, often perceived that this fashion of setting up Greek orders in front of their buildings was an offence against reason. Accordingly, in many buildings, such as theatres, amphitheatres, and palaces, they *engaged* the orders in the building itself; that is to say, they made use of columns as buttresses to give greater footing to the parts that were weighted, while they also thus obtained an external or internal decoration. It must not however be supposed that the Romans were the first to discover this application of the

THE THEATRE OF MARCELLUS, ROME.

THE BASILICA OF THE GIANTS, AGRIGENTUM.

orders ; the Greeks made use of engaged orders : in fact they had frequently so employed them, and one of the most remarkable examples of such employment is the temple or basilica of Agrigentum,—called the "Temple of the Giants." But I do not suppose the idea ever occurred to the Greeks of superimposing engaged orders, in the Roman fashion—as on the exterior of the Theatre of Marcellus, the Coliseum, and many other buildings. In engaging the orders in the building the Greeks proceeded on a principle quite contrary to that which actuated the Romans on a similar occasion. The idea the Romans had was that of erecting buttresses presenting a decoration which custom had made familiar. They raised one, two, or three stories ; they piled one, two, or three orders one above the other (fig. 7), like so many superimposed buttresses. They reasoned so little when it was a question of giving to an object a form suited to its nature, that they placed upon each of these orders its complete entablature, just as if each of them had to terminate the edifice. If in this case the engaged columns A might serve as buttresses and afford a decoration which was at the same time useful, it must be acknowledged that the projecting entablatures, B, extending from column to column, were rather injurious than otherwise to the stability of the building, and that their overhanging weight must tend to weaken the masonry. Here there was an error of judgment, and consequently a want of taste. It was bad reasoning, or no reasoning at all.[1] What does it matter, some will say, —provided this decoration pleases the eye ? for that is the true and only aim of Art. It must however be allowed that in architecture there exist rules imposed by the natural laws of statics, and that without being architects we can recognise the importance of these rules. Thus every one can see that a column should not be more slender at its base than at its summit. The eye instinctively recognises these laws, without requiring the intervention of reason. Reason only confirms, extends, and explains feelings that arise spontaneously within us ; just as in every nation written laws only define the instinctive sense of good and evil, justice and injustice.

The Greeks, when they engaged the orders in the building, proceeded on a true principle. Since in their view the order was nothing other than the expression of the structure,—the means of support ;—when they deemed it necessary in certain cases to

---

[1] The Romans were not always thus false to the true principles of architecture. Around the *Arenas* of Nîmes, for example, the two superimposed orders which serve as buttresses between the arcades of the two stories of that edifice, on the outside, are treated as veritable buttresses ; the lower order consists of projecting piers, the upper of engaged columns ; the cornices only go round each pilaster or column, and do not form, as in the theatre of Marcellus or the Roman Coliseum, those projecting girdles, overhanging so heavily and uselessly around the building.

form a solid enclosure between the columns,—as had been done before them by the Egyptians and Assyrians,—this wall, this enclosure, was merely a thick partition.   To erect, as in the great Basilica of the Giants at Agrigentum, columns as stable points of support,—piers or buttresses supporting the entablature and roofing—and to shut in all or part of the intercolumniations (fig. 8) with a slighter construction—a simple enclosure, in fact—was to

Fig. 9.—Early example of Arch built immediately on the Column.

reason most wisely ; but to take as the Romans did at a later day, the voids for the solids, the partitions for the part of strength, and the buttresses for a mere decoration, was,—with all due respect for the Romans, and for those who copy them without serious examination—to reason barbarously.   Having departed so far from the path of reason, the Romans went still farther ;—they made arches beneath the projecting entablatures of the engaged orders (see fig. 7).   This, as I have already remarked, would seem to a Greek the last degree of aberration; it would show an utter ignorance of the forms of Greek architecture.

In the great buildings, however, that were erected by the Romans towards the close of the Empire, on the eastern coast of the Adriatic, and in Asia, the architects began to build the arch directly on the columns (fig. 9). But this innovation was probably due to the Greeks. Whenever they were able, the Greek artists, without contemning the methods employed by the Western Romans—subjected them to their invariably rational judgment. But it is time to investigate a question highly important in the history of Architecture. We acknowledge the existence of a Byzantine art; we assert that this art is an off-spring of the active spirit of the Greeks; I have even gone so far as to assert above that Byzantine art was a Renaissance. But whence had the Greeks derived the elements of that Renaissance? How had Greek art as it existed in the time of Pericles been made to undergo this transformation? Under the Empire the Greeks in Greece itself as well as in Italy saw themselves constrained to adopt the pompous taste of the Romans; how can we account for the fact that on the establishment of the Eastern Empire the Greeks found themselves in a position to apply novel forms to the Roman structure without any apparent process of transition? The key to the arts of the Middle Ages both in the East and West is to be found in the investigation and solution of this question. Let us therefore try to lift the veil. There is reason to believe that at a very remote period the Greeks had derived the elements of their arts from Asia and Egypt; but in the time of their greatest splendour, that is to say from the destruction of Athens by the Persians, to the end of the Peloponnesian War, they scrupulously avoided adopting anything from the Asiatics, with whom they were incessantly at war. During this period—so short and brilliant—the arts of the Greeks radiated far and wide, and their influence extended to the Bosporus, and probably over a part of the coast of Syria. There, however, long previous to that glorious epoch, there existed a powerful civilisation, possessing arts marked by a vigour altogether primitive. Phœnicia and Judæa built, traded, and colonised, long anterior to the historic times of the Hellenic peninsula. After having stifled the last vestiges of Greek independence, the Romans extended their Empire as far as Syria and Persia; when the Greeks, having no longer to struggle against the Orientals of Asia, became through commerce the natural intermediaries between the Levant and the West: they performed the function which later on the Venetians assumed in regard to Asia and Western Europe. In Syria, on the coasts of ancient Phœnicia, and in Judæa, they found arts whose development they had aided perhaps unconsciously, but which, far more than those of Greece, preserved traces of primitive grandeur; there they found one of the sources from which the Romans had doubtless borrowed as far back as the time of the Republic,—the source of Etruscan art.   This requires explanation. At the epoch when the importance of Rome began to make itself felt in Italy, the Etruscans possessed a well-developed art.   They employed vaulting—not vaulting constructed of pise rammed on a centre, but the arch formed with voussoirs of cut stone; they built with huge blocks, laid without the intervention of mortar or slips; they decorated this construction—the outgrowth of influential traditions—with slightly projecting pilasters, disks and mouldings, which are neither Egyptian nor Assyrian.   Recent discoveries,[1]—contested we must admit, (but what discoveries are not contested by those who did not make them?),—recent discoveries, I say, have brought to light certain remains of buildings assumed to be Judæan, and therefore having near affinities with the Phœnician arts whose connection with those of Etruria is very close.   We observe a similar method of construction, mouldings similar in principle, decoration of a similar kind, and, which is still more remarkable, arches made with immense blocks of hewn stone.

M. de Saulcy, to whom archæologists owe these important discoveries—the subjects of controversy I allow—has kindly submitted to my inspection the collection of photographs and notes which he made in Palestine.   If the archæological worth of these documents is matter of discussion, no one can doubt the accuracy of the photographs; and for the practical architect—to him who has seen stonework hewn and built by the hand of man, who knows how it is worked, and how it is laid in place—photography acquires the importance of fact.   Its testimony discloses, or seems to disclose, the remains at Jerusalem, of the platform—consisting of enormous stones—upon which stood the temple of Solomon; and on one of the sides of this platform appears the springing of an arch, which formed at one time the bridge of communication between the temple and the palace.   Here (fig. 10) is a faithful representation of these remains.   This would appear to be the bridge destroyed by the Jews when Pompey besieged the temple of Jerusalem in 64 B.C.[2]   Above these accurately jointed and

---

[1] The remains to which we are about to call the attention of our readers—copies of which M. de Saulcy has collected and described—were not discovered by him, for they had been known for some time.   But the honour is truly due to him of having discovered their probable date.

[2] " And without further delay (the party of Aristobulus) occupied the temple, broke down the bridge which connected it with the city, and resolved to defend themselves there. The others received Pompey and placed in his power the city and the royal palace " (with which this bridge formed a communication).—Flavius Josephus, *History of the Jews*, Book xiv. ch. viii.

shaped blocks of stone are apparent, at B, the restorations of the time of Herod—admitted to be so by M. de Saulcy,—and at C some walling of the Middle Ages. Without proposing to enter into the discussions raised concerning the date of these constructions, I shall confine myself to stating what any one may verify. In the first place, the enormous blocks composing this platform, consist of the jurassic limestone of the country, which is very hard and durable ; and taking into account the mildness of the climate, it must be admitted that between the date of the setting of these blocks and our own century a very consider-

Fig. 10.—Remains of Arch, Platform of Solomon's Temple.

able period must have intervened to allow of limestone of this kind to have decayed, or rather for its softer beds to have perished, as shown in the annexed figure. Moreover, the construction B is evidently Roman, and the walling, built of stone identically the same as that of the arch, is perfectly sound : consequently between the date of the construction B and that of the work beneath, several centuries must have elapsed. And lastly, these blocks are not hewn conformably with the method in use under the Empire ; the faces are coarsely dressed, and around the beds and joints may be observed a wide chiselling like that which is found on the few remains of Phœnician masonry. The beds and joints are beautifully dressed, perfectly true and without mortar. "Titus," says Josephus (Book vi. ch. xlii.), "having entered (the city of Jerusalem, after the siege) admired the fortifications among other things, and could not repress his astonishment at beholding the strength and beauty of those towers which the tyrants had the imprudence to abandon. After having attentively considered the height and breadth, and the extraordinary size of the stones, and with what art they had been fitted together, he exclaimed : 'God has indeed fought on our side !'"

If this arch and the walls that serve for its abutments do not date from the primitive construction undertaken by Solomon, and carried on during several centuries after him,[1] it must be admitted that they belong to the restoration or reconstruction undertaken by Herod under Augustus. But in that case what date can be assigned to the Roman work whose remains are seen at B ? It is plain that these latter works must have been executed by some one ; but it does not appear that between the reign of Herod and the siege by Titus the temple was either rebuilt or restored from its foundations ; and after the time of Titus the Romans do not appear to have done anything to the temple of Jerusalem. That these blocks were laid in Solomon's time there is no positive proof ; but that they are of a date anterior to the Roman rule cannot reasonably be doubted ; and this is all I wish to establish. I am well aware that in Syria— at Baalbec, for example—are found remains built with huge blocks, and that these works are attributed to the Romans ; and in accordance with this hypothesis it has been concluded that the Romans sometimes employed these unwonted methods, and that they might therefore have been the constructors of the enclosure of the temple of Jerusalem. This reasoning rests on imperfect observation. The basements of the temple of Baalbec belong to an edifice anterior to the temple built under Hadrian.

---

[1] This is what the historian Flavius Josephus says about the basement walls of the temple of Jerusalem. He remarks that they were successively extended. Solomon built only the retaining wall towards the east. "But in process of time, as the people continued to bring earth in order still to widen this space, the summit of the hill was considerably enlarged. Then the wall which was on the northern side was pulled down, and a still further space was enclosed as large as that covered by the temple. . . . To give an idea of the magnitude of this undertaking, not to speak of the perimeter on the top, the basement walls of the temple were raised to a height of three hundred cubits, and in some places more ; but the enormous cost of these foundations was not apparent, because the valleys having since been filled up, their level had been raised to that of the narrow streets of the city : the stones employed for these basements were forty cubits in length. . . ."—*War of the Jews against the Romans,* Book v. ch. xiv. In fact the blocks of this basement, which still rises to a great height above accumulations of considerable depth, are of extraordinary dimensions ; the wall-stones average 5 feet 4 inches in height, and from 16 to 24 feet in length, sometimes more.

These primitive constructions are not disposed as regards the aspect in the same manner as the Roman temple ; and in the

Fig. 10 *bis.*—Masonry of the Platform of Solomon's Temple.

subterranean chambers the junction of the Roman construction with the primitive basement built like that of the temple of

Jerusalem of enormous blocks, is plainly visible. These primitive vaults are arched, and the Roman barrel-vaults are built above them. The arch of Solomon's Bridge may therefore belong to the Phœnician epoch.

But it may be objected that to base an entire theory upon a fragment of such slight importance—two or three courses of stones, huge, it is true, being all the data—is at least hazardous. It may be so. These fragments, however, are not the whole of the data; almost the entire base of the platform, and a part of the enclosure of the temple of Jerusalem still exist; and at some points these remains are of great height. Here (fig. 10 *bis*) is the southern face of the south-east corner of this enormous basement. Does this look like a work of the time of Herod the Great—of a king who was devoted to the Empire, who had such constant relations with the Romans, who built the city of Cæsarea dedicated to Augustus, who contributed from his own resources to the erection of the city of Nicopolis built by that Emperor, who had himself visited Rome, and who maintained ambassadors there? Do we not, on the contrary, find in this basement the traces of an altogether primitive art? Does not the setting back of the layers (*battering*), in conformity with the method pursued by all primitive nations, indicate a very high antiquity? This gigantic masonry, these projecting ledges, and —I repeat it—the perished beds of these blocks, are not they proof of an age long anterior to the time of Herod? But if this corner is of the age of Solomon, or his immediate successors, the arch, a view of which has been given (fig. 10), is likewise of that age; for the appearance of the stones, and the manner in which they are hewn and laid, is the same in this arch as in the other most ancient portions of the platform of the temple.

Are not the Etruscans, like the Carthaginians, with whom they had evident relations, the vestiges of a Phœnician colony, from whom the Romans of the Republic derived their earliest notions of the art of building?

But in the basement walls of the platform of the temple we see only masonry, without any appearance of sculpture; and if this masonry belongs to a very remote period, as proved by the colossal dimensions of the blocks, the manner in which they are hewn, and their jointing, which presents frequent *décrochements* (notchings),[1] there is here nothing indicating a distinctive art.

---

[1] It should be remarked that all primitive masonry is cyclopean, namely, composed of irregularly-shaped blocks, laid in the form in which the quarry furnished them by means of a bevel—or *decrochés*. It is cyclopean when the stone can only be extracted in pieces, whose faces are not parallel. But in countries like Judæa, where calcareous stone is found in parallel layers in the quarry, it is clear that the builder employed stone in the form in which nature provided it. These layers, however, are of unequal thickness, and, in order to build with them, it was frequently necessary to notch the beds, or else to thin many of

There exist, however, near Jerusalem, a considerable number of tombs hewn in the jurassic limestone, which covers a great part of Palestine.   M. de Saulcy maintains that these tombs date from the times of the kings; his opponents assign them a much more recent date.   But first, the Romans under the Empire were not in the habit of hewing their tombs in the living rock; secondly, even in the time of Constantine, tradition, which should always be consulted, referred them to the Judæan epoch; and thirdly, the style of the architecture of these *hypogæa* is foreign to Roman Art.   Among these tombs let us take as an example one of the most important,—one which, in certain architectural

Fig. 11.—Tomb of the Kings, Jerusalem.

forms, and even in certain mouldings, most nearly resembles Roman Art under the Empire—the Tomb of the Kings (fig. 11). The two pillars left in the solid which existed at A are destroyed. We have here, it is true, the triglyphs of the Greek Doric order; but who has proved that the Greeks did not originally derive this feature from the Phœnicians or the Jews?   As to these palms, garlands, disks, grapes, and especially this large bordering under the architrave, and which returns at right angles at the corners, they are ornaments which are neither Greek, nor Assyrian, nor Roman.   A detailed examination of the sculpture, even more than the *ensemble* of the monument, will suggest the

the blocks, a proceeding not adopted by primitive builders.   We can, therefore, merely by seeing a piece of masonry, always tell whether it belongs to a primitive civilisation or to a civilisation advanced in the practice of the arts and the crafts.

idea of an original art. Observe (fig. 12) this portion of frieze, these triple palms, the angular manner in which they are carved ;

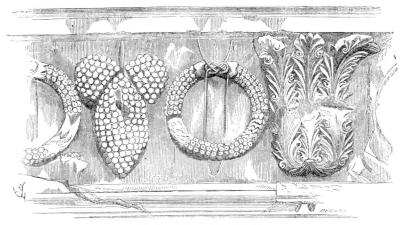

Fig. 12.—Portion of Frieze, Tomb of the Kings.

these bunches of grapes, these garlands suspended from knotted cords. See again (fig. 13) these fragments of the bordering formed of olive and vine leaves. Neither the Greeks nor the

Fig. 13.—Portions of Bordering, Tomb of the Kings.

Romans—most certainly not the Romans of the debased period —ever produced sculpture of this style. Is another example required, possessing a more original character ? Here (fig. 14) is a portion of the tympanum surmounting the opening of the Tomb of the Judges, likewise hewn in the rock. If there exist anywhere sculptured ornaments having any affinity with these, it is evidently the Byzantine sculpture of the fourth, fifth, and sixth centuries. Will it be asserted that these hypogæa date from that era? But in that case, for whom and by whom were they made? And if it be granted that they are anterior to the fourth century, were they even regarded as not earlier than the Herodian period, is it not evident that the Byzantine Greeks borrowed largely from this school of art? In these sculptures—and it is a fact to be noted—we observe the entire absence of any representations of human beings or of animals; on all the tombs we find the same *style of work*—an execution sharp, exact, flat, undercut, full of character, and at the same time presenting a delicacy of modelling, a finish, a *primitive*

Fig. 14.—Part of Tympanum, Tomb of the Judges.

chiselling, shall I call it?—characteristics, in fact, the very reverse of those which distinguish the sculpture of the Lower Empire, which is weak, heavy, projecting, and monotonous, absolutely devoid of style, and clearly denoting a worn-out art degraded to a trade. I address myself to artists; and it seems to me that to them at least the primitive character of the sculpture in question cannot be doubtful.

But we will suppose that these tombs date from the Roman period—that they are of the time of Herod the Great—an hypothesis for which some show of proof might be adduced, since, when speaking of the rebuilding of the Temple by that prince, Josephus in his *Ancient History of the Jews* (Book XI. chap. 14) says, "The architecture of the porticoes (of the Temple) was very similar to the rest; stretched above were to be seen hangings of divers colours enriched with flowers of purple, with columns between two, from the cornices of which hung vine branches of gold, with *their bunches and their grapes*, so admirably wrought that the art in these works was in nowise inferior to the material." Herod had employed Asiatic artists to build his temple; and they possessed a traditionary art of their own, in which there was no Roman element. Moreover, Josephus is very careful to let us know how very jealous the Jews were of their nationality; how impatient they were of foreign influence; and Herod, who was anxious to preserve his popularity,—warned by the injurious results of his attempt to introduce Roman fêtes and usages into Judæa,—would have been very careful not to introduce a foreign style of art in the building of the Temple. If the tombs at Jerusalem were of the time of Herod, they would none the less preserve the evident stamp of a local art; and that is all we postulate.

Let us however follow the chronological classification dictated by tradition, and examine next the works attributed to Herod the Great. It is known that Herod restored the temple, and even in great part rebuilt it. Subsequently to him nothing more was done to this building till its destruction by the army of Titus. By Titus the city was razed to the ground, except two towers; he rendered it a solitude, and it was not till the time of Hadrian that the Jewish city was re-peopled, though it never entirely emerged from its ruins. We can well imagine that however great may be the ardour of the destroyer of cities, they may well be discouraged when walls have to be thrown down such as those of which I have presented portions (figs. 10 and 10 *bis*). The prophecy, "There shall not be left one stone upon another," was difficult of accomplishment by the hand of man. There exist not only considerable remains of the platform and of the original enclosure of the temple, but also portions of sculpture; and at some points of the enclosure are plainly discernible the remains of works of later date than the gigantic masonry of which illustrations have been given above; and these remains in point of structure resemble Roman work; they cannot however be of any other period than that of Herod. It is fortunate for the history of art that of this enclosure there remains a gate decorated with sculptures; and although this sculpture and the architectural forms denote an art very much more developed than that of the tombs of the Valley of Jehosaphat, it nevertheless bears the imprint of that original art whose existence it is of such importance to prove. I give (fig. 15), also from photographs, a view of this fragment of the gate (blocked up subsequently to its erection, probably during the Middle Ages) of the temple enclosure, which can only be attributed to Herod. Here

GATE OF THE ENCLOSURE OF THE TEMPLE, JERUSALEM.

THE GOLDEN GATE, JERUSALEM.

again the ornamentation and the architectural features are of a character foreign to the Roman Art of later times,—a finely wrought arch, enriched with extremely delicate sculptures, is set in front of a lintel, which is relieved by a second arch. It will be observed that the lintel, like the blocks of the platform of the temple, presents a very wide chiselling and a projecting ledge. The faces, however, are well dressed, and the stones laid close-jointed without mortar. If these sculptures are of the time of Herod (which their position seems to compel us to infer), the celebrated *Golden Gate* is evidently of the same period ; for its sculpture is identical with that of the gate of the temple enclosure, which I have just given. M. de Saulcy has no hesitation in regarding the Golden Gate as one of the works of Herod. The construction of the jambs is quite Roman, the two arches which close it are slightly segmental, and the sculpture is most exquisitely treated ; preserving that Judaic character whose importance I just now endeavoured to establish. Here (fig. 16) is a detail of this sculpture. The acanthus palms of the capital, with their heads abruptly turning over, exhibit a firmness and vigour of execution which is altogether unlike the sculpture of the period of the Lower Empire. The capitals of the jambs are not surmounted by an entablature ; but the arches spring from the abacus, as in the gate of the temple enclosure. The ornamentation is undercut, sharp and delicate, and has a remarkable likeness—though of a more vigorous character—to the Byzantine ornament which is to be found in the capitals of St. Sophia and in a variety of objects fabricated between the sixth and twelfth centuries at Constantinople—such as diptychs, manuscript covers, ivory, boxes, etc. Now, are we going too far in saying that the Greeks, disgusted by the decline into which Art had fallen at the close of the Roman Empire, finding themselves in habitual contact with the inhabitants of Syria, and unable to revert to their ancient Art—for the Greeks never retrograded—took these, to them novel elements, and withdrawing themselves from the Western World, where they were not understood, set themselves to form a new Art out of that of Asia, viz., Byzantine Art. The character of the sculpture and the manner in which it is treated make this evident to me ; but I must endeavour to enable my readers to share this conviction. Those last fragments just given must be either of the time of Herod the Great, of Hadrian, or Constantine. Although Roman Art of the time of Hadrian was tending to approach ancient Greek types, that effort was limited to perfecting the execution without a modification of the general character of the architecture. Even in Jerusalem there exist remains of Roman architecture of the time of Hadrian, such, for example, as the fountain known as *St. Philip's;* and these remains are as Roman in their details and general design as the edifices of Rome itself. Would any one venture to maintain that these gates and the tombs hewn in the rock (for these are certainly the productions of the same art) are of the time of St. Helena? But we know what Roman Art was under Constantine; it had reached the last stage of debasement, as regards execution: if therefore the architecture of Constantine in Syria excelled that which was to be found in the West at the same epoch, it was because there existed in Syria at that time a genuine school of architecture, and our argument in favour of the influence of the arts of Syria on the works of the Greeks is valid.

The Greeks became ardent converts to Christianity, and naturally so, for it had been presaged by their philosophers. They were the first therefore to betake themselves to the land which had been the cradle of the new religion,—an easy matter to them moreover, as the country was a neighbouring one. When Christianity began to overspread the territory of ancient Greece, intercourse with Palestine became frequent and necessary; and considering the versatile spirit of the Greeks, it was also natural that they should seek the elements of a new art in those places which had witnessed the birth of the new religion. Psychological considerations therefore combine with the investigation of monumental remains, to render it probable that Byzantine Art derived some of its decorative constituents from Palestine. I am aware of the prejudices that oppose this hypothesis: we have none of us forgotten the opinions of Voltaire respecting the Jewish people: but Voltaire had no conception of the nature and value of the primitive arts of Syria; and I suggest that his very persistence in endeavouring to depreciate that people and the wit he employs in making it ridiculous, should put us on our guard against his views on the question. One does not take so much pains to destroy that which has no veritable basis; and the warmth of Voltaire's attack on this inconsiderable Jewish people is an indication of its real importance.

The Greeks always had the faculty of quickly assimilating the elements they derived from others. They were always magnificent pirates, casting all they took—whether things or ideas—into their melting-pot, to transform them into a Greek product, and exhibit them as such to the astonished world, which was then no longer able to refer them to their origin. How many more or less ingenious suppositions have there not been made as to the origin of ancient Greek and even of Byzantine Art, though the latter is much less distantly remote from us and is more easy to analyse! How many hypotheses have been suggested since archæology became a science! I do not assume to have indicated, as if it were its exclusive source, the origin of

that Byzantine Art in the few lines above written ; I limit myself to mentioning facts.   From the day when the Romans had
stifled Greece beneath their powerful hand, Greek Art became a
trade ; it was Roman Art that was introduced into Greece as
everywhere else : that the buildings erected after that epoch
were in a higher style of execution than those erected in Italy,
Gaul, Spain, and Germany, is indisputable ; but still they were
Roman buildings : and this is so evident even to persons least
acquainted with architecture, that in Attica, for instance, whatever the purity of the execution of edifices built since the era of
Roman domination, the gaze is involuntarily withdrawn from
these edifices which would excite admiration eveywhere else.
From that time, I say, until Constantinople became the seat of
the Empire, there is no longer any vestige of Greek Art ; if anything was accomplished it was in obscurity : then, all at once, at
Byzantium the arts of architecture, sculpture, and painting are
seen taking a fresh start, clothing themselves in new forms,
developing new principles, and assuming a decided character.
But the Greeks must evidently have derived these new elements
from some quarter ; and the only monuments that present—in
their decorative principles at least—striking analogies with this
Byzantine Art are to be found in Palestine on that ancient
Jewish soil.   The monuments, whatever opinions may be entertained respecting them, are anterior to Byzantine Art, properly
so called, and during the last three centuries of the Empire the
Greeks ; formerly at war with the Asiatics, had friendly relations
with them.   The inference is readily suggested.   But even
granting that these monuments in Judæa are of the later Roman
period, they bear no resemblance to the Roman Architecture
of the Lower Empire, either in general design or in the
details of the sculpture : so that, supposing them to be of a date
posterior to Herod the Great, that is to say, the period of
Augustus, the influence of a local art is perceptible ; and for this
influence to have left traces, we must admit the existence of an
anterior art.   Thus we are turning in the same circle, and are
obliged to acknowledge that in Syria, dating from the Phœnician-
Judaic epoch, there was a native art which was neither that of
the Assyrians or Persians, nor the original art of the Greeks.
Under the Empire we find, it is true, some traces of this
influence in the Roman buildings ; but it must not be forgotten
that from the time of Augustus the Romans were constantly
extending their dominions eastwards.   Though Roman architecture at Balbec, Palmyra, and on Syrian soil exhibits traces of that
art which I consider indigenous, the structure and decoration
remain Roman in point of execution ; the mouldings are covered
with ornament, but this ornament is invariably Roman : Byzan-

tine Art proper could not originate in this art which was manifesting decline: for a renaissance is never based on degenerate types; on the contrary, it can only secure a long career by reverting to primitive types. I would not assert that the Greeks found the elements—new to them—of Byzantine Art, in Judæa alone. Possibly the whole of Asia lent its contingent : all I wish to prove is this, that Byzantine Art bears no resemblance to Greek Art, that it infused novel principles into Western Roman architecture, and that some of those principles are to be found conspicuously written on ancient Jewish soil.

Let us now examine what those new principles are. The Greeks, who in the times of classic antiquity had invented the orders, or had at least reduced them to their proper proportions, seeing how the Romans had used and abused their conceptions, gave up the orders. They had recourse to other principles ; the orders, which were only adapted to the trabeated system, could not, in the view of the Greeks, continue to be used after the introduction of the arch into architecture. They only employed the lintel, when they did employ it, beneath the arch. The columns exchanged their regulative character as dictating the form of the building, for the subordinate function of vertical supports for the arcades,—of rigid monoliths carrying arches pierced in thin walls. They often employed the detached pilaster instead of the column, as may be seen at St. Sophia's, in Constantinople, in the great lateral openings.[1]

The greatly projecting mouldings of the cornices of the Greek and Roman orders were completely abandoned and were replaced by string-courses and mouldings in low relief ; the greatly projecting mouldings being thenceforth confined only to the crowning of the edifices. The use of the orders being discontinued, the proportion of the columns as well as that of the capitals became arbitrary. Carrying the principles of Roman construction to their ultimate consequences, the Byzantine Greeks came to regard the *walls* only as screens,—as enclosures or partitions. The structure consisted solely in the vaultings reciprocally counterthrusting and concentrating their pressures on certain isolated points and piers supporting these vaultings. This kind of construction is very frankly developed in the great church of St. Sophia. Byzantine Art is not, therefore, as sometimes asserted, a result of Roman Arts in their decline ; it is an art which carried the principles of Roman construction to their utmost limits, which laid aside the decorative borrowings of the Romans and gathered fresh ones more truthful and more con-

[1] See for example the two pilasters standing outside the Church of St. Mark, at Venice, on the side of the Piazzetta, and which tradition reports to have been brought from St. Jean d'Acre. These pilasters appear to belong to the early Byzantine period ; they are covered on their faces with wreaths.

sonant with the principles of that structure, and which applied them with Greek intelligence. It is an art not in its decline, but, on the contrary, rejuvenescent,—rendered capable of entering on a long career of excellence and of becoming the parent of principles hitherto unknown.

I have said that the Nestorians, after the condemnation of their leader, took refuge in Syria, in Persia, and Egypt; their sect spread itself abroad in Asia and carried with them the principles of Byzantine renaissance and certain elements of art peculiar to them. The Virgin, in their view, was only the mother of Christ, not the mother of God. They recognised in Jesus Christ two natures; one divine, the other human. The tendency of this heresy in its bearing on works of art was towards the honouring of God, not by the representation of the body which he had assumed, but by the representation of his works. The Arabs, who appropriated the arts imported by the Nestorians, carried this doctrine still further and maintained that no animated beings of any kind ought to be portrayed, either in sculpture or painting. Thus limited, Art was constrained to seek its ornamentation in floral forms, in organic objects, or geometrical combinations. Among the Arabs, therefore, the study of geometry became the principal element, not only of the architectural structure, but also of its embellishment. Thus Greek Art, transplanted by the Nestorians, was departing as far as possible from ancient Greek Art in point of form, as it was also departing from it in its principles.

When therefore in the time of Charlemagne, the West was beginning to cultivate the arts, three principles presented themselves from which it might select the elements needed. It had in its midst the vestiges of Roman Art; it borrowed all it could from Byzantine Art, and was affected by the influences of Arab Art, to the extent of its connection with Spain, Syria, and the coasts of Africa.

Latin in virtue of its ancient traditions, Gaul[1] was scarcely such in its essential characteristics, as I remarked above. It was attracted by the Byzantine types of Art, and was feeling itself drawn towards the study of the mathematical sciences cultivated by the Arabs. As early as the tenth century its architecture was already manifesting tendencies very superior to

---

[1] If I should appear, especially to our neighbours on the other side the Rhine, to give an exaggerated importance to Gaul, it is because I am desirous of tracing—as far as data will allow—that people which in the West seems in remote times to have already presented a marked national character. Tacitus, in his book *De Moribus Germanorum*, chap. xxvii., thus expresses himself:—" Julius Cæsar, whose authority carries such weight, says that the Gauls were formerly more powerful than the Germans (*Validiores olim Gallorum res fuisse, summus autorum, C. Julius tradit*);" we might thence infer that the Gauls had formerly passed into Germany. Certainly the Germans have largely indemnified themselves for this.

the practical means at its command. Barbarism is still traceable in the execution, but it no longer appears in the conceptions. We perceive the effort of very advanced artists, but it is seconded

Fig. 17.—Column employed as a Buttress, Church of St. Remy, Rheims.

only by rough unskilful workmen. The principles were already developed, and they differed completely from those of classic Greek architecture, and those of Roman architecture under the

Empire. Thus the Greeks only employed the lintel on vertical points of support. The vault dictated the Roman structure, and the orders remained independent of that structure. The Byzantines had made a step in advance; they had endeavoured to give the orders, or rather the columns, a real and useful function in their vaulted buildings; with them, however, the columns remained in the condition of accessory members—as supports for screen-work in a structure still altogether Roman. The Westerns, at the time when Romanesque architecture began to develop itself, made the column an integral part of the structure of their buildings,—an indispensable member; but then they were compelled to cease to regard the proportions of the classic column. They no longer treated the column otherwise than as a vertical support to which they might give an indefinite number of modules, according to its function. This was a breach of conformity with the classic mode; but is there only one mode in the world from which we may never deviate under penalty of falling into barbarism?

We have seen how the Romans superimposed the engaged columns in edifices consisting of several stories, and how in that case, if the column performed the function of a buttress, such a strengthening was rendered useless by the weight of the overhanging entablature. As early as the tenth century (perhaps before this epoch) we see the architects of the West suppressing the intermediate entablatures of these superimposed orders, and of two, three, or four columns placed by the Romans, one above the other, making up one pile of shafts or a single column or cylindrical buttress, with only one capital, and an entablature at the summit of the building. When there are several stories, they are indicated by string-courses between the columns; and the latter indefinitely lengthened or set back at each story, rise from the ground (fig. 17).[1] Here we have a new principle, the result of sound reasoning. We have already seen how among the ancient Greeks, when two orders were superimposed, the upper order was only the prolongation of the under columns; as, for example, in the temple of Neptune at Pæstum, in the temple of Ceres at Eleusis, etc. (fig. 18). The Greeks, therefore, had felt that two orders superimposed should form a whole; that there should be a perfect connection between them; that they should be and appear to be only two stories of the same building, and not two superimposed buildings. The architects of the Romanesque period were unacquainted with the architecture of ancient Greece; they were familiar only with Roman or Byzantine Art; but starting from the point at which they found themselves, they reasoned as the Greeks did, and were unwilling that several

---

[1] Ancient part of the Church of St. Remy, at Rheims.

stories of a building should simulate two, three, or four buildings, one on the top of the other. They thus did away with the Roman orders; but they reasoned aright. The whole question, therefore, resolves itself into this : Whether the conclusions resulting from right reasoning equal in value an ordonnance resting on a basis of false reasoning. With the help of the ancient art, whose remains they possessed, and by recourse to Byzantine Art, the western peoples originated principles of their own ; and if they were in uncertainty as regarded the selections of forms during the Romanesque period, they showed no indecision in the principles deduced from an increasingly rigorous course of reasoning. For barbarians, this was not a bad beginning.

The architects of the West were no longer able to build with materials of large dimensions ; they had not the means either of

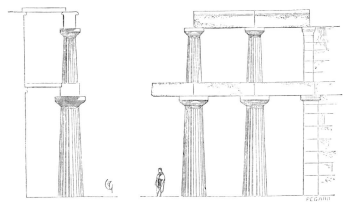

Fig. 18.—Example of Superimposed Column, Temple of Ceres, Eleusis.

transporting or raising them. Moreover, the Romans had bequeathed to them vast edifices, built of very small courses of rubble and of brick ; but we have seen that the Roman structure was always a naked body, clothed subsequently with marble, stucco, or worked stone, and decorated with monolithic columns. The Romanesque architects frankly determined to abandon the distinction between the body and the dress. The construction itself was to become the architecture ; the necessities of that construction were to dictate the form. For example, the Romanesque architect proposes to erect a nave with two aisles, in the style of the basilica ; he is unable to erect columns of single stones to carry the nave walls, so he does not trouble himself about giving these columns or pillars, which he will be compelled to build with low courses, the proportions of the Roman column. He will make square or round columns, of short and massive character (fig. 19) ;[1] or, on the other hand, if he wishes to dissimulate

Fig. 19.—Romanesque Nave Arcade.

the heavy appearance of these supports, he will form a clustered column (fig. 20).[2] But he will soon propose to vault the aisles, retaining the timber roof over the nave. He is aware that lateral vaulting will tend to thrust the pillars inwards; that these pillars must consequently be very strong. Then (fig. 21) he forms a square pillar to which he attaches an engaged column A to carry the cross arch of the aisle vaulting, and two other columns of the same height B to carry the archivolts supporting the longitudinal wall; next, as an interior buttress, and to receive the roof principal, a fourth column C which rises from the ground to the top of the wall. Here he still reasons most justly, though he disregards the proportions of the ancient orders. Meanwhile he will copy, with various degrees of success, Roman or Byzantine capitals or capitals composed with Byzantine ornament.

The Romanesque architects had lost the tradition of those excellent Roman mortars which enabled builders to form a masonry as homogeneous as a block of concrete; they did not know how to make hydraulic limes, and they built on eminences generally at a distance from the great water-courses that furnished good sand; they felt that they could not depend on the cohesion of the inferior mortars they were using; and they compensated for this defect, resulting from deficiency in material

[1] Church at Vignory, Church of St. Etienne at Beauvais, Church at Turnus, etc.
[2] From the nave of the Church of St. Remy at Rheims, tenth century.

resources, by combinations of masonry which were rigid or elastic as the case required. To quote an example of the difference

Fig. 20.—Romanesque Clustered Column.

thence resulting :—the Romans did not hesitate to build a wall on two arches whose extrados met at the springing, because

(fig. 22) the whole combination A B C, although consisting of
sloping beds, formed one compact mass by reason of the perfect
cohesion of the mortar ; but if this mortar was only slightly

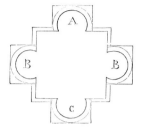

Fig. 21.—Section of Romanesque Nave Pier.

cohesive, the wall would evidently slip on the extrados E F, and
would only rest on an acute angle F.   Accordingly the Romanesque architect designed his pillars as I have just described, and

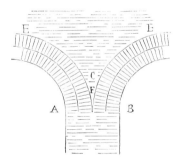

Fig. 22.—Springing of the Arches on a Roman Pier.

(fig. 23) resting the two arches A on the two spreading capitals
B, he leaves between the extrados of these two arches the
entire piece C, which he strengthens by an engaged column.
By this means the arches become independent of the pier which
rises from the ground in courses whose beds are horizontal.   It
will be objected that this is not architecture but construction :
we have in fact reached that period in the art when the construction and the architecture cannot any longer be regarded
apart ; when architecture is only a construction combined in such
a manner as to satisfy material wants, while at the same time it
necessarily pleases the sight by the well-balanced assemblage of
materials fashioned and placed exactly in accordance with the
required forms and dimensions.   It was when Western genius
subjected itself to this principle that it manifested its veritable

tendencies and its essential excellencies ; for then its borrowings from previous schools of art became fewer and fewer, it drew everything from itself ;—constructive system, general arrangements, harmony of proportions, mouldings, sculptured or painted ornament, architectural statuary. I shall certainly not make this independence a ground of reproach against the masters of the Middle Ages.

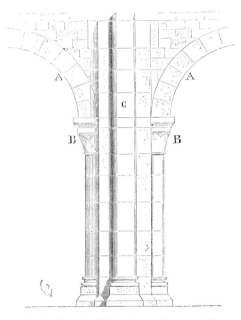

Fig. 23.—Springing of the Arches on a Romanesque Pier.

In my opinion, it may be said respecting any nation : " Show me its architecture, and I shall be able to appreciate it at its true worth." Until the most recent times there have existed, between the peculiar genius of nations and their architecture, relations so intimate that the intellectual and moral history of those nations might be deduced from a study of their buildings ; and as in these Lectures I have imposed upon myself the obligation never to advance an opinion without adducing the facts on which it is based, I may be allowed to justify this assertion. We have already observed how faithfully the arts of the Ancient Greeks and Romans reflected the genius of the respective nations. During the period in which the barbarian peoples were engaged in violent conflict, the traditions of the West lost their original character ; but we do not find these barbarians contributing any new æsthetic element. When, however, the violence of this ferment had subsided, the nationalities gradually regained coherence; their indelible character reasserted itself after the mêlée ; and it was not till then that architecture began to be developed among them. In Gaul it was the monasteries that devoted themselves to this art, and stamped it with their own character. But in the eleventh century the monasteries were not what they subsequently became,—assemblages of men forming themselves into isolated corporations in the midst of a regularly organised community, living luxuriously and uselessly on estates that had been given them or which they had gradually acquired. The monasteries of that day were, on the contrary, asylums in which men disgusted with anarchy, fleeing from turbulence, anxious to escape the tyranny of brute force, and to find tranquillity and repose, could take refuge with a view to work ; secluded from a world in which anarchy and abuse prevailed both in the upper and lower classes of society. The monastic orders of that period consisted of those who were eager to escape from barbarism ; accordingly they were recruited quite as much from among the nobler and wealthy class as from those in humbler station. These men therefore formed a regular government in the midst of a society incapable of governing itself; and such institutions were as useful, even necessary, in times when every principle of authority and discipline was disregarded, as they would be injurious, and even dangerous, in the midst of a well-regulated and well-governed society. These incorporated bodies collected together the remains of ancient architecture, put themselves in communication with distant nations, and drawing illumination from those which had preserved the benefits of civilisation, imparted it to those which were still plunged in darkness.

We find their architecture strictly in accordance with the part they played. In less than a century—the period intervening between the tenth and eleventh—it developed itself so as to be able to fulfil this part ;—it was unpretending in principle and means of execution, yet it was a fit embodiment for the splendid ambition of those who, at the time of the Reform of Cluny, aimed at nothing short of governing the world. This monastic Romanesque architecture proves itself a distinctive and genuine art, by preserving its identity of feature in the poorest chapel —in the monastic dependency buried in the depths of a desert as decidedly as in the immense and magnificent basilica of Cluny ; an architecture capable of producing edifices on the grandest and the humblest scale, with the same methods ; an architecture whose characteristic is the combination of small resources,—

in this resembling the religious corporation with whom it originated. Meanwhile the feudal fortress preserved the traditions of Ancient Roman construction, because it was erected in the same manner, *i.e.* by means of forced labour or requisitions. Even as early as the close of the eleventh century, we find the monks, then at the summit of power, indulging the ambition to make a display; sacrificing to luxury, though without changing their architectural methods. Their magnificent edifices were frequently constructed in haste, and carelessly; while the lay nobility—who up to that time did not make a point of displaying their riches, but who thought only of protecting themselves with walls—built substantially, and were not seduced by the love of luxury which gained possession of the monasteries. Saint Bernard, perceiving the danger, undertook his reform of Citeaux; and this movement had an immediate effect on the architecture of the buildings belonging to that monastic order. While we detect among the Clunisians of the twelfth century amid the Romanesque severity of outline a decided penchant for rich effects, an indulgence of fancy in the forms adopted, a marked refinement in sculpture, accompanied by a deterioration in point of substantiality of execution, we observe among the Cistercians, on the contrary, the marks of a severe rule; we see in their manner of constructing, care, regularity, inflexible formulas,—nothing superfluous, nothing but the fulfilment of the material requirements, but these provided for in such a way as we might expect from those who had no other aim than the performance of duty. The remains of Cistercian architecture present building and building only, but well and solidly constructed; they may be recognised at first sight from this character alone. During the Romanesque period, then, we observe various and distinct architectural expressions just as in the political life of those times we find various societies moving parallel to each other, but not one consolidated social unity. There was an architecture of the Black Friars, an architecture of the White Friars, and there was feudal architecture; but there was not an architecture distinctive of the period, because there was no national unity; yet each of these systems of architecture was a distinct expression of the manners, tastes, habits, and tendencies of those with whom they originated.

It was not until the end of the twelfth century that the spirit of nationality began to make itself felt, as the result of efforts more or less successful to secure the enfranchisement of the communes, of the scholastic discussions, the study of ancient philosophy, and the progress of monarchical power. The Encyclopædic spirit, and the application of the exact sciences engaged the attention of enlightened men; and the influence of the monks then disappeared for ever from the history of art.

Architecture fell into the hands of laymen ; and in the course of a few years it abandoned the Romanesque traditions, not only in respect to structure and material execution, but even in sculpture —rejecting what belonged to Byzantine or Ancient Art : it was invariably to the flora of the fields and woods that it had recourse for its decorative subjects. In its statuary it made a point of imitating nature, and abandoned those hieratic types derived from the East, which the monastic schools had so scrupulously preserved. Then, in all the cities of the royal domain, was formed a nucleus of artists truly national, whose emulation induced such a rapid development of the new art, that the same generation witnessed its birth and its maturity. The architecture of the beginning of the thirteenth century is the purest and most exact reflection of the ideas of the nation at that epoch. The desire for political consolidation and union, the tendency to investigation, to the acquirement of knowledge, and to the immediate practical application of what had been acquired, and the reaction against religious corporations were distinctly expressed by that architecture : men reasoned on every question that presented itself ; they examined everything ; they had a firm belief in the progress of science, and exhibited a daring boldness without pausing a single day in their rapid career. In this general movement individualities soon disappeared, and architecture assumed the form of a science. We must not forget that architecture was then cultivated only by laymen belonging to the common people, having under them guilds of craftsmen. It would seem that the middle class of society, amidst powers at war with each other, felt the necessity of association, of organising itself on principles proper to itself, which should render it, so to speak, independent of the past, and allow it to follow an entirely new path. This class of artists and craftsmen, not being able to claim political rights, and not hoping to rival the power of the feudal noblesse, strove for enfranchisement by work ; they made architecture a kind of freemasonry, to which initiation was requisite—an initiation that was constantly made more difficult : this middle class felt that they possessed no material vantage-ground,—that study and the practice of the arts could alone secure them a moral independence : they devoted themselves passionately to that study ; they made the means of execution complicated and subtle, in order to remain masters of the art, and to limit the secular and clerical noblesse to the services of the initiated alone. To believe that the architectural art of the thirteenth century— the architecture called *Gothic*—was an art not closely connected with the state of society of that period, is to misunderstand altogether the national spirit of these times. For the rise of that architecture was but the awakening of the ancient Gallic

spirit : a spirit which pursued an idea with passionate enthusiasm; which, while constantly aiming at independence, was secretly
concentrating the forces necessary to secure it; which could
deliberately and persistently wait its opportunity,—notwithstanding all that may be said of its levity,—and which forced a
way to light and liberty through every available issue.   Gothic
Architecture, at its commencement, was a protest against monastic
influence ; it was the first and most vigorous reaction of knowledge, examination, and inquiry into facts against tradition.   Its
monuments, whose principles of construction were entirely novel,
and whose decorative elements had ceased to be traditionary—
its monuments, I say, are before our eyes ; their stones speak ;
they do not express "suffering," as we were recently told by the
Académie des Beaux Arts, but, on the contrary, enfranchised
labour,—the triumph of an intellect which feels its power, which
acts, which is asserting its independence, while ironically concealing its secrets from blind or indifferent masters, and which
is conscious that it will one day become in its turn the ruling
power.   Developing itself with incredible rapidity, and arriving
at its culmination half a century from its commencement, this
art, as soon as it was recognised as dominant, exaggerated the
expression of its own principles ; it followed out rigorously a
logical process that led to abuse : but from the thirteenth to the
fifteenth century it did not deviate one moment from the courses
it first entered upon ; it brought its practical appliances to a
perfection, such as no art at any time had achieved : as regards
structure it arrived at a formula ; in decoration at a servile and
ultimately *outré* imitation of nature : it carried realism to such
an extent as to adopt ugliness in statuary—studied ugliness—as
a type of humanity.   The execution, however, did not decline,
as it did in Roman art : there was exaggeration and abuse, but
not decadence.   So that when, in the sixteenth century, there
was a desire to return to the imitation of Classic architecture,
skilful workmen, capable and well-instructed architects, were to
be found, versed in all the resources of their art.

But what do we observe in Italy during this period, comprised between the thirteenth and the fifteenth century ?   At
first great indecision ; an art or rather arts which are making
their first essays and are subjected to very various influences ;
no fixed principle, no relation between the structure and the
decoration ; a love of luxury of *appearance*, combined with a
barbarous execution, indicating decadence ; we no longer find
the ancient sculpture, nor, as in France, the free imitation of the
local flora ; it is a compromise, destitute of style or character,
between Roman and Byzantine traditions, and the influences
of the Northern arts.   It is only at the beginning of the fifteenth

century that we find—not an architecture, indeed, but—architects in Italy. It would seem that from the day when that country was torn from the Roman Empire, it became the very type of disintegration. We observe rival cities disputing the soil with each other ; and a similar isolation presents itself in the æsthetic world ;—we find artists, but not principles ; individualities were sometimes distinguished, but they were only individualities : thus the study of the art of architecture in mediæval Italy brings to light only biographies, not a history, and therefore no profitable instruction. The Italians of the Middle Ages, failing to create an art, as they had failed to constitute themselves a nation, naturally reverted to the imitation of Roman art ; this movement took place a century before the corresponding revival in France, and was essentially an individual rather than a general movement. If the Italian renaissance is the subject of study, what is it that will occupy our attention ? Will it be the renaissance of Brunelleschi, that of Michelozzo, of L. Batista Alberti, of Bramante, of Baldassare Peruzzi, or of Sansovino ? The works of these masters, whatever merit they may possess in themselves, are individual works, not having those relations to each other—that filiation which we delight to discover in the art-products of a country ; relations which are so striking a feature in our own country, from the Garonne to the English Channel, during the course of the sixteenth century. Through the influence, however, of the Italian masters of the fifteenth century, we find the young French nobility, on their return from the campaigns of Charles VIII. and Louis XII., bent on erecting Italian palaces. And you will see how shrewdly the inveterate spirit of the French artists contrived to manifest itself—how Gauls remained true to Gallic tradition.

From the thirteenth century to the beginning of the fifteenth, Architecture was an art so complete and connected, and so entirely subject to the control of a corporate body, that no external influence could affect it : neither the clergy in the construction of churches, nor the secular nobility in the erection of palaces and castles, nor the rich bourgeoisie in the building of their houses, attempted, or could attempt to submit art to their fancies ; art was absolutely independent : it was a power to which recourse was had when it was needed, but which could not be directed ; it acted freely and governed itself : in fact, the architects of the time formed a corporate body, which in the domain of arts possessed its privileges and franchises which no one thought of interfering with. Besides, during the period of the Middle Ages, every one kept within his own sphere ; the clergy sought to maintain and to augment their prerogatives ; secular feudality defended itself against the encroachments of

royal power, and was constantly at war with the clerical feudality
and the inhabitants of the cities and towns; while royalty was
engrossed with the endeavour to increase its political power.
But neither clergy, laity, nor king dreamed of interfering with
matters of art; consequently they neither perceived nor feared
that new and independent power which was elevating itself by
daily labour. They found artists and craftsmen, but did not
govern them. At the close of the fifteenth century, the nobility,
on their return from Italy, prided themselves on their appreciation
of art : they made it a subject of study, and the passion for
Italian works led to the formation of that body of *amateurs* which
has ever since had so powerful and injurious an influence on art.
On their return the French noblesse desired to substitute
luxurious abodes in the foreign style for their old chateaux and
manor-houses; and dreamed of nothing but porticoes, colonnades,
galleries, and symmetrical façades. The old Gallic artists therefore having completely exhausted all the resources with which
the principles of Gothic Art could furnish them, adopted the new
tastes of their clients. In the thirteenth century, it was the
artists alone who had led the way in æsthetic progress; in the
sixteenth century they accepted a style of art imposed upon
them. But adopting only a foreign exterior, they preserved the
national genius in essentials; the edifices they built were still
Gothic in general arrangements and structure; but to please
their employers they arrayed the old body in a new dress, consisting of fragments borrowed from the Italian renaissance.
Since the ancient orders were called for, they adopted them
almost exclusively as a mere decoration; the local flora was
replaced by arabesques, and prismatic profiles by Italian mouldings. Jupiter, Venus, and Diana, with nymphs and Tritons,
were substituted for angels, saints, and personages clothed in the
costume of the day. The owners of the chateaux and manors were
delighted; and the artists who at that time had scarcely any
firmer belief in angels and saints than in Diana or Mercury, were
not less satisfied at being disembarrassed of the worn-out garb
of Gothic Art, which in point of form had reached the last limits
of the possible. But the principles of art,—those methods which
were the outcome of many centuries of experience,—these did
not change; and the architects who were so ready to obey the
fashion in exchanging their old Gothic ornaments for a dress of
foreign importation, did not borrow from the Italians either
methods of construction or general arrangements of plan. They
continued to draw Gothic plans and to construct like their predecessors, to cover their buildings with high roofs, to crown them
with conspicuous chimney shafts, to build their porticoes low to
afford shelter from the rain, to make mullioned windows, narrow

and numerous staircases, build great halls flooded with light for large gatherings, and small apartments for daily use ; to care little for symmetry, to flank the main buildings with towers or pavilions, to provide for defence, to detach the parts of their buildings from each other in case of need, and to proportion the windows to the apartments they were destined to light. Meanwhile noble amateurs loudly applauded, because they saw Italian columns and porticoes, arabesques and Caryatides on the façades of their palaces ; and everybody said—and it has been foolishly repeated from that time forward—that these edifices were the works of the Jocondes, the Rossos, the Primaticcios, and Serlios !

It is worth remarking that most of these artists joined the party of the Reformation as soon as it began to make proselytes in France. Amid all its glory, the sixteenth century was in France a period of protracted and sometimes tragic mystification. We deceived each other ; every one paraded sentiments opposed to his real inclinations or interests. Though religious questions were made the occasion of civil war, both Catholics and Reformers were the most incredulous of mortals. The Reformation found its chief supporters among the higher classes who had everything to lose in a social revolution, and who did not apply the Reformation to their own morals. The common people were fanatical adherents of religious tradition, though they had nothing to lose and everything to gain by change ; they mingled republican sentiments with the defence of ecclesiastical traditions and with loyalty to the most despotic of Catholic kings. Royalty was feeble and hesitating at the very moment when energy was especially needed. And he who succeeded in restoring order, Henry the Fourth, was the most ingenious and the shrewdest mystifier of all. The arts of the time were the faithful image of this chaos of ideas. We behold confusion, want of unity and of harmony between principles and appearances, and an exaggerated importance given to details ; the execution often negligent, and always affected, tame and undecided. A few distinguished individualities arose amid this disorder, but they left no trace behind them. They were flashes, but not light. This period, so brilliant in its early years, closed amid ruins. Meanwhile a civic spirit had arisen, the sense of political duty had been developed, and progress had been made towards national unity. At the very commencement of the seventeenth century we observe that a revolution had taken place in the arts : the spell of Italian fascination had been broken. There arose on French soil buildings for civil purposes impressed with a novel character ; we no longer observe the disordered fancies or mystifications of the renaissance, nor yet Gothic traditions ; nevertheless the old Gallic spirit reappears in all its energy. The architecture of this period is reasonable, and free from superfluous ornamentation ; it is severe, well studied in point of structure, and exactly appropriate to the requirements. With a kind of Puritan affectation it aims at employing only such means as are absolutely needed, though without pedantry ; and while preserving a dignified ease the construction is clearly, even ostentatiously exhibited. The intention is that it should be seen and appreciated ; solidity is made a point of, though without clumsiness : we have the architecture of men of sense comparatively free from illusions, well-informed, and liking richness of effect without ostentation, and comfort without effeminacy ;—in fact, tending to regain that character of independence which it had lost during the preceding age, and which it was on the point of losing yet again.

The architecture of the period between the end of Henry the Fourth's reign and the majority of Louis the Fourteenth may still be called French Architecture ; and next to that of the twelfth, thirteenth, and fourteenth centuries, it is the architecture which best deserves this name. In going over a chateau or mansion of the time of Louis the Thirteenth we seem to live among those who inhabited it. These edifices are the proper architectural habiliment of the social life of the period—the last to leave a profound impression on the history of the development of intelligence and of the arts,—the last to be distinguished at the same time for the firm and independent character that adorned it, and for a most lively and elegant spirit, combined with that good-humoured irony which is peculiar to our country. The long reign of Louis xiv. succeeded, though not without a struggle, in stifling this final effort of the French spirit in the arts. Louis xiv. took an interest in architectural works ; but his direction of the arts was influenced by tendencies which were opposed to their development; for the moral independence of the artist is essential to their life. In his time, the good and wise traditions of construction were lost, the workmanship became more and more careless, masons built badly, carpenters lost the art of framing timber with intelligence and economy, sculptors no longer had that firm hand, that refinement of sentiment and feeling for truth which they still possessed at the commencement of the seventeenth century ; their heavy chisels produced only works of a monotonous description, destitute of character, and pompous without grandeur ; the old trade guilds were extinct ; what was characteristically French in our arts was effete. I have been sometimes accused of severity and even of injustice towards the arts of the age of Louis the Fourteenth ; and though that age has left sufficient remains of its grandeur to be able to dispense with my admiration, I should wish to justify my opinion. It is because I behold in Louis XIV. a great king that I regret to find in him a spirit little disposed to further the true development of the arts. When a sovereign refrains from interfering with questions of art and leaves them absolutely free, he cannot be deemed responsible for their progress or decline during his reign ; but when an absolute monarch makes it his ambition to exercise an influence in every sphere of life,—even over the productions of intellect among his subjects,—it is surely allowable, I submit, to consider him responsible for the enfeebling of that intellect ; and no one will dispute the fact that architectural art was in a more flourishing condition at the time when Louis XIV. attained his majority than at his death. It was with his architects as with his ministers and generals. He began by calling to his councils such men as Colbert and Louvois, and ended with the Chamillarts and the Ponchartrains. He found De Brosse, Le Mercier, Blondel, and François Mansart intrusted with public works ; he ended by confiding them to Perrault and Hardoin Mansart,—the last dignified by his uncle's name but sharing none of his abilities. Louis XIV., that king so thoroughly French, so jealous of foreign influences, regarded the arts only through a Roman medium, and what a medium ! He had the ambition to rival ancient Rome ; yet his well-balanced mind, so capable of self-restraint, so moderate in all things, so correctly appreciating what is right and suitable, stifled, in the sphere of art, the natural and original genius of that French people whose political unity he cemented, and whose dominion he extended. After the middle of the sixteenth century, art in France was evidently bewildered ; its history is a perpetual contradiction ; it lost its way. Under Catherine de Médicis both people and artists had an aversion for the Italians and for everything that came from Italy ; and yet they imitated Italian arts. Under Henry IV. and Louis XIII. they swore by Classical Antiquity, yet the arts resumed their peculiar French character. Under Louis XIV. the nation thought only as Louis XIV. thought. The heart of that king was as soundly French as ever beat in a royal bosom, yet he would have Roman architecture ; he insisted on being represented in painting and sculpture always as a Roman Emperor. Under Louis XV. political prosperity and the arts declined together. Philosophers spoke in the name of reason, yet the arts were never less subjected to reason than at that epoch. Under the Republic the national spirit was developed even to delirium : yet our national edifices were thrown down, and models were sought for our buildings from Rome—the city of our former conquerors. While crying " Death to the aristocrats ! " people were endeavouring to reproduce the architecture of the aristocratic civilisations of antiquity. I would not encourage an exclusive patriotism in matters of art. The arts, in whatever part of the globe they are developed, belong to humanity : I fully admit the principle that they have no country. But each nation, or, to speak more correctly, each centre of civilisation (for political boundaries do not always coincide with those of characteristic nationality), has, as I have already said, a genius of its own which must not be disregarded ; and it is because during the last three centuries we have too often failed to appreciate our own genius, that our arts, after so many variations, have become hybrid, and can no longer be recognised as connected with any particular time or people. It is commendable to cherish a cosmopolitan spirit,—to acknowledge all men as brethren,—and to admit that ideas without any exception are the property of all ; but facts are continually demonstrating that the French brain differs in its construction from that of our neighbours, the English and the Germans. Let us profit by the ideas of our neighbours, but let us take care to have some of our own,—since this is by no means impossible ; and above all let us be on our guard against the supposition that simply because other nations are or have been endowed with rare intelligence and creative originality, it is absolutely forbidden to us to have any. It is not for me to characterise contemporary art,—though what it is capable of becoming is a proper object of inquiry : to its future development we should all give our best energies ; for I cannot admit that as long as a France shall exist worthy of the name, the arts can perish. The sap is latent ; a few clear days and a gleam of reason will suffice to send up its reviving influences even into the feeblest branches.

Perhaps I have dwelt too long in this Lecture on the period of transition from the arts of Antiquity to those of modern times ; but it must not be forgotten that we have to contend with deeply-rooted prejudices. If these prejudices only tended to create a misunderstanding respecting certain historical facts—to perpetuate exclusive prejudices in the study of art—I should perhaps not have devoted so much space to the consideration of the Byzantine Arts, the principles of the arts of the West, their tendencies and value. But these prejudices entail, in my judgment, a more serious inconvenience; they produce a complete misunderstanding of the nature of modern western genius ; they thrust us, who of all western nations have the greatest capacity for the culture of the arts, completely into the background. This is unjust and ill-advised ; it prevents us from profiting by the efforts of our predecessors, and nullifies the well-reasoned and useful results of ages of experience. Mediæval art among us had only one drawback ; that of being developed too soon. Art had its *Eighty-nine* in 1170 ; at that era it had completely freed itself from all that could shackle its independence and its national character : it had recast its traditions ; it had admitted principles as *liberal* as could be desired, and had discovered a new and indefinitely extended path while it established very decided and reliable methods. Born under feudalism, —a system which had no affinity with the French character ; born among the laity,—the people,— it shared the fortunes of feudalism, and fell with it, though essentially antagonistic to it. It was involved in the ruin of mediæval institutions ; but is that a reason for not restoring to that truly national art the position it justly claims ? Is the fact that for more than three centuries it was misunderstood and vilified, a reason for not reinstating it, and for not looking to its principles—which are so liberal and so conformable to the spirit of our time and country—for elements which may be useful to us in the present day ? Are not our character and tendencies always the same ? Does national character change ? Does not daily experience demonstrate,—and perhaps more clearly at the present than at any former time,—that neither conquests, nor institutions, nor political boundaries, nor diplomatic combinations produce any effect in modifying the spirit of the races that occupy the globe ? Our Arts, which are so brilliantly developed in the interval between the twelfth and the fifteenth century, are our own—the fruit of our own labour and genius ; and we may go on deducing useful results from the principles underlying those arts, to-day, to-morrow, nay as long as we continue to be what we have been and still are. The civilisations of the ancient communities perished, because the latter were constituted only of masters and slaves. In the ancient world we do not find what we now call a nation,—that is an association of provinces united by the same spirit, the same thought, and all whose members are interested in and contribute to the preservation of the general body. In the ancient world we see absolute monarchies supported by a theocracy, oligarchical or aristocratic republics, and a rude, uncultivated populace—the mere dregs of society—a body of slaves. All inspiration, all intellectual movement, all sense of dignity and independence come from the upper stratum. Our community is not of this character : the nation has formed itself by its own efforts, in spite of institutions imposed upon it as the result of conquest; it has raised itself by its inherent power; and even in our days, on great occasions, it often acts contrary to the calculations of the most skilful and experienced. Happy is he who comprehends its genius and instincts, and is not afraid to trust them. Feudalism, secular or clerical, was distinct from the nation,—it was not of it ; it neither knew nor saw the labours that were being carried on among the people ; feudal power made use of those labours but did not direct nor fetter them ; or, if perchance it thought the control of them to fall within its province, its efforts were always made too late, proving that it was not aware of the progress that was taking place.   The entire history of our arts is an exemplification of this principle ; and here we may also see what prevents them from perishing, in spite of three centuries of oppression.   The reaction is ripe ; we possess all the elements for its development ; for during the last twenty-five or thirty years our artisans and workmen have shown themselves eager to co-operate with every endeavour made to revive our national arts.   In our own times, as in all former periods, it is from below that the movement proceeds ; it is in the workshop and the studio that the labour is being undertaken : the old spirit of the lay craftsmen of the twelfth century is being gradually awakened, for in France the humblest workman reasons and desires to understand what he is doing ; and he conceives a passion for works in whose general plan as well as in the details he can detect a logical sequence.   Our workmen are, in fact, of the same stuff as our soldiers : both classes devote themselves the more enthusiastically the more clearly they comprehend the object of their devotion and the more elevated that object is. But we shall have an opportunity later on of appreciating the value of this fact, of demonstrating the importance of the elements we have at command, and of investigating the means of availing ourselves of them ; for our age has not yet exhausted all its creative powers.

LECTURE VII.

THE Architecture of the Ancients was long studied without any account being taken of the effects produced by the colouring of the form ; whether this colouring was produced by mosaic, marble veneering, or painting on stucco. The Orientals and Greeks, and even the Romans rejected the principle that the naked material of which an edifice was constructed should remain visible. The Greeks coloured white marble when they employed that beautiful material. However slight that colouring may have been (though everything leads us to suppose that it was on the contrary strong and vivid), its result was none the less that of concealing the real material under a kind of tapestry independent of that material. I am not one of those who would allow that the Greeks could have adopted a false principle in the execution of works of art ; and if we find them adopting modes of procedure that are apparently strange, and to which we find it difficult to accustom our eyes, I should rather believe in the imperfection of our senses than in an error on the part of these masters in art.

It is now some time since archæologists and artists made clear, even to the most incredulous, that all the Greek monuments had a colouring both outside and inside, laid on a thin coat of stucco when the stone was of a coarse grain, and on the smooth surface of the marble itself, when the building was of that material. This indisputable fact leads us to suppose that the Greeks did not regard the form alone as sufficient for architectural effect, but considered that this form should be completed, aided or modified by a combination of various colours. No lengthened experience in matters of art is needed to show what an influence colour has on form, and even on proportions : if, for example, we were to colour black the metopes and the wall of the *cella* of a Greek temple, we should obtain an effect quite different from that which would result from leaving these metopes and the wall white, and covering the cornice, the triglyphs, the architrave, and columns black (fig. 1), all the real dimensions and proportions remaining the same. The result of the first method of colouring would be to give breadth to the order, and importance to the architrave, the triglyphs, and the cornice; that of the second, indicated at B, would be to make the columns appear more slender and lofty, while the entablature would lose in importance. Colouring therefore greatly influenced the effect produced by architecture; and in the present day we cannot form a correct judgment of the ancient Greek buildings without taking the colouring into account. An order that seems to us heavy might have appeared slender; another whose proportions seem delicate would present a firm and solid appearance.

1

A   B

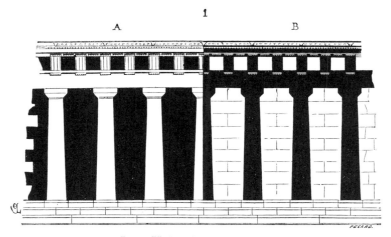

Fig. 1.—Effect of Colouring on Proportions.

The senses of the Greeks were too delicate to allow of their failing to understand the advantage that could be gained from the recognition of this principle in architecture, or neglecting so powerful means of visual effect in giving a different signification to form—shall I say—by dint of variety of colouring. We are subjected to the sway of deeply-rooted prejudices, so that our senses refuse to recognise facts which are nevertheless in strict consistency with natural laws. In sculpture and architecture we have been long accustomed to admit the effect of form as the only legitimate one, as if an object in relief must on that account dispense with colouring. On what is this sentiment based? I will try to give the reason; and the question is especially interesting, inasmuch as this sentiment is the result of new principles whose importance is perhaps not duly appreciated. We have here another of those innumerable contradictions which in our times have led art astray. Some uncompromising admirers of Classic Architecture insist on the rejection of colour as an aid to form, although the ancients always admitted this means of effect : and in their unwillingness to admit of colour in architecture, they are carrying to excess the tendencies of the mediæval architects who gave to structure an importance previously unknown. To show more clearly what I mean, it is as if one should say, " I approve of no other mode of architecture but that adopted in classic times, but with the understanding that the most powerful appliance for producing certain effects befitting the object, and which was actually used by the ancient architects, shall not be employed ; I think it right to exclude the architectural methods employed during the Middle Ages, but I maintain that the results to which those methods have given rise ought permanently to exercise a dominant influence over our architecture."

The Asiatics coloured their architecture.

The Egyptians coloured their architecture.

The Greeks coloured their architecture.

The Romans coloured their architecture, either by painting or by the employment of materials of various colours.

The Arabs coloured their architecture.

During the Byzantine and the Western Romanesque period, the colouring of architecture was continued.

During the period called Gothic, architecture was coloured as a result of traditional influences ; but in consequence of the refinements in structure introduced by the leading architects of this epoch, the colouring of buildings was gradually abandoned, with a view to render the complicated and skilful combinations exhibited in the construction conspicuously evident. Painting was no longer architectural, and was thenceforth applied only in exceptional cases.

Among all the ancient nations, and during the earlier mediæval centuries, an edifice was not considered complete until colour had been called in to enhance the effect of form. But from the thirteenth century onward, architectural form in France can dispense with this complement ; form becomes effective simply as the result of structural combinations ; geometry bears away the palm from painting ; painting is regarded as a luxury, a sumptuous addition, a decoration ; but architecture can and does dispense with it. These two arts, architecture and painting, though essentially connected, tend constantly towards separation ; till at last we find paintings hung on whitewashed walls, without the painter and the architect having foreseen, respectively,—the one that his painting would be hung up in such or such a building,—the other that his building would receive such or such a picture.

That regard for harmony without which art cannot exist, has long been lost to us. The architect ought to be also a painter and sculptor to such a degree as to enable him to comprehend the advantages to be derived from these two arts which are allied to his own; the sculptor and the painter ought to be sufficiently alive to the effects produced by architecture not to disdain to contribute to enhance those effects. But this is not the case now : the architect erects his building, and gives it certain forms that are suitable to it; then, when the building is finished, it is given over to the painter. The chief object of the latter is to secure attention to his painting; he cares little for that general effect which even the architect himself has not considered. The statuary is at work in his studio, and his bas-reliefs or statues will some day or other take their place in the building. The architect, the painter, and the sculptor may each have displayed remarkable talent in his own department, yet the work as a whole may produce only a mediocre effect : the statuary is not proportioned to the building, or it presents an effect of agitation when the eye seeks repose; the painting overpowers the architecture, or seems to have no relation with it; it is sombre where we could wish for a light effect, garish where sobriety is desirable. These three arts conflict with, instead of aiding, each other. As a matter of course, the architect, the sculptor, and the painter accuse each other of the non-success of the result as a whole. We are unacquainted with the relations that existed between architects, sculptors, and painters in classical or mediæval times; but the aspect of the extant monuments assures us that such relations existed, and that they were direct, continuous, and intimate. I do not believe that the artists were the worse by the connection, while it is certain that art gained by it. Traces of this alliance between the arts continue to appear during the seventeenth century, at least in the interior of palaces; the galleries of Apollo, at the Louvre, of the Hôtel Lambert, and even that of the Marbles at Versailles, offer us the last specimens of a harmony between the three arts,—which must advance in union if they would produce great effects. This invaluable alliance was broken from the moment when architecture shut itself up in the prejudices of the schools, when the painter produced pictures and not painting, and the sculptors statues and not statuary. The museums and the galleries of amateurs were filled, and the public buildings were stripped of their proper ornament; the opinion was established that architecture allowed only stone in its cold and naked whiteness; and those who would have refused to live in apartments not hung with gaudily-coloured papers, rejected all colouring in the temple erected to God or the hall of a palace. Moreover, since the opinion pre-

vails among us that the arts ought to be encouraged, painters
have been commissioned to execute pictures, and these pictures
have been hung up in edifices which their painters had never seen
—painted and hung in utter despite of the forms of the architecture, the dimensions of the interiors, and the direction of the light.
Sculptors were commissioned to carve statues, which they were
well capable of doing; but they had no notion as to where they
were to be placed. We cannot, therefore, boast ourselves of being
a people endowed with sensibility in matters of art, since we have
ceased to be convinced of the necessity of that harmony between
arts, whose very nature requires that they advance in concert.
During all the best periods of art, sculpture and painting have been
the decorative dress of architecture,—a dress made for the body
to which it is applied, and which cannot be left to chance. But
to preserve that authority which it had acquired over the other
arts, it was necessary above all things that architecture should
respect itself, and render itself worthy of that decorative dress
which was formerly deemed indispensable to it.

At the present day we behold the remains of Classical
Antiquity in a state of ruin, all bearing the marks of barbarism,
violence, and devastation. These ruins are often buried in dust
or mud, and surrounded by shapeless débris; but the ancients,
when such beautiful structures were first erected, were not
indifferent as to their surroundings, but carefully selected their
position; they took care to provide a gradual and skilful transition from the highway to the sanctuary of the divinity; and at
Athens and Rome the temples and palaces never rose absolutely
from the mud of the streets as is the case with most of our
public buildings. That exterior colouring of buildings which
would appear ridiculous in our country (as it is ridiculous to see
a person dressed in a brilliant costume in the street) was in
ancient times a very important architectural element, owing to
the care that was taken to render those edifices secure from
injury of any kind, the due preparation of their site and the
accessories by which they were surrounded. We find these
sentiments of respect for a work of art very strongly developed
among the Orientals. It appears to us consistent that a pagoda
should be coloured from its base to its summit with brilliant
colours, inlaid work, and enamelling, when the pagoda is approached only through a series of courts, narrowing in dimensions
and increasing in magnificence, elaborately paved with marble
and adorned with shrubs and fountains. The sumptuous decorations of the Egyptian sanctuaries can be understood when we consider that those pylones, porticoes, and halls whose magnificence
increases as we advance, had to be passed before the temple itself
was reached. And we can appreciate the brilliant colouring of

the Greek temple when we see by how many artistic objects it was surrounded ; when we imagine to ourselves the sacred woods and enclosures and the thousand accessories whose presence led up to that last and most finished expression of architectural art.

We have been too forgetful of the consideration that works of art require a *mise en scène*. The ancients never abandoned this principle ; the Middle Ages often endeavoured to adopt it, though with evidently inferior success, especially in France : for in Italy we still recognise the influence of pagan traditions ; and this will largely account for the effect produced by the architectural works of that country; whereas, taken by themselves, these works are often much inferior to what we have in France. There is an art in setting off a work of art, though for a long time we seem to have ceased to think so. We will frankly allow that this kind of negligence, which belongs to our national idiosyncracies, results from a noble and admirable element of character, but this result might be avoided without sacrificing the advantages of the principle in which it had its root. To effect this we must gain an exact acquaintance with our special aptitudes, and lay aside certain prejudices, crude or obsolete doctrines, and vulgar prepossessions against which we artists, through weakness or ignorance, have not the courage or the means boldly to struggle.

Mingled perhaps with other elements of character we possess those qualities which are most adapted to the development of the arts, and of architecture in particular ; yet not only are we unable to take advantage of them, but we allow them to be crushed under that tyranny of vulgar prejudices which enslaves us, because we wish to appear other than we really are, and neglect the precious endowments that have fallen to our share. We erect a public monument, but we give it an unsuitable position and undesirable surroundings ; we do not know how to present it to the public ; it may be a *chef-d'œuvre*, but we have managed so as to expose it to desecration. We have not had the sense to respect our work, consequently no one else respects it ;—what else ought we to expect ? The most insignificant buildings of the Middle Ages or of modern times, built in Italy, are always placed with a view to effect ; the picturesque plays an important part. For this we have substituted symmetry, which contravenes our genius, is irksome to us and fatigues us ; it is the last resource of incapacity. Neither the Acropolis of Athens nor the Forum of Rome, nor that of Pompeii, nor the descriptions given us by Pausanius, present us with symmetrical groupings of buildings. Among the Greeks symmetry is consulted in regard to a single building,—though exceptions are abundant,—never in a group of buildings. The Romans themselves, who admitted this principle in the arrangement of architectural masses, never sacrificed utility, good sense, or the necessities of the structure to it. But with what art did the Greeks dispose their public buildings! What a just appreciation of effect—of what we now call the picturesque! an object of contempt to our architects. And why? Because the building as drawn on paper generally takes no account of the place, the aspect, the effects of lights and shadows, the surroundings, or the variations of level—which are, however, such an aid to the display of architectural forms; because the architect, even before considering how he shall faithfully satisfy the requirements of the programme, makes it his first thought to erect symmetrical equiponderant façades,—a great box in which the various services will have to find their place afterwards as best they can. There is no need, I think, to cite examples to prove that this is no exaggeration. A glance around us will be all-sufficient. Still, if we erected these great regular boxes on platforms, or terraces, or vast basements, as the Romans always did in similar cases, and as was done in our own country at Versailles and St. Germain, in the seventeenth century; if we gave them proper surroundings, and endeavoured to give effect to such dignity as may attach to them as an ensemble of symmetrical lines, by isolating them from the other buildings of our cities, there would be a reason, or at least an excuse for this fondness for symmetry; but no, these huge piles are lost in masses of buildings, their basements are in the gutter, their façades can be seen only one at a time, and it is only on paper, and looking at the plans, that we can give ourselves the satisfaction of thinking that the right wing is exactly of the same length and breadth as the left. The Romans—but above all the Greeks—never adopted a symmetrical arrangement except when it could be recognised at a glance,—that is in a space sufficiently limited for the eye to be satisfied, without the aid of reasoning, by a balanced disposition of the structure. But if we have to go half a mile or more to enable us to see that the façade on the north side—supposing we have a visual memory sufficient for the purpose—corresponds with that on the south; if we have to leave one court and enter another to perceive—continuing the supposition that our memory does not fail us—that these courts are exactly similar, I ask what purpose is served by abandoning common sense, inconveniencing the internal arrangements of the building, and thwarting the requirements of the scheme, to obtain so puerile a result, which only serves to amuse a few curious idlers?

What authority can be appealed to in support of these so frequent examples of absurdity? Mediæval traditions? Certainly not. Classical Antiquity? But Classical Antiquity is quite opposed to them. On what authority then do they rest? On certain academic formulas, very modern, but crude and out of harmony with our national genius, which is essentially independent and prone to reason ; formulas in accordance with which we erect inconvenient buildings, wearisome to look at, but which allow of every one's making himself a judge in questions of architecture, and are therefore on that very account extolled as infallibly correct.

In visiting the ruins of Greek cities, we see how scrupulously the architects of the most brilliant period of art took advantage of the site to set off their monuments. They loved Architecture as art, but they were also lovers of nature—of light ; they used coquetry—if I may be allowed the expression—in the arrangement of an edifice : they avoided monotony,—they dreaded ennui! They were severely critical as savants and artists,—they were full of respect for principles and forms ; but they were also skilful decorators ; they had exquisite taste in regard to the *mise en scène.* The Greek architect does not level the rock on which his edifice is to be built,—he embellishes it and takes advantage of its asperities ; he modifies its form with good taste and with a profound appreciation of the ultimate effect. Look at Athens and Corinth, but especially those ancient cities of Sicily, Agrigentum, Selimus, Segesta, and Syracuse. Who has not said to himself on seeing the remains of those cities, "How fortunate were the men who were thus able to ally art with the beauties of nature, and who could so thoroughly enjoy that alliance?"

The Roman is not swayed by these sentiments, he is sensible to beauties of another kind. At the outset he takes a pride in subjugating nature, and he subordinates it to his penchant for order and grandeur. With a view to render these two distinct principles clearly appreciable, we have, in two figures (2 and 3) given a view of the temple of Juno Lucina, at Agrigentum, as restored, and a bird's-eye view of a Roman temple of the imperial epoch, with its porticoes, its exterior enclosures, its entrances, its ample and sumptuous arrangements.[1] In the present day we have to bargain for the sites of our public buildings ; or if we isolate them, we surround them with bare spaces which by their

[1] Of the temple of Juno Lucina at Agrigentum there is still extant the great platform placed on the east side of the rock, and the whole of the building in ruins. Our view is taken from the city side,—the temple being built on a long ridge of limestone rocks which served as ramparts. These rocks were, on the inner side, covered with monuments hewn in the stone. On visiting these ruins now buried in rural seclusion, we perceive that the Greek architects had the talent of skilful landscape gardeners, and that this talent did not injure their art. As regards the Roman temple, which, it may be remarked, resembles many sacred edifices of the Imperial epoch, it is engraved from a medal dedicated to Jupiter the Avenger by the Emperor Alexander Severus. On the reverse we read IOVI.VLTORI. P. M. TR. P. III. COS. P. P. (Bibl. imp., cabinet des médailles.) Vid. *Architectura numismatica,* or *Arch. medals of Clas. Antiquity,* by T. L. Donaldson, London, 1859.

PERSPECTIVE VIEW OF RESTORED TEMPLE OF JUNO LUCINA, AGRIGENTUM.

FIG. 3.

FIG. 3.—VIEW OF A ROMAN TEMPLE, OF THE IMPERIAL EPOCH.

vacuity of aspect dwarf such edifices and give them no help in the way of surroundings. If we have taste, we do not know how to give effect to it, and think we have done enough for our great public monument when we have surrounded it with a railing stuck upon a stone plinth.

I remarked above that this carelessness in regard to setting off a work of art,—completing it,—was the result of a noble element of character. In fact we are always seeking,—gaining glimpses of the good and pursuing it,—but we do not make a point of holding it fast, for we are eager to get beyond the good to the better ; so that being always in a hurry—out of breath— our enjoyment is constantly adjourned to the morrow ; it will come, we suppose, but it never exists at the present moment. The true history of our arts, as also of our civilisation generally, may be summed up in these few words. In this also we do not resemble the Romans, the most practical of the nations that have figured in history. It must be remarked that this disposition gives rise to the strangest blunders in the study of the arts among us. We express a principle, which gives rise to another, and so on ; we do not set to work to follow out the application and developments of the first ; we press on leaving unfinished the work we had commenced : meantime, a people of calmer temperament, or one more attached to the interests of the moment, lays hold of that first principle which we had abandoned, develops it, studies it, and perfects its results. Sooner or later, fatigued with our unceasing pursuit of the best,—harassed, and our resources exhausted,—those developments carried out by others present themselves on our road ; we are rapt in admiration, and set ourselves as zealously to work to imitate the results, often ill-deduced, of those principles which we had formerly abandoned, as we had been eager in the pursuit of fresh ones. It is easy to perceive how much confusion these singular re-adoptions introduce into our ideas, and how difficult it becomes to disentangle the true from the false,—inspiration from imitation, —amid these diverse elements. To this state of things we may trace the reason why in the present day we have so much difficulty in deciding what we want and what is really appropriate to us in point of art. The Greek world presented nearly the same spectacle, but their invincible love of form saved them ; they advanced ; they became subject to various influences ; but they transformed all they touched, as the result of their instinct for the beautiful, and always remained the masters of those to whom they were politically subordinate.

Let us then follow, step by step, the progress of our arts in this corner of Western Europe, from the Carlovingian epoch down to modern times. Neither in Italy nor in France do we find more than a few remains of the buildings of the eighth and ninth centuries; and these remains present only an amorphous art,—a hybrid product of Roman traditions and Oriental influences. In the tenth century we find the invasions of the Northmen arresting the progress of a civilisation which was but just beginning to revive. It is not till the eleventh century, under the influence of the monastic establishments—especially the Clunisian—that we perceive an art in actual process of development on a new and independent track.[1] These monks began by settling, wherever it was possible, on sites formerly occupied by the Romans. The plan of the Roman *villa* continued to exercise an influence over the arrangements of their monasteries. In the programmes of their buildings the aspect, the site, and practical requirements take precedence of symmetry, and the Clunisian monasteries, like the Roman *villæ*, are only a judicious and well-arranged agglomeration of buildings destined for various purposes. The style adopted by the monks of the West is nearer the Latin than any other, nevertheless from the eleventh century onwards we find new elements introduced into the art. It is at this epoch that the history of Architecture requires to be analysed with especial care ; for all that is properly our own in architecture is derived from these first essays. It is needless to remind the reader of the supreme influence of the Abbey of Cluny during the tenth and eleventh centuries, *i.e.* under the rule of the Abbots St. Odo, Aymard, St. Marieul, St. Odilon and St. Hugues ; of the privileges enjoyed by this Abbey, which was independent of power secular or episcopal, and was subordinate only to the Pope ; of the numerous journeys undertaken by the monks in all the countries of Europe; of the reforms of which they became the devoted apostles in every part of Christendom, or of the considerable labours which they undertook. It was a real government,—the only one that followed a regular and consistent course in those ages of public misery and depression of all the other powers. The order of Cluny, taking the lead in intelligence and learning, the only one that kept up a constant intercourse with Italy, Spain, and Germany, and which was introducing its "rule" in every quarter, had need of an art that should correspond with the dignity of its mission. Moreover, it must be considered that at that time all minds of the nobler order,—all who thought that humanity should endeavour to rise above barbarism,—were eager to enter the monasteries of Cluny, and thus contributed their quota of intelligence to that vast religious and civilising association. At Cluny, therefore, and, as the consequence of the constant intercourse kept up between this centre and the

---

[1] See, in the *Dictionnaire raisonné de l'Architecture française du Xe au XVIe siècles*, the articles Architecture, Architecture Religieuse, Monastique ; Construction.

establishments distributed through Italy, Germany, and even the East, was formed a kind of reservoir, into which flowed the divers springs of art that had been collected in various quarters, to form a new current. It was thus that the traditions of Roman art laid the foundations of an influential school of architecture. Cluny, Tournus, Vezelay, Saint-Martin-des-Champs in Paris, and La Charité-sur-Loire, preserve remarkable specimens of this Clunisian art, which is the only one that in the eleventh century deserves the name of architecture. The masons, the stone-cutters, the sculptors of Cluny, possessed methods characterising a school whose efforts and whose greatness cannot be ignored,—a school based on Latin arts, but which bears the impress of original genius.

In the literary productions, instructions, and constitutions that issued from Cluny there is a logical consistency,—a clear and practical intelligence which strikes an attentive reader ; in perusing these documents we recognise the work of lettered men, accustomed to a rational exercise of authority, to administration, to the difficulties which the government of men presents ; convinced of their intellectual superiority, and possessing the patience and moderation that belong to real strength. In the eleventh century the Clunisians could honestly believe, and not without reason, that the government of the world was destined inevitably to fall into their hands ; and this will partly explain the struggles of Gregory VII. against the imperial power. The monk Hildebrand on becoming pope had remained the friend of the Abbot Hugues ; who, however, was not on that account less attached to Henry, and who often mediated between these illustrious rivals. This fact is a sufficient indication of the political spirit of those great abbots of Cluny during the eleventh and twelfth centuries. That real uncontested power, that taste for intellectual labours, that moderation, that dignity of power—have left their mark on all the Clunisian monuments of that period. We trace the influence of the " rule ; " but it is not the narrow rule of the cloister ; it is something that reminds us once more of the Roman. It may be affirmed, to the credit of the Clunisians, that they were able to form schools of master-builders and sculptors ; whereas the Romans had only the structure of their edifices to contrive, taking all that belongs to decorative art from the Greeks. I am willing to suppose that the Clunisians summoned from Byzantine or selected from among the Greek artists who had found an asylum in Italy, sculptors and painters to adorn their edifices : but where in Italy, at the end of the eleventh century, was there a building erected like the church of Vezelay ? Who then had introduced those mouldings so bold and so pure in·style ? In what European country do we find at the close of the eleventh century a composition analogous, *e.g.* to that bay of the nave of Vezelay, of which Plate XI. gives only a feeble idea ? For it must be observed that this architecture contemplates simply a practical result, not the gratification of the eye by a geometrical design. Do we not find here the impress of an original style ? What has this composition in common with the examples left us by Classical Antiquity ? In these Clunisian buildings (but especially in such as were produced during the period called Romanesque), we already see the genius of the architect abandoning worn-out traditions and inventing new forms; he subjects these forms to reflection,—decoration to construction ; as regards that construction, he wishes that it should show itself ; and while he renders it conspicuous, he makes it elegant and even refined. The Clunisian architecture is a manifest result of the Clunisian spirit,—while, on the other hand, the establishment of Cluny presents itself in the Middle Ages as for its time the truest and most practical expression of Christianity. To repudiate falsehood in every department is to be consistent with the spirit of Christianity,—to regard form only as the logical manifestation of a practical requirement : the Christian treats everything according to the value of the idea of which it is the embodiment. Everything in his view should have a necessary function,—fulfil a duty (if I may thus express it), and reach perfection without deviating from these laws ; and it was as men of taste,—though as yet possessing little more than its barbarian rudiments—that the Clunisian artists first applied these principles. The Clunisians were on the point of realising a Renaissance in the Middle Ages ; they revived the taste for letters ; they had administrative and governmental ideas of a character very comprehensive for the times in which they lived; they were legislators, diplomatists, politicians, savants, artists : if they did not succeed in accomplishing what they attempted, it was because they constituted only a clerical aristocracy amid the peoples of Europe ; but could they aspire to be anything else considering the social condition of that period ? To them perhaps is owing that great national movement which caused their disappearance from the scene at the end of the twelfth century ; and this fact suggests one of the most interesting subjects for investigation in the history of the results of intellectual effort since the termination of the Classical period. The Clunisians, in consequence of the influence they exerted in secular affairs, their love of arts and letters, and their relations with European sovereigns, had been naturally led to display in their monasteries a luxury till then unknown. It was against this luxury that St. Bernard protested in the twelfth century ; he saw that monastic institutions were becoming perverted, and he endeavoured to arrest the evil.

How interesting it is to read the letters of the Abbot of Cluny, Peter the Venerable, to Bernard, written to urge him to be more moderate in his attacks, and to regard with an impartial eye the White and the Black Friars in his religious houses. Peter in his correspondence with Bernard exhibits himself as a man of the world, enlightened and tolerant, and who anticipates in the reaction provoked by Bernard only additional peril to the monastic order in general; he exhorts him to charity:—" Different colours," he says in one of his letters, " different dwellings, dissimilar customs, are adverse to love and are contrary to unity. The white friar looks on the black friar, and regards him as something monstrous. The black friar, observing the white friar, considers him an amorphous monstrosity. Novelties produce an irritating effect on a mind in which other habits are deeply ingrained ; it is disinclined to approve what it is not accustomed to see. Such is the impression experienced by those who take account of external things and do not pay attention to what takes place in the depths of the soul. But the eye of reason, the eye of the mind, does not see in the same manner ; it perceives, acknowledges, and comprehends that a diversity of colours, usages, and dwellings, is of no account among the servants of God, since, as the Apostle says : ' Circumcision availeth nothing, but a new creature ;' and ' there is neither Greek nor Jew ; male nor female, barbarian, Scythian, bond nor free ; but Christ is all and in all.'

"This is what men of discernment see, acknowledge, and comprehend clearly ; but all are not so ; there are few to whom this intellectual discernment is given. It is necessary, in my judgment, that we should put ourselves on a level with the inferior, and conduct ourselves towards them with a kind of selective precaution, in the spirit of him who said : ' I am made all things to all men, that I might gain all.'"

But I must stop, or I might go on to quote the whole letter, which is a masterpiece as displaying a truly Christian spirit, good sense, good taste, and sometimes fine irony. Peter the Venerable and Suger were an embodiment of the intelligence of the twelfth century. The ardent Saint Bernard anticipated the influence of arts and letters upon the mind of the peoples of Europe ; he feared the return of the Pagan Art, and thought he foresaw form gaining the victory over doctrine, philosophy over faith. He was a man of genius, endeavouring to sound the abyss, but misunderstanding the spirit of his contemporaries. He could scarcely retard the course of the torrent during his own life. Peter the Venerable almost presents the aspect of an ancient philosopher : there is something of Cicero in his cast of mind ; but with the dignity, the resignation, and the calmness of the true Christian. Suger is the statesman,—taking no part in monastic contests; perceiving the danger, but thinking it more prudent to evade it than to fight hand to hand with it like Saint Bernard. This digression is necessary for the understanding of what follows.

The Clunisians had schools in their monasteries; and not only were these schools required for the instruction of the monks themselves, but they were also open to the laity. While the Clunisians had among themselves architects, sculptors, and painters, they also taught these arts to the world outside; for in the building and decoration of their churches and sumptuous abbeys, they were obliged to have recourse to lay workmen, as the Clunisians in the twelfth century were above working with their own hands. The more the Cistercians affected to despise the plastic arts, the more elaboration was displayed by the Clunisians in their buildings, furniture, and dress: the struggle had commenced; and the Clunisians, like all who have attained a high degree of civilisation in a community still characterised by rudeness, regarded their rivals as barbarians, and combated their excessive puritanism by introducing the study and the love of the arts among the people at large as far as the circumstances of the times allowed. Their architecture, towards the middle of the twelfth century, bears the impress of remarkable elaboration; but in thus raising laymen to the rank of skilful artists and craftsmen, and giving them a taste for the arts and skill therein, they developed in them native inspirations which had hitherto remained latent. In fact in the Clunisian buildings from 1120 to 1140 we see a new principle arising: the traditions of the Romanesque period are impugned; the attempt is made to solve certain problems by abandoning the methods of Classical Antiquity, and adopting a course of independent reasoning. It would seem as if in France whenever the traditional path has been abandoned for a new idea, the course of change has been rapid: we had an example of this a century ago; and in the twelfth century we were the same people as in the sixteenth and the eighteenth. About the year 1135 the Abbots of Vezelay were having the narthex of their church built, in which, though Romanesque in plan, details, profiles, and sculptures, we observe new principles of construction, which foreshadow an independent style of art.[1] It was at the same time or nearly so, that the Cathedral of Langres was being built; in which, as regards the system of construction, if not in the details, which are almost Roman, the Romanesque methods are abandoned. In 1144, Abbot Suger was completing the Abbey Church of St. Denis; and in the parts of

[1] See in the *Dictionnaire de l'Architecture française* the articles Architecture Religieuse, fig. 22, and Construction, fig. 19.

the building dating from that time, we observe the architectural revolution accomplished : not only is the round arch abandoned, but the system of construction called Gothic has been invented. Whence had Suger got his master of works? Was it from among his monks? Was the master a layman? Friar Guillaume [1] tells us only that the illustrious Abbot "summoned from different parts of the kingdom workmen of all kinds, masons, carpenters, painters, blacksmiths, founders, goldsmiths, and lapidaries, all renowned for skill in their several arts." But nowhere, in the France of that day, and certainly not elsewhere, were structures being erected like St. Denis ; we must remark also that Suger wished that the edifice should be quickly built ; he was urgent that it should be finished, fearing that his successor would not continue the undertaking. On the 5th of June 1140, King Louis le Gros laid the first stone of *the foundations*,[2] and on the 11th of June 1144 was present at the consecration ; the church was finished. Now this new church was as long as the present one, though not so broad ; and this haste will explain the negligence exhibited in the erection, the inadequacy of the foundations at some points, and why the nave and the transept had to be rebuilt a century later ; but it also indicates to us the idea of rapidly achieving an extraordinary result, of astonishing the multitude, of striking a grand blow. The object was accomplished ; for all his contemporaries, including the Abbot of Cluny himself, Peter the Venerable, saw in the work undertaken and accomplished by Suger one of the marvels of the West. But why this haste?

Suger was a man of discernment ; he could not fail to see that the monastic system was approaching its decline ; and though he introduced a severe reform into his abbey as early as 1127, and was content with a poor cell for himself, (in consequence of a letter of St. Bernard's in which the Abbot of Cîteaux inveighed against the license prevailing among the monks of St. Denis,)[3] he felt that the glory of the Royal Abbey must be renovated by some great undertaking, that something more and something other must be done than the Clunisians had effected,—though without affecting the contempt expressed by the Cistercians for art ; in fact that, on the contrary, the religious orders ought to be in the van of progress and of new ideas—that they should attract the multitude by a display of art hitherto unknown.

[1] Life of Suger, Book ii.

[2] "Ipse enim serenissimus Rex intus descendens propriis manibus suum imposuit, hosque et multi alii tam abbates quam religiosi viri lapides suos imposuerunt, quidam etiam gemmas, ob amorem et reverentiam Jhesu Christi decantantes : *Lapides pretiosi omnes muri tui*" (*Suger's letter*).

[3] In this letter (18th in Mabillon's edition) Saint Bernard says that "the interior of the monastery was filled with men-at-arms, and women, that business of all kinds was transacted there, and that quarrels were frequent."

In fact it is in this that the arts developed in France, in the twelfth century, differ in all respects from those of Classical Antiquity. We find Western society at that time under the dominion of a kind of fever, and the arts bear traces of its influence. In ancient Rome political revolutions and intellectual movements had no sensible effect on the arts; the latter followed their own course, and were not mixed up with public affairs. In France, in the twelfth century, the communes are in revolt, the feudal régime suffers from the hand of this very Abbot Suger the first assaults; the royal power begins to recover from the depression into which it had fallen; the great reform of Cluny is sending forth its last scintillations; the clerical power of the religious orders has become effete; it is a source of embarrassment—an obstacle to the unity of the ruling power. We find Suger distinguishing himself in the middle of this century by a conduct exhibiting political prudence,—which in troublous times is the distinctive mark of a prescient mind,—an exact appreciation of men and of events, and at the same time great moderation; and it was during the government of this minister that in the very centre of the kingdom of France we see the arts completely changing their direction, and finally abandoning the last remnants of clerical Romanesque tradition to enter on a completely new path. It was under the administration of Suger that the Bishop Beaudoin II., a friend of the Abbot of St. Denis, built the Cathedral of Noyon, about 1150, and this cathedral presents analogies of a very striking character to the parts still extant of the Abbey Church. It was also about the same time that the Cathedral of Senlis was built, and it was in 1160 that the Bishop Maurice de Sully began the Cathedral of Paris with a novel plan and arrangements.

Dating from the Roman period, the cities of Gaul in the central and northern provinces had lost, together with their municipal institutions, those buildings which were their visible embodiment. When, in the twelfth century, some of them endeavoured to reconquer their ancient privileges and took the communal oath, they were obliged to hold their meetings in the public places; for in those unhappy times, except the churches and castles, there were no edifices large enough to hold an assembly of citizens. Among the powers against which the communes rose in revolt, the abbeys were necessarily the most persistently hostile to the movement; while the lay lords, the bishops, and the sovereign declared themselves sometimes the protectors, and sometimes the adversaries of the newly asserted liberties, according as they found it their interest to protect or to repress them.

In the twelfth century the bishops saw their authority seriously weakened by religious establishments depending only on the Holy See, freed from all diocesan authority, attracting to themselves the gifts of the faithful, covering the land with conventual or parochial churches, establishing their influence more and more securely in the court of the sovereign, the castle of the noble, and the dwellings of the peasants. Only one resource remained to the bishops, viz., to take advantage of the communal movement,—the secular spirit which was beginning to develop itself,—so as to regain, at least in the cities, that diocesan power which was escaping from their grasp. From 1160, therefore, they used their utmost efforts to be able to afford to these cities, in which the communal spirit had shown itself, vast edifices in which the citizens might assemble around the episcopal throne. Then their concessions to that spirit were liberal; adopting architectural programmes of a contrary character to those adopted by the abbots, they purposed that their cathedrals should present vast interiors, easy of access, with no partitions, having only an altar, an episcopal throne, and few or no chapels;—that is to say, buildings fulfilling very nearly the functions of the Roman basilica.[1] And in fact the people responded to the appeal of the bishops, contributions flowed in, and in a few years the cities of Paris, Sens, Chartres, Rouen, Bourges, Reims, Senlis, Meaux, Amiens, Cambray, Arras, Beauvais, and Troyes, witnessed the erection of great cathedrals which are still existing, though seriously modified in their original arrangements. Laymen alone, already organised in craft-guilds, were called in to design and carry out the plans; and entering fully into the views of the bishops, they not only followed the new programmes that were presented to them, but adopted a new system of construction, and new forms in architecture and in sculpture. They advanced rapidly in the study of geometry and drawing, and made a point of having recourse to nature in all that belongs to statuary and decoration.

In this art was manifested the special genius of the French nation,—a genius foreign to the civilisations of antiquity, as it is to those of Italy and Germany in modern times. Until the rise of the secular school in France, we find the architecture presenting traces of Roman and Byzantine Art. Construction proper and decoration were still derived from Classic Antiquity: if the influence of Western taste was discernible, it was not yet strong enough to set aside traditions that were still vital; the religious establishments, while they modified, could not help preserving those traditions. The secular school of the latter part of the twelfth century abandoned them completely, and replaced them by principles based on reflection. These principles may be summarised as follows : equilibrium in the constructive system by opposing active resistance to active pressure, the

---

[1] See, in the *Dictionnaire de l'Architecture française*, the article "CATHÉDRALE."

outward form resulting only from the structure and the requirements ; ornamentation derived solely from the local flora ; statuary
tending to the naturalistic, and seeking dramatic expression.
These principles must be thoroughly appreciated at the outset,
if we would gain any understanding of the French secular school.
Begging my reader's best attention I present (fig. 4) a trans-

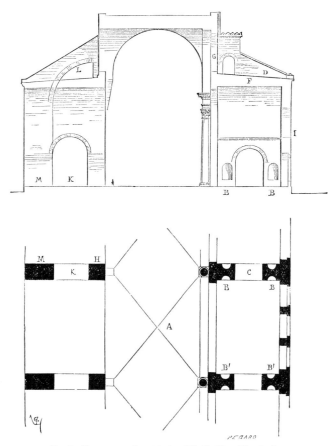

Fig. 4.—Transverse section and plan of the Basilica of Constantine.

verse section and part plan of a Roman hall,—the Basilica of
Constantine,—as an example.   This hall is built entirely of rubble-
work with brick facings coated with stucco, except the columns
and their entablatures, which were of marble, but which were in
fact only a decoration, as the building could stand without the
great interior orders.   The central nave A consists of a series of

groined vaults, built according to the Roman method, namely, by means of intersecting half cylinders. These vaults are of rubble,—thus forming a concrete mass without elasticity,—inert, like a huge tortoise-shell cut out of a single block. These vaults however required to be kept up; for if they had not been compressed between immovable masses the enormous weight would have occasioned cracks, and the vault thus dislocated would have fallen to pieces. Buttresses B were therefore erected opposite the meeting of the vaulting groins pierced in their lower part by an arch C; and between these buttresses which rise to D, were turned barrel vaults, likewise of rubble, covering the spaces BB, B′B′, supporting the terraces F, and facilitating the formation of openings for light, G, beneath the central vault. The wall I, also pierced with openings, is only an enclosure supporting nothing. If we removed from this building all that is unnecessary to its perfect stability, we might, as shown in the left-hand plan and section, reduce the inside piers to the vertical supports H, further enlarge the openings K, omit the column, and throw over a flying-buttress L opposite the thrust of the upper vaults, and direct that thrust on the buttresses M. These are the really effective elements of the structure.

It must be acknowledged that, adopting the Roman method, it was impossible to apply it in a manner more simple, strong, economical, or dignified in point of appearance. But we have elsewhere shown how and why this method of building, which was so well suited to the political and administrative organisation of the Romans, was not practicable in the west under the feudal régime. The secular architects of the end of the twelfth century were compelled to make use of the means at their command: and even had they regarded the Roman method of building as the only desirable one, it is not probable that the entire political organisation of their time would have been changed to please them. In fact, in order to build a hall such as that figured above, it was first necessary to provide a considerable space for the preparations, as it was not possible to erect such a building in parts; it was necessary to *level up* regularly the whole surface of the building; it was necessary to make and fix at the same time the wooden centres intended to support the bedding on which the concrete vaults had to be turned; it was necessary that these centres should be of sufficient strength and near enough together to enable the bedding to bear the weight of the concrete; it was necessary—the centres being fixed (and we may imagine the enormous quantity of wood they required)— that the vaults should be rapidly made,—for concrete-work, if it is to be homogeneous and strong, must be executed uninterruptedly; it was necessary therefore to have at disposal very considerable stores of gravel, brick, sand, but particularly lime. And it must be observed that brick and lime are not raw materials—that a baking process is required. The Romans alone had the organisation required to build such an edifice. Let us imagine ourselves in France in the twelfth century : we are not absolute masters, we lack the space necessary for building ; objection is made to our having it, and it is conceded only after considerable opposition ; we are not supplied with immense stores of timber by vessels solely employed to transport it for our use ; on the contrary, we have to go and seek our framing spar by spar, among twenty proprietors, from each of whom we shall only get a few pieces ; or, on the other hand, we must buy it, and if it is known that we want it, since there is no fixed market price we shall have to pay dearly for the timber. Suppose again that we cannot have stone brought to us by means of requisitions, by disciplined soldiers or by slaves, but that it must be sought for in various quarries from different proprietors, be transported at our own expense or by voluntary aid ; that the lime is supplied at intervals and in small quantities ; that our workmen are forced labourers who do as little as possible, or of men to whom wages must be paid, and that every now and then the lord of the manor takes away these men to go and fight against his neighbours. Should we, under these circumstances, build an edifice such as the Basilica of Constantine ? or, if we commenced it, could we finish it ? Should we not fall short of timber and lime before the work was half done ? or if after many delays we finally succeeded in erecting it, would it possess the qualities necessary for its perfect stability ? under conditions such as I have mentioned, should we not, on the contrary, if we were prudent and well-advised, subdivide our work, avoid encumbering the site, apportion the labour so that it may be suspended or recommenced without imperilling the whole ?—try to economise our materials, since they are difficult to procure, and endeavour to obtain great results by means of limited resources. Let us see then how we should proceed to erect a hall analogous to the Basilica of Constantine. Our quarries afford us abundance of freestone ; so we shall not waste our time in making and burning bricks. Stone, however, is an expensive material ; we shall therefore be economical with it, and shall only use the quantity necessary. Instead (fig. 5) of raising a buttress of brick and rubble-work, pierced at its base by an archway, we shall put two stone columns AA' and an exterior buttress B. Instead of turning a barrel vault of rubble-work at right angles to the nave, we shall put an intermediate column C, and build two groined vaults AD, EC over each bay of the aisle. Raising a wall GG astride on the coupled columns the remaining outward part of

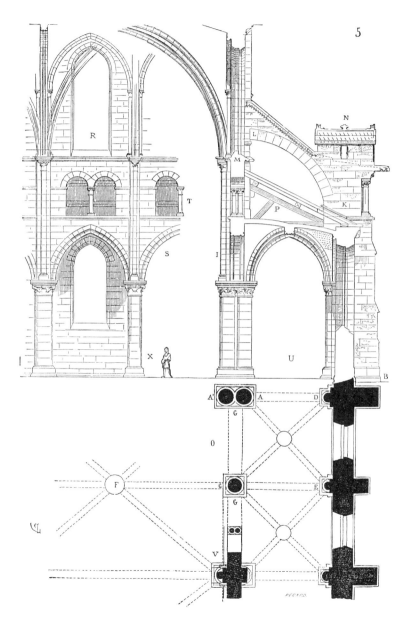

Fig. 5.—Example of twelfth century construction.

the double capital A will serve as support to the springer of the transverse-rib AD, and that of the capital A will receive the attached shafts I running up the wall to carry the central vaulting, which will be groined, but divided by a transverse rib CF. Instead of raising solid buttresses to abut the thrusts of the central groined vaulting, we shall only erect a pier K on each buttress B, and throw over a half arch, KL, replacing the inert resistance which the solid wall would have afforded by an active resistance,— active inasmuch as it acts by pushing against a wall M which tends to depart from the perpendicular by the thrust of the central vault. But as we are not satisfied of the sufficiency of the abutment K to resist the combined action of the vault thrusts directed against the flying buttresses, we surmount the pier K with a weight N, which insures its stability. Our climate scarcely admits of those concrete terraced roofs, cemented or paved, such as the Romans formed in Italy; we shall therefore elevate the central vaulting sufficiently to allow of a roof P beneath the upper windows R, and with a view to relieving the arches S as well as lighting and ventilating the timber roofing P, we shall pierce openings at T over the arches. We shall soon perceive that the coupled columns AA′ are useless, and that we may replace them by a single cylindrical pillar, since the pressures—if the structure is as it should be—fall between these two columns. But we are well aware that this construction, consisting of props from the ground and thrusts met by active counter thrusts, cannot have the firmness of base,—the inertia of the Roman structure; that movements may occur, and that consequently the vaulting should not consist of a concrete and homogeneous mass, but should have a certain elasticity to enable it to yield to the strain without rending. Moreover, we have not at our command either the quantity of timber required for the centering of Roman vaults, nor the materials suitable for their construction. We content ourselves with forming the transverse and diagonal ribs on centres; and these arches themselves become permanent centres enabling us to turn portions of concave vaulting from one to another according to every required curve without making use for this purpose of intermediate centering.[1] If circumstances render it necessary, we can, on this plan, suspend our works, recommence them, execute them all at once or in parts without disadvantage to the solidity of the edifice.

We reflect deeply on what we are doing, and consult our

---

[1] See the Article CONSTRUCTION (voutes) in the *Dictionnaire raisonné de l'Architecture Française.*—In figure 5 we have represented at A the ground-plan, at V the plan of the piers above the columns, at U the transverse section of the edifice, and at X the longitudinal section of a bay. The Cathedral of Arras was built on this plan. In the nave and choir of Sens Cathedral may still be seen constructive arrangements analogous to those given here.

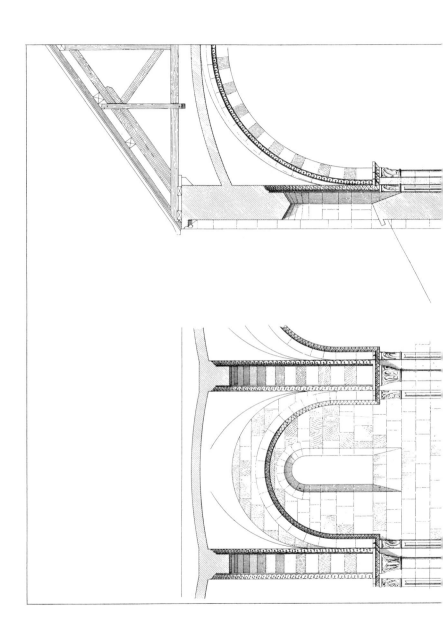

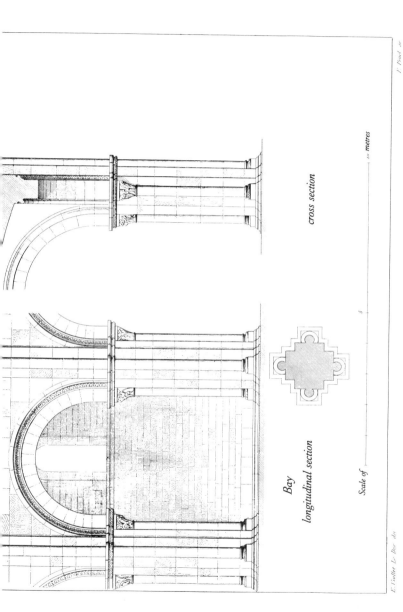

cross section

Bay
longitudinal section

Scale of ———————————— 5 ———————————— in metres

PLATE XI.   Nave of Church, Vezelay

reason only without concerning ourselves about traditions or time-hallowed forms. The diagonal ribs being naturally the longest,—those whose diameter is the greatest,—we retain the semicircle for these; and with a view both to lessen the thrust of the other ribs and to raise their apex nearly to the level of the key-stone of the diagonal ribs, we trace the transverse ribs, the arches, and the wall-ribs, with two portions of arcs, which intersect at the height we desire to give them. Thus we are no longer restrained by the necessity of making groined vaults on a square plan,—that is vaulting resulting from the intersection of two equal or nearly equal cylinders. Every plan, whether drawn on a parallelogram, a quadrilateral, a triangle, a regular or irregular octagon, can be vaulted by our method. We have freed ourselves from the rules imposed by the Romans, and more or less adhered to by the Romanesque architects. I can readily conceive that there should be those who prefer the section of the Basilica of Constantine to that of an analogous hall built at the end of the twelfth century. The later conception is more complicated, demands more skilful combinations, and a larger amount of reflection; but is it on that account more barbarous? From the section of the Basilica of Constantine we can never produce anything but the section of the Basilica of Constantine. We have here an art matured,—perfect, if you will,—but unalterable; this is its final expression; whereas the combinations presented in the section, figure 5, are capable of endless developments; for this reason, that the equilibrium of balanced forces affords us every variety of combination and opens before us ever new paths. It is not necessary to repeat here what we have said elsewhere, or to recall attention to principles which have been already treated at considerable length.[1] Let us examine the features of the new architecture belonging to the Western secular school, at the close of the twelfth century. The tendency to substitute rational for traditional methods was apparent in the structure of the edifices of this period; it was also apparent in the forms and in the decoration. We observed that the Greeks had only admitted the vertical point of support, weighted vertically by the mono-lithic lintel, and that the Romans had long employed the arch and the lintel without troubling themselves about harmonising these opposite principles; that at the termination of the Empire, aided by the Greeks, they had admitted the arch resting immediately on the column, but without uniting those two principles. The Romanesque school had already taken an important step by seeking combinations in which we see the column subordinating itself to the arch and becoming merely an accessory of minor importance (see Plate XI.) Among the early Gothic

[1] See the *Dictionnaire raisonné de l'Architecture Française.*

architects we find the arch absolutely determining the support; the arch determines not only the structure but the form; the architecture is dictated solely by the arch. The Romans did in numerous instances subordinate their structures to the arch,— to the vault;—but, I observe, once more, in their architecture every support is an inert mass, and their vaulted buildings are, as it were, hollowed out in a single block; they are enormous castings; whereas the architects of the twelfth century assign a function to each part. The column is a real support; if its capital is expanded, it is to sustain a load; if the mouldings and ornaments of this capital are developed, it is because such development is necessary. If the vaults are divided by ribs, it is because these ribs are so many sinews performing a function. Each vertical support depends for its stability on being stayed and weighted; every arch-thrust meets another which counteracts it. Walls, as supports, no longer appear: they have become mere enclosures. The entire system consists of a framework which maintains itself, not by its mass, but by the combination of oblique forces neutralising each other. The vault ceases to be a crust—a shell in one piece; it is an ingenious combination of pressures which are really in action and are directed on certain points of support disposed so as to receive them and transmit them to the ground. The mouldings and ornaments are shaped with a view to manifest this mechanism. The mouldings fulfil exactly a useful function; externally they protect the architectural members by throwing off the rain-water,—the simplest form of section being adopted for that pupose; internally they are few, only indicating the different levels, or frankly jutting out for the purpose of corbelling or footing. The ornaments are designed solely from the local flora, for the architects wish everything to be of home production, and borrow nothing either from a foreign art or from the past; they are moreover adapted to their place, always apparent and easy to understand; they are subordinated to the architectural form and the construction; they are worked before they are set in place, and take their position as members essential to the whole.

At the decline of the Empire,—in Gallo-Roman buildings, for example,—the sculpture is scattered at hazard, as it were, on the walls, the pilasters, even the shafts of the columns; it would appear that at that time when a building had been erected, carvers were set to work on the rough stone scarcely faced, and which they covered with ornaments or figures as closely as they could cram them without regard to beds and joints.

The Romanesque architecture towards its decline,—especially in the west of France,[1]—was falling into the same abuse of

---

[1] As in certain buildings in Poitou of the twelfth century.

ornament. The secular architects of the French school completely broke with these habits, which always indicate the
declining phase of art. The ornamentation became sober and
rational, it only occupied special parts of the architecture, was
never redundant, and could neither be lessened nor augmented
without destroying the general harmony.

We often judge of these buildings from their present appearance, without considering that in the course of some seven
centuries they have undergone changes or mutilations; and we
thus charge the architects who designed them with the faults
and defects that have resulted from subsequent additions or
dilapidations. On the other hand, we judge of the buildings of
antiquity from the ruins still standing; and imagination, supplying what is wanting, creates for itself beauties which really did
not exist. Many Roman buildings would gain nothing from
being restored; and what remains to us of them is precisely that
which constitutes their grandeur and beauty—the structure. I
will not say this of Greek architecture, which, on the contrary,
to be appreciated at its true value, must be supposed complete
and surrounded by all its accessories. As since the renaissance
we have drawn our inspirations much more frequently from
Roman than from Greek architecture, we have thus neglected
one of the most valuable points of excellence which we had
in common with Greek art during the Middle Ages. The
Roman is but little sensible to contour,—to the conspicuous
appearance of a work of Art, and his buildings often present an
unattractive outline; if we imagine the mass of those great
edifices which belong to his genius, as restored, we shall perceive
that—dimensions apart—this mass must have formed lines and
profiles that are far removed from Greek elegance. In their
architecture—I say it once more—the Greeks took account of
the light, the transparency of the air, and the features of the
environment; they paid particular attention to the arrangement
of the angles of the buildings, which stood out *en silhouette*
against the sky or against the blue depth of the mountains. It
is evident that they did not study these important parts of the
architecture in view of mere geometrical relations, but took into
consideration with the most thoughtful and artistic judgment
the perspective effect; it was as real artists that they combined
these effects, being well aware that buildings, when actually
constructed, are not seen in geometrical relations. Calculations
such as these which suggest themselves to a man endowed with
a just and delicate sense of form do not enter into the mind of
the Roman; we observe, on the contrary, that to him the geometrical study of his building has been his sole consideration,—
that a positive and practical view is his only determining motive.

The imitation of Roman architecture has unavoidably led us back to the method adopted by the Roman architects, and we have come to design our plans and elevations on paper without bestowing the least thought on the perspective results of the realisation. But we did not always act thus; we once possessed, like the Greeks, a very delicate and well-trained feeling for effect; we liked to let our imagination dwell on the effect of our architectural forms in profile, and were long under the impression that buildings are more often viewed obliquely than perpendicularly to one of their faces. The Greeks were fond of architecture, and while walking or going to business, would take pleasure in looking at their public buildings; they made a point therefore of their presenting an agreeable aspect from every point of view, and especially of their outlines being always attractive. While we were "barbarians," we had the same artistic weaknesses; but now that it has been clearly demonstrated that we are Latins, and people of sense, we pursue our callings without being affected by the outline of a building; if we want to see it that we may keep ourselves *au courant* as regards the productions of our time, we go and stand right in front of it, in the middle of the façade; and woe to the architect if one side is not absolutely like the other, for symmetry is almost the only excellence of which we are sensible. Our architects have gradually lost the habit of representing their buildings in perspective, or at least they limit their graphic studies to geometrical relations. I cannot think that the Greeks proceeded thus, and it is certain that our architects in the Middle Ages took into account the effects produced by accidental points of view; this is evident from the treatment of the square returns of their buildings, the way in which the angles and the profiles of the cornices are managed, and pyramids with octagonal base —for example—placed on prisms with a square base. It is demonstrated to us in those architectural planes which so effectively intersect each other in perspective, while their geometrical representation could not exhibit such results or even allow them to be surmised.

There is one other artistic element which we share with the Greeks, but which we have almost lost since we have imagined ourselves to be Romans, and that is appreciation of form. Our lay school of the twelfth and thirteenth centuries possessed this sense in a very high degree; and while these two styles of architecture (I mean that of ancient Greece and that of the Ile-de-France in the twelfth century) are contrary to each other in principles, and consequently differ greatly in results, we find striking relations between these two arts in everything that concerns elaboration of form, in the mouldings, the ornamentation, in certain effects of detail, in the study of the general outlines and the vigour of the parts which have to do both with construction and decoration ; certainly there is no imitation, nor anything like identity in features, but there is a connection between the mode of feeling and expression. If we have not taken advantage to the same extent as the Greeks, of the effect to be derived from colouring applied to buildings, we have discovered effects resulting from variety of forms, of which they were ignorant ; for we may frankly acknowledge that we are more sensible to form than to colour,—that we are draughtsmen rather than colourists : during the twelfth, thirteenth, fourteenth, and sixteenth centuries we possessed distinguished schools of statuaries and architects ; the seventeenth century abounded in excellent engravers, while our painters have never been able to rival those of Italy, and our decorators have never equalled oriental works in combination of colours. We were formerly, and should be still—if we were allowed to be so—a people specially endowed with those gifts which characterise the architect.

For some years, indeed, it has been acknowledged that there appears in the works of the secular school, at the close of the twelfth century, an art very profound and elaborate,—possibly too elaborate ; a noble inspiration and principles fruitful in applications ; but there has been as yet no serious study of the characteristic form of that art ;—a form which is the most vivid expression of our genius, which is versatile, facile, and skilful in invention ; acutely reflective, and presenting a mixture of lofty conception with a simplicity which is rather affected than sincere, but mobile and restless, and greatly preferring appearance to reality.

A people formerly civilised, but which for several centuries finds itself oppressed by barbarian conquerors, oppressed by feudalism secular or clerical, and to which the light can penetrate only through the mantle of the monk, which nevertheless in a few years succeeds in developing a complete art whose principles are logically deduced,—an art in which all is new from the structure to the form ; a people which having originated this art, pursues its developments with ardour in increasingly logical sequence, without deviations or reactions ; a people that accomplishes this presents a fact that is perhaps unique in the history of the arts, and gives more than sufficient proof of its being endowed with a very extraordinary instinct. To recapitulate : We find that in the middle of the twelfth century, the political and social condition of that little corner of the Western World which then constituted France was such as to break the connection between the arts and the monastic establishments. A secular school,—purely secular,—is formed ;

it reacts in the first instance against the monastic spirit in
substituting the investigation of new principles for hallowed
traditions; these new principles are based not on the improvement of traditional types, but on science,—on the observance
of laws hitherto unrecognised in the art of construction. This
school, deriving its inspirations from within itself, and constituting
a kind of free-masonry, does not deviate for a moment from the
line it has traced out for itself, while leaving the individual his
liberty; it abandons not only the methods of construction
adopted by the Romanesque architects, but their mouldings,
their sculpture, and their mode of decoration; it attracts to
itself all the other bodies of the state, and in a quarter of a
century transforms not only the other arts but the handicrafts
generally; it is so powerful (and we must not forget that it is
secular,—that its members are the people), that its assistance is
sought in every quarter,—to build the castle, the city mansion,
the palace, the hospital, and the fortress, as also to erect the
church and even the convent, which has allowed art to quit its
confines. The individual artist uses his inventive power, but
does not attach his own name to his work : the work belongs to
the corporation which has succeeded in making the only conquests
in its power,—independence in intellectual labours, ideas of
liberty, investigations in various branches of knowledge; its
tastes, its preferences, its hatred of injustice and oppression, and
even its penchant for satire,—all are expressed by it in those
buildings which it is allowed, perforce, to construct according
to its own fancy. It has secured for itself a complete liberty
in works of art, which it abuses without restraint or interruption; and it is through this abuse that it decays, having
carried its science and the excessive development of its principles
and perfection in execution to the utmost limits of the possible.
But what connection is there between the emancipation of the
artist,—an emancipation in accordance with the national genius,
—the emancipation of the industrial classes—and the political
régime of the Middle Ages? Why—I ask once more,—should
we confound those who were incessantly striving after intellectual
development, and improving the practical appliances of an art
exclusively their own, and of which they made themselves the
masters, with the petty tyrants who occupied the soil of the
West, when these tyrants were unable to exercise any influence
over that association of artists and craftsmen, were powerless to
develop or arrest its progress, and were only too happy to
employ its intelligence and labour? Was it these artists and
craftsmen that had produced the social condition amid which
they were living? Was it by vague theories or by insurrections
that they endeavoured to escape from it? No; it was by work

—by union in work—not by endeavouring to pass beyond the circle which destiny had marked out for them, but by enlarging this circle as much as possible ; and can we be so ungrateful as not to recognise these efforts ? We erect statues to certain artists of mediocre merit, who were only plagiarists of arts foreign to our country and manners ; and are we not bound to cherish, at least in our hearts, a profound sense of gratitude towards men who in so humble a position were the first to give a visible form, which was both original and novel, to national unity, and the revival of intellect, art and science ? Will any one venture to deny this power of the secular French school of the close of the twelfth century ? Let us examine what the Romanesque or monastic schools were a little earlier. It must not be supposed that those schools had fallen so low that a reform in art had become necessary ; on the contrary, they were in a flourishing condition, and they produced works of rare elegance ; but these schools were divided.

At the commencement of the twelfth century, Cistercian buildings did not resemble Clunisian buildings, the architecture of Poitou did not resemble that of Normandy, and the latter differed essentially from the architecture of the Ile-de-France, which in its turn was diverse from that of Auvergne and Limousin ; Lyonnais and Burgundy possessed a Romanesque art which was not that of Champagne ; and these schools had a vitality of their own, their methods of execution were of a very superior order, and they had an original character, resulting from the genius of the populations of these provinces themselves, or from local traditions, or from the influence of powerful abbeys.

In Burgundy, the Romanesque architecture of the twelfth century is entirely Clunisian ; in Champagne it is rather Cistercian, in Auvergne it is delicate and elegant, affected by local Roman traditions and Byzantine influences introduced through Perigord and Limousin ; in Poitou it is confused, loaded with sculpture, and still preserving the impress of Gallo-Roman art ; in Normandy it is severe, methodical, scientific, powerful, elaborate in point of structure, but with less sculpture ; we observe the stamp of a practical, calculating people, with little sensibility to form, having regard for principles, and not restrained by traditions : in the Ile-de-France, this architecture is refined, sober, pliable, and already characterised by that reserve which is the impress of cultivated taste. In Saintonge, the Romanesque architecture of the twelfth century is a perfectly faithful reflection of the tranquil and gentle character of the Western provinces—a mixture of delicacy and firmness ; its style approaches perhaps the most nearly that of the Greek art of the Byzantine period : it possesses the charm, the elegance, and purity in details, and the delicate and free execution by which that art is characterised. Let us take an example, Plate XII. ; let us study this exterior of the aisle of the Church of St. Eutropius at Saintes. Could we not imagine ourselves looking at one of the buildings to be found on the shores of the Adriatic, though showing more intelligence in construction, and a more decidedly Greek character in the execution of the details ? The lower windows light a crypt, and the bays of which the aisles consist are indicated in the exterior by those relieving arches which make the vaults penetrate as it were through the wall. The architect succeeded in giving dignity to his arrangement by dividing the lights ; he considered, and justly, that the archivolts of the windows concentric with the arches would give too much importance to these openings ; his taste led him to perceive that concentric arches of different diameters, successively repeated, produce a disagreeable effect on the eye ; he preferred tympanums pierced by circular windows which, by giving light to the interior, indicate on the exterior that the vaults rise as high as the great *relieving arches.* The whole construction consists of small materials which could be raised and laid without the assistance of machines, human strength being sufficient. The mouldings are extremely delicate, and are designed by a consummate artist ; the ornaments are only an embroidery whose purity and pleasing arrangement set off the mouldings without altering their character ; nevertheless, with such limited resources and simple means, this architecture has an air of grandeur ; it is easy to understand, and clearly explains its intention. This is a specimen of the productions of one of the best schools of the West at the beginning of the twelfth century—taken from a hundred not less remarkable examples ; and if we compare this art with the Western Italian architecture of the same or nearly the same period,—the outer aisle of the Cathedral of Pisa for example, which does not at all indicate the interior structure, whose proportions are comparatively unattractive, its aspect being frigid and monotonous, and presenting in the details an exceedingly poor execution,—mouldings imitated from the debased Roman style,—in which quarter I would ask, do we find science ? in which quarter do we discover art ? It is true that the aisle of the Cathedral of Pisa presents a marble casing, and that the building is raised on a noble flight of steps of the same material, in an admirable position, whereas the Church of St. Eutropius at Saintes has been thrice despoiled, its basement is sunk in heaps of accumulated soil amid briars and dirt,—and it is in France.

I have spoken of the details,—the mouldings with which this specimen of architecture is decorated ; and I think it needful

Scale of ——————————— ;; metres

PLATE XII.   Aisle, Church of St. Eutropius, Saintes

E. Viollet le Duc. del.

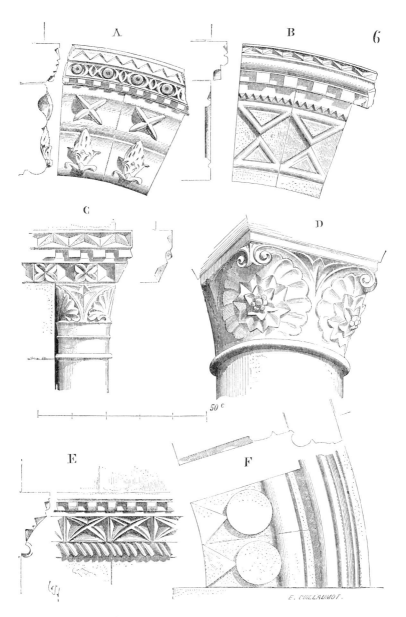

FIG. 6.—Details from Saint-Eutropius at Saintes.

to give a few examples here, figure 6.[1] To any one who is at all acquainted with the effect of mouldings in architecture, or who has meditated on the profound elaboration and delicate grace of the Greek mouldings of Classical Antiquity and of the Byzantine period, an analogy will be manifest here in point of method, sense of effect, and the relations of lights and shadows. But it would be useless to expatiate on points requiring such subtle appreciation, and which are exclusively matters of taste ; artists will understand me, and demonstrations would prove nothing to those who are destitute of artistic feeling. It was about the same time that the Clunisians built the nave of Vezelay, of which we have given a bay, Plate XI. The Romanesque of Burgundy is as robust, even rude, as that of Saintonge is refined and delicate. At Saintes the capitals are short, slightly developed, and covered with sculptures resembling goldsmith's work ; the mouldings are flat, composed of a great number of members, the ornamentation is only an embroidery, the proportions elongated, almost slender. At Vezelay, on the contrary, the construction is composed of large stones, the proportions are sturdy, the capitals massive, and widely expanded to carry arches without members ; the mouldings are bold and simple in design, the sculpture is vigorous, and bold even to rudeness, but full of style : we recognise an art that is conscious of its power and asserting its mastery. The Norman school resembles neither of those just mentioned ; but if we would see Norman architecture of the Romanesque period that has retained its original character during the twelfth and thirteenth centuries, we must quit France and look for it in England. It was there that it found its development at the close of the eleventh century. The Normans were skilful builders; it was not however until late that they endeavoured to construct vaulting of great span ; in fact not till it had been long known in Burgundy and the Ile-de-France.

For instance, even till the close of the twelfth century they placed only timber roofing on the naves of their great churches ; but they imparted to their vertical constructions a monumental character which is not seen elsewhere. Endowed with a genius which was subtle and practical, though prompting them to daring undertakings, the Normans left a stamp of their own on their buildings. It is easy to demonstrate this in the original

---

[1] The moulding A is that of one of the upper archivolts, the moulding B belongs to the arches of the upper windows ; the detail c presents one of the capitals of those windows ; and D one of the great capitals of the columns receiving the large archivolts. The mould-ing E gives the string-course serving as a sill to the windows, and the drawing F the archivolt of the windows of the crypt. Each of these arches has mouldings and details of sculpture different from the rest. The archivolts of the windows of the crypt alone are all alike.

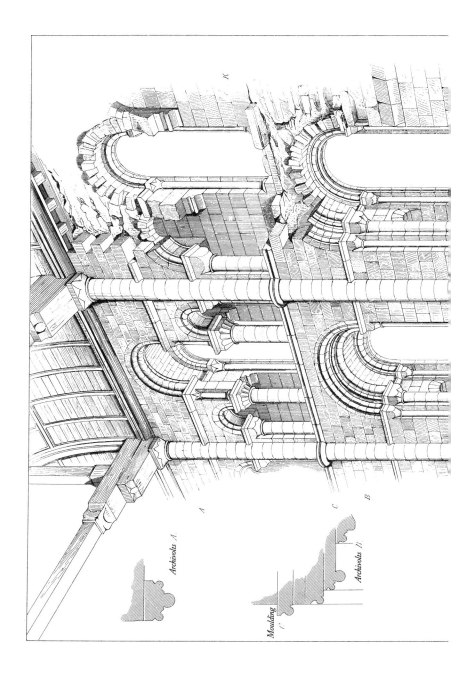

Archivolts A.

A

Moulding

C

Archivolts B.

B

C

K

E. Viollet Le Duc. del.

Gibert sculp.

PLATE XIII.　Transept of Peterborough Cathedral (England)

portions of La Trinité and St. Étienne at Caen, in the remains
of the Churches of Saint Wandrille and of Jumièges, but
particularly in the edifices built on the other side the Straits of
Dover. The transept of Peterborough Cathedral, for instance,
built about the middle of the twelfth century, is a perfect
specimen of the Norman style in its best days—Plate XIII.
We observe excellence in the masonry, and careful execution,
but an absence of sculpture ; a system of construction based on
sound reason and knowledge, a delicate sense of proportion,
mouldings of no great variety, but well designed for the place
they occupy, and an elaborate study of imposing decorative
effects. Plate XIII. shows on the right, the system of construction adopted : the walls are solid in their lower part,
ornamented on the interior by an arcading G, which is only a
surface decoration. At the second range of windows, at I, the
architect has reserved a passage in the thickness of the wall to
facilitate the inspection and repair of the glazing. At the third
range of windows the construction becomer still lighter ; there
the wider passage K forms a gallery open to the transept.
Under each tie-beam of the timber roof, engaged columns, rising
from the ground, divide the combination into bays. If this
architecture departs more widely from Roman art than any
other of the Romanesque period, it must nevertheless be confessed that it wants neither grandeur nor science.

While the Romanesque architecture of Burgundy is sturdy,
bold, full of vigour, that of Normandy dignified and relatively
scientific, and that of the ancient Celtic populations of the West
refined, elegant, and elaborate, we find the architecture of the
Isle of France, towards the beginning of the twelfth century,
simple, sober, Latin in construction and form, subordinated to the
materials employed, and already bearing the impress of a severe
taste, as remote from exaggeration as from timidity. The basins
of the Middle Seine, Oise, and Lower Marne still present a great
number of buildings belonging to this period, which are very
beautiful in design, and displaying intelligence in construction
and sobriety in sculpture. That which most particularly distinguishes this province from all those of modern France is
variety. In Auvergne, for instance, all the buildings of the
eleventh century resemble each other, and appear to have been
all built on the same pattern and by the same workmen. In
Burgundy and in the Haute-Marne—the country of the ancient
Ædui—we observe the same fact. We find in Norman architecture a certain number of ideas and principles which suffer no
variation. It is the same in Poitou and Saintonge. On the soil
of the Isle of France, on the contrary, we observe even as early
as the Romanesque epoch a freedom and variety in type which

indicate incessant efforts to escape from the fetters of tradition. It is these efforts that developed the architecture which Suger —as I remarked above—appears to have inaugurated as an innovation at once bold and scientific. This new architecture was soon adopted by other provinces with characteristic modifications. Thus we find the Burgundians adopting it as early as the close of the twelfth century ; these new methods accorded with their active and enterprising spirit ; nor were the Normans slow in appropriating them ;—as for the provinces of the Centre and the West, they have never understood nor adopted them ; their inert disposition, and—a consideration which must not be left out of sight—the perfection which Romanesque architecture had attained among them, checked the desire for innovations. The style of architecture called Gothic was not introduced into these provinces till a much later date—towards the close of the thirteenth century ; and it was then only a foreign importation, —an irresistible movement to which they were obliged to yield.

In a highly civilised society, whose government and laws are fully developed, the arts exercise only a feeble influence ; to such a society they are only an affair of luxury, incapable of modifying its manners and customs in any respect. But we should be greatly mistaken if we supposed it thus with a social condition still in process of formation ; here, on the contrary, art supplies a powerful aid in the development of civilisation ; it becomes one of the most effective agents in producing unity, especially when there exist points of affinity between the races forming the population and ancient local traditions. Art in France, as early as the commencement of the thirteenth century, was an instrument used by royalty to develop its efforts in the direction of national unity ; and, in fact, wherever its influence made itself directly felt, it was manifested in the construction of a cathedral—a civil quite as much as a religious edifice—built according to the new principles which were first adopted in the centre of the royal domain. Civil and military architecture followed step by step the progress of ecclesiastical architecture ; and in the city in which a Gothic cathedral was erected, we find buildings for civil purposes constructed at the same time—houses and fortifications—in which Romanesque traditions were totally abandoned. If there ever was a renaissance of art in France it was at this epoch, when the secular spirit resumed that active part which was proper to it, and when arts and handicrafts began to develop themselves freely in the midst of a nation in which the consciousness of its vitality was reviving, and which was reconstituting itself after ages of darkness and misery. I cannot, within the limits I have marked out for myself, enter at large upon the principles and spirit of French architecture in the thirteenth century,—a work which has been done elsewhere ; I will therefore confine myself to pointing out those excellencies of that art which are properly our own, and which may find their application at all times and in every state of society.

An art whose form is sufficiently pliant, and its principles broad enough to accommodate themselves to all the changes which civilisation occasions, is no ordinary product of intelligence ; we have therefore a deep interest in thoroughly mastering those principles and studying that form. In that state of scepticism into which we have fallen as regards art, it matters little enough to us whether one school or another gets the upper hand,—whether the buildings erected for us are pseudo-Greek, pseudo-Roman, or pseudo-Gothic. But what does matter to us is, that our buildings should be erected in conformity with our customs, our climate, our national genius, and the progress that has been made in science and its practical application : in fact— to put the matter frankly—I maintain that it is impossible to erect a Greek or Roman building with certain materials furnished us by modern appliances,—iron, for instance ;—whereas the principles and methods introduced by the secular architects of the close of the twelfth century adapt themselves, without effort, to the use of these new materials as also to the multitudinous requirements which our social condition tends ever and anon to create. And what is still more important, economy is in our days a necessity, on account of the multiplicity of the needs that have to be considered ; we can only adopt the absolute and limited principles of classic art by adopting its methods, and thus involving ourselves in expenses which are out of proportion to our resources, or, if we resolve to change those methods we are untrue to its principles, and produce none but works that are valueless in point of art. To make Roman columns of brick or wood, or even of small courses of stone plastered with stucco, and to surmount these columns with lintels of jointed stones secured to iron stays, instead of employing blocks of granite and marble, is to adopt methods other than those of the Romans, and to pervert a wise, nay, an excellent principle, substituting for it a mere appearance which is ridiculous, ephemeral, and expensive, relatively to the value of the result ; it is, moreover, a sin against taste, for taste consists essentially in making the appearance accord with the reality.

The architects of the secular school of the Middle Ages,— notwithstanding the penchant we have always manifested for *appearances*,—subjected form, and, in fact, appearance generally, to the processes and materials employed. They never gave to the hall of a castle the form of a church, to a hospital the aspect of a palace, or to a city mansion the semblance of a country

manor : everything is in its appropriate place, and exhibits the
character suitable to it : if an interior is spacious the windows
are large ; if an apartment is small, the openings are proportioned
to the space they are intended to illuminate ; if a building is
divided into stories, this is indicated on the exterior,—in fact,
sincerity is one of the most striking excellencies of primitive
Gothic architecture ; and it must be observed that sincerity is
one of the conditions essential to style in the arts, and is also
one of the conditions of economy in point of expenditure.   Moreover, these architects were daring ; their structural combinations
exceeded the limits of the material appliances at their disposal ;
they anticipated the industrial progress of their age ; appliances
failed them rather than theoretical knowledge and imagination.
If an architect of the thirteenth century could return among us
to-day he would be astonished at our industrial resources, but he
might perhaps think that we scarcely know how to make use of
them ; if material appliances fell short at that time when art was
capable of taking advantage of a great advance in industrial
development, our professed respect for "sound doctrines"
(which, however, no one takes the trouble to examine) forbids
us the use of those appliances which exist in abundance in the
nineteenth century ; the result of this state of things is the
isolation of the artist : instead of taking advantage of and appropriating all that might further his purpose, he holds himself
aloof from the progressive movement, he perverts the new processes which it affords him to subject them to forms which are,
without sufficient reason, pronounced immutable, instead of
modifying those forms in accordance with the extent and nature
of those processes.

The architect complains that the age has no taste for fine
works of art, because he is unwilling to endeavour to produce
fine works of art with the appliances which this age furnishes ;
he complains that engineers, for example, are encroaching on the
domain of art, and that they sometimes produce works devoid of
art ; but he will by no means consent to quit an obsolete routine
and devote his intellect and artistic skill in the interest of novel
requirements.   I acknowledge, however, that all architects do not
thus stand aloof from progress, and that most of the defenders of
those narrow doctrines regarding art, are to be found in that very
august body who are designated *amateurs;* for everybody thinks
himself something of an architect,—a circumstance which, while
it honours architecture, is in some respects detrimental to it.   I
think that architects adopting really liberal principles, and freed
from the prejudices of the schools and the opinions that have
obtained popular currency, would soon reduce mere dilettanti
to their proper level.   The great point is to put a little reason

into what we do,—to proceed as did our predecessors who really did reason ; in the long-run reason is sure to be in the ascendant ; —*in the long-run*, I say.

The architecture of the secular school of the thirteenth century is a real architecture ; it is applicable to all purposes, because its principles proceed rather from a course of reasoning than from a form. Form never shackled those architects who, in the thirteenth century, erected that vast number of churches, palaces, chateaux, and civil and military edifices ; yet the least fragment of a structure of that period indicates its origin,—is stamped with the seal of its time.

It is desirable to show at the outset that it is impossible to separate the form of the architecture of the thirteenth century from its structure ; every member of this architecture is the result of a necessity of that structure, as in the vegetable and the animal kingdom there is not a form or a process that is not produced by a necessity of the organism : amid the multitude of genera, species, and varieties, the botanist and the anatomist are not mistaken as regards the function, the place, the age, the origin, of each of the organs which they separately examine. A Roman building may be stripped of all its decorations or deprived of its external form without prejudice to the construction ; or (as has been the case with the Pantheon at Rome, for example) a Roman edifice may be clothed with a form that has no necessary or intimate connection with the structure. It is impossible to remove decorative forms from an edifice of the thirteenth century or attach any to it, without detriment to its solidity—its organism, if I may so express myself. This principle, which is easy to understand, and which any one may verify by examining that architecture with some care, proves to us that, in spite of its complicated appearance, the art of the thirteenth century is of such a character as to adapt itself to the requirements of the construction, or to those of external form. Gothic architecture, at the culminating point of its excellence, has therefore been reproached with being nothing but construction ; the challenge is sometimes addressed to us : "Show us the form, give us the rules by which that form is governed : we see the construction ; but prove to us that the form is not the pure fancy of artists, who allow themselves to be guided by their capricious imagination." The only reply I can offer is : That form is not the result of caprice, since it is only the expression—embellished, I allow —of the structure ; I cannot give you the rules by which the form is governed, inasmuch as it is of the very nature of that form to adapt itself to all the requirements of the structure ; give me a structure, and I will find you the forms that naturally result from it, but if you change the structure, I must change

the forms—not indeed in their spirit, for that spirit consists in
their expressing the structure, but in their appearance, since the
structure in question is a changed one.

To a Roman these considerations would, I allow, have appeared too subtle ; the Roman found it much easier to prescribe
a structure and to leave the dress to decorators, without troubling
himself to ascertain whether the dress was the only one appropriate to that structure. But a method which proceeds quite
differently, and which in so practical an art as that of architecture, aims at subjecting the form to the requirements of the
construction and the necessities of the case, cannot certainly be
regarded as bad. Moreover, it must not be supposed that this
intimate alliance between the structure and the appearance is
appreciated only by artists and savans ; it is pleasing to every
eye, because the eye has an instinctive sense of what is reasonable. In Greek architecture, an order in which every member
fulfils a useful and necessary function, satisfies the eye even of
those who are utterly ignorant of the requirements imposed by
the laws of statics. Similarly, groined vaults, reciprocally
counterthrusting, while springing from a slender column, as
in the refectory of Saint-Martin-des-Champs, satisfy the eye ;
because without being aware of the counteracting effects of the
collective thrusts, it instinctively comprehends that this column
may be slender with impunity, since it only requires to present
a rigid vertical line of support as a resistance to the neutralised
thrusts.

A little further illustration will, I trust, enable all to perceive
that the architects of the secular school of the twelfth century
were not merely subtle reasoners and geometricians of some
ability, but possessors in an eminent degree of that faculty of
delicate perception which we observe among the Greek artists.
I said just now that the eye has an instinctive sense of reason
(I mean the eye of those who *do* see, and who see without prepossessions—the eye of the general observer, in fact). That
singular phenomenon which we call " optical illusion," is only an
instinctive perception of certain laws that are confirmed by
scientific observation ; as if God had endowed the human eye
with the faculty of perceiving by intuition what reason will
eventually formulate as a law. And why should not our eyes
be possessed of a special instinct,—as our mind is, which, ante-
cedently to any law, possesses the sense of justice and injustice,
of right and wrong ?

Thus, for example (fig. 7), we set up a framed truss A, consisting of a tie-beam and two blades—the primary roof-principal,
that is. The framing being in place, however straight and
horizontal the tie-beam, the tie-beam will appear to curve down-

wards in a sensible degree towards the centre ; it is an optical illusion which all who see clearly may verify. If I add a king-post B to my principal, this vertical line connecting the apex of the triangle with the middle of its base destroys the illusion,—the tie-beam no longer appears curved ; and in fact by means of this king-post I can actually prevent its bending. The optical illusion therefore warns me of the real defect in my principal ; it impels me to discover the only means of remedying that defect ; the illusion induces the examination of what

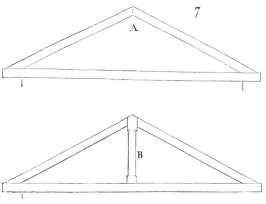

Fig. 7.—Primitive roof-principal.

experience proves to be the law. This is very elementary ; let us proceed to examples of greater complexity. If, figure 8, I erect a perfectly vertical pier, and if, from the side of that pier, at C, I spring a vaulting arch, even supposing the pier to remain absolutely perpendicular, this arch CD, will seem to push out the pier at the point opposite the springing C ; especially if at A I have another arch turned in the contrary direction ; it is an illusion, but this illusion which offends my eye urges me to seek for some arrangement at the springing of the vault at C, which may destroy this disagreeable effect. An excessive augmenta-tion of the thickness of the pier would certainly be a means of obviating this effect ; but I cannot, nor do I wish to give this pier greater thickness than is necessary. I therefore seek for and discover the combination adopted by the architects of the twelfth century, figure 9. By this interruption of the lines at the level of the springing of the lateral arch I have destroyed the illusion. The pier is slighter and appears vertical ; it has the semblance of supporting more firmly than the other that rises unbroken. Experience now comes in to prove that the illusive effect on my eye was only a presentiment of the law to be discovered. In fact the effect of the thrusts of the arches AB is counteracted by the vertical weighting AC. Moreover, as there is a flying buttress CD, counteracting the thrust of the upper vaulting, that thrust resolves itself into a vertical pressure which increases that of the pier AC. The result is that all the thrusts are concentrated in a vertical line passing down through the axis of the column E. Consequently I need only give that column a diameter sufficient to support the vertical pressure passing through its axis. As the capital A has to receive the

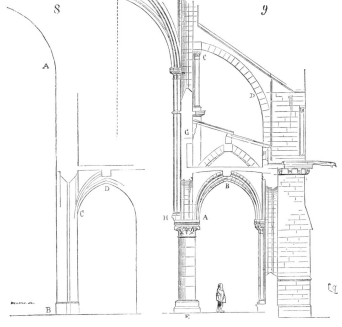

FIGURES 8 and 9.—Example of construction, twelfth century.

springers of the archivolts supporting the wall G, the springers of the three rib-arches (a cross rib and two diagonal ribs) of the lateral vaulting, and some horizontal courses composing the pier which goes up to support the upper vaulting, I require a large bearing surface. I design the capital therefore in accordance with this important function; it is massive, outspreading, and formed of thick courses; its profile will express its function, its ornamentation will have a character of vigour, and instead of *weakening* the stone, will on the contrary help to give it strength at the point where it is weighted.

Thanks to the principle of elasticity which characterises my method of construction, the column may even diverge from the perpendicular without the least detriment, precisely because it has not a bearing surface large enough to enable a slight movement to flush its edges. By means of the projections of the capital and of additional corbelling H—if required—I bring the collective pressures of the upper vaulting to bear on the middle of the under-column ; and so far from destroying the impression of strength demanded by the eye, these corbellings will, on the

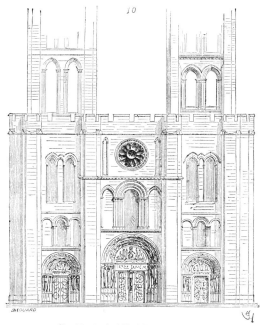

Fig. 10.—Ancient West Front of St. Denis.

contrary, give a character of vigour to my construction ; and the ornamentation and mouldings will be designed with a view to enhancing the effect produced by the structure.[1]

That perfection of the senses which characterised the Greeks was manifestly the cause of their adopting combinations of lines which subsequent experience has enabled us to recognise as laws of stability. If we build a façade whose two outer lines are perfectly vertical, the façade will appear wider at the top than at the base, figure 10 ; this again is an illusion, and one by which the eye is most unpleasantly affected.[2]

[1] For fuller details respecting constructions of the kind in question see the *Dictionnaire raisonné d'Architecture* under the head of CONSTRUCTION.

[2] Ancient western front of the Church of St. Denis. The same defect is observable in several fronts dating from the end of the twelfth century,—that of the Church of Notre Dame at Mantes, for instance.

In the façades of their buildings the Greeks were always careful to make the outer lines converge ; in building the peristyles of their temples they did not even content themselves with giving the angle columns the inclination proper to the column, they exceeded this inclination,—that is, they proceeded as indicated on a slightly exaggerated scale in figure 11. They

11

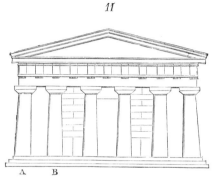

FIG. 11.—Inclination of angle columns in Greek Architecture.

not only inclined the angle columns inwards, but made the intercolumniation A B narrower than the others, and gave these

12

FIG. 12.—Doorway, with perpendicular jambs.

angle columns a greater diameter ; because they were well aware that these angles seen nearly always diagonally, stand clear out against the sky or luminous background, and that the light diminishes the solid parts which it envelopes. It is certainly a very delicate instinct of the eye which has, in this instance, suggested the statical law. Similarly, when an opening has to be made into an edifice—an opening whose background is dark,—if we erect the jambs of the opening perpendicularly (fig. 12), the orifice of the opening appears wider at the top than at the base; therefore the Greeks did not fail to give an inclination to the jambs of their doors and windows, fig. 13. There again we have a requirement of the eye which is in conformity with the laws of statics; for while a certain width is necessary for the passage of a door,

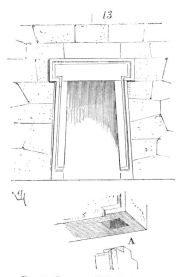

FIG. 13.— Doorway with inclined jambs.

that width is not required for the whole height; and by thus drawing in the jambs we lessen the bearing of the lintel. and stay the open part. Our architects of the twelfth century, while adopting architectural forms widely differing from those of the Greeks, and a system of construction whose principle was opposed to theirs, were notwithstanding guided by the same instincts. They always narrowed their façades towards the summit; not by the inclination of lines,—which is only admissible when monostyles are employed,—but by successive settings back of vertical lines, since they built with courses. In the openings to Greek buildings of earlier date, the two jambs, figure 13, are two pieces of stone or marble, placed on end and slightly inclined towards one another; the lintel is in one piece; this is the elementary construction ; and when, later on, the architects constructed their jambs with built up courses, they preserved the form of the primitive structure. Then (I refer to the prior construction) the two jambs were furnished with tenons at their upper extremities (see A figure 13), fitting into the lintel, which would necessarily

Fig. 14.—Side door of the front of Senlis Cathedral.

overlap the interval of the jambs, in order to leave the mortise the requisite strength. There again is the origin of the *overlapping* of the lintel of the Greek doorway. The Architects of the twelfth century did not construct their openings with jambs in a single piece ; the jambs consist of courses built up, but the

lintels are made of a single block. We do not find those architects copying the Roman door with its architraves, which is but
a commonplace and unimportant reproduction of the Greek doorway; but reasoning like the Greeks and wishing to lessen the
bearing of the lintel, they build the jambs vertically, assist the
bearing of the lintel by means of corbels, figure 14;[1] and, still
further to insure the lintel from breaking, and to enable them to
erect heavy masonry above it, they turn over a relieving arch,
leaving the jambs and the lintel free and unweighted. The
Greeks had contrived to relieve the lintel by narrowing the
opening at its summit and by means of courses laid corbel-wise
above the lintel; the architects of the twelfth century achieved
the same end by diminishing its bearing with the aid of two
corbels and putting a relieving arch above the lintel. In both
cases it is the same instinct that rules, and the same law that
is derived from that instinct; and yet the forms resulting there-
from are not only dissimilar but even opposite in character, in
virtue of a difference in the application of the principles. Both
follow the same inspiration proceeding from their refined nature,
and arrive at results opposite in form though identical in principle.

We have seen how careful the Greeks were to consult effect;
how fully they appreciated what we call *the picturesque;* how
they reached the perfection of art by means that may be called
recondite; what a delicate sense they had for contour, and how
this feeling found expression in a very close and subtle study of
natural laws and the instinctive requirements of the eye. We
find the same refined faculty in our French school of the twelfth
century, with less of simplicity in the means, and less grandeur
in the results, but with a quantum of the unbounded hardihood
of modern times.

The Greeks gave especial attention to the design of the angles
of their edifices: and in fact the angles of an edifice constitute
its profile, its outline, its external form,—that which is impressed
on the memory. The mere geometrical drawing can never give an
idea of the effect which the angle of a building will produce when
seen, as is most frequently the case, from an accidental point.
To design and draw it the architect must represent it to himself
in imagination,—must foresee it in execution: some Greek edifices
whose geometrical elevation in drawing is heavy and ungraceful
produce quite a different effect in execution. I will take as an
example the Pandrosium of Athens (fig. 15). The drawing in
elevation, of this little portico, presents an immense entablature,
which seems to crush the Caryatides that support it; the basement appears naked; but if we examine the building itself, we
find these supports assuming such importance, through the purity

---

[1] Side door of the front of the Cathedral of Senlis; latter end of the twelfth century.

and firmness of the sculpture, and there is so much ease and majesty in the figures, that the heaviness of the entablature disappears, and it presents exactly the dimensions befitting the whole. The statuary is so treated that columns would appear less solid. Had the architect of the Pandrosium not been gifted with the delicate sense of effect here displayed, had he supported the angles of his portico on two pilasters, leaving the Caryatides as intermediate supports, his work would certainly have been sound and faultless in point of construction ; but then he would only have obtained an ordinary outline,—not that angle contour at once so bold and so delicate ; he would not have engaged the eye, and his building would have left no trace on the memory. An artist subjected to the commonplace laws that are now accepted as classical traditions, would never have dared to present the angle Caryatides in profile,—especially not those of the second line ; he would have turned the face of those of the angles diagonally, and would not have failed to give a quarter turn to the Caryatides of the second line, so that they should always present their faces to the outside and their backs to the inside of the portico. Support an entablature on a statue placed edge-ways !—monstrous ! Nevertheless, apart from the execution of this monument—which is admirable—the whole merit of the design consists in the original idea of the six figures advancing in the same direction just as if they were bearing a canopy on their heads. There is a repose in the figures which suits their character as supports; and thanks to this original arrangement, there is an energy,—a living thought in this edifice which strikes the imagination.

It would be an error to suppose that it was artistic instinct alone that guided the Greeks in their designs ; these always bear testimony to a profound judgment. Thus, in this portico of the Pandrosium, we observe that of the four anterior figures, two—those on the left—are posed on the right ; two—those on the right—resting on the left leg. The statues, used here as supports, exactly serve the purpose of angle-columns in the portico we have drawn, fig. 11, directing the pressure towards the middle of the edifice. Suppose that in the erection of this portico the architect and the sculptor had not been actuated by the same idea ; that the sculptor—as too frequently happens in the present day—had not worked in conjunction with the architect, and that instead of arranging the figures as shown at A fig. 15 *bis*—namely, resting on the outer leg—he had posed them indifferently or alternately, as shown at B, the entablature would not have appeared well supported, and the little fabric would have seemed in danger of giving way. Here we have an example of those grand rules of art founded on a cultivated sense of the

True, which neither the architects of the Renaissance, nor those of the age of Louis XIV.—who claimed to have gone back to Classical Antiquity—ever suspected; whereas we find them applied by the artists of the best period of the middle ages, though adapted to forms of their own. But what neither the latter nor the artists of the Renaissance ever succeed in deriving

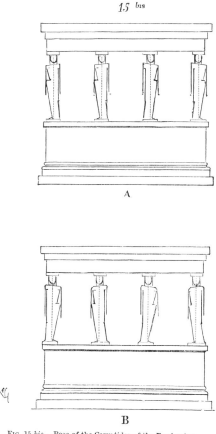

FIG. 15 *bis.*—Pose of the Caryatides of the Pandrosium.

from the ancients is that air of calmness,—that serenity which pervades every work that issues from the hand of the Greek. I cannot say how the Greek architects would have set to work to give a pleasing outline to the angles of very lofty buildings consisting of several stories; but assuredly they would have solved the problem skilfully, and would have given us valuable instruction on this point ; but if we examine the architectural *chefs-d'œuvre* of the French School we discover in the treatment of the angles a special ability analogous to that which is apparent in the Greek artists,—methods of producing effect resulting from the same natural instincts and a faculty of observation not less delicate.

It is very evident that our architects were deeply impressed with the necessity of accentuating the angles by features standing out in bold relief, and graving themselves on the memory by forcibly attracting the eye ; with them the results of reasoning are—as is invariably the case—in accord with the requirements of feeling. It must be observed at the outset, that these architects possessed materials that were strong and hard, but rather thin in the bed ; they had not at their disposal either the marble of Pentelicus or the blocks of granite which the Romans procured from Corsica, the Alps, and the East ; they were absolutely compelled to erect considerable buildings with thin courses of stone ; whereas the Greeks erected small buildings with enormous blocks. This condition would naturally influence the forms given to the architecture even in the vertical parts. The artist's instinct makes him feel that the piling up of thin courses, whatever the firmness of those courses and the solidity of the supports, does not present the firm and rigid lines which the eye demands in a building. He therefore desires—more especially at the angles—to obtain pure lines that mark an outline sharply. He inserts, fig. 16, in the angle, a shaft of a single stone ; he even detaches it from the angle so as to lighten it—giving it at the same time an aspect of firmness. In buildings that are very high and consequently consist of a great many courses, this method of placing at the angles, stones on end, rigid as a prop, not only has the advantage of satisfying a requirement of the eye, but of stiffening the angles and directing the weights and settlements towards the centres : the Greek artists reasoned in this way when they narrowed the openings of their buildings at the top and inclined the angle columns inwards.

Whether his instinct or his eye guided the artist before the intervention of reasoning, or whether the reverse operation took place, certain it is that our secular architects employed, as a means both of decoration and of construction, stones placed on end and in courses, with remarkable skill. They soon became aware that by propping very lofty buildings composed of thin courses liable to settle and give out, with pieces of tough stone placed on end, they gave those buildings perfect stability without having recourse to enormous masses of material ; and that by substituting weight for footing they in like manner insured that stability without cumbering the ground space with piers or walls of great thickness. Suppose we have to build an isolated wall thirty feet high with brick or thin courses of stone, and that we cannot give this wall a greater thickness than one foot, it is

Fig. 16. – Inserted Angle-column.

evident that to keep it upright, it must be stayed with buttresses at frequent intervals; but it is desirable to have as much clear

space as possible at the base of the wall, and we purpose ornamenting it.   There would be only one means of giving stability
to such a wall, which would be to flank it on the two faces
(figure 17) with shafts of very rigid material—cast-iron for
instance—and if necessary, to superimpose these shafts, setting
them back somewhat, and connecting them with the body of the
wall by intermediate tie-blocks A, and weighting them at their
summit B with arches turned from one to another.   It is certain

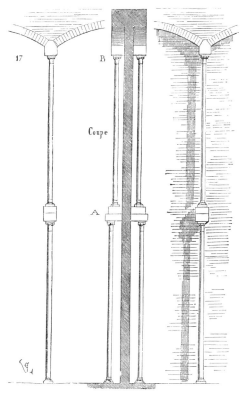

Fig. 17.—Method of staying a Wall.

that this construction, dictated by the laws of equilibrium and
statics, may be made to offer a means of architectural ornamentation.

In the architecture of the Lower Empire and in Byzantine
architecture, we perceive that these methods of obtaining stability
were already beginning to be adopted, though timidly.   The
merit of having systematised them is due to our Western archi-

tects. Thus, in the lofty towers of our Cathedrals, as at Laon and Senlis, we observe that the architects, in their desire to give rigidity to these structures, whose height as compared with their base is very great—carried up their angles with stones on end ; which form a decorative feature, while at the same time they stiffen the angles, since they direct the settlement towards the middle.

In the construction of the Basilica of Constantine, shown in figure 4, the architect did not exhibit a very sound judgment when he placed his rigid support—his monolithic column of granite or marble—beneath the springing of the great vault. This rigid support would have been much better placed outside against the buttresses ; for had there not been an enormous concrete homogeneous mass of material in this building of super-abundant strength,—in the event of a settlement, the rigid support set beneath the springing of the great vaulting would have had the effect of making the whole structure give way outwards, since the outside was more compressible than the inside. Let Classic Antiquity have its due meed of admiration ; but let not that admiration be a blind one ; let it not prevent us from recognising the superiority of certain well-considered prin-ciples that are the offspring of the modern spirit. There exists no structure better fitted to exemplify the wide differences that separate Romanesque art from French art of the secular school than the front of the Cathedral of Paris. Having in view the erection of a colossal edifice to exceed in size all the other build-ings of the city—an edifice that should exactly fulfil all the requirements of a Cathedral, at a time when a Cathedral subserved purposes both civil and religious,—when it had a kind of political significance,—it is hardly possible to conceive a design more imposing as a whole, more sound in construction, or more skilfully executed in its details. Every one knows the front of Notre Dame de Paris ; few perhaps realise the amount of know-ledge, taste, study, care, resolution, and experience implied by the erection of that colossal pile within the space of at most ten or twelve years. Still it is an unfinished work ; the two towers were to have been terminated by spires in stone, which would have completed and rendered intelligible the admirably designed lower masses. Here we have indeed Art, and Art of the noblest order.

It is desirable to furnish the readers of these Lectures with a drawing of this front in its entirety ; though the drawing cannot render the effect that would have been produced by the building itself ; photographs will, however, supply the defects of geometrical elevations. But since I have been speaking of the angle arrangements of edifices standing out in relief,—of the

outlines which assume so much importance in the eyes of the
spectator, of the simultaneous employment of stones set flat-wise
and on end, both to give rigidity to the structure and to remove
the monotonous aspect of a building composed of courses of equal
heights, and of the intimate connection between the construction
and the decoration, I could nowhere find a combination of these
various excellencies more complete, homogeneous, or skilfully
designed.   First observe—what is of rare occurrence in buildings,
particularly when they attain very considerable dimensions—that
the architect has managed to divide his front by grand horizontal
lines, which, without cutting it up into sections, form so many
resting-places for the eye ; that these divisions are made by an
accomplished artist, inasmuch as they present spaces that are unequal, sometimes plain, sometimes ornamented, varied in their
details, and yet presenting perfect unity in the entire effect.   We
have not here, as is so frequently to be seen in Roman, Byzantine,
or modern buildings, the piling up of features that seem introduced
at hap-hazard, and that might be changed, modified, or omitted
(see Plate XIV.)   Each division has its purpose ; thus in the
massive basement open the three doorways with their wide
embrasures, and their richly embellished arches.   To connect
these three doorways and to relieve the hardness of the lines of
the buttresses, four projecting canopies supported by monolithic
shafts, shelter four colossal statues, without however interrupting
the lines of those buttresses ; since the shafts recall them vividly,
by lines of light on either side of the statues.

Above this basement, which, despite the profusion of sculpture
spread beneath the arches, preserves an aspect of gravity and
strength, there extends across the whole breadth of the front a
gallery—a portico composed of hollowed lintels, supported on
monolithic shafts surmounted by large capitals ; in each opening
is placed a colossal statue of a king.   The architect, without
interrupting his portico, took care to render apparent the
projection of the buttresses ; this cincture, which is of great
severity in design and execution, and is low in proportion to the
height of the front, has the effect of its actual dimensions restored
by being surmounted by a balustrade which recalls the size of
the human figure.   Above, the buttresses continue upwards with
offsets ; but the three divisions of the front are set back to a
considerable depth to leave a broad terrace over the Gallery of
the Kings and to aid in giving this gallery great importance as a
decorative line.   In the central division, beneath deep round
arches, opens the rose-window, which indicates the nave and the
level of the interior vaulting.   In the side divisions are pierced
couplet windows, lighting the interior of the first story of the
towers, and made to participate in the general scale of the front

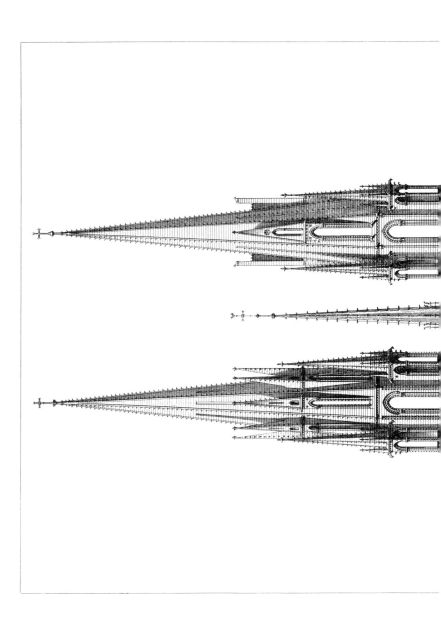

Scale of |_____|_____|_____| 50 metres

PLATE XIV.   Completed Front of Notre Dame de Paris

by the arches which environ them. Two small panelled roses occupy the tympanums beneath these arches and repeat the compartments of the central rose-window. Over this story, kept lower than that of the basement, there runs a grand foliaged cornice which returns round the buttresses and makes them stand conspicuously out from the mass ; and this is the starting-point of the two towers. And here we recognise the genius of the artist. It is always difficult to start two towers,—that is to say, two solid, thick masses, on a front whose general aspect presents a plain surface. The embrasure that remains between these two towers leaves an unoccupied space in the middle of the front, where the eye requires on the contrary a solid and dominant point ; for the pyramidal form is one of the necessities of the eye, because it is that which indicates perfect stability. Therefore, raising the two towers abruptly on this nearly square lower mass, the architect connected the towers by a lofty open gallery, which, continued along their faces and thus very useful for passing round, was formed of large monolithic columns and rich arcadings ;—the whole surmounted by a bold projecting cornice and a balustrade that once more recalls the size of the human figure and restores to the gallery the full effect of its real height. By this device, therefore, the architect has relieved the abruptness of the transition from the solid to the open. Within the embrasure remaining between the two belfries, the gallery standing out against the sky and the gable of the nave rising behind the belfries, take off the hardness of the outline produced by the open space ; so that we have a kind of transition between a solid mass and the sky. Placed in front of the two towers this gallery obviates the difficulty of setting two isolated bodies on a solid body ; it has the effect of preventing the eye from exactly noting the point where from a single mass the edifice divides into two masses. It makes the façade of Notre Dame a homogeneous whole instead of a front on which two towers have been set up. Forming a portico in the divisions between the buttresses, the arcading becomes solid against the buttresses, and is continued round them as a facing : and here again the architect gives proof of sound taste and a thorough knowledge of effect. It would not do to thin the buttresses by a decoration injurious to their solidity, and in order to prevent the continuity of the gallery from being broken they had to be incorporated with it. It was necessary to consider the angles of these buttresses, which stood out in relief against the sky ; and they must have a crowning, since this gallery forms an elevated passage way around the belfries. Again, it was requisite that the piers of these belfries should not appear to start from the gallery as a distinct work having no connection with it. The fulfilment of all these requirements presented serious difficulties, especially as this was the part of the front which, from its position and importance, must attract attention. Observe, therefore (Fig. 18), how the architect of Notre Dame succeeded in overcoming these difficulties.

First, on attentively examining the masonry, we shall see that the monolithic columns define the angles, if I may so express myself; that they agreeably intersect the horizontal construction of the buttresses, while leaving it apparent; that the open arcading between the buttresses is richly ornamented, while on the buttresses it takes a more severe character and participates in their structure; that the angles above the capitals grow out with a kind of vegetal form that leads the eye up to the bold projection of the cornice, which is necessary to obtain a passage-way; that this expansion of the angle indicates a crowning; that, lastly, in order to avoid the hard effect of the returns of the balustrades and their abrupt set off beneath the piers of the towers, and to form a transition between the projections and settings-back, animals were sculptured at the extremity of the angles of these balustrades.

While the front of Notre Dame de Paris in its present condition is very beautiful, it must nevertheless be admitted that everything has been so admirably arranged for carrying the eye up to the stone spires, that their absence is to be regretted. There is a superfluous strength in the construction of the towers, since they support nothing. How elegant would their skilfully planned piers, their large and boldly arched windows, and the superstructure—somewhat heavy as a crowning—have appeared if the spires had been built. Plate XIV. shows those crownings, of which the two existing towers are merely the base. If we examine this drawing (giving here only the general mass—the outline—without pretending to complete the original architect's design) we can appreciate the admirable proportions of the great open gallery,—evidently too high for the towers had not the latter been designed for spires; and we recognise the felicitous arrangement of the terminations of the buttresses of these towers —terminations that now seem indecisive and not in harmony with the severity of the lines below. We see how the architec- tural arrangements pass gradually from the horizontal to the pyramidal lines of the summit. If we cover over the two spires shown in Plate XIV., we shall readily perceive that every part in the front of Notre Dame was designed to lead up to the spires, —to prepare a base for them; and if from the examination of the general features we proceed to the details of the building, every one who understands construction will be amazed when he sees what numberless precautions are resorted to in the execution,— how the prudence of the practical builder is combined with the

Fig. 18.—Upper Gallery— Front of Notre Dame de Paris.

daring of the artist full of power and inventive imagination;
while in examining the mouldings and the sculpture we remark
the use of reliable methods, a scrupulous adherence to principles,
a perfect appreciation of effect, a style unequalled in purity by
modern art, an execution at the same time delicate and bold,
quite free from exaggeration, and owing its merit to the study
and love of form.   Whence, we may ask, did the artists of that
time acquire all these excellencies if not from their own imaginative faculty?   Who had taught them the art of producing
imposing effects?   Who had suggested to them these novel
forms?   In what school did they acquire that perfect sense of
fitness?

The front of Notre Dame also renders conspicuous an excellence belonging exclusively to French architects at the time
when France possessed an architecture of its own; that of
variety in unity.   At first sight the portals appear symmetrical;
nevertheless the love of variety is evident; thus the doorway on
the left is unlike that on the right.[1]   The north tower (that of
the left) is sensibly larger than the south.   On that side the
arcading of the great gallery is more severe and solid than that
of the other; whence we may conclude that—according to a
custom generally followed—the two stone spires would present
dissimilarities in the details, though designed to present two
equiponderant masses.   We know how imperatively variety is
required by our western genius.   It is evident here as in other
edifices built up at once in the same period, that the architect
could not resolve to produce the same detail twice : in erecting
two towers he gave a different drawing for each; and the increase
of work he thereby imposed on himself was of no account with
him in comparison with the *ennui* he would have experienced in
letting his workmen execute two colossal towers exactly alike.
Many find fault with these dissimilarities that contravene absolute
symmetry; but it cannot be denied that in this craving for variety
there is manifested an intellectual effort—a constant seeking for
the better,—an emulation, shall I say, which is in accordance with
our Western character.   As we might naturally expect, this
diversity is still more observable in the details; thus, although
similar in their general form, all the capitals of the same ordonnance are varied.   While conforming to the general design, every
sculptor aimed to give something of his own.

In point of conception Romanesque art comes far short of the
imposing grandeur of Notre Dame de Paris; in the details it
diverges still further from the forms adopted by the secular

[1] The main part of the decoration of the right doorway consists of fragments of
sculpture of the twelfth century.   It appears that in rebuilding the front of Notre Dame the
architect wished to preserve the finest remains of an earlier building.   (See the *Description
de Notre-Dame, par MM. de Guilhermy et Viollet-le-Duc,* 1856.   Bance.)

artists. The secular school may be regarded as a kind of reaction of modern ideas against tradition,—a vigorous effort towards civilisation such as the modern mind conceived it, namely, incessant progress.

But, it will be said : There is only one front in Europe like that of the Cathedral of Paris. This is true ; and though a multitude of examples proves nothing in point of art—though there is but one *Iliad*—it cannot be asserted that in the domain of art and poetry a *chef-d'œuvre* arises in utter isolation—that it is an exception : it is in fact only the *résumé*—the expression— of an order of ideas. On the contrary it is part of the prerogative of epochs that are favourable to art to have the power of grouping together the features of all in a single combination. Besides, we do not know what the secular artists of the thirteenth century might have achieved if they had had the opportunity and the means of erecting other buildings equal in importance to the front of Notre Dame. It is the only one that was able to be erected by a nearly continuous effort ; and yet it remains unfinished. At Laon, Senlis, and Amiens we find conceptions of the same date; but mutilated, altered, or unfinished,— each having its special type, and exhibiting special beauties.

It is characteristic of periods favourable to the arts, that these have been developed universally during their continuance— dignifying the cottage of the peasant as well as the palace, the humble village church as well as the cathedral of the opulent city. A perfume of art exhales from the least pretentious Greek building as well as the most magnificent temple, and the small houses of Pompeii, built of tufa and brick, are as much works of art as the public buildings of that city. An age which considers art as only an affair of luxury —an appanage of the higher classes, or an envelope suited only to certain public edifices,—may be distinguished for good government, but it is certainly not civilised ; and painful dissensions may be anticipated for it. Intellectual enjoyments, like material enjoyments, when confined to a privileged few, excite envy and anger. When but a few knew how to read, the ignorant multitude, when they succeeded in getting the upper hand, burned books with as much rage as they burned sumptuous chateaux in which the material luxuries of life were collected. Let reading become a universal acquirement, and books may be sure of remaining uninjured on the library shelves. To make art a thing of luxury, or to associate it exclusively with wealth, is therefore very dangerous to art and to the few who enjoy it. It is then important to all to concede to art the claims it makes to universal predominance ; to give it its place every- where, to instil into the minds of all—of artists especially,—that in architecture art does not consist in the employment of costly marbles, or the accumulation of ornaments, but in distinction of form and the truthful expression of the requirements ; for it costs no more to cut a moulding according to a judicious principle and a good design than to work it without regard to its position or the effect it should produce.

In the thirteenth century the art invented by the secular school was essentially democratic ; it was universally diffused, and the villager might be as proud of his church, or the simple knight of his manor-house, as the citizen of his cathedral or the sovereign of his palace. It is not enough for the artist to admire the arts of the past ; while to copy them is an admission of incapacity : he must comprehend and be penetrated by them, extract from them results applicable to the times in which he lives, and regard form only as the expression of an idea. Any form whose *raison d'être* cannot be explained, cannot be beautiful ; and in architecture any form that is not suggested by the structure should be cast aside.

These principles, which I cannot regard as too restrictive, were rigorously observed by the French secular school,—especially at the time when it began to be developed,—and their application is especially conspicuous in the simplest structures. Let us take as an example one of those small Burgundian edifices, built of rubble-work, in which dressed stone is employed very sparingly ; let us enter the church of Montréale,[1] a village church. Here we find nothing superfluous ; the architecture is simply the construction ; the walls are of rubble-work, the pillars only of dressed stone, and yet we find in this simple edifice an art full of elegance ; the few mouldings are of an incomparable beauty, and executed with a perfection equal to that of Greek mouldings of the finest period. The sculpture, very scantily diffused, is boldly treated, and harmonises with the simplicity of the building. Let us examine (fig. 19) one of the aisle wall-piers ; a column engaged a third of its diameter, supports the transverse vaulting arch A. In order to get a footing for the wall-ribs B, the springing of the vault-groin C and the second rings of the transverse arch, the architect surmounted the pier D with two moulded corbel-courses ; he was aware that if he carried up the engaged pier D plumb with the wall-rib E, his column would altogether lose its value, and stone be uselessly employed. His reason and instinct suggested this very simple arrangement, which also afforded him a decorative feature. Observe how the moulding G of the abacus is relieved by deep hollows, with a view to producing sharp shadows in an interior where the light is always diffused, without taking anything from the strength required for this thin course

[1] Six miles from Avallon. The church of Montréale dates from the end of the twelfth century.

which has to bear weight—some piers H are square, with the
angles taken off for convenience of passing. Observe the judicious
composition of these bases,—how from the square socle the intermediate course I leads to the polygonal section; how finely
curved and firm in character are the angle-stops K;—how the
form accords with the construction. When with means so simple

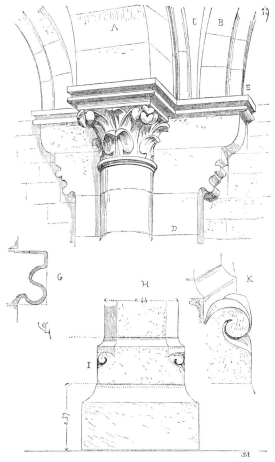

[FIG. 19.—Aisle Wall-pier—Church of Montréale.

art succeeds in manifesting itself, it is an art complete and full of
instruction. Numerous details are suggested which find their
place elsewhere, and I should be exceeding the limits of this
work if I endeavoured to analyse them all. It will suffice to

point out some with a view of showing how the architects of the secular school at the beginning of the thirteenth century proceeded in their endeavour to adopt novel forms.

As an example, let us take the mouldings ; for mouldings in architecture have a twofold importance ; they subserve a practical and an æsthetic purpose,—practical inasmuch as they have a function to perform,—æsthetic, since the architect aims to give these mouldings a form and character expressing that function. When a moulding exactly serves the purpose assigned it, and pleases the eye by a shape that is perfectly appropriate to that purpose, it possesses style. Whenever we find an architecture characterised by mouldings fulfilling these conditions, it claims the position of an art highly developed, refined and thoughtfully elaborated. When, on the other hand, we find a style of architecture overlaying its buildings with mouldings whose design cannot be justified by reason, and which serve a purely decorative purpose, that architecture is wanting in one of the most essential qualities of style. Now of all the styles of architecture with which we are intimately acquainted, it is only the architecture of the Greek and that of the secular school of the Middle Ages whose mouldings satisfy reason and taste alike. I regret that I cannot say the same of Roman Architecture ; it does not possess this excellence except when it almost servilely imitates Greek or Etruscan art. Roman mouldings of the Imperial Epoch, dating from Trajan, ceased to be more than copies— increasingly feeble—of Greek mouldings. On the other hand, the mouldings of the Italian or the French Renaissance of the fifteenth and sixteenth centuries are only a confused tradition of classic art in its nobler periods—degenerate types, drawn at random by artists and viewed with indifference by the public. In my opinion the Romans attached but little importance to a matter which they regarded only as a detail more or less felicitously conceived, but devoid of signification. During the Romanesque period in France, on the contrary, we see the architect carefully studying this highly important part of his art ; he purified—if I may use the term—the mouldings bequeathed by the architecture of the debased period, but he did not entirely forsake them ; we observe that the Roman types always served as his starting-point ; this however ceases to be the case towards the end of the twelfth century when the mouldings, together with the method of construction and the sculpture, assume completely new forms.

We will cite a few examples. The Greeks did not put a base under the Doric column ; they reserved this lower architectural member for the Ionic order. Still the placing of a base beneath the column is of very early date in Greece ; the columns of the front of the treasury of Atreus at Mycenæ had bases nearly

approaching in character the mouldings in use among the Persians
and the Assyrians. The Ionic order, which was more ancient
than the Doric, had bases; but the Ionic order was evidently an
importation from Asia; while the Doric order appears to have

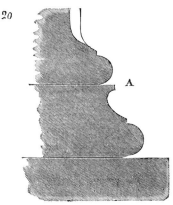

20

A

Fɪɢ. 20.—Base-moulding—Great Portico of the Erechtheium.

originated on Greek soil. In appropriating the Ionic order, the
Greeks, according to their invariable habits, transformed it—
refined it,—while they left it its traditional members; it was
repugnant to their sense of fitness to put at the base of a column
a projecting socle that could only be in the way; accordingly,

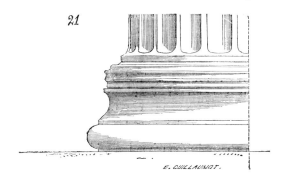

21

E. GUILLAUMOT.

Fɪɢ. 21.—Base-moulding—Small Portico of the Erechtheium.

while retaining the base in the Ionic order they were careful not
to give it a square plinth; the base of the Ionic order of the
Erechtheium is round like the shaft of the column; some columns
—as that of the great portico—present the profile (fig. 20); the
others, those of the smaller one thus, (fig. 21). Mouldings so
attenuated and edges so sharp, are suitable only for marble;
furthermore it must be supposed that the Greek *gamins* were less

destructive than ours, or else that they were not allowed to enter the porticoes, or they would not have failed to break the angles of these sharp edges for amusement.   Certainly these mouldings are much more beautiful than those of the Asiatic columns ; but I must say that the edge A of the base (figure 20) does not appear to me to be justified either by reason or taste.   All I can understand by it is, that the architect wished to get a sharply defined shadow beneath this thin edge in order distinctly to isolate the upper torus.   We will pass over the Roman base of the Ionic and Corinthian orders, with which all are familiar, and which under the empire had a square plinth, whose four projecting angles easily break under the weight, and are only an obstruction to the feet.   We proceed to France, and first remark that even as early as the Romanesque period there existed in the base-mouldings certain analogies with the Greek base-mouldings, (fig. 22).[1]   The course A is round, and rests on an octagonal socle B.

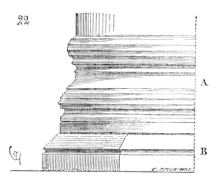

FIG. 22.—Romanesque base-moulding—eleventh century.

Probably the Romanesque architect who drew the profile of this base was unacquainted with the Erechtheium of Athens. He might have seen Byzantine mouldings shaped to this section ; but it is evident that his instinct led him to give up the Roman mouldings,—of which at that time there was no lack of specimens in the neighbourhood,—and especially to abandon the square plinth for bases resting on the ground.   Here we see attempts, in which, however, no method is observable.   At the end of the twelfth century the base-mouldings change and assume a particular shape ; the lower torus is flattened, as if to rest better on the plinth, which reappears ; the latter however is frequently canted at the angles ; and an appendage is placed on the angles of the square of the plinth AB inscribing the lower torus.

---

[1] Base of a column of the choir of Saint-Étienne at Nevers (eleventh century).

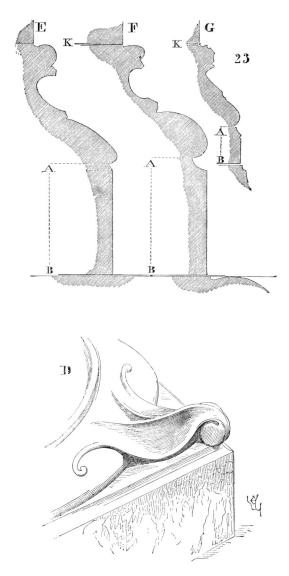

FIG. 23.—Base-mouldings.—End of the twelfth century.

Here (figure 23) are some base-mouldings of this period; the moulding E is from the Church of Montréale (Yonne), the moulding F from the choir of the Church of Vézelay; that G from the Hôtel de Ville at Saint-Antonin (Tarn-et-Garonne) as the bed of the shaft of the column is at K,—to prevent flushings and avoid sinkings the shaft has no *apophyge* or hollow conge ; the upper torus stands clear out, and the face of the upper listel is sloped to make it apparent, the base being placed beneath the level of the eye. The *scotia* is deeply sunk, but sufficiently full at its incline to give strength to the mouldings ; the listel beneath the scotia is also sloped to present a conspicuous face,— the lower torus, by its flattened shape, is well engaged with the

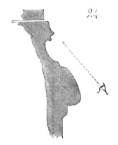

Fig. 24.—Base-moulding of elevated shaft.

plinth : then come the appendages (claws) represented at D, which assume various forms usually derived from the vegetable kingdom, and which strengthen the unoccupied angle of the plinth. We shall here remark also the upper torus of the base G, which is fluted horizontally, like the torus of the Greek base ; I should add that these bases are in every case worked in hard stone, with an exactness and perfection of form such as our most skilful workmen can scarcely equal. But in Roman Architecture, whether

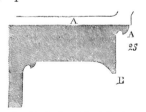

Fig. 25. – Section of Greek Cornice.

an order be placed on the floor or whether it forms an upper gallery and is intended to be seen from below, the form of the base is not changed, whereas in our buildings we observe that the mouldings are adapted to the place they occupy. If a column is considerably elevated above the floor, the mouldings of the base are modified (fig. 24) to make its various members visible.

The Greek cornice is perfectly adapted to its position ; it always crowns an edifice, and its upper surface A, figure 25, supports a gutter, beneath which is a first drip A, and a second B ; but what is to be thought of the Roman cornice that divides

two stories, and whose upper surface, figure 26, receives the rain,
holds the snow, and compels the droppings which fall on A to
traverse the entire surfaces A B before they reach the drip B,

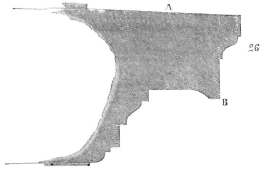

Fig. 26.—Section of Roman Cornice.

which obliges them to quit the stone? Our architects of the
twelfth century did not put a cornice between two stories, but a
simple string-course, whose section is shaped, fig. 27, so as to
throw off the rain-water as soon as possible. When they wanted
to mould an arch, they were careful to choose the moulding

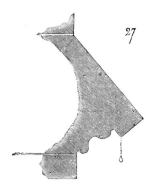

Fig. 27.—String-course, Twelfth Century.

which would best indicate the strength that arch should have,
cutting away as little stone as possible and avoiding sinkings.
The Greeks, and in a still greater degree the Romans, seem to
have been regardless of economy in stone and labour. All stones
come from the quarry in the form of a parallelopiped; if, therefore, we desire that in the building a stone should carry a projection, that projection must be got out of a thickness of stone
reduced. Thus, for example, figure 28, wishing to give to a face
stone the moulding A, we must reduce the surface of the front

by the thickness B C. This is a sacrifice of stone, and also
involves labour, both which might be avoided by putting the
bed at D instead of at E. The Greeks thought, not without
reason, that every basement should spread—should attach itself
to the ground, so to speak; and hence they made a point of
charging the basements with a moulding, which gave an idea of
stability, not only by its form but by the absence of beds between

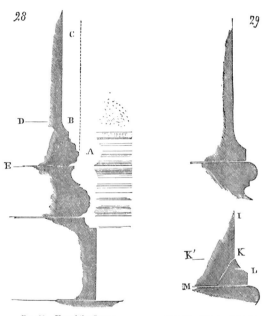

FIG. 28.—Use of the Conge.   FIG. 29.—Misuse of the Conge.

the vertical face and the spread at bottom; this was a result
of the system of Greek construction, derived from the
simplest laws of statics. But when, in the twelfth century,
the primitive system of stability was replaced by a system of
stability obtained by counteracting forces—by equilibrium
—it became useless and even dangerous to give the lower
parts of supports a footing or a projection which would injuri-
ously affect that system of equilibrium. It is readily understood
that when a column had only a weight pressing vertically
to bear, it was reasonable to give an apophyge to the lower
bed of the shaft, figure 29, which afforded a foot—a spread,—to
the shaft; but when the columns or pillars had to support
weights pressing obliquely and reciprocally neutralised, so as to
resolve themselves into a vertical pressure, the result could not
be calculated upon with sufficiently absolute certainty; it was
necessary to allow for the movements to which every equilibriated

system is liable in seeking its centre of gravity; when in the event of an inclination of the line ɪ ᴋ the projection reserved at the base of the shaft occasioned the flushing of the apophyge. It was at ᴋ′, therefore, and not at ᴍ that the bed of the column had to be placed. With the bed at ᴋ′, the apophyge—the spreading form of the moulding ᴋ ʟ—was an absurdity; hence we observe that at the close of the twelfth century the base-moulds assume the shape represented in figure 23.

In the Romanesque school there was already a marked tendency to subordinate the mouldings to the construction; and in this respect that school was in advance of the Roman archi-tecture of the Empire, which did not much concern itself with bringing form into harmony with structure. What the Roman-esque architects had perceived was constituted a law by the secular architects of the twelfth century. From that date onwards,

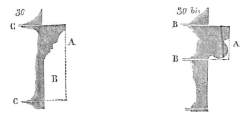

Figs. 30 and 30 *bis.*—Comparison between Roman and Mediæval Mouldings.

mouldings were designed:—First, with reference to their purpose; second, in strict accord with the thickness of the courses; third, so as to necessitate the least possible sinking of the stone,—that is with the smallest loss of material; because the material itself is costly, and because the more has to be cut away, the more expense is incurred. Never does a projecting moulding form part of a face, as is too often the case in Roman architecture. The Roman, fig. 30, when he has procured stones in the condi-tion in which they come from the quarry, wishes to work a string-course; he will draw the section ᴀ, will leave the beds at ᴄ, and will lose all the sinking ʙ; the architect of the twelfth century, figure 30 *bis*, will form his string-course of a thin course ᴀ, having the beds at ʙ, and in drawing his moulding will lose the least possible space, and will not have to make any sinking. This rule is absolute, and admits of no exception; the examination of a few buildings of that period will enable us to recognise it. It will be granted that this judicious use of material in building is praiseworthy. In contemplating the basilica of the Giants, at Agrigentum, and observing that not only the external engaged columns, the interior pillars, and even the great caryatides, consist only of courses of stone with a number of vertical joints;

that the materials in the building, in proportion to the dimensions of the edifice, are mere wall-stones, I am obliged to recognise the fact that the Greeks desired above everything to obtain such forms as were esteemed beautiful by them, without concerning themselves about the means they made use of. I allow that they clothed this structure with stucco, laid on with a view to conceal the discrepancy between the construction and the appearance; I admire the form, I place myself at their point of view, and would refrain from blaming them; nevertheless, if I see a building in which the architect has succeeded in obtaining forms that are likewise beautiful, while subordinating them to the structure; if I perceive that this structure and the nature of the material employed have reacted on the form, my admiration is excited here also, and my reason is satisfied. More than this, if the Greeks had adopted these last principles, it is probable that they would have been led on to do what our artists have done, for their mode of reasoning is the same; but starting as they did from opposite principles, they necessarily obtained dissimilar results. I see in the case of the Greeks excellent artists, who in their buildings considered the construction (which it must be observed was of a very simple order, and could be applied only to very simple buildings) as a means to which they attached no further importance. I see, in the case of our Mediæval architects, skilful builders obliged to construct vast and complicated edifices, and who had the skill to give their structures forms that perfectly harmonised with them, by the most simple means.

The Greek wishes to secure the form, and subordinates the structure to it; the Greek had the genius to discover a form as beautiful as it was simple,—his construction is simple, and nothing can be more logically consistent. The secular architect of the twelfth century is led by the force of circumstances, by the modern spirit, and by new requirements, to adopt a very delicate and complicated structure; he takes care not to conceal it; on the contrary, he seeks to express it by the most natural forms; and here again nothing can be more logically consistent. I am perfectly willing to admit that the age of Pericles was nobler than that of Philip Augustus,—that it would have been more desirable to be a contemporary of Ictinus than of Pierre de Corbie; but regrets or wishes of this kind will be of no great service to us; we shall not succeed in annihilating the intervening centuries or the new ideas, novel requirements, attempts and discoveries which they have brought with them. We may reasonably be astonished, then, to hear it said that to progress we must retrograde twenty centuries. Rather, if we would advance, we must be well acquainted with the distance that has been travelled, and what the ages have accumulated on the road;

and the stage covered by the twelfth and thirteenth centuries is one of the most instructive in the history of the arts, since it saw the rise of a prodigious intellectual movement in the direction of modern ideas,—a movement called forth by the secular spirit reacting against tradition, seeking for novel methods and applying new forms to them. Should we then assert that this school discovered the final and most complete expression of our art? Certainly not; the stage of progress which it traversed was a noble one, and progress cannot demand that it should be ignored. "But,"—it may be objected—"we allow that the period in question was marked by power, and that it gave a considerable impulse to the arts; since that time, however, a still further advance has been made; will you take no account of what has been done since, and would you—you who maintain that we ought not to retrograde—blot out six centuries, and bring us back to that art of the past?" To this I answer that a regress of six centuries and one of twenty is nearly the same thing, and that those who in the sixteenth century proposed to revive the arts of Classical Antiquity, had reasons for the attempt whose validity I shall endeavour to make appreciable; but that to imitate or perpetuate this return in the present day is to compel a young and robust body to live among corpses—to inflict on it a premature death. We admire tombs, but we do not live in them. It is one thing to read the works of a man who is dead, it is quite another thing to attire ourselves in his shroud. Our object should be, not to go back to the time of Pericles, Augustus, or Saint Louis; but to investigate those periods of history during which art was a living expression of civilisation, and during which it had the energy to develop new principles; our object should be to derive advantage from their accumulated treasures,—not to lose a fragment of them,—to recognise those various principles, and to fix the attention of the artist on those which are eternally true, applicable, and vital.

The Greeks lived under a beautiful sky, which was free from those fogs which obscure our atmosphere; they were settled in a country intersected by mountains and gulfs, and abounding in building materials of marvellous beauty. They adopted the architecture which best accorded with the climate and the materials at their disposal. They attained such an intellectual development as was possible in a country of small extent, and amidst communities which were only associations of traders and thinkers; they advanced the arts as a union of enlightened amateurs is capable of doing. And all this is calculated to call forth the envy and the regret of every succeeding generation to the end of time; but I would ask: What analogy is there between that specially favoured community and our vast Christian nationalities? Greek unity was a dream that never was able to become a reality, at least in the times of Classical Antiquity. Those small states united only when pressed by a common danger menacing their existence or freedom. The danger once passed, they were in conflict with each other. Struggles between them became more and more frequent as civilisation advanced. In the West, on the contrary,—and by the West I mean France only, —the dominant, the principal idea, has been unity; the arts have been among the most powerful means of securing that unity; and on this ground alone they would deserve to be studied, even if they had no bearing on present requirements. What we must admire in the Roman architecture of the Empire is the manifestation it offers of a powerful organisation; but we frequently observe in this manifestation a disdain for the form of art, and an evident contempt for the personality and liberty of the artist. On the contrary, we perceive that, during its best period, the Greeks subjected art to criticism; if they wished to render their buildings as a whole the expression of the require- ments proper to the political or religious programme that had to be satisfied, and to preserve the majesty proper to archi- tectural masses, they did not on that account sacrifice the details, and did not believe that it was beneath the dignity of the artist to devote study and rational reflection even to the shaping of the least important mouldings. In the Romans I behold skilful administrators, with liberal ideas, not enforcing their own views in art, and scarcely troubling themselves about questions that are peculiar to its domain. I admit, in fact, that this manifest disdain on the part of the Roman for that which is proper to the artist—that which attaches him to his art as to a creed—has a certain grandeur, especially since—to repeat what I have said before—if the Roman despises, at least he does not persecute,—does not meddle with questions of art; the Roman stands aloof from forms of faith; he requires nothing more than respect for the law and submission to his administrative and political system;—these apart, he cares little whether you satisfy the programme prescribed by adopting one form or the other; that is your affair, not his. Nevertheless, art resembles forms of faith in this;—it is not enough for it to be tolerated; it claims sympathy, it seeks it, nay, challenges it; if it is developed amid a community that contents itself with not being hostile to it, and which affords it no stimulus either in the way of adhesion or criticism, it declines; and it is this which explains the decay of forms of art in a powerful and flourishing empire, such as was the Roman empire until the time of Constantine. On the con- trary, we have no reason to expect a decline of the arts among a people naturally endowed with artistic power, as the result of an attempt to constrain or even to direct them. Constraint gives that elasticity to the arts which it gives to all beliefs.

In France, as in Greece, the artists whom the age has endeavoured to ostracise have always on that very account acquired the greatest influence over the arts of their time. The establishment of an official art, which the Romans were able to effect in the first century of our era, would be attempted in vain by any power in France, since among us there is fortunately a leaven of investigation and criticism in the domain of the arts, which is universally diffused, especially among those classes of craftsmen whose services are to us architects indispensable. The triumphs of architecture have been confined to those epochs when this art has really been under the control of artists, and when they have been able to exercise it with independence. Indeed every person of intelligence who considers the material difficulties connected with the execution of even the least ambitious architectural undertaking, arising from the nature of the programme presented, the materials to be employed, the expenditure, the space, and so forth ; the conditions imposed by art, proportion, and harmony that have to be satisfied ; the multiplicity of details involved in every problem of construction however simple ; the experience that is required of the general effects to be produced by the combination of materials that have to be shaped, fabricated, cast, forged, or worked separately : every person of intelligence, I say, who considers all this, must conclude, that if we would have an architecture, architects themselves must be left to resolve these complicated problems, without being harassed by an absolute but vague control, to which they may perhaps submit, but with repugnance, and to the injury of their work. We should also consider that, in order to justify their claim to that independence which is necessary to the due exercise of their art, architects must have made themselves so fully conversant with the means of execution that these shall never occasion them any difficulty. In studying the architecture of the ancients, particularly that of the Greeks and French mediæval architecture in its best days, we readily perceive that the masters of the art were masters of the means of execution, and that when a novel requirement presented itself, they would seek to invent new modes of procedure without, on that account, abandoning the principles of their art. The Greeks had brought the means of execution to such a high degree of perfection, they were so thoroughly versed in them, so absolutely masters of them, that in no case was their imagination or their genius,—if we prefer to call it so,—shackled by material exigencies ; among them there was no weakening of the conception manifestly produced by the study of the execution, though,—it must be confessed,

—the processes employed by the Greeks were very simple. The secular masters in art of the Middle Ages had, on the contrary, been led to the adoption of very complicated methods, without any detrimental result to the character of their conceptions; they preserved their liberty, because, however complicated might be their methods of execution, they were based on profoundly intelligent principles which allowed of the greatest conceivable variety of constructions, and constituted the architecture properly speaking: conception and execution were in this school one and the same thing. We proceed otherwise in the nineteenth century; and it is not uncommon to meet persons declaring themselves competent judges, and even artists themselves, who believe that a project conceived by an architect may —without any injury to the value of the work—be executed by subordinates independent of the direct intervention of the author. An architectural work, like all other works of art, is the result of an intimate harmony between the conception and the means of execution; and to imagine an architect's conceiving a design whose means of execution are to be suggested by some one else, would be as absurd as to imagine a dual musician,—one the composer, the other the writer of the score. The competent architect, who conceives a design, necessarily sees in imagination the materials to be employed, and their form and dimensions; he estimates their capacities and nature; he constructs in his own mind that which it will require several years to build; and the sheet of paper before him presents to his imagination a vast work-yard where masons, stone-cutters, carpenters, blacksmiths, tilers, joiners, sculptors, etc., are at work; just as the musician, in writing an opera, hears the various instruments of the orchestra, the choruses and the voices of the singers. But if the public are to recognise in the musician's score or in the building erected by the architect an original work of art bearing the impress of personal talent, the musician himself must have written all the parts of the opera, and the architect must have indicated to his workmen the various details that form the whole; it is also desirable that the musician should direct the rehearsals, and the architect superintend his workmen. It should be constantly borne in mind that of all the products of human skill, art is that in which imperfection is least to be endured: but to approach perfection in art, we only want a man of genius, or, failing such, a man of talent, with the stipulation that this genius or talent shall be allowed the liberty of developing itself, and of using all the resources which nature and knowledge have provided for it, —a principle that has never been questioned at those epochs which are regarded as having been favourable to the arts.

LECTURE VIII.

CAUSES OF THE DECLINE OF ARCHITECTURE——CERTAIN PRINCIPLES AFFECTING
ARCHITECTURAL DESIGN——THE RENAISSANCE IN THE WEST, AND PAR-
TICULARLY IN FRANCE.

SINCE architecture belongs almost as much to science as to art
properly so called, and as its conceptions are very largely
dependent on reasoning and calculation, it must be allowed that
Design is not the result of a mere process of imagination, but is
subject to rules methodically applied, and that it must take
account of the means of execution, which are limited.[1] If the
painter or the sculptor is able to conceive and execute at the same
time, and without having recourse to extraneous co-operation, it
is not so with the architect. On the one hand, the requirements,
the expenditure, the site, restrict him within certain limits ; on
the other hand, the nature of the materials and the way in which
they must be employed. If the architect is to design, he must
before all things take account of the various elements that will
affect his work. It would seem therefore that if architects are
to be duly trained to design, they should, when a programme of
the requirements is submitted to them, be made acquainted
with the various conditions that must be complied with in its
execution.

This is not the way in which architects are accustomed to be
trained, at any rate among ourselves. We ought however to be
consistent in the matter. On the one hand, it is alleged that
architects involve the private individuals or the public bodies

[1] M. Quatremère de Quincy's *Dictionnaire d'Architecture* may be consulted ; under the word
COMPOSITION it will be observed that the distinguished author does not treat of architectural design very fully. We find however this remarkable passage : "Nothing is more
important for the architect when engaged in design than to have his attention constantly
directed to the means by which his designs are to be realised. The student of architecture,
therefore, cannot be too early trained to consider his designs with reference to the means
of execution. The study of design should be something more than a mere imagining on
paper of the several parts of a plan commending themselves to the eye on account of their
variety and symmetry, or of elevations that seem to promise effective combinations or novel
outlines and aspects. It will often happen that all these attempts, of which the imagination is prodigal enough in drawings, will result in producing designs that cannot be executed
at all, or whose realisation would involve an enormous outlay."

who intrust works to them, in enormous expense ; that they are disinclined to study the material requirements of the programme or its practical execution ; that their aim is rather to erect buildings that will do honour to themselves, than to fulfil all the conditions imposed by the needs and habits of the day ; that they are always imitating the forms of bygone times, rather than trying to discover an architecture appropriate to the age in which we live. On the other hand, they are subjected to a course of instruction—under the direction of the State—by which they learn nothing more than the production of designs according to programmes that are generally very vague and often very remote from the architectural requirements of the time ; while they are not aided in their work by any information relating to the cost, the locality, the materials to be employed, or the local modes of building. This course of instruction does nothing more than present to the pupils certain architectural forms, interpreted with more or less ability, belonging to a period of the arts anterior to our own time, to the exclusion of others ; it almost ignores the bold innovations that have been suggested by the employment of modern appliances : it has been revolving in the same circle for years ; and at its close, as the highest reward for an implicit submission to its precepts, it sends young architects to Rome or Athens, to enable them to produce, for the hundredth time, a restoration of the Coliseum or the Parthenon. In fact we reap what we have sown ; and we surely should not complain of architects since we *make* them what they are. Alter the teaching if the results do not satisfy you ; or if you maintain that the teaching is good, do not complain of the results. It is true that side by side with the instruction circumscribed within these narrow limits, there is a complete liberty ; but very few can avail themselves of it, for reasons which it would be useless to indicate here. Besides, this unrestrained liberty has also its inconveniences, sometimes impelling those who enjoy it into eccentric paths ; so that between the academical oligarchy on the one hand and the anarchy resulting from the entire absence of method on the other, architects know not where to seek what everybody is calling for,—an art characteristic of our times. It is even a matter of surprise that in so deplorable a state of things, architecture should still retain so honourable a position in France : this proves how richly we are gifted with the faculties that qualify for the study and practice of this art, and to what a degree of eminence we might restore it if efficient instruction were to be had and if it became liberal ; if it did not limit itself to a kind of initiation or rather protectorate such as that which was accorded to their clients by the Roman patriciate. It is during periods of decline that we see schools broken up into sects fanatically exclusive,

holding to formulas instead of principles ; abandoning the broad
paths of reason, or, under the pretext of dignity, shutting themselves up in complete silence, and requiring of their disciples
nothing but an unquestioning submission to dogma, or rather the
shadow of dogma. In this state of things what is sought for is
no longer the great interest of art,—which can only live and be
advanced by intellectual activity and free discussion, by the
continual introduction of new elements, and by liberty subjected
to the control of reason,—but the triumph or the predominance
of a sect.

During no period since the thirteenth century and the reign
of Louis xiv. have so many buildings been erected in France as
in our own age. Nevertheless (and in this particular I do but
repeat a universal sentiment) the new edifices that fill our cities—
in point of design at least—do not appear to be based on any of
the principles recognised during the best epochs of art, still less
on new principles.[1] In these buildings, which however have been
erected at great expense, and in which the material is employed
with a profusion that may be called excessive, and often in a way
that contravenes its nature, there is no harmony,—nothing to
indicate the needs and tastes of the civilisation of this age ; they
abound in reminiscences, suggested moreover by no rational
motive, of ancient architecture, Greek or Roman (especially
Roman), or of that of Italy or France in the sixteenth and seventeenth centuries : but the finish of the execution, and the beauty
of the materials employed, cannot make us forget the want of
ideas, and the absence of methods easy to comprehend, as well as
of unity and character ; qualities which distinguish the arts of
all periods, however inferior the position they occupy in history.
These defects are so obvious as even to shock persons unacquainted
with the theory and practice of art.

Have we then reached such an incurable stage of decline that
we cannot hope to see architecture free itself from the rut in
which it has been dragged along ? Is the evil irremediable ?
Are we reduced to the necessity of copying the Romans, very
badly—the Greeks after a fashion which to those acquainted with

[1] It would, however, be unjust not to acknowledge that among these recent buildings
there are some of very considerable merit in point of art. I should mention as in the first
rank, the central Market-halls of Paris, which indicate so clearly the purpose to which these
great structures are appropriated. I believe that if all our public buildings were erected
with the same implicit deference to the requirements of the case, and the habits of the
population—if they indicated the means of construction as boldly—they would have a character proper to the age, and would also find for themselves beautiful and intelligible forms of
art. In the example referred to, there has been a compliance with the requirements of the
programme and of the materials employed, and the result has been, in my judgment, a very
fine building. Perhaps there may have been no deliberate intention to "produce a work of
art." It were therefore to be desired that such an intention should be abandoned from this
time forward ; this would perhaps be the readiest way to secure works of art that should
be the real expression of our civilisation.

Greek architecture must seem puerile,—the Middle Ages—the Renaissance—the age of Louis XIV. and even the poor buildings of the close of the last century, and to return once more—because we can do nothing better—to the Romans, and recommence the cycle of imitation? Are there not, outside or above these various forms of the same art, certain immutable principles, fruitful in consequences, and which are susceptible of new expressions, if new requirements should arise? Are these principles impenetrable mysteries, accessible only to a small number of the elect? Are they not, on the contrary, accessible to all?—No: decline is not absolutely inevitable; the evil is not without remedy; but it is high time to consider the state of things, to make use of all the vital elements that are still at our command, to quit the mere interests of the schools and to devote our attention entirely to the great interests of an art which has always been considered in the case of every people the most striking expression of its civilisation. The whole field must be subjected to intelligent scrutiny, and we must not hesitate, if necessary, to grate upon prepossessions, however respectable they may seem.

Let us not ignore the popular judgment; we shall do wisely even to regard that judgment as sovereign, in the last resort, for the very sufficient reason that after all, if we erect public buildings, it is for the public, which makes use of them and pays for them. I am quite ready to admit that we must seek to enlighten that judgment, although it is never so far astray as some are willing to suppose; but this cannot be done by carefully concealing from the profane the principles of the art, by making architecture a kind of free-masonry,—a language incomprehensible to the multitude. For since the last century architecture has been a mystery whose rites (if it has any) are veiled from the eyes of the public. From its sanctuary there issue monuments whose sense or use nine persons out of ten do not comprehend, but which are accepted, because the interpreters of its doctrines declare them conformable to its rules, without ever explaining those rules—and for good reasons. Sometimes however that public, which is looking on and has to pay for all, becomes a little impatient; it would be glad to comprehend; and then it is told once for all that it understands nothing about such matters, and that its influence has been deliberately ignored from the beginning; that if it considers what has been constructed for it neither beautiful nor convenient, it must blame itself for bad taste; that the guardians of the dogma—the only competent judges—are content, and that this must suffice. In an age such as ours, when new ideas are daily brought to light, and when all things—even the very foundations of society—are subjected to discussion, one thing alone remains unshaken,—the inscrutable dogma of architecture, guarded by a mysterious Areopagus. Outside however, there are voices calling for an architecture proper to the age, an architecture of our own, a comprehensible architecture, an architecture conformable to our civic habits. The Areopagus—of course—utters no response to these indiscreet clamours ; it closes its doors and exacts from its adepts a submission so much the blinder as the multitude without are noisier. What then is to be done ? To whom shall we have recourse ? The authorities, or rather the government, who do not profess to be artists, and who have something else to do than engage in discussions on art, prefer to transfer their responsibility to the guardians of the doctrines which are declared by themselves the only sound ones, and the result is considered to be for the best in "the best of possible worlds." Besides, where can we find a touchstone ? "The public are not satisfied," you say. "But it is only certain malcontents who say that,—some journal whose supporters have nothing given them to build. Where do you find your discontented public ? As for myself, I have heard nothing but a concert of praises around the censured building. Have not there always been envious people ? France is an admirable country ; the city of Paris is its worthy capital ; nowhere in Europe will you find a more enlightened or a worthier administration : the Académie des Beaux Arts is an assemblage of the élite of our architects who choose each other ; it is consequently the most liberal of the institutions in this home of enlightenment and art. Of what then do you complain, O Public ? " To this, no answer is possible.

The director of a theatre, however, is obliged to pay some respect to an audience that hisses a piece—though the latter has been received with acclamations by the most respectable reading-committee—because hisses entail a question of receipts. A poor picture in an exhibition, though enjoying the highest patronage, remains a poor picture still, and the painter will have to keep it. A literary work, though well befriended, if it is found tedious, stays on the bookseller's shelves. But when a building is erected, what can be done with it if it is a bad one ? Shall it be demolished ? That would be an expensive solution of the difficulty. Shall it be made the best of ? This is the wisest plan.

In the domain of letters, of painting, of sculpture, the appeal to the public is *bonâ fide ;* between the work of the artist and that public there is no intermediate authority ; monopoly and ostracism are therefore impossible. Had they the wish to be so, the *Académie Française,* the *Académie des Inscriptions,* the Academy of Moral Sciences, those of Painting and of Sculpture, could not be exclusive ; for public opinion—whose competence extorts recognition when the appreciation of literary works, of history, philosophy, painting or sculpture, is in question,—succeeds sooner or later in obtaining for the authors or the artists it approves, the opening of the most venerable portals ; in our days we have seen remarkable examples of this fact ; but it cannot be thus with architecture. The architect cannot build a public edifice in his studio ; a direct appeal to the judgment of the public is therefore denied him. If he has the misfortune not to coincide with the opinions of the Academical body, it may happen that though endowed with talents of the highest order cultivated by the profoundest study—if this has been conducted outside the *Villa Medici*—he is not able to furnish proofs of his merit, for he will find adversaries in his way often powerful enough to oppose their *veto.* " Be one of us, or be not at all !" has always been the supreme maxim of every corporation placed beyond the control of public opinion. " The schools," wrote one of our brother architects not long ago, " are intolerant from conviction." But a corporation that recruits its members within its own limits, and is responsible for its teaching doctrines and judgments only to itself, is what is called in French a *coterie.* Supposing the ablest and the most sincere of men placed in this position ; just because they are sincere, learned, and firmly convinced of the truth of their opinions, they will close the barrier against all who do not share their views or prejudices. To require any other course of conduct from them would be nothing less than an insult to the dignity of their character and the sincerity of their convictions ; but this being the case how can we hope to succeed in bringing to light principles not admitted by the school, forms which it repudiates, endeavours which it regards as revolutionary ? How can we attain an art having the vigour of youth or of rejuvenescence, the product of an examination of the various opinions and tendencies of our civilisation and of the changing requirements of the day ? Architecture is, after all, only a form given to ideas ; it is, as a certain poet has said, a book in stone. If the French Academy had the will and the power to hinder the publication of certain new or resuscitated ideas ; if it could compel the world of letters to express only a restricted number of authorised conceptions, expressed in phrases that have been in use for a couple of centuries,—would it be reasonable, I ask, to complain of the monotony of literary productions, or of their being incomprehensible and useless ? Should we not then act more wisely to read nothing but ancient works and to write nothing new but legal instruments and tradesmen's bills ?

In France the arts are loved with a moderate affection by the higher classes, but there is an enthusiasm for them among the lower classes ; their influence is recognised ; but it is on the condition that this influence is not imposed from without, that it is freely exerted, that it is open to discussion, and does not seek to assume the tone of an indisputable dogma. As regards architecture in particular, in presence of the large number of persons concerned in its development, a perspicuous chain of reasoning, a clear demonstration, suffice to nullify the hollow phrases—however elegantly turned—which are poured forth in support of the exclusive doctrines of the schools.

It is an opinion somewhat widely diffused that artists have not a practical mind—that they are prone to indulge in illusions. I should not notice this prejudice here if it had not the injurious effect of placing the enlightened public who take an interest in Art in a position absolutely false towards artists, and artists in their turn towards that public. Artists, and architects especially, are of all people the least impelled towards illusions,—they are, on the contrary, the most practical, for the simple reason that in their case every work of imagination is immediately rendered into a real product. Every work of art implies a visible form in which it is embodied, a means of practical realisation, and a manual labour, which bring us back immediately to the sense of the real, the possible,—of that which lies within or beyond human power to accomplish. Artists are therefore amenable to reason ; and a school of art, if it would be something other than a protectorate compelled to surround itself with dependent clients—if it would be really a school—should derive all its influence from discussions, the exchange of ideas, and the emulation resulting from rival principles, freely manifesting themselves under the control of public opinion.

The obscurity that is made to involve all questions relating to architectural art has a tendency to hasten its decline ; and while in France we are sometimes disposed to boast of superiority over the other nations of Europe in art products, serious and liberally sustained efforts are made in open day, in England and in Germany, to rival and even surpass us. Whilst we still succeed —thanks to our natural aptitude—in studying architecture without teaching, our neighbours have established schools which, far from being exclusive, boldly investigate all the original arts of the past, to find the elements of a new formation. While our laureates lock themselves up in the *Villa Medici*, the young English and German architects are gleaning everywhere, in France, Italy, and Greece, studying the methods of those countries, comparing them, visiting building-works and endeavouring to understand the various phases of art. Private associations are forming museums of architectural casts and copies, which are placed within the reach of the humblest workmen.[1]

---

[1] It must be confessed however that in England a movement has taken place in favour of exclusive doctrines. In a recent discussion the House of Commons decided that the

From the above considerations I conclude that in France architecture is the art which above all others presents conditions favourable to the prolongation of mediocrity, if the questions that concern the principles of this art,—vital questions, —are not brought under the view of all,—if instruction in it does not enter on liberal paths. Believing that a country really possesses an art only so far as every one can comprehend and discuss, if not practise it, I shall endeavour to raise the thick veil with which our architecture and the teaching of it have been concealed, with a view of making it a kind of hieratic art bound by supposed dogmas which have not and never have had an existence,—a formula void of principles,—a hieroglyph whose meaning the initiated themselves cannot interpret—simply because it has none. I remember how excessively the celebrated Champollion was amused by some drawings brought from Egypt, in which the draughtsmen, perhaps in their haste to leave the desert, had reproduced certain fragments of hieroglyphs as a decoration over the entire surface of a column, so that "*Ra-men-cheper*, son of the Sun, the joyful heart," was recorded to have "despoiled the city of *Arat-tou* of all its corn and cut down all its plantations" thirty-two times following—which would seem a difficult achievement. And it is in some such intelligent fashion that we see the forms of ancient architecture reproduced in our days.

Our aim then should not be to know what relative proportions the Ancients or the Moderns have thought proper to give to the "Orders;" how an architectural member requires to be treated ; what are the conventional relations actually recognised or conjectured between the parts and the whole of an ordonnance. We should make it our chief endeavour to explain how reason should dictate architectural forms, whatever be the phase of civilisation ; how, since reason is common to all, every one must consequently possess an aptitude for recognising in what respects an edifice is good or bad ; how the public, which judges by instinct and is yet on the whole seldom mistaken, though it cannot define the causes of the censure or approval it expresses, may succeed in compelling the masonic fraternity to discuss and defend their principles, if they have such, or to justify their judgments if they pronounce any. Our aim must be to explain the various methods that have been employed at certain epochs favourable to the development of art, for realising the interpretation of a given programme.

Italian style of the Renaissance should be adopted in the Government offices. But when a political body concerns itself with questions of style in art, no danger need be anticipated ; a style can no more be decreed by a government than the form of a hat ; and in England this victory of Lord Palmerston will probably result in the commencement of the buildings thus voted in the style of Palladio, and that will be all.

The main features of architectural programmes change but little, for the needs of mankind in a civilised condition are the same with very trifling variations; but climate, traditions, manners, customs, tastes, cause these programmes to receive a particular interpretation, according to time and place. The requirements of a theatre, *e.g.* are the same both for the Athenians and the Parisians, as far as the purpose of the building is concerned. What were these requirements, and what are they still? Places for a large body of spectators, arranged so as to enable all to see and to hear; a stage and an orchestra for vocal or instrumental performers; rooms for assembling and apartments for the actors; *promenoirs* for spectators; commodious arrangements for entrance and exit. And yet a modern playhouse by no means resembles a theatre of Bacchus. Why? Because side by side with the requirements which indicate simply the object of the building, there are others dictated by the manners and customs of the society that prescribes them. The mere fact that the scenic representations of the Ancients took place in daylight, and that ours are given at night, obliges the two edifices—the Ancient and the Modern—to differ essentially in point of structure, internal arrangements and decoration. If to the cardinal points of difference just noted we add the innumerable details which our habits in respect to theatrical arrangements impose—such as scenic effect, machinery, the division of the house into stalls and boxes, etc.,—the result is the production of an architectural work which has little in common with that of the Ancients but the name. Here then we have a programme given at Athens and Paris respectively, to satisfy the same requirements; yet this programme, from the mere reason that our habits are not those which the Athenians adopted, produces in the case of the two peoples two buildings greatly differing from each other. We may therefore regard it as a principle that in every architectural programme there is a basis that varies little,—which is destined to satisfy requirements almost identical in character in all phases of civilisation—and a form prescribed by the habits of the time; that architecture is none other than the expression of this form: that the usages of society during any period must not be made to submit to certain architectural arrangements; but that these arrangements must be the outcome of customs and habits, which are necessarily variable. No one, I imagine, will dispute this principle. Practically, however, it would seem to have been forgotten more than once since the commencement of the present century.

Since architectural design should be suggested simply, 1*st*, By the requirements of the case, 2*dly*, By the habits of the civilisation of the time, it is essential in designing to have a definite programme and a correct appreciation of the customs, usages,

and requirements of the civilisation in question. But, I repeat
it, while architectural programmes change comparatively little in
these substantial conditions, the habits and manners of civilised
peoples are continually being modified; consequently, architectural forms must vary indefinitely. An architectural programme
of the time of the Roman Empire and one of modern times would
both require that a hall should be lighted by windows; neither
can go beyond this prescription; but a Roman window does not
resemble a window of modern date, and cannot resemble it,
since the usages of the two periods differ. Certainly in both the
buildings—the Ancient and the Modern—the window will be an
opening made in the wall; but the mode of securing the light,
of closing and glazing the opening, and the consideration of it
simply as a means of giving light to the interior, or as also
affording an outlook,—will produce designs of very different
character, if the architect knows how to take account of the
customs of his time. Architecture assumes a character, if besides being the faithful interpretation of the programme, it also
clothes itself in the form that suits the customs of the period.
If the latter condition is not fulfilled, a people does not possess
an architecture, in my opinion; the architect compiles but he
does not design.

The architecture of the Egyptians, that of the Greeks, that
of the Romans, and that of the Middle Ages in the West, perfectly fulfil the conditions mentioned; and these arts have, therefore, left indelible traces in history. Among the Egyptians we
observe that the architectural design is a product of the building
requirements and the customs of the people; it is simple. The
building, whatever its extent, has never more than one axis, its
services presenting always a continuous range of apartments. In
the temple as in the palace, each part forms an approach to the
next, beginning with the first court, the first enclosure covered
or uncovered, and proceeding in succession to the sanctuary or
the terminal hall, which is nearly always the smallest and most
closely shut in. The richest ornamentation is reserved for the
interiors. Outside we observe little more than a casing of simple
aspect,—mere masses : the porticos do not open outside but on
closed courts. Here we observe the influence of a system essentially theocratic. We find even the Greeks discontinuing this
practice. Among them a public building—even a sacred one—
is constructed for the public; it does not conceal its riches, it
displays them. The mysterious appearance of the Egyptian
edifice is no longer to be found. We see a building characteristic
of a republic, not a theocracy. We find no palaces in the Greek
cities, but houses, temples, and a few public edifices, such as
gymnasiums, theatres, and porticos ; monuments that are rather

enclosures, architectural arrangements open to the sky, than buildings properly so called. Roman architecture under the Emperors has a completely different character. The Romans, it is true, adopt the temples from the Greeks, while they copy their palaces from the Lucumones and the Asiatic princes; but in their public edifices, such as amphitheatres, thermæ, and basilicas, the arrangements are dictated by their own genius. What particularly attracts our attention in Ancient Architecture, whether Oriental, Greek, or Roman, is the perfect accord that exists between its character and the manners and customs of the people, and the methods of construction adopted by them.

I have already pointed out, in our preceding Lectures, those profound differences that render Roman architecture and that of the Greeks two distinct arts, chiefly as regards the construction. This difference is not less marked as regards the designing. The Greek gives comparatively little attention to what we call the plan, while to the Roman the plan, or rather the design for the plan, is the chief concern; the plan is the literal rendering of the programme, and the architecture is subordinated to it. The Romans were not artists; it was natural that they should wish, above all things, to comply with the material requirements of the programme prescribed. This method has ever since been regarded as a sound one; and if among ourselves it has been often departed from, it is because we are rather more of artists than the Romans were, and are ready to sacrifice our material requirements to satisfactions of a higher order.

Through not being agreed on principles and defining them clearly, we are continually falling into the strangest contradictions. We propose to ourselves to proceed as did the Romans (so at least it has been assumed since the seventeenth century), while we are impelled by instinct to introduce considerations of a purely artistic order into our architectural compositions. Thus hesitating between two opposite principles, we end in producing works that are destitute of that straightforwardness which in architecture marks the position of having "made up one's mind." In fact it is very difficult to be Greeks and Romans at the same time. The Greeks sacrificed much to form, the Romans everything to utility,—to necessity, public or private. Each of these methods has its commendable side; but to wish to follow them both at once is, perhaps, to wish for what is impossible; it is to satisfy neither the artistic feeling of the Greek, nor the reason of the Roman; it is the way to habituate ourselves to erecting buildings destitute of character.

Most assuredly for us Western peoples of the nineteenth century there is only one right method of design in architecture, —that is, to comply with the conditions of the given programme, and then to make use of what we know to find a form for all the requirements imposed by the habits of our times; a form moreover which must be beautiful and durable. But all who have long studied architecture, without being previously imbued with the prejudice of the schools, have been able to perceive that a form which was the simple expression of a necessity,—were it even a commonplace one,—acquired from this very circumstance a special charm.

Since every part of an edifice or construction should have its *raison d'être*, we are, in spite of ourselves, attracted by every form that indicates its object, as we are interested by the sight of a beautiful tree, all whose parts,—from its root clinging to the soil, up to its remotest branches that seem to seek the air and the light,—so clearly indicate the conditions of life and duration of these great vegetable growths. But if each part of a building should express the requirement that dictated it, there should exist intimate relations between these parts; and it is in the combination of the whole that the artist develops his natural abilities, knowledge, and experience. And while an acquaintance with various architectural compositions, ancient and modern, may then be brought in to aid the artist, by enabling him to see how others have proceeded before him, it is also sometimes a cause of embarrassment; it brings before his mental vision a thousand forms, good in themselves, but which conflict with each other, and which, as they cannot have undisputed possession, draw him into compromises as the result of which the work loses all character. I am far from complaining that our age possesses treasures of art in greater abundance and variety than any previous age; besides, were I to lament it,—good or bad,— nothing could avail to make circumstances otherwise; but the wider our acquaintance with what has been actually realised in art, the more order and firmness is required in our own minds to be able rightly to make use of it; and the more necessary does it become to subordinate those memorials of art,—which in many cases have been accumulated without respect to order or measure, —to thoroughly fixed principles, just as strictness of discipline is required in an army in proportion to its numbers and the heterogeneous character of the troops composing it. In our days, therefore, if we would produce an architectural design, it is more than ever necessary to adhere with ardent firmness to the true and invariable principles of art, and methodically to class the knowledge we have acquired of the creations of the past.

If an architect, in designing a plan, does not see the whole edifice before him; if it does not present itself complete in his brain; if he reckons on the abundant materials he possesses to

apply to each part in succession a suitable form, the work will
remain undecided; it will be wanting in unity, freedom, and
character; and it will be decidedly bad, if, before studying the
arrangements of the plan, he has resolved to adopt such or such
a front, such or such a composition which has struck his fancy,
or which is prescribed him by others who are strangers to art.
Forgetfulness of these immutable principles, which are, as it were,
the moral sentiment in art;[1] want of method in study and the
classing of the remains of ancient art; and deference to the fancies
of the moment, have filled our cities with buildings justified
neither by reason nor by taste, although their execution is sometimes of a high order.   In the ancient world,—with rare exceptions,—and even during the Middle Ages (in France at least) we
notice among architects a constant observation of the laws that
constitute good taste, *i.e.* the absolute subjection of form,—of
appearance,—to reason.   When we forget these principles, we
may have more or less skill and repute as decorators according
as we interpret well or ill the fashion of the day ; but we are not
architects.

It was quite natural that when the requirements to be satisfied were simple, and were not obscured by the multiplicity of
details introduced by peculiarities of custom infinite in variety,
—architecture should be simple.   The Greeks, who were, *par
excellence*, endowed with taste, knew that in imposing on their
architects very complicated requirements, they could not expect
them to adopt a simple form : so that, if there is one thing
especially noteworthy in the monuments they have left us, it is the
extreme simplicity of the requirements of the social customs they
indicate, and consequently of the plans adopted.   But to think of
applying, in modern times, forms which were the natural results of
very restricted requirements, to the exigencies of our social state,
is to set ourselves an insoluble problem.   The Romans, who were
a practical people, demanded much more : their architectural programmes are, as compared with those of the Greeks, complicated,
extensive, and varied ; thus their architects adopted new arrangements and modes of construction in harmony with those new
requirements; and if they borrowed certain forms from the Greeks,
it was rather in the way of interpretation than imitation.   Those
forms often embarrassed them ; so they modified,—or if we will
call it so,—debased them.   The Western peoples of the Middle
Ages, almost as practical as the Romans, but more artistic, finally
abandoned the Greek forms, which had been deformed or inap-
propriately applied by the Romans, and adopted forms of their

---

[1] I think I have sufficiently insisted on the value and bearing of these principles in the
preceding Lectures,—principles which, I may add, may be summed up in these few words :
Absolute respect for the True.

own which are the genuine expression of the manners and customs of their time. These are facts sufficiently attested by the studies of the last twenty years. If the programmes of Greek buildings, whether of the religious or civil order, were too simple for Roman edifices; if the programmes imposed on the architects of the Middle Ages differed so widely from all those of preceding times that these architects thought themselves obliged to seek new forms and a novel mode of construction; and if our modern requirements are so complicated that they forbid us the adoption of even mediæval architecture, it is difficult to understand how,—by what singular logical deduction,—we should be induced to resume, in the present day, the architectural forms or mixture of forms of the Romans; or how *à fortiori* we could, without running counter to our habits, apply to our public or private buildings the arrangements of plan that were suitable in Ancient Rome. In fact, the more clearly we demonstrate the excellence of these arrangements as having been perfectly adapted to their purpose, the requirements imposed, and the manners and daily habits of the Romans,—seeing that their manners and habits do not resemble ours,—the more carefully we should avoid reproducing those arrangements in our cities of the nineteenth century.

If need required, it would be possible to live in a château or a house of the fourteenth century; but what Frenchman of modern times would wish to inhabit a Roman house of the time of the Emperors, or what sovereign would find himself conveniently installed in the Palatine? While it is well to examine by what means civilisations anterior to our own succeeded in satisfying the architectural programmes of their time—while this must be allowed to be an *exercise* intellectually beneficial, —it is desirable that such study should not draw us into imitation. That which should deeply impress our minds is the perfect agreement of the programme and the customs of the times with the design,—not the design apart from the programme and the customs in question. Changes, and modifications, and complications of the social element must, in all reason, induce proportional changes, modifications, and complications in architectural design. It would seem, however, according to certain systems very recently adopted, that form (and one style of form in particular) should always take precedence of vivifying principle,—that is, the application of reasoning to things of art. According to these schools, the requirements of the age, the tastes and intellectual characteristics of our country, the efforts of artists outside such or such limits, our materials for construction, the mode in which they are employed, and the whole field of modern industrial appliances, are of very little account. We may observe that the fashion of confining art within certain

limits cannot be applied to our houses, and that if we are subjected to the Academic rule in our public buildings, we have
been hitherto at liberty—apart from municipal regulations—to
accommodate our dwellings to programmes dictated by our
customs; so that in our cities, side by side with our houses,
which are perfectly adapted to those customs, we see newly-built
edifices that seem to belong to a civilisation which has but slight
affinities with our own. In most of these public buildings the
architecture is a matter of prescription, as in the case of a hieratic
art to which was attached a sacred tradition. Let us not shrink
from acknowledging the fact that many of our public buildings
seem erected, not to satisfy any definite or previously recognised
necessity, but to present to the eye an effective architectural
spectacle. In view of our public edifices, those who accuse our
age of falling into *positivism* are evidently mistaken. An attractive design is produced, a plan is drawn in obedience to
academical rules which do not invariably accord with reason,
and forthwith walls are built decorated with columns and banded
with cornices; then, when this heap of stones has been covered
in, worked down and sculptured, presenting an assemblage of
forms borrowed,—no one knows why,—from the remains of
Classical Antiquity or the Renaissance, the question comes of
allotting the huge building to a use of some sort.

"Shall it be a God, a table, or a bowl,"

a palace, a Government office, Barrack, an Assembly Room, a
stable or a Museum? Sometimes it will be all these in succession without difficulty. I say without difficulty, but I am wrong.
It is now that the architect's embarrassment commences. Windows must be cut through floors and partitions, stairs must wind
their way through dark stair-ways, considerable spaces must be
lost because they cannot be lighted, while available apartments
are too small; gas has to be used at mid-day in galleries, and
closets are flooded with sunshine, carriage-porches have to be
placed before doors which were not constructed with a view to
any such, and outside or inside blinds fitted to windows little
adapted to receive them; small apartments have to be "entre-
soled" that they may not look like wells, and the ceilings of
large rooms raised to make them habitable; suites of rooms receive none but borrowed light from arched porticos through
which nobody passes; that is, people must be condemned to live
in apartments without air or light, for the satisfaction of giving
the public *the sight* of magnificent galleries. But apart from this
perversion of internal arrangements for the honour and glory of
external architecture, do we not sometimes see a façade which on
paper *geometrically drawn*, is splendid, produce a quite different

effect in reality ? And this because the architect has not taken into account the effect in perspective, or has not considered that the sun will never cast those shadows which he has so skilfully drawn on his plan at an angle of 45°; or, it may be, because he has not foreseen the effect of an unlucky outline brought into hard relief against the sky,—an outline cleverly obscured in the drawing under light tints. The architects of the Ancient World, those of the Middle Ages, and even those of the Renaissance, were certainly less skilful draughtsmen than ours, they cared little whether the arrangements of the plans were *Academically* sanctioned,—in fact, troubled themselves little with the geometrical aspects, except when diagrams were in question ; and when the plan was drawn they endeavoured to subordinate architectural considerations to it. When treating these on paper they did not deceive the more or less intelligent amateurs they had to do with, nor did they deceive themselves, by geometrical elevations, which are nearly always misleading ; but they certainly sought to get a clear notion of the effects that would result in the execution. To do this they needed something quite different from a course of instruction limited to the study of architectural designs that were never to be realised ; they had to acquire the habit of seeing and comparing : they had to study not only theories, but their applications, and not limit the horizon of architecture to the walls of a studio, or even a city, were that city Rome itself.

Certainly we are not limited in point of means ; the elements of good work are supplied us in profusion ; one thing alone is wanting ;—a true, wide, and liberal training, based on principles, not on certain degenerate forms ; training that shall teach us to see and to profit by what our predecessors have done, instead of shutting our eyes against whole periods of art,—that shall consider seriously the application of our appliances and develop the minds of our students instead of carefully environing them with old prejudices which are abandoned by all persons outside "the School."

To make architecture a "mystery," an art shut up within certain conventional methods which the profane can neither see nor comprehend, may be, it is true, the means of preserving a kind of monopoly advantageous to those who enjoy it ; but is it not to be feared that some day the initiated will be left alone with their mysteries ? and have we not already, in these times of rapid change, been witnesses to defections and alarming symptoms pointing to such isolation ? Not to mention those who have introduced rival schools, have we not seen a great deal of work that was formerly intrusted to architects, pass into other hands ? Has not the school, while remaining absolutely riveted to those methods which it no longer takes the trouble even to explain,

seen starting up at its side those "specialities" which are daily
tending to take possession of some new fraction of the domain
of architecture? If the School said, "Let us see architecture
perish rather than abandon a principle!" I could understand
such a doctrine, barbarous though it be. But what is that
principle? It should, at any rate, be defined : but we are still
waiting for this definition. If there is an official school of architecture, there is no such thing as a teaching of architecture. To
have acquired the right of conjugating the verb "*Etre élève de
l'Ecole*" is a privilege assuredly ; but it is perhaps no sufficient
defence against the invasions which on all sides threaten the
domain of architecture, and tend more and more to narrow its
boundaries.

Let us return to design. The first condition in effective
design is to know what we wish to do. To know what we wish
to do is to have an idea ; to express that idea, we require principles and a form, that is to say, rules and a language. The
laws of architecture can be understood by every one,—they
appeal to common sense. As regards the forms,—the means of
expressing one's thought as subjected to rule,—a long course of
studies, theoretical and practical, is needed for learning them,
and a spark of the sacred fire. In the next place, design requires
a conformity to the immutable laws of architecture, which are
reducible to common sense, and then the finding in our mind
and at our finger-ends a form that will enable us to express
what our mind has conceived and our reason prescribes to us.
We cannot require of an architect that he should possess genius ;
but what we have always a right to demand of him is reason and
comprehensible forms. It has happened, however, that simple
formulas applicable at most to a style long anterior to our own
times, have been taken for laws of architecture, and that thus
invariable principles,—principles superior to all form,—have been
tortured into subjection to the narrow exigencies of one among
those forms. Some minds of a more liberal order have, it is
true, sought to form an eclectic school,—to give a welcome to all
the forms that have been recognised from Classic times down to
our own days ; but, in their practical application, these liberal
ideas produce only a *macaronic* language (if I may be allowed
the term) whose meaning no one can decipher. Besides, it is
very difficult, however impartial we may be, to allow an equal
position to every form of art : on many occasions we must make
a selection : now selection means preference, and preference is
exclusion. The architects of Classical Antiquity, those of the
Middle Ages and of the Renaissance, who happily for them were
less learned than we, had no need to trouble themselves with
these subtleties ; they all set out from invariable principles, and

to express their ideas they had a form, recognised in their day, which was more or less pliable, but was always appropriate to those principles. They possessed a single language, and we have several ; if they paid any attention to the forms adopted in previous ages, they applied them only after having adapted them to the standard of their time. This fact may be observed at the epoch of the Renaissance and, later on, at the beginning of the seventeenth century.

The architects of the sixteenth century, who admired the remains of Roman Antiquity, and who sincerely believed themselves imbued with the spirit of the ancient form, through habit and tradition indulged in a liberty so complete, and knew so well how to submit to the necessities of the times, that they transformed but did not imitate those Roman arts. It was a language which they translated, so to speak, unconsciously ; intending, perhaps, to speak Latin they spoke French : but in this involuntary translation they felt the influence of ancient art, which gave a peculiar tone, singularly piquant, to the architecture of this period. When we examine what remains to us of the châteaux and palaces designed and built in the sixteenth century,—such as Chambord, Madrid, Ecouen, Anet, some parts of the Louvre, and not a few others,—we clearly perceive that this architecture grew up under the shade of Roman Antiquity ; yet it is a distinct art, which is consistent with our earlier traditions, which belongs to its own age, is thoroughly French, and in perfect harmony with the manners and tastes of the time,—which renews or rather continues an ancient form and makes it its own. How did it do this ? By rigorously following out the principles of the olden time, the principles which had not ceased to be carried out in practice by Classical Antiquity and the Middle Ages : not by forcing those principles into accordance with these renovated forms, but on the contrary subjecting these forms to those principles.

To come closer to our subject, we may observe, for example, that in both the civil and ecclesiastical buildings of the Renaissance, the design of the ground-plans is altered only as far as new habits require it. The plans of the palaces, châteaux, houses, or churches, differ but very little from those of the fifteenth century, which again were but reproductions, with some slight modifications, of the arrangements of the fourteenth and thirteenth. The ground-plan—that which determines all the others—is invariably the arrangement required by our civil or religious habits ; the idea is always accommodated to the requirements of the time, it does not seek its starting-point elsewhere ; but when his idea has to be expressed, the architect takes possession of a foreign form, yet knows how to adapt it to the idea, because he proceeds methodically, and because he is above all a man representative of his times, and does not cherish the belief that a formula should be respected in preference to the faithful expression of practical requirements. As early as Louis XIV.'s time this method had been abandoned : the colonnade of the Louvre proves this, for there the architect's first thought was to erect an order imitating the Roman Corinthian, without concerning himself with the rationality of that order or its adaptation to the palace to which it is attached. This plan of reversing the reasonable order in architectural designs,—that is to say, giving to form—a particular form—precedence before the simplest expression of a practical requirement, seems to us to be leading architectural art to its ruin ; and experience daily proves that we are not deceived, for our public buildings are more and more losing the character befitting their purpose. Architectural design, instead of being a logical deduction from the various elements which ought to be taken account of in a building,—*e.g.* the requirements, the habits, the tastes, the traditions, the materials, the method of employing them,—has been reduced to an *Academic* formula. This method, supported by a theory more and more vaguely enunciated, not by a true understanding and practical acquaintance with an art whose character is never defined, and which consequently cannot be discussed,—which constitutes, I say it once more, a mysterious initiation, or rather a kind of protective patent, acquired by a blind submission,—brings architects into a state of isolation if they submit to it, or leads them into the most extravagant vagaries if they free themselves from it. It entails moreover the serious disadvantage of giving a handle to the advocates of the "practical," who are disposed to see in works of art only a useless and ruinous luxury, having interest but for a very small section of society. How, in fact, can we defend the inconvenient magnificence of most of our public buildings, against those who have so little difficulty in demonstrating their irrationality; and who, though unprofessional persons, can see that these architectural forms are out of harmony with the arrangements of which they are the casing ?

We have seen that the Greeks had the power of giving to their civil and ecclesiastical buildings forms suitable to their destination, and that the Romans themselves had remained faithful to this true principle. During the Middle Ages, in France, we find architects adhering to it with absolute fidelity. While a Roman house does not resemble a public building, a temple a basilica, or a theatre a palace, our mediæval churches, châteaux, *hospices, hôtels-de-ville,* palaces, and houses present a great diversity in their arrangements, forms, and aspects. While the mediæval architects approve of symmetry in buildings that

present a perfect unity of purpose,—in churches, *e.g.*,—they pay
no regard to it in a château, which is only an agglomeration of
parts used for very various purposes ; in this (as I have already
said) these architects conform to the principles of the Roman
villa, in which the separate parts presented an agglomeration of
constructions having each a form suitable to its purpose.   These
principles having been recognised as sound during the period of
Classical Antiquity, why should they be regarded as bad during
the Middle Ages ?   Why this inconsistency ?   But our authorities
carefully abstain from giving reasons ; they praise in Italy
under the Emperors what they blame among ourselves under the
kings of the third race, because the object is to impose a form,
not to explain principles.   But why should this form be insisted
on and that other repudiated ?   Because the first is known and
has been studied, while the second would require to be known
and studied ; and because artists who are convinced that they
have reached the goal of progress do not like to have that goal
pointed out to them as only a halting-place beyond which there
remains a long road to be traversed.

I do not think it necessary to say much here of those mediæval buildings, of which I have treated at length elsewhere.[1]   I
shall resume the history where art enters on its modern path
while preserving certain elder traditions which could not be
discarded all at once.   I examine the buildings of the sixteenth
century, the epoch at which architecture had reached its climax
in point of material execution ; when society was undergoing
a transformation and tending to destroy the last remnants of
feudal bondage, clerical and secular, and when the study of
antiquity was beginning to be attentively, seriously, and con-
secutively pursued.   But we have first to combat a prejudice
(and at each step we observe such prepossessions, when the
history and practical development of our art is in question) : it
has been said and frequently repeated that the French architects
of the Renaissance drew their inspiration, at the beginning of the
sixteenth century, from the arts of the Italian Renaissance ; it
has even been asserted that many French buildings of that date
were constructed by Italians.   This latter opinion—which, I may
remark, is supported by no proof—has been signally refuted in
our day.[2]   As respects the former, a glance at our sixteenth-
century buildings will convince us that the French art of this
period did not go to Italy for its examples ; for these buildings
are not Italian either in the arrangements of the plans, or in
style, or in methods of construction.   Besides, we should be

[1] See *Dictionnaire*, etc.
[2] See M. de la Saussaye's remarks on Chambord.   *Les Grands Architectes de la
Renaissance*, by M. A. Berty.

LECTURE VIII.

strangely mistaken if we considered the French Renaissance as dating only from the reign of Louis XII.; it began to make its appearance before 1450, and that in a form entirely French. I cannot clearly account for the belief that our arts are derived from foreign sources. There are provinces in France all whose Gothic buildings are still referred to the English; the cathedral of Cologne,—which is a copy of those of Amiens and Beauvais, and is of later date by nearly fifty years,—has been regarded as the prototype of Gothic art; and lastly, the château de Chambord, and certain parts of the Louvre and Fontainebleau, were asserted to be the work of Italian artists: an art of our own is conceded to us, at the earliest, not till Louis XIV., that is to say, at the very moment when we were beginning to lose our originality. "Assuredly," said Philibert de l'Orme to his contemporaries, "the advantages of one's own country and kingdom are always, but particularly in France, less prized than those of foreign lands. I firmly believe that there will not be found any kingdom or country better furnished and provided with variety of stone for building than this. In fact, nature has been so bountiful there that it seems to me one could not find a nation possessing finer building materials than the French. But most of them are accustomed to think nothing 'good' (as we said above) unless it comes from a foreign country and is very costly. This is the natural disposition of the Frenchman, who in such matters sets a far higher value on the artisans and products of foreign nations than on those of his own country, however ingenious and excellent the latter may be." We must confess that things are much the same in our own days as regards the appreciation of architecture, and that art in our country must be endowed with strong vitality since it still offers some resistance to these prejudices, and to the constant restraint and the enervating régime to which it has been subjected for nearly two centuries.

What is conventionally termed the Renaissance was not an accidental occurrence that could be retarded or advanced, or was dependent on political events. The Renaissance was rather a continuation of the Roman organisation than a return to a forgotten system. To explain this fact, which is unique in the history of the civilisations of the world, it is necessary to give here some explanation respecting the singular position in which the dominion of the Romans had placed Europe.

Ever since the first century of our era, the Roman Empire had been a compound of elements so diverse that it was not possible to discover in it a national spirit, still less that of a race, but only a vast political and administrative organisation, much more calculated to stifle the special idiosyncrasies of the peoples than to develop them. From the time of Nero, in fact, it was

the barbarians, or at least those who were so called, who were
the sole conservators of the decrepit Empire,—aiding it either by
their strength of arm or by constantly contributing vital elements
amid the purulent body of which Rome was the centre.   The
Roman Empire contained everything except Romans; the legions,
the generals, the senators, the emperors themselves, from the
close of the first century downwards, were strangers to Rome, and
often even to Italy.   We can now understand why Rome should
not have possessed an art, but only a commonplace formula of
art, tending necessarily to a deeper and deeper degradation as
regards the execution.

The results of recent studies in Germany, England, and
France,[1] have clearly exhibited the special aptitudes of the three
great races of man for intellectual production.   But Rome, composed as it was from its origin of a confused mixture of these
races, had not been able to give a clear and definite impulse to
the arts ; it had contented itself with imitating and collecting
Etrurian, Celto-Tyrrhenian and Hellenic art-productions and
those of the Semites of the coast of Asia, while subjecting them
to a powerfully 'practical' spirit.   From this medley it had
succeeded in deducing (when edifices of public utility—the only
buildings truly Roman—were required) certain formulas generally
applicable, but which, from the very circumstance that they were
generally applicable, did not possess, in point of form, any of
those excellencies which as artists we love to find so vividly
expressed in Egypt, Asia Minor, Greece, and Etruria.   When the
Germans—whose tribes have preserved a comparative purity of
race—ceased in the fourth century to guard the frontiers of the
Empire, when, even allying themselves with the torrent of invaders from the North, they flung themselves upon the dead
body of the Empire, what has been called Roman art was lost,
together with its political and administrative organisation—since
that art was in fact only one of the branches of this administration.   However, these peoples of the North whom we have been
taught at college to call barbarians—to say nothing of their
having performed a meritorious act, in the eyes of humanity, by
coming to introduce young and vivacious elements where death
was reigning—were destined, by this very contribution of a
purer blood, to restore to the arts a distinctive character.   If
the Teutons, the Lombards, the Franks, the Burgundians, and
the Goths were not artists when they came down upon Gaul,
Italy, and Spain, it is not less certain that they introduced a very

---

[1] See, as a *résumé* of these results, M. A. de Gobineau's *Essai sur l'inégalité des races
humaines*, Paris, Didot, 1855.   The study of the question investigated in this remarkable work cannot be too strongly urged on architects who interest themselves in the
history of the arts.

active ferment of art into the stagnant mud of the Roman Empire. They introduced an energetic infusion of Aryan element into the incurably corrupt and inert medley which Rome had formed from the vital principles of the West and South of Europe. It must, however, be acknowledged that the traditional prestige of Rome was still such, that these Northern nations, in establishing themselves in the provinces of the Empire, thought they could not do better than preserve or even copy the public buildings of the Romans. Clovis, moreover, assumed the title of Augustus; and before him the first barbarian chiefs held the position towards the people of the Provinces of magistrates acting under the authority of the Emperor,—the supreme dominion being still considered as belonging to the Empire.

Charlemagne had no other idea but that of restoring this Roman Empire, and he wished to accomplish in the eighth century that Renaissance which developed itself spontaneously in the fifteenth. But under Charlemagne the Aryan elements were still too powerful to make this return possible ; and after him, when the feudal disintegration took place, we see arts arise which borrow very little from the Romans,—which develop themselves in an opposite direction, arrive at a high degree of perfection, and are a marked expression of an Aryan element introduced among those Gallo-Roman races, which, in the Northern provinces, where that art attained its complete development, had remained almost entirely Celtic. That the Renaissance might be accomplished,—in other words, that Western Europe might become disposed to return to the political and administrative ideas of the Romans,—the element introduced by the white races of the North must be swallowed up in the confused medley effected by the Roman Empire. This is what happened in the course of the fifteenth and sixteenth centuries. Regarding the Renaissance therefore, not in its details, but as a great social fact, we may find in it the continuation of the Roman organisation which had been interrupted for many centuries by the influx of those powerful white races of the North whom we see at the remotest epochs invading India, Asia Minor, Egypt even, and Greece, and ultimately—on two distinct occasions —Western Europe. By what strange impulse of self-contradiction do we admire the Aryan-Hellenes, who are the fathers of the arts of Greece, and regard as barbarians the Aryan-Germans, the Aryan-Franks, and the Aryan-Scandinavians, who, breaking in upon the path of Roman decline, became the fathers of our Western mediæval arts ? I admit the cogency of the evidence that the Aryan-Hellenes, Semitised in Greece, found themselves in such fortunate relations of intermixture as to have produced arts superior to what the world had seen or will ever see again. But if the Aryan element introduced into the Roman Empire was less pure, and the conditions of intermixture less favourable, it must nevertheless be acknowledged that this last infusion of white blood suspended the dissolution of Western Europe, and was able to impart new strength to its social state, and introduce a new form of art; and that if that dissolution was only respited (I am speaking exclusively of the arts) this is no subject of congratulation, nor a reason for precipitating the final crisis. I am well aware that I shall be accused of treating the Romans more harshly than they deserve; but let me be clearly understood: I greatly admire the Roman power, as a governing, administrative, and military power; not less do I admire the Roman legislation, and especially the respect shown by the Romans for all that assumes a legal form; but if the arts are in question I must be allowed to class the Romans much below the beautiful civilisations (beautiful from an artistic point of view) of India, Asia, Egypt, and, above all, Greece. The necessary elements were wanting to the Romans (elements of race) for producing arts clothed in an original and distinguished form; they were admirable builders,—nothing more; all that is not mere building in Roman edifices is Greek, Etruscan, or Asiatic, but not Roman. It is the same with poetry: there is no Latin Epic; for whatever may be the beauty of the *Æneid*, it cannot be regarded as a sincere epic. Virgil evidently does not believe a word of what he writes, any more than the Roman architect of the time of Augustus believed in the Orders—at least as forms consecrated to Diana or Apollo. But Homer, or the reciters of the songs of the *Iliad* (whichever view we take of its authorship) had a firm belief in its heroes; the author identified hmself with them; and so the *Iliad* from the first time it was sung to the present has been a soul-stirring poem; and as long as a thinking being shall remain on the earth, the *Iliad* will always be the liveliest, the most touching, the most beautiful, sincere and noble expression of the emotions of the human heart. Well, during that mediæval period which has been so greatly depreciated by those who admire the Romans in all and for all, we discover both in the plastic arts and in poetry some glimpses of that Aryan genius of the Greeks. The *Chanson de Roland*, which dates from the eleventh century, is to the Romances of the thirteenth and fourteenth centuries what Homer is to Virgil,—a *bona fide* epic,—not a mere intellectual product, but one in which, though the language is imperfect, the nobility of the sentiments and thoughts, and the knowledge of the human heart it displays often render it comparable with the best passages of the *Iliad*. But the men who sang and listened to these passages could not pass for descendants of the Latin races. In point of human dignity and of art they occupied a grade infinitely superior, especially if we compare them with those Romans of the period of decline who spent their time in writing lectures on grammar, lipogrammatic poems, epigrams, madrigals, and the rest of the intellectual trifling so much in vogue at the time. And similarly our Western buildings of the twelfth century, notwithstanding the frequent rudeness of their construction, and even the practical deficiencies of the artists, display a sincerity, an appreciation of the true, a severity of principle and a choice of form, much superior to that degenerate, feeble, uniform, vulgar art which overspread the Latin world during the second and third centuries. Certainly the idea of continuing that degraded Roman art could not arise in the minds of men who were endowed with a much greater capacity for art than the Romans had ever been even during their best period. Less cultivated certainly than were the Latins of the period of the Decadence, they might be astonished at and be seized with admiration for the vast remains of Roman power; but by the very nature of the blood that flowed in their veins, imitation was impossible to them.

The great revolution that took place in the arts at the close of the twelfth century, and of which we spoke in the preceding Lecture,—a revolution as the result of which the domain of the arts passed entirely into the hands of the laity, that is to say, into the hands of the Gallo-Roman races, somewhat modified by the element contributed by the white races of the North,—was a first step towards a return to the Latin arts; and although the architecture of this epoch had no relations of structure or of forms with that of the Romans, although the modern analytic and scientific spirit was tending to take the place of the degenerate Latin traditions and the poetical conceptions of the earlier part of the twelfth century, yet we can already foresee that those secular arts of the thirteenth century were fated to fall back into the deep furrow made by the Romans. However, the Renaissance, and the French Renaissance in particular, still preserves so considerable an admixture of those elements to which the splendour and originality of the arts of the Middle Ages were due, that it occupies a respectable position in the history of Western Europe. Those arts of the Renaissance were developed under favourable conditions such as will not be realised again; but while we are demonstrating the increasing vulgarity of modern arts, we must not the less endeavour, as far as possible, to stay our steps on the road to decline, and to try whether new paths are not still open to us.

The task is ungrateful,—I cannot pretend to think it otherwise,—and I would rather share the faith of those who firmly believe that architectural art is progressing; that out of the state of uncertainty and hesitation in which we find ourselves, there will arise—as was the case at certain epochs in the Greek world, and in the thirteenth and fourteenth centuries—an original and novel art, perfectly appropriate to our civilisation ; but, without asserting this to be impossible, I may, I think, be permitted to doubt it, and to give my reasons for this doubt. Whether in ancient or modern history architecture has exhibited a brilliant development only as the result of certain social shocks in which intermixtures or antagonism of races have played an important part,—intermixtures or antagonism which in other spheres also exercise a powerful influence on intellectual production. I do not see that we are thus favourably circumstanced. We have traditions confused or not rightly appreciated, and in which no one believes ; means of execution in numberless variety, and powerful industrial appliances : but, to direct these means and use these appliances what have we ?—The negation or the forgetfulness of the simplest general laws ; the exclusive spirit of a school, or individual fancy ; the disputes of coteries in which the public find no interest ; gifted individualities, which, when they happen to arise, are sought to be ostracised ; and rival camps of imitators of the past—who are wrangling over formulas while making no attempt to come to an understanding respecting principles. We may, however, discover, side by side with or below this confused condition of the republic of architectural art, a certain patient labour, a conscientious analytical study of the works left by our predecessors, the basis of a new doctrine, relinquishing tradition and relying on the most rigorous principles,—something analogous perhaps to the movement which made the arts of the twelfth century quit the convents and intrusted them to the hands of the laity ; but will this intelligent *democracy*, which is endeavouring to emancipate itself, find that support which greeted its predecessors ? Are our times favourable ? Is there in our *blasé* state of public feeling an energetic sympathy for works of art ? Have we not reached, in matters of art, that point at which society in Byzantium found itself, when it was engrossed with the disputes of the Schools while the enemy was storming the ramparts ?

In all intellectual questions there is a constant struggle between tradition more or less firmly established, and the tendencies of minds disposed to innovation. The secular school of the twelfth century, aided by circumstances altogether favourable, had enough energy and faith in its principles to substitute, in the space of a few years, for the expiring monastic traditions, an art which it had been able to form in its own bosom, and which adopting a form, eminently flexible, accommodated itself to all the transformations which the habits of society can undergo. This art, which resulted from the intellectual emancipation of the industrial classes in the cities, which was essentially democratic, and which put examination and reasoning in the place of theocratic tendencies, soon degenerated into an abnormal development of its own principles : through the very circumstance that it was democratic, it knew not how nor was it able to stop : proceeding from deduction to deduction it ended in a geometrical formulary. As early as the close of the fourteenth century it had reached the utmost limit which its principles could attain. Only one outlet remained to Architecture,—that which had been long abandoned by the Gallo-Roman races,—and this it eagerly followed.[1]

Our architects of the Renaissance, while endeavouring to restore the forms of the ancient Roman world, succeeded in maintaining their individuality,—and we cannot praise them too highly for doing so. Thanks to the practical spirit that distinguishes us (when we are left to ourselves), they continued to attach great importance to the material means placed at their disposal, the requirements of contemporary customs, traditions, the influences of climate, and the convenience of those for whom they built. Not only do the buildings they have left us prove how faithfully they adhered to their principles, but their writings also, and particularly the Treatise on Architecture by Philibert de l'Orme. This author, in fact, gives the foremost place in his book[2] to the proper carrying-out of the works, to counsels applicable to those for whom buildings are erected, to questions of aspect and salubrity, the various branches of knowledge required by the architect, the liberty that ought to be granted him, the employment and choice of materials, and the study of arrangement and adaptation. " So that," says he, " it would in my judgment be far better for the architect to neglect columnar decorations, proportions, and façades (which all who set up for builders study the most), than to disregard those admirable laws of nature which affect the convenience, use, and profit of the inhabitants, and not the decoration, beauty, or magnificence of

---

[1] There is so little clear understanding in reference to the history of the arts in France, that we find the defenders of democratic tendencies considering what is called *Gothic* art as a reflex of the feudal régime, and therefore condemning it unheard. The men of the seventeenth century, with Louis XIV. at their head, understood their position better when *they* expressed contempt for French mediæval art ; but it will be confessed that it is strange to hear the partisans of the supremacy of intellect—the adversaries of despotism and privilege—reason in regard to art exactly as did the "Grand Roi" ! The arts invariably count among the most energetic manifestations of the mind of a people and of its aspirations. Louis XIV. was true to his character when he sought to crush Mediæval Architecture beneath that of the pseudo-Roman type : conversely, those who assert their sympathy with the triumph of democratic intellect are scarcely consistent when they fail to perceive that in this mediæval architecture we find ingenious appliances accommodating themselves to every phase in the progress of society, and that judicious application of materials, strength, and means which we in our days so highly extol as the *ne plus ultra* of civilisation.

[2] *L'Architecture*, by Philibert de l'Orme. Paris, 1676.

the dwellings, which are made only to gratify the sight, without bringing any advantage to the health and life of the inmates. Do we not observe, I would ask, that for want of forethought in adaptation, aspect, and arrangement, a dwelling renders its inhabitants melancholy, sickly, morose, and disquieted by annoyances and inconveniences of all kinds, whose causes are generally invisible and untraceable?" What wiser precepts could we suggest than these?

Philibert de l'Orme, as well as his predecessors in the art, regarded the selection of a good aspect for building as one of the first conditions in design; and the faithful observance of this principle explains most of the irregularities remarked in the châteaux and palaces of the Middle Ages : it is moreover in accordance with the traditions of Classical Antiquity, for we should mistake if we took for granted a systematic contempt for the rules of symmetry. Symmetry is a requirement of our visual instinct, —a requirement which they always endeavoured to satisfy when it did not contravene more practical obligations. It is certain that the architects of the Middle Ages had not the same idea respecting symmetry as the ancients : what they sought for was rather the balancing of masses and details than their exact similarity.

It is necessary, I think, to give a clear exposition of these two systems—each of which has its advantages and inconveniences,—for when their application is in question there would seem to be some misunderstanding respecting them. We have seen (and it is needless to return to the subject) that the Greeks believed it necessary to make every building conform to the rules of symmetry, but that they did not think of arranging several edifices, each having its separate destination, in a symmetrical order; in this respect they used liberty in their private habitations, and their houses consisted of an agglomeration of erections diverse in design, which, as a whole, are not subjected to the rules of symmetry. The Romans accepted this wise principle, and their palaces and houses exhibit a suite of arrangements which may be symmetrical separately, but which are not subordinated to an *ensemble* symmetrically designed. They knew how to make the best of the ground assigned for the building, and occupied it with plan arrangements skilfully locked into each other ; but they did not dream of enclosing services that had no relation to each other in a casing of uniform aspect.

The Palatine of Rome, for example, must have presented both in its exterior and interior the aspect of a monumental city—a collection of palaces—not of a palace in the modern acceptation of the word. We may say the same of the imperial structures of Spalatro, Palmyra, etc. The perspective views given us in ancient paintings always exhibit combinations very irregularly arranged of buildings regular in themselves; and we should not find in all Roman Antiquity—and most certainly not in Greek architecture—arrangements such as at Versailles, for example the Place Vendôme or the Louvre of modern times, or the Place Louis xv. with its buildings of the Garde-Meuble, the Rue Royale, and the Madeleine. This plan of ancient Rome does not present in any of its Regions such symmetrical arrangements of public establishments; its buildings are symmetrical only in reference to themselves and as far as the requirements of their programmes and the character of the ground allow. Adhering to this principle even in the form of the buildings themselves, the Romans allotted a particular building to each service; that building is complete, has its special treatment, its separate roofing, and the height that suits it; and in the architecture of the Romans we never see various halls of any importance, included together under a single roof, presenting a uniform treatment outside.

It must therefore not be asserted that we are following the traditions of Classical Antiquity in contriving to give a symmetrical envelope to services of very various kinds—such as large halls, private apartments, staircases, vestibules, banqueting or ball-rooms, chapels, galleries, offices, libraries, museums, etc. On the contrary it must be allowed that we are much further removed from those traditions than were the mediæval architects. I am not arguing now, but simply stating facts whose certainty every one can verify. A Roman palace, like one of modern times,—that is to say, a royal dwelling, in which must be provided very large halls for assembling, easy means of communication, as also rooms for living in, public and private arrangements, state-apartments, and those required for the daily needs of life,—imposed on the architect a programme consisting of parts whose character was too varied to allow him to give all these parts a similar dress without offending reason. This has been attempted, I allow, from the seventeenth century to our own times, but certainly not in accordance with ancient traditions; and if it is an innovation, and if our architecture prides itself upon it as an advance on anterior arts, I think it is mistaken. The Romans, nevertheless, like the Greeks, loved symmetry in the parts; thus if they built a temple, the edifice was perfectly symmetrical; if a hall, it was treated symmetrically without and within; if an *atrium*, a xystus, a basilica, the principal axis divided the composition into two similar parts as far as possible. In the details the same principle was applied; all the capitals of the same order were similar, as also all the modillions of a cornice. Here the Middle Ages differ perceptibly from Classical Antiquity; and though in a château of the fourteenth century, as in an ancient *villa*, the various services presented forms appropriate to their purpose, the details of the architecture were infinitely varied in each of the chief features of the château, whereas uniformity was sought in each of the chief features of the *villa*.

We must however not deceive ourselves on this point : that uniformity in details is much less considerable in Ancient Classical buildings than is supposed. It is well not to pay too much regard to the drawings of restorations of classical monuments ; in these speculative representations, the balance, in a case of doubt, is nearly always inclined to symmetry.

For my own part, I have often been surprised, in examining the ancient monuments of Italy and France, to find conspicuous irregularities where restorations on paper had given me reason to expect perfect symmetry ; irregularities which were not always the result of the character of the site, but which seemed much rather an accommodation to a detail of the programme or a fancy of the artist. In fact, perfect symmetry, as now understood, did not exist in the architectural *ensembles* of the Romans ; there was a symmetry—though this is much more absolute among ourselves—in the details, but with a certain liberty which the Academical school no longer allows : affording, it must be owned, a great relief to architects ; for it is pleasant to think, when you have designed a capital or a bit of a frieze, that you will have nothing to do but allow the sculptors to reproduce this design—the work of one day—twelve hundred times ; which will take them three months. The restless spirits who wish to disturb such a state of things are greatly in the wrong ; that is obvious enough. Lazy routine is a powerful sovereign by reason of the numbers of its subjects, and finds defenders everywhere ; it is madness to struggle against it.

Among the Romans, a particular treatment was in the earlier period assigned to each class of structure. The architect adopted a different method in designing a vaulted structure and one covered with timber, respectively. The very plan showed whether such or such a building or hall was to be vaulted or ceiled with timber. On examining the plans of the Thermæ of Antoninus Caracalla or Dioclesian, we not only perceive that these buildings consisted of a combination of large and small rooms covered with vaulting, but we can even recognise the form and structure of each of these vaults ; while a glance at the plan of the basilica Ulpiana informs us that this edifice was surmounted by an open timber roofing ; thus therefore the mode of construction exerted an influence over the architectural designs of the Romans. Moreover the purpose of each building or part of a building indicated to the Roman architect the proper dimension and form whether in area or height. This is evident alike in the Thermæ, the palaces, and the simplest and most ordinary dwellings. We

observe the same true tendencies in Mediæval buildings, although
the form of the architecture and the methods of execution are
different. In the Middle Ages, as under the Roman Empire, the
structure and purpose of a building are manifest from the very
ground-plan ; the ground-plan determines the whole : it is there
that the power of the architect who designs is exhibited in its full
energy ; for in drawing his ground-plan the architect has really
had the solid edifice present to his mind's eye; and the arrangement of the details, when this first labour has been accomplished,
is little more than an intellectual pastime. What pleases and
must please in Roman buildings is their frankly determinate character,—the clearness with which the details are subordinated to
the whole. The same excellencies, under different forms, reappear
in the good architecture of Mediæval times ; that is to say,
ground-plans strictly dictated by the programme and subordinated
to the conditions of the construction : nothing redundant,—a
conception clear from the foundations upwards, and methodically
followed out,—impulses of genius frequently exhibited, but alway
regulated by the reason and knowledge of the practical builder.

Already, however, towards the commencement of the fifteenth
century, systematic knowledge was tending to take the place of
the individual genius of the artist; the methods both in general and
detail designs were becoming circumscribed by geometric formulas,
very ingenious, but calculated to stifle the artist beneath the mere
practitioner. Then it was that on the banks of the Loire and
in the Valois the powerful Dukes of Orleans became the patrons
of a novel school which sought gradually to break with the
old worn-out forms of Gothic art. Thus in the year 1440 we
perceive the Renaissance beginning to manifest itself and buildings assuming a novel dress: the principle remains the same; the
general design is not altered ; it continues to be the expression
of the manners of the day, and of tradition ; but the outward
form is changed. This movement received a vigorous impulse
when a member of that illustrious branch of the Valois, Louis XII.,
ascended the throne. But at that time, though Architecture was
adopting a new style of ornamentation,—forms very freely
copied from Classical Antiquity,—in structure and general design
it remained French, and continued subordinated to the habits
of the time. Even under Francis I., though the Gothic form
became extinct, the principle scarcely underwent a change. The
plan of Chambord is that of a French mediæval château ; the
Abbey of Thélême, projected and described by Rabelais, is Gothic
in plan ; and the château of Boulogne (called the château of
Madrid), which then appeared a bold innovation, bears no resemblance either to a Classic or an Italian palace of the sixteenth
century. The château of Madrid may be regarded as the first

attempt in a mixed style,—on the one hand reflecting the traditions of the Middle Ages, and on the other the requirements of a court that was seeking to break with the usages of the past. Such however is the strength of the preconceived idea that our Renaissance buildings are derived from Italy, that a learned writer, well versed in the study of the arts of the Renaissance,— M. le Comte de Laborde—appears to think that the conception of the château of Boulogne is attributable to the celebrated Italian designer of faïence, Della Robbia. As a conscientious historian, however, M. le Comte de Laborde does not altogether ignore the name of the *master-mason*, Pierre Gadier ; but, as usual, classes the French artist in the second rank,—with insufficient reason, in my opinion. This is what he says respecting the building of the château in question :—

"Jerome della Robbia was the creating artist, the man of genius and taste" (we shall see presently that this is a gratuitous supposition); "Pierre Gadier, the master-mason, was a subordinate workman" (why subordinate ?), "but in reality the actual builder; and while, in this association of two men so variously gifted, we have art on the one side and handicraft on the other, it is yet possible to perceive and to define the sort of compromise that was established between them. Guided by his imagination, Jerome della Robbia would have given to his arcade of two stories an uninterrupted line, and to his apartments a communication by means of a wide flight of stairs ; Pierre Gadier, on the contrary, divided this front, 250 feet long, into three blocks, by pavilions which, rising from the ground, presented their plane surfaces to the eye as breaks and points of rest, giving value to the enriched portions, and, at the same time, serving as staircases for the numerous winding stairs called *vis* de Saint Gilles, the remains of the toys of our mediæval architects."[1]

It is evident from this passage that the title of master-mason given to Pierre Gadier, places him, in M. le Comte de Laborde's view, in the rank of a "builder," or "clerk of the works." But the title of master-mason was applied to architects down to a very late date. Pierre Trinqueau, the architect of the château of Chambord,—as is sufficiently proved by M. de la Saussaye,[2]— had the title of master-mason, and had, as such, the "care and carrying out of the buildings" intrusted to him. As regards Della Robbia, without lessening his merit as a modeller of faïence and a decorative sculptor, he might very well assist Pierre Gadier, and yet leave the latter his liberty as architect. I do not know what design would have resulted in case the Italian artist had taken upon himself what M. le Comte de Laborde

---

[1] *The Renaissance of the Arts at the Court of France.*
[2] *The Château de Chambord*, by L. de la Saussaye. Lyon, 1859.

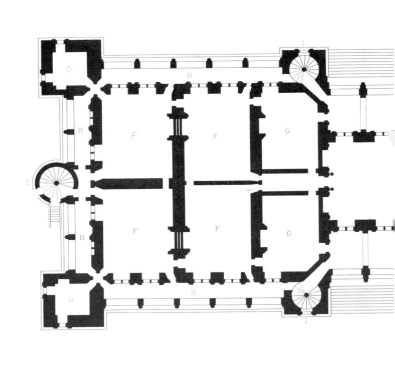

PLATE XV.   Plan of the Main Floor of the Château de Boulogne (called
the Château de Madrid)

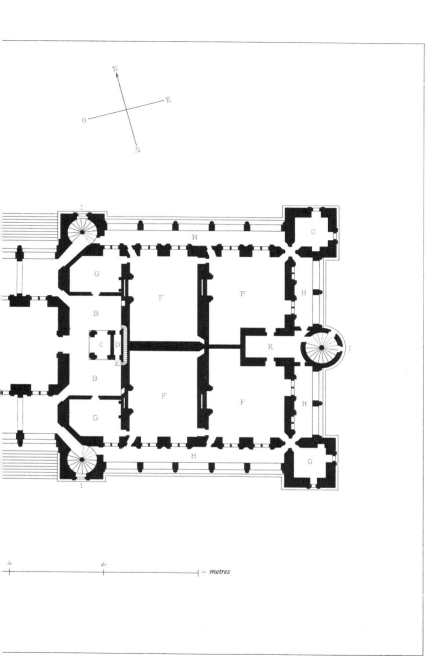

Axis

E. Viollet Le Duc del.

Scale of |⎯|⎯|⎯|⎯|⎯|⎯⎯⎯

PLATE XVI.   Front of the Château de Boulogne

15   70   25 metres

terms the trade of Constructor,[1] of which, to all appearance, he had no idea; but, judging by the plans and elevations of the Château of Boulogne, it is clear that souvenirs of Italian architecture had no great influence on the design of this building. I am, however, prepared to acknowledge that influence, if any one can point to a single Italian palace having the appearance of relationship with the Château de Madrid. Certainly there were porticos at Boulogne, and Italian palaces likewise had them; but our châteaux of the fourteenth century were also provided with them to a sufficiently marked extent. The portico has been a feature of the architecture of every country and of all times; that decoration in faïence itself, which ornaments the whole exterior of a façade, is not used in the same manner in Italy; in fact we have here a novel application of a foreign craft, the honour of which may be attributed to Francis I. or to his humble master-mason. We may observe that P. Gadier died in 1531, and that he was succeeded by Gratian François and his son Jean, neither of them Italians. The building was continued by De l'Orme, who employed Pierre Courtois of Limoges[2] to complete the faïence work. With respect to the winding stairs, regarded as a relic of the *toys* of the Middle Ages, I remark that they are very useful toys when we wish to contrive a way to the upper stories in a small space: might we not with more reason give the name of *great toys* to those double flights of stairs which take up unnecessary room in our buildings, and which, by their exaggerated monumental character, always remind me of those preambles of the poets, announcing in pompous strains the fine things that never come. In Roman architecture, which people are so ready to exalt as a model to be followed, the stairs were never made a feature of more than secondary importance; while in the same architecture, winding stairs were in use long before the date of those of Saint-Gilles. It is true that Primaticcio was intrusted with the completion of Boulogne, and he naturally brought back his countryman, the faïence modeller, Della Robbia. However that may be, and irrespective of the faïence, Boulogne is a French château in plan, elevations, construction, architectural details, and interior arrangements.

The design of this château, therefore, merits our particular attention, since it is the primitive type of all our fine *maisons de plaisance* of the sixteenth and seventeenth centuries, which are so remarkable in point of plan and style of architecture. The Château de Boulogne, of which we give, Plate XV.,

[1] This distinction, made by one of the most enlightened amateurs of art in France, between the "creating artist" and the "Constructor," sufficiently shows how little known and appreciated architectural art is in our days.

[2] See the notice of the Château de Madrid in the excellent work of M. A. Berty, *La Renaissance monumentale en France.*

the ground-plan, included a vaulted half-underground floor, a ground-floor, a first, second, and third story, besides a story in the mansard roof. In Paris, the north aspect is disagreeable; accordingly the architect took the precaution to place his château so that every side might in turn be warmed by the sun's rays. What was especially required at that time in a seigneurial habitation was a large apartment,—the *hall*, or place of gathering, central and accessible to every one, with its dais, or portion reserved for the noble and his intimates; next, suites of apartments, independent at need, each comprising a large chamber and a wardrobe—a room corresponding to our modern dressing-rooms and boudoirs. Numerous and independent stairs were also required,—*toys* if we will, but *toys* enabling each inhabitant to leave his quarters or re-enter privately. Here we have still the traditions of the feudal habitation.

The plan of the Château de Madrid is exactly conformed to these requirements. In fact, we see first at A the great central hall, with its inner hall B; in the middle of the latter stands a vast fireplace C, around which a considerable number of persons can move or sit. The architect even took the precaution of leaving a passage D at the back of the fireplace, which afforded a means of passing from one side of the inner hall to the other without disturbing the persons who, seated around the fire, occupied the space left between it and the great door. Moreover, a small secret staircase E forms a communication between this inner hall and that of the first floor. At F and F' are eight large chambers with their wardrobes G, all separate, and communicating with the porticos H or with the large hall. At I, six staircases, which, rising from the bottom, communicate with the various suites of rooms and the porticos or terraces. The chambers F' have also a common antechamber K. The porticos contrived in front of these chambers, shallow and very open, allowed light and sunshine to penetrate into these apartments, and afforded a covered communication for entering them without passing from one room into another. The porticos erected in front of the great hall being, on the contrary, very wide, added to the pleasantness of that place of gathering by affording an exterior covered promenade. Moreover, while the architect has endeavoured to give a perfectly symmetrical appearance to the mass of his building, he has disposed his doors and windows in accordance with the arrangement of the rooms, and without in the least caring to make the piers correspond in their axis with the pillars of the portico. He did not hesitate to make those crooked passages which, from the porticos or the chambers communicate with the stairs and angle wardrobes, and which facilitated passing and the servants' duties. Here again the traditions of the feudal château are perceptible:

the doors, windows, and corridors are placed according to the requirements of the inmates; it mattered little whether a room was out of square, whether an opening was oblique, or a line of axis was disregarded. In elevation, the architect compensated for these defects (if they are such) by arrangements of detail which gave him features that were spontaneous and pleasing, though they might not be approved by architects devoted to the worship of the so-called Academical plan. Two large flights of steps (another tradition of the feudal château) led down from the two sides of the great hall to the terrace of which the château occupied the middle. And it may be observed that this plan of placing a portico in front of a wall pierced with openings, having no relation to the centres of the piers, is a Classic method, much practised by the Greeks. Note that the lateral porticos were not vaulted, but covered by panelled ceilings of stone and glazed terra-cotta; that thus the architect was not obliged to put pilasters against the walls of the rooms opposite the pillars of the portico, while the two porticos of the great hall, being wider, and their pillars thicker, were covered by means of cross-arches, receiving ceilings divided into compartments, and that here the architect set the pillars of these porticos opposite the centre of the piers, in order to contrive the pilasters needed for the starting of the cross-arches. Again we recognise the influence of the Gothic tradition of the baronial castle in the angle turrets; flanking the façades, and giving lightness and variety to the block of the building.

If we only consult the programme of requirements, we shall perceive that it is exactly observed in the planning of the Château de Madrid: 1*st*, A well-considered aspect; 2*d*, Numerous apartments grouped as closely as possible to the place of assembly,— the great hall; 3*d*, Facility for communication and service; 4*th*, The means of making apartments communicate with one another, or of rendering them independent; 5*th*, Great depth of building, with the coolness in summer and warmth in winter thence resulting; 6*th*, Porticos sheltered from the wind by the arrangement of the angle turrets, widely open and shallow, so as not to throw a gloomy shadow over the windows of the rooms; 7*th*, A vaulted and well-lighted basement story, appropriated to the kitchens and domestic offices. For a prince like Francis I. this was not a grand residence, such as those of Fontainebleau or Chambord; it was a pavilion where he might stay with a small court; but it was a delightful retreat, in the midst of a park no less than five miles in circumference; and it would offer still, even with our customs—a few slight alterations being made—a sumptuous château, perfect in its arrangements and pleasant to live in. The plan of the ground-floor is repeated almost identically in the first floor.

The elevation of the Château de Boulogne, given in Plate XVI., is quite worthy of the ground-plan.[1] Every part is frankly expressed : the interior arrangements are plainly apparent outside, even to the number of apartments ; the sky-line is picturesque, and the varied architectural features—rendered brilliant by the glazed terra-cotta, decorating the friezes, the interspaces of the arches, the crownings and upper piers—are, if I may use the expression, aided and strengthened by the turrets that afford firm points at the angles. This château bears no resemblance to ancient Roman architecture ; it in no way recalls the Italian palaces of Florence, Rome, Venice, Sienna, Brescia, Verona, or Padua in the fifteenth and sixteenth centuries, nor is it like a baronial residence of the best period of feudal architecture ; still, if it has any connection with the past, it is with the old French habitations, so admirably adapted to the requirements of those who built them, so little known in the present day, and so little appreciated, because we only possess remains of them which are hardly at all studied.

If we take the trouble to ascertain exactly what the court of Francis I. was when reduced to the personal intimates of the king, we shall see that the Château de Madrid must have been perfectly suited to the customs and tastes of that court. It was adapted for the brilliant gatherings of a select society, and enabled every member of it to enjoy complete independence. Each guest could go from his apartment into the gardens without his absence being remarked. Even in the great hall, which was repeated on the first floor, this privacy was respected ; for if the sovereign wished to have around him only a few courtiers, he withdrew into the inner hall, while the other persons of the court were amusing themselves or conversing in the great hall. During the heat of the day, one of the porticos afforded a cool promenade on the north-east side ; if, on the other hand, the weather was cold, the south-west portico allowed the occupants to enjoy the benefit of the sun's rays. Note besides that these two porticos, occupying the space between the projections of the buildings, sheltered the persons walking in them from draughts. From these porticos access could be gained unobserved to the private apartments on every floor; the smaller hall could also be entered without crossing the great hall. It is evident that such ingenious arrangements, indicative of special usages, had been denoted in the programme of requirements furnished to the architect.

What chiefly deserves our study is the careful manner in which the architect has complied with this programme ; how he

---

[1] That the elevation may not be too reduced in scale we give only a half of one of the principal façades.

has made everything subservient to it, how in his hands the architecture became pliant and submissive, and how, in fine, the artist, while scrupulously respecting definite requirements, preserved his independence.

On a much larger scale, and of a more monumental character, Chambord (figure 1)[1] presents us with an analogous plan : a large central hall, cruciform, in the middle of which rises an immense flight of double winding stairs, giving access to every floor ; then a number of smaller suites of apartments forming entre-sols, all having their own stairs and communications with the great hall. Chambord was built some years before the Château de Boulogne.

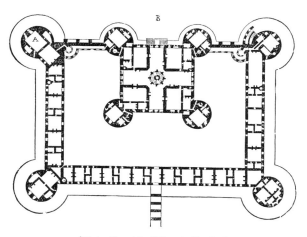

Fig. 1.—Plan of the Château de Chambord.

The Château of la Muette, on the contrary, presents on a smaller scale than that of Madrid a plan accordant with the same programme.

The Château de la Muette (figure 2)[2] was also erected by Francis I., "lequel," says Du Cerceau, "après avoir fait bastir le chasteau de Saint-Germain-en-Laye, voyant iceluy luy estre tant à gré, comme d'estre accompagné d'un bois si prochain, il choisit un endroit en iceluy, près d'un petit marescage, distant de deux lieues dudit chasteau, où les bestes rousses, lassées de la chasse, se retiroyent ; et y fit dresser cette maison, pour avoir le plaisir de voir là fin d'icelles, et la nomma *la Muette*, comme lieu secret, séparé et fermé de bois de tous côtez. Toutefois, estant bastie royalement, elle ne se peut tenir si muette ni cachée, qu'elle

---

[1] Drawn to a scale of half a millimetre to a metre.
[2] To a scale of $\frac{1}{500}$.

n'apparoisse outre le bois de sa grandeur." [1]   Here the programme was necessarily given by the king, who desired a quiet

2

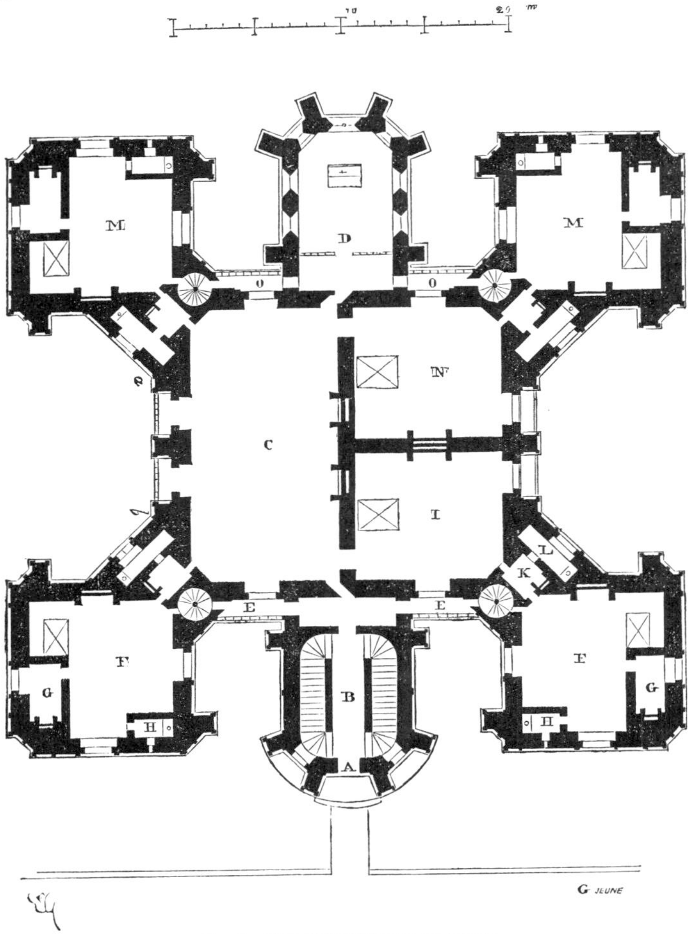

Fig. 2.—Plan of the Château de la Muette.

retreat in the depth of the woods, in which to end a day's hunting

[1] "Who, after having built the Château of St. Germain-en-Laye, finding the same an
agreeable residence on account of its vicinity to the neighbouring forest, chose a site in
the latter, near to a little marsh about two leagues distant from the said castle,—a place
where the deer retreated when spent by the chase ; and there he built this house in order
to have the pleasure of observing their end, and named it *la Muette*, as being a place of
retirement secluded and shut in by woods on all sides. Being, however, built in royal
style, it was not so retired and hidden as not to make some show above the wood by reason
of its size."

with a few intimates; and it would appear that this strange design exactly fulfilled the conditions of that programme.

The ground floor was raised on a basement story which contained offices (fig. 2); the entrance of the château was at A, approached by a small bridge; on either side of a passage B were two flights of steps with landings, the object of which will be presently explained. From the passage B an opposite entrance led somewhat obliquely (these oblique entrances were not then considered inconvenient) into the great hall C, which had an outlook on three sides, two balconies, two fireplaces, two entrances into large bedchambers, and a door opening into the chapel D. The two open galleries E led from the passage B to two winding stairs rising from the bottom, giving access on the ground-floor to the suite of apartments F, each consisting of a bedchamber, a wardrobe G, and a closet H. The wardrobe and the chamber were warmed by fireplaces. From one of these suites of apartments, or from the great hall, there was a communication with the suite of apartments I, also containing a wardrobe K and a closet L. Two other suites of apartments M, equally complete, communicated with the great hall, or the suite N, or the exterior, by means of winding stairs, which, descending to the basement story, enabled the occupants to come in or go out without passing through the great rooms. The open galleries E and O, ending in the four winding stairs, were necessary: for the great hall occupied the height of two stories; or rather the château consisted of five stories above the basement, and there were only three great halls one above the other; so that of the first four stories of apartments, two were entre-sols relatively to each of the two great halls. This entre-sol arrangement of apartments presents itself likewise at Chambord; it was, moreover, a very natural one; for the height which suits a hall 60 feet long by 30 wide would not be appropriate for a room 20 feet square. Externally this arrangement of the great halls comprising two stories of apartments was frankly indicated by the arcades of the front *ab;* for it must be observed that the construction of the Château of la Muette was similar to that of the (old) Château of St. Germain-en-Laye; it was in great part built of brick, and consisted, for the central block, of arches resting on buttresses, sheltering the windows and balconies. As at St. Germain, also, the whole upper story was vaulted (hence the thickness of the walls and the buttresses) and covered with a paved terrace for the enjoyment of the woodland view. The double flights of the great staircase gave access therefore both to the three floors of the great halls and to the five floors of apartments by means of the intermediate landings and the central passage. In the design of this plan also we find that subtlety which the mediæval artists had exhibited when called upon to erect those châteaux which were at once fortresses and agreeable places of residence ; but we already observe tendencies towards symmetrical arrangements and absolute ideas, and especially conceptions of a new order struggling to free themselves from the restraint of traditions.

But during that sixteenth century, so agitated, active, and brilliant, many undertakings were commenced, while few were completed ; and it would often be very unfair to judge of the architecture from unfinished conceptions,—from parts of general designs that were never carried out. Thus we have no idea of what would have been the Louvre of Francis I. and Henry II. The original plan of the entire design, of the Palace of the Renaissance, does not exist,—perhaps never had an existence ; for the buildings were erected piecemeal, as the Louvre of Philip Augustus and Charles V. was demolished.

Other palaces, such as those of Blois, Amboise, and Fontainebleau were only ancient châteaux adapted to novel requirements, and whose original plan therefore could not be altered. That of St. German-en-Laye, even though entirely rebuilt, except the chapel, which is of the thirteenth century, was in fact only a residence erected on the foundations and basements of the feudal castle. These are not conceptions belonging in point of arrangement to the period of the Renaissance.

In 1564, Catherine de Medicis, wishing no longer to inhabit the Château des Tournelles, where Henry II. had died, selected a residence that was already celebrated for its salubrious situation, outside the city, on the banks of the Seine, and where the Duchess of Angoulême, mother of Francis I., had recovered her health. This house had taken its name from the tile-kilns by which it was environed, and which had been established there since 1372. Catherine purchased this house and the land surrounding it, and Philibert de l'Orme was commissioned to build a vast palace intended for the residence of the queen-mother. The ground-plan of this palace has been left us by Du Cerceau.[1] The design, it must be allowed, is a very singular one, grandiose in its composition,—one in which the classical influence most certainly makes itself felt, and in which moreover French tradition is disappearing. It is not easy to conceive how a princely establishment could have found accommodation in this monumental pile, ill suited for habitation in its arrangements when compared with those of the châteaux mentioned above. Philibert de l'Orme was unable to erect more (see Plate XVII.) than the block of building comprised between the letters A and B on the garden side ; moreover, his design has been so altered since, that scarcely any traces of his work exist in the building as we now see it.

---

[1] *Des plus excellens bastimens de France.*

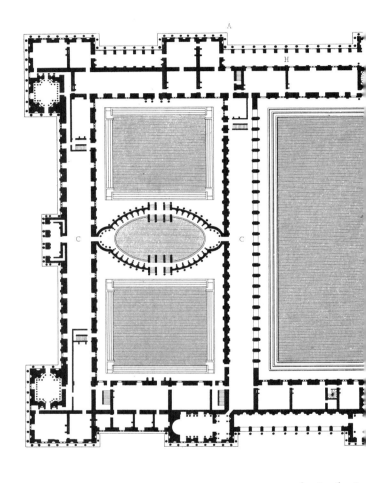

A

H

C   C

Scale of

PLATE XVII.   Plan of the Palace of the Tuileries, as Designed by
Philibert Delorme

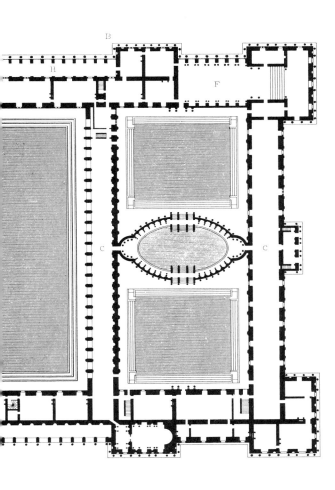

B

H

F

C   C

_____ _____ _____ *10 metres*

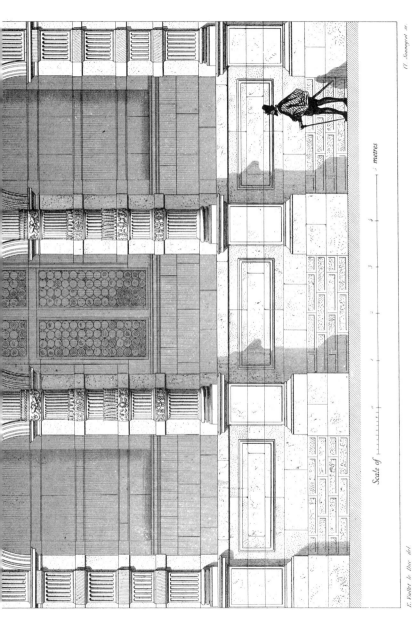

E. Viollet le Duc del

C. Stannigret sc.

Scale of [⎯⎯⎯⎯⎯⎯⎯⎯⎯⎯] metres

PLATE XVIII.   Part Elevation of Philibert Delorme's Palace of the Tuileries

The ground-plan resembles that of an Asiatic palace rather than of a French château. We must suppose it to have been the intention of the architect to place dwelling-rooms over the immense galleries c; in any case the troubles of the Ligue obliged Catherine to suspend the works, and she never inhabited the Tuileries. However ill adapted for habitation may have been the plan of Philibert de l'Orme, it must nevertheless be admitted that according to his design the palace would have been more habitable than the Tuileries as it now exists,—a kind of endless gallery cut by partition walls, without courtyards or offices, without private passages, and with no convenient staircases.

Let us look for a moment at the design of Philibert de l'Orme. The principal entrance of the palace was naturally placed on the city side at D, near the site of the present triumphal arch erected by Percier and Fontaine. There existed a large palace-court E, bordered at the ground level on the two sides by two porticos or open galleries. Four smaller courts, separated by two amphitheatres, were probably appropriated to habitation. What could have been the purpose of these two amphitheatres? I could not say : possibly for giving fêtes or ballets, which were so greatly in vogue at that time ; one of them might perhaps be intended for a riding-school. The great hall was at F, and its arrangement is very admirable. The royal residence placed on the garden side was reached by a magnificent flight of stairs which still existed in the middle of the seventeenth century. The porticos H, next the garden, supported a terrace which the present generation has seen, though its arrangement had been altered. But without discussing the worth or genuineness of the plans left us by Du Cerceau (for I am inclined to think that in the execution Philibert de l'Orme, who was a thoroughly practical man, would have considerably modified them), let us take a part of the building which he erected on the garden side, and examine its architectural composition in detail (Plate XVIII.)

In the domain of the arts we are so habituated to exaggerations,—to taking the great for the grand, obtrusive luxury for richness of effect, noise for harmony,—that we find it difficult to regain the right point of view, whence it is possible to appreciate what is delicate, moderate, refined, and impressed with the seal of good taste. Philibert de l'Orme was probably the artist most distinguished among his contemporaries for a thoroughly sound taste, a true sentiment for art, and severity in point of principles. This appears not only in his performances as a practical architect, but in his written work, which cannot be too frequently consulted in times like ours, when the arts are gone astray, abandoned to the strangest caprices or confined to a routine so little justified by the advanced position of contemporary science. In the works of Philibert de l'Orme we recognise an attentive and careful study of proportions and harmonious relations which seem to be of the simplest order, but which nevertheless are the result of a perfect knowledge of his art and of the means at his disposal : we see apparent in the composition of the ground floor portico of the Tuileries, towards the garden, the good side of the French genius—few novel ideas, the adoption even of old ideas, but a special character, and a subtle and delicate reasoning.

The composition of this gallery, as a whole, is merely an adaptation from ancient Roman art; but the point wherein the French artist manifests himself is the structure of the portico, which is not only frankly expressed, but is made a decorative feature. Carrying up his building in courses, Philibert de l'Orme has indicated each of them in the jambs, and particularly in the Ionic columns, by a special ornamentation. In these columns each fluted stone drum is separated by a thin course of marble delicately chiselled. The carving of the stone is deeply sunk and sharp, while that bestowed on the marble bands is flat and fine as the material on which it is cut. It is also on the marble drums that the symbols commemorating the affliction of Catherine are figured. It would appear that the refined feeling of the artist had determined him to represent on a durable material, and on that alone, the regrets of the widow of Henry II. : broken mirrors and plumes, clubs (emblems of strength) entwined with knotted cords (the emblem of widowhood) and faded laurels.[1] Moreover the proportion of the order, with its high stylobate forming an enclosure between the archways, and its delicate entablature formerly surmounted by a balustrade, is most felicitous. The inner wall of the portico was pierced at every second archway by a mullioned window ; between them, in the recesses corresponding to these windows, the masonry of the jambs, so well divided into high and low courses, was repeated. The first story—set back and on a line with the rear of the porticos—formed a mansard attic, above which appeared the roof.

Our engraving obviates the necessity of a longer description. The lines of this attic story standing out against the dark mass of the roof formed a rich crowning. We have here a truly palatial architecture, grand and noble in its massing, and refined in its details. Between these two galleries, the wide double winding flight of stairs,—considered one of the wonders of the Renaissance,—was crowned by an elegant cupola, flanked by four spire-

---

[1] Apropos of this our readers may observe that among these ornaments the piers and windows of the first story present the well-known cipher said to be an H and a D, beneath a crown : Henry II. and Diana de Poitiers. It will be allowed to be improbable that after the death of Henry II. these two initials would be seen carved on a palace built by Queen Catherine. The probability is that this cipher, repeated so often on the buildings erected under Henry II., is composed of the two initials H and C,—Henry II. and Catherine.

lets. The two extremities would be terminated—as the plan indicates—by two pavilions intended for habitation. Being suitably proportioned, these pavilions did not overpower the delicate architecture of the central part, as did the two pavilions of Jean Bullant after the death of de l'Orme. In my opinion, what remains of Jean Bullant's work (in other respects greatly disfigured) will not bear comparison with the few fragments yet existing, though greatly mutilated, of Philibert de l'Orme's lower gallery.

The history of the building of the Louvre and the Tuileries during the sixteenth and seventeenth centuries is calculated to render us cautious in our judgments respecting the designs of the Renaissance architects. It is with the utmost difficulty that an architect's original conception can be distinguished amid those numberless intrigues and harassing confusions which changed the designs and the designers at intervals of every few years. What we now see of these palaces (I refer to the oldest parts) is the result of such various conceptions and strange superpositions, that the work of the individual artist cannot be traced, but merely a few scattered portions showing exquisite taste,—such as that gallery of the Tuileries,—the south-west interior angle of the court of the Louvre,—the ground-floor of the gallery of Apollo, and that next to it on the Quay. It is therefore rather in the illustrated works and writings left by our Renaissance architects that we must search for the sentiment that guided them. I cannot resist the pleasure of once more citing a few lines on the subject by Philibert de l'Orme, which very clearly indicate the tendencies of the author's sensible mind in reference to the outward form and the appropriate decoration of buildings. Besides, what was said by our brother architect, with so much truth, three centuries ago, is more than ever applicable at the present day :—

" I have always been of opinion that it would be better for the architect to know well what is necessary for the health and preservation of persons and their property than how to make ornaments and decorations for walls or other parts. The reverse of this is now the case ; for many who make building their profession and call themselves architects and directors of works, do not study these requirements, perhaps because they are ignorant how to do so ; and if the subject is mentioned it is quite a novelty to them. And what is worse, I observe that in many cases our nobles who build attach more importance to producing a magnificent ornamentation in the way of pilasters, columns, cornices, mouldings, bas-reliefs, marble inlays, and the like, than to the situation and nature of the site of their dwellings. I do not say that it is improper to make very handsome decorations and

ornamental façades for kings, princes, and nobles, when they wish
for such. For these give great pleasure and contentment to the
eye; especially when such façades are designed symmetrically
and in true proportion, and the ornamentation well adapted to
its place, as is proper and reasonable. Delicate ornamentations,
for instance, should be confined to cabinets, warmed chambers,
baths, galleries, libraries, and places most frequented by the
nobles, and where they principally take their pleasure, and not
used in the façades of outbuildings, vestibules, porticos, peristyles,
and such like places. I know no one who would not allow that
they would be out of place in a kitchen or in places where
servants lodge. But such ornamentation should be composed
with great architectural art and dignity, and not of foliage nor
of bas-relief, which only gathers dust and filth, or harbours
bird's nests, flies, and similar vermin. Moreover, such ornaments
are so fragile and perishable that when they have begun to
decay, instead of pleasing they become excessively displeasing
and dreary-looking, and cause ennui instead of delight. I consider all this so much money spent to no purpose but that of
occasioning in aftertime a melancholy disgust. Therefore I
recommend the architect, and all those who make building their
profession, rather to study the nature of the sites than to produce grand embellishments, which most frequently serve only
for snares to entrap men, or that which is in their purses. Truly,
it is far more honourable and useful to know how to plan a
habitation well and render it healthy than how to cover it with
embellishments without reason, proportion, or measure,—most
often from mere caprice, *without being able to say why.* I consider, however, that both should be understood, and that everything should be placed with due regard to convenience and good
taste, as may be required, so as to render dwellings at the same
time healthy and beautiful. But to return to our original
subject, the ornaments and decorations of façades should be
appropriate and *correspond with the interior of the building;* the
divisions of halls and rooms and the openings of windows and
casements should not produce a repulsive effect on the exterior
of the building. At the same time, I should not wish the said
exteriors or ornamentations to prevent the right dimensions
being given to a hall or room, or the doors, windows, and fireplaces from being put in the most convenient and necessary
places, *without embarrassment being occasioned, i.e.* by such
means as art and nature suggest. . . ." [1]

We have truly here the man who built the Château d'Anet,
who left his mark in the palace of the Tuileries, who erected
many charming residences at Lyons, and who designed the

[1] *L'Architecture* de Philibert de l'Orme, liv. I. ch. viii. Paris, 1576.

monument of Francis I. at St. Denis. These right-minded,
critical, moderate minds, however, are not generally those to
whom the greatest works are intrusted.[1] Nevertheless it would
appear that the principles laid down by Philibert de l'Orme
bore fruit; for after his time architecture with us became less
and less subject to caprice—the almost absolute mistress of the
greater number of our architects during the first half of the
sixteenth century—and adhered to principles of increasing
severity. It is true that the latter years of that century scarcely
favoured an inclination for useless luxury, and that the higher
nobility of France—in great part Protestant—were too much
occupied to concern themselves with building sumptuous habitations. Accordingly in a collection published by Du Cerceau
(Jacques Androuet) we see a number of designs for country
houses in which the highly rational principles that are
laid down by Philibert de l'Orme, are scrupulously observed.[2]
This work gives specimens of rural dwellings, from the most
modest up to small châteaux, among which are to be found plans
that are charming in point of design, and elevations whose
principal merit consists in a perfect "conformity between the
exterior, and the interior" as insisted upon by De l'Orme.

Devoid of ornamentation, the façades owe their merit to a
certain movement of lines given by the ground-plans, the
judicious arrangement of the roofs, and an exceeding delicacy in
the proportions. In the text accompanying the plates, moreover,
Du Cerceau, as a practical architect, gives the estimated cost of
each of the dwellings, together with the explanations necessary
for their construction. Many of these plans remind us once
more in miniature of the general arrangement of the Châteaux
Madrid and la Muette, viz., a large central hall, around which
are grouped several private apartments. If the king was content with one immense room that served as a place of gathering
all day, and even as a banqueting-hall, with still greater reason
would the gentry consider that arrangement sufficient for their
requirements: the hall in fact was the living-room; it was the
reception and dining room; it was there that the wet days and
the evenings were passed in conversation. None stayed in his
own apartment except to sleep, dress, or when indisposed.

Here (figure 3) is one of the plans from this collection of
Du Cerceau. The manor-house is placed—according to the
custom of that period—on a platform having the appearance of
a defensible post, and surrounded by a moat filled with water.

[1] See *Les Grands Architectes français de la Renaissance*, par Ad. Berty, 1860. In this
excellent work we find a great many documents affording valuable information respecting
our architects in the sixteenth century.

[2] See the *Livre d'archit. de Jac. Androuet Du Cerceau . . . pour seigneurs, gentils-
hommes et autres qui voudront bastir aux champs, etc.* Paris, 1615.

It must be mentioned that the architect took care to provide a trellised walk on the parapets of his curtains and bastions, thus forming a belt of verdure round the habitation, and a shady promenade.   At A is a small raised court with its flight of steps : here we still find a tradition of the Middle Ages : this is the seigneurial court.   The great hall is at B, arranged so as to command the prospect : it is lighted on four sides, and yet communicates with four suites of apartments on the ground-floor and two

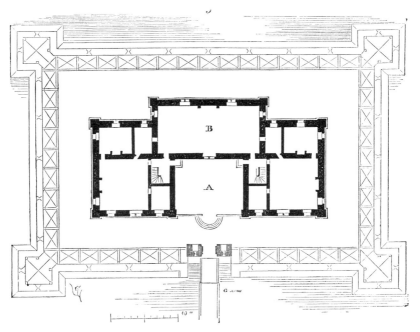

Fig. 3.—Plan of Renaissance Manor-House.   End of sixteenth century.

flights of stairs that ascend to similar suites on the first floor. Each of these has its wardrobe and separate entrance.   It will be observed that the lower landings of the staircases serve as vestibules to the great hall as well as to the two principal rooms. Certainly when we consider the habits of the times, it is impossible to find a more convenient or simple arrangement, or that lends itself to an architectural design more felicitous in elevation.   In fact, if we examine it we see in this elevation a charming manor-house (fig. 4) whose internal arrangements are perfectly indicated by the exterior.   It was then an invariable rule,—as also during the Middle Ages and classic times,—to give a special roofing to each block of building; a course which allowed the architect great liberty in placing the several parts of the dwelling, and which afforded the means of gaining very picturesque effects. Later on it was discovered that this custom of the builders was not sufficiently grandiose, and so all the services of the building—large rooms and small—were included within one uniform roofing. At the same time, there can be little doubt that the different parts of a dwelling thus distinguished by these special roofs present an effective architectural grouping, however modest the building. Many nineteenth-

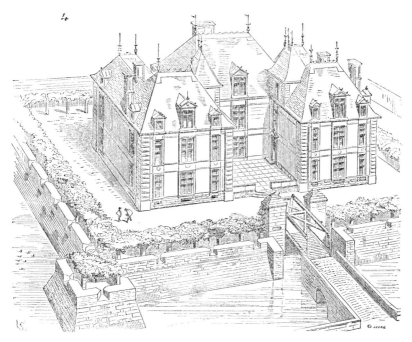

Fig. 4.—View of Renaissance Manor-House. End of sixteenth century.

century country-houses of the bourgeois are of larger size than this manor-house, but very few have so dignified an appearance.

The principal excellence of the architectural works of the Renaissance,—selecting the period from the middle of the fifteenth century to the reign of Louis XIII.,—consists in a certain "distinction" which is found only exceptionally in edifices erected since. What we understand by "distinction" is none other than the reflection of a correct taste thoroughly and habitually permeating society. Greek antiquity always displays this rare artistic virtue in its highest degree. I incline to think it too delicate for the Romans, while it is natural to the French architects of the sixteenth century; it is a natural gift, in fact, for if "distinction" is sought for,—if it is produced only by an intellectual effort,—it leads direct to mannerism and affectation. It is no great achievement in architecture to display magnificence; in fact, nothing is easier, if we have money. The difficulty is to give a perfume of art to the commonest or simplest things; it is to know how to preserve sobriety, even in the midst of splendours. The architects of the Renaissance did not, any more than their brethren of the profession now, live as *grands seigneurs*, but neither did they form a pedantic and exclusive coterie disposed to consider as barbarians all persons placed outside this coterie: if they did not give themselves aristocratic airs and contented themselves with the position that was assigned them amid the society of the time, they at least knew how the noblesse lived, what they liked, and what they wanted: they knew how to conform to the tastes and wishes of their clients without bringing formulas of art to contravene them, but also without in any measure abandoning principles when a requirement or a fancy had to be complied with. Ever since the day when architects, united in an Academic body, began to discuss questions relating to forms of art with the outside world, making light of principles, and opposing conventional rules of art that are purely arbitrary to programmes of requirements, architecture has entered on a path which must gradually separate it from the spirit of the age; people have learned to do without it, because it has begun to be intolerant, perverse, and even tyrannical.

It is interesting to observe, during the first years of the sixteenth century, what trenchant airs the Italian artists who came into France assumed, how they disdained all our home-sprung art, and how their haughty ways led to their dismissal; and how the noblesse who were amateurs in building came back again to their French architects. It was in fact because at that time our architects had known how to interpret exactly the tastes of the society in which they lived; not thinking of imposing a form of art upon it, they sought on the contrary to adapt the forms in use to satisfy its tastes and habits.

Louis XIV. and his ministers, consequently, used to amuse themselves by discussing with architects questions purely æsthetic; and it is curious to observe the reasons which at that early date these artists used to give for adopting or not adopting such or such a form, while neither party troubled itself respecting suitability, the requirements of the times, the arrangements of buildings, or what would render a building agreeable, or even habitable. There is a very curious book on this subject with

which artists cannot be too well acquainted : the memoirs of
Charles Perrault, brother of the architect of the colonnade of the
Louvre and the Observatoire.[1]

Charles Perrault was *First Clerk of the Royal Buildings,*—in
modern language, Director of State Architecture. He had
naturally enough the highest opinion of his knowledge in matters
of art, and he has left us very valuable information respecting
what took place at the court of Louis XIV., apropos of the
project for finishing the Louvre under the superintendence of
the Cavalier Bernini,—a project happily not carried into execution,
notwithstanding the wish of the king and the boastful pretensions of the celebrated Italian architect. Charles Perrault, who
wished to have the execution of this project intrusted to his
brother, and succeeded in his endeavour, at least partially, as
every one knows, thought the Cavalier the most unreasonable of
men (in which he was not mistaken) and procured his dismissal.
But what is instructive in the matter is the list of reasons on
which the first clerk of the king founded his objections to
Bernini's plan. Let us hear him : " The Cavalier did not enter
into any details ; he thought of nothing but building great rooms
for comedies and banquets, and gave himself no trouble respecting matters of convenience, dependency, and arrangement needing consideration in the various apartments : details whose
number is incalculable, and requiring an application which the
quick and eager genius of the Cavalier could not bestow ; for
I am persuaded that in point of architecture his talent scarcely
went further than was required for theatrical decorations and
machines. M. Colbert, on the contrary, wished for exact information, and to know how the king would be lodged and the
arrangements of the service duly provided for. He thought, and
with reason, that good accommodation should be secured not only
for the sovereign himself and all royal personages, but for all
the officers, even of the humblest rank, whose services are not
less needed than those of the highest rank ; he was incessantly
preparing and writing memoranda of all that ought to be observed
in the distribution of the several apartments, to the great
annoyance of the Italian artist. The Cavalier did not and would
not understand all these details, fancying it unworthy a great
architect like himself to descend to these minutiæ."

These are golden criticisms ; but when we examine the
designs of Perrault and that part of his plan which was executed,
we are inclined to ask ourselves whether the excellent reasons
that were alleged against Bernini's plans would not have been
equally valid against Perrault's work. In fact, if the good sense

---

[1] *Mémoires de Ch. Perrault de l'Académie française, et premier commis des bâtiments du Roi.* Avignon, 1659.

and the perspicacity of Colbert and Charles Perrault's *memoires* and intrigues happily delivered us from the Louvre of Bernini, which would have left nothing remaining of that of Henry II., it is not less certain that the architecture of the physician Perrault was not of a kind to adapt itself to a royal habitation. It was an affair of orders, colonnades, and peristyles, not an attempt to produce a really well-arranged palace. The king, weary of being harassed, chose Perrault's design, because it seemed to him " more beautiful and majestic," certainly not because he thought it, or could think it, more sensible. " The envy of the masters of the profession in Paris," adds the First Clerk of the Buildings, was inevitably roused against this resolution, and gave rise to sorry jests, such as that architecture must be in a very sad way since it had got into the hands of the physicians." There was better reason for this belief on the part of the masters of the profession than they dreamed of. Nevertheless architectural life among us had a persistent vitality: reason, good sense, found an opportunity of asserting themselves in spite of that mania for formulas of art which was mistaken for art itself. The close of the seventeenth and the eighteenth century have left us some very remarkable architectural works, in which we find dignity, well devised arrangements, and a certain sober elegance in which for some years we have been rather too deficient.

When in the arts the wholesome teachings of reason—the pure stream whose source is truth—are assigned the second rank, while formulas occupy the first, we rapidly reach decline. The Renaissance, at its origin, had not altered the general arrangement of plans and elevations further than was required to suit new customs; it remained faithful to the methods of design adopted by the mediæval architects; it innovated in applying to public or private buildings a style of decoration borrowed from the arts of Classical Antiquity and the Italy of the fifteenth century : but the main features were still those of the French architecture of the preceding ages. Thus, for example, in their buildings each successive story was distinguished by its special series of features. Determining to apply the classic orders to their architecture, the first architects of the Renaissance placed orders one over the other according to the number of stories in a building : this method may be observed in the Château of Chambord, Madrid, the Louvre, Ancy-le-Franc, Tanlay, Anet, and many others. If this method was suggested by reflection, and was logical, it had nevertheless the disadvantage of giving a monotonous and paltry aspect to edifices of any kind. These superposed orders, whether very rich or very plain, divided buildings like a chess-board : presented, at a distance, an assemblage of horizontal lines (the entablatures) and vertical lines (the pilasters or columns) which fatigued the eyes by their uniformity, especially in a country like ours, where variety and unexpected effects are particularly grateful.

Philibert de l'Orme had in his day endeavoured to avoid this defect in the design for the palace of the Tuileries : he had only a lower order, surmounted by a truncated story, forming a kind of high crowning over the architectural division of the ground-floor ; he had besides even endeavoured to give to that lower order a special physiognomy, breaking the vertical lines of the pilasters and columns by very frankly indicated horizontal courses. An essay of the same kind had been made originally (before the superpositions of stories under Henry IV.) at the gallery of Apollo and the gallery with the square return on the quay of the Louvre. But this was only an ingenious method of disguising the coldness and uniformity of those vertical and horizontal lines that divided the façades into equal compartments ; it was no new principle. If we examine the public buildings erected during the second half of the sixteenth century, we shall remain convinced that architects were seeking for new combinations,—that they were feeling the need of giving an aspect of dignity to their edifices, by obviating the effect on the eye of the divisions resulting from the superposition of stories. Jean Bullant had already endeavoured, in certain parts of the Château d'Ecouen, to free himself from the architectural divisions produced by the succession of stories. He had adopted in the court of this residence a kind of Corinthian casing which rises to the entire height of the edifice. Yet, remarkable as this order is, in point of execution, it is only a study, an appendage, an architectural *morceau*, with no relation to what surrounds or follows it.

We observe in the ancient outbuildings of the Château de Chantilly a very manifest desire to give dignity to an architectural composition by raising an order of Corinthian pilasters through two stories (figure 5).[1] This method had the advantage of greatly increasing the apparent size of the small building to which it was applied, but it would have been very difficult to discover any rational meaning in it. However, the architects of the sixteenth century could not suddenly abandon the rigorously logical method of their predecessors ; the influence of the old French school was still vital among them ; they were men of taste, carefully avoiding vulgarity, in fact aiming at that distinction which lends a charm even to the commonest things. It is easy to discover traces of the struggles that took place in the minds of the architects of the second half of the sixteenth century, when they wished to satisfy both their reason and the craving

---

[1] *Vid.* Du Cerceau's *Des plus excellens bastimens de France.*

5

Fig. 5.—Treatment of a two-storied building—Château of Chantilly.   Sixteenth century.

Fig. 6.   LECTURE VIII.

PART OF THE EXTERIOR OF THE CHÂTEAU DE CHARLEVAL.

FIG. 7.   LECTURE VIII.

PART OF THE COURT FAÇADE, CHÂTEAU DE CHARLEVAL.

for the abandonment of that monotonous course which the system of superposed orders compelled them to pursue; they then made every imaginable attempt to disguise that monotony; we see them adopting treatments composed with caryatides, terminals, piers with sculptured subjects, ornamented panels, and pilasters with arabesques. These expedients were wanting in dignity, and in spite of the architect's skill a variation on the old theme of superposed orders was the only result.

Androuet du Cerceau, in his work entitled *Des plus excellens bastimens de France*, gives us the designs prepared for the construction of the Château de Charleval, near Les Andelys. This château, which King Charles IX. had begun, "would have been," says De Cerceau, "the noblest of French buildings." The foundations were scarcely completed; but the designs for it which are extant are of great interest, both in the general arrangement of the plan and the style of the elevations, in which we see the unprecedented attempts of an architect who wishes to discover a positively dignified combination, without abandoning the logical principles of his predecessors. In the exterior elevations of the buildings of the yard (the first court), fig. 6, we observe the great order of Doric pilasters exactly performing the functions of buttresses—stone ties. To render this function more manifest, the author of the plan has even divided these pilasters by sinkings. Taking the order as supplying buttresses, it was possible without shocking reason to cut the order by a floor. We should observe that the cornice is continuous, and does not project at each pilaster,—the friezes stopping beneath the projection of the drip. These details excepted, we have here again a treatment which belongs entirely to the mediæval system of civil architecture. But on the interior façade of the same building, which seems to have reached some height, the architect of the Château de Charleval determined not only to give greater prominence to the great order, but also entirely to mask the presence of the floor above the ground story; and adopting this resolution, which is contrary to the logical principles of the mediæval architects, he has accomplished his design with remarkable skill. In fact (fig. 7), the floor above the ground story, which would naturally be placed at the level A, is cut by arched niches, so that the eye does not suspect its presence, and is obliged to take in this façade of two stories from top to bottom as if it were *one*. The architect has carried his skill (admitting his principle) so far as to interrupt the arcades of the portico, and to open small square windows between them, which set off all the lines and give an extraordinary grandeur to the piers left at every second bay. The porticos were then perfectly sheltered, and the cellars could be lighted by shafts contrived beneath the sills of these small square bays.

This was the work of a consummate artist, and I know of nothing in the palaces of the Italian Renaissance that approaches the noble aspect of this front.

It is certain, therefore, that at the close of the sixteenth century some architects were bold enough to reject the plan of orders corresponding with stories, and to adopt, in the exterior of the edifice that included several floors, a single order starting from the basement and reaching the upper cornice. This is the style which has been called the "Colossal order." This expedient had an immense success; architecture thus treated was thought to have a certain air of grandeur and a majestic aspect which made all that had been done during the first half of the sixteenth century seem paltry. This plan, however, was at first adopted only for very large buildings,—façades of great extent;—it became a regularly recognised method in architecture towards the middle of the seventeenth century.[1] We shall readily understand that this *majestic* style of architecture should have been greatly prized by King Louis XIV., whose notions respecting the arts did not go beyond the idea of external grandeur,—an idea which, I would most readily admit, had its advantages, and is invariably exhibited in all that was built under the auspices of that prince. Moreover, the Renaissance, which had taken the place of mediæval art at the moment when that art had exhausted its resources, had exhausted itself still more rapidly; in less than a century it had reached its ultimate expression. It was, however, impossible to return to the Gothic, which had fallen into utter disrepute; novelty was absolutely necessary. Ever since that time, architecture has been autocratic, it has become an art to which convenience has had to bend, as best it might; the "Colossal order" is in the ascendant: it gives law both in public buildings and in private habitations. Sometimes we find a trace of reaction against this tyrannical fashion—as in the Hôtel des Invalides, for example; but it is only exceptionally, and we observe that till the end of the last century the Colossal order does not cease to predominate. The Garde-Meuble and the Mint at Paris still preserve the Colossal order, and these latest examples of this style are not the worst. The result was that, after all, uniformity in the detail of the Renaissance had been exchanged for uniformity on the large scale. There would have been no harm in this, if the Colossal style had not the disadvantage of being out of scale with everything, and not lending itself readily to convenience.

In my view, two or three rows of superposed windows placed between pilasters or columns forty or fifty feet high cut but a

[1] In the Château de Vaux, for example, built for the superintendent Fouquet, by the architect Le Vau.

poor figure ; these buildings would seem to have been erected by giants to be inhabited by dwarfs. This is the effect produced by certain antique edifices appropriated by moderns,—*e.g.* the Temple of Antoninus Pius in Rome, between whose columns the stories of the Custom-House have been built. This want of harmony between the style of architecture and practical requirements has so greatly embarrassed the architects of recent times that they have been led by degrees to seek for relations of proportion, between the windows, *e.g.*, and those colossal orders, and have come to make those windows colossal also, though they have had to cut them by floors and partitions half way across their height and width. If passers-by are gratified in this last case by examining these majestic façades, the inmates behind are scarcely so, and do anything but bless the architecture and the architects. Such, however, is the result of the neglect of true principles. But, whatever may have been the errors and the exaggerations of mediæval art in its decline, it never was so completely out of harmony with the habits of life. In those Gothic buildings of the fifteenth century, which are most overloaded with details, ornamentation, combinations of prismatic surfaces, mouldings, and perforations, we always find a rigorous observance of the programme : of the convenience of the inhabitants if it is a mansion; of that of the public if it is a town-hall or a hospice. The first architects of the Renaissance, in adopting a new form—without troubling themselves to examine whether this form had any relations to our modern civilisation and habits—thought that they had only to change an old worn-out dress for a new and elegant costume, and that the body and soul would preserve complete liberty beneath it ; they believed this, and, in fact, at first their expectation was fulfilled ; but soon the dress became the chief concern, and the body, and consequently the mind, were embarrassed by it. At length a privileged company was formed which ultimately forbade all styles of dress but one, whatever the body to be clothed ; thus the difficulty of discovering new combinations was evaded, and the not less troublesome one of studying the various forms adopted in former ages and recurring to them in case of need.

But while architecture went astray towards the close of Louis XIV.'s reign, through starting from false principles, it ended at least with dignity. The buildings of that period belong to a people possessing an art still influential and having a character of its own.

If the exterior architecture indicates a threatening decline, if it aims at a *majestic* effect on all occasions, if it becomes more and more out of harmony with social needs,—it at least preserves longer in interior decorations a truthful character, often expressing with rare felicity the manners and habits of the society of the time. Down to the close of the last century, the interiors of palaces, public buildings, mansions, and châteaux, were designed and executed by artists who preserved something of the sound traditions of art; and no one can enter a saloon of the time of Louis xv. without finding himself transported into the midst of the society of that epoch.

We may be allowed to doubt whether it will be the same a hundred years hence with those who see the interiors of our palaces and mansions. It will be difficult for them to find the impress of our customs, ideas, and daily life. But we will leave to posterity the task of unravelling as they can the strange confusion of our modern arts, and explaining that pretentious grandeur, that poverty of invention, which is concealed beneath the mass of gilding and ornament filched from every quarter: this will be their business,—it is not ours.

At the beginning of the sixteenth century, Italy had attained a high degree of magnificence in the internal decoration of public and private buildings. The *libraria* of the Cathedral of Sienna, some of the interiors of the Palazzo Vecchio of Florence, the *stanze* of the Vatican, the Villa Madama, the vaulting of the sanctuary of Santa Maria del Popolo, the Vatican library, and the Farnesina at Rome, and several palaces at Venice and Genoa, offer to us examples of interior decoration whose judicious composition and admirable execution have been, and will continue to be, a subject for inexhaustible study. And what is the principle from which the artists who produced these works never deviated? It is, in a word, this: in these interiors, the form of the architecture—of the structure—is never disguised or lost under the multiplicity, the extent, the size, or the excessive magnificence of the decorative details. This was one of the traditions of Classical Antiquity, which, as far as we are aware, never thought of covering the interiors of its temples, palaces, or houses, with decorations masking the real structure under their redundant magnificence, their dimensions not harmonising with the scale of the building, or their lavish profusion. Since in France we are privileged to possess a body presiding over the teaching of architecture, and which considers the study of Greek and Roman antiquity as the only desirable one, why does it not recall its students and adepts to a principle so thoroughly judicious? Why, in following one of those contradictory proclivities so frequently observed in matters of art, does it repudiate the study of the modern arts which have followed that principle strictly, and assert that we are following *Classical* ideals while we ignore Classical examples—*i.e.* the examples left us by antiquity? Are we not thence justified in supposing that in that focus of

art which is called the School of Architecture in France, personal
considerations bear sway in all these matters in preference to
principles, and that the interest of art is altogether lost sight of?

In the preceding lectures it has been clearly shown that the
exterior decoration of Greek architecture was only a beautiful
and well-studied form given to the construction; but the latter
is always manifest, as the skeleton is always manifest below the
muscles of the body. The fragments of decoration that have
remained to us from the flourishing period of Greek art never
depart from this principle. Under the Roman Empire, if the
decoration is sometimes foreign to the structure of the building
itself, it nevertheless frankly manifests its own structure. A
Roman edifice, built of rubble-work and bricks, receives a decoration of marble which has no absolutely necessary connection
with that edifice; but the decoration is a kind of second structure, whose richness does not belie the material used nor the
manner of using it. I shall be repeating here what I have already
said (but there are certainly truths that need to be repeated
even *ad nauseam* before they are recognised): Greek architecture
is an unclothed body, whose visible forms are imperatively dictated
by the structure, and these forms are as beautiful as it has been
ever given to man to devise, whereas Roman Architecture is a
clothed body; if the dress is properly fashioned it neither embar-
rasses nor distorts the form of the body; but whether it is well
or ill suited to the body, it is always a dress, which as a dress
is rational and appropriate; rich for the rich, simple for the
poor, and whose decoration disfigures neither the style nor the
form. During the Middle Ages, in France at least, it is still
the structure that is decorated, it is the naked body to which an
attractive form is sought to be given; and it is in this particular
that the Architecture of this period stands in such close relation
to Greek art.

The Renaissance endeavours to reconcile the two principles:
the body and the dress are one and the same thing, because
the architects of those times, attracted by the mere external
appearance of Ancient Roman art—the only one they had been
able to study,—and not perceiving that this form was merely an
envelope, not the real structure, continued to follow the traditions
of the Middle Ages, which, I repeat again, did not separate the
structure from the decoration.

We are told by certain travellers (I do not vouch for it as a
fact) that there were tribes of savages living naked under a
tropical sun, who on seeing Europeans for the first time imagined
that our dresses made part of our bodies, and were astonished
beyond measure when the white men took off their hats. Well,
the architects of the seventeenth century (whom, be it understood,

I am far from comparing with savages) saw in Roman Architecture, which was composed of masses of rubble faced with stone, marble, or stucco, a homogeneous whole, which they thought to imitate with the means of construction adopted in the Middle Ages. Thus, in spite of their eager wish to resemble the Ancients, it was in endeavouring to reconcile these opposing principles that they invented an original architecture. However, this confusion did not last long; and even in the time of Philibert de l'Orme and among his brethren of the craft, Architecture was manifestly inclining towards the Antique structure;[1] since the Roman form was absolutely insisted upon, it was logically consistent to subject the construction to the form. Nevertheless, it is so difficult for the traditions of an art to be lost, and their traces are so deeply impressed, that even at the close of the sixteenth century we find the two principles at variance in the same buildings; we see the structure still decorated,—the naked body with the form that suits it,—and side by side with this a shred of clothing borrowed from Roman Art. The savage has put on a coat, but he has no breeches. Moreover, the idea of first erecting the mass of the building—a structure put up like a block—and clothing it afterwards, or even as it was being raised, with a decoration of stone or marble, not absolutely necessary to its stability,—could not enter the mind of an architect during a period subsequent to the mediæval school; and this method by no means harmonised with the appliances available then, and which were very inefficient as compared with those of the Romans. They felt obliged to erect a building which should reflect credit on their invention, while they were bound to produce a copy on a very diminutive scale of that Roman architecture which, executed according to the antique fashion, would have swallowed up in a few months the means at the disposal of any private persons or even princes in the sixteenth century. The funds which King Henry II. had at his command for all his royal buildings would not have been sufficient to erect, even in ten years, such an establishment as the Thermæ of Agrippa or those of Antoninus Caracalla.

In fact, such an edifice, or rather group of edifices, as the Thermæ of Caracalla, of which we have given the plan, if decorated with Roman magnificence, would in our days cost thirteen millions sterling: for these structures cover a surface of about 50,000 square yards, and they would certainly cost on an average £260 per square yard, if we take account of the columns of granite and marble, the entablatures and casings in marble, the bronze screenwork, the mosaics, the painted stuccos, the subterranean works, the excavations, the lead roofings, the ornamental sculpture, the statues, the bas-reliefs, etc. Thus, although the Renaissance

[1] See the Chapel of the Château d'Anet, and the tomb of the Valois at St. Denis (Marot).

architects did not employ either those enormous masses of rubble or costly materials which the Romans used, although they contented themselves with an appearance, and their buildings were of small dimensions, compared with the Roman buildings, they were scarcely able to finish any.

The farther these architects deviated from the mediæval methods, and the more nearly they sought to approximate to those of the Roman Empire, the less capable were their financial resources of coping with the demands of the architectural style they were attempting to resuscitate. This will explain the reaction which began to make itself felt as early as the beginning of the seventeenth century, after the Wars of Religion, in favour of mediæval methods of construction. We observe at that epoch a return to simple walls pierced with openings, floorings and roofings of timber for municipal buildings and private habitations ; the vast arched porticos are abandoned ; châteaux like those of Saint-Germain, la Muette, and Challuau, covered by terrace-roofs supported on vaulting buttressed by thick walls pierced with arcades, are no longer designed ; we see a return to wooden wainscoting in the interiors, and an avoidance of that ornamented stucco-work with which artists sought to imitate the grand marble decoration of the Roman architecture of the Empire. In the exteriors, the superposition of orders, whether as pilasters or columns, which were so much in repute towards the middle of the sixteenth century, was discontinued ; they were contented with bands of stone and intermediate brick facings, the string courses and cornices had their projections reduced, and the openings ornamented by pilasters covered with arabesques were abandoned. In the interiors, architecture assumed a severer and more tranquil aspect, clearly indicating the method of construction. After the attempted imitation of classic remains, and having undergone the influence of the Italian Renaissance, it recovered its French physiognomy in perfect harmony with the society of the time. What it did not recover was excellence in execution.

Many causes had contributed to produce a deterioration in the workmanship. During the Middle Ages, simply because the construction, the decoration, and the apparent form were inseparable, the masters of the works were accustomed to give full-size diagrams of the construction, with the mouldings and ornaments; and each stone was finished, moulded, and sculptured before being laid. It is not possible to erect a Gothic building without employing this method, which had the advantage of forming very skilful and intelligent masons and excellent stone-dressers, and of obliging the sculptor to make the decoration suit each piece of stone. The habit having been the growth of centuries, although the new form adopted did not require the employment of these processes, they continued to be followed for some time after the commencement of the Renaissance ; but the new mouldings and the carvings could be executed with more exactitude, and with less expense, in place : the workmen, therefore, began to lay the stones merely cut to their rectangular section. Thenceforward the necessity of making the jointing accord with the various members of the architecture was no longer imperiously felt ; and it must be noticed that whenever the immediate necessity of observing a principle ceases to exist, the principle, however valuable, is lost.   Even in the middle of the sixteenth century we see skilful architects,—intelligent and scrupulous respecters of good methods, such as Philibert de l'Orme,—conforming their masonry to the form of their architecture : but they are exceptions.   In Philibert de l'Orme's time, many of his professional brethren intrusted the stone-jointing of a façade to the workmen, then afterwards had the mouldings and ornaments cut in the more or less roughly-shaped stone, already in place. This negligence often issued in a total want of harmony between the jointing and the architectural feature.   As the mason's function no longer required a complete understanding of the piece of work to be jointed, it became degraded, and fell into the hands of ignorant workmen, and most of our buildings dating from the close of the sixteenth century are jointed in contravention of common sense, and even of the conditions of stability.   This fact may be observed on a large scale in the Church of St. Eustache in Paris.   For the same reason, the sculptors, obliged to cut their ornaments on the building, and consequently less rigorously superintended, and being often aware that their decorations would be scarcely seen, got into a careless style of execution.   Besides, it was desirable to have the scaffoldings taken down which their presence alone prevented from being removed ; they were hurried, there was an impatience to get the work out of hand, and they were glad enough to have done with it ; so that the carving remained incomplete or coarsely executed ; besides, it was no longer necessary to carve it between beds ; it was continuous work, that took no account of the jointing,—cut on the building itself as on a mere block.

By degrees that school of sculptors which was so distinguished during the Middle Ages, and even during the first half of the sixteenth century, became weak, lost all feeling for monumental art, and sunk down to a mere trade.   The types which under the inspiration of ancient art and French traditions had been so graceful, and often even so pure, at the commencement of the Renaissance became debased, and were nothing more than indeterminate incisings without decision, style, or character.   On regaining a certain degree of vigour, a new youth, at the end of the reign of Henry IV., and under that of Louis XIII., Architecture succeeded in exacting from its workmen, masons, stone-dressers, and sculptors, more study, care, and respect for things of art. But during this period the chief effort of architects would seem to have been directed to interior decoration.

In fact, the Renaissance had not given a well-characterised physiognomy to secular architecture in interiors; it either continued to follow the manner of the preceding century or indulged in mixed designs, in which the hand of skilful artists, of people of taste, could be recognised, but which were deficient in general effect, and especially in dignity. The best times of the Renaissance had been of so short duration, and had been followed by so many agitations and disasters, that neither princes nor private persons had had time to complete the habitations commenced by them; still less had they been able to finish the decorations of their interiors; and the artist, amid so many troubles and interruptions, would have had great difficulty in adopting a complete art applicable to halls, apartments, or places of assembling. It will be readily acknowledged that while we may modify a system of architecture in exteriors—in façades—the task becomes more difficult when it is required in a few years to adopt a new mode of disposing and decorating the interior of public buildings or habitations,—that is, to change the habits, the tastes of daily life, the entire social element. A nobleman who might have asked his architect to give a classic character to the façades of his residence, would in many cases have been far from pleased that his bedroom or the hall of his mansion should be so arranged as to compel him to change his fashion of life. This very natural feeling will enable us to understand why the plans of the châteaux of the Renaissance preserve in their interiors all the arrangements of a château of the fifteenth century.

But after the Wars of Religion, peace having been almost re-established in the kingdom, the noblesse began to recover themselves; having for some time lived a life of warfare and privation, there had been a break in their ancestral usages. And thus, as soon as they could get their châteaux rebuilt or restored, we see them adopting by preference a system of interior decoration severe, calm, bearing the impress of dignity and unity, very superior, in my opinion, to the style, overcharged with details or poor to excess, indeterminate and confused, which was in vogue under Francis I. and Henry II.[1] The interiors of the apartments bear-

---

[1] I should wish that the judgment I feel bound to pronounce here on the interior decorations of the Renaissance should not be misunderstood. We have some very admirable interiors dating from this epoch, such as the gallery of Henry II. at Fontainebleau; but this is an undisguised imitation of Italian art applied to the traditions of the great halls of the French mediæval château. In the gallery of Francis I. in the same residence

ing the name of Anne of Austria, at Fontainebleau ; some parts of the ancient apartments of the Luxembourg and of the Hôtel Mazarin, now the Bibliothèque Nationale ; certain parts of the Hôtel Lambert, especially the gallery, and the ground floor of the wing of the Louvre called the gallery of Apollo, present noteworthy specimens of that French architecture of the commencement of the seventeenth century which was appropriated to the interiors of palaces. We observe a rich effect without confusion, a perfect harmony between the sculpture and the painting, details adapted to the scale of the whole, and above all an air of dignity to which the internal decorations of the Gothic period and the Renaissance had not accustomed us.

Under Louis xiv. art preserves the beautiful arrangements of the preceding period, which we still find in the interiors of the Châteaux de Vaux, in the gallery of Apollo at the Louvre, and even in certain parts of Versailles ; but the taste for the grand sometimes degenerates into turgidity, as may be seen in Le Pautre's work ; the execution becomes feeble, and the sculpture and the painting lose more and more their monumental character and launch out into exaggerations. From turgidity and the striving for magnificent effect at every turn, by one of those abrupt changes of fashion which are so common in France, we come to excessive meagreness, and an excess of delicacy in the details. We see no more good outlines ; all the interior decoration is only a kind of flexible dress taking forms which are most inconsistent with the real structure. Elegance alone continues as the last reflection of our arts in their best days, the surviving expression of our national character.

In the designs for palaces, châteaux, and houses, architects towards the second half of the seventeenth century concerned themselves but little with internal arrangements, the convenience and comfort of the inmates ; they sought for grand effects in their interiors, long suites of apartments ; they sacrificed convenience to splendour, so that in fact the interiors of the habitations of the sixteenth century date can be much more readily appropriated to our customs and ideas of comfort than the residences of the time of Louis xiv. At Versailles, all except the king were badly accommodated : there were no private entrances nor

---

we shall find the defects here pointed out. There is a complete want of harmony between the details and the dimensions of the gallery ; there are sculptures which are charming, it is true, in design, but whose projections and importance as apparent supports are by no means justified by the ceiling with its delicate compartments of woodwork. It must be understood that I am speaking here of the gallery of Francis I. as it was before its restoration ; at present these defects are still more glaring. The want of definite character and effect are very apparent in the cabinet of Francis I. in the same château. However graceful these panels and small pilasters of wood may be, there is no *ensemble* in this interior which reminds us of the wainscoted rooms of Louis II., but presents a wearisome straining after effective combinations.

staircases; there were many sombre apartments; there were no wardrobe-rooms. The memoirs of the times have left us some curious details respecting the inconvenience of most of the accommodations. Even for the state apartments, the arrangements for service were inconvenient, and many of the suites of rooms opened one into the other; but these discomforts of the interior were concealed behind the great symmetrical façades of the palace, and these were the objects that seemed to be chiefly considered. From the inconvenience of the internal arrangements in the private buildings of the close of the seventeenth century the conclusion has been drawn that the apartments of the preceding periods must have been still more inconvenient. But this inference is not just. During the fifteenth and sixteenth centuries architects not only paid attention to internal arrangements, but subordinated the designs for the exterior to them. The usages of life dictated the arrangement, and the arrangement suggested the form of the building. This was the dominant principle in all architecture in the times of Classical Antiquity and the Middle Ages. When Academical doctrines took upon themselves to direct the arts this principle was practically set at defiance, although none dared to deny its truth or importance.

LECTURE IX.

ALTHOUGH in Paris and some large cities we see in our own
day public and private buildings erected, whose execution
is good, and in which we recognise the presence of considerable
knowledge and the successful solution of certain problems of the
art, it must be admitted that in the provinces and small towns
many are constructed in defiance of the most elementary principles of Architecture. Between the better houses in Paris and
the average *mairies* erected in the provinces, we find not merely
the distance which separates luxury from poverty, but the abyss
that yawns between a refined civilisation and the basest barbarism,—not the barbarism characteristic of an undeveloped social
condition, but that which forebodes dissolution. Architects
whose duty it is to examine the various designs for buildings
destined to be executed in the departments, will bear witness
that I am not exaggerating in saying that, out of twenty of these
designs, one may be tolerable, one-half are below mediocrity, and
the other half exhibit an utter ignorance, I will not say of art,
but of the ordinary methods of building. Now there was never
a time in France, previous to the commencement of this century,
when such a state of things existed.

To say nothing of more ancient times, the houses and
churches of least pretension in France during the Middle Ages
belonged to art as decidedly as the lordly château and the
episcopal cathedral. These works, whether great or small,
sumptuous or modest, issued, so to speak, from the same
practised hand, and were the result of the same knowledge.
Architectural art has by degrees retired from the extremities, to
vivify only the centres of population ; and the greater the
abundance of the resources it accumulates, and the more pretentious the display it makes in the great cities, the more con-
temptible is the figure it presents everywhere else.

This is a deeply ingrained evil, arising from several causes : 1st, an administrative organisation which is little adapted to spread a taste for the arts among the people generally ; 2d, the entire absence of instruction ; 3d, a degradation of taste in the upper classes. As long as the Provincial system lasted, there were as many capitals as governments, and each of these capitals was the centre of a school of architecture. Orleans, Poitiers, Rouen, Troyes, Limoges, Bordeaux, Toulouse, Lyons, Dijon, etc., had their schools and artists, as Paris had, and these schools possessed an originality of their own ; even regarding them as only secondary, they must have had the effect of giving life to the province, and they sent forth branches into the most obscure localities. The governors of these provinces were powerful nobles, who in virtue of their position as well as their education, took a pride in giving a certain distinction to works erected during their government. The spirit of the trade-guilds was sustained, especially among the artists and members of the *building crafts*, and through the guilds the local traditions remained in the hands of the most capable ; they were acquainted with, aided and criticised each other.

It was in the reign of Louis XIV. that the freedom of these provincial schools was first subjected to restraint. Louis XIV. established a system of general direction in the arts, as well as in government ; all independent action on the part of the Provinces was precluded, freedom was utterly stifled. Lebrun (the name of the individual is of little importance) became the superintendent-general of all art production in France. This system had for a time the effect of giving a great impulse to architectural undertakings, and a character of unity accordant with the spirit of this reign ; it was moreover, a revival of the system established under the Roman Empire ; but, as was the case under the Roman Empire, architecture thus officially directed, and becoming part of the administrative machine, soon lost all vigour of style.

Under Constantine we may see to what the official art of the Empire had been reduced ; and the public buildings erected at the close of the reign of Louis XIV. are not equal in point of art to those which belong to the first half of the seventeenth century. Every product of intellect,—and I do not imagine that the part played by intellect in matters of art will be contested,—finds development in proportion to the freedom allowed it. Art, which is more a mental than a mechanical growth, withers as soon as it quits the free air of independence ; transplanted to a hot-house it loses all healthy tone, in fact it dwindles alike in bud and fruitage.

Now in our days architecture is subjected to a kind of

intellectual government, still more restrictive than was that established by Louis XIV.; it has never had its *Eighty-nine.* Isolated, little understood and ill defined, it has exchanged the yoke of the Lebruns,—a domination which was at least characterised by a certain amount of grandeur and originality,— for another which is vulgar and narrow, and which does not accord with the genius of our time nor even with that of our country. It is forbidden to follow such or such a path, but receives no instruction as to which it should choose ; it is instructed as to what it should not learn, but no one ventures publicly to explain to it what would be desirable to be known. Of the official, self-satisfied, tyrannical, but at all events power- ful direction of the Lebruns, there remains only a slavery under masters as numerous as unqualified.

Architecture, driven hither and thither among the official world, the amateurs, academicians, professors of the art who pro- fess nothing, archæologists, partisans of Classical Antiquity or of the Middle Ages, men of science, political economists and enthusiasts, is obliged, in order to exist, to make a concession to one, to avoid quarrelling with another, to live in fear of silent persecution of coteries, gropes its way, listening to advice from every quarter and seeing everywhere hostility or envy ; and when its work is finished the result is that no one is satisfied, and all the city exclaims, " Why do not our architects produce an architecture characteristic of the age ?   Here we have another anomalous building, and without the smallest claim to beauty!!"

People want to have an architecture proper to our country and our time, yet of all the styles of architecture which our youth are permitted to study, that which is the native growth of our soil is specially excluded and even proscribed ; an architecture characteristic of the time is expected, yet we send our youth, after a totally insufficient course of preliminary training to study the monuments of Ancient Rome and Attica—monuments whose study could be of use to them only after a solid foundation of severe criticism and extensive knowledge had been laid.

If an architectural work is planned suggesting new ideas, it is subjected to the criticism of persons who by their conviction or rather their want of conviction are opposed to any innova- tion and even to the novel application of recognised methods. It is acknowledged that the arts of Greece present types eternally beautiful, and whose principles are eternally true : yet those who insist on making these principles dominant, even by constraint and without allowing them to develop themselves, forget that the Greek artists produced their *chefs-d'œuvre* only under the ægis of liberty, and that the arts of Rome were in a state of continuous decline from Augustus to Constantine.

In the present day we have immense resources furnished by manufacturing skill and increased facilities of transport ; yet instead of making use of these means with a view to the adoption of architectural forms adapted to our times and civilisation, we endeavour to disguise these novel appliances by an architecture borrowed from other ages. It is complained that artists have no ideas, and everybody insists on imposing his own upon them. If men of science are consulted they offer their advice on questions of art, and a mining engineer will discuss the form of a capital. If a mere trustee is consulted respecting the ways and means, he volunteers the statement that he does not like pilasters, that he will not have buttresses at any price ; he prefers plain walls, which cost more ; and then when the building is finished, he will declare that the architect is incompetent, that these flat walls look like a barrack, and that they must be decorated with engaged columns, which are in fact buttresses.

There is an *école d'architecture* in France, but there is no course of architectural lectures delivered in that school ; or if by chance such a course is given, it limits itself to a few generalities concerning one phase of the art. Respecting the carrying out of architectural works, the organisation and administration of labour, the history of civilisation in France, the comparison of the various styles or groups of styles of architecture, their relation to civilisation, their development or decay, and the causes of such growth or wane ; the art of economising resources by employing the materials peculiar to the various localities, and the judicious application of those materials to the forms they are adapted to receive ; the importance to an architect of being ready and able to explain and justify his design by sound reasons in a clear and logical form of expression ; and the wide and catholic principles which, when they have free scope, must develop energetic intelligence, and clothe those principles in new forms—not a word is said.

Amateurs can only acquire a sound taste (which in architecture especially is identical with sound reasoning) by contact with artists ; but if they would form the taste of influential patrons, architects must be able to explain to them the reasons which lead them to adopt such or such a method ; if these conceptions are to be admitted or defended, they must be defensible. How can we hope that architects who have been always accustomed to make use of forms whose meaning and reason have never been explained to them, but which have been imposed on them under pain of ostracism, should be prepared all at once to explain their conceptions ? What answer can you give to the nobleman or proprietor who declares that he will not have such or such a design of front, when you do not know yourself why you have adopted this rather than another? Besides, have you not been obliged to stifle every sentiment of independence? Has the Academical dictatorship to which the School of Architecture has been subjected allowed you to reason or discuss? When a bourgeois of the most ordinary taste and understanding, for whom you are preparing a plan, says, " I do not like this *sort of thing*," you have nothing to say in reply; since this "*sort of thing*" stands on the paper without your knowing why you put it there.

Habituated by degrees to this mute submission on the part of the artist, the connoisseur instead of consulting becomes capricious; he soon begins to fancy that the architect, not knowing how to defend himself, recognises the excellence and soundness of his taste. Men never become tyrants till they find drudges willing to resign themselves to their tyranny. For want of solid and rational instruction, the architect has allowed the amateur to give himself up to every whim of his fancy, unchecked by those clear views and sound reasons which it was the architect's business to urge. For want of enlightened connoisseurs, the architect who indulges any promptings towards independence is silenced at the outset, and thus we run adrift in a vicious circle, finding no support or guidance anywhere. Even supposing that the *Ecole d'Architecture* in France were on a level with the requirements and the progress which our age is daily accumulating, it is none the less, in virtue of the principle on which it is organised, a kind of Academic palæstra in which a chosen few attain to high positions simply by waiting for the prizes to drop into their mouths. As to the great body of the students, after having been engaged for ten years in preparing designs of impossible and indescribable buildings, they have no prospect in view but a position in the provinces, or occupation with private undertakings. And it must be acknowledged that they have been in no wise prepared to fulfil these functions. They have few practical ideas, many prejudices, no knowledge of the building materials which our country affords or of the modes of using them, that profound disdain which results from ignorance of the Arts proscribed by the School, and which are difficult to study and to master; no idea of the conduct and administration of building-works, no method, and a mania for building *monumental structures*, when what is required is simply to erect substantial and commodious buildings which shall be adapted to their respective purposes. Thus students who have been diligent, but who have not had the chance of obtaining the scholarship for residence in Rome, entertain a repugnance, which is very natural on their part, to practise their profession at a distance from the metropolis; they prefer remaining at Paris, and finding some employment there of an inferior character, but in which they have no responsibility, rather than entering on the career of a provincial architect when they have no practical experience. Hence we have a superabundance of architects at Paris and a great lack of them in the Departments.

In a School of Architecture it is not sufficient to teach the principles of the art (and not even these are taught in Paris); but there should be developed in the minds of students the sense of personal responsibility, the knowledge of their functional duties, and a well-assured authority founded on the study of all the branches of industry to which the architect is obliged to have recourse. In virtue of that somewhat southern temperament which characterises us, we are rather too fond of leaving the guidance of our individual judgments to an authority of some kind. Many intelligent men in France who are otherwise competent recoil from the burden imposed by personal responsibility; thence it results that we have always excellent soldiers, and to this may be attributed the success of those religious establishments which our customs, our legislation, and social condition seemed to have for ever abolished. We have, however, enough of northern blood in our veins to struggle against this tendency, which is an impediment to all intellectual progress, and which, should it gain the upper hand, must soon lead us to decline.

It would seem reasonable that the result of our architectural training should not be limited to sending out, once a year in September, *one* architect officially pronounced competent, but that it should diffuse instruction and a sense of the duties which an architect's functions imply among those young men who are capable of rendering themselves of use to the state and to private persons, and give them an exact acquaintance with the interests they will have to guard while maintaining the dignity of the art.

What should we think of a military school organised in such a manner as to form only Marshals of France, leaving to mere chance the training of captains and lieutenants?

If in the provinces competent architects are gradually disappearing, we must attribute this in great measure to the system adopted by the *Ecole des Beaux Arts,* a system whose principle it is to present every year a laureate at the *Villa Medici,* but which takes no pains to form a body of useful artists, acquainted with their duties and with the innumerable details required in the practice of their art. Have we a real desire to possess an architecture? We must form architects—that is to say, men who are able to sustain that independence which is necessary to the interests of art as well as to those of individuals and of the State, by an appeal to knowledge thoroughly sound in character and very liberal in its range. If it is acknowledged that the School is and always will be powerless to form such men in a social condition such as ours; if personal considerations are, in the domain of art, always to carry the day against questions of general interest and principle, rather let us determine to close it and to leave to private interests the task of training the architects required by a great country : this course would at any rate have the advantage of not keeping up illusions in the public mind, of giving complete liberty to instruction, of not giving an official countenance to manifest mediocrity, and of leaving to every one the initiative and the responsibility in the choice of his studies.

This by way of preamble ; but in order to show the real position which is offered to the architect in the middle of the nineteenth century, we shall have to examine the nature and the extent of the acquirements which the architect of the present day ought to possess. These acquirements are of two kinds,— some theoretical, the rest purely practical. Theoretical acquirements which, less than a century ago, were very limited, have been remarkably extended as the result of archæological researches and the discoveries thence resulting. If these discoveries served only to satisfy curiosity, we should not speak of them here, but made as they have been in that analytical spirit which is characteristic of our age, they ought to have,—indeed, really have,—a considerable influence on the arts, and especially on architecture. Thus no one disputes the fact that an extensive knowledge of geometry is the groundwork of all architectural labours ; now the study of archæology proves to us the application that has been made of geometry to styles of architecture which are very different in appearance ; this study shows us the points which these styles have in common, how they start from the same principles, or how, to speak more correctly, the architecture of nations that have played an important part in the history of the world are only the varied results of one dominant principle. We shall by and bye return to this demonstration. The architect ought not only to possess a large acquaintance with descriptive geometry, but also to be sufficiently familiar with perspective to be able to draw a design or parts of a design in every aspect. Perspective should be a practical science to him to such a degree that, in designing his geometrical projections, he can realise in thought the effect which the prominent or elevated parts will produce at different planes of distance, the character of the site, the declivity of the roofing, the thickness of the walls, etc. When the horizontal plan had been determined, the architects of former days were accustomed to prepare a set of perspective elevations, and in this they proceeded wisely and spared themselves deceptions. And if the practice of perspective is useful, that of marking shadows is not less so ; not indeed the conventional shadows sanctioned by custom, but the shadows actually produced by the sun on the building in the place it is destined really to occupy. The ancients, and the artists of the Middle Ages and of the Renaissance evidently paid attention to these effects ; it is only in our time that architects have erected façades with a northern aspect, covered with delicate details in low relief, which the sun never deigns to bring into prominence, and which are consequently so much trouble and money lost. We pointed out in the First Lecture how the Greeks took account of the light, and with what delicate feeling they took advantage of shadows. The artists of the Middle Ages were no less skilful in disposing the salient parts of mouldings and the reliefs in the sculpture, according to the direction of the light. These refinements are, it is true, rarely understood in our days, and an architect never thinks of giving this reply to any one who should ask him to reproduce in a northern aspect a façade whose effect is striking because it faces the south : "The aspect being different, the effect which has struck you cannot be obtained here." He says nothing in reply, the façade is built, and the amateur who wished for its reproduction is greatly surprised to find a sombre monotonous mass instead of the brilliant play of lights and shades which had charmed him. He calls the architect a blunderer, and the charge is not altogether an unjust one.

The architect should not be satisfied with amassing piles of drawings and sketches in his portfolios ; he must also reason while he is drawing. If he sees an edifice whose aspect strikes him, let him carefully sketch and measure it,—nothing can be more desirable ;—but he must also get a clear idea of the *causes of its attractiveness;* for a beautiful edifice situated at A on a height, surrounded by trees or buildings of moderate height, and presenting a particular orientation, will be unattractive at B on level ground, surrounded by lofty structures, and with a different orientation. The orientation of the Greek temples was a matter of deliberate choice, as was also that of the mediæval churches ; and while considerations connected with religion had some influence in determining it, it must be acknowledged that artists also took advantage to a great extent of the importance attached to its selection. When proportions are in question, the locality and the scale are matters of still graver importance. In Classic times public buildings were relatively large as compared with private houses ; besides they had always their special connections, they were never placed at haphazard; they were surrounded by accessories which enhanced the effect of their dimensions. The same observation holds good of our cities in the Middle Ages. The houses were small, and every building that was destined for religious or municipal purposes assumed a considerable relative dignity. Under these favourable conditions, the building being "mounted" (if I may so term it) had proportions of its own, whose harmony was not put out of countenance by a crowd of unsympathetic neighbours. In our large towns these conditions are not taken into account. A public building is required and a site is sought for it surrounded by houses all of equal heights, and the architect says to himself: "Suppose I were to erect façades in the style of those of the beautiful palace of ——; but the palace in question is 70 feet long, and you have 140 feet to occupy; that palace faces a square of limited extent, surrounded by low porticos surmounted by a single story, and your building is on a quay or a boulevard 100 feet wide; and while the windows of that palace are five feet wide, yours must be ten." But all this goes for nothing, the treasures of the portfolio are drawn forth, and with their aid inspiration commences; that is, you distort that unfortunate model,—admirable in its original position,—to produce a nondescript work. The commendable method is to draw, to collect materials in great abundance, not with a view of taking bits from them or patching them together without reason, but to make ourselves acquainted with the means employed by the masters of the art to produce a certain effect in a given place and under special conditions. We know all that has been said and written respecting architectural proportions since the time of Vitruvius and, perhaps, before him. But all may be summed up in this principle, viz., that there are proportions which were regarded as beautiful in ancient times, and that we cannot do better than recognise them as such now. But, in the first place, of what ancient times are we speaking? We certainly observe proportions recognised by the Athenians,—for the Orders, *e.g.,*—proportions independent of the dimensions; but I do not see that these proportions (of the Orders) were rigorously followed for a century and a half among the Hellenic people. Their artists, who were so highly gifted, appear to me to have established a harmonic system, but not a formula as, later on, did the Romans, who were veritable "engineers."

Going further back and examining the monuments of Ancient Egypt, we also recognise the influence of a harmonic method, but we do not observe the artists of Thebes subjected to a formula; and I confess I should be sorry if the existence of such formulas among artistic peoples could be demonstrated; it would greatly lower them in my estimation; for what becomes of art and the merit of the artist when proportions are reduced to a formulary? The Italian architects of the Renaissance period undertook, in their books at least, to establish absolute proportions for the Orders, but for the Orders only; as regards the *ordonnance,* we see that they were guided by their taste and feeling, or what reason and necessity prescribed.

In the Middle Ages, however, incontestably, and probably in those of Classical Antiquity, certain methods were adopted according to which the proportions of buildings were determined. We have but little information on the subject; the loss of traditions, the utter decay of official instruction, have allowed the clew which formerly guided architects in the labyrinth of those *mysterious* branches of knowledge with which the professional guilds were formerly so familiar, to slip from our hands. For two centuries the architectural methods employed by our predecessors in the art, and which had enabled them to produce masterpieces, have been regarded with anything but respect. We are apt to revenge ourselves on knowledge which we do not possess, by despising it; but in the nineteenth century contempt is not demonstration. For geometrical methods which had been elaborated and consecrated by long experience, we have substituted empirical formulas whose origin and reason it is absolutely impossible to assign, precisely because these formulas have been transmitted to us only at second or third hand. Those modest *maîtres des œuvres* who have been somewhat looked down upon by our *Patres Conscripti,* did not profess to imitate the arts of Classical Antiquity; but we suspect that they were nevertheless much more thoroughly acquainted with certain noble principles of art than we of the present day are, and that they even reduced them to practice. This we shall try to prove, but we must go back to a somewhat remote date; I shall, I trust, be pardoned for doing so, as the importance of the subject justifies the reference. Plutarch says :[1] " And there are good grounds for supposing that the Egyptians intended to compare the nature of the universe to the triangle, which is the most beautiful of all, and which Plato seems to make use of to the same effect in his books on the Republic, composing a nuptial figure; and this triangle is such *that the side which makes the right angle is three units in length, the base four, and the third line, which is called the hypothenuse, is five,* whose power equals the powers of the two others that form the right angle; thus we should compare the line that falls perpendicularly on this base to the male, the base to the female, and the hypotenuse to that which is born of the two."[2] We shall presently return to this demonstration whose importance is considerable, as will be seen.

The obscurity into which the maxims of the *Grand Siècle*

---

[1] *Treatise on Isis and Osiris.*

[2] It is evident that the right-angled triangle whose base is 4, the square of which is 16, and the side 3 whose square is 9 has for its hypotenuse a line $=5$ whose square is 25, *i.e.* $16 + 9$.

have thrown us, and which are as little based on reason as they are absolute in character, has, however, been pierced in our days by some German *savants*, and, among ourselves, by a small number of engineers. M. Henszlmann, in his work entitled *Théorie des proportions appliquées dans l'architecture*, has opened the way to discoveries of incontestable value; and although we cannot, in view of the monuments themselves, adopt all the parts of his system, it is nevertheless certain that he is paving the way for those who are willing to follow out his principles. M. Aurès, chief engineer *des ponts et chaussées,* in his *Nouvelle théorie déduite du texte même de Vitruve* (Nîmes, 1862), has lately published some very singular results respecting the relative proportions of the orders. This author proves to a demonstration, *e.g.*, that the Greeks took their modulus at about the centre of the column, and not at the base, as was formerly supposed. He thus succeeds in proving mathematically the exactness of the measures given by Vitruvius. But this is not what chiefly concerns us now. It is useful to know the proportions which the ancients gave to the orders; but it is probably still more advantageous to discover what were the generating principles of the proportions adopted in Classic architecture in the Middle Ages, and even at the Renaissance,— though the latter often loses sight of the pure traditions, and gives itself up to caprice. It would be self-deception to imagine that proportions, in architecture, are suggested by instinct. There are absolute rules and geometrical principles, and if these principles accord with *ocular instinct,* it is because sight is a sense resembling hearing, which cannot encounter a discord without being offended, however little one may be acquainted with music. A discord offends my ear: I cannot say why, but a teacher of counterpoint will give me a mathematical demonstration that my ear *ought* to be offended.

It would be strange certainly, if architecture, which is the offspring of geometry, could not demonstrate geometrically how it is that the eye is annoyed by a defect in the proportions of a building, though I do not regard the empirical methods of Vignola and his successors as a demonstration. We must therefore consider the question from a higher and especially a more demonstrative point of view. The above-quoted passage from Plutarch shows that the triangle was regarded by the Egyptians, who were very good geometricians, as a perfect figure. The *equilateral* triangle is that in particular which completely satisfies the eye. It presents three equal angles, three equal sides, a division of the circle into three parts, a perpendicular let fall from the vertex dividing the base into two equal parts, and the formation of the hexagon inscribed in a circle and dividing it into six equal parts. No geometrical figure affords more satisfaction to the

mind, and none fulfils better those conditions that please the eye,
—viz., regularity and stability. Now we see that the equilateral
triangle was employed by the Egyptians to give such a proportion
to important parts of architecture as should please the eye. If
they had to construct pillars destined to carry a lintel, leaving
(as is often the case in their oldest edifices) as many voids as solids
(fig. 1) the proportions of the height of these pillars in relation to
their width and to the voids, are often determined by a series of
equilateral triangles (see drawing A) : for these piers are so

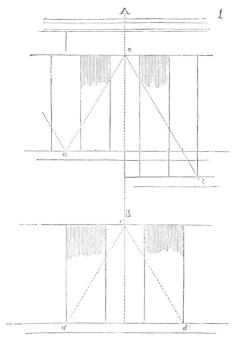

Fig. 1.—Method of obtaining Proportions.

divided that either the axis of each of them meets the summit
of the triangle as is seen at *aa*, or at least—if more slender
dimensions have been intended—that the base of the equilateral triangle never goes beyond one of the sides of the
pillar, as the drawing indicates at *b*. Thus they satisfied a
requirement of the eye, which demands that the part borne
and that which bears it shall not go beyond the angles of
an equilateral triangle. If we run counter to this principle, as
indicated at B, we abandon the conditions of a good proportion.
The eye will then remark a want of stability, for it requires that

the axis *c* should find laterally two solid points of support, at an equal distance at the base of the triangle, *i.e.* at *dd'*. Similarly (figure 2) the façade of a basilica, for example,—that is of a building consisting of a nave and two aisles—inscribed in an equilateral triangle, will give a satisfactory proportion in its *ensemble*. If openings have to be made in the gable, and these

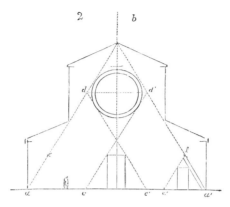

FIG. 2.—Method of obtaining Proportions.

are arranged so as to be inscribed in equilateral triangles, these voids will be felicitously proportioned in reference to the façade. The eye will instinctively draw the lines *a a' b, c a' d', a c' d, e' a' f,* without finding them traversed by voids,—in fact, on the contrary, marked out by them ; and this requirement of the eye will be in harmony, as it always is, with the rules of stability. The Greeks were not unacquainted with this simple principle. Thus (figure 3), if we take the order of the temple of Corinth (see the drawing A), we see that the equilateral triangle, whose vertex is placed under the axis of the abacus at *a*, has its two other angles on the axis of the two columns on the right and left at their foot, at *bf*. When the Dorians wished to secure a more slender proportion (see drawing B), as in the order of the Temple of Concord at Agrigentum, they did not allow the angles of the equilateral triangle to project on the exterior line of the shaft of the column ; or if they decided to give a greater opening to the intercolumniations, as in the order of the Temple of Egina (see drawing D), they selected not the lower but the upper side of the abacus for the vertex of the equilateral triangle.

The equilateral triangle is not the only figure that has been adopted as the generator of proportions ; the pyramid with a square base whose vertical section from the vertex, parallel to one of the sides of the base, gives an equilateral triangle, has also been used. The section of the pyramid through one of the diagonals of the base will give the triangle *c d e* (see drawing G), and this

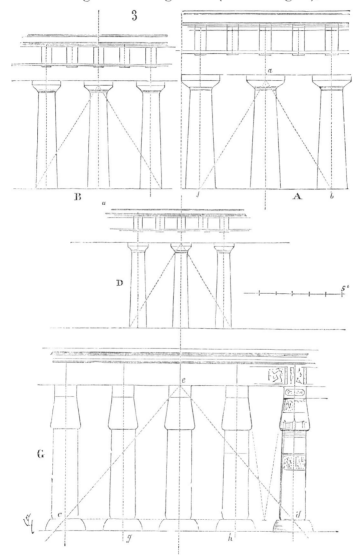

Fig. 3.—Method of obtaining Proportions.

triangle is adopted in some colonnades in the ancient monuments of Egypt, and especially in the portico of the Temple of Khons at Carnac (20th dynasty), as shown in our figure.

Whether this triangle,—taken on the diagonal of the square base of a pyramid whose vertical projection, parallel to one of the sides of the square, is an equilateral triangle,—appeared to give inclined lines that were pleasing to the eye, the dominant outline of a pyramid of this kind, being rather that produced by the diagonals than that produced by a vertical projection parallel to the base ; or that the equilateral triangle appeared insufficient, as too acute in vertex to determine the proportions of buildings of great extent ; it remains certain that if we apply this triangle *c d e*, which is taken vertically on the diagonal of the square base of a pyramid generated by an equilateral triangle, to the Parthenon, for example, we are led to curious observations. We see that this triangle is exactly included within the two vertical lines, let fall from the middle of the exterior line of the angle columns, and the extreme apex of the pediment (fig. 4) and that the sides of this triangle at the point where they meet the lower

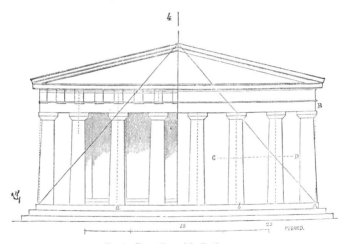

Fig. 4.—Proportions of the Parthenon.

line of the architrave, give the two axes of the third columns on the right and left ; that if we then divide the interval *a b* into three equal parts and mark off one of these divisions on the right and on the left, we shall have obtained the axes of the six central columns ; that the angles A of the triangle give the plumb-line, B of the architrave ; that the horizontal line C D, drawn at the intersection of the sides of the triangle with the axis of the second column, gives the height which has served to fix the relative proportions of the edifice—in a word, its modulus.

In a building consisting of isolated points of support bearing a lintel, the eye is not satisfied with the mere rigidity of these points of support, and their competent strength : it seeks for mutually dependent unity among them,—solid points at the lower extremity of oblique lines according to a certain angle suggested by reason ; for when this angle is transcended, the conditions of stability are no longer fulfilled. In the drawing G of figure 3, for example, the artist felt that if he wished to have a series of points of support closely approaching and slender, it was not possible for him to make the two sides of an equilateral triangle fall on the axis of the columns *gh* or even on the extremity of the exterior line of their shafts. He therefore adopted, in determining the axes *c d* of the second columns the widest possible opening of the angle,—that given by the vertex of the triangle, taken on the diagonal of the square base of a pyramid generated by the equilateral triangle. The eye, which in every building instinctively looks for points of resistance which guarantee its stability, being habituated to follow certain oblique lines which satisfy it, because their inclination accords with the laws of statics, is in fact satisfied if these points of resistance are well emphasised. In this respect the Athenians satisfied the requirements of the eye in an admirable manner by inscribing the whole façade of the Parthenon in that triangle whose two sides give so complete an idea of stability, and likewise placing the axes of the intermediate columns at the intersection of those sides with the architrave. These are two points of stability placed on the sides between the vertex of the triangle and the base, as if to direct the vision. Of all architectural monuments those which are isolated, and whose character is not so much that of utility as of art in and for itself—the triumphal arches built in such numbers by the Romans, for example— should most endeavour to present a perfect harmony, the result of an attentive study of proportions. In their case, in fact, we have not an imperious necessity dictating the relations of heights to breadths and fixing the dimensions of the voids : the programme leaves the artist full liberty—and if he does not succeed he has only himself to blame. A great number of triumphal arches erected by Roman vanity are known to us ; and though many are distinguished by a certain grandeur of aspect, majestic masonry, or beauty in details, there are few that are completely satisfactory as regards their proportions. The Arch of Trajan which was rebuilt under Constantine presents ill-determined proportions, that of Septimius Severus much too heavy, that of Orange offers a vile outline, bearing a cumbrous mass on slight piers. The Arch of Titus at Rome, small as it is, presents on the contrary an agreeably proportioned mass, which completely satisfies the eye. Let us then inquire into the principle of proportion adopted in the design of this structure (fig. 5).

Here the equilateral triangle was the generator. The key-stone of the arch is placed at the vertex of an equilateral triangle, whose base *a b* is determined by the distance which separates the two axes of the two piers. The space of the opening *c d* to the spring *e f* of the arch is a perfect square. The lower bed of cornice-course passes over the vertex of an equilateral triangle of which the diameter *e f* is the base. The lower bed of the attic cornice passes over the vertex of an equilateral triangle whose base *g h* extends across the entire width of the structure on the

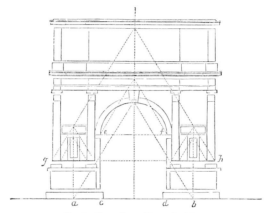

FIG. 5.—Proportions of the Arch of Titus.

upper bed of the bases of the columns, whose profile, continued on the pier, presents a well-marked level. The square niches, placed between the columns on the face of the piers, have their lintel on the vertex of equilateral triangles for which the inter-columniation gives the base. The tablets themselves, placed above these niches, do not rise above the apex of equilateral triangles whose base is given by the width of the piers comprising the columns. It is scarcely conceivable that chance should have furnished these geometrical combinations, or if we may suppose that the architect of the Arch of Titus by a delicate artistic instinct obtained these combinations without having recourse to the processes given here, it must be acknowledged that this instinct was singularly in harmony with geometrical analysis. There exists in Provence at St. Chamas near Marseilles, a small Roman arch built on a bridge. This struc-ture, which preserves in a higher degree than the monuments of Imperial Rome a very delicate perfume of art and whose pro-portions are excellent, is entirely included in an equilateral triangle (fig. 6). There the curve of the arch has a tangential relation to the two sides of the triangle conformably to the rule indicated in our figure 2. Chance cannot furnish these results.

Besides, on applying these methods to structures belonging to the Middle Ages, the Renaissance, or our own times, we find the proportions nearer to perfection in the degree to which they are in harmony with analogous data. The façade of Notre Dame, in Paris, for example, is inscribed in an equilateral triangle whose base is formed by the distance which separates the axes of the two extreme buttresses, the cornice under the great open gallery being placed on the vertex of the triangle.

Let us now return to the text of Plutarch quoted above. The Great Pyramid of Cheops, at Gizeh, is designed according to the method given by the author, as has been clearly shown by M. Daniel Ramée in his *Histoire générale de l'Architecture,* and

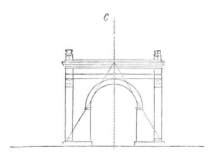

Fig. 6.—Roman Arch at St. Chamas, Provence.

demonstrated by M. Jomard in his *Description de l'Égypte.* It will be necessary to give the demonstration here (fig. 7). At the extremity B of the line AB, which is divided into four parts, erect the perpendicular BC equal to three of the divisions of the base AB. Join AC. The line AC (the hypotenuse) will contain five such parts, *i.e.* the length of the base $+\frac{1}{4}$ of this length. This is the triangle *par excellence* of the Egyptians as stated by Plutarch. From the point D, the centre of the base AB, erect a perpendicular, give it a length equal to half the hypotenuse AC, this line DE will be the half of five parts, *i.e.* two parts and a half. Joining the points AE, BE by two lines, we have the triangle given by the Great Pyramid of Cheops ; the line DE being its height, and AB one of the sides of its square base. A perpendicular to the hypotenuse drawn from the angle B will likewise give the height of this pyramid, for the line AF is equal to one of the sides AE, BE. Producing the perpendicular BF to the circumference of the circle in which the triangle ABC is inscribed, we get the chord HB. Letting fall a perpendicular from the point F on the side BC of the triangle, we get a length FK. If we divide each of the four parts of the base AB into two, and each of these subdivisions into six, we get 48. Dividing the perpendicular BC in the same way, we get 36. Dividing the two and a half parts of the height DE we get 30. If we proceed to divide the hypotenuse in the same manner we get 60. Now 60 $= 5 \times 12$; $30 = 2 \times 12 + 6$ (the half of 12); $36 = 3 \times 12$; $48 = 4 \times 12$; we have thus dimensions measurable by 4, by 3, by 5, and by $2\frac{1}{2}$. If we divide each of the parts of the base AB into 100, we get 400 ; and cutting BC in the same way we get 300 ; in DE, 250 ;

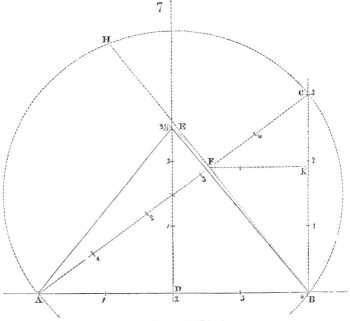

Fig. 7.—The Egyptian Triangle.

the chord BH gives the number 480 ; the part AF of the hypotenuse 320 ; FC, 180 ; the perpendicular FK gives 144, or 12×12. Thus by means of this figure we get decimal and duodecimal divisions.   In a case of proportions, the duodecimal system has the advantage of being easily divided into halves, quarters, and thirds ; the combination of the two systems applied to our figure gives useful results.   Thus, the base AB, divided by the duodecimal system into 48, has a proportional relation to the chord BH divided by the decimal system, which gives 480, or 48.   Perhaps the architects of the ancient world made use of this figure ; it is certain, as we shall see presently, that the masters of the Middle Ages made it the generator of some of the great buildings.

Take, for example, the Basilica of Constantine at Rome, and on the transverse section of this edifice place the triangle ABE given above. We see (fig. 8) that the apothemes AB, AC, fix the axes of the outer walls B and C, and the height of the cornice of the great order by their intersection with the face of the walls pierced with great arches forming the aisles at D and F. These sides AB, AC give also the springings G and H of the small arches of the aisles. The two columns IK being placed, raising from the axis of these columns above the bases an equilateral triangle IKL, we have the height of the intrados of the keystone of the arch of the tribune. Taking the half *ab* of one of the four divisions of the

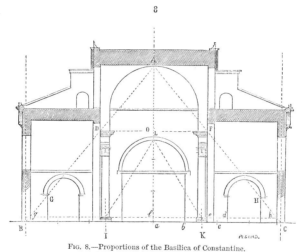

Fig. 8.—Proportions of the Basilica of Constantine.

base of the triangle ABC, we have the piers of this tribune. The point *c*, which divides one of these sections at the quarter, gives the axis of the pier *ed*. According to this drawing the interval between the two wall-faces at the level DF is to the height OA as the interval of the wall-faces *gh* taken above the level of the bases is to the height *l*A. Here, as in the Parthenon and the Arch of Titus, the eye finds points of stability A D G *g*, which are so many landmarks taken on a side of a triangle which the ancients regarded as perfect. The artist has, however, intervened. One of the conditions to be fulfilled when we wish to give agreeable proportions to a range of architectural features, is to avoid similarities,—equal lengths or surfaces in direct relation to each other. The artist has taken good care not to divide the side *g*A into two equal parts. The ratio of *g*D to DA is 29 to 21, and the Egyptian triangle taken as a generator of proportions has the advantage,—its base being to its height as 4 to $2\frac{1}{2}$,—of avoiding in its very principle those identities of widths and heights which are the most displeasing of all. In fact, the eye comprehends dimensions only by contrasts. The nave of a church appears lofty because it is narrow in proportion to its height, or wide because it presents greater width than height. But if you get a perfect ratio of width to height, you have the key to the proportions that shall be given to your building. The *Egyptian* triangle was considered by the Ancients as perfect, and must often have served as a standard of proportions. By its divisions it facilitated architectural design as shown above. Unfortunately there are so few ancient Classic buildings complete in all their parts, that it is difficult to apply this method with certainty to the proportions of a great number of them. It is not so with regard to the Middle Ages, at the epochs when art was passing from the cloisters into the hands of secular artists. At that time, whether because the architects were acquainted with certain ancient writings; or because certain traditions were preserved in their original purity among them; or that a principle or mystery known only to the initiated, or to adepts, was retained among them; it is certain that we find in their system of proportions, applied to architecture, laws evidently derived from certain principles of Classical Antiquity, although those artists had no idea of imitating the form of ancient architecture, and the very starting-point of their system of construction was, as I believe I have demonstrated elsewhere, absolutely foreign to the system adopted by the Greeks or the Romans.

Let us take one of the oldest buildings of the secular school that is really French, one of those in which the Gothic form appears as early as the twelfth century. Let us take the Cathedral of Paris (fig. 9),—a transverse section through the nave of the building. The total width of the church being given, let AB be the half of that width; it is divided into four equal parts. Starting from the axis A the first division gives the face of the wall of the great nave above the columns; the second, the interior face of the columns of the double aisle; the third, the axis of the outer wall, above the sills of the windows; the fourth, the extreme outer face of the first course of the buttress on the level of the interior floor. Taking as a base of operation the upper part of the bases of the piers of the nave, on this horizontal at the point A we erect the perpendicular AC, on which we mark five divisions equal to each of those of the base AB; this is the total height of the nave. We connect the end D of this line,—whose ratio to the half of the base line is as 5 to 4, —by the line BD. We have thus the half ABD of the *Egyptian* generating triangle. The intersection of this side BD of the triangle with the perpendicular erected on the first part of the

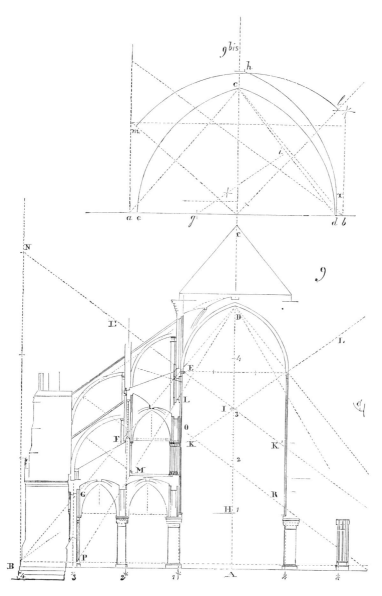

SECTION OF NOTRE-DAME DE PARIS.

base gives at E the springing of the upper vault, with the second the level of the sill F of the windows of the gallery, and with the third the level of the crown G of the windows of the outer aisle. The first division H of the perpendicular, erected at the point A, gives the springing of the arches of the aisles, whose centre points are raised twelve inches above the capitals. The third division I, also on the vertical line, gives the level of the crown of the gallery vaults. The hypotenuse KI (see the demonstration applied to fig. 7) gives the inclination of the copings of the flying buttresses whose centres are placed on the axes 1 and 2. If now we take AD as the height of an equilateral triangle, we see that the side PD of this equilateral triangle, cutting the section lines of the construction partly determined, gives at L the lower point of the rose windows placed under the great windows, at M the floor of the gallery, and at P the interior face of the outer wall. Lastly, a line RO parallel to the hypotenuse L'K' gives in crossing the point of level of the crown of the gallery vaults, the former inclination of the outer triangles of these vaults. Naturally the gables and roofs exactly follow a triangle like the Egyptian triangle whose half is ABD. If chance has led to these results, we must acknowledge that chance gives rise to singular coincidences. To draw the upper vaults (see fig. 9 *bis*); *abc* being the Egyptian triangle from *b* to *d* and from *a* to *e*, a distance is marked equal to the thickness of the voussoirs of the cross-rib; joining the points *d* and *c*, and erecting a perpendicular *ig* at the bisection of this line, the point *g* where this perpendicular meets the base line *ab* is the centre of the cross-rib of which the arc *dc* is the intrados. As regards the arc *ml*, it gives the half of the diagonal rib, and the arc *xh* the intermediate cross-rib. We shall see (fig. 9) that the height of the central nave, under the crown, is the half of the hypotenuse, *i.e.* that this height is equal to IN.

Let us now analyse the transverse section through the nave of the Cathedral at Amiens. It has been said that in St. Peter's at Rome, Michael Angelo placed the Pantheon on the Basilica of Constantine. I do not know whether the thought suggested itself to Michael Angelo; it would not be a mark of genius to place one building on another; but it would be a mark of genius to give harmonious proportions to a building whose height was double the width of another building whose proportions already presented a perfect whole. This is what the architect of Notre Dame d'Amiens accomplished with rare skill. All who enter this cathedral are struck with the apparent grandeur of the whole and the perfection of the respective proportions. Entering the vast interior, the eye is satisfied at once; it understands without effort a conception originating in a single impulse of a

superior mind. Is this harmony the result of a series of tentative efforts? Is it the effect of happily hitting off the details
in harmony with the general design? I have no great faith in
luck, especially in architectural design; nor am I more inclined
to believe in happy hits—that is to say, of their coming of mere
instinct. If a work is good, it is because it springs from
a sound principle, methodically carried out. The transverse
section of the nave of the Cathedral of Amiens (fig. 10) presents a harmony of proportions obtained by means of two
Egyptian triangles superposed. The base AB of the lower triangle ABC rests on the top of the bases of the nave piers; here
again we find the same foundation level of the design's geometrical scaffolding. This base AB has for its length the distance
which separates the two exterior faces of the outer walls of the
aisles. The apex C gives the height of the under bed of the
string-course D, made conspicuous by a wide ornamentation,
which runs without interruption all round the interior of the
edifice. This base AB, divided into four, gives at the points
1 and 3 of the division, the exterior face of the great piers,—
i.e. these points *a* are given by the tangent *gh* (see pier P).
These four divisions being each bisected by the points 0, 1′, 2′, 3′,
the subdivision 1′, by means of a parallel to the line AC, determines the point of meeting E with the line BC, which is the level
of the astragal of the capitals of the engaged columns XXX. The
parallel at AC, drawn from point 1, determines the crown F of
the wall ribs of the aisle vaults. The parallel drawn from point
3′ gives the inclination of the aisle window-sills. The parallel
drawn from point 2 determines in meeting a horizontal line
drawn from the point F, the edge of the keystone of the wall
rib *f*; the parallel drawn from point 2′ determines at *e* the face
of the engaged pier, by its point of meeting with the horizontal
drawn from the point E, the thickness of the pier of which the
detail is figured at P having been previously decided by the proportion of the weight which this pier supports. The vertical GC
being divided into five, each of these divisions, in accordance with
the drawing of the Egyptian triangle, is equal to one of the
eight of the base AB. The first division 1 gives the level of the
aisle window sills; division 3 determines the astragal of the
capitals of the central cylindrical part of the piers given in detail
at P. For we shall see that if the capitals of the engaged
columns X and of the central pier have the same abacus, the
astragals of the great cylinder are lower than those of the
columns.

On the level A′B′, which terminates the first ordonnance, that
of the aisles, the architect has resumed his lower base AB, and
has marked it by the internal jambs of the openings which pass

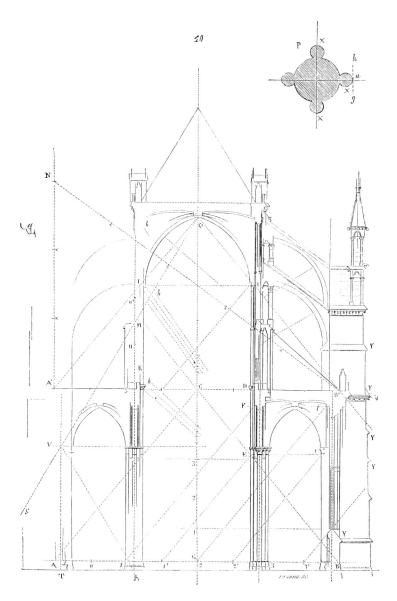

SECTION OF THE CATHEDRAL OF AMIENS.

through the buttresses. On this base A'B', he has raised a second Egyptian triangle A'B'C'. The sides A'C', B'C' of this triangle, meeting with the face K of the walls or spandrils have given the point I the height of the springing of the arcs, whose point C gives the crown. In drawing these arcs he has followed the method adopted in Notre Dame de Paris, *i.e.* he has set off on the horizontal line II interiorly, the thickness of the arch-stones of the cross-ribs. The axis R of the piers having been prolonged, the centres of the flying buttresses OO' have been marked on these axes, C' being taken as the vertex of an equilateral triangle whose side is C's, the meeting of this line C's with the axis R has determined at M the height of the upper passage of the triforium ; and its meeting with the axis T of the outer wall of the aisle at V, the springing of the vaults of this aisle. The line VR, also the side of an equilateral triangle, determines, by its intersection with the axis R, the floor-level and consequently the height of the bases. The slant of the roof is likewise that of an equilateral triangle. Here the hypotenuse B'N gives the height of the nave from the upper part G of the bases to the crown C' of the great vaults. All the profiles drawn at *b* are so arranged as to be perfectly developed, taking B as the point of vision. But we shall return to this principle. As to the inclined lines of the coping-stones of the flying buttresses, they are drawn parallel to the hypotenuse B'N. This *Egyptian* triangle has so completely served the purpose of generator for the whole design of the building that the slopes Y of the weatherings are all cut parallel to the hypotenuses AC, BC, as if to determine their inclination the designer had worked by running a set-square over the various parts of his diagram and starting from a general line of base.

It is certain that many processes of detail have escaped our observation in the drawing of this section, and that all the divisions, even the minutest of them, have been obtained by means of intersection of vertical lines with the parallels to the hypothemes. But if this principle is not contested, it may yet be asked why these geometrical methods give satisfactory proportions. It is simply because they establish a constant and harmonious relation between the lengths and the breadths.

We must recognise, it is true, as did the Egyptians, that the triangle generated by the sides 4, 3, and 5,—the sides 3 and 4 forming a right angle,—is a perfect standard. Also that the relation of 5 in height to 8 in breadth satisfies the eye. Now, while it is difficult to *prove* why a visual sensation is pleasing or displeasing, it is at least possible to define this sensation. As I said above, *dimensions* become *proportions* sensible to the eye,— that is, comparative relations of lengths, breadths, and surfaces,— only as far as there are dissimilarities between these dimensions.

The relations of 1 to 2 or of 2 to 4 are not dissimilarities, but equal divisions of similars, reproducing similars. When a method of proportions obliges the designer, so to speak, to give divisions which are as 8 to 5, *e.g.* 5 being neither the half, nor the third, nor the fourth of 8, sustaining a relation to 8 which the eye cannot define, you have already, at the very outset, a means of obtaining the contrasts which are necessary for satisfying the first law of proportions. The eye is a very delicate instrument, even in the case of those who have never tried to understand what makes a system of proportions good or bad; for the simple reason that the eye is that organ of the senses which is most exercised, and that it acts independently of reasoning. Now, whenever the eye is able to establish a relation between measures in a building; whenever it observes, in despite of the intellect, that such or such a void is equal to such or such a plenum,—that such or such a height is equal to another,—it recognises a relation of similarity, not a relation of proportion : it is engrossed, it is occupied with calculation, and is quickly fatigued. So true is this that, for example, in this nave of the Cathedral of Amiens, although it is very difficult to verify the fact that the great decorated string-course, which exactly bisects the height of the nave, is placed in the middle of the line falling from the crown of the upper vaults on the bases, yet I have often heard persons who had no knowledge of the art find fault with this horizontal cincture bisecting the nave ; and the reason is that in this work, whose design is otherwise admirable, there is here a defect in proportions.

The architect has performed two distinct operations, applied one over the other, and he did not think that his double process, whose results are connected by the intersections given by the equilateral triangle, would leave any traces; it is apparent, however, to the least practised eyes, and is more conspicuous as all the other parts of the edifice present those felicitous relations which are secured by dissimilars. But in these dissimilarities there must be an order, a unity; it is not enough to fix on dimensions different in point of height and breadth, set side by side according to mere caprice ; it is necessary that these dissimilarities should proceed from a general principle ; and it is in this respect that the determination of proportions by triangles is advantageous, because it furnishes points of articulation which direct the eye instinctively to this general system, although it does not comprehend the method followed. There can be no proportion without unity, and there is no unity without plurality; pluralities imply not *similars* but differences.

The Greeks (for we must always recur to them when we wish to get light on questions relating to the arts) had two philosophical schools, as they also had two schools of art, the Dorian or Pythagorean and the Ionian school. Of these two schools the former insists on absolute unity, excluding all difference : *all is one ;* the second, which is purely empirical, recognises, on the contrary, infinite divisibility, difference without identity, phenomenal being without dominant reason, movement without a unique motive power. From these two schools, I say,—of which the principle of the one is Theism, of the other Pantheism,—the Athenians deduced a system applicable to the arts ; taking the principle of unity from the Dorians, and empiricism from the Ionians, while subjecting architecture to an absolute standard,— a unique generator,—left to the artist, *i.e.* to individualism—that liberty which leads to difference, to variety. An admirable combination, which produced *chefs-d'œuvre* among them, as it did during one of the periods of those Middle Ages, with which we are little acquainted, and over which thick veils of obscurity have been thrown as if to separate it from that other Greek period with which we ultimately succeed in discovering such intimate relations of kinship.

In fact, in the veritable architectural school of the Middle Ages, there is no empiricism,—no outward form without a principle,—but there is at once unity and plurality, not only in the system of proportion, but even in the most minute details. As in Greek architecture, the principle of creation is one ; but the artist is the creator, who moves freely within the limits of the principle. We have here a natural law, which the Greeks had recognised as true by the mere power of their intelligence, and which modern scientific investigation has explained, so to speak, mathematically.

In fact, in organic nature, for example, we discover *one* principle. From the serpent up to man the principle is rigorously followed out ; it is the very variety of the applications of the principle that causes its unity to be recognised ; and when we consider that, in each individual, every increase of a part of the whole is made at the expense of the other parts, that each of these individuals has only its share of organs, as it were, which can be developed only in a relative proportion, so that the animal which has no feet will be endowed with an excessively developed vertebral system ; that other one which has enormous lower limbs, will have but embryonic arms ; that the horse, for example, each of whose limbs has only a single colossal finger, has allowed the others to be atrophied or to disappear ; when we consider, I say, the rigorous unity of this principle of creation, we are tempted to ask ourselves whether man, when he undertakes to create, should not proceed in the same manner, and whether he has not, in fact, proceeded in the same way during those periods

in which he has produced works of lasting value.   Now, on the
one hand, it cannot be denied that geometry is the starting-point
—the ground-work—of architecture ; that among geometrical
figures the most perfect is the triangle ; that of all triangles
those which are best accommodated to the laws of statics and to
proportional divisions are the equilateral triangle and the triangle
whose base is to the height as 4 to $2\frac{1}{2}$, generated by that other
right-angled triangle which gives 4, 3, and 5 ; and that, consequently, the adoption of these triangles and the intersection of
their sides with vertical lines, supply us with divisions subjected

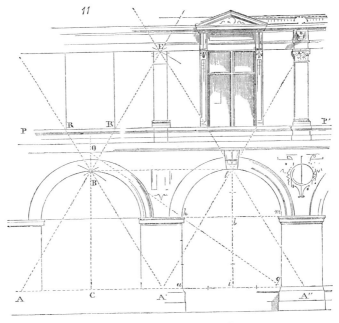

FIG. 11.—Method of obtaining Proportions.

to a single principle, points which remind us of the inclinations
of the sides, and proportions necessarily derived from these
generating figures.   On the other hand, we understand how the
application of these triangles to architectural designs obliges the
designer to make his heights bear a certain proportion to his
breadths ; and that, consequently, the more space one part of
these heights or breadths occupies, the less he has left for the
others ; though there is always a relation between these parts,
however different they may be from each other.
      Let us take an example.   Let fig. 11 represent a façade con-

sisting of a ground-floor forming a portico, and one upper story.
A A′ A″ being the axes of the piers of the portico, we erect the
equilateral triangle AA′B ; the point B will give us the intrados
of the crown of the arches of the portico. Dividing the height
CB or *i l* into five parts, and from the point *i* taking two of these
parts right and left on the base, we shall have the points *a g* of
the piers. From the point *b* as a centre, taking *bl* as a radius
(two parts), we draw the arch *hlm*. We have remaining, from
a to *h*, three parts, joining *g* and *h*, the base *ag* measuring 4,
and the perpendicular *ah* 3, the hypotenuse *gh* will measure 5,—
a length equal to *il*. In this arcade, therefore, we have unity in
the measure, and plurality in the parts,—relations and dissimilarities ;—the proportion 3 to 5 in architecture, as in music, is a
harmony : *ah* measuring 3 ; *gh* and *il*, 5. The lines AB, A″*l*, produced, will meet at the point E ; and the triangle B*l*E is similar
to the triangle AA′B. Let us place the upper cornice at the level
E. Producing the line *gh* till it meets the vertical CB produced,
we get the point O, which will determine the under-side of the
string-course at the height of the floor of the first story. We
shall also observe that *ag* is to *gh* as *cg* is to *go* and *ah* is to *co*;
we have therefore relations of proportion between the breadths
and the heights. Having fixed the height P of the sill, from the
points of intersection RR′ of the horizontal PP′ with the sides AE
of the large triangle AA″E, we shall erect two perpendiculars
which will give the jambs of the windows. Thus, the points A, B,
R′, E will be points of articulation indicating to the eye this line
AE, the side of an equilateral triangle ; we shall have established
a connection and a relation of proportions between the two stories ;
they will evidently form parts of a whole ; we shall have a unity
of *ensemble,* and a dissimilarity of dimensions, and relations of
proportions between the parts.

We will exhibit one more example of a unity in the whole,
realised under unfavourable conditions. The façade of a château
has to be erected, consisting of a ground-floor with one upper
story only and dormer-windows, high roofs and wings lower than
the main building (fig. 12) ; dividing the lengths of the façade
into twenty-two parts, we take four for the central pavilion, and
three for each of the two wings. At A we see how we should
proceed ; as we are evidently unable to give a point of articulation at the vertex B of the great equilateral triangle, we content
ourselves with drawing a semicircle with *a* as centre and *ab*
as radius. Occupying the point *c*, we shall again determine
a relation between the total breadth and the height.

We do not propose here to give models, but only to explain
a method in an age when method in architecture has been
entirely abandoned. It is evident that no application of a

method, whatever that method may be, can make up for want of observation, or for deficiencies in knowledge or taste. While adopting these mathematical means, the artist will always preserve his liberty and individuality. Moreover, in the execution there will be as many different applications as there are examples ; and it is this consideration which shows how dangerous is the *classic* definition of *the orders ;* it professes to give an immutable *process,* a perfect formula to substitute a *modulus* for reasoning—to substitute the *absolute* for the *relative.* But in architecture every part is relative to the treatment of the

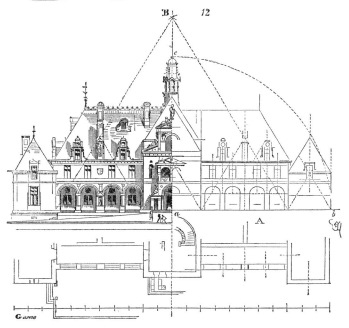

Fig. 12.—Method of obtaining Proportions.

whole. This principle, which was followed among the Greeks, was also found among the artists of the Middle Ages. In a mediæval building all the parts are interdependent, each member occupies a position determined by and relative to the whole ; and this is the reason why the buildings, religious and civil, of that period, appear larger than they really are.

It will be necessary to examine some of those architectural arrangements which exceptionally influence the method of pro-portions. The Greeks (at least in the buildings which still exist) have generally only a single ordonnance ; that is, the fronts of their edifices are erected on a single plane. They have not left us any buildings consisting of several stories or of superposed ordonnances or of recessed façades. And it will be readily understood that while it is easy to adopt a method of proportion for a façade presenting itself to the eyes in a single vertical plane, it is much less so to apply that method to buildings which not only have several stories, but façades in several planes, some standing out in relief against the rest. In this case a method of proportions carried out in a geometrical drawing is distorted in execution by the effects of perspective. The eye being a portion of a sphere whose centre is the point of vision—the *pinule*—all objects are represented as on a curved surface. Thus (fig. 13) let A be the visual point, and BC a pole divided into four equal

13

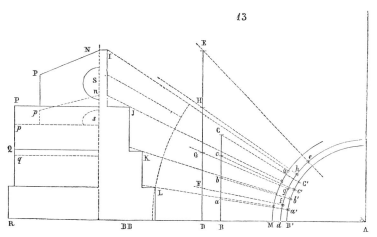

FIG. 13.—Influence of Perspective effect on Proportions.

parts, Ba, ab, bc, cc. These parts will be represented to the eye by four unequal parts, B$'a'$, $a'b'$, $b'c'$, $c'c'$. If therefore we wish the pole to appear divided into four equal parts, it will be necessary (the point of vision being at A and the pole at DE) to join the points E D by two lines at the point A, to divide the arc of the circle de into four equal parts, df, fg, gh, he; to carry lines from the point of vision through these points f, g, and to produce them to meet the pole DE. We shall thus have marked on this pole four unequal parts, DF, FG, GH, HE; DF being the shortest and HE the longest. There will, however, necessarily be a relation of proportion between these four parts. But if we have to design a façade consisting of several vertical planes standing one back from the other as shown in section BB perpendicular to this façade, and if we wish the four stories to appear of equal height to a person whose point of vision is A, it will be necessary to draw these stories so that the lines AI, AJ, AK, AL, may divide the arc of the circle MO into four equal parts. Then this façade which in geometrical elevation gives the drawing NPQR, will be only the dotted line *npq*R, and the round window s will give only the appearance *s*. When therefore we have to proportion the parts of an edifice, it will be of the greatest importance to take account of the point or points from which it will be possible to see it, and the diminishing effects of height, retreat and projection. But as the architect is often unable to prescribe the heights or arrange the recessings,— as he is obliged to comply with a programme and to submit to the requirements imposed by the uses to which the building is destined,—he must endeavour to restore the effect of desirable proportions by leading the spectator to surmise what cannot be seen, but which must exist, through a skilful arrangement of details, so as to magnify. what would seem too small, and diminish what would appear relatively too great. It is on such occasions that the competent artist will employ the ample resources furnished him by architectural art—art I say—not mere formulas.

The information we have respecting the interiors of Greek edifices is very incomplete. The dwellings and public buildings of Pompeii, which for the most part belong to the more recent period of the architecture of Magna Græcia, are those of a city of no great importance. It is only by inference that we can gain any idea of the interiors of the dwellings or public buildings of Athens; but we cannot suppose that the Greeks employed in their interiors architectural forms appropriate to the exterior. In an interior the field is limited; there can be no distant views there. Projecting features assume a considerable development, and are so many obstacles which prevent the eye from embracing the *ensemble*. If the Romans placed complete orders in enormous interiors, such as the halls of their Thermæ, it does not appear that they employed them in halls of moderate dimensions. The interiors of the Baths of Titus, of the Palatine of Pompeii, and of Hadrian's Villa, are not intersected by salient cornices or by obstructive pilasters or columns; the decoration consists exclusively of fine stuccos ornamented with sculptures in low relief and paintings. We may well suppose that the Greeks of Attica adopted a similar method, and when they placed orders in the interiors of temples,—the Parthenon, for example,—they gave them dimensions, very small as compared with those of the exterior.

In Persia, where traditions of remote antiquity were so long preserved, we observe that the interiors were decorated only by paintings or faïence, or mosaïcs, or moulded reliefs of a very delicate kind, which do not in any way alter the form of the halls or absorb the attention. A system of proportions which may be good when applied to a façade seen from a distance and illuminated by a direct light, would be out of place in the decoration of an interior ; and though the section of a great interior may be designed, as we have seen above, on a system of monumental proportion—for the sake of general effect—because the section lines of an interior are the first thing to catch the eye, when we come to the elaboration of details, the method which was good for the outside is bad for the inside. Moreover, it was scarcely before the end of the sixteenth century that architects in Italy and France thought of placing in the interiors of their building architectural features which had been designed only for exteriors.

While expecting to produce surprising effects by forced contrasts, architects have only diminished the effect of the real dimensions. Thus the interior of St. Peter's (at Rome) appears small at first sight, and some of our modern halls embellished with columns and entablatures make us wish to clear away all these superfluous pillars so as to restore the real form and dimensions of the interior. As light plays a very important part in architecture, it is evident that an entablature admirably designed with a view to produce a certain effect on the exterior where the light comes from above, will produce a very different one in a situation in which only a reflected light can be obtained. The finest Corinthian capital which defines itself so well, and which is so elegant seen in full sunlight at a distance under an angle of illumination of forty or fifty degrees, loses all its effect in a reflected light and seen from below. The Greeks were not unacquainted with these natural laws, for we observe, *e.g.* that the bas-reliefs placed in the interior of the portico of the Parthenon are sculptured so as to produce their effect under a reflected light. The Greek Doric capital was so designed as to preserve all its effect whether lighted from above or by reflection. Besides, its flattened corbel, of such delicate line, was often decorated with painted ornaments, and by its inclination presented a surface distinctly visible in an interior. But I can scarcely think that previous to the Roman dominion, the Greeks placed Corinthian capitals and entablatures in the interior of a hall ; that (with a view to keep to the terms of a formula) they placed architectural features in a position in which they cannot but mar one another and produce confusion, or at least crowd each other out of sight.

If the object which an architect ought to have in view in designing the architectural features of a hall is to make that hall appear smaller or less lofty than it really is, I allow that this object is perfectly attained in our days; but if the contrary ought to be aimed at, it is desirable to examine the means furnished by our art for enlarging, not diminishing, apparent size.

Gothic architecture, said M. Raoul Rochette in 1846,[1] " presents disadvantages which cannot be justified by the laws of taste, or be reconciled with the conditions of modern civilisation. In the distribution of the architectural members, there prevail *none of those principles which have become rules of art simply because they are the result of experience.* WE SEE THEREIN NO SYSTEM OF PROPORTIONS ; the details never bear any relation to the masses ; everything is capricious and arbitrary, alike in the invention and employment of the ornamentation ; and the *profusion of this ornamentation on the front of the churches as compared with its entire absence within* is a striking defect and a veritable absurdity." Without inquiring what are the disadvantages in architecture that could be justified by the laws of taste, and without troubling ourselves about the meaning attached by the *Académie des Beaux Arts* in 1846 to the words *veritable absurdity*,—taking the sense of the passage—we find it to contain an eulogium on Gothic architecture. The distinguished perpetual secretary had perceived that the architecture employed for the interiors of mediæval buildings was not the same as that applied to the exteriors ; and yet here we really have a principle that has become *a law of art because it was the result of experience* and also of good sense and taste. In fact, while on a façade of very considerable width and height,—a part that can be seen under various aspects, from a distance and close by, frontways and obliquely,—it is necessary to multiply the projections and the effects of light and shade, in order to engage the eye and delineate the whole by a succession of points of articulation skilfully placed ; while it is desirable to consider the various aspects and combine the features in such a way as to present agreeable and varied effects both frontwise and in profile, from a distant and near view, it is otherwise in an interior : for the architecture of the interior of a hall is seen only from the inside, so that its surface is limited relatively to the heights, and the spectator moves on a horizontal plane ; the limited surface over which the spectator's view ranges must therefore be taken account of by the architect.

It is my firm conviction that the Greeks observed this principle ; I perceive that the Romans on the other hand too often disregarded it ; but we have the proof that the Mediæval architects recognised it. Accordingly, whatever the dimensions

---

[1] *Considérations sur la question de savoir s'il est convenable, au* XIX⁰ *siècle, de bâtir des églises en style gothique.* A paper read before the Académie des Beaux Arts in 1846, and forwarded to the Home Secretary.

of their interiors, we observe, *e.g.* that one single ordonnance rises from the base to the springings of the vaulting. When they employ the column, it springs from the ground and supports the vaulting. If in buildings presenting a transitional phase, such as Notre Dame de Paris, the Cathedral of Noyon, Sens, and Senlis, and certain churches dating from the end of the twelfth century, architects placed the vaulting shafts on a lower range of pillars, they had sufficient good taste to give to this lower feature dimensions relatively inconsiderable, to make it serve the purpose, as it were, of a base or socle. But when this architecture is developed, when it acquires a perfect consistency, as at Reims, Amiens, Bourges, Chartres, etc., in proportion as the exteriors are made bolder in outline, with ornamented and accentuated projections (advantage being taken of the effects produced by direct light),—the interiors are brought into harmonious unity by reducing all projections and generally simplifying the decorative features. In these edifices the exterior invites the spectator to turn his gaze from point to point, to shift from place to place, and to enjoy very varied and manifold effects ; while in the interior everything is contrived so as to produce a single impression—that of repose and grandeur. Sculpture is sparingly employed ; vertical lines, whose effect is to increase the apparent height, are multiplied. The details are kept within the scale of the human figure ; everything concurs to produce unity of effect. And when we come to the analysis of these details, we perceive that all the members, all the mouldings, were designed for the positions they respectively occupy, and with a view to the effect required in those positions. If the Cathedral of Amiens had become a heap of ruins, we might by examining each fragment assign its place by means of the geometrical formula illustrated by figure 13.

M. Raoul Rochette complained of the poverty of the interiors of our churches as compared with the *fronts ;* but these interiors were only decorated with painting, stained glass (which is a kind of painting), and by furniture, usually of great richness. It is indisputable that the interiors of Greek buildings were also decorated by painting and movable objects rather than by architectural features of a complicated character or presenting numerous projections. The principle involved is too manifestly true, too natural, for artists of the Hellenic race not to have observed it. But what was the *cella* of a Greek temple compared with the interior of Amiens Cathedral ? A surface of a hundred square yards beside one of seven thousand. Most certainly I do not call attention to this difference here as a mark of superiority ; art is independent of the dimension of buildings, and no one would assert that the Madeleine will bear comparison with the little temple of Theseus ; but neither can it be disputed that the dimensions impose on the architect problems correspondingly difficult to resolve. If much consideration is required for giving felicitous proportions and a suitable decoration to a hall thirty feet in length by eighteen in width, it requires still greater study to preserve an aspect of unity, harmony, and dignity in an interior four hundred and fifty feet by one hundred and fifty. Now the difficulties thus involved were surmounted by the architects of the Middle Ages in the designs for their civil and religious edifices. To say nothing of the churches, the great halls of Sens, Poictiers, Montargis, the Palais in Paris, the Château de Coucy, as also the great hall of the Château de Fontainebleau, though of a much later period, sufficiently prove that the mediæval builders knew how to give a perfect unity to the architecture of their interiors, and that this unity was obtained by means different from those employed in the designs for the exterior.

The Romans, in moments of happy inspiration, or (as I should be rather inclined to think) when they left full liberty to the Greek artists and did not thrust in their love for sumptuous display between the artist and his work, themselves adopted this principle. Some of the halls of their Thermæ, but especially certain interiors of moderate dimensions, show that they were now and then able to employ the architectural features specially adapted for interiors.

The Greek artists who were employed by the Romans exercised an injurious influence on Roman architecture. The Greeks, unable to do better, "managed" their conquerors or "protectors," —the Roman policy considering it good taste to affect towards the Greeks the part of protectors rather than that of victors. The Greeks, then, "managed" their protectors, not by opposing the refined rules of their art to the Roman taste for ostentatious display and colossal bulk, but by indulging to the utmost the desire of these *barbarians* for costly materials and workmanship.

The Romans were but little concerned to appropriate to themselves or transmit to posterity the ideal refinement of Greek art which they did not comprehend ; but they considered it their interest to appear the most powerful nation of the earth,—to produce an imposing impression by the use of choice materials difficult to work, and a profusion of ornament. Accepting this desideratum of the Roman barbarian, the Greeks carried that profusion so far that they soon debased the art of which they had made themselves the subservient instruments. When that Roman art had fallen so low, had become so vulgar, so pompously insignificant, that it was no longer possible to restore it, the Greeks remoulded it for themselves ; but in so doing they did not retrograde; they did not servilely reproduce the Parthenon at Byzantium in the fifth century; they preserved as a valuable acquisition what the Romans had succeeded in discovering, and they re-clothed that thoroughly Roman form, for which a permanent recognition was secured, with a dress much more appropriate to the structure than that adopted under the Empire from Augustus to Constantine. The Greeks, the veritable pioneers of *progress* in all departments, advanced even while working for their powerful patrons; under subjection, they abandoned their Ionian and Dorian traditions; they took Roman architecture for what it was, gave it orderly arrangement, and of what was merely construction they succeeded in making an art. Instead of weeping incessantly on the steps of the Parthenon, like the Jews on the walls of Solomon's temple, they evolved Byzantine art from the debased Roman art of the third century. The Athenians can scarcely be called inventors, but they were endowed with the power of elucidating, combining, and purifying. They were admirable adapters, because they passed everything that came in their way through the crucible of an intelligence that was at once elevated and logical. Under Pericles they gave proof of this ability in art and in philosophy; from the essays, more or less meritorious, of the Ionians and Dorians, they evolved the Parthenon; and from the school of Pythagoras, Parmenides, Zeno, and the Ionian empirical system, arose Plato and Aristotle. Later on, this Greek race found even in its impoverished blood energy sufficient to develop from the effete art of Rome, in its decrepitude, the vigorous sapling called Byzantine architecture, the parent of the only styles of architecture deserving the name since the time of Constantine.

Successors of the Greeks in the West, during the Middle Ages, and, like them, lovers of progress, we advanced and formed an integral art from disjointed ruins. We too, like the Greeks, did not know where to stop; and, after having reconstituted an art, and then ridden it to death by the abuse of the employment of its own principles; after having had our sophists, we have put ourselves again under the protectorate of the Romans, probably to depress still more the level of their architecture. When we are tired of this last washed-out rag of classical disguise, we shall perhaps do as the Greeks did, and falling back on our own natural powers, discover a novel application of that art whose last remains we shall have exhausted. Among the numerous contradictions by which modern society is distracted, that which we witness in the domain of architecture is not the least remarkable, impelling as it does the defenders of Classical Antiquity (or those who assume this position) in a course diametrically contrary to that followed by the ancient Greeks. If we regard the Greeks as erratic in art, and the Romans as true artists, we are consistent in ignoring the architectural productions of the Middle Ages ; but if the Greeks were really artists, the Romans were evidently barbarians seeking to become refined by contact with their *protégés;* and in that case it is the Greek genius that should survive in the domain of art ; but the Greek genius is the reverse of immobility : rather than not go forward it prefers to descend,—sure of rising again further on, and finding new horizons.   The Greeks did not ignore Roman architecture; when the debilitated Empire committed itself to their hands, they regenerated and rejuvenated it ; and with such success that this resuscitated art was able not only to live, but to supply elements to the whole of the West and a portion of the East.   Let us not forget that in raising only the question of art here, we find the Greeks and the Romans adopting principles absolutely opposed the one to the other.   I shall not discuss whether, in their political life, their government, or their grade of civilisation, the Romans were superior or inferior to the Greeks, or whether the unification of the Romans was or was not an immense gain to humanity; but it is certain that this unification was repugnant to the genius of the Greeks as it must be to that of every artistic people.   Though subjugated, the Greeks always considered themselves superior to the Romans by the whole distance that separates a tragedy of Sophocles from a municipal regulation.   Artistic peoples have been exclusive peoples—forming restricted societies.   The Greeks and the Egyptians,—the artistic races of the Ancient World, —manifested to the last only contempt and dislike towards foreigners and barbarians.   The cosmopolitan Roman was not, nor could he be, artistic.   We possessed arts in France at the feudal epochs, because isolation has proved itself, up to this time in the world's history, at any rate, favourable to the development of art.

The part played by the Roman in the history of civilisation is sufficiently grand and magnificent to excuse us from awarding him more than what is fairly his due.   In matters of art the Romans proceeded as they did in all other things, especially in the domain of law.   Having in the early part of their history founded their legislature on absolute principles,—as in their Laws of the Twelve Tables, for instance,—they became aware during the early period of the Empire, that this legislation, applied with literal rigour, was repugnant to the customs and spirit of the nations constituting it ; they therefore instituted their *prætors,* who were interpreters of the law, leaning rather to equity than to the letter.   Similarly, in the domain of philosophy, they had Stoics of their own who regarded all subjects, not from the point of view of a fixed system, a written law, but with due allowance for diversity of intelligence and the circumstances, traditions, usages, and ideas of the times. We can thus understand how they should have allotted a place to the Greeks in the construction of their buildings,—a construction which was the written law, the letter; but which was able to admit of very various applications. That the Romans should have done this is in perfect accordance with the spirit of those great civilisers and levellers; but that the Greeks should accept the part conceded to their art, logical, elevated, and absolute in its principles as it was, is not to be admitted. The Greeks *worked* for their masters; but they never unveiled the principles of their exclusive art, because they felt sure that those rulers would not have admitted them, simply because they were exclusive. On both sides, the two races, while seeming to blend their structure and art, remained fundamentally, down to the time of Constantine, what they had been previous to Paulus Emilius,—antagonistic in sentiment; and that antagonism manifested itself anew on the establishment of the Roman Empire at Byzantium. Neither the benignity of Adrian nor the wise and moderate spirit of the Antonines availed to make the Greeks regard the Romans as other than barbarians. The Greek worked for the Roman without having any faith in what he did for that powerful master; he sold or lent his hands, but he kept deep within himself his principles and his devotion for art, in hope of some day displaying them openly. We have here matter for reflection, since happily we have still within us something of that Greek spirit in our republic of the arts; the antagonism still exists.

The Romans do not appear to have been sensible to harmony of proportions; they were an ostentatious people, who would have sacrificed the most felicitous proportions for the gratification of setting up—with no good reason for doing so—a few columns of marble, granite, or porphyry. If the Roman structure always produces a grand effect, it is because it is truthful and well-considered, and because, on that very account, it satisfies the eye. But the decorative dress that covers it often deprives it of majesty and dignity,—never gives it any. The generally very conscientious work of the students of the French Academy at Rome, will furnish a proof of this to those who cannot by an effort of imagination restore certain ancient Roman ruins which would corroborate it. The drawings of Roman ruins are always more satisfactory than the restorations; and, for my own part, I believe that if we could see some of those ancient monuments preserved intact,—abstracting the immense interest they would have for us, and setting aside the dimensions of the masses and the richness of the materials,—we should in most cases experience that impression of disappointment which is caused us by the

view of the interior of St. Peter's at Rome, or of St. Mary of
the Angels,—a disappointment which is only the result of a defect
of proportions in the architectural features clothing these immense
structures.   If we relieved the interior of St. Peter's of those
huge stucco pilasters, those entablatures wide enough to ride
along, those monstrous statues, those incrustations in the way
of panels, and those tasteless embellishments that break all the
lines, we should produce an interior which would appear what it
really is—colossal.   The vast size of the interior of St. Peter's
is only apparent in the evening twilight, when nothing but the
masses can be seen.   In full daylight its dimensions cannot be
appreciated, unless, by placing the hand above the eye, the gaze
is confined to the pavement—which presents a plain unbroken
surface, slightly ornamented with compartments of marble and
porphyry obscured by a film of dust.

The artists of the Byzantine Empire were still Greek enough
to supply rigorously that law of the predominance of masses ;
and it was observed in the architecture of the Caliphs, the Moors,
the Persians, and the Romanesque builders of the West during
the first period of the Middle Ages.   I should be the last to say
that this second-hand art is comparable to that of the Greeks,
nor should I say that the sophists of the school of Alexandria
are equal to Plato, or that the *Chanson de Roland* rivals the *Iliad*
in every point ; but I remark once more, we must move onwards,
—regrets cannot constitute life.

In order to explain, as before, by a drawing, the transformation to which the Byzantine architects subjected Roman architecture, let us take an example (fig. 14).   At A is drawn the
section of one of those Roman halls disposed in bays, whose construction is good, simple, and grand in effect.   Observe, however,
that the column B is out of scale with the dimensions of this
hall ; that its complete entablature breaks the view, and hides a
considerable part of the transverse arches C, or of the spandrels
D ; that, to the spectator at H, the column takes the length of
the chord *ab*, the entablature that of the arc *bc*, and the half-
vault that of the arc *cd;* that this length *cd* is reduced by the
importance of the points of support *a,b,c,* and that, consequently,
the development of the vault which should preponderate, and
which does in fact preponderate, in the geometrical drawing, is
partially lost.   Observe again, that in the proportions of a vaulted
hall the importance of the thing supported should bear such a
relation to that which supports, that the latter shall not appear
stronger than is necessary.   Now, in the example presented here,
it is evident that that which *supports,*—namely, the column
with its entablature,—assumes an exaggerated importance relatively to its function, since the parts of this support occupy

together the space *c d.* Moreover, it is a fact that projecting members, such as the cornice E of the order, when viewed from an inconsiderable distance, assume a relative extent greater than they really have. The eye is arrested by these projecting angles and mouldings, and instinctively develops their surfaces to such a degree that a slightly projecting cornice, such as that shown here, acquires an importance it would not have if seen from a much greater distance.

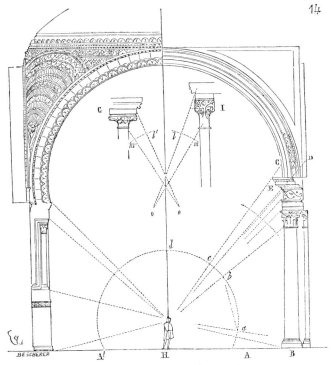

FIG. 14.—Comparison of Byzantine and Roman Architecture.

Without materially modifying the structure—the frame of the hall,—the Byzantine architects, freed from the traditions of the forms preferred by the Romans, would have modified its proportions according to the drawing A′. In lieu of the great column, they would have erected—which is more rational—a pier, and would have lightened that pier by engaged shafts, or angle columns without entablature,—for an entablature has no business in an interior. For the better development of the transverse arch, they would have exceeded the semicircle and would have constructed pendentives by means of superposed arches as a transition from the square to the circle instead of the groined vaulting. To increase the apparent size of the interior they would have covered certain parts with a delicate ornamentation in low relief and in harmony with the structure. They would thus, while preserving the general form of the Roman structure, have reverted to that Greek principle which always subordinates the ornamentation to the chief lines, and enhances their effect instead of marring it. Our spectator H thus contemplates proportions generally satisfactory. The vault—the thing supported—resumes its importance in relation to the thing which supports. The eye is no longer undesirably occupied by projecting entablatures, but from the floor to the top of the vaulting embraces a whole that is nowhere interrupted, and the ornamentation does not render the masses unintelligible; on the contrary, it explains them.

It is evident that in this example of interior architecture we are very far removed from our halls of the seventeenth century, in which we see gigantic figures, vases, and garlands borne on cornices of threatening projection.

But this return of the Byzantine architects towards a refined sense of proportions went still further. As soon as the orders had ceased—as in Roman architecture[1]—to be anything more than an accessory decorative member, when of themselves they no longer constituted the building, and their proportion was consequently no longer absolute, but relative, that proportion should, logically, be variable. The Romans, like true barbarians, priding themselves on being connoisseurs—who sought to bind the captain of a vessel to replace, *at his own expense,* the *chef-d'œuvres* of Greek art transported from Corinth to Rome, if his ship should founder—doubtless affected to retain the *orders* in their architecture, notwithstanding their being alien to its style, because they imagined that in retaining them they were giving proof of taste ; they made themselves more Greek than the Greeks, as the classicists of our days make themselves more *classic* than the ancients.

The Romans were necessarily *classic*, in the modern acceptation of the word ; for nothing assimilates better with administrative direction than classicism, as we now conceive it, and nothing is more contrary to the administrative spirit than discussion. There is reason for supposing the Greeks to have been indifferent administrators. The orders therefore—especially the most ornate, the Corinthian,—were preserved by the Romans

---

[1] It must always be observed that when we speak of Roman architecture, we refer only to buildings veritably Roman, to the exclusion of temples derived more or less from Greek architecture.

down to the times of the Lower Empire, with the rigour of a law ; but when architectural Rome fell into the hands of the Greeks, they renounced the orders whose proportions they themselves had originated. As in Roman architecture the order had ceased to be anything more than a decorative feature, they treated it as such, and variously transformed it, or, to speak more correctly, they entirely suppressed the orders and preserved the column and its capital, rarely its entablature (which no longer served any purpose, since the order had ceased to constitute the structure and the cornice to be the rain-drip of the roof), and adapted the proportions and form of the column and its capital to the position they occupied. For instance, were a column placed in the interior of a building at a great elevation as compared with its distance off, they either widened the corbel of the capital, as seen at G, fig. 14, so that the corbel gained in development as seen from the ground, or they lengthened the corbel in order to restore to it its duly proportionate height, which its elevated position in relation to the spectator caused it to lose, as shown at I. In fact, to the spectator placed at o the arcs lm, $l'm'$, are equal. Here we again find the Greek with his freedom and his logical mind. Now, while the Romanesque architects of the Middle Ages almost ignored these novel principles of proportion, the secular architects of the twelfth and thirteenth centuries in France applied them with a geometrical rigour which is interesting to observe. The system of proportions was therefore abandoned by the Greeks themselves, as soon as, free to exercise their own judgment, they were able to treat Roman architecture according to their unfettered instincts. The period when the largest edifices scarcely exceeded 500 square yards in extent had passed away ; the new phase of civilisation required them to cover vast areas, and they were obliged to make use of what was good and practical in Roman architecture. The last of the Greeks accepted these conditions, and while accepting them they did not seek to pervert their old art, so beautiful and so enduringly venerated ; they frankly adopted another, and made their intelligence, their logical mind, subserve the requirements of the times. We have here a grand lesson, if we knew how to profit by it. But what course did the Latins of the Renaissance adopt ? They reverted, not to this Roman art reformed by the Greeks of Byzantium, but to the Roman art of the Lower Empire, embellished by expatriated Greeks and subjected to a kind of governmental regulation. It may be truly said that the Italians, from the fourth century to the fourteenth, ceased to have an architecture ; that, subject sometimes to Byzantine, sometimes to German influences, and fluctuating between forms of which they comprehended neither the origin nor the principles, they were little capable of producing an art. Resuming as well as they could the old official art of the Empire, they could not at any rate be accused of losing by changing. But with us of the West the case was very different. We, who are usually classed *en masse* among the Latin races, but whose turn of mind so little accords with that of the Latins, possessed an art that was subject to its own rules, derived from no foreign source ; yet we have been seeking to import those Italian copies of an art rightly contemned by the Greeks—whom forsooth we greatly admire ! Let those who can, explain these contradictions. Meanwhile a well-supported sheltering and tenacious routine does duty for explanations.

But Greek genius was destined to be long dominated by the Barbarians—for in fact that subjection continues still ; active intellect, enthusiastic for progress in accordance with logical deduction, was to be reduced once more beneath the control of organised force ; formulas were to override intelligence, and it was fated that formula should even stifle, by a seeming return towards one of the forms sanctioned by Greek genius, that inspiration which in the West had not been utterly extinguished.

Greeks were to be made the instruments of hindering the free advance of architecture, of contravening that progress of which they had been the apostles, and of subjecting that art once more to the enervating influences of Roman dictation. At Byzantium even, as soon as an effort had been made to bring form into harmony with structure, there was an endeavour to arrest the march of progress, and the most enlightened minds— the seekers of the better, the Nestorians,—were exiled ; and they went far away from the capital of the Eastern Empire to lay the foundations of an art more rational still than that of Byzantium ; never failing, however, to take account of the advance that had been made,—never plucking out any of the landmarks already set up.

The Greeks of classic antiquity (*i.e.* the Greeks of Attica) did not adopt the vaulted construction in their buildings. But having been for several centuries the subject skilled artisans of the Romans, they had become familiar with that kind of structure, while they had not sensibly modified its principles or form. In these the Romans brooked no interference ; the Roman structure was a matter of governmental regulation, and the Romans regarded the Greeks only as tasteful decorators. At Byzantium, and in the buildings erected under the Eastern Empire, only one innovation had been made in the system of vaulting,—the pendentives. This was a considerable one, it is true, and it was a very logical deduction from the mixture of the barrel vault and the hemispherical vault,—a deduction which seems to have originated with the Greek genius, which found itself more free in Byzantium than at Rome.[1] With respect to the semicircle, no one thought of abandoning it ; it remained the generator of the arch generally, of barrel vaulting, groined vaulting, and of the cupola. If however we consider one of the three triangles described above, namely, the equilateral triangle, the triangle taken on the diagonal of a pyramid with a square base, whose vertical section—from the summit parallel to one of the sides of the base—is an equilateral triangle, and the triangle which we call *Egyptian*, as three generators of proportions, we are led to give the arch a form other than that of the semicircle, as all those three triangles give an angle at the summit of less than 90°.

Suppose, for example, we take the *Egyptian* triangle as generator of proportions (fig. 15), its base AB being the diameter and

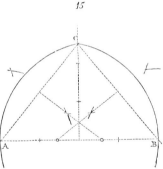

15

FIG. 15.— The Pointed Arch.

the springing line of the arch ; if we wish the apex of this arch to reach the summit C, we must necessarily,—making use of the compasses to draw the arch,—seek on the line AB not one centre, as in drawing a round arch, but two centres, which will be the points of intersection of perpendiculars from the middle points of the lines AC, BC with the springing line AB. We shall thus have drawn a curve of two segments, composed of arcs of circles that will follow the system of proportions imposed by the triangle ABC. This is what is now called, but very improperly, the *ogive* (pointed arch)[2]. It is quite certain that the schools that issued from that of Byzantium, subsequently to the sixth century,

[1] It is in fact strange that the pendentive, which is so natural a consequence of the hemispherical and the barrel vault, was not adopted in any known Roman building previous to St. Sophia at Constantinople. Hence there is every reason for ascribing the credit of this so logical result to the Greek artists of Byzantium.

[2] See the article OGIVE in the *Dictionnaire raisonné de l'architecture française.*

adopted this arch, which the Western architects of the twelfth century in France turned to such admirable account, since they made it the starting-point of a new system of structure. But it may be remarked that, in Classic times, Greek genius attained a relative perfection only by a series of experiments tending always in the same direction. Thus, by how many successive modifications of the Doric order was that perfection attained which is exhibited in the Parthenon! We recognise many, though we do not know them all.

From the great temple of Selinuntum to the Parthenon, the gradation is insensible; it is always the same order; the order once originated, nothing was added to it, nothing subtracted from it; yet perfect proportion was obtained only after a course of improvements introduced by the observance of a logical method that was undeviating and determinate. Similarly, the scattered débris of the Greek school, mingled with Roman traditions, and subjected to Asiatic influences, were still sufficiently complete, after the establishment of the Eastern Empire, and the internal discords of that Empire, to infuse into the architectural works they were called upon to engage in, that refined and rational sense of proportions in which they had always excelled. And it should be carefully noted that those arts which arose in the East and in Egypt, and in which we find the precious Greek vein, lose nothing that has been once adopted, and do not retrograde ; they take that which exists and improve it.

Since the close of the Roman Empire, the irrational mingling of the arch and the lintel in the same architectural composition had often been discarded. The Greek artists, still subject to the Empire, had sprung the arch directly from the column ;[1] but it was the Roman arch,—the semicircular arch with its concentric mouldings. Already the springer of these arches, wider than the diameter of the column, explained the spreading of the capital by making use of it. But this semicircular arch would appear flat, crushed, and heavy on the slender proportions of the Corinthian column ; nevertheless, it was at that time a novel idea, based on correct reasoning. Besides, the Greek artists had not leisure to seek the quintessence of proportion under masters as barbarous as they were magnificent. Such studied refinements might perhaps have had some success under Hadrian, but under Diocletian they would be lost labour. After the advent of Islamism, these remnants of the Greek school found themselves in presence of other barbarians who left them greater liberty, because they manifested no taste or preference in matters of art ; Greek feeling regained its love for elaboration of form and delicate observation of proportions ; it endeavoured to associate

[1] See the Sixth Lecture, fig. 9.

the arch with the column, and sought curves other than that of the semi-circle; and we see that these essays frequently produced architectural ordonnances singularly beautiful in their lines and proportions.

At Cairo, in the year 21 of the Hegira (A.D. 641), the mosque of Amrou was being erected.   It must be remembered that this Amrou had, at the request of Philoponus the grammarian, begged Omar to preserve the valuable library of Alexandria, after the taking of that city.   The Caliph answered : "The contents of

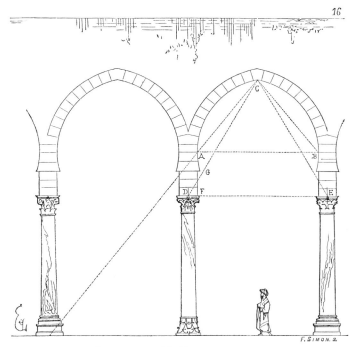

FIG. 16.—Portico of the Mosque of Amrou, Cairo.

the books of which you are speaking to me, accord with what is written in the book of God, or they do not accord with it.   If they accord with it, the Koran suffices, and these books are not needed.   If they do not accord with it, they must be destroyed." The books were burned, but certainly the mosque of Amrou at Cairo was built by no others than the Greek artists who had taken refuge in Egypt ; and it was built with marble columns taken from great Roman buildings.   This mosque consists merely of immense porticos erected around a court.

Here (fig. 16) are two bays of a portico, and we see that the

Greek architects (for no one will suppose that Omar had architects with him), employing columns of which edifices built under
the Empire had been despoiled, raised arches on these capitals
that were novel in form, having a complex curve, but with lines
indicating a delicate sense of proportions.   All the travellers
who have visited the mosque of Amrou agree in saying that the
effect of these bays is most pleasing; that nowhere have they
seen a great portico nobler in proportions or more elegant in
aspect.   The method of striking these arches is as follows : AB
is the line of level of the centre-points, and ABC the *Egyptian*
triangle.   The arch is struck according to the method given in
figure 15.   The point C being taken as the vertex of the equilateral triangle DEC, the base of that triangle gives the upper
level of the abacus of the capitals.   The Egyptian triangle gives
the centres of the arch and its diameter in relation to its height.
The equilateral triangle gives the general proportion of the arch
above the capitals.

To avoid the weak line that would be produced by a perpendicular FA, let fall from the springing A of the curve, the architect
continued the curve of the arch below the point A to the point
G ; he thus obtained a stop above the parallelopiped which surmounts the capital,—a stop which, in execution, gives an appearance of peculiar firmness to these arches.   Here we have Greek
architects who, building for conquerors with the débris of buildings which their own countrymen had erected for former masters,
discovered sufficient vitality in their genius, so often oppressed
and humiliated as it had been, to apply once more to the work
of improving upon the art with which they were occupied.

Driven from Byzantium in the fifth century, the Nestorians
emigrated, for the most part, to Persia : and there, appropriating
the arts which they found languishing on the soil, and adhering
to the traditions of Roman structure, they erected buildings in
a new style, while they preserved established arrangements,—
buildings of extreme elegance, and in which proportions were
very carefully studied.   To these Nestorians alone can we attribute the tincture of art acquired by the tribes who followed
Mohammed when he began the conquest of the entire East.   The
Semitic races—the Arabs—have no aptitude for art ; and what
is commonly called Arab architecture is only an offshoot of Persian
architecture modified by the Greeks,—that is to say, the Nestorians.   We know how brilliant was even this last emanation
of Greek genius.   I repeat here purposely : Greek genius does
not invent ; on the intellectual side of art it co-ordinates, establishes relations, deduces consequences, and carries reasoning to
its utmost limits ; on the material side, it has the faculty of
investing with the most true and beautiful expression the form

it is treating, modifying it without changing its principles; it never creates monsters; in those products of its imagination that are furthest removed from the natural order, it subordinates itself to a harmony so exact and well-conceived that these products assume the appearance of reality. Mathematical knowledge was diligently cultivated by the Greeks of the Lower Empire, who in this respect only carried out the already very extensive discoveries of their predecessors. As the new masters of the East excluded all imitation of organic nature in the art which they willingly left the Nestorians to practise, the latter, destined, like their predecessors, to work under barbarian rulers, entered energetically upon the only path that was open to them; and geometry became the originating principle of every form, and even of every ornament. Architecture saw itself despoiled of its richest antique decorations; figures, statuary, and inspirations from the flora of the country were no longer admitted. The square and compass became supreme; and yet with these means, apparently so restricted,—with so dry a theme,—the artists whom we call *Arabs* succeeded in producing marvels. It was natural, however, that the study of proportions should then become one of the most efficacious means of giving a pleasing appearance to buildings. In fact, in this architecture of the Caliphs, proportion is everything, because nothing masks its defects; ornamentation lends its aid in rendering the harmony of that proportion manifest, but it is effective only in the mass; it engages the attention only as embroidery on a tissue; it pleases without distracting. A singular destiny is that of this Greek art: so living, so splendid, yet nearly always in a state of subjection, and never failing to find the means of satisfying the most contrary tastes; no problem appeared insoluble to these indomitable labourers for intellectual advancement; always seeking, they were always finding; always in subjection, their intelligence never failed to influence their masters, and contributed to their posthumous fame. They had been the instructors of the Romans, and they became the instructors of the barbarian hordes of Arabia; and this last effort of their genius had also an influence that survived even to the fifteenth century, and made itself felt on the confines of the West.

Hitherto we have only treated of proportion considered absolutely, independently of the system of construction and the purpose of the buildings: we have exhibited only the general aspect of those principles of harmony applied to architectural effects, and have even purposely selected buildings of very various character, belonging to times separated by long intervals or by differing civilisations. We have thus shown that in this art there are laws which depend on human genius whatever be the element in which it is developed. But there are others which are evidently an inference from material facts, such for instance as the nature of the materials, the mode of using them, the particular customs resulting from climate, from the aptitudes of particular races, from comparative wealth, from taste for luxury, from necessity, or from the degree of refinement characterising the people in question. Though we find the same principles of proportion among the ancient Greeks as among the artists of the Middle Ages, it is not less evident that the Greek temples have no analogy, at least apparently none, with our Gothic churches. A rational method, however, in virtue of its being a method, and because it is rational, should produce opposite consequences, as soon as it is applied to elements that are themselves of an opposite character. We do not accuse of inconsistency a person who complains of heat in July and of cold in January ; his organism is no less identically *the same* because he feels differently in different circumstances. We can only accuse of inconsistency those who should walk about in summer covered with furs, and in the winter dressed in linen, and who should wear a long dress at the gymnasium and a short one during a funeral ceremony. While there are general laws, there are also laws special to particular times, places, and means at disposal ; and it is the confounding of general with special laws that has long prevented a mutual understanding respecting architectural questions. Some would have us wear nothing but furs, others nothing but linen, and will not concede the propriety of a change of dress according to circumstances.

The Greeks had reasoned correctly in adopting the column, the raised stone, the *stylus* supporting a *rail* or lintel, and in giving to this column a proportion relative to itself—to its function. The Romans reasoned very indifferently in retaining the relative proportions of the column, applied to vaulted buildings, in which the *Order* served only a secondary purpose. The Greeks of Byzantium having admitted the principles of Roman structure, wisely ceased to regard the *Order* as a type whose proportions were fixed.

Among the Western nations during the Middle Ages, the columns became independent of the *Order* ; it is elongated or shortened according to the function it fulfils in the general system of architecture ; it is slender or stout according to the material employed, since no satisfactory reason can be imagined for giving the same diameter to a column of granite as would be required for one of vergelé[1] under the same pressure. To say that the columns of the nave of Notre Dame are not in good proportion, because they have no relation to the proportions adopted

---

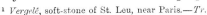

[1] *Vergelé*, soft-stone of St. Leu, near Paris.—*Tr.*

in the orders of Greece or Rome, implies a singular method of appreciating proportions ; for it is evident that proportions are nothing else than relations between the parts and the whole, and that these relations must be imposed by the whole on the parts, not by the parts on the whole. In Greek architecture, or rather in the Greek temples, the part (*i.e.* the *Order*) was the whole, and the proportions of the *Order* necessarily determined those of the edifice ; but when the *Order* ceased to be anything more than one of the parts of the whole, it lost its character of *Order* and assumed that of a subordinate member : in proof of which we have the fact that it abandoned the entablature and was reduced to a column,—a point of support. That column itself exchanged its own proportion for one that bore a relation to the place it occupied or the function it fulfilled, or to the nature of the material in which it was worked; its capital and base underwent the same variations, in point of height, breadth, and strength, according to the general ordonnance of which these members formed a part. This was rigorously logical. But in art we may reason correctly and yet produce only unpleasing works, if the selection of form is not made the corollary to a rigorous course of reasoning. The French architecture of the fifteenth century is only the result of a true principle pushed to its extreme limits ; and that architecture is unattractive by reason of the forms which the absolute application of its principle caused it to adopt. It became a mere demonstration,—a geometrical diagram ; it is a problem proposed and solved, not a conception of art.

When the *Order* ceased to constitute the whole—the entire ordonnance of the edifice,—it ceased to be, because it no longer had a rational purpose. The *Order* ceases to appear in the outgrowths of Roman architecture reconstituted by the Greeks on novel principles. There is no trace of the order in the architecture attributed to the Arabs, any more than in the Western architecture of the Middle Ages ; and these arts must be considered from quite another point of view, although certain general laws of proportion are common to classic and to mediæval architecture, as above demonstrated. Geometry became the sovereign mistress of the latter art ; and it was not without reason that the architects of our Western edifices, from the twelfth to the fifteenth century, included in a single personification architectural art and geometry. Nevertheless, while bringing geometry to bear on every architectural conception, in the general design as well as in the details, the great Oriental artists —the remnant of the Alexandrian school,—as well as our Western artists in France, still preserved so true a feeling for form that this latter, to the vulgar at least, still appeared to be the supreme law in every work of architecture ; but only in the debased periods do these works betray the geometrical methods by which they were designed. But in this, the special genius of the two races is fully manifest, and we have clear evidence here that the architects of the West never imitated those of the East, though both drew from the same source.

While the Greeks were not inventors, the men of the West were so in an eminent degree. The Arabs, or their instructors in art, the Nestorians, did not change the Roman system of structure ; they only modified its envelope ; the geometry to which they had recourse did not cause them to discover a new system of construction ; its functions were limited to giving novel curves to the arches and controlling all ornamental design ; it afforded an intellectual pastime, and engaged the eye by wonderful combinations, whereas in the West geometry began by subverting the Roman structure, which no longer seemed satisfactory in point of science ; it was continually proposing new problems, bidding architecture recognise laws of equilibrium until then unknown ; it proceeded with an inflexible logic from the general design to the details, assumed the control of the form of the material, and dictated the smallest moulding ; and it advanced so rapidly and so far in its bold march, that in the space of two centuries it had succeeded in depriving the artist of all individuality. It proceeded like the inexorable laws of crystallisation ; and to appreciate the difference between the two arts which both became the slaves of geometry, let us enter the Alhambra, for example, one of the latest edifices due to the civilisation attributed to the Arabs, and what do we see? A concrete structure, like the Roman, Classic ground-plans, walls of brick —masses that maintain themselves only by the adherence of the mortar,—and slight porticos whose delicate marble columns and spandrels of earth and reeds support wainscoted ceilings. In all this there is no attempt to invent a structure different from that which existed in Rome and which may still be seen at Pompeii. But these masses of pise, brick, lath, and plaster, are covered with stuccos presenting to the astonished view the most skilful geometrical combinations that could be imagined. Those who inhabited these palaces—given to contemplation, loving to reflect, lost in dreams amid these aimless combinations, luxuriating in vague reveries—certainly did not belong to the active, logical, and practical family of the West. If we enter the Cathedral of Amiens, or any of our most perfect mediæval buildings, the first impression we experience is a sense of unity : we first appreciate the general effect ; no detail engages the eye : it is clear and grand ; but if we study the method of execution we are soon struck with surprise at the number of geometrical combinations that must have contributed to the conception of the framing of the edifice.

In the Arab building, geometry adorns the dress; in the Western mediæval edifice it sustains the body. In the Arab building, geometry began its task when the decoration was in question;—the very moment when it ceased to intervene in mediæval architecture, in which all decoration is inspired by the flora, at any rate from the thirteenth century downwards. In France we barely discover traces of the intervention of geometry towards the close of the twelfth century in certain decorative parts; and these traces belong to traditions which are very

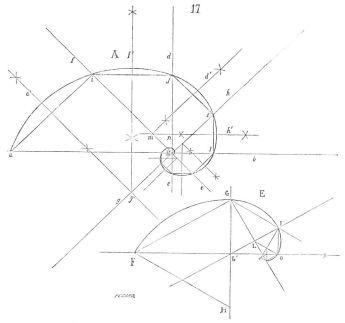

Fig. 17.—Volute lines of French Twelfth-Century Capitals.

ancient, in fact anterior to the Roman period. Thus, to cite an example, we see at the angles of some large capitals of the second half of the twelfth century, certain volutes that have a peculiar character. They are like great leaves, with a vigorous line curving inwards at their extremity.[1] Now, in studying the curves which these volutes follow, we perceive that they are drawn by the aid of a geometrical method. Thus, fig. 17 (at A), the eye of the volute being at B, the horizontal line *ab* was drawn;

[1] Choir of Notre Dame de Paris, Saint Julien-le-Pauvre, Noyon Cathedral.

then, from the point B, the perpendicular line *cd;* dividing the
four right angles into two equal angles, the lines *ef, gh* were
drawn.   From the point *a*, the starting of the curve, a perpendicular *ai* was let fall on the line B*f;* from the point *i*, a perpendicular *ij* on the line B*d;* from the point *j*, a perpendicular *jk* on
the line B*h;* from the point *k*, a perpendicular *kl* on the line B*b*,
etc.   Erecting a perpendicular from the middle of the line *ai*, its
intersection with the line *gh* gave the point *g';* a second perpendicular from the middle of the line *ij* also meets the point *g'*, and
the point *g'* is the centre of the arc *aij*.   Erecting a perpendicular
from the middle of the line *jk* it will meet the line B*f* at the
point *m*, the centre of the arc *jk;* erecting a perpendicular from
the middle of the line *kl*, it will meet the line B*d* at *n*, the centre
of the arc *kl*, etc.   Thus was obtained a figure whose vigorous
curve reminds us of certain volutes of primitive Ionian art.
Other volutes were obtained by means of the equilateral triangle
(see drawing E in the same figure).   FGH being an equilateral
triangle, the arc FG was drawn with the point H as centre.
Dividing the side GH into two equal parts, the second equilateral
triangle GG'I was described upon the half G'G of that side ; and,
taking the point G' as centre, the arc GI was drawn.   Proceeding
as before, upon the side G'I of the triangle G'GI, with the middle
point L as centre, was drawn the arc IO, etc.   It was not the
Romans who transmitted these methods of design to the artists
of the twelfth century ; they were derived from another and a
more remote origin.

We must penetrate as far back as early Greek antiquity,—
that of Ionia, in particular,—to find analogous designs ; just as
we are constrained to recognise striking relations between certain
Greek decorations in Asia Minor, and certain decorations of the
end of the twelfth century in France.   If we consider the mouldings, we find a singular kinship between these arts, so widely
separated from each other both by time and distance.   The
principles of drawing are the same, and the line is often identical.
It is not necessary to have seen many Greek buildings, Ionian
and Dorian, to perceive that in the architecture of these populations the designing of mouldings was regarded as one of the
essential parts of art; and that the designs were not the results of
caprice, but of just reasoning and a refined sense of form.   All the
mouldings of the beautiful Greek architecture had been caressed,
shall I say, with studious love.   Now, in the designs for mouldings, two conditions must be observed : the function they have to
perform, and the effect to be produced in the place they occupy.
A moulding is good only in as far as it exactly fulfils these conditions.   The material employed may modify the design without
thereby changing the principle.   It is natural to give greater

delicacy and even thinness to a moulding cut in marble than to one worked in a friable stone; but this is a question of more or less sharpness given to the angles,—of more or less depth given to the sinkings. The principles are the same for both. But it would denote a condition of profound barbarism to give, for example, to mouldings of joiner's work the section adapted for those that suit stone or marble,—to mouldings inside a hall the section adapted to those outside it. The artists of the Middle Ages did not, any more than the Greeks, forget these very natural laws; I would say again that the former pushed still further than their predecessors the rigorous observance of prin-

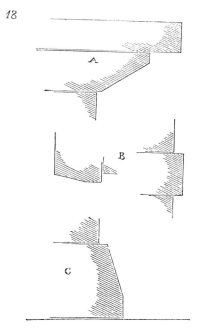

Fig. 18.—Elementary Cornice, String and Base Mouldings.

ciples, at any rate as far as we can judge from the few Greek ibuldings that remain. With the Greeks, as in our architecture of the twelfth century, the moulding serves three purposes: it either supports a projection, or it forms a footing, or it marks a height, or defines an opening. In the first case the moulding is a cornice; in the second a base, a basement, a plinth; in the third a string-course, a jamb, a frame. Except for these three functions, a moulding has no rational purpose; accordingly, it does not appear otherwise in good Greek architecture, any more than in French mediæval architecture. These functions being thus determined, mouldings are reduced to three elementary arrangements, which are indicated by the three diagrams A, B, C (fig. 18),—shapings, shall I say, dictated by the necessity of the structure. But this shaping admitted, it remains to give these projections the forms suitable to their purpose, and the place they occupy. They have a use, and should produce a certain effect in accordance with that use. The cornice, if external, should protect the outer walls, and throw off the rain-water far from their surface ; as all the under part is in shade, it should be worked in such a manner as to appear sufficiently strong to sustain the projection. The string-course is only a cincture, indicating either the level of a floor or a change in the building of the faces ; it is a projecting course which should appear able to resist a pressure and clearly mark a separation. The enframing moulding, the jamb moulding, stay the faces and strengthen the partitions of a void. The base, plinth, or socle sustains all the weight, forms a footing on the ground, and serves as a transition between the horizontal and the vertical plane.

Examine some of these mouldings designed by the Greek architects. Figure 19 presents mouldings of capitals, antæ, and cornices. A is the cornice moulding of the temple of Castor and Pollux at Agrigentum ; this is an exterior moulding ; beneath the gutter *b* is hollowed out the throat *c*, intended to hinder the rain-water from spreading along the drip ; then comes the drip *d*, which arrests the light and also throws off the water. The numbers *e* are sharply accentuated in order to give dark lines beneath the shadow thrown by the drip. These mouldings therefore serve a purpose, and are intelligible to the eye. The great gutter moulding will catch the luminous rays at *g*, and will also present two dark lines above that line of light to give it projection. Similarly, buried in the shadow cast by this gutter moulding, a second dark line *c* will bring out the transparency of that shadow. If we direct a luminous ray on this moulding, at an angle of 45°, for instance, we should remark that the artist obtains two fine luminous lines, at *h* and *g*, separated by dark lines ; and a third dark line at *c*, to limit, as it were, the shadow thrown by the gutter ; and beneath the great shadow of the drip other strongly marked lines which variegate that broad belt of shadow with ledges and grooves admirably calculated to intensify it here and diminish it there, as they court or shun reflected lights.

Here, then, we have study of effect together with provision for a requirement. The moulding of the antæ of the temple of Neptune at Pæstum, drawn at B, completely buried in the shadow of the pronaos, is, on the contrary, designed to receive a reflected light, as indicated by the wide ogee moulding *b'* ; there again we remark the sunk-in dark line *c'* beneath the reflected light taken

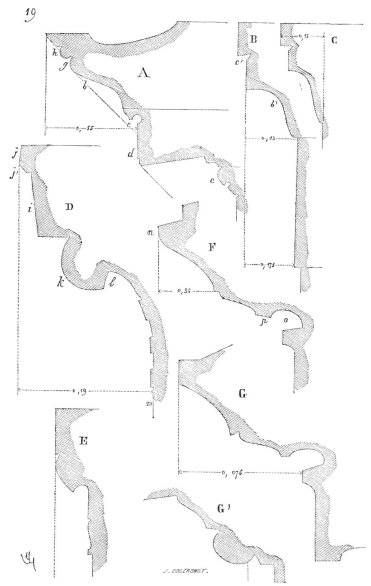

FIG. 19.—Greek Mouldings.

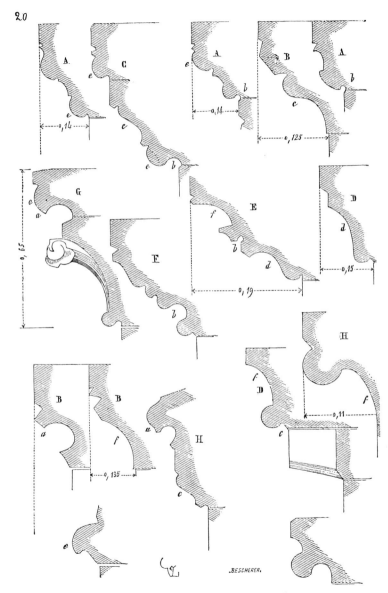

FIG. 20.—Twelfth and Thirteenth Century French Mouldings.

by the upper member. The same may be said of the moulding c, crowning the architrave of the interior order. The moulding D of the propylæa of Eleusis is likewise designed in reference to a reflected light. It will be observed that the upper fillet j falls slightly back in order to show out the reflected light of the chamfer j'', that the face i inclines a little to take the light, that the torus k recedes near the horizontal part of the abacus for shadow and to set off the projection of the latter, that this torus is abruptly cut to produce a sharp shadow at l; that, lastly, between the vertical face m and that shadow l, there is a transition accentuating a reflex increasing in brightness as it approaches the torus, and that this reflex is cut by shades and bright lines so as to fill up the curved surface and give it value. The section E of a portion of frieze from the temple of Ceres at Eleusis gives us another example of the delicacy with which the Greeks designed their mouldings intended to receive only reflected light.

Let us conclude this examination of cornice-mouldings with those from Pompeii. F is an exterior moulding almost entirely buried in shade, except the edge n of the upper ogee. A strong black o, behind a fillet p, receiving a bright reflex, occupies this shade. The moulding GG', taken from the Triangular Forum, is designed according to the same principle as that marked A, but with a more decided accentuation.[1]

While the Roman cornice-mouldings remind us of these in point of mass, it must be admitted that, in the details, they exhibit neither the refinement nor the appreciation of effects which we observe here; in them we miss those sinkings that bring out the lights, and especially the transparency of the reflected shadows. The outlines are weak and indeterminate, the curves indifferently studied and conventional; and, whether these mouldings are intended for interiors or exteriors, was not a matter of much concern. In the mouldings of our French architecture of the secular school of the twelfth and thirteenth centuries, it is difficult not to recognise the influence of the principles which guided the Greek architects. In figure 20 we have a proof of this. Here we see the same delicate study of the curves, the same elaboration of contrasts, the use of the same means suited for obtaining certain effects of light and shade, reflected lights, and intensification of shadow. We observe the same consideration of the purpose which the mouldings should subserve. This is not derived from Roman art,—most certainly not from that Gallo-Roman art, which had sunk so low in all that belongs to the execution of architectural details.[2]

[1] See the result of M. Uchard's researches, published in M. Daly's *Revue d'architecture*, vol. xviii. pl. 49 and 50.

[2] The mouldings A belong to the first half of the twelfth century, and are from the interior of the nave of Vezelay (cornices, or rather projecting abaci of the inside capitals).

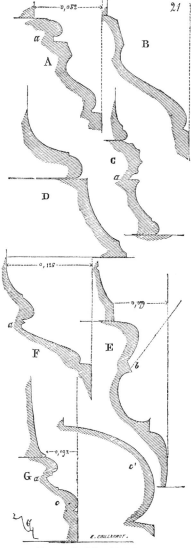

FIG. 21.—Greek Base Mouldings.

The mouldings B are from the old tower of Notre Dame de Chartres (exterior) [about 1140]. The moulding C crowned externally the choir aisle of the Cathedral of Paris (about 1165). The exterior mouldings D are from the church at Montréale (about 1180), (Yonne) ; the moulding E of a balustrade from the interior of the church at Vezelay (about 1190) ; the moulding F from the porch of Vezelay (about 1135) ; the exterior moulding G from the same church (about 1235) ; the exterior moulding H (same period).

The drips a, the dark sinkings b, the ogee c, the doucines d, the toruses e, and the cavettos f, remind us of Greek mouldings. In execution these mouldings are designed for the place they occupy and the function they fulfil; but as the light is less brilliant in our climate than under the skies of Greece or Italy, these mouldings are more relieved, rely less on the clearness of the reflexes, and repeat more frequently those black lines which set off the projections. As the buildings of the Middle Ages were larger, and the mouldings placed higher, it was also necessary to consider their distance from the eye. In the base mouldings the analogy is yet more striking.

Here (fig. 21) are some Greek base mouldings.[1] These mouldings are evidently designed to be seen from above. They spread out on the ground, lead the eye from the vertical line to the horizontal plane, and are only accentuated by the fine scotias a, or by sinkings that give sharp shadows to define the toruses. It will be observed how, in the moulding E, the upper torus is flattened in its lower part to disengage the fillet b. The shape of the lower torus c of the moulding G, which we give to a larger scale at c', should also be remarked.

Let us now take some base mouldings of the twelfth and thirteenth century columns in France (fig. 22); but first we should give the section of a torus of a Doric capital turned upside down. We give, at A, that of the capitals of the temple of Metapontum. The lower torus of the column bases round the choir of the Cathedral of Paris, drawn at B, exactly reproduces the section of the Doric capital of Metapontum,—a section obtained by means of three circular arcs. Even the double fillet a of the capital is preserved at a' in the base, only it is single. The upper torus of this base B is slightly flattened in the upper part, as in most of the Greek mouldings (fig. 21). As to the mouldings CC', from the columns of the old tower of Notre Dame de Chartres, they are singularly like the Greek mouldings BE of figure 21. The moulding G is from one of the column bases of the choir of the abbey church of Vezelay.[2]

The socle mouldings E likewise reproduce the section B of fig. 21. Like the Greeks, these lay artists of the twelfth century considered that the toruses of bases should not be drawn with a single sweep of the compass; that they should have a footing on the ground and be outlined by the sharp shadow of a well accentuated scotia. At c, figure 21, we give the section

---

[1] A, from the antæ of the temple of Diana, the propylæum at Eleusis; B, from the antæ of the propylæa at Eleusis; c from the temple of the Wingless Victory, Athens; D, from the temple of Apollo at Bassæ, Phigalia; E, from the Triangular Forum at Pompeii; G, the same; F from Pompeii.

[2] See article BASE and GRIFFE in the *Dictionnaire raisonné de l'architecture française, du* XIe *au* XVe *siècle.*

of an Ionic base moulding of the Wingless Victory ; the large
torus of this base is fluted horizontally ; this type is reproduced
in the Pandrosium of Athens and in other Ionic buildings of the
time of Pericles.   Now we find this same fluted torus in a certain
number of French twelfth-century buildings, especially in the

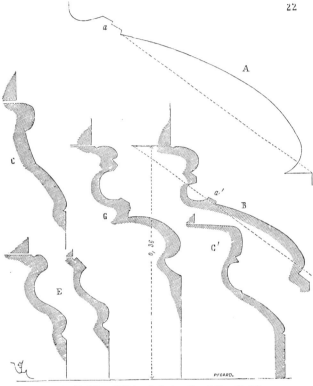

Fig. 22.—Twelfth and Thirteenth Century French Base Mouldings.

southern provinces.   Figure 23 gives at A the section of a
column base from the town hall of Saint-Antonin (Tarn-et-
Garonne) ; the upper torus *a* of this base is fluted horizontally,
and it is easy to perceive that all the mouldings of this base
have a strongly marked Greek character.   The base moulding
B from the church of Déols (Châteauroux) likewise presents, as
do many of the mouldings of this province belonging to the
twelfth century, a Greek base moulding.   The column shafts of
Berry were during this period often turned and scored horizontally, as may be seen at *b*.   These scorings are also found on
column shafts of the period of the Sassanian dynasty, and even
much later, as for instance in the Alhambra of Granada.   I will

CAPITAL FROM THE CHAPTER-HOUSE, VEZELAY.

add here, to complete what relates to column bases, that when the artists of the twelfth century placed circular toruses on a square plinth they were careful to strengthen the projecting angles with *claws*, which abut those angles and perfectly clench the mouldings ; a precaution which the Romans never took, and which certainly belongs to the logical genius of the Greeks, as it does to our own. I allow that the coupling of these names, Athens and Saint-Antonin, Pompeii and Déols, will sound strange to some ears ; but what can I do to help this ? There are the buildings : I may be blamed, if you like, for having looked

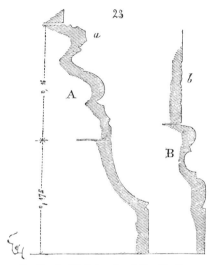

Fig. 23.—Twelfth-Century French Base Mouldings.

at them ; but every one may do the same. We shall have other similar remarks to make ; and the relations between Greek and French art of the twelfth century are not limited to mouldings, they are to be found also in the sculpture. Here, for example (fig. 24), is a capital from the chapter-room of the abbey church of Vezelay (about 1160), which bears more similarity to the Greek than to the Roman style—particularly that which prevailed in Gaul.[1] If a pupil of the *Ecole des Beaux Arts* found this capital in Macedonia or on the shores of the Bosporus, the Academy would certainly pronounce it a very fine one ; but it is so unfortunate as to be *in situ* within a hundred and twenty miles

[1] If the reader will turn to figure 16 in the *Sixth Lecture*, he will be convinced of the striking relations which exist between the sculpture of the capital of Vezelay given here and that of the Golden Gate at Jerusalem. Admitting that this frieze is of the time of Herod the Great, or even of the time of Hadrian, in either case it was certainly executed by Greek artists.

of Paris, and of supporting vaulting that is still intact. It has the misfortune to belong to the twelfth century, and of having been carved by an artist of our own country.

The artists who designed these mouldings and carved capitals in France in the twelfth and thirteenth centuries were certainly but slightly, if at all, acquainted with the monuments of Attica, Ionia, Magna Græcia, or Asia Minor; they were not archæologists; but they reasoned, they had affinities of race with those old civilisations of the western side of Oriental lands; they loved the beautiful, profited by traditions, and perseveringly advanced. They abandoned the Roman structure, which had ceased to suit the customs of the times; they sought a structure harmonising with their requirements, their materials, and their social conditions; and reasoning as the Greeks had reasoned (for there are not two ways of reasoning), they gained, in the execution of details, results analogous to those obtained by the ancient Greeks. Even granting that this sculpture owed its character to an influence originating in the east, it cannot be denied that in the West there is sculpture of all kinds, and in particular very inferior Roman sculpture of the time of the Lower Empire; the French artists at any rate selected their models and selected those which reflected Greek feeling. But, as I said above, after the first years of the thirteenth century, French architecture abandoned that traditional sculpture and frankly adopted the local flora; in this again it reflected the Greek method; it did not copy the model, the example; it started from the same principle of incessantly adopting new elements.

In the state of doubt and uncertainty into which the architecture of our period has fallen,—amid so many equally irrational doctrines—it is necessary to bring a careful criticism to bear on the subject, and to learn what are the principles in virtue of which that art was developed amid the civilisations which preceded our own. From what has just been said, we may conclude that Greek art and Roman art have no essential relationship; that while Roman architecture was suited to a great cosmopolitan people such as the Romans were,—while it was the true expression of that vast civilisation,—it was not the *architecture of artists*, but the architecture of universal Empire; that if Greek architecture was splendid, if we admire and assume that we understand it, we cannot at the same time admire Roman architecture; that to wish to adopt both is to wish to admit at the same time rigorous principles and indifference respecting principles,—*i.e.* to believe and not to believe; that Roman art necessarily sank into decrepitude, because it borrowed forms from every quarter without seeking to bring them into harmony with the principles of its structure; that Greek art furnished, and will furnish as long as the human race occupies the earth, new elements, because it is nothing other than a true application of forms to means and requirements ; that we Western architects, by the logical turn of our mind, are more inclined to proceed like the Greeks than like the Romans ; and that while through one of those reactions which history frequently exhibits, we have fallen back under the domination of the Romans in what regards the arts, we, as did also the Greeks, retain, deep-seated in our minds, the sense of the true in art, ready to allow it to take a new flight as soon as the hand of the latest *barbarians* shall have been withered by contact with the truth.

LECTURE X.

WE must not shrink from recognising the fact that in architecture, shackled as we are by prejudice and traditions, and accustomed to confusion, both ideas and principles are wanting to us. The more our buildings are loaded with details, and the richer they are through the variety of their constituent elements, the more do they betray forgetfulness of great principles and the absence of ideas in the artists who contribute to their erection.

The studios of our architects are full of instructive appliances, books, and drawings, but when called upon to design even the most unimportant edifice, though all material means are in abundance, the artist's intelligence is inert, and refuses to create anything new. His invention languishes under a surfeit of undigested data. Talents, study, and often beautiful execution are conspicuous in many quarters; but rarely an idea, still more rarely the observance of a principle. Our public buildings appear to be bodies destitute of a soul, the relics of a lost civilisation, a language incomprehensible even to those who use it. Is it then to be wondered at if the public remain cold and indifferent in presence of works void of ideas, too often destitute of reason, and which have no other claim to distinction but their cost?

Is the nineteenth century destined to close without possessing an architecture of its own? Will this age, which is so fertile in discoveries, and which displays an energetic vitality, transmit to posterity only imitations or hybrid works, without character, and which it is impossible to class? Is this sterility one of the inevitable consequences of our *social* conditions? Does it result from the influence on the teaching of the art exercised by an effete coterie? and can a coterie, whether it be young or old, acquire such a power in the midst of vital elements? Assuredly not. Why then has not the nineteenth century its architecture? We are building everywhere, and largely; millions are expended in our cities, and yet we can only point here and there to a true and practical application of the very considerable means at our disposal.

Since the Revolution of the last century we have entered on a transitional phase ; we are investigating, searching into the past, and accumulating abundance of materials, while our means and appliances have been increased. What then is wanting to enable us to give an original embodiment and form to so many various elements ? Is it not simply method that is lacking ? In the arts, as in the sciences, the absence of method, whether we are engaged in investigating or in attempting to apply the knowledge we have acquired, occasions an embarrassment and confusion proportional to the increase of our resources ; the abundance becomes an obstruction. Every transitional period however must have a limit ; it must tend towards an aim of which we get a glimpse only when, weary of searching through a chaos of ideas and materials brought from every quarter, we set to work to disentangle certain principles from this disorderly mass,—to develop and apply them by the help of a determinate method. This is the work that devolves upon us, and to which we should devote ourselves with uncompromising persistency— struggling against those deleterious elements which are invariably engendered during all transitional periods, just as miasmas exhale from matter in a state of fermentation.

The arts are diseased ; architecture is dying in the midst of prosperity, notwithstanding the presence of energetic vital principles ; it is dying of excesses and a debilitating régime. The more abundant the stores of our knowledge, the more strength and rectitude of judgment is needed to enable us to make a productive use of them, and the more necessary is it to recur to rigorous principles. The disease from which architectural art suffers dates from a remote period ; it has not been developed in a single day ; we see it increasing from the sixteenth century to our own times ; from the time when, after a very superficial study of the architecture of ancient Rome— certain of whose externals were made objects of imitation—our architects ceased to make the alliance of the form with the requirements and the means of construction the chief consideration. Once out of the way of truth, architecture has been more and more misled into degenerating paths. Endeavouring at the commencement of the century to reproduce the forms of classical antiquity, without taking any trouble to analyse and develop their principles, it has been incessantly hastening to its decay. Then, in the absence of the light which reason alone can furnish, it has endeavoured to connect itself with the Middle Ages and the Renaissance ; but still only superficially adopting certain forms without analysing them or recurring to their causes, seeing nothing but the effects, it has become *Neo-Greek, Neo-Roman, Neo-Gothic* ; it has sought its inspiration in the caprices of the age of Francis i., the pompous style of Louis xiv., and the decadence of the seventeenth century ; it has become the slave of fashion to such a degree, that in the bosom of the *Académie des Beaux Arts,*—that classic domain, as it is esteemed,—we have seen designs made presenting the most grotesque medley of styles, fashions, epochs, and means of construction, but not suggesting the least symptom of originality. The reason is that originality is impossible apart from truth. Originality results from the direct irradiation of truth on an individual mind ; and though the truth be one, the medium which receives has a refraction happily as infinitely varied as humanity itself. So that whatever efforts may have been made in recent times to bring together such a number of styles and influences, and to satisfy all the caprices of the moment, that which strikes us most in all our modern public buildings is their monotony.

There are in architecture—if I may thus express myself—two indispensable modes in which truth must be adhered to. We must be true in respect of the programme, and true in respect of the constructive processes. To be true in respect of the programme is to fulfil exactly, scrupulously, the conditions imposed by the requirements of the case. To be true in respect of the constructive processes is to employ the materials according to their qualities and properties. What are regarded as questions purely belonging to art, symmetry and external form, are only secondary conditions as compared with those dominant principles.

It was all very well for Indians to erect in stone *stoupas* representing piles of wood ; for the Greeks of Asia Minor, the Carians, or the Lycians, to produce in marble monuments simulating wooden shrines ; for the Egyptians to construct temples of enormous stones, whose form was evidently borrowed from structures of reeds or pise : these were traditions, deserving respect, of primitive arts replete with historic interest, and curious, but which it would be ridiculous to imitate. The Dorians and Greeks of Attica had already freed themselves from those swaddling-clothes. We find the Romans erecting substantial public buildings, whose forms are absolutely the expression of the means of construction adopted by them, and which derive their beauty from that frank sincerity of expression. The Romans exhibit a mature growth of intellect ; they are no longer children ; they reason. Our predecessors in the Middle Ages go still further than the Romans in this direction ; they discard even that concrete architecture—the moulded hive of the Romans ; they desire an architecture in which all the appliances for strength are apparent, where every element in the construction originates a form ; they adopt the principle of active resistances ; they introduce equilibrium into the structure ; in fact they are

already impelled by the genius of modern times, which loves to
assign to every individual product or object a distinct function,
though tending to one common end. This continuous and
logically consistent labour of humanity ought to be followed up ;
why then should we abandon it ? Why do we of the nineteenth
century, proceed (and certainly with far less reason) as the
Egyptians proceeded ? and why should we reproduce architectural
forms belonging to another civilisation, or to a comparatively
primitive condition, with materials that are unsuitable to the
reproduction of those forms? What theocratical institution compels us thus to insult common sense, and to repudiate the evident
progress of former ages and the genius of modern social system ?

The nineteenth century, in common with all those periods of
history that have been fertile in great discoveries and favourable
to moral or material progress in certain directions, has thrown
itself with a kind of passionate vehemence into the path of investigation. It introduces the analytical spirit into the study
of the sciences, philosophy, and history. It makes archæology
more than a speculative science ; it undertakes to deduce
practical knowledge from it—perhaps even a great system of instruction for the future. Never could the axiom, "The youngest
are the oldest," have been so justly applied as to the modern
world. In the study of natural phenomena and of philosophy
the spirit of method has already produced remarkable results,
but this spirit of method has not hitherto been applied to
archæological investigations respecting the arts ; materials have
been amassed in great abundance, but the discoveries made have
remained undigested and unfruitful. Yet over this heap of
accumulated materials premature discussions have been raised,
because no understanding had been come to respecting principles.
It is therefore of essential importance to apply a rigorous method
to this knowledge of the arts of the past ; and I do not know
that we can do better in this matter than to abide by the four
principles of Descartes, and which he deemed sufficient, " provided," he remarked, " that I made a firm and constant resolution
not to neglect them in a single instance." The first, he adds,
" was never to receive anything as true which I did not clearly
know to be so, *i.e.* carefully to avoid precipitancy and pre-
possession, and not to include more in my conclusions than what
presented itself so clearly and distinctly to my mind that I had
no reason to doubt it.

" The second, to divide each of the problems I was investigating into as many portions as possible, or as should be requisite
for a complete solution.

" The third, to follow a certain order in my thoughts,
beginning with those objects which are simplest and most easy

to understand, and ascending as by gentle degrees to the knowledge of the most composite,—supposing an order even in the case of those which do not appear naturally consecutive.

" The last, to make such complete enumerations and general reviews in every field of inquiry as that I should be certain of omitting nothing."

No wiser precepts have been uttered, nor any more applicable to the present subject. If we follow these precepts in the study and practice of art, we shall discover an architecture appropriate to our age, or at least we shall prepare the way for those who follow us ; for an art is not made in a day. In fact, if we bring to the study of the arts of the past a spirit of examination sufficiently earnest and enlightened to distinguish the false from the true, and to deduce primordial principles from traditions, we shall in the first place have cleared those arts from the various influences that have successively modified their expression, and we shall succeed in finding those expressions which best accord with immutable principles ; we shall then consider these expressions—or forms, if we prefer the term—as those which are nearest the truth. We shall be able to recognise them as types. If we would advance from archæology to an immediate application of what it places at our disposal, that preparatory clearance is necessary ; it enables us to distinguish that order of study which is purely speculative from that which tends to a practical result.

For instance I ascertain that most of the still existing ancient buildings of Asia Minor only present in stone forms borrowed from timber-work ; I may study these monuments as presenting traditions of considerable interest, but I cannot make a practical use of the result. I see how a race of men transported from a woody country into one destitute of wood has preserved the tradition of its primitive arts ; I ascertain the tradition, but at the same time I perceive that the tradition is contrary to the elementary principles of architectural art. In the same way, if I examine the buildings of Thebes, I find the strangest contradiction between the forms and the means of construction adopted : I see men proceeding to build in stone, and with appliances of prodigious strength, imitations of huts made of reeds and mud. This procedure is extremely curious, it has produced the most surprising results, it may even be very beautiful, but I do not find in it any suggestion applicable amid such a civilisation as ours. It is only when we find ourselves in the country occupied by the precursors of Western civilisation that we begin to meet with races knowing how to bring form into harmony with principles. The Greeks were the first to introduce into the art of architecture the spirit of investigation, logic, and

reasoning, which is superior to tradition. Between the buildings
of Greece and those of India there is an interval as great as
that which separates Plato from Buddha. But while rejecting
Buddha and admiring Plato,—in fact, just because I admire
him,—I would not in the middle of the nineteenth century erect
buildings such as were constructed in his time. The Greeks,
while setting principles above form, and subjecting even form
to principles, point out the way to us ; and the more charmed
we are by observing what a vivid expression the remains of the
Acropolis of Athens present of Athenian civilisation in the time
of Pericles, the less shall we seek to imitate the form of these
remains, since our social condition and public and private habits
differ essentially from the social condition and habits of the contemporaries of Socrates.

In the study of the arts of the past, therefore, we should
observe a clear distinction between a form which is only the
reflection of a tradition, a form adopted without consideration,—
and a form which is the immediate expression of a requirement,
of a certain social condition ; and it is only the study of the
latter that issues in practical advantage,—an advantage not consisting in the imitation of this form, but in the example it affords
of the application of a principle.

Conformably, therefore, to the first principle laid down by
Descartes, as applied to the study of the various arts of former
ages, while on the one hand it is perfectly clear that there is no
reason for imitating in stone a structure of wood or of pise ;
and that consequently I ought to repudiate, as starting from a
false principle, every order of art which, in subservience to mere
traditions, thus allows itself to deviate from truth in its expression, on the other hand I should most attentively consider by
what means certain races of people succeeded in giving a
character to their architecture, while adapting the latter to
their requirements, usages, and the materials at their disposal.
Thus directed, archæological studies should greatly aid us, for
they bring before us as many varieties of form as there have been
differences in civilisation and in the methods employed ; they
render our intellect versatile, and ought to give it an aptitude
for applying, not the forms we see, but the principles that
produced those forms ; so that in fact the study of the arts of the
Greeks, if it be conducted in a spirit of criticism and examination,
leads us to deviate as widely from architectural forms adopted by
that people as our modern civilisation diverges from theirs.

Passing to the second precept, I shall, however, examine
whether among the examples which come successively under my
review certain rules are not apparent that are immutable and
independent both of the social conditions and of the employment

of materials : and the result will show that the harmony of the proportions is in fact established on the basis of certain geometrical formulas, and that these formulas reappear in phases of art apparently very different, as I was able to demonstrate in the last Lecture ; that similar requirements, the necessity of resisting the same destructive agents, and the desire to produce the same visual effects, caused analogous mouldings and outlines to be adopted after the lapse of centuries, and by peoples who had had no acquaintance with each other.   Carrying the investigation to its extreme limits, and continuing to proceed by analysis, I shall show that since the nature of man is one, there is an identity between all the products of his intellect, when the latter allows itself to be guided by truth,—an identity such that certain forms of art always reproduce themselves under the artist's hand ; and that the reason of their thus reappearing is that they are true ; for it is the characteristic of truth to reach similar consequences by very different paths.   I shall also prove that these similar consequences may be very different in appearance as being the result of a series of inferences deduced from different conditions. I will explain myself.

I have at command materials of great size and strength, and have to erect a building which is but small as compared with the dimensions of those materials ; it is but reasonable, therefore, that I should not waste my time in cutting up these materials into small fragments to construct it.   I therefore erect *posts*— vertical supports or columns—on which I place cross-beams, lintels, ceilings.   But massive materials are difficult to extract, to transport, to shape, and to put in place ; I shall, however, employ them for the divisions of openings or for a portico.   But if I have to build a wall behind this portico,—the wall of a *cella* for instance,—I shall procure materials of moderate dimensions, and shall have no difficulty in cutting and placing them.   I built the divisions of my portico with large stones, because I thus secured admirable conditions in point of stability, and avoided thrusts and dislocations ; but I have constructed my wall with small stones because this is an easier and quicker method, and one which affords sufficient solidity.   This wall, however, is pierced by a door; it has corners; I therefore procure large stones to form the jambs of the door, and have some placed vertically at the angles of the wall, so as to keep up and stiffen those parts of the building which are constructed of small materials.   I thus get a building erected strictly in accordance with the simplest laws of statics, and which is accommodated to the conditions imposed on me by the programme and the nature of the materials.

The programme is a different one.   I have, on the contrary, to erect an immense edifice with stones whose dimensions are not larger than those just employed. The problem is not that of covering bays with lintels of two or three yards in length and supporting these lintels and the ceilings at a height of six or eight yards, or of providing a hall of twenty or thirty square yards in area ; but of crossing spaces of ten to fifteen yards, erecting tiers of galleries, and providing several covered spaces,—in short, constructing a large church instead of a Greek temple. It is evident that I must change the whole system of construction ; but I shall still employ monoliths and even lintels : by means of these monoliths I shall give solidity, as the Greeks did, to a structure built of small materials. I shall be able, with the help of these clusters of monoliths, to maintain enormous walls in their vertical plane ; I shall be able to resist the pressure of vaulting and obviate the results of settling.

Instead of lintels of stone and ceilings of timber-work, I shall have to construct vaults. I shall endeavour to find a system of vaulting that most nearly approaches a ceiling, not in point of appearance but in result,—that, namely, which causes the least thrust while bringing the weight of the whole to bear on certain chosen points of support ; and thus proceeding according to the reasoning adopted by the Greek architects, employing the same means and starting from the same principles, I shall ultimately produce structures very different in appearance, because I shall have had very different requirements to satisfy. This however will by no means prevent me from adopting the system of ornamentation and the moulding which the Greeks would have adopted according to position and purpose. I go still further : I observe that the Greeks, in the construction of their temples, endeavoured to shore up the building, so to speak : I observe that they place the larger materials without, and the smaller within ; that they even gave the angle columns an inclination toward the centre of the edifice and the horizontal lines a depression towards the middle, so as to bring all the pressure to bear on the interior. Having an immense edifice to construct, I shall proceed on the same principle ; but as the materials at my command are very weak in proportion to the dimension, it will not be by depressions and slight inclination of piers that I shall be able to counteract the outward thrust of the structure,—I shall have recourse to flying buttresses—abutments—*i.e.* an exterior system of shoring.

Bringing the spirit of method therefore to the study of the parts of such buildings as come under my observation, I shall become aware that principles identically the same produce results very different in appearance, because the conditions which have had to be complied with were different, and that nevertheless in obtaining these diverse results, the genius of man, being unique, has proceeded in the same manner and has adopted the same expression in many of the details.

The third precept explains the necessity of a true or imaginary classification; and in this our author seems to have indicated the nature of the studies of which we must avail ourselves in producing an architecture. In fact, while in the speculative study of archæology there is only one method of classification—the chronological,—it is not so when we are endeavouring to give this study a practical aim. The examples we have collected should in this case be associated according to their several kinds, and the analogous application of immutable principles. We shall thus discover three classes of architecture : wooden architecture, concrete architecture, so well understood by the Romans, and the architecture of jointed stones, carried to perfection by the Greeks. Concrete architecture led to vaulting and all its consequences ; the architecture of jointed stone gave rise to the lintel—statics in their simplest expression. From these last two divisions the Middle Ages succeeded in producing a composite art in which the influence of both is simultaneously manifested ; and this composite art—from the very fact of its endeavouring to reconcile two principles, opposed, or at any rate very alien to each other—has given rise to a new principle of which ancient architecture had been ignorant, that of equilibrium,—a principle which is more applicable than any former one to the various exigencies of our modern social condition.

As to the fourth principle, it only indicates the necessity of collecting the greatest possible amount of data, so that we may know what has been done, and profit by the experience acquired ; for it is of importance that we should not be spending our time in seeking the solution of problems already resolved, and that we should always start from a level already reached. But the multiplicity of such data will be dangerous to the architect, if he has not succeeded in methodically classifying the materials he has collected. There are styles of architecture—the Egyptian, for instance—whose apparent forms do not always accord with the structure. I would not be understood to say that these forms should not be carefully studied, but that in studying them we should observe that they are more suitable to a construction of pise and wood overlaid with stucco than to one consisting of large stones. On the contrary, another style of architecture—Roman architecture under the Empire, for instance,—derives its principal merit, the beauty of its forms, from the perfect harmony that exists between the structure and the appearance ; but the very fact that this is the principal quality of that architecture warns us not to apply its forms to a different order of structure.

From a large collection of examples thus classified it becomes possible to ascertain what are the forms suitable to such or such a structure; we no longer run the risk of getting into that confusion of styles, methods, and forms which renders most of our modern edifices incomprehensible and repulsive. A certain school, weary of the more or less faithful imitations that have been produced of the various styles of architecture anterior to our age, considers it possible to compose a new architecture by selecting from all of them what has appeared good; this is a dangerous error. A *macaronic* style cannot be a new style. Its adoption gives proof of nothing more than dexterity, intelligence, and acquirements of no great profundity; it is never the manifestation of a principle or an idea. Compositions of this kind, even the most successful, remain isolated, sterile works, incapable of being the origin of a new epoch in the arts. Only simple principles are productive; and it may be remarked that the simpler they are the more beautiful and varied are their products. I refer my readers to what was said in the preceding Lecture respecting the organic creation and vertebrate animals. A very simple principle is certainly manifest in the creation of such a reptile as the adder! Yet how many varieties may be traced between the serpent and man! What a number of consequences, always logically deduced, and by a series of scarcely perceptible transitions, occupy the interval between these two beings!—And what is simpler than placing a stone horizontally on two vertical supports? Yet from this so simple principle what a numerous train of deductions were drawn by the Greeks! When the Romans sought for or were otherwise able to discover the principle of the moulded vault—the hive structure—they certainly started from a simple principle; but what combinations did they not obtain by working out this primitive conception? And when the French architects of the twelfth century added to this principle of the concrete vault that of elasticity and equilibrium, what did they not accomplish? Did they not in less than a century reach the extreme limits imposed by the conditions of matter?

We have then three styles of architecture,—the first two setting out from principles alien to each other, and the third adding a new principle to the first two,—which have succeeded in discovering forms rigorously deduced from their respective principles, and leaving definite and characteristic modes of art.

And if we examine the philosophical side of the question, we observe that the Greeks, divided into small republics, chose that style of architecture which best suited their social condition. Relatively few in numbers, considering themselves superior to the rest of the human race, exclusive, composing a kind of select society, and enthusiastic for refinement and beauty of form, they naturally repudiated in architecture all that could tend to vulgarise it. In their eyes grandeur did not consist in the extent or dimensions of a building, but in choiceness of proportions and purity of execution. Thus all their buildings are small if we compare them with those of their neighbours, the Asiatics, but especially those of Imperial Rome.

We observe also that the Romans, impelled by a social idea the very opposite of that of the Greeks,—assimilating the nations to themselves, summoning them to join them, and inducing or compelling them to become Romans,—adopted on their part that style of architecture which best accorded with this cosmopolitan spirit. They seemed to be erecting buildings for the whole human race; and they constructed them by methods which any chance workmen might employ at Cologne or Carthage indifferently.

If the Greeks introduced anything into Roman architecture, it was, as we have often remarked, a dress, not a principle. What did the Western spirit do in France, at Paris,—the centre of European intelligence in the twelfth century? It introduced a modern element amidst the degenerate traditions of the Empire. It took account of mechanical forces, employed materials according to their nature, and only according to their nature; it sought for those laws of equilibrium which were to be substituted for those of inert stability,—the only laws known to the Greeks, or even the Romans. It studied how to economise material and to elevate human labour; with unity in the masses and leading features it admitted variety in the details,—that is, individuality amid regularity,—as it likewise allowed of liberty in the means of execution, with a unity in the conception. Impelled by the genius of innovation, this spirit broke with all traditions and aspired to subjugate the material; it soon sought for the ornamentation with which it embellished its buildings in the flora of the fields, which it carefully studied. It rendered a great ecclesiastical edifice an encyclopædia of knowledge instructing the crowd through the eye. Observing and experimentalising, it accomplished in architecture that which Roger Bacon attempted in the sciences—a veritable revolution. Every new erection was a step aiding it to rise towards the aim of its endeavours, and constantly ascending, it soon reached the limits assigned it by the material elements at its disposal.

What would these artists have done if they had had the materials and the means which we possess? And what could not we do if, instead of playing the dilettante with all the arts without examining their principles, we determined simply to start from the point at which they arrived, and the principles they recognised ? We must not close our eyes to the fact that in architecture we are now submitting to the authority of the ancients as in Philosophy the school of the thirteenth century submitted to the authority of Aristotle without examination, in fact, without a real acquaintance with him. But what said that monk Roger Bacon in 1267 respecting the authority blindly accorded to the master ? Let us hear him :—

" Scarcely half a century ago Aristotle lay under the suspicion of impiety, and was proscribed by the schools. To-day he is exalted to an absolute sovereignty ! What is his claim to this distinction ? He is learned, they say. Be it so, but he did not know everything. He did what was possible in his time, but he did not reach the limit of wisdom. . . . ' But,' say the school, ' we must respect the ancients !' Doubtless ! the ancients are to be respected, and we should show our gratitude to them for having prepared the way ; but we should not forget that the ancients were men, and that more than once they were in error ; in fact, the number of their errors was proportioned to their antiquity, *for the youngest are in reality the oldest :* recent generations ought to surpass their predecessors in intelligence, since they inherit all the labour of the past."[1]

Does not this language exactly apply to the School of our days, which insists on our forgetting all that the Middle Ages have taught us ? Did not the same Roger Bacon, that monk of the thirteenth century, a most worthy rival of the artists of the time, say also in his *Opus tertium*[2] when earnestly inveighing against the scholastic routine ?—

" I call *that* experimental science which is distinct from argumentation ; for the strongest arguments prove nothing as long as their conclusions are not verified by experiment.

" Experimental science does not receive the truth from the hands of any superior sciences ; it is she that is the mistress, and the other sciences are her servants.

" She has the right, in fact, to command all the sciences, since she alone certifies and sanctions the results.

" Experimental science is therefore the queen of the sciences and the goal of all speculation."

And further on :[3] " In every investigation the best possible method must be employed. Now this method consists in studying the parts of a science in their necessary order, giving the first rank to that which should really occupy the first place, putting the easier before the more difficult, the general before the particular, the simple before the compound ; we should also select for our study the most useful subjects, in consideration of the shortness of life ; lastly, we must expound science with all possible clear-

---

[1] *Compendium philosophiæ*, cap. 1. [2] Douai manuscript. [3] Cap. xiii.

ness and definiteness, without any admixture of what is doubtful or obscure. But nothing of this is possible without experimental verification, for we have indeed various methods of gaining knowledge, *i.e.* authority, reasoning, and experimental verification; but *authority has no value if its grounds are not explained;* it does not make us understand, it only makes us believe; it overawes the mind without enlightening it. As to reasoning, we are able to distinguish sophistry from demonstration by *verifying the conclusion experimentally and practically."*

This, then, was the reasoning of those men in the Middle Ages, the builders of those edifices which we in our days sometimes admire, but with which we are so little acquainted. In these lines Roger Bacon sums up the principles of the secular school of architecture that had arisen on the last tradition of Romanesque art—*method, examination, experiment;* his whole system is comprised in these three words.

Let us return to the precepts given by Descartes : "Never to receive anything as true unless it has been evidently recognised as such." If this precept is applicable to Philosophy, it is still more so to an art such as architecture, which rests on laws of matter or laws purely mathematical. *It is true* that a great hall, a very long, wide, and lofty interior, ought to be lighted by windows larger than those which suffice for an ordinary room ; the contrary is false. *It is true* that a portico supported by arcades or columns, is built for the purpose of sheltering persons from rain, sun, and wind ; the relations between the height and width of this portico ought therefore to be such as will afford protection against atmospheric agencies ; the contrary is false. *It is true* that a door ought to be made for the purpose of going into a building or going out of it ; the width of such door ought therefore to be accommodated to the greater or smaller number of persons who have occasion to go in or out ; but however dense a crowd may be, the persons composing it are always under seven feet in height ; or, supposing them to carry lances, banners, canopies, or flags, even with these accessories, they will not require a height of much more than five or six yards ; to make a door five yards wide and ten high is therefore absurd. *It is true* that a column is a support,—not a decoration, like a frieze or an arabesque ; if then you have no occasion for columns, I cannot understand why you furnish your façades with them. *It is true* that a cornice is intended to keep the water from the face of the wall : if therefore you put a projecting cornice in an interior, I cannot but say that it is unmeaning. *It is true* that a staircase is necessary for reaching the upper stories of a building : that this staircase is not a place of rest but of passage, and that if you give it a relative importance out of proportion to the apartments to which it leads, you may produce a magnificent flight of steps, but you commit an absurdity. *It is true* that the thing which supports should be proportioned to the thing supported, and that if you build a stone wall or pier two or three yards in thickness to carry floors that would be easily supported by a wall one yard in thickness, you produce a work that cannot be justified by reason, which satisfies neither my eyes nor my understanding, and wastes costly materials. *It is true* that vaulting ought to be maintained by buttresses, whatever form you give them; but it is a falsity to introduce salient pilasters, engaged columns, and buttresses, if there are no thrusts to which resistance must be opposed. It is needless, I think, to continue this parallelism. Following this simple method of reasoning, of which any one may see the force without being versed in architectural art, and passing in review the styles of architecture adopted by the ancients, in the Middle Ages, and in modern times, it will be easy to assign them their true value. We shall see that the Greeks (taking into account their social condition and the climate in which their buildings were erected) remained faithful to those primitive principles which originated in mere good sense; that the Romans often deviated from them; that the lay architects of the French school of the twelfth and thirteenth centuries rigorously observed them and that we have almost abandoned them. We may therefore class the various styles of architecture and the studies relating to the monuments produced by them according to that first precept, which is based on the true expression of the requirements and necessities of the structure. Thus a house at Pompeii of insignificant dimensions, the gate of a city, a fountain or a well, may sometimes possess a value superior in point of art to that of a palace. Being thus able to separate the true from the false, we shall succeed after mature examination in recognising the various modes of expressing it employed by our predecessors: for in architecture truth is not sufficient to render a work excellent; it is necessary to give to truth a beautiful or at least appropriate form,—to know how to render it clear, and to express it felicitously;—indeed, in the arts, although we make use of the most rigorous and logical reasoning, we often continue obscure and unpleasing, we may, in fact, produce what is ugly. But while conceptions based on the soundest reason sometimes produce only repulsive works, true beauty has never been attainable without the concurrence of those invariable laws which are based on reason. To every work that is absolutely beautiful there will be always found to correspond a principle rigorously logical.

Having first directed our course of study in conformity with this primary principle, let us pass to the second: "to divide,"

says Descartes, "each of the problems I was investigating into as many portions as possible, or as should be requisite for a complete solution." We remain here still on the domain of speculative study ; we are engaged with analysis pushed to its extreme limits. In fact, if we examine ancient buildings, we find them to be complete, finished, composite works. We are obliged, if we would understand them in all their parts, to proceed in an order the reverse of that in which they were produced. Their author proceeded from his primitive conception to the execution in its final form,—from the programme and the means at disposal to the result ; *we* must start from the ultimate result and ascertain successively the design and the programme and means of execution ; we must dissect the edifice, as it were, and verify the more or less complete relations that exist between that apparent result which first engages our attention and the hidden methods and reasons that have determined its form. This second part of our studies, which is long, irksome and arduous, is the best exercise we could engage in if we would learn to design, to create. To arrive at synthesis we must necessarily pass through analysis. And the more complicated a civilisation is, the more concealed from view are the sources to which the buildings it erects owe their conception and execution, and which contribute also to secure their permanence. While the analysis of a Greek temple requires only a few days, it is not the same with the hall of one of the Roman Thermæ, or, *à fortiori*, one of our French cathedrals ; and since our modern civilisation is very complicated, while it is desirable to commence our studies with the analysis of the simplest works of classical antiquity, we must not stop there ; we must certainly go on to analyse more complete works, and learn how in former ages architects succeeded in solving problems more and more extensive in their bearing, encumbered with details and replete with difficulties ; and in raising buildings possessing, if I may so express myself, an organism much more delicate, and especially more complicated.

To insist on limiting the studies by which architects are to be trained, to certain monuments of classical antiquity which have not even come down to us in their complete state, or to more or less successful imitations of those monuments, is not the way to obtain what is asked for everywhere—an architecture of the nineteenth century. It is better to take account of that long series of efforts which have developed new principles and methods, and to consider all human labour as a chain whose links are connected in logical order.

The third precept introduces us to the application of principles, for its import is that we should " follow a certain order in our thoughts, beginning with those objects which are simplest and most easy to understand, and ascending as by gentle degrees to the knowledge of the most composite,—supposing an order even in the case of those which do not appear naturally consecutive." In fact, if by analysis we have proceeded from the compound to the simple—from the complete work—the apparent result,— to the means and causes that have produced this result,—it will become easier, when we are desirous of designing in our turn, to proceed in order, and to give precedence to fundamental con- siderations with a view to reach the consequences that will follow from them. The fundamental points of consideration in architec- ture,—those which decide everything else,—are none other than the programme and the material means of execution. The pro- gramme is only the statement of the requirements. As regards the means of execution, they are various ; they may be restricted or extensive ; whatever they are, we must know them and take account of them : the same programme may be complied with by the use of very different means, according to the locality, the materials, and the resources at our disposal.—Great Assembly Halls to hold two thousand persons have to be built in different localities. But at A we are furnished with materials of superior quality ; considerable sums are placed at our disposal ; we have durable stone—marble or granite. At B we can procure only brick and wood ; our resources are at a minimum. Shall we give these two halls the same superficial extent ? Evidently we must, since we have to accommodate two thousand persons at both A and B. Shall we make them alike in appearance ? Certainly not, since the means at our disposal at B are not the same as we have at A. While thus complying with the same programme we shall have to adopt two very different methods of architecture, for if, having only brick and deal, we simulate a structure of stone or marble, by means of stucco and paint, we make a very sorry use of art. Compliance with a programme and the determining of a plan of structure are not enough to produce a work of art ; a form is also requisite. The pro- gramme as well as the structure will exert an influence on the form ; but while scrupulously respecting the first, and paying attention to the second, we may nevertheless adopt very diverse forms. And which is the one most appropriate to our civilisation ? Probably that which is most supple and pliable ; that which will lend itself the most readily to the infinitely varied details of our excessively complicated life. Where shall we find, if not models, at least precedents of such a form as will answer to all our exigencies ? Will it be in Greek antiquity ? Or perchance in Roman antiquity ? Rather in the latter. But it may be asked, How can we make Roman antiquity our starting-point if we

employ iron ?   Should we not rather choose those works of the
lay school of the Middle Ages ?   Had not its artists a presentiment of the resources furnished us by manufactures, mechanical
science, and the abundant facilities of transport to great distances ?   Are there not, for example, the closest relations
between the recently constructed Library of St. Geneviève and
the great Salle du Palais in Paris, which was burnt at the beginning of the seventeenth century ?   Has the classical character
that has been given to the modern hall added anything to the
merit of the work ?   Has this not rather contributed to injure
its unity by a mingling of elements foreign to each other, and
combining forms originating in two opposite principles ?

Applying the third precept of Descartes in designing, the
programme being satisfied and the structure determined, what
have we to do in proceeding from the simple to the compound ?
1st, We must know at the outset the nature of the materials
to be employed; 2dly, We must give these materials the
function and strength required for the result, and the forms
which most exactly express that function and strength; 3dly,
We must adopt a principle of unity and harmony in this expression,—that is, a scale, a system of proportion, a style of ornamentation related to the destination of the structure and having a
definite signification, as also the variety indicated by the diverse
nature of the requirements to be complied with.

What then is implied in an acquaintance with the materials
to be employed in a building ?   Is it to know whether the stone
will resist frost or not?   whether it will bear a certain pressure or not ?   Is it to be acquainted with the fact that
wrought-iron will endure considerable tension, while cast-iron is
rigid ?   Yes, certainly ; but it implies more than this.   It is to
know the effect that can be produced by the use of these materials, according to certain conditions ; a stone placed on end, or a
monostyle, has a quite different meaning for the eye from that
of an erection in courses ; a casing of great slabs does not produce the effect of a facing of small flat bedded stones.   An arch
consisting of extradossed stones has an appearance quite different
from that of an arch of notched voussoirs.   A jointed lintel has
not the strong look of a monolithic lintel.   An archivolt of similar section built in several concentric rings, possesses other
qualities and produces a different impression from those resulting from one built in a single ring.   A perfectly close-jointed
masonry, such as that of the Greeks and Romans, suits forms
that cannot be made consistent with a masonry between whose
joints there is a layer of mortar.   Three stones with mouldings,
forming a door or window casing, environed by a plastered wall,
answer to a necessity, and consequently exhibit an architectural

form that is comprehensible and has a good effect ; but a casing
jointed in horizontal courses shocks reason and the eye.   In the
same way stone-jointing, which does not coincide with the various architectural members, whose beds are not placed immediately above and below the string-courses, socles, base-mouldings,
etc., destroys the effect which a design should produce.   To give
the materials the function and strength suitable to their purpose,
and the forms that most exactly express this function and
strength, is one of the most important points in design.   We
can give a special style, a distinction, to the simplest structure,
if we know how to employ the materials exactly in accordance
with their purpose.   A simple band of stone, placed in a wall,
thus becomes an expression of art.   A column, a pillar, shaped
with due regard to the resisting power of the material in relation
to what it has to sustain, cannot fail to satisfy the eye.   Similarly a capital whose contour is designed with due regard to that
which surmounts it and the function it performs, always assumes
a beautiful form.   A corbelling which plainly shows its purpose,
will always produce a better effect than an undecided form which
hides the strength needed by this architectural member.   The
adoption of a principle of unity and harmony in the expression
of the various requirements indicated in a programme,—that is
to say, a scale, a system of proportion, a style of ornamentation
in harmony with the purpose of this structure, which has a
meaning, and which also displays the variety proper to the
diverse nature of the requirements to be satisfied,—this is the
point in architectural design in which the intelligence of the
artist develops itself.   When the conditions of the programme
have been satisfied, and the system of construction has been
determined, when we have been able to apply in our methods
a sound process of reasoning, so as to do neither too much nor
too little, and to assign to each class of materials the function,
appearance, or, if we choose to call it so, the form suitable to its
properties and use, we must search for and discover those principles of unity and harmony which should govern every work of
art.   This is the rock on which nearly all our architects, since
the sixteenth century, have made shipwreck ; they have either
sacrificed the requirements, and the judicious employment of the
materials to a form that is symmetrical without being rational, or
they have not known how to give an appearance of unity, a *one-
ness* of conception to the buildings, while satisfying the programme and employing the material judiciously.   But since that
epoch the first of these defects has certainly been the most frequent, and the one against which architects have been least on their
guard.   The architecture of the close of the seventeenth century,
which has been extolled to excess, and which is still substantially

in the ascendant in art, furnishes us with the most exaggerated specimens of this deplorable system. In no age or country has a fanaticism, as I may call it, for symmetry—for what was then called *ordonnance*—been carried to such an extent as in the reign of Louis XIV. It was the mania of the sovereign, and every one gave way to it; he had moreover found a man, a second-rate architect and a vain creature, usurping the name of artist, who humoured all his whims, flattering, on every occasion, his taste for a pompous uniformity, and who, consulting his own interest, thus stifled the last vestiges of originality still remaining in our French architecture.[1] One of the most striking examples of this departure from good sense, and consequently from good taste, is the Château de Clagny, built by Hardouin Mansard (the second-rate artist of whom we were just speaking)—a château which

---

[1] A curious anecdote related by Saint-Simon supplies a noteworthy illustration. It will show us the nature of Louis the Fourteenth's taste in architecture. ". . . The King was greatly interested in his buildings, and he had a sure eye for exactness, proportion, and symmetry, but without corresponding taste, as we shall see. This Château (Trianon) had scarcely begun to rise above the ground, when the King perceived a defect in a window that had just been completed, on the line of the ground floor. Louvois, who was naturally of a surly disposition, and who had been, moreover, so spoiled by his master as to resent any censure on his part, maintained most positively that the window was all right. The King turned away and went to another part of the building.

"Next day he met with Le Nôtre, a good architect, but most renowned for the taste displayed in the gardens which he has begun to introduce into France, and which he has carried to the highest pitch of perfection. The King asked him if he had been at Trianon. He said he had not. The King explained to him what had offended him, and told him to go there. The next day he asked the same question and received the same answer: the day following also: in fact the King perceived that he dared not run the risk of discovering that he was wrong, or of finding fault with Louvois. He was angry, and ordered him to present himself the next day at Trianon when he should be there, and when Louvois too should be present: there was no possibility of escape.

"The next day the King met them at Trianon. The window was talked about. Louvois kept to his assertion: Le Nôtre said not a word. At last the King ordered him to take the line, and measure, and report the result. While he was thus occupied, Louvois, furious at this scrutiny, was giving full vent to his anger, and sharply maintaining that this window was exactly like the rest. The King was silently awaiting the result, but he was vexed. When the examination had been quite completed, he asked Le Nôtre what he had ascertained, and Le Nôtre began to stammer out a reply. The King lost his temper and commanded him to give a direct answer. Then Le Nôtre confessed that the King was right, and said that he had discovered a defect. He had no sooner finished when the King, turning to Louvois, said to him that his obstinacy was intolerable, and that had he himself not been persistent, the building would have been spoiled, and all would have to be taken down as soon as it was finished. In a word, he rated him soundly. Louvois, exasperated at this censure, of which the courtiers, workmen, and valets had been witnesses, returned home furious. He found there Saint-Pouange, Villacerf, the Chevalier de Nogent, the two Tilladets, and some others of his intimate friends, who were greatly alarmed to see him in this condition. 'It is all over with me,' said he, 'I am ruined with the King; considering how he has treated me about a mere window, I have no resource but a war, which may turn his attention away from his buildings, and may render me necessary to him, and by —— he shall have it! In fact, a few months afterwards he kept his word, and in spite of the King and the other powers, he rendered it general. It ruined France at home and did not extend her domain without, in spite of the prosperity of her arms; on the contrary, it was productive of shameful results."

I am willing to admit that Saint-Simon is not a very reliable witness, that he has no liking for Louis XIV., and that this window was not the primary cause of the war that was terminated by the Peace of Ryswick, but the anecdote is not the less substantially characteristic.

in Louis the Fourteenth's reign was esteemed a masterpiece. It must be allowed that the programme is good, and the arrangement pleasing, but how greatly has the architect perverted that programme to clothe it with a symmetrical architecture ! Thus the great gallery of the right wing presents, outside, the same features as the left wing, which contains only bedrooms and closets. The windows overlooking the court, designed to light wardrobes, are identical in appearance with those made in the building at the back, to light state-rooms. The façade of the chapel is a repetition of the façade of the bath-room, arranged as a pendant, and to complete the absurdity, the orangery is a copy of the wing opposite which contains only servants' rooms. The programme is satisfied certainly, but with what peculiar concessions to symmetry,—to what was then called the dignity of the *ordonnance*. On the first floor the defects are still more striking, and the monumental style of the architecture inconveniences all the domestic arrangements. The staircases concealed in the mass of the building are small, ill-lighted, and inconvenient ; the great hall of the central building absolutely breaks the communication, on the level, between the two wings ; partitions intersect windows, and pilasters are met with where there are no interior divisions. I take this château as a specimen ; but the greater part of the princely residences of that date are no better : everywhere we find the arrangements dictated by the requirements completely out of harmony with the architectural appearance. Certainly neither the Greeks nor the Romans, who are extolled as excellent architects, any more than the men of the Middle Ages, proceeded in this fashion. The *villæ* of the ancients and the French châteaux down to the sixteenth century, are a proof of this. That aspect of unity which has obtained in architectural works since the sixteenth century has been secured only by contravening the programmes and the methods of construction ; or if occasionally there has been an endeavour on the part of architects to free themselves from the blind tyranny of symmetry, they have readily fallen into a kind of contempt for form ; and absolute and irrational rules have been replaced by the absence of all rule ; for, while the principles they adopted were incapable of delivering art from this tyranny, they were equally at fault when there was an attempt to create something new : those who know not how to defend themselves against a power which exercises an unreasonable dominion over them cannot be qualified to govern themselves. In modern architecture, therefore, unity means only uniformity ; and when there has been an attempt to avoid the latter, nothing but disorder has resulted. Nevertheless—I repeat it—the ancients, as also the mediæval artists, subjected their works to principles of unity without ever sinking into uniformity. Each building, however little it may differ as regards the programme and means of construction, has a physiognomy peculiar to itself, although we easily recognise by inspecting its general features and its minutest details, that it belongs to such or such a period. If archæological studies afforded no other result than that of enabling us to lay our finger on the logical forms that belong to each style of architecture in the past, from that of Greek antiquity down to the Renaissance, they would render us a considerable service at a time when we are in the habit of bringing together forms that are alien to each other according to the fashion or caprice of the moment.

"This principle of unity and harmony in the expression of the various requirements indicated in a programme" is therefore neither symmetry nor uniformity; still less is it an undigested medley of various styles and forms of which it is impossible to give a rational explanation, even if such a medley were skilfully composed : it is in the first place a rigorous observation of the scale. But what is the scale? It is the relation of all the parts to unity. The Greeks adopted as their scale, not an absolute, but a relative unity,—what is called the *module;* this becomes evident in studying their temples ; for it is certain that in their private dwellings the Greeks kept in view the absolute scale, which is the human stature. But regarding it as relative, the scale, by the very fact that it was the module,—that is, a component unity,—established a harmonious relation between the parts and the whole in every building.[1] The Greek temple on the large scale is simply the small one viewed through a magnifying glass. The parts and the whole, in the smaller as in the larger, present the same harmonious relations ; a perfectly logical method when the *order* alone constituted the building. We find the Romans, who had to satisfy programmes much more extensive and complicated than those of the Greeks, adopting in their buildings the absolute scale, that is, an invariable unity ; only instead of taking the human stature for this invariable unity, it is an *ordonnance* with which they start. In their large edifices there is always a small order which serves as a scale, and gives an idea of the real dimension of the whole. Often,—in the exterior of the Thermæ of Diocletian at Rome, for example,— the small order has really no other function than furnishing a point of comparison to enable the spectator to appreciate the grandeur of the masses. The niches occupied by statues, and which are seen in profusion on the exterior and interior walls of

---

[1] On this head I may perhaps be allowed to refer to the article ÉCHELLE in the *Dictionnaire raisonné de l'architecture française,* an article in which I have thought it well to institute a parallel between the Classical system and that of the Middle Ages.

their buildings, are not a mere decoration; the adoption of this detail involves an absolute scale intended to suggest the real dimensions of the edifice.

With the Byzantine architects the column is made the scale, whatever may be otherwise the size of the edifice; the column, with slight variation, preserves certain recognised dimensions, and thus serves as a constant point of comparison, enabling us to appreciate the volume of the structural masses and the importance of the voids. With the mediæval architects of France the only scale admitted is man; all the points of the building have reference to his stature—as has been sufficiently demonstrated elsewhere[1]—and from this principle necessarily springs the unity of the whole; it has also the advantage of presenting to the eye the real dimensions of the building, since the point of comparison is man himself.

If, while adopting the principle of the human scale, we employ a system of geometrical proportions, as the architects of Antiquity and those of the Middle Ages[2] evidently did, we unite two elements of design which compel us to remain true as regards the expression of dimension, and to establish harmonious relations between all the parts. We have here, therefore, an advance on the system of the Greeks, which had only employed the module and not the invariable scale. Why, then, should we deprive ourselves of this resource which we owe to the genius of the mediæval artists?

In the best periods of Classic art, the ornamentation, which forms an important part of architectural design, was never anything more than the embellishment of the body after the latter had been completely formed. Now, the ancients employed two modes of ornamentation. The one consisted in not contravening the form adopted, but clothing it with a kind of drapery more or less rich: this was the system employed by the Egyptians, among whom the ornamentation, properly so called (statuary excepted) never presented a projecting outline,—a relief,—but contented itself with enveloping the geometric form as would an embroidered stuff, a diapered covering. The other, on the contrary, was, as it were, independent of the architectural form; it was attached or applied to it, modifying by its projections the particular shape of that form. It was then no longer a drapery spread over the form; it consisted of flowers, leaves, ornaments in relief, designs borrowed from the vegetable and animal kingdoms. The Greeks, who derived much from the Egyptians and the Asiatic populations among whom architectural decoration was

---

[1] See the article by M. Lassus in the *Annales Archéologiques*, vol. ii.; *De l'art et de l'archéologie*, and the article mentioned above in the *Dictionnaire raisonné de l'architecture française*. [2] See the preceding Lecture.

little more than draping, began by drawing their inspiration from
these examples; but their judgment, so correct in matters of art,
soon made them feel that this kind of ornamentation, however
subordinated to the architectural form, tended to contravene it,
and to destroy its character; they therefore soon abandoned this
method, and employed sculptured ornamentation only as an
accessory *attached* to the form, independent of it, and leaving
it apparent in all its purity. And with what exceeding sobriety
they used sculptured ornamentation! We observe rows of pearls,
of eggs, and of *feuilles-d'eau* running horizontally along some of
the members of a cornice; sometimes metal laid on, bas-reliefs
enclosed within the rigid lines of the architecture; and when,
later on, they designed,—*e.g.* the Corinthian capital,—it was a
corbel which they enveloped with stalks of acanthus, angelica, or
fennel. This system of *engrafted* ornaments naturally com-
mended itself to the love of display characteristic of the Romans;
and they pushed it to excess, in fact to such a degree as to
conceal the architectural form beneath the superabundance of
foliage, garlands, arabesques, and symbolic decorations. The
Byzantine artists made a compromise between the two systems,
but with an evident leaning towards the ornamentation which
enveloped the form without distorting it. Asiatic influences are
profoundly manifest in their works, and still more evidently in
what is called Arab Architecture does the principle of draping
again obtain. We see it abandoned in France towards the end
of the twelfth century. At that time we find sculptured ornamentation attached to the architectural features as if it were
nailed on; and it is wholly derived from the local flora. In no
case, however, does it contravene the architectural form; on the
contrary, it helps to bring it out,—a result obviously attested
by an examination of the interior pillars of the Cathedral of
Paris. In no architecture, Greek included, is ornamentation
added to the form better allied with it; far from distorting it,
it lends it a vigorous aid.

The attempt to reconcile the two systems just described, in
architectural design,—that is, embroidering the architectural
form in one part and attaching ornaments in another,—is a sin
against unity; it is rendering the two systems mutually injurious.

"In the last place," says Descartes, "to make everywhere
enumerations so complete and reviews so comprehensive that I
may be sure of having omitted nothing." This precept is applicable to studies generally, but still more to the case of architectural design; for it is in the consideration of the programme, of
the requirements to be met and of the means supplied that it is
desirable to undertake those "so comprehensive reviews." It is
not enough to have succeeded in conveniently disposing the

services of a public building or a private dwelling; to have succeeded in giving these arrangements the aspect befitting each of them; there must be a connection between the parts: there must be a dominant idea in this assemblage of services; the materials must be judiciously employed, according to the qualities; there must be no excess on the side of strength or slightness; the materials used must indicate their function by the form we give them; stone must appear as stone, iron as iron, wood as wood; and these substances, while assuming forms suitable to their nature, must be in mutual harmony. This was easy for the Romans, when they merely built with rubble-work, with brick and marble facings; it is very difficult for us, who have to make use of materials which possess different and even opposite qualities, and to which must be given the appearance befitting these various qualities. "The so complete enumerations" of what has been done before our time, especially by the mediæval architects, are therefore useful if we would advance and not fall below the works of our predecessors; for, I say once more, it would seem as if those men had a presentiment of the appliances which our age affords. There is in the works of our French mediæval architects of the secular school, at the time of its first development, such complete cohesion, so close a connection between the requirements, the means, and the architectural form; there is such an abundance of resources provided for the solution of the numerous difficulties inherent in the complicated requirements of our civilisation, that nowhere else could we find a precedent more fitted to facilitate the task we have to perform. To attempt in the present day to find in the good architecture of Greek or even Roman antiquity anything more than valuable instruction in a few very simple principles applied with inflexible logic; to attempt to copy, imitate, or even to get ideas from the forms given by the expression of those principles, is gratuitously to involve ourselves in inconsistencies the more glaring as our requirements become more complicated and our resources more extensive. During the seventeenth century, so great was the enthusiasm for Roman architecture that every imaginable inconvenience was put up with for the sake of being Roman. That Roman art might not be trammelled but have its free scope, people were most sincerely willing to be made uncomfortable. However unreflecting this enthusiasm may have been, and however mediocre its expression, it was a belief, and is worthy of respect; but it cannot be disputed that there is now more scepticism in reference to art than was the case in the time of Louis the Fourteenth, and that no one among ourselves has sufficient faith in Greek or Roman architecture to induce him to sacrifice to it the least particle of comfort or the most trifling convenience.

Of what use then to us are those incessantly copied, and moreover badly copied, Classic forms?   What business have we with them?   They embarrass us artists; they have not the adaptability demanded by modern requirements; they are very expensive; they have very little interest for the public; they cut the strangest figure amid certain modern arrangements which we are obliged to adopt; they have the disadvantage of perpetually contravening our habits and methods of building.   Why then this persistence in retaining them, or rather in so misapplying them? Whom are we trying to please in thus expending immense sums in reproducing forms of which no rational explanation can be given?   The public?   The public does not appreciate them, and scarcely troubles itself about them.   Is it some twenty persons in Paris?   This is paying dearly for the pleasure of a few.   Is it done from respect for art?   But what art?   A falsified, distorted art, reduced to the condition of a language that no one understands and that is no longer subject to its own rules.   That from respect for art—in order to preserve for the world a type of eternal beauty, the original being mutilated and destroyed,—we should erect with the utmost care in Paris, on Montmartre, a facsimile, in marble, of the Parthenon, built exactly as the Parthenon is,—this I can comprehend; it comes under the category of the museum,—the perpetuation of an ancient text.   But to stick up Greek Doric columns on the first story of a railway station, engaged between Roman arches,—all pointed with mortar or plaster of Paris, and built of soft stone, with jointed lintels: where, I ask, is the reason, the use, the sense, the object of so strange a proceeding?   Have we not here rather a sign of contempt than of respect for art?   Who would be gratified if we were to go and engrave lines from Homer on the walls of a warehouse?

We shall not have an architecture until we thoroughly make up our minds to be consistent,—to appreciate the works of the past at their relative worth, and "make everywhere enumerations so complete and reviews so comprehensive that we may be sure of having omitted nothing;" when we have good and substantial reasons to oppose to the fancies of amateurs; for good sense has always prevailed in the long-run.

Let us therefore thoroughly examine our methods and the customary forms of our architecture; let us compare them with the methods and forms of Classical architecture, and see whether we have not gone astray,—whether everything has not to be commenced anew,—if we would discover that Architecture of our time which is so loudly called for even by those who deprive us of the only means by which it could be produced.

I say nothing of Greek architecture,—some of whose features

may have been taken indiscriminately and applied without definite purpose to our modern edifices, which have no affinity with those of the Greeks,—and come to the architecture of the Roman Empire,—the only one that has exercised any serious influence on the designs of our buildings since the seventeenth century, and the only one which in certain special cases can afford us practical examples. When I analyse a Roman building, such as the Coliseum, the Thermæ, the palaces, the theatres, what first strikes me is the strong and rationally conceived structure, designed by thoroughly practical men. Now of what does this structure consist? Of masses of rubble-work forming a perfectly homogeneous concrete body, in front of which, and sometimes below them,—in the Coliseum for instance,—a construction of dressed and jointed stonework. In this case the stonework serves as a casing, and often furnishes supports to the main structure, the real core of the edifice. But while the rubble-work, the masonry of gravel, brick, or rough stones, is firmly united by an excellent mortar, not a particle of lime is to be found between the jointed stones. Roman building therefore exhibits two quite distinct methods of building : one derived from construction in pise, which presents as it were a series of excavations in a mass of tufa; the other enveloping this cellular body and derived from the Etruscan and Greek jointed stone building. Little artistic though the Romans were, they never confounded the two systems; they coupled them,—united them ; but invariably left to each its appropriate character. The Coliseum is only a concretion of cells in rubble-work, sustained, enveloped, and covered with masonry of dressed stone, close-fitting and set without appearance of mortar. These supports and this envelope of stone takes forms which are appropriate to dressed stone, while the rubble-work affects forms suitable to a casting.

This mixed system was not always adopted. Often, as for instance in the Thermæ of Diocletian and of Antoninus Caracalla, and in the Basilica of Constantine at Rome, the entire mass is of rubble-work, and only cased with brick ;—it is a single block variously hollowed, which the architect covered (without regard to the construction) with slabs of marble, painted stucco, and mosaics. If in some cases solid hewn materials indicate a structure and really form a substantial part of the building, they are monolithic columns of granite or marble and entablatures of marble firmly built in beneath the springing of the vaulting, appearing to give solidity, and in fact giving rigidity to these rough and inert masses of rubble-work. But while the Romans gave a section of eight superficial yards to a rubble-built pier of a great vaulted hall, and while they also strengthened and shored that pier, by means of the granite column placed against it, they would not have been so stupid as to give the same section to that pier had they built it of wrought stone; and they would not have added to that pier of wrought stone a monolithic column of granite to shore it, since, being formed of courses laid close-jointed, no settlement was to be feared. These Romans, who possessed the financial resources of the known world, never incurred useless expense, never lavished materials in pure waste, and made a meritorious use of those they did employ. If they built a Basilica covered with a timber roof they would erect mono-lithic columns of granite on marble bases, and on these columns they would place capitals and lintels of marble; but they would not waste their time or their money in building on this under colonnade a wall of wrought stones; forming relieving arches of brick over the lintels, they would raise the wall with unwrought stones or bricks and coat it inside and out either with slabs of marble or with stucco. If neither marble nor hard stone had been at their command, they would have adopted another plan; either they would have constructed a basilica without aisles, or, on the other hand, instead of columns they would have erected square piers of brick or rubble-stones, and would have crowned them with arches likewise of brick.

It cannot be disputed that Roman architecture derives its principal merit from this judicious employment of materials; it invariably displays power and intelligence; and the imposing character of its ruins and the profound impression they leave on the mind, are due as much to sound reasoning as to grandeur of conception on the part of the builders.

The sixteenth century undeniably produced some charm-ing fancies; the architecture of Louis xiv. is not wanting either in majesty or grandeur; but it is not by reverting to the art of that time or its expression, that we can succeed in con-stituting an architecture of the nineteenth century. If we would produce anything new in art, we must pay regard solely to principles, and classify the works of the past according to a rigorous method, so as to appreciate each at its relative worth; we must therefore make ourselves acquainted, and thoroughly acquainted, with those works of the past, and study them without either exclusive preference or prejudice; we must lay aside once for all those prepossessions of the school which are ruining art among us, for the benefit of a coterie which endeavours to maintain its predominance by exacting a blind submission to dogmas which it does not even explain. I am well aware that in the course of time we cannot fail to overcome these inert obstacles which oppose the advance of knowledge and the judicious and impartial analysis of the past; but during the last quarter of a century how many young artists have we not seen losing precious years in efforts without purpose or practical results! and if some few more pliant, more fortunate, or more favoured than the rest have attained a high position, what have they produced? Only pale imitations or confused compilations of reminiscences, masking poverty of invention, and absence of idea beneath a profusion of details. And, as the total result for the public, inconvenient edifices, in which the requirements are not expressed nor even provided for; which respond neither to its intelligence nor its tastes; an enormous outlay which sometimes surprises but never impresses it.

We Frenchmen have our defects; but we have also some good qualities; we are logically minded and practical, with a passionate fondness for variety. Our quasi-official architecture is absolutely illogical, utterly unpractical, and patronises that uniformity which is supposed to be one of the elements of beauty. It would seem as if, in architecture, the grave Minerva had given place to the goddess of *Ennui*, and that in order to be truly classic we must sacrifice to that pallid divinity. The façades of our buildings, symmetrical in despite of the requirements, reproduce hundreds of times the same columns with the same capital, the same window with the same architrave, the same arcade, and the same frieze for nearly a mile in length.

I allow that the architect finds this an advantage; that the idler gazes with wonder at this persistent repetition of one model; but it cannot be denied that the public—the great active and intelligent public which fills our streets and places of resort—wearies of passing these miles of monotonous architecture, and sighs for some incident to occur amid these, to its thinking, excessive classical perfections. Observe, moreover, that nothing was more picturesque or more diversified than the collection of buildings presented by a town in classic times, among the Greeks and even among the Romans; and that among ourselves during the Middle Ages and the Renaissance, the taste for variety—for the unexpected—was gratified at every step. It is only since the reign of Louis XIV. that this wearisome and monotonous system has been substituted for those elder traditions, under the pretext of magnificence. Now if magnificence was in place under the somewhat fastidious régime established by *le grand roi*, it has no affinity with our customs in the nineteenth century,—and most certainly none with our tastes. We no longer wear huge perukes, and we do not ornament our pantaloons with ruffs of Alençon lace. We have customs dictated by comfort and a sanitary régime, public and private, that do not harmonise with the pompousness, the irrational pretension, the architectural forms borrowed without rhyme or reason from other periods, that are displayed in our palaces and mansions.

If we want to have an architecture of our own time, let us first provide that the architecture shall be ours, and not seek everywhere else than in the bosom of our own social state for its forms and arrangements. That our architects should be acquainted with the best examples of what has been done before us, and in analogous conditions, is highly desirable, provided they unite with this knowledge a good method and a critical spirit. That they should know how the arts of former times faithfully reflected the social conditions amid which they were developed is also most desirable, provided that this knowledge does not lead to an unconsidered imitation of forms that are often foreign to our usages. But that, under pretext of maintaining such or such a doctrine, or perhaps merely for the sake of not troubling the repose of some twenty individuals, we fail to deduce the practical results from those studies which could be gained by paying regard to principles rather than to forms, is reprehensible. The architect must not only be well informed, but must make use of his knowledge, and must derive something from his own powers; he must determine to ignore the commonplace notions which, with a persistence worthy of a nobler cause, have for nearly two centuries been promulgated respecting architectural art.

The architecture we desiderate must take account of the ideas of progress proper to the age,—subjecting those ideas to a harmonious system sufficiently pliant to lend itself to all the modifications, and even consequences of progress; it cannot therefore confine itself to the study and application of purely conventional formulas; for instance, those relating to the orders, or those derived from what are called the laws of symmetry.

Symmetry is not a general law of architectural art any more than equality is a law of society. We assert the equality of all men before the law; but equality is not the law, for we do not acknowledge an equality in intelligence, in aptitudes, in physical strength, or in wealth among all the members of a social body. Symmetry insisted on as a general dominant law is none other than a kind of communism, enervating art and debasing those who observe it.

Because you build all the houses of a street or of a square after the same pattern, and require your architect to make all the windows of a façade just alike, regardless of the very various arrangements which the building contains, you conclude that you are showing respect for art. No such thing; you are putting it on the rack; you become its torturer; you stifle its noblest quality, that which consists in the free expression of its wants, its tastes, its individuality. There is no art without liberty ; for art is the expression of thought ; but what is the expression of thought if you are compelled to repeat what your neighbour says, or to call that white which you see to be black ?

That a town-council should interfere to limit the height of the houses or their encroachment on the street by municipal regulations is perfectly legitimate ; but that it should use its authority to oblige twenty architects to adopt in twenty houses the same cornice-moulding or the same window, or the same height of string-courses, under pretext of symmetry, when each of these houses is differently arranged within, is scarcely justifiable. Be assured that those superior intellects which, without any practical knowledge of the arts, have a certain influence on their direction, would never have been involved in this lamentable imbroglio of errors and false principles, if artists themselves had not urged them forward on this downward path, by crying up doctrines opposed to immutable reason ; representing architecture as a kind of recipe applicable to every purpose and to every programme,—a common formula which all may apply without having recourse to reason.

Symmetry cannot be accredited with the qualities which go to constitute a law ; it is at most, and only in certain cases, a gratification to the eye : but harmony and equilibration are laws which must be defined and applied in architecture.

In the preceding lecture we explained some of the harmonic laws of proportion ; as respects the laws of equilibration, they are illustrated in the noble edifices of classic times and of the Middle Ages ; but equilibration is not symmetry, for it admits of variety. Like things do not require balancing, for the simple reason that they are similar. Nothing is more common than for a programme rigorously observed to give an irregular disposition of plan ; but it is for us artists to contrive that this irregular plan shall in elevation present a balanced ensemble,—that the edifice shall not appear deformed or unfinished.

Suppose, for example, that we have to build a small town hall, containing offices on the ground-floor, and a large hall on the first floor, and having a belfry. It is evident that if for the sake of symmetry I place the belfry-tower in the middle of the front, I cut the large hall in two ; or I must have recourse to complicated, fictitious, and expensive means of construction (for in architecture, falsehood is often very costly). I determine to be truthful. I place (see the plan fig. 1) the tower at one of the ends of the building, with an entrance porch below ; I build the staircase outside, at A ; the offices and the mayor's room will be on the ground-floor at B. On the first floor I have every facility for obtaining an anteroom above the porch, and a spacious, well-lighted hall in the body of the building. In the roof space I contrive muniment and store rooms. Thus settled, in elevation C the belfry tower is boldly treated; it is a strong and massive feature; it strengthens one end of the building, and rises to a considerable height. Then comes the great hall amply lighted;

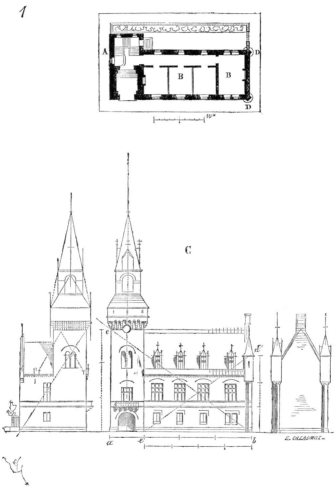

Fig. 1.—The principle of Equilibration.

and to strengthen the corners D of the front opposite to this tower, and enable them well to resist the thrust of the relieving arches of the great windows, I erect a turret—an angle pier—a buttress or vertical mass; in this way I terminate the gable and balance the façade, which is in nowise symmetrical. The eye in fact perceives that the left corner occupied by the tower is thicker, more massive and lofty ; that the portion lighted is not weighted, and that this front, perforated with wide openings, is terminated at its extremity opposite to the tower by a weight acting vertically. The building is not symmetrical, but it is balanced, especially if we can so contrive that the base $a\,b$ shall bear the same proportion to the height $a\,c$ as that of the length $e\,b$ to the height $b\,d$.

I have to erect a square structure : it consists of four buildings around a court : The site is not level, the angle A (fig. 2) being very much lower than the three angles B. It is necessary

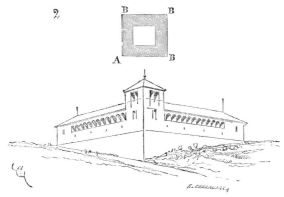

Fig. 2.—The principle of Equilibration.

to place at some point of the edifice an elevated outlook, a tower or an extra story. Shall I erect this tower in the middle of one of the sides ? No, but on the angle that occupies the lowest point of the site, at A (see the perspective view). The eye will in fact demand that the extra story be placed at the corner of the building, which by the form of the ground requires the most solid construction. Thus the edifice is balanced ; it would not be so if the extra story were placed in the middle of one of the sides, supposing the site to be unlevel.

Look at the antique paintings representing *villæ, i.e.* collections of buildings ; if we examine the buildings themselves we shall be struck with the delicacy of observation displayed by the architects of classical antiquity as regards the balancing of the masses. And our mediæval buildings—our castles, abbeys, hospices, and even our mansions—what numerous examples do they not present us of the application of this principle of equilibration ? These buildings are firmly based, and they present a most pleasing appearance to the eye. Look at the house of

Jacques Cœur, at Bourges : the Hôtel de Cluny at Paris : look at all those old feudal castles, and the châteaux of much more recent times : Blois, Chenonceaux, Ecouen, Azay-le-Rideau. Is it to symmetrical arrangements that these edifices owe the charm that engages us ? Certainly not ; but rather to skill in balancing the masses. This, I allow, is a more difficult achievement than continuing the lines of a building,—than repeating the same window and the same pier a hundred times over,—than fatiguing the eye by the uniformity of the masses. But it is art ; and none will assert that art—as the chief condition of beauty— must be easy to produce.

The laws of architectural equilibration do not apply only to the masses ; we observe that the ancients regarded them as essential in the design of the details, and that the mediæval artists applied them with consummate intelligence. Let us take

3

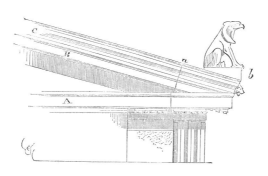

Fig. 3. –Treatment of the lower angle of a Greek Pediment.

only two examples ; for we shall have occasion, in the investiga- tion of the practical methods of the art, to return to the question. Every one knows how the mouldings which form the angle of a pediment on a Greek peristyle are disposed (fig. 3). The cornice drip A surmounted by a fillet slopes up at B on the face of the tympanum of the pediment, and its slope is terminated by a doucine or ogee C, forming the coping of the roof, returning partly or wholly to form a horizontal gutter along the side walls. However great the respect we entertain for the architecture of the Greeks, we must remark a radical defect in this arrangement : It is the drip stone B, cut at an acute angle, and surmounted by a moulding, which to the eye would seem as if it must slide on the slope of the pediment. At the angle of the entablature, where the eye seeks for horizontal masonry capable of hindering the

sliding, the form adopted only presents an effect of weakness and
a defect of combination. To insure the requisite strength, the
jointing of the masonry has to be in contradiction with the apparent form, as shown at *a*. The refined sense of the Greek artists
must have been offended by this defect; for there is evidence of
their having frequently left at the angle of the crowning cymaise
a small block *b*, surmounted by an ornament or a figure, in order
to give weight,—an appearance of solidity,—a horizontal line
partially obviating the disquieting effect to the eye of the sharp
cutting of the inclined drip, and the apparent tendency of the
cymaise to slip. More frank in their combinations,—above all,
more truthful,—our architects of the thirteenth century, when

Fig. 4.—Lower termination of a Twelfth-century Gable.

they had to terminate the lower portion of a gable, sought and
discovered combinations which decidedly expressed both the
return of the mouldings and the weighting which it is necessary
to give to these angles, as may be perceived by examining figure
4, representing one of these gable slopes. Such a gable base
balances its mass, and is moreover perfectly logical. Perhaps at
the other angle there might be a staircase turret, or a tower ; in
that case the eye will none the less be reassured by this decided
finish, so frankly expressing a termination. Equilibration is in
fact the art of making a finish where symmetry is wanting ;
and when the architect has no other resource than the adoption

of symmetrical arrangements to give an air of finish to his work, it differs little from that of those machine looms which reproduce with such remarkable precision the corresponding sections of the design woven in them.

While, therefore, properly speaking, there are no laws of symmetry, or while the laws of symmetry express merely the result of a mechanical labour, there are laws of equilibration in architectural art,—laws which the architects of classic times and those of the Middle Ages strictly observed ; these laws of equilibration, like the laws of proportion, are only the outward expression of statical laws. Geometry and calculation constitute, therefore, in architecture, the fundamental basis of art ; with these as a basis we shall be able to get rid of the pitiable vulgarity of so-called classic forms ; and if our engineers, who are excellent geometricians and accurate in calculation, concerned themselves less with designing those classic forms, too often introduced into their constructions in disregard of what common sense would dictate, they would undoubtedly produce works of artistic merit. Laws based on geometry and calculation, and resulting from a nice observation of the principles of statics, naturally give rise to true expression,—sincerity. Now, sincerity endows every work of art with a charm that engages the most cultured mind as well as that which is least so. Though we have depraved the taste of the public by the falsity that pervades architectural productions, when that public chances to find a truthful work, —one that appears what it really is,—its attention and interest are awakened. Whatever clearly explains itself, pleases and engages it, in France at any rate. The various materials we use possess different properties ; and if we succeed in expressing these properties by the forms we give to our materials, not only do we thus open a vast field for variety, and take advantage of infinite resources, but we likewise interest the public by this constant endeavour to give every object the form that befits its nature. Is it not, moreover, the duty of artists to enlighten the public taste when it goes astray ? Is there not a kind of baseness in deferring to people's errors, especially when these are manifest ? Not to deceive is the first rule which persons of taste lay down for themselves ; how then can we credit with taste artists who in their works heap falsehood on falsehood ? The word is strong, but the thing itself is monstrous. The so-called classical architecture which prides itself on perpetuating the traditions of antiquity is a deception ; while one of the noblest qualities of ancient architecture is that of never deceiving, either in regard to the material or the mode of using it. To begin with, this formal architecture, supposed, very erroneously, to be derived from the classic arts, might with some care preserve a truthful character, whenever an edifice has to be built without regard to expense; but when the means are limited, to what untruths must not the architect have recourse, in order to give his building the pompous appearance recognised as classic! Plaster columns and cornices; wooden beams simulating stone-lintels; lath and plaster ceilings simulating timber-framing and carpentry; stucco simulating marble; plaster ornament simulating sculpture; lathed vaults simulating plastered masonry. The pervading principle of this architecture is simulating something, —deception in form and material. But without descending so low—though we often do descend to this,—let us look at some of our great modern buildings, erected at great cost; do we not see that the masonry in nowise accords with the form; that the beds of the courses do not coincide with the heights of the bases, string-courses, and entablatures; that after a few years, as each stone takes a different tint and each bed becomes apparent, the jointing of the structure does not accord with the form adopted; that the *simulated* lintels are cut in the most disagreeable fashion by the joints of the stones which compose them; that the outer mouldings of the arches do not extrados the arch-stones, whose joints stray into the spandrels; that the bas-reliefs show beds cutting the sculpture; that the enormous windows simulating openings which in the ancient buildings were destined to remain unfilled, are partitioned by glazed wooden framing which destroys the effect they were intended to produce; that the string-boards of stairs pass across windows, and that stories which appear outside to form a single ordonnance, are cut by the floors of entresols; that the roofs are concealed by parapet walls; that iron floorings are coated with plaster to represent wooden ceilings; that immense rooms are lighted by several stories of windows, so that on the outside these interiors of 30 feet in height appear divided by several floors; that the wood is often painted in imitation of stone or marble, and the stone of wood; that inside there are as many false doors as real ones; so that you do not know where the entrance is, and open a sham door supposing it leads into a room,[1] while enormous chimney-pieces are erected to contain small fireplaces? What name can we give to these eccentricities? Falsehood: no other is applicable.

If we seriously desire to invent an architecture, the first condition to be fulfilled is not to deceive, either in the general design or in that of the smallest details of the building to be

---

[1] Have we not seen in a modern edifice, built with perhaps excessive luxury, doors symmetrically represented in a staircase whose landings are naturally at different levels; so that of four doors thus symmetrically placed, two open into empty space? On seeing this architectural freak, some one suggested that people one wanted to get rid of might be very conveniently shown out by these doors, opening on corresponding precipices.

erected.   Certainly, in the present day, the determination to be
absolutely sincere would produce very novel and probably very
fascinating results.   Besides, we should thus be putting ourselves in perfect accord with the methods pursued in the good
periods of antiquity; we should be making ourselves really
classic, in the sense of obeying the invariable laws of art.   Having
at our disposal novel materials, having machines formerly
unknown, powerful appliances much more developed and
complicated than those of the Ancients, a tolerably complete
acquaintance with what has been effected amid various civilisations in the past, and with all this, a determination to be sincere,
—to comply absolutely with the requirements, to take the
materials for what they are and for what they will allow us to
attempt, having regard to their properties, making some little
use of science and a good deal of our reason, seeking, above all,
to forget false doctrines, and to put aside some prejudices, we
might then be able to lay the foundation of an architecture of
our time; and if we did not discover it immediately, we should
at least be preparing the way for our successors.

Not the least important law in architectural design,—one
that concerns more directly art *per se*, and which is too often
disregarded,—is that of *fitness;* and it must be acknowledged
that while we erect buildings without sufficient regard for the
general rules of proportions, while deception is habitual with
us in the manner of observing the programme and using the
materials, we nearly always disregard this law, which I call that
of propriety or fitness.   To give to a house raised on shops which
absolutely destroy its basement the aspect of a palace; to
ornament its front with Corinthian pilasters resting on woodwork, behind which peep forth hats or stockings, is an evident
contravention of this law; to erect in the same town and during
the same period, a Gothic church, a second of a Renaissance
character, and a third of a pseudo-Byzantine style, is not easily
reconcilable with propriety (I mean artistic propriety): seeing
that for churches we either preserve a traditional style because
the worship is a tradition equally belonging to every period, or
on the other hand, adopt a new style suitable to the novel
requirements of a worship undergoing modifications; but it is
not readily conceivable that the same form of worship should
accommodate itself to architectural forms that are foreign to one
another.   Which will be the most orthodox, the Byzantine form
of church, that of the Renaissance, or the neo-Gothic?   But
why allow it to be supposed that one can be more orthodox than
the other two?   To make the front of a Mairie *simulate* the front
of a church built as a pendant; a small theatre beside a large
one appear a fragment detached from the latter; to crown a

court of justice with a cupola like a mosque : all this manifests contempt for or at least ignorance of the laws of fitness which govern matters of art. If in a vast palace you exhaust on an accessory all the means adopted to express richness, what will you do when you come to the principal part ? If, beginning with the vestibule or the staircase you lavish the resources afforded by art and material, what will you give the public after this introduction ?

And the law of fitness, be it remarked, extends to everything, —to the whole as well as the details : we fail to observe it if we erect porticos where no one passes, and which we are obliged as a matter of precaution to close ; for we do not benefit the public by this shelter, while we render the rooms which have these windows beneath its arches very dismal ; we fail to observe it, if, behind façades covered with sculpture carved at great expense in stone, we decorate the interiors with plaster-work simulating wood carving, bronze, or marble ; we also disregard it if our interior decoration affects a style out of harmony with that followed for the outside.

As regards the mode of decorating buildings, the architect should never lose sight of this necessary gradation ; he should not expend all he can afford on the front or on the vestibule ; sobriety should be observed, even where conditions of the greatest richness are admitted ; for in art, richness only acquires value by contrast and a judicious use of its resources. What, in fact, are those palace interiors which are now presented to the gaze of a public which is soon wearied after a first surprise ? Accumulations of ornaments, gildings, and paintings almost invariably concealing poverty of design, ill-considered proportions and disconnected masses ! The effect is like that of varnish on a roughly formed object, or embroidery on an ill-shaped figure. Dress up a deformed person, and you will never succeed in producing a noble carriage. Be assured that it is the same with architecture. When by lavishing sculpture and gilding you have tried to disguise an awkward assemblage of lines, unpleasing proportions or vulgar forms, you will only have succeeded in amusing the public for a moment.

The memory will retain only a confused recollection of the whole,—often nothing more than a feeling of deep disgust at the splendours so tastelessly lavished ; a longing to find some square room with smooth white-washed walls. Nothing in the arts leads more quickly to satiety than the abuse of richness ; especially when the richness does not adorn—while leaving it apparent,—a beautiful form ; nothing so nearly approaches absolute sterility. It is only by lines intelligently combined, forms easily comprehended, and general striking effects, that a deep impression is produced on the mind, and a conception acquires the dignity of a work of art. And in this the Ancients are our masters. While you depart from these principles, therefore, do not say that you are the only supporters of classical art, and while you borrow from the age of Louis xiv. some tinsel ornaments, without reproducing the sense of form whose traces are still apparent in its monuments, do not talk of venerable traditions ; for the public, weary of these gilded rags covering miserable bodies,—of this art without character, and utterly commonplace,—will end by asking to be taken back to the colourless, cold reproductions of classical art in vogue at the beginning of the century, but which were, at any rate, not ashamed of their baldness, and did not conceal their poverty of conception beneath a splendour borrowed from a few old mansions of the Marais or the faubourg Saint-Germain.

As a résumé of this lecture, we will conclude by recapitulating the conditions essential to the formation of the architect : Method in the study of the arts of the past—this study being always subjected to the crucible of reason : Observation of certain laws when we come to synthesis,—to design,—laws, some of which are purely mathematical, others belonging to abstract art. The former are corollaries of statics, and relate particularly to construction ; the latter concern proportions, the observance of effects, decoration, fitness deduced from the requirements, the purpose, and the means at command.

Archæological study has proved to us that each period of art possesses a special style,—that is to say, a harmony, a unity in the general conception and the execution of the details. There never was, and never can be, an art not based on this fundamental condition. Either we must adopt one of these known styles, or we must form a new one. If you would produce an amalgamation of the various known styles, the Archæologist comes and analyses your mixture, and proves in the most logical manner that it is composed of contradictory elements that are incongruous and mutually injurious ; and inasmuch as knowledge has something to say on the question, its dictum must be duly respected. What some have called Eclecticism in art,—the adaptation of elements derived from various quarters to the composition of a new art,—is, in every respect, barbarism ; it is what was attempted after the ruin of the Classic arts before the rise of the secular school of the twelfth century. When in the eleventh century the Romanesque architects took a ground-plan from the Romans, details from the East, débris from the old monuments of the Empire, a dome from the Byzantines, and timber-framing from the Northern peoples, there was no one to label these often incongruous fragments according to their derivation. But we have now too much knowledge to attempt such a proceeding ; in our times we should not make those admixtures with that naïveté or good faith which thus gave a harmonious tone to the most heterogeneous combinations : in fact, ignorance alone was capable of giving shape to this confused mass of elements. Science can classify them, but for the very reason that it does classify, it is unable to mingle them. It soon perceives that only two or three essential principles are to be found among them, and a very limited number of ideas pertaining to each of these principles ; but that to attempt to harmonise these principles in a single expression of art, or not to regard the ideas as derived from the principles, would be a deliberate lapse into barbarism.

It would be an unworthy office to object to archæological studies : we believe in fact, that they are calculated to serve as a solid basis for modern art ; but at the same time we must not close our eyes to the danger they entail, especially as Archæology would seem of late to be exerting an influence rather on the material than the intellectual side of art. If we would derive advantage from the study of the past, we should not occupy ourselves so much with inquiring whether the metopes of such or such a temple were coloured blue or red ; whether the bronze enclosures were inlaid with silver ; whether gold fish were painted at the bottom of azure-floored *vivaria;* whether the eyes of such or such a statue were incrusted with enamel or precious stones,—as with investigating the reasons which led to the adoption of such or such a style of decoration, or obtaining a precise and comprehensive idea of the civilisations a few of whose manifestations we have succeeded in deciphering. The numberless and puerile details with which the study of classic and mediæval times is occupied in the present day too often cause it to lose sight of the chief object,—that of investigating human nature, its efforts, its tendencies, and the means it has employed to manifest its thoughts, taste, and genius. It is of trifling importance to us to know the composition of the pomades used by the ladies of Greece and Rome ; but it is of great importance to us to know what was their social and domestic status, how they spent their leisure, and what was the degree of their mental cultivation. I see no harm in painters knowing the number of rows of pearls the Satraps wore on their necks, and whether they wore laced-up boots, shoes, or sandals, provided they first learn what a Satrap was. Archæological studies will be advantageous to the arts provided they first lead us to ascertain the dominant principles, the causes and the logical order of facts ; when observations respecting details,—trifling results,—offer themselves, they should certainly not be thrust

aside, or even neglected; but it is well to give them their due
place, and not accord them a greater importance than they deserve
in human history. In a word, the part played by Archæology
should not be that of narrowing the mind of the artist, but on
the contrary, of enlarging it, by showing him certain grand invariable principles which always rule in the products of intelligence. But in the nineteenth century there is a serious question
which is daily assuming greater importance, and which will
eventually take precedence of all the rest: the question of
expense,—the financial question. The greater the increase of
prosperity in a particular civilisation,—the greater the extent
of wealth,—the more are people inclined to make a judicious use
of their means ; and useless expenditure excites public disapprobation. When all are possessors of property every one knows
the value of things and criticises the misapplication of the public
money, which is in some sort the property of each. In a word,
what every one occasionally finds fault with, is not that too much
is expended, but that it is unwisely expended, or that the best
use possible is not made of the public resources. Now, in a
nation like ours, buildings form a large item in the budget ; it
is therefore of consequence that they should be useful, substantial,
and beautiful, and cost no more than the value they represent ;
for we like to get full credit for the sacrifices we make, when we
are rich and know what we have a right to expect. Is architecture prepared to give satisfaction to that spirit of true economy,
which is certain to have a vigorous extension? I think not.
Moreover, a singular phenomenon is witnessed in our days,
which are so fertile in contradictions. On the one hand, those to
whom the expenditure of the public money is intrusted are for
the most part strangers to art, and often cherish the conviction
in secret, if they dare not openly avow it, that what is called the
mania for building is the ruin of a state, and that if we were
wise, we should limit ourselves to the erection of mere sheds, fit
to last some fifty years, for all our public offices. They are
horrified, and not without some reason, at seeing enormous sums
expended in the erection of buildings whose destination is not
altogether fixed, and which assume architectural forms whose
adaptation no one can perceive. In their view, the architect is
simply an enemy of the public prosperity,—a spending machine
that makes short work of the purse when it has clutched hold
of the strings. On the other hand, our architects, directed by
the School, and enjoying its special patronage (I do not say instructed by it, for it does not instruct), are not prepared for
refuting these charges ; on the contrary, the tendency of their
education is fully to justify them, since not a word is ever said
to them about the direction of works or the judicious employ-

ment of materials, or the application of architectural forms and means of construction to the requirements of the case; but they are trained to produce designs that cannot be executed, and which are of a monumental character, no regard being had to the method of securing a wise economy. Thus in one quarter of Paris the State is educating young men as architects, who in another quarter will incur the most bitter suspicion, and whose tendencies will be deliberately counteracted. The State will charge the architects with ignorance of that which has not been taught them in a school maintained and protected by it, of which it is the master, and whose tendencies, hitherto at least, it has not thought fit to alter. It should, however, be observed that building has never ruined States during periods when architecture was in perfect harmony with national habits and wants, and was subordinated to the requirements of the case, the judicious use of the materials, and the necessities of the times. The buildings erected by the Romans in the provincial towns did not ruin them, but on the contrary contributed to the spread of civilisation and of ideas of order, wealth, and comfort. France was not ruined at the end of the thirteenth century, during which it rebuilt all civil and religious edifices on entirely new plans. This was because those buildings then represented an idea, or were erected to satisfy real wants, and did exactly satisfy them. Their degree of richness depended on their distinction; and it was impossible to mistake a palace for an hospital, or a guildhall for a princely mansion. The architectural forms were in harmony with the necessities of the times. In a word, architecture was then a pliable art, applicable to everything, understood by all, and not a conventional formula foreign to the social condition, to the times, and to practical appliances. It changed as did customs, and, free in its expressions, it had not yet been subjected to the enervating régime by which we now see it oppressed.

END OF VOL. I.